How to get a Job in Computer Animation

Create an Amazing Demo Reel and get It to the Right People

By Ed Harriss

EdHarriss.com, Inc.
"Helping Animators into the New World"
PO Box 90154, Raleigh, North Carolina 27675 -90154
www.EdHarriss.com

How to get a Job in Computer Animation
Create an Amazing Demo Reel and get It to the Right People

©2003, EdHarriss.com, Inc.

Version 1.22
ISBN 0-9743230-0-4

Printed in the United States of America

This text last revised: September 14, 2003
For updates to this book please visit:
www.GetA3DJob.com

Trademarks

EdHarriss.com, Inc
PO Box 90154, Raleigh, North Carolina 27675 -90154
www.EdHarriss.com

Our Thanks To:

Editors: Chris Haire, Elaine Harriss and Bernard Lebel.

Technical Editors: Chris Haire, Bernard Lebel and Leonard Teo.

Support: Will Mendez, Raffael Dickreuter, Bernard Lebel and Alan Jones

Quotes: Dan Ablan, Mark Ainslie, Alec Bartsch, Kevin A. Bjorke, Doug Brooks, Juan J. Buhler, John Coldrick, Michael Defeo, Paddy Eason, Per-Anders Arvid Edwards, Ben Fischler, Steph Greenberg, Jonn Gorden, Deke Kincaid, Gordon Farrell, Brian LaFrance, Bernard Lebel, Anthony Milas, Porl Perrott, Josh Reiss, Alex Scollay, Alex Smith, Bruce Steele, Leonard Teo, Leigh van der Byl, Jayson Walton, Dean Warren, Chris Wise, Bill Zahn.

Error Correction: Christiaan Moleman and Brian Parchim.

3D Career De-Mystified: David Gould, Markus Manninen, Stefan Marjoram, Dennis Price, Carlos Saldanha, Jason Schleifer, Leonard Teo, William Vaughan

Cover Art: Pete Draper

Pete Draper is a full-time freelance CG artist with over 10 years industry experience. Originally starting out as a fine artist and graphic designer, Pete discovered several 3D programs for his old Archimedes computer and 3D Studio R3 in his University's CAD laboratory.

After channeling his love for art into this new medium, he graduated and joined a local company producing multimedia for CBT applications which enabled him to focus on all aspects of 3D production, before joining companies aimed more at film, TV and DVD production.

Now located in the South West of England, Pete has gone back to his freelancing roots, something he did throughout college, university and early employment. Previous positions as Lead and Senior Artist and Head of Media enables him to provide sound advice with regards to tips and techniques when working with 3ds max. This expertise can be found in the publications he writes for, such as Computer Arts and 3D World magazines, in which he is the resident 3ds max expert. He has also contributed to 3ds max 4 Magic from New Riders publications.

Freelancing now gives him the opportunity to produce work for a wider range of clients and therefore a broader range of work from title motion graphics to Special FX, historical reconstructions to concept print work, commercials to in-house training, book tutorials to architectural visualization.

This image was originally published in 3D World Magazine (www.3dworld-mag.com) issue 31 to accompany a "Demo Reel" article. Pete can be contacted through his web site: http://www.xenomorphic.co.uk

Preface

Why I wrote this book

I wrote this book to help those of you that want to pursue a career in computer animation and those of you that are already in the animation industry but need to switch jobs or are in between jobs. Knowing what you need to do to get a job from the very beginning will make it much easier for you to focus. For many 3D artists, the road from classroom to career (or job to job) is shrouded in mystery. This book will unlock the secrets that you need to know in order to create a killer demo reel and get it into the right hands.

Redundant passages

I have included what some might call "redundant passages" in this book. I did this assuming that many readers will thumb through this book, read the sections that they find interesting, but never read the book in it's entirety. Or they will read the entire book one time. Then, some time later, they will refer to this book in order to research items that interest them. To accommodate everyone, if an item is of importance to more than one area, it will be mentioned in more than one area.

Accurate information

Every effort was made to ensure that the information in this book is as accurate as possible. However, this business changes rapidly and some of the information may be out of date before the book even gets printed. Keep this in mind as you venture out into the world to hunt for your first (or next) job. Please investigate any information that is critical to your livelihood before jumping into anything.

Liability and responsibility

This book is designed to educate and entertain. The author and the publisher have neither liability nor responsibility to any person or entity with respect to any loss, damage caused, (or alleged to have been caused) directly or indirectly, through the use of the information contained in this book. If you do not wish to be bound by the previous statement, send this book back to where you bought it for a full refund of the purchase price. (Excluding shipping.)

Phil disclaimer

I use Phil as a generic person in this book. He's fictitious; none of the people that are mentioned in this book are actually named Phil. So, if your name is Phil, relax…. I'm not talking about you. =)

General disclaimer

The characters and events portrayed and the names herein are fictitious and any similarity to the name, character, or history of any persons is entirely coincidental and unintentional. This book contains many stories of characters and incidences from my own experience and others like me who have successfully gone through the process of getting a job in computer animation. Also included are many short quotes from animation industry professionals as well as some of my personal views, which are the un-credited quotes.

Copyright

Directory disclaimer, terms of use and other legal mumbo jumbo

entities featured in the directory are accurate and up to date. If your company listing is incorrect, if your details change, or you wish to be removed from the directory at a later date please email us at EdHarriss@EdHarriss.com

EdHarriss.com expressly disclaims all or any warranties, express or implied, relating to the directory or any other products or services obtained through use of the directory, including in particular any warranties of satisfactory quality or fitness for a particular purpose.

Companies should note that all such information is entered into the directory strictly under the terms of this disclaimer. EdHarriss.com takes no responsibility for the information, illustrations, copy, etc., appearing in the directory. All complaints with regard to the aforesaid should be addressed to EdHarriss.com.

EdHarriss.com will not be liable under any circumstances whatsoever for any direct, indirect, consequential, punitive or special damages arising from the use of EdHarriss.com's directory. EdHarriss.com reserves the right, at its discretion, from time to time to make changes to the information provided in the directory. You are, therefore, advised to check the information provided to you in the directory. Any reliance that you place on the accuracy of that information is at your own sole risk. All of the data in the directory is subject to change without notice by EdHarriss.com. EdHarriss.com reserves the right, in its sole discretion and without any obligation, to make improvements to, or correct any error or omissions in, any portion of this data. EdHarriss.com acknowledges that you are entitled to use the information provided in the directory for your own personal, private use. You may not use any data or information provided through the directory in connection with any business or commercial undertaking that is liable to compete directly or indirectly with EdHarriss.com. The directory contains information and text that are protected by copyrights, trademarks, service marks, or other intellectual or proprietary rights owned by EdHarriss.com or other third parties. Any other use of the directory or any of its contents is strictly prohibited, including without limitation, modification, deletion, publication, transmission, distribution, uploading, posting, reproduction, redistribution or any other dissemination without the express written permission of EdHarriss.com or the applicable rights holder. The content contained in the directory may not be used by third parties for telemarketing, direct marketing, commercial mass e-mail or by representatives or e-mail spamers. All trademarks and copyrighted information contained herein are the property of their respective owners. The data and information contained in the directory and the trademarks, logos and other intellectual property used in conjunction with it are the property of EdHarriss.com or other third parties.

No license of any such property or intellectual property rights is granted to you as a result of your use of the directory. EdHarriss.com may, in appropriate circumstances and in its sole discretion, delete the entries of entities that infringe or otherwise violate the copyright rights of others, and may remove the record of

Image copyright information

About the author - Ed Harriss

Ed Harriss has been working professionally in the computer animation industry for over 10 years. In that time he has worked in many of its different sectors: video games, special effects, commercial production, corporate animation, technical visualization, medical animation, web graphics, animation instruction, trade show graphics, magazine advertising, and much more. He has given lectures and taught classes at many different schools and conventions from coast to coast. In his spare time he writes articles for magazines such as: Highend Magazine, 3D World, Digital Production, 3D Artisan, Graphics Live, and 3D Magazyn.

Currently Ed works as a Technical Director and 3D Artist at SAS Studio Productions, in Raleigh, North Carolina. He is the president of the local Research Triangle SIGGRAPH chapter. He also produces training videos for aspiring SOFTIMAGE|XSI artists and teaches SOFTIMAGE|XSI over the internet via Mesmer Inc.

We want to hear from you!
Please tell us what you thought about this book

This book was written for you and people like you. Therefore your reaction to our book is very important to us. What could we have done to make it better? What should we include/leave out in our next edition? What did you like/dislike about this book? If you have suggestions, opinions, comments or anything else you like to say, please feel free to contact us. You can contact us via e-mail, snail mail or fax. If you do, please include the book's title, ISBN number and your contact information. (e-mail, address or fax number.) We take your comments, as well as all the others like yours, and do our best to implement them into the next version of the book. If you are the first one to report an error or to make a suggestion, we will acknowledge you in the next printing. (Unless you specify otherwise.)

Due to the extremely high volume of mail we may not get back to you immediately. You can be sure that your e-mail will be answered.

Email: EdHarriss@EdHarriss.com

Fax: 1-603-691-6470

Mailing address:

EdHarriss.com
90154
Raleigh, NC 27675-90154
United States

How to contact us:

Through our web site:
www.EdHarriss.com

This is where you will find information about our other books, videos, classes and book errata. Here is also where you will find information on purchasing these books, videos and classes, both domestically and internationally.

Please feel free to e-mail us at:
EdHarriss@EdHarriss.com

... if any of the following statements apply to you.
- You have comments or questions about the book.
- You noticed errors in the book and would like to report them.
- You have a suggestion that would drastically improve the quality of this book
- You are an educator and are interested in educational discounts on this book.
- You are a member of the media that would like a copy of this book for review purposes.

Interested in bulk purchases or corporate sales?
EdHarriss.com provides discounts to those that are interested in purchasing multiple copies of our products. Please contact us at Edharriss@EdHarriss.com for the latest discount information.

Mailing address:
EdHarriss.com
90154
Raleigh, NC 27675-90154
United States

Fax: 1-603-691-6470

Demo Reel?

Who should read this book?

Intro: What is this book about?

This book is designed to help get you a job in the exciting world of 3D computer graphics. In this book you will learn about: the different types of jobs that are available, what companies are looking for, how much you should get paid, creating a great demo reel, how to get it into the hands of the right people, what to do once they've got it, the software and hardware requirements for 3D animation, how to pick an animation school, and much more.

Who should buy this book?

1. Students and beginners that are trying to break into the business, both self-taught and students enrolled in school.
2. Instructors that want to teach their students how to prepare for the real world and what to expect.
3. Professionals that are thinking about switching careers, changing companies or have lost their job and need that edge to get another one.
4. Anyone who thinks that they might want to get into the world of computer graphics and wants to know what it will take to get there.

How this book is organized

Each section covers a major aspect of getting or keeping your job in the 3D graphics industry. Since this book will probably be referenced over and over during your job search, each section is divided into smaller chunks that are clearly labeled to make it easier to find information quickly and decide if you want to read a particular section or not. (If you are in a hurry this can really save you some time.)

Table of Contents

Chapter 3: Demo Reel: Designing   45

The Wonderful World of Computer Animation

1

What is computer animation?

Simply put, it is animation that is created with the help of a computer. Computer animation builds on the two-dimensional animation techniques pioneered by Walt Disney. These techniques create the illusion of motion using a sequence of still images, rather than having actors captured in live action film. There are two main types of animation: two-dimensional (2D) and three-dimensional (3D). While this book is geared toward helping 3D animators find a job, many of the basic principles can be applied to job hunting 2D animators as well.

When computers became powerful enough to generate quality graphics, new techniques were developed to speed up 2D animation. These new techniques would replace most hand drawn animation with computer-generated images. Instead of drawing pictures, animators would use software to do much of the work for them. (Specifically the in-between frames.) At the same time 2D animation started to adopt computers, the 3D animation industry was being born.

| Wireframe | Textured | Rendered |

3D animation allows an artist to create 3D models of virtually anything within the computer. Initially the models have no surface color, looking a lot like clay. Those 3D models are then wrapped in color, much like you would wrap a gift in wrapping paper. This is called texture mapping. This makes the models look less like clay and more like real objects. These textures are usually obtained from photographs or generated by a computer program. The artist then moves the position and adjusts the shapes of the 3D models to create realistic motion. (Animation) It could be a car driving down the street or a person walking up a flight of stairs. Once that is finished, the 3D models are typically lit accordingly. (Night scenes would be lit with dark bluish lights and day time scenes would be lit with bright yellowish lights.) The final step is to render the image. The computer will take all of the 3D work that the artist has done and create a 2D image that can be viewed on the appropriate output device. (Television, film, paper, etc...)

Animation has been around a long time, but computer animation is still relatively young. Traditional 2D Animation became popular at the beginning of the twentieth century. It wasn't until the 1960's that computer scientists, with the help of artists, started to experiment with 3D computer animation. In 1982 the world was exposed to its first heavy usage of computer animation via the feature film "Tron". Immediately following "Tron" was another theatrical release called "The Last Starfighter." Both of these movies had a tremendous amount of computer animation in them. Unfortunately neither of them made a lot of money at the box office. The general feeling is that if they had, more of them would have been made and the computer animation industry would be much farther along than it is today. Instead, investors didn't want to have anything to do with movies containing computer animation. It wasn't until 1989 that 3D animation had a good chance to catch on again. This time, in the movie "The Abyss" it was used to create a living being made entirely of water. Then, in 1991, the world of computer animation began to be taken seriously with the release of "Terminator 2: Judgment Day". This movie was filled with computer animation, most notably its computer-generated villain, the T-1000. When "Jurassic Park" came out in 1993 it was obvious that 3D computer animation was here to stay. This movie was incredibly popular and, together with "Terminator 2," generated a tremendous amount of interest in computer animation. So much so that computer animation has now become a "must have" for most big motion pictures made today.

It was around the "Jurassic Park" era that the first video games which employed 3D artists began to emerge. In 1992 Sega's Virtua Racing was released. It did so well that Sega released another game, Virtua Fighter, based on the same technology in 1993. As with motion pictures, just about every game released today has some form of 3D in it. Many games are entirely 3D.

Today, computer animation has changed the way we watch movies and play videogames. It is almost impossible to distinguish between live action and computer-animated scenes in today's movies and television shows. Video games are also becoming more and more realistic as time goes by. With computer animation still in its infancy, it is a very exciting time to enter this field. For a more detailed account of the history of computer animation, there is a great book called "Cg 101: A Computer Graphics Industry Reference". More information on that title can be found in the "Resources: Books" section of this book.

What is the 3D industry?

The world of 3D computer graphics is not limited to movies, television and videogames, even though they are the three most popular and largest areas in the computer graphics industry today. Many other sectors such as engineering, manufacturing, medical, architectural, industrial, corporate, law, print, internet and research make extensive use of computer graphics as well.

Practically everything around you has been influenced directly, or indirectly by computer graphics. For example: your electronic devices, furniture and automobiles were probably designed in 3D before they were built. The magazines you read likely have 3D graphics in them, whether it is in the ads or the magazine content itself. When you are browsing the internet, practically every site has

"Of course they always tell you to make changes - that's because you always tell them how easy it is to make changes."

some 3D element or elements in it somewhere, and if not, there are plenty of completely 3D sites out there that make up for it. For detailed information on 3D animation job areas see the chapter on computer animation jobs and which ones are right for you.

Why should computer animation interest me?
Why would I want a career in it?

If you enjoy creating art or animation then there is no better job than 3D graphics. Today's hardware and software allows you to create graphics very quickly with high quality results. This "instant feedback" is one of the aspects that makes computer graphics so enjoyable. After getting their first job, many people enjoy it so much that the workday seems to pass in an instant. Imagine doing what you love, all day long and getting paid for it! One of the best things about the computer animation industry is that it is fun! Unfortunately this is also one of the worst things about the computer animation industry. Because the jobs can be so much fun, people tend to stay late and work more hours, especially the newer employees. Over the years this has resulted in longer hours for many of the animators out there. Many companies are now expecting their employees to work late all the time. While long hours are expected on special occasions, as when deadlines are tight, they should not go on forever. (But there is a good chance that they will.) Be prepared, as a 3D artist, to work longer hours than your friends who are not 3D artists. On the average you will probably only have to work an extra hour or so every day. Many 3D artists are not prepared for the fact that they will more than likely never have a "9 to 5" job.

3D animation can be a very satisfying profession, but it has a very high burnout rate. During the course of your 3D career, you will hear about many people switching professions because they just can't take it. The work is very intense, requires a tremendous amount of concentration, involves re-doing a lot of jobs to meet client expectations and usually has you working long hours. It is not as bad as it sounds though. There are plenty of companies out there that treat their employees well, jobs that are not that difficult and clients that are not morons. But it may take you a few jobs before you find a place that fits this description, as companies like that don't often have a very high turnover rate.

Job cycles

Jobs in the most popular areas of computer animation (film, TV and video games) usually come around in cycles. For example: When a major gaming console starts to be come incredibly popular, game companies start creating a larger number of games in order to cash in on the current trend. At times like this there will be a lot of game jobs. When the game console becomes outdated and consumers lose interest, the game companies start laying off people. Many artists will have to move to a different company or into a different sector of computer animation till another "game industry" hiring cycle starts back up. The same thing happens with TV and film jobs. A set of TV shows might end long production runs or a series of movies may wrap up. This will leave a large number of animators out on the street. Sometimes these dry spells only last a few weeks; sometimes they can go on for months, even years.

While this is the way most of the companies out there work, there are exceptions. There are plenty of companies large enough and diverse enough to keep most of their employees practically indefinitely. If you are looking for a stable (possibly lower paying) job, then a large company with a diverse workload would be a great place to shoot for. Otherwise, be prepared to look for a new job, on the average, every two or three years.

What areas are there in the 3D industry?

When people talk about computer animation jobs they often mention "the big 3" areas: television, movies and video games. However, there are a lot more jobs areas out there. In fact, there are probably more people working outside of those three areas than inside. For example: industrial, architectural, forensic, corporate and medical animation are all very large sectors of the animation industry. Since they are not as glamorous, do not receive as much press, or are as popular as animation for entertainment, they tend to be overlooked. Many of these jobs are perfect for entry-level employees, as they tend to get fewer applicants. For detailed information on 3D animation job areas see the chapter on computer animation jobs and which ones are right for you.

What sorts of jobs are there?

Just as there are different areas for a 3D artist to go into, there are different jobs as well. Most people think that there are only a few job types: Animation,

Modeling and Rendering/Texturing. But there are so many more jobs. For example: Roto-Artists, Technical Director, Match Mover, Lighting Artist, Compositor, Character Animator, Effects Animator, Production Assistant, Art Director, etc. For more detailed information on specific 3D animation jobs see the chapter on computer animation jobs and which ones are right for you.

How much money can I expect to make?

For many people, this is the ultimate question. The rest are not as concerned with money simply because they enjoy animation so much. But, they are interested in making enough to be comfortable. Regardless, everyone wants to know what sort of "standard of living" they can expect if they choose computer animation as their career. For the most part, your pay will allow you to achieve a typical middle class income. Unless you are extremely talented or very lucky, you will not become rich doing computer animation. If you can keep a job you will not starve or have to struggle to pay your bills.

The amount you make will vary greatly from country to country and even from area to area, within each of those countries. Every country has primary markets and secondary markets. Primary markets are the areas with the greatest concentration of animation production companies. Secondary markets will have a smaller number of animation companies, which are often geographically spread out. Generally speaking primary markets usually pay the highest, while secondary markets pay slightly less. Using the United States as an example: Los Angeles, New York and San Francisco would be considered primary markets while parts of Texas, Florida, North Carolina, Illinois, Georgia and the Washington D.C. area would be considered secondary markets. There are animation companies outside these two markets. However, they don't always have as many jobs or the best pay. But, since they are usually overlooked by job hunters, there often is less competition. For more specific information on salary, have a look at the "How much should you make?" section of this book.

Importance of education

Education is a very important step in getting a computer graphics (CG) job. There are basically three educational paths available to you: attending a university, attending a specialized school or teaching yourself. Everyone has different needs when it comes to education. Which one is right for you?

Education: university

A university education will typically consist of a broad education where you will learn many things that have nothing to do with your future job. Believe it or not, that is one of the main benefits of attending a university. When you graduate you will be a well-rounded individual that will be able to tackle a wide variety of problems relatively easily. Another benefit is that you'll have a long time to develop your skills, as typical university degrees take at least four years to earn.

Education: specialized training facilities

A specialized school will consist of a more focused education where you will learn exactly what you need to hit the ground running the instant you graduate. These schools also tend to react faster to hardware, software and industry changes. As a result, your education will probably be a little more "up to date" than a traditional university education. Schools like this will also offer you more "hands on" instruction. Since the classes tend to be more focused, there will probably not be any history, language or philosophy classes. These schools are also an easy way, for people who already have a job, to change careers quickly or refresh their skills.

Education: self-taught

What about teaching your self? It can be done, but you have to be very dedicated to do it well. If you are the type of person that needs someone standing over your shoulder or someone giving you deadlines in order to get things done, then the self-taught route is not for you. However, if you are good at scheduling your time, able to learn from reading manuals, (rather than having some one show you), have the dedication and the equipment, then the self-taught route might just be for you. Many people go the self-taught route and flake out after a few months. Don't let this happen to you. If you even think that it might, then go to school instead. There is something to be said about having others around you when you are trying to learn CG.

None of these three routes are "better" than the other. In fact, some of the best CG artists out there are often a result of a combination of these three educational paths. Different people have different needs. There are pros and cons to each of the three types. The university route will take you longer and might not give you the specific knowledge that you need to know, but you'll have more time to develop your demo reel and you'll learn things that you'd never learn in a specialized school due to time constraints. Going to a specialized school might increase the chances that you'll get a job immediately after you graduate, but the broad range of knowledge that you'd gain at a university might be more important to you down the road. If you go the self-taught route, you'll save a lot of money and you'll be able to learn exactly what you want, but without structure and interaction with other CG artists you might not be able to learn what you need to become good enough to get a job.

Once you've chosen a school type, how do you choose which school to attend?

In the back of this book is a list of computer animation schools. Go through this list and pick out the schools that you'd like to attend. Ask around on the internet, and anywhere else you might find industry pros, for information on the schools you want to consider. Find out which schools have graduates that are working at respectable companies. Make a chart of how much each school is going to cost. How long does it last? Are they accredited? Do they offer financial aid? What sort of resources do they have? Does the school provide all of the necessary equipment needed for the student to learn and work in the industry? Is the program long enough for you to get a thorough education? Do they have an advisory board with members from the local animation industry (the type that helps review courses so they can keep up with the changes in the industry)? Do they invite members from the local animation industry to talk to classes about the needs of the industry, their companies, and how to apply for a job? Do they help the students prepare their graduate portfolios or reels and help market them to the industry? Once you have the answers to these questions, take the list and mark off all but the top choices. Visit each school. Talk to the staff as well as the students and use that information to make a decision.

I can think of at least a couple of cases here at PDI of people who were hired right out of school, and are now key players in their departments.

It all comes down to the person's reel, motivation and attitude. A good interview process can detect the good people even if they have no experience or recommendations (we go through a full day interview here where you get to talk with the people who would work with you, then those people compare their impressions and decide whether you get the job or not.) When I came to PDI this was one of the things that made a good impression on me. I had this little booklet of 3D tools I had developed, and PDI was the only place where I got meaningful questions about the tools, their purpose, use, etc. The farthest the other places went was to say "Wow! Nice presentation..."

We have hired people out of the school in the past and I expect we'll do that in the future...

Juan J. Buhler
PDI/Dreamworks
www.PDI.co

What skills do I need?

Different areas of computer graphics require different types of skills. But there is one skill that is common to all areas of CG. It is called, for lack of a better title: the "artistic eye" or "foundation art skills". Whether you are a character animator or a compositor you have to know what looks right and what looks wrong. This is something that most people learn through countless hours of practice, not from reading a book. Rarely are they born with this type of talent. There isn't a fool-proof way to gain an artistic eye either. It is different for everyone. Traditionally it is achieved through drawing, sculpting and painting, either in the real world or in a computer.

For all areas of computer animation, there are specific skills that are needed as well. For example, character animators need to have a good sense of timing, weight, balance and motion while modelers need to have a good understanding of mass, volume and geometry. The basic requirements for every area of computer animation can be found in the "Different Types of Computer Animation Jobs: Which one is right for you?" section of this book.

Computer animation hardware and software

The price of computer animation technology is dropping rapidly. Gone are the days when a single computer animator needed hundreds of thousands of dollars worth of equipment and software just to produce and output a single animation. For the beginner, an animation setup can be had for a few hundred dollars. Even an extremely high-end professional setup can cost less than ten thousand dollars.

On the one hand, this is a good thing. It is allowing many people who would have never had this type of access before, to obtain a career in 3D computer animation because they are able to afford the equipment. On the other hand, it is increasing the number of 3D computer animators that are applying for work. As a result employers now have thousands of prospective employees from which to choose from. This makes it tougher for animators to get work, making the need to stand out in the ever-expanding sea of unemployed 3D artists more important than ever.

What sort of hardware and software will you need to start learning computer animation?

In order to answer that question, you'll need to decide which of these three categories you fall into.

1. The beginner/budget animator.
2. The intermediate level or hobbyist animator.
3. The advanced level or professional animator.

The beginner/budget animator computer

For the beginner or the animator on a budget, all you need is a computer with a 3D accelerated video card and a piece of 3D software. Just about any computer manufactured in the past year or so will work, with the exception of machines running the Macintosh operating system and the Linux operating system. They make very good graphics workstations and they will do 3D. They also have some very good computer animation programs available for them. However, the range of animation programs for the beginner is much wider on Windows machines. Having said this, Macintosh machines and software are usually only recommended as a cost saving measure to 3D beginners who already have a Macintosh. For people running Linux machines on Windows compatible hardware, installing a copy of Windows is highly recommended.

What is a 3D accelerated video card? Why do I need one?

A video card translates your computer's output into something that can be displayed on a monitor. Computer animation programs are very taxing on your video card. Every time you move geometry around on the screen your 3D card has to redraw it. The more geometry you are working with the slower it will redraw. If you are using a video card that has no 3D acceleration (an oddity these days) or has poor 3D acceleration, things will get very slow very quickly.

The video card is one of the key components in a computer animation system.

Just having a fast video card is not always the answer to this problem. Sitting between your 3D application and your video card is a small program called a driver. This program translates all of the work you do into information the video card can understand. Some 3D accelerated video cards have such poorly written drivers that they cause your 3D application to crash frequently.

If you want to be absolutely sure that you have a *"good"* video card, then there is an easy way to find out. For *most* 3D programs the video card will not matter as *almost* all video cards on the market today can do 3D well enough for a beginner. However, some 3D software requires specific cards to perform properly. It is best to check the software company's web site before buying a video card. Of course, you might not know what software you'll be using. You might also be thinking that a higher price means a more stable video card. This is not always the case. Don't buy something expensive as your first video card. It will cost you a fortune and may not work out in the end. This is why beginners should just use the one that comes with the computer or buy a cheap video card the first time around. If it does not work very well, then upgrade.

"Tonight we will attempt to answer the most difficult question ever conceived - Which 3d application should I learn?"

Which 3D application should you choose?

There are a lot of 3D applications on the market. If you don't have a specific application in mind, how will you decide which one to start with? This can be a very difficult task. Ask yourself if there is a specific company or group of companies that you want to work for. If so, see if you can find out what they are using and choose that application. Keep in mind that it may take you a couple of years (or more) to reach the skill level needed to get a job at one of these companies and 3D software can come and go rather swiftly. By the time you are ready to apply, they may have switched to something entirely different. As you are learning 3D, check on the general health of your particular application. If the company stops updating it frequently or goes out of business, it may be time to re-train. :)

There are other ways to choose a 3D application.

1. Ask your friends what they use. If all of you use the same application, then it will be very easy to bounce ideas and suggestions off of each other, making the learning curve much easier to handle.

2. Call up an animation instructor at one of the local colleges and ask them what they teach/recommend.
3. Read magazines, internet newsgroups and chat forums to see what is being used for the type of work that you'd like to get into.

If you still can't make a decision, try creating a list of the applications that seem interesting to you. See if it is possible for you to "test drive" any of these. Most major 3D software companies offer free trial versions of their applications. The only downside is that these free versions usually have some of their functions disabled or restricted. For example, they might save their images with a watermark or there might be a watermark on the interface. It may render only small images or it may not render at all. It may save your file in a format that is incompatible with any 3D program but the trial version. Even though you might have a dual cpu machine, it may only use one cpu. Certain scripting functions may be disabled or scripting may be removed completely. Every company that offers trial versions uses different limitations to cripple the software. Make sure you are comfortable with the limitations beforehand.

If these limitations are too much for you, there are alternatives: Freeware and academic 3D applications. Most companies offer full versions of their 3D software at a fraction of the cost to students and teachers. Often there is no real difference between academic and professional software. The only catch is that it is not legal to make money with the academic version. Additionally, some companies will not sell you an academic license unless you can prove that you are a student.

Freeware 3D applications

If you are not a student, and cannot get an academic version, then there are still restriction free 3D software alternatives available to you: Freeware 3D applications. These are fully functional 3D packages that are absolutely free. One of the most popular pieces of 3D freeware is called Blender. It is available for download at www.blender3D.com. Others are listed below.

Anim8or: www.anim8or.com
Blender : www.blender3D.com
Gmax: www.discreet.com/products/gmax
Loq Airou: www.quelsolaar.com/loqairou
Moonlight3D: http://moonlight3D.net
Wings3D: www.wings3D.com

Budget 3D applications

But as with most everything, you get what you pay for. While these free programs are very good for the "starving artist" animator, they simply cannot compete, in most areas, with the large commercial applications. The time will come when you will outgrow freeware and trial versions. If you feel that you need something more powerful but do not want to spend very much money, then there is a "class" of 3D applications just for you: Budget 3D applications.

Amapi Designer: www.eovia.com
Amorphium Pro: www.electricimage.com
Carrera: www.eovia.com
Hash Animation Master: www.hash.com
Pixels 3D: www.pixels3D.com
Plasma: www.discreet.com
Strata 3D: www.strata.com
TrueSpace: www.caligari.com

All of these programs are less than $800 USD. Some, such as Amorphium Pro, can be found for as little as $150 USD.

Paint programs for beginners

As a beginner artist you are going to need something for editing images, something better than the paint program that came with your computer. The same rules you used for choosing a 3D program apply to choosing a 2D program as well. Find out what is being used by the professionals in the area you are most interested. As with 3D programs, there are freeware paint programs as well. Some of them, like CinePaint, are so good that you might not need to buy a paint program until later on in your 3D career.

Free paint programs

CinePaint: www.cinepaint.org
ImageForge: www.cursorarts.com/ca_imw_d.html
PhotoPlus Freeware: www.freeserifsoftware.com
Ultimate Paint: http://www.ultimatepaint.com

Paint programs that are $100 or less

Corel DRAW Essentials: www.corel.com
Digital Image Pro: http://pictureitproducts.msn.com
ImageForge Pro: www.cursorarts.com
Lview Pro: www.lview.com
Paint Shop Pro: www.jasc.com
Photogenics: www.idruna.com
PhotoImpact: www.ulead.com
PhotoPlus: www.serif.com
Photoshop Elements: www.adobe.com
PhotoStudio: www.arcsoft.com

PhotoSuite: www.roxio.com
Pixel32: http://pixel32.box.sk

Paint programs that are $100 or more
Deep Paint 2D: www.righthemisphere.com
Painter: www.corel.com
Photoshop: www.adobe.com

Of course there are many more options in both the 2D (paint) and 3D software categories. These lists contain only a few of them, but they represent a very good cross section of the most popular software on the market today.

The intermediate level or hobbyist animator
At this level you will either progress from beginning animator to intermediate animator or realize that 3D is not for you at all. If you decide to quit and you followed the advice laid out in this book, at least you won't be out a tremendous amount of money. If you continue to grow as a 3D artist, you will eventually need more powerful software and hardware.

Do you need a new machine?
As a beginner, it was relatively easy to purchase hardware. Practically any computer would do. Now that you are growing as a 3D artist, you will want your tools to grow with you. The first step is to evaluate your machine. It is fast enough to run current 3D animation software, or is it getting a little out of date? How will you be able to tell if your computer is fast enough? This is actually very easy. By the time you become an intermediate animator, you will probably have enough experience with 3D animation to know if you are waiting too long for a preview or if the geometry in your viewport is not responsive enough. If you are still questioning your computer's speed, then take a look at the hardware requirements laid

"If the jumper cables don't work, I'll pour in some more anti-freeze."

out by your 3D software manufacturer. Often they list "recommended" hardware and "minimum" hardware specifications. If your machine is better described by the "minimum" hardware specs than the "recommended" hardware specs, then it is probably time to buy a new machine or upgrade.

There are also many sites on the internet that benchmark computer speeds using 3D programs. They provide scenes for the users to download and instructions on what to do with the scenes. Users then follow those instructions, note the time that it took for the 3D program to execute them and send that in to the benchmark site along with a description of their machine. These sorts of sites can be a very good way to gauge the speed of your computer compared to the rest of the world. If your computer is at the top of the list or even in the middle, it is safe to say that it still has some life left in it. If you are near the bottom of the chart it may be time to upgrade. These types of charts are also helpful when that time comes. Look at the machines that are getting high scores. This will take a lot of the guess work out of buying a new machine, since it is obvious that these machines perform well. If these types of machines are within your budget, the decision will be easy.

The importance of RAM

If your machine is only a year or so old, then it will probably still be worth upgrading. The most cost efficient upgrade you can buy is memory. (RAM). Animation software uses a lot of RAM. The larger your projects the more RAM it uses. If your computer runs out of RAM, it will start to use the hard drive to temporarily store bits of information that would otherwise reside in RAM. Since your hard drive is much, much slower than your RAM, it makes working on and rendering your projects painfully slow. This can cause your computer to perform certain functions thousands of times slower than it would if you had the proper amount of RAM. As you can imagine, a slow computer with a lot of RAM could easily outpace a faster computer with a small amount of RAM.

There are many different types of RAM and they come in different shapes and sizes. Also, there are different rules depending on the type of RAM your machine uses. For example, some types of RAM will not let you mix different sizes together and some work better when there is an even number of RAM chips. Some RAM may be physically identical to others but have different internal characteristics. Be sure to check your computer documentation before buying RAM to make sure that you are not wasting your money.

Not only is RAM rather cheap, it is also very easy to install. On most machines it just slides into a RAM slot much the way a piece of toast slides into a toaster. Once it is installed, there are safety latches that keep it from working its way out of the slot. Every computer is a little different; so make sure you read your manual or do some internet research before replacing or upgrading your RAM.

Video card upgrades

Another easy way to upgrade is to replace your video card. As mentioned earlier, a bad video card can slow down your interactive workflow and even crash your 3D programs. Replacing an older video card with a faster one can really improve your productivity. (Especially on large projects.) Putting in a new video card is almost as easy as replacing your RAM. It, too, slides into a slot, much like RAM does. The only difference is you'll probably have to install new drivers when you install your card. How do you choose a video card? There are quite a few video card vendors and manufacturers on the market today. They come and go rather fast. The best way to decide on a card is though research, usually conducted on the internet.

Researching video cards

What should you look for in a video card? There are six things that you should consider regarding video cards, stability, speed, dual monitor support, video out, support/warranty and misc. features.

Stability

The single most important feature is stability. A video card that runs all day with out crashing your 3D application is invaluable. Many vendors will try to sell you video cards based on benchmarks. They will tell you that their card is 10% faster than any other card on the market. While a very fast card would be nice to have, that 10% speed increase is useless if you lose hours worth of work due to constant crashing, so look for stability first.

Speed

The second most important feature is speed. Some companies do not make very fast 3D cards. Their specialty might be geared more toward video production, print design or other 2d work that does not really require heavy duty 3D performance. Because these companies do not focus on 3D, their cards are often poor choices for 3D animators. On the other hand, there are quite a few companies that make cards with very good 3D acceleration. Find out which companies fall into this category and focus solely on them.

Dual monitor support

Many video cards support more than one monitor. This spans the desk top across

two monitors, allowing the user to have a very wide workspace. Today's modern 3D software requires a lot of screen real estate. Often certain functions require you to have many dialog boxes open simultaneously in order to perform them efficiently. It usually does not cost very much more to get a video card that supports dual monitors. This will push the overall price of your computer up because you'll have to buy another monitor, but it may improve your animation experience so much that it is worth it. If you have not bought a monitor yet, consider getting 2 smaller monitors rather than one large one. The cost may be so close that it is possible to do this and stay within your budget.

Video out

Many video cards offer a "video out" option, allowing you to plug a television into the video card. This will display the output from your computer on the TV screen. This feature is ideal for animators that want to record animations from their computer onto tape, for making their demo reel.

Support and warranties

What will you do if your video card goes bad? Some companies have excellent support, while others make it close to impossible to obtain a replacement. Check out the reputations of each company from which you are considering buying a card. Have they been around a while? Do they make quality products? Do they respond fast enough to customer inquiries? Answers to these questions are usually not found in a magazine or in an online video card review. A few well-placed questions on a 3D animation forum or mailing list will probably get you an answer in no time.

Misc. features

There are a lot of features that are often overlooked, like the size of a video card. Some cards are very big. As a result they might not fit into your computer case. Always measure the area around your video card slot before buying a card. Another good feature is 3D application specific presets. Many video card drivers come with settings that optimize performance with most of the popular 3D applications. Not only do these presets improve performance, but they help to prevent crashing as well. Color correction is also a good feature to have. Monitors have controls for adjusting their display, but the control you get from within the video card is much better. This allows you to adjust your display so precisely that it matches your output, i.e., TV, film, print, etc. How loud is the video card? Many people forget that lots of video cards have cooling fans on them. You have to sit next to your computer all day. If noise is an issue, then you might want to ask around to see if any of the cards that you are choosing are noisy.

Is your computer still too slow?

If you've upgraded your RAM and you've upgraded your video card and your computer is still too slow, you might want to upgrade your central processing unit (CPU.) This will definitely be the most difficult upgrade. Many non-computer savvy people will be better off taking their machine to a computer shop for this upgrade. Often CPU upgrades involve moving tiny switches inside the computer to get the new CPU to work. One wrong move and you could ruin your computer.

"My Computer is too slow, it is time for a new one."

Of course, if your computer is non-upgradeable then you should have probably bought a new one in the first place. If you have not, hopefully the new video card and new RAM you bought will work in a new computer.

Do you need a new computer?

If you are going to buy a new computer rather than upgrade, here are a few tips. Buy as much RAM as you can afford. If your budget will not allow you to buy the absolute best CPU and a lot of RAM, then consider getting the next best CPU so you can afford the RAM. Remember, even a computer with a very fast CPU will practically grind to a halt if it runs out of RAM.

If your budget will allow for it, get a computer with two CPUs instead of one. You might want to check to see if your application supports two CPUs before you do this. But it is not required. Why? Having two CPUs has more benefits than just speeding up your 3D application. It allows you to perform multiple CPU intensive tasks simultaneously. For example: You can render a preview of your current animation while you work on an image in your favorite 2D paint program, check your e-mail, surf the web, manage files or work on another animation entirely.

If your program does support two CPUs then purchasing 2 CPUs may benefit you in more ways than you think. The main benefit is gained in rendering. Two CPUs are almost twice as fast as one CPU when rendering. So, if you plan on doing a

"With Phil here as our fall-back, our animation systems are virtually fool-proof."

lot of heavy rendering, you will want to consider getting two CPUs. You also might "save money" by getting two CPUs. A two CPU machine usually has a greater lifespan than a single CPU machine, i.e., people tend to keep them longer because they are much like having a computer that is twice as fast as current single CPU machines. Another way a two CPU computer can save you money is with regard to rendering licenses. Many rendering engines are sold at a fixed price per computer regardless of how many CPUs are in the machine. In this case, having a two CPU computer is much like getting another rendering license for free. If those licenses are thousands of dollars, but the second CPU will only cost you two or three hundred, it makes sense to buy two CPUs.

There are machines available that have more than two CPUs. Performance does not usually double when you go from two CPUs to four. You will probably see a sixty to seventy-five percent increase. These machines are a lot more expensive. Often it is cheaper to buy two computers than to get a machine with four CPUs in it.

Additional hardware

In addition to a computer, you might want to purchase a few other items. A scanner or a digital camera will make texture map creation much easier. With one of these items you will no longer be limited to the images you already have digitized or can find on the internet. Another really helpful accessory is a drawing tablet. This is an item that looks like a thick piece of paper. It comes with a plastic pen. Moving this pen across the tablet will move the mouse across the screen. Pressing down on the pen is much like pressing down on one of your mouse buttons. A drawing tablet will help you the most when working in 2D paint programs. Many say that using a mouse to operate a 2D paint program is like painting with a brick. Some people find that they like using a tablet with 3D programs as well. Tablets come in many different sizes. The larger they are, the more they cost. See if you can try out some of the different sizes before you buy one. Some people cannot work on the smaller ones, while others say that the large tablets make their arms tired.

Drawing tablets are invaluable.

There is usually a direct correlation between tablet preference and the size of the drawings that you like to make. Most people that like to "draw big" will want a larger tablet, while people who doodle in the margin of their books and create many small sketches often prefer smaller tablets.

3D Software for intermediate users

As with your computer, you've probably outgrown your "beginner" 3D software too. When you were a beginner, cost was very important. You did not want to invest thousands of dollars in a 3D program only to find that you were not really cut out to do 3D animation. Now that you are an intermediate level 3D artist, you'll need to spend a little more to get a more powerful 3D program. There is a whole new level of 3D software that you should consider.

Which 3D programs are available? What can I expect to pay?

Unlike beginner 3D software, the programs listed here usually have a maintenance program associated with them. Here is how it works. Every year you can pay a maintenance fee to the software manufacturer in addition to the purchase price. This fee entitles you to free support and free upgrades. Sometimes it also includes special training materials and courses. You are not required to pay a maintenance fee. But if you don't, then you will be charged for software upgrades and support. Often these charges can add up to much more than the yearly maintenance fee. Additionally, you won't save any money by waiting a few releases to upgrade. For example: You have version 5 of a piece of software. Over the past 2 years you have not upgraded and you didn't have a maintenance contract. During that time three releases have come out. (5.5, 6 and 7.) You have finally decided that it is time to upgrade. You've noted that every time a release came out the company charged $500 for it. This does not mean that you can buy the latest release for $500. This means that it will cost you $1,500 to upgrade. ($500 for every release you skipped.) If the maintenance fee was $500 a year, then keeping your maintenance current would have saved you $500!

There are basically two price levels for 3D software: "high-end programs" that cost more than $4,000 USD and "low-end" programs that cost less. The prices of these programs sometimes fluctuate. Some of them are so expensive, that it is much like buying a new car. When purchasing those programs, it is entirely possible to haggle with the reseller and get a better price.

3D software programs that cost less than $4,000 USD

3D Studio Max: www.discreet.com
Cinema4D: www.maxon.net
Electric Image: www.electricimage.com
Lightwave3D: www.newtek.com

Houdini Select: www.sidefx.com
Maya Complete: www.aliaswavefront.com
Shade: www.expressiontools.com
Softimage|3D: www.softimage.com

3D software programs that cost over $4,000 USD

Houdini Master: www.sidefx.com
Houdini Escape: www.sidefx.com
Maya Unlimited: www.aliaswavefront.com
Softimage|XSI Essentials: www.softimage.com
Softimage|XSI Advanced: www.softimage.com

How do I choose a 3D program?

By the time you become an intermediate 3D artist, you will probably have a good idea what program you want to concentrate on, but this does not mean that you have to limit yourself to just one. Many 3D artists are skilled in two or three of the most popular programs. This really helps them get work as they have a wider range of marketable skills.

Note to beginners: Once you have chosen a 3D application, stick with it till you feel you've become an intermediate user. It is not recommended that beginners dive in and learn multiple programs at the same time. It is difficult enough for many beginners to grasp the basic concepts of 3D, much less the different ways each program deals with those concepts. Once you've learned one 3D program, it will be much easier to learn another.

If you don't know which 3D program(s) you want to concentrate on, then use the same steps listed in the beginner section to decide: asking friends, colleagues, and professionals; doing research on the internet, in chat forums and mailing lists; getting demo versions and test-driving programs, etc.

The plugin dilemma – both a blessing and a curse

Often cheaper programs rely heavily on third party tools (plugins) to perform many of the tasks that are already built into the more expensive programs. If your demands on the software are not very heavy then you can usually get away with this type of program. However, if you plan on producing very complex, mission critical work that often extends past the programs limits, you might want to consider something a little more complete.

Plugins are an excellent solution to many of today's 3D problems. However, many third party plugins come with varying levels of support, compatibility and stability. What if you need plugin A and plugin B to produce effect C. If plugin A will not work with plugin B then the effect either becomes impossible to produce or requires cumbersome workarounds. Another thing to consider is that plugins are expensive. Many times the cost of the plugins plus the cost of the application makes it much more expensive than its higher priced counterparts. The cost savings gained through the use of a lower priced program is often an illusion.

On the other hand, software that supports a wide variety of plugins can do jobs that no other can. The more plugins available, the more options you have. Low budget software coupled with a few exceptional plugins can outshine even the most expensive software in some areas. This combination is often used for special situations where no other option is available. Another huge benefit that programs with large plugin communities enjoy is the freeware plugin. The more plugin developers a 3D program has, the more likely there will be free plugins. This is a major benefit. Most of the time, downloading, installing and learning how to use a free plugin to do a particular job can actually take less time than doing the job manually. Furthermore, next time you have to perform that same job, you've already got the plugin.

Paint programs for intermediate users

As an intermediate artist you are going to need something for editing images, something better than the free programs you used as a beginner. There are a lot to choose from. As with 3D software, you will have to try them out and see if they will work for you. Many companies offer downloadable "trial" versions of their paint software. If you are really low on money, you'll probably want to choose an application from the "$100 or less" category. However, 2D paint programs from the "$100 or more" category do not cost that much more and they are well worth the money. You should seriously consider upgrading to one of the "$100 or more" 2D software packages.

Paint programs that are $100 or less

Corel DRAW Essentials: www.corel.com
Digital Image Pro: http://pictureitproducts.msn.com
ImageForge Pro: www.cursorarts.com
Lview Pro: www.lview.com
Paint Shop Pro: www.jasc.com
Photogenics: www.idruna.com
PhotoImpact: www.ulead.com
PhotoPlus: www.serif.com
Photoshop Elements: www.adobe.com
PhotoStudio: www.arcsoft.com
PhotoSuite: www.roxio.com
Pixel32: http://pixel32.box.sk

Paint programs that are $100 or more

Deep Paint 2D: www.righthemisphere.com
Painter: www.corel.com
Photoshop: www.adobe.com
Qpaint: www.quantel.com

Compositing software

Compositing is a process where at least one image is super-imposed onto another. The most common example of compositing is shown every day during the weather forecast. The graphic of the weather map is displayed and the meteorologist is super-imposed on top of it. It looks like the meteorologist is standing in front of a giant television screen, but in reality, they are standing in front of a giant green screen. The computer is taking everything in the shot that is green and replacing it with the weather map. In the end the meteorologist is composited into the scene. There may be another layer composited on top as well. Perhaps it is the name of the meteorologist, the local time or the station ID.

Tools like this are commonly used in computer animation to assemble elements that have been created by different 3D artists or at different times. As an intermediate artist you are going to need something to composite images with too. Until now, when you wanted to assemble pieces of a render into a final image, you probably used a paint program. If you were lucky, a compositing program was included with or built into your 3D application and you might have used that instead. If your built in program works well enough for you, then you can probably skip this section. However, if you don't have a compositing program at all, you are going to need one. As a general rule, beginners don't do much compositing. This is why compositing is not mentioned in the "beginners" section of this chapter.

Which one do I choose?

The logic behind choosing a compositing program is very similar to that used when choosing a 3D or paint program. (Considering costs. Asking friends, colleagues, and professionals. Doing Research: on the internet, in chat forums and on mailing lists. Getting demo versions and test-driving programs, etc...)

There are two very different types of compositors, node based and stack based. The type of compositor used is often determined by the user's preference. Each type requires a slightly different type of thinking and therefore attracts a different type of person. Taking each type of compositor for a test drive is the only way to determine which type is best suited to you. Keep in mind, just because a person prefers one type to another does not mean that they cannot operate both. It is a good idea to learn one of each as it will make you more flexible in the long run.

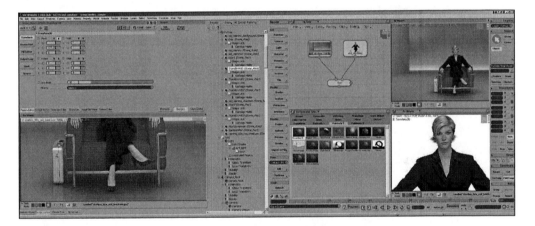

SOFTIMAGE|XSI FXTree is a node-based compositor

Node based compositors

A node-based compositor uses individual nodes to represent images and effects. These nodes are connected together with lines that represent the flow of information. For example, if you wanted to composite a rendered image of a plane onto an image of a sky you would need at least three nodes: one representing the sky, one representing the plane and one that composites those two together. This particular node is usually called an over node, since it composites one image *over* another.) Softimage FxTree, Apple Shake and Digital Fusion are three examples of node-based compositors.

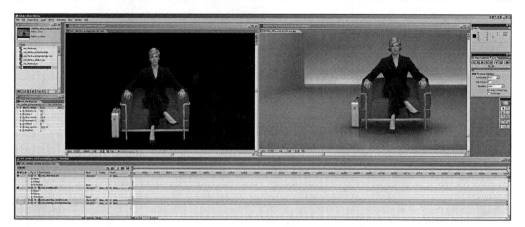

Adobe After Effects is a stack-based compositor

Stack based compositors

A stack based compositor works by stacking one image on top of another. Images at the top of the stack will cover up images at the bottom of the stack. For example, in the plane example above, you would want to put the sky image at the bottom of the stack and the plane image on top. Adobe After Effects, Newtek Aura and Discreet Combustion are examples of stack-based compositors.

Compositing programs come in four levels:

Free, moderately priced, expensive and very expensive.

Compositors that are $0 :)

Cinelerra: www.heroinewarrior.com/cinelerra.php3
Jahshaka: www.jahshaka.com

Compositors that are $5,000 or less

After Effects: www.adobe.com
Aura: www.newtek.com
Combustion: www.discreet.com
Digital Fusion: www.eyeonline.com
Houdini Halo: www.sidefx.com
Liberty: www.libertydesigntools.com
Shake (Mac): www.apple.com/shake

Compositors that are $5,000 to $12,000

FX Tree: www.softimage.com
Nuke: www.d2software.com
Qeffects: www.quantel.com
Shake (Linux): www.apple.com/shake
Xpress: www.avid.com

Compositors that are $12,000 to $500,000 plus

Avid | DS: www.avid.com
Flame: www.discreet.com
Inferno: www.discreet.com
Henry Infinity: www.quantel.com
IQ: www.quantel.com
Media Composer: www.avid.com
Piranha: www.ifx.com
Symphony: www.avid.com

Operation specific software: 3D Paint Software

As an intermediate user, you will more than likely want to try out some "operation specific" software to help tackle tasks that your 3D program may not handle. For example, many 3D programs come with a built in 3D paint system. A 3D paint system allows you to paint directly on a 3D object, rather than a flat texture as you would in a paint program. If your software does not have a 3D paint program or the built in program is lacking, then you might want to consider one of the 3rd party 3D paint programs listed below.

Amazon: www.ifx.com
Deep Paint 3D: www.righthemisphere.com
Flesh: www.dnasoft.com
Studio Paint: www.aliaswavefront.com

Tracking Software

Some 3D programs also include tracking software. Tracking software allows you to take live footage, extract the motion of the camera that shot it and apply that motion to the camera in your 3D software. If your software does not have a tracking program or the built in program is not very good, then you might want to consider one of the 3rd party tracking programs listed below.

Bojou: www.2D3.com
Icarus: http://aig.cs.man.ac.uk
PFTrack: www.thepixelfarm.co.uk
Match mover: www.realviz.com

Landscape generation software

Sometimes you just need a landscape and you need it fast. Believe it or not, there is a category of 3D programs out there just for that. They are called landscape generators. They produce relatively decent results considering the very short amount of time it takes to produce these results. These programs are nowhere near as flexible as the 3D animation software you are currently using, but they are fast and do not cost very much.

Bryce: www.corel.com

World Builder: www.digi-element.com

Terragen: www.planetside.co.uk

Vue d'Esprit: www.e-onsoftware.com

Advanced users

By the time you have become an advanced user, there is a good chance that you will have had an animation job or will be enrolled in a graduate level educational program. As an advanced user, you will probably have a specialty, animation, modeling, texturing, lighting, rendering, etc. Most advanced users tailor their computer for that particular job. For example: A technical director that does a lot of tasks involving file manipulation, compositing and rendering might need very fast, very large hard drives but could do with a slower than average video card. An animator that is interested in fast visual feed back but rarely pushes their hard drives to the limit would be perfectly happy with slow hard drives and a top of the line video card. As an advanced user, you will probably have been exposed to enough computer hardware and software that you will not need any help when purchasing a computer.

Back up your work

Regardless of what level of animator you might be, it is imperative that you back up your work. Beginners are especially guilty of thinking "it can't happen to me". There are many different ways of backing up your work, from creating disks of your work to elaborate backup systems that backup your entire machine in the middle of the night. It really does not matter what you choose, just make sure that it gets done.

I've got my computer and software, now what do I do?

Once everything is up and running you'll need to start learning how to use the software. Just about every animation program on the planet comes with tutorials. Do those tutorials! Many people start by picking around the interface till they begin to understand how the program works. You can learn how to perform a lot of functions this way, but you might not learn the best way to perform those functions. Often doing a tutorial is just as much about workflow as it is about where the buttons are and what they do. Once you have gone through the tutorials, consider doing them again. 3D software is very complicated and trying to remember how to do something you have only done once can be almost impossible.

Read the manuals. This can be the most difficult part of learning a piece of software. Some manuals are thousands of pages long. If you are serious about learning your software, read everything. If you do it in your spare time, it will not take you as long as you think. Try reading them each night before you go to bed, on long trips, the bus, the subway, or an airplane. Once you have finished doing the tutorials start working on small projects. Put what you have learned to use. It will help you remember it later on. There is no need to put off working with the software till after you have read the manuals.

Create some small motivational projects for your self. If you are interested in doing television commercials, then create an animated commercial. Record some audio from a commercial that you particularly like and do a simple animation to it. But remember, the audio for the television ad will probably be copyrighted. Using this copyrighted audio in your own personal experiments should not get you into trouble. Just don't try to make money off of it as the material belongs to someone else.

If you are interested in working in the games industry, then make some video game style characters and objects. Keep in mind that most games rely on a technology that renders them in real time. As a result their geometry and textures have to be created in a specific way so that they will work with the current level of gaming technology. This level is constantly rising and its limitations are changing. If you are interested in doing video game art, it is recommended that you do a little research before you start.

If you are interested in doing special effects for television or movies, then set up small effects shots. If you see a particular effect in one of your favorite movies then try to emulate it. The possibilities for these personal projects are endless.

If you feel that you have gone as far as you can with your current project or that you have worked on it for too long and are tired of it, start a new one. Some projects are doomed to fail. Perhaps they were not set up properly or the initial idea turned out to be a bad one. If this is the case, move on. Hanging onto a doomed project is one of the biggest mistakes beginners tend to make. Don't waste your time. Create more projects. Not only will a new project inspire you, but you will also learn much more and much faster working on many projects than you will on one.

As you create these projects, show them to industry peers, either over the internet or in person. Continue to refine the good ones and throw out the bad ones. With a few good projects created, you have the beginnings of your demo reel, which is your key to getting a job in computer animation!

*"We're not that different, Phil. You want
a better salary and I want a better animator."*

Demo Reel: Basics

What's the single most important thing you need to get a 3D Animation job? Your demo reel!

Most people need a demo reel to get a job. There are a handful of superstar animators that can land a job based on who they know, or more likely who knows them. But that is not going to happen to the average "Joe animator," you. You need to make one in order to get work. Unfortunately, just having a good reel is not enough. Not only do you need to get it into the hands of the right people but they have to watch it too. It's not as easy as it sounds. There are a lot of dangerous traps that you'll want to avoid and there are loads of great opportunities that you won't want to miss. Not knowing where these two things are and how to find or avoid them can keep even the best demo reel from doing its job or being seen by the right people. You'll find many, many examples of these "traps and opportunities" scattered throughout this book.

What is a demo reel?

A demo reel is most likely a videotape containing a short collection of the best work that you've ever done. Think of it as a commercial for yourself, a sales tool. It's the single most important tool you'll ever use when getting a 3D-animation job, especially if it's your first one. You've got to make it as good as you

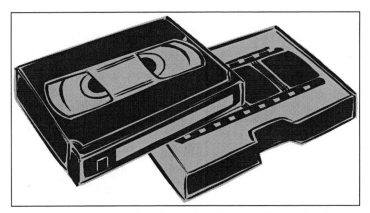

For years VHS has been the demo reel standard

possibly can. It should be designed to show off just how much talent you have. It also needs to demonstrate to the employer that your skills would be a valuable asset to their company and that you should be called in for an interview. You might be one of the most talented people on the planet but if that does not show in your demo reel then you're not likely to get that job and your talent will be wasted elsewhere.

Length

The first and most simple rule of demo reels: keep it short, three minutes or less, but not too short. Ten seconds is probably not enough. Put your best work on first and leave something that is fairly good for the very end. If you put your best work last (or even in the middle) then the person that looks at the demo reel may eject it before they get to the good animation. If you have 15 minutes of great demo reel material then try to narrow it down to two or three minutes. I have heard of people getting jobs with reels that were under 30 seconds, but that is very rare. However, in this case the 30 seconds contained incredibly phenomenal work.

I think if it was up to two seemingly equally talented candidates, one with a long demo reel showing good work and one with a short reel including a carefully chosen selection of their absolute best work, I'd be more impressed with the short reel simply because he or she took the time to be more discriminating. But that's only one factor that goes into hiring a person and it's easy to get theoretical. Personality and background can go a long way to tip the scales from one side to the other.

Mark Ainslie
Senior Animator
Guru Animation Studio
www.gurustudio.com

If you really want some of your longer pieces to be included on your reel then try putting them at the end. Put excerpts and (if you have them) other works that are of equal quality at the beginning. This way people have the option to watch the "best of" portion at the beginning without sitting through an entire piece.

Your reel length can be a little different based on a reel you are sending to get hired at a studio/production house vs. a reel you are sending to do a show for a client for getting a job somewhere, [but] the 1-2 minute rule is a good one. Even if you show all your extended shots later on the reel, you should throw together a 1-2 minute montage at the start. Any recruiter is only going to watch 1-2 minutes of a tape, and then make their decision. If you put all extended sequences (30seconds to 1 minute) then most likely a decision about you will be made based on the first project or 2 that you show. A 1-2 minute reel that includes a variety of your clips gives a great overview of your work. Fast. And this is what someone watching your reel really wants to see. They'll decide if they like a shot of yours based on 1-10 seconds. If they see something they like in 10 seconds, 1 minute more of that project won't change their mind.

When I put together my last reel, I had 14 shots from 6 projects in a 1-minute montage. It wasn't everything that I've worked on, but it kept things short and was a good representation of my recent work. When I went to interview I had extended footage with me.

When creating a reel to present a body of work to a client, it's a little different. Usually they are up for a more extended show. So it's good in this case to have a more extended montage, and definitely throw extended examples on a reel.

Also it's good to have a burn-in title (watermark) over the footage you send out or else sometimes (rarely) you'll find an unscrupulous client (or person from a client agency) is showing your work as their own. Just recently I heard another story about a producer who showed work that was done by the brother of the person to whom they were showing the work too!

Josh Reiss
P I X A R
www.Pixar.com

Don't Repeat!
It's not a good idea to repeat anything on your reel except your name and contact information. It will only look like you are trying to meet some sort of artificial "time requirement" for your reel. This will make the viewer think that you are just adding "filler." The viewers have rewind buttons on their VCRs. If they want to see a section of the animation over again, let them choose to do so and not be forced to.

Mediocre work
If you have to think twice about putting something on your reel, leave it off. Don't include older work or "middle of the road" quality work just to make your reel longer. It will only bring the overall quality of your reel down and lower the chances of getting a job. You are only as good as the worst piece on your reel. Employers will remember the worst thing you did because it will stick out. It is also an indicator showing what your "minimum quality work" will look like. If the quality of work is below their standards then they might think twice about hiring you.

Try to be different
There are a million demo reels with spaceships on them. You are not the first one to animate a space battle or dinosaurs or robots or tanks. If you are a student, or you are making your demo reel at home, then chances are you can do whatever you want. Pick something that you enjoy, something that other people have *not* done over and over. This expression of creativity has the potential to impress the viewer and help your reel stand out from the crowd. The easier it is for them to remember your work the better your chances of getting hired.

© CHARLES BARSOTTI

"It's his creative time."

Music

You might not want to include shots on your demo reel that require sound to be appreciated. Often your demo reel will not be watched with the sound on. But when it is on you'll want to make sure that you have not chosen music that will give the viewer a headache. (Heavy rock and grating hardcore techno is probably not a good choice.) On the other hand you don't want to put them to sleep with some very slow ambient or classical music either. Try to edit your reel so that the cuts will match the beat of the music. Edit your reel so that exciting shots appear when the music becomes more intense and slow peaceful shots are paired up with softer portions of the music.

I think demonstrating the ability to put together an exciting demo reel, with good use of music, good editing, good title graphics, etc., is all to the potential employee's credit. It shows a hint of creativity, and an interest in the context of the material that bodes well for that artist's all-round usefulness. We all want to work alongside interesting people with more to them than the ability to write a really great wet rock shader. I'd watch it once with the sound up and see if the reel sucks you in, and if it does, THEN turn down the sound, and watch it with the magnifying glass out, and a finger on the pause button.

And, I have to say, I wouldn't want to work alongside anyone who put, say, Chris de Burg [(cheezy 80's pop music)] on their reel.

But I still stand by what I said about respecting the ability of someone to cut a great reel of their work to music, and produce something exciting and involving to watch. Sure, you then need to have a good look at the shots themselves, and find out what it was that the person actually contributed to each shot. But - I would be wary of a mute reel of great shots just cut together with black spacing, no titles. Lack of initiative I think. If I had to choose a person to animate an action sequence, I'd pick the one with the funky reel of great shots over the one with the dreary reel of great shots.

Paddy Eason
The Moving Picture Company
www.moving-picture.com

Formats

NTSC is the standard television format for the United States, but if you are sending your work to a foreign country then you should have your reel converted into a different format. (PAL or SECAM) These are the three most common standards in use around the world. A recording made in one format is usually incompatible with machines that are designed to play a different format. However, it is relatively easy to convert your reel from one format to another. After the conversion, the tape can be viewed on the appropriate equipment. Almost any video duplication bureau will be able to convert your demo reel for a small fee. If this sounds like something that you're going to have to do, then take a look at the NTSC, PAL, SECAM section of this book.

How many reels should you make?

How many reels should you send out? It may take 100+ demo reels to get your first job. Until you land your first gig, treat job-hunting as if it were your full time job. But, with this said, don't just send out demo reels blindly. Target companies that you can work for. For example, if you are a poor modeler then you probably don't want to send your reel to Viewpoint, a company that mostly builds custom models.

Clearly list the position that you are applying for

Put the position that you are applying for at the beginning of your reel, on the cover and on the labels. This way it will be easier for your tape to make its way into the hands of the person that hires for that department. It wouldn't do you or the employer any good if you are applying to be a modeler and your tape gets sent to the character animation department.

If people don't know what job you are applying for then it will be hard for them to place you. Let's say you want to be a character animator. Not only is your animation good but the characters on your reel just happen to have great textures too. If you don't specify which position you are interested in, you might accidentally get hired as a texture artist, while the animator position is filled by someone else. This probably wouldn't be the ideal situation for you, especially if you don't really like texturing. Of course, this is much better than not getting a job at all. But imagine how you'd feel if you found out that you could have had the character animation job if your reel had just gone to the right department.

Include a shot list

A shot list is just that: a list of all the shots on your reel with information that details your contribution to that particular shot. If you don't include a shot list there is no way that the employer will know what you did or didn't do, making it much harder to decide if they should hire you or not. Without a shot list they might assume that you are trying to say, "I did everything on this reel," which could be really bad, especially if you didn't do all of the work yourself or if some of the work that you didn't do is really low quality. The last thing you want is to lose a job because they thought the animation was horrible, when you were the texture artist on that job.

Try to put at least some of the shot information, on your reel. A simple text overlay, shown at the appropriate time saying "Modeling and Textures" or

"Animation and Rigging" will suffice. This will help demonstrate your ability to communicate visually, not to mention printed shot lists can be tough when large groups of people are watching the same reel. It is difficult for a dozen people to watch a reel while one person tries to read the shot list and keep up with the video. While on screen information like this is important, don't leave the printed shot list out of your demo reel package entirely.

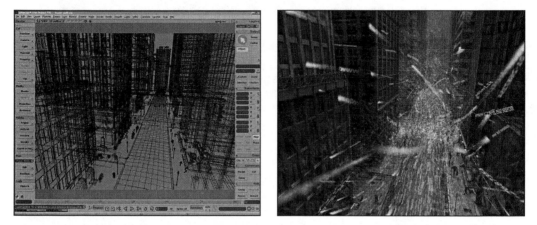

Visual information, that shows just what your contribution to the shot was, can really help the viewer understand just what you did.

I invest a lot of time and effort making "how-to" breakdowns of the shots on my own reel, and every interviewer without exception has told me how much they appreciate that. It helps to reveal how much work went into something that might otherwise be invisible, as well as showing exactly what contribution you made to each shot. I'd highly recommend that approach for TDs, lighters, effects animators, and compositors.

Alec Bartsch
Lead Lighter and Technical Director
The World of Tomorrow
www.illusionati.com

What should you include on a printed shot list?

1. What was it done for? (Film, TV, games, etc.)
2. What types of tools did you use to complete your work? (Software, hardware, off the shelf, proprietary?) Of course, you might want to leave this off too. Depending on the situation. (See the section called: "Should you list what software you used?")
3. Break down every shot. Did you work on the entire thing? Did other people help you? If so, what did you do and what did other people do?
4. Use this opportunity to expose computer graphic (CG) elements. Show them "Turning into wire frames" so that people can see what was real and what was CG.

A perfect reel to me would be one that includes final material with prudently-trimmed development material to show what the individual contributed, listed in the same order as the c.v. so that the points made are clear and easily communicated. This sort of reel is incredibly rare.

Kevin A. Bjorke
Computer Animation
www.botzilla.com

Watch every single tape

There is one thing that you absolutely have to do and it's not any fun at all. Watch every single one of your tapes… and not just the beginning either. Watch the entire video. There is nothing worse than sending out blank or severely damaged tapes.

Whee, what fun…
Watch every single tape.

I've seen demos that had the title card, a couple of seconds of animation and then nothing but snow. I've also seen reels that looked perfectly normal on the outside but something went wrong with the internal workings of the videocassette. As a result, the video was so full of artifacts that it was impossible to watch. I've also seen videos where the tape has snapped in two. Of course, those are unplayable and a reviewer definitely is not going to take tie time to sit down and try to splice the tape back together. They are just going to throw it away and put the next tape in.

After you've watched your reel, rewind it! An un-rewound demo reel has a much higher chance of going unwatched than one that has been rewound. There is a reason that video stores used to charge you when you brought back tapes that were un-rewound. Aside from greed, it was just a hassle.
Be kind, please rewind. ;)

Videos that you've had converted to foreign formats will probably be impossible for you to watch. Depending on how much you've got riding on these videos, you might consider buying a low-end multi-format VCR so that you can watch them. These VCRs do not cost much more than a good single-format VCR. If you are low on money, look around for a used one. If you are really low on money, rent one. If you are broke, see if you can borrow one, or at least borrow time on one.

Use a new tape!

The ideal tape is new and short. If you do record your demo reel on a used videotape, something I don't recommend by the way, try to have it erased. If you don't have access to a bulk tape eraser make sure that you record over

Choosing the right tape is important

anything else that might come on after your demo reel is over. There is no way of knowing whether that animated TV show you taped 5 months ago will get watched or not. What if they think you worked in it? It is, after all, on your tape. If they call you in for an interview and only then find out that it was a mistake and you had nothing to do with the show, it will seriously hurt your chances for a job. But more than likely the people viewing your reel are smarter than that. (One can only hope.) They will be able to tell the difference.

Leaving old television shows on your reel just doesn't look very professional. It might make the reviewer think that you weren't serious enough about making your reel and in turn might not be serious about getting a job. Sometimes, when you record your reel using a really cheap VCR, the older content will leave artifacts or show "ghosted images" through the newly recorded content. This is rare, and might not lose you the job, but it certainly won't help. There are, however, times when leaving old content on a video can automatically lose the job for you.

On two different occasions I've seen demo reels that were recorded over pornographic material. That's fine, as long as that material is totally erased. (Because you never know who might see this video.) This material was not erased and it did not bleed through the newly recorded content, but it came on immediately after the applicants end title card faded out. Personally, I don't care what the applicant watches in their spare time, but in this case the individuals that were doing the hiring were offended by what they saw and threw the tape in the trash. (And one of them had pretty good work on it.)

Then there was this showreel of a cute young redhead who briefly worked at the Mill in London. She never made it past the stage of Runner before being fired but when she was fired, and her showreel was finally watched, it revealed an 'art' piece at the end of her and some guy in a very compromising position. As I said, she was very cute :)

Porl Perrott: porlp@btinternet.com

What brand should I buy?

Most of the time brand does not matter. Try to buy the cheapest tapes you can find. If you are worried, buy a brand name like Fuji, TDK, Sony or Maxell. But don't buy all of them at first. If you find a place that has very cheap tapes and are the exact length that you want, buy three or four. Inspect the tape shell. Compare it to some of the other VHS tapes you've got lying around. Does it seem strong enough to survive its trip through the mail? If so, then make test dubs of some of your animations. Take the tapes around to different VCRs and see what they look like. If they are good, then buy the as many as you need. If not try again with some slightly more expensive tapes. There is no reason to go out and buy really expensive videotapes to dub your reel on to. At the most, a demo reel gets watched 10 or 15 times. (And that number is pretty rare) This is not enough to wear even some of the cheapest tapes out. If it looks good the first time, it will probably look good the 15th time.

Pull the record tab out

After you've dubbed your reel make sure to take out the record tab. This is the little plastic tab located on the lower left hand side of the tape spine. Once you've taken this tab out the tape cannot be recorded over unless a special VCR is used or the hole created by the missing tab is filled again. Believe it or not, there are a lot of VCRs that have the record button right next to the play button. Many VCRs have "One Touch Record" that, when pressed, start up a timed recording instantly. It is really easy to wipe out a demo reel with one of these "features." Don't let this happen to you.

 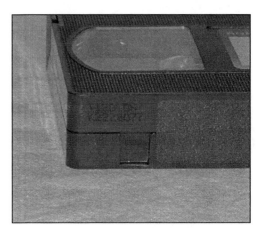

Removing the record tabs isn't the easiest task. (Imagine trying to remove 100.) You either need a very small screwdriver, some thin keys or extremely tough fingernails. If you don't have a small screwdriver, don't want to cut your fingers to shreds or ruin your keys you can use a "paint can" opener.

These can be found at just about any store that has a paint department. They are only supposed to be given to customers that are purchasing paint. But most of the time, if you ask, they will just give you one. This tool is perfect for removing record tabs. It has a bent tip that is just small enough to slide behind the tab. Once behind the tab, a small tug is all it takes. Not only will this tool prevent you from scraping your fingers and breaking your fingernails, but it will also speed up the tab removal process. Once you get going, it only takes a second or two to do each tape. You can easily do a hundred demo reels in just a few minutes.

Next time you are in a hardware store, pick up a "paint can" opener. You'll be glad you did.

Make sure all extra items included in your demo reel are secure

Make sure all extra items in the tape case are secured to the case somehow. It's not very much fun to open up a reel and have 10 things go spilling out onto the floor. If you plan on putting multiple items inside your case, then try to find one that has a pocket to hold all of them. If you have a lot of items then you might also think about getting a non-standard tape case that will hold it all, but don't over do it. If the case is too large and unwieldy then it won't be easy to mail or carry around. Usually smaller is better. This is discussed further in the chapter called: "Demo Reel Packaging and Mailing".

The "backup" résumé

As we all know, computer graphics companies are always a whirlwind of activity. People are busy and things can get lost very easily. This is why you might want to tape a copy of your résumé to the inside of your tape case. Of course if you are using a standard tape case a normal 8.5" X 11" piece of paper will not fit. I suggest reducing your résumé's font size and printing it out again. A good size for your "backup" résumé is 7.25 inches by 4.25 inches. You'll probably be able to print two of these "miniature" résumés on a single sheet of standard paper. (Some printers cannot print that close to the edge.) Try printing them out with a thin black border around each. This will make it much easier to cut out, it will keep your lines straight and everything will look a lot more professional.

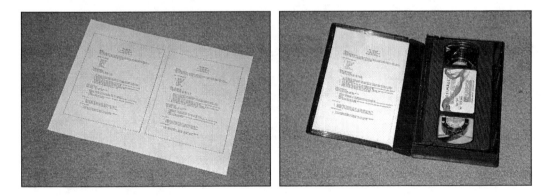

Creating small "backup" resumes to attach to the inside
of your tape cover can help the reviewer tremendously.

Make everything look the same

If you are including multiple pieces of information along with your demo reel, there are a few things you can do to help the reel reviewer keep track of it all. First, make everything look the same. Use the same font everywhere: the reel labels, your résumé, your cover letter and anything else you might include. Use the same color of paper. White is best, but paper with a hint of color can be fine too. Don't use dark paper or something that is hard to look at, fluorescent paper, for example. It won't photocopy or scan very well and is sometimes hard to read even if you are looking at the original. Making all of your materials look similar is a lifesaver when trying to match résumés with reels. Imagine this: A reviewer is carrying a large stack of demo reels and résumés. They trip, sending everything flying all over the place. Putting it all back together again is going to be a nightmare. But, your materials will be easy to match up, since they all look the same. After a long afternoon of reviewing reels, one of the hardest parts is getting organized afterwards. Picking up and matching all the pieces together will be a lot quicker if they are easier to identify.

Using an icon or a still

Some people like to put a small still image from their animation in the corner of their tape labels, résumé and cover letters. While this looks nice, and it certainly makes is easy to identify your work at a glance, it can cause problems when your résumé and cover letters get scanned or photocopied. This sort of thing is a double-edged sword and its use must be carefully controlled. It can be a good idea to use a still on the tape label. But you might not want to put it on your résumé or cover letter. The problem leaving it off your résumé or cover letter is that they will not look exactly like the tape label any more. With a little work you can minimize this problem. Try making a smaller still or using creative design to separate the still from the text. For more detailed information on this topic see the "cover letters and résumés" section of this book.

Sounds like a waste of time doesn't it?

You might be wondering, "what's in it for me? Sounds like a lot of extra work, I should be spending more time on my reel, not all this other stuff." Your reel is very important. You want to make viewing it a pleasant experience. All this might not seem necessary to you, but it is. Don't think you have time? Then do all of this work while your animation is rendering. Still not convinced? Ok, then think read this scenario.

An awesome reel was sent in that only had the animators first name on the label. The label said "Phil's Demo Reel." There was no contact info anywhere, not even on the tape. But, all was not lost because, included with it was a resume that contained all of the important information. Unfortunately the tape and the resume were completely different looking from each other. The tape label used some strange wavy font and the resume and cover letter used Arial. This would have probably been fine if it had been the only reel that had come in that week. But there were a lot more and during the weekly "demo reel viewing session" his reel and resume got separated. A few of the reels were so bad that they were sent down to tape recycling immediately after being viewed. Their corresponding resumes and cover letters were thrown away. Phil's resume accidentally got thrown away too, but his tape got put in the "prospective employee pile." A short time later the prospective employee pile was narrowed down to a few select people and it was decided that everyone in that pile should be hired. Everyone in that pile got a job except for Phil. Not because he wasn't any good, but because they couldn't get in touch with him. Two important lessons are learned here. Make your resume and cover letter easily associated with your reel. Put your contact information on the tape label and in the demo reel.

Demo Reels: VHS versus CD-ROM

Which is best? VHS or CD-ROM?

Many people think, "It sure would be awesome if I put my demo reel on CD-ROM. There could be interactive menus, a cool interface, great sound and graphics too! It'll be great, every one will love it. I'll get the job for sure then!"

Think again.

At the time of this writing CD-ROM demo reels are not considered a good idea unless you are applying for an interactive content creation position. Even then it's not always the standard. VHS is the standard tape type and PAL, NTSC or SECAM will be the standard format, depending on where you are sending the tape.

CD-ROM demo reels are usually more hassle than they are worth. Imagine you are the interviewer and someone sends you a CD-ROM demo reel. You walk over to your computer and put it in. It does not work. So you throw it in the trash because you don't have time to figure out why. Why don't you have time? Because you've just picked up the stack of 100 VHS demo reels sitting on your desk and have to watch them too. You know that they will probably work and each video won't eat up any more than 5 min of your time. A VCR is a VCR. They are not as different from each other as computers are. It's like fast food, it's not great, but you know what you are getting, it will do what it's supposed to (fill you up) and you know that it won't take long (which is why it's called fast food).

Still not convinced? Here are some of the problems that can cause a CD-ROM demo reel to "not work."

Say you made the CD on a Windows machine. It might not work in an SGI, a Mac, a SUN, a Linux or even in another Windows machine. This could be because you made it an executable file that only works in Windows. Maybe they use Windows NT, 2000 or XP and you made it in Windows 95 (shudder) or Windows 98 or Windows ME and as a result it won't load or is incompatible. It might be that you used director to make the content and the director plugin doesn't load. Many SGI,

Linux and MAC machines can't play certain types of Windows created CD-ROMs at all. It is possible to make a "Hybrid" CD-ROM but even then it still might not work. If you've never done it before and don't have an SGI, a Linux machine or a MAC around to test it on, then you'll never know.

If the CD-ROM does manage to open up, and your interface springs to life then there is a chance that the video files won't play. If that doesn't happen, then everything up till then is useless. Not only have you wasted the reel reviewers time but you've probably annoyed them as well. Your movies might not play because the right codecs are not installed on the computer. Even if you include the codec on your CD-ROM it is unlikely that they will want to install it just to look at your CD-ROM. Some of the operating systems out there don't even support a few of the most popular codecs. Obtaining an install for your codec for all your target operating systems might be impossible. Then there is the issue of formats. What do you choose? Mpeg, QuickTime, Avi? Maybe a proprietary format like Bink or Smacker? What happens if you send someone a movie that requires Quicktime and they don't have it installed? Again, I doubt that they will install it just because you've sent them a CD-ROM demo reel that requires it.

Let's say that everything goes well and the reviewer is able to watch your videos. If they have a really fast computer then your animations might play back too fast. If you are trying to get a character animation job and your timing looks bad because the animation is playing back 5 times faster that it was on your machine then you are probably not going to get the job. With VHS you know your animation will play back at a certain rate, it will never change and you can control it ahead of time.

The person watching the reels might not have time to navigate through your "super cool menu system" so they don't bother. Maybe they do get the CD to work, but in the end can't figure out how to work your menus so they never get to see your animation.

Not everyone is a good person nor do they have good intentions like you. There have been at least 2 instances where "Demo reel CD-ROMs" were just an easy way for some malicious individual to sneak a virus into the company. Maybe it was someone that didn't get hired earlier, or it was a previous employee that got fired. Perhaps it's an individual from a competing CG house or someone that has no morals and wants to "take out" the competition. Regardless of who it is, they'll probably never put their real name on the CD and the chance of finding them is going to be pretty slim. But the main problem is not persecuting the person that did it; it's recovering from the damage that was done. (Lost work, down time, overtime for employees repairing the damage, etc...)

Some companies don't even have the computers on their desks at all, just a monitor, keyboard and a mouse. At places like this, the computer might be kept in a "clean room" or a "machine room" where access to the CD-ROM drive is very limited. Rarely, if ever, is anyone going to go through the necessary steps to watch your CD-ROM if they have to walk into another room just to insert it into the computer. Some places don't even keep these machines in the same building. If that is that case, then the chance that anyone will watch your disc is probably less than 1%.

While the "clean room" scenario mentioned previously is pretty rare, this one is even more so. Believe it or not, some of the people out there that do the hiring don't even have computers at all. (Or they have a computer, but it does not have a CD-ROM drive.) It's hard to believe, but there are people like this. They might just have a palm pilot, a sub-notebook, or something like that. Think about it. How many people do you know that have a VCR? How many have a computer? The number is probably close to the same, but there is always someone that has a VCR but does not have a computer. To them, a CD-ROM reel makes a great coaster!

What happens if your CD-ROM gets scratched or broken in the mail? It might not play at all then. I've seen VHS tapes fall down stairs, get stepped on, sat on, and still play fine… (Try that with a CD) But, keep in mind: just because they are more durable does not mean that they will play the tapes if they get dropped. But their chances are probably much better than a CD.

Most companies watch demo reels as a group so they can pick out people they want to interview. Often this is done in a conference room or a client room. This type of room usually looks like a small theatre with a TV and a VCR. (Often there is no computer or computer access is difficult.) These companies are very busy, they often watch reels only when they have a little free time, like lunch or during a break. They try to watch as many as possible in as little time as they can. They don't want to leave any out, because they might miss that "golden demo" that they've been looking for. Even though don't want to miss any, they are going to skip over a CD-ROM demo reel. They are comfortable, everyone is probably eating and they don't want to go crowd around a computer and watch someone try to figure out how to work this CD-ROM demo reel. Some companies just say "VHS only, no CD-ROMs please." Now what do you do? If you didn't make a VHS demo reel, you don't have a chance at that company.

I would have to say that when reviewing a stack of "reels" it is a pain in the neck to get the group of reviewers to go over to a workstation or other location to see the odd one or two DVD or CDROM "reels". They tend to make their way to the bottom of the pile.

Michael Defeo
Model dept. Head
Blue Sky Studios
www.blueskystudios.com

Many post houses and production companies are not the cleanest places. I don't mean that they are dirty, I mean that people are so busy that their desks are often covered with papers, manuals, magazines, food, etc... It's really easy to lose a CD-ROM in the mix. A VHS tape on the other hand is big. It's much harder to lose than a CD-ROM. Also, since it's so big, it will stick out in the pile of "stuff" on their desk. This will serve as a constant reminder to the reviewer that they need to watch it so that they can get it off their desk.

CG professionals are busy. Make your reel easy to watch.

Making a CD-ROM demo reel takes a lot of your limited time. It's not easy to make and it's very easy to screw up. You are better off spending your time making your animation better or working a little extra to make some cash to pay for good transfers or buy equipment for laying your demo to video. But, if you are determined to make a CD-ROM demo reel, then make sure that you send a VHS version along with it.

You might be thinking:
"What about a DVD or a Video CD?"

It's better than a CD-ROM but still not ideal. When played in a computer, a Video CD (VCD) reel is likely to run into the same problems that a normal CD-ROM style demo. A VCD is usually a CD that uses MPEG compression to store the video and audio. A VCD can be played on a lot of stand-alone DVD players and on almost all computers with a DVD-ROM or CD-ROM drive. But you need a software-based decoder/player. It is unlikely that anyone is going to want to install the decoder just to watch your VCD.

What about a DVD or A VCD? No, at least not yet anyway.

In my experience with VCDs I've seen about a 25% failure rate when it comes to playing them in a stand-alone DVD player. Since you are not around to see if "Company A" has a VCD compatible DVD player then I'd steer clear of VCDs. The only time I have seen a VCD that was 100% effective is when it is played in a portable DVD player. (The kind that looks like small laptop computer) A friend of mine did this at SIGGRAPH one year. He carried it around and showed his demo to prospective employers. Since he had total control of the creation and playback of the VCD, it worked great. That trick actually got him a job.

What about DVD? Maybe DVDs will be a good idea in the future, but at the moment it's just not as widely accepted as VHS. A lot of companies have DVD players, but not all of them have one in the demo reel viewing area. You can make

DVDs in your computer at home, but the burners are much more expensive than regular CD-ROM burners. Also, blank DVDs are more expensive than blank CD-ROMs. Even after spending all that money there is no guarantee that it will play in all the DVD players out there. I think that DVD demo reels will be the standard in the future, but as of this writing, they just aren't there yet.

Format issues are exactly why I'm going wait on doing a DVD reel. Cost isn't the issue. Add that to the schlep factor and I would simply say don't bother doing DVD reels until the formats are 100% standard and you can count on "Joe Studio X" having DVD players lying around. By schlep factor I mean that if I have to schlep over to the other side of the studio to the fancy client Dog & Pony suite to view an artist's DVD reel, I'm probably not going to do it until I have some spare time, which is basically never.

VHS? I've got 3 within my line of sight, so a reel WILL get looked at.

Ben Fischler - Technical Director and Animator
WildBrain - www.wildbrain.com
www.benja.org

There are some advantages of using VHS aside from compatibility. With tape, the quality is not as good as it is with most forms of digital displays. Because of this, the quality of your render does not need to be that high. If you have a deadline and don't have time to get your demo rendered with "the best possible settings" then do a short test using a lower setting and lay it off to tape. If it looks good then go with that instead. If not crank, it up a notch and try again. As long as your animation renders finish on time and it looks good, it does not matter what settings you use. Also, shuttling through VHS on a frame-by-frame basis is not as easy as it is with CD-ROM or DVD. If you make some mistakes in your reel they will not be as easy to notice.

As someone sending out reels: The thing I like about the idea of a DVD reel is that you have a great master with which you can make VHS reels to send out (I wouldn't send out DVD reels). I say this because it's currently a pain in the ass to find a free dBeta to make VHS dupes of or update my reel, but if I had the DVD master I could make copies at my leisure.

As someone watching reels: Use VHS. Where I currently work there's not a readily accessible DVD player, but there are VCRs *everywhere* (there's one sitting beside me right here). This is true of all the places I have worked in the past, as well.

Dean Warren
Technical Director
Nelvana Ltd.
www. Nelvana.com

Demo Reel: Designing

Gathering your animation

Where do you get all of the segments used to create your demo reel? If you haven't learned to archive your projects properly, then when it comes time to make your demo reel, you might have lost or be unable to find certain pieces. Improperly archived work will make the demo reel creation process more stressful and time-consuming than it should.

One of the most important steps in archiving anything is to make sure that everything is named properly. To prevent cross –platform problems do not use spaces in your file names. If you have a file called "ARS Flood scene 9.scn" then rename using underscores to "ARS_Flood_scene_9.scn" This will ensure that no matter what type of computer you are working on now, future computers or different operating systems will be able to open this file. Avoid using common names like "render.tga" or "test.jpg."

Try to use names that will make sense to you in case you have to decipher them 8 months down the road. Let's say that you worked on a series of commercials for Acme Corporation. In this series you did ads for rockets, grenades and motorcycles. The "grenade" commercial had 23 different shots. When you are working on version 8 of shot 14 you might want to name it "acme_grenade_shot_14_v8." Of course this is just an example. As you work you will develop naming convention specs that make more sense to you. Regardless of how good you think your naming conventions are, it is still good to have a cheat sheet. When you are done with a project, write up a small text file that describes them, what you did in them and what the naming conventions mean. Make sure you do this relatively soon after the project is over. If you wait too long, it will no longer be fresh in your memory and you might have forgotten important elements of the production.

When you are archiving a project, make sure that you not only get the models, but that you get the textures, shaders, background/live action plates and all of the other materials that went into producing it, including the software that you used to create the work, if possible. Applications come and go. What if you need this data a few years from now and nothing you use will open it? It won't be a problem for you. Just install the "ancient" software, load up your files and save them out in a different format.

Demo reel creation is not the only reason for archiving projects. If you need a certain effect or model that you've already created, it will be a breeze to find if you've archived it properly. This sort of workflow can really impress an employer. There is no good way to put "I am very good at keeping up with/archiving my work" on your demo reel. But your archival process might be a good subject to bring up at an interview.

If you create your work with future archiving in mind, you'll save yourself a lot of trouble in the long run. It's a good idea to render out a sequence of video resolution images regardless of what the job's target resolution was. Storing them as a sequence of frames (or in a format that uses lossless compression) that are always the same resolution will allow you to integrate them very easily into a demo reel. Imagine trying to make a demo reel from multiple sources that are all different sizes. Some of them might have been compressed with QuickTime, some saved as an Avi and some in mpeg format. In the end, a few of them will look great and others will look blocky with compression artifacts and size interpolation issues.

Reel content

The type of job that you are applying for should dictate what you include on your reel. If you are applying for a job as a character animator then think twice about including "Flying Logo" work, unless the flying logos are animated in such a way that it shows good timing and animation skills. But the opposite is not always true. If you are applying for a flying logo job, then you might think about putting your flying logo work on as well as your character work. They'll probably think, "If he can do character animation then flying around logos should be a breeze for him." Not that flying logo work is bad, but character work is usually much more difficult and most of the people out there know this.

While this goes with out saying, you should also have good work on your reel. Companies are not going to hire every applicant, only the exceptional ones. Even if a company is not hiring at the moment, they might pick you up if your work is beyond amazing. How do you know if your work is above their expectations? Just look at anything that they have done. If your work is just as good or better than theirs, you should have no problem impressing them. Their work has a minimum level of quality that must be maintained. They will probably not hire employees whose work dips below that. If you fall into that category, then you will need to work a little harder before you apply there.

Things that should not be on your reel

Just as there are things that should always be on your reel regardless of what type of position you are applying for, there are also things that you should never (or almost never) put on your reel. Don't put every tutorial animation you've ever done on your reel. In fact you should probably not put any animations of tutorials on your reel. Most working professionals can spot a "tutorial animation" a mile a way. Not only does this look cheesy but it automatically puts you into the "extreme novice" category. (Not a good thing if you ask me.) Don't show any "plugin animations" either. That is, don't put anything on your reel that only looks interesting because you used some "cool new plugin" to make the effect. Anything that you can do with the push of a button or that takes just a few seconds will probably be frowned upon. Most people will say "Hey, he just used "super duper multi-quantum plugin X" to do that effect, it probably took him 10 seconds! That doesn't show any talent... what a joke!" This is especially true if you use an automated character animation plugin or program. You didn't really do the animation, you just pressed a few buttons, so don't try to take credit for it. If you get hired to do character animation and you can't really animate but you managed to fool the employer into thinking that you can, then you'll eventually get into big trouble. The first time you are asked to animate something that does not have built-in motion, forcing you to you create it from scratch, you'll be busted.

I've received demos from people, which consisted of tutorials from my own books. I guess some people don't do their homework before sending a reel.

Dan Ablan - www.danablan.com
AGA Digital Studios, Inc. www.agadigital.com
Chicago

No more tanks, space ships, robots, etc... please. (We've seen enough already.) Don't fade your name in and out for 45 seconds at the beginning of your reel either. Reviewers don't have 45 seconds to spare and will probably start fast-forwarding your video, running the risk of passing over vital portions of your demo reel.

"At one of my previous jobs we hired a guy because his reel had some work on it that was the same 'style' as the project we had coming up. He didn't know the software that we used but we hired him and were going let him learn it as the project ramped up. After a couple of months (more than enough time to transition to this new software) he was still not able to produce anything useful at all. This was puzzling because the work on his reel led us to believe that he should be able to produce at least something. So the boss gave him a little "test." He asked him to create a model that was almost identical to one on his demo reel. He couldn't even do that. This sent up a red flag and forced us to do a little more background research on him. We found out that someone else did 75% of his reel and that the remaining 25% was done with a 'tutor' sitting right next to him. This way he could just ask how to do things and what buttons to push, rather than figure them out himself. Needless to say, he was fired. The sad thing is that he couldn't understand why he was let go. They told him that his position had been "downsized." Then turned around and brought in a new employee the next day."

Procedural graphics

"Procedural type" graphics programs usually fall in the same category. If you used a landscape generator that makes great renderings at the touch of a button, then you probably won't be qualified to be a terrain modeler. Here's why. Years ago, before procedural landscape generators could create decent looking terrain, there was a company that needed a terrain modeler. A demo reel came in to that company that had some very nice landscape fly-though animations on it. The terrain looked pretty good and there was a lot of it. When the person that made it was asked if he modeled all of the terrain, he said "yes." When asked how long it took him to make everything on the tape he said, "Just a few weeks." This was an incredibly short amount of time to create such a huge volume of work with a wide variety of landscapes. When asked what he used to model the landscapes he said "It's beta software, I'm a tester and I can't discuss it because of my NDA. Sorry." He managed to convince the person doing the hiring that he had modeled everything on the reel. Of course, in his mind he had modeled everything, he pressed the "create tree" button and the "create mountain" button, etc…. He was a newbie and didn't really understand that he was actually "lying" about his skill level. (Yea, right!) He got hired and, unfortunately for him, couldn't produce anything useful. Eventually he was let go.

There is an exception to the "No procedural software" and "No plugin animations" rule. If you wrote the procedural software or the plugin that was used to create the imagery,you should put that on your reel. Good computer animators that are also good programmers are very rare and extremely valuable.

Color bars

Don't put color bars on the beginning of your reel, unless you are applying for a position where your job would include color control. In the early days of computer graphics people always put color bars on their reels. But not any more. Now, it's just one more thing for the reviewer to fast forward through. Color bars were usually put on there to help the viewer adjust the TV so the color could be viewed correctly. If you think that anyone watching your reel is going to adjust his or her TV set so that your reel looks good, think again. This almost never happens. If they did this for every tape that came through the door then they'd never finish watching half of the reels. I did see one reel where the color bars were used in the animation and it was pretty interesting. But it was put in the middle of the tape so that the reviewer didn't fast forward over it thinking that it was "another video with color bars at the beginning"

Transitions

When editing your reel, don't put a lot of "stock" wipes and transitions on there just because you think they look cool. If they serve the story or if they were created by you then they belong on there, otherwise, leave them off. You might have just discovered that neat spiral shaped transition button in your editing application, but most everyone out there has been using (abusing?) it for years. Demo reel reviewers are tired of seeing these things used poorly over and over again. Bad transitions won't ruin your chances for a job, especially if the content on your reel is great, but if it irritates the reviewer then it certainly won't help. If you aren't good with transitions or have not used them very much then just use fades and cuts.

Stolen work

This should almost go with out saying but, never put other people's work on your reel unless you worked on the project with them and never put work on your reel that you had nothing to do with. Seems pretty straightforward, doesn't it? You'd be surprised how this happens more than you think.

I once got a reel when I was at Disney Imagineering that had *my* work on it. Pretty amusing. I let the guy know he was busted, but I don't know what happened from there. I believe *he* got the work either from a reel I sent a company, or from one of the software companies whose reels my work appeared on. I *was* amused until one day I realized that if my work was being passed off by someone else, and a company got a reel from him before me, they might think it was *I* who lifted it. The only way around that is to take that material off your reel and replace it with newer stuff. But it still stinks when that happens.

Steph Greenberg
CG Character Animator
www.casadiablos.com/steph

Not everyone out there is a "good person." The CG community is not very big. If you try to pass off work that was done by someone else as your own, you will get caught, maybe not today, maybe not tomorrow, but soon. When this happens it will become very hard for you to get a good job in CG again.

Often people get away with stealing work, passing it off as their own and getting a job with it. They think they are safe once they get the job, especially if it's with a large company where they can just "blend in" and hope that it will never be noticed or that it will be forgotten. Actually the exact opposite is true, the larger the company, the better the chances of catching someone like this.

At my last place of work I had to interview a guy applying for a computer graphics teaching job. His reel consisted of the example QuickTime files that were supplied with a particular software package edited together to a piece of techno.

He used the "foreign language" thing to get around my questions about the origin of the material (where a foreigner speaks English perfectly well for most of the conversation but starts to talk nonsense when answering direct and potentially revealing questions). Also, on two separate interviews (no, I didn't ask for a second one, my boss did :-) he gave differing answers to those questions. The first time I eventually got out of him that yes, these were the example files, but that he had gone through tutorials and other such-like himself to generate the animations personally. This was obviously untrue, because the probability of getting all the animations absolutely identical in every way is somewhat unlikely. The second time he said he hadn't done any of them, but that he did know how to use those features and could generate such things if I paid him to.

I politely suggested to him that using other people's work on his demo reel is a bad way to demonstrate his skills to a company who is looking at hiring, even going as far as explaining to him why (as he didn't seem to understand when I said just that). When I had explained it all, he seemed quite offended and taken aback, and gave me more of that "foreign language" pigeon-english thing.

He also had a bunch of "work" he'd developed - course material and such, but he wouldn't let me see it.

...unless I paid him $10,000. (I'm not kidding, and the really sad thing is that I believe he had conned someone in a government department into purchasing this stuff to later develop courses around - I doubt this could ever happen however as I'm familiar with the process and if it was to be given the official stamp it would need to be independently verified by persons in the industry - but it's unfortunate for the person who okayed the purchase).

He did do me the tremendous honor of getting an inch thick binder of this stuff, and flicking through it with his thumb and fore-finger - presumably so I could look at it in awe and wonder and think "Wow, look at that, it must be genuine, because there sure is writing on EVERY page!" I offered to write and sign an agreement stating I would never use or divulge any information, even just so I could see one page - he refused.

He eventually walked out seemingly quite offended when I suggested we sit down together and work on an object he had pointed at and claimed he could model. The modeling technique he was going to use was called the "mesh spline" technique. A non-computer animator in the room at the time picked up that this guy seemed to be using non-existent jargon words.

He was keen though - he did submit some *obviously* original material when asked (he claimed it was 17 seconds of animation, but it was actually the same two 1-2 second shots cut together at different points). 'Nuff said.

(And you can't say I didn't give him a damn good chance!! :-)

Anthony Milas
antt@paradise.net.nz

How not to get a job as a 3D animator by Bruce Steele
(with many contributions from Glassworks 3D)

· Don't rewind the tape, leave that for us to do, honestly, we're not as busy as you.
· Phone up to tell us you have a show reel and your going to send it; we need to know that.
· Ensure you send it to the wrong person or department and, for that personal touch,
  make sure you spell their name wrong.
· Just send the same unchanged letter to every company and be sure to ask us about job
  opportunities at some other company.
· Put everything you've ever done on the tape, especially if it's really awful.
· Put all the good stuff at the end, we will happily sit through several minutes of rubbish to
  get to the good bits; we won't chuck it in the bin after 30 seconds.
· Don't make a VHS, show how clever you are by using a multimedia CD or DVD.
· Make sure you use an obscure multimedia-cd format that only works on your computer.
· Be sure to have a chrome flying logo - we rarely see flying logos - we'll be impressed.
· Failing that, show us some X-Wing and Tie-Fighters (or computer circuit boards).
· Try to find some way of using images of yourself on the show reel.
· Make sure you use some really bad keying; we especially like blue or green edges.
· Save on electricity by having only one dim light in your scene and don't bother to under
  stand TV gamma or check your VHS. We'll assume it all looks fantastic on your computer.
· Please include bad copies of characters and scenes from the movies to show us just how
  much better you are than ILM or PIXAR.
· Ensure that we have no way of knowing what work is yours by having 18 of your mates
  work on your show reel too. We'll give you all a job.
· Have rolling credits with lots of names at the end just like in the movies, we like that.
· Have a long title sequence at the start so we won't notice the rubbish in between.
· Take on such a large project that you can't finish; it demonstrates how you can still miss a
  deadline even when you have total artistic freedom, six months and no client.
· Try to make sure you have stuff on your reel that is not your work.
· Especially try to include some work we did and pass it off as your own.
· Try to include in-jokes and bad humor; we will be laughing so hard we won't look to close
  ly at the quality of the animation.

· Be sure to include a techno sound track to make you stand out from the crowd.
· Don't put any contact details on the tape. Put that on a bit of paper so it won't get lost.
· Avoid a one-page CV. Use several pages and tell us about your hobbies.
· In fact, write lots of stuff on paper. Then even if your work is crap we'll give you a job.
· Finally, write an angry letter telling us how we've missed out on the opportunity of employing the next John Lasseter. We won't stick it up on the notice board so everyone can have a laugh at what a plonker you are, honestly....

The scary thing is that every one of these suggestions are based on actual events!

Should I put a "story" on my reel?

How much impact does a good story in a show reel have on your chances to get a job? Not as much as you think. Is it necessary to have the most amusing reel in the world, or can you get by with just good scenery, nice models and clever animations? There is no way to be 100% certain. However, a story is more important on some types of reels than others.

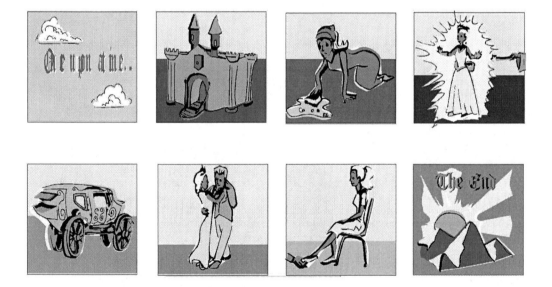

If your reel has a story and the story is good, then you might be one of the fortunate ones that gets their reel passed around to other people. This is basically free advertising for you and can really help you get a job. Your reel will be seen by people that would have otherwise never have seen it. If you are one of these lucky ones, you are almost guaranteed that some one will call on you simply because of the sheer number of people that will see your reel. Also, if you have a reel like this, making it available on the internet will really increase your chances of getting a job. Many animators pass links to good demo reels around to each other, increasing your exposure with little or no effort at all.

If you are going for a job as a character animator, a story will help you more for that than it will for any other type of CG job. Character animators must be able to successfully convey emotion in their work. It will be easier for people to understand the types of emotions the animator is trying to convey if those emotions are surrounded by a story. Humor can be very helpful. If you know how to make people laugh, put something funny in your demo reel. It will definitely make it more memorable. But what if you don't know how to make people laugh or aren't any good at telling a story? Re-do one! There is nothing wrong with re-doing a story that you have read/seen somewhere else. Just make sure that you credit the original source.

There are times when you might not want to do a story or you might want to pick a different one. For example: You've chosen a story and are finding that it is difficult to animate. It is getting in the way of doing your best work. In this case, either you need a new story or you need to forget the story idea altogether. The story is not getting you the job, the animation is. Don't sacrifice quality just for a story on your demo reel.

Multiple versions

Some people are fortunate enough that they can either have multiple versions of their reels made for different types of prospective employers or have the equipment (and knowledge) to do it themselves. If either of these apply to you then there are a few things you need to keep in mind.

If you've done a lot of different types of animations then pick the ones that have the same style as your target company. Think about the type of work that your prospective employee is doing and try not to send them work that might prevent you from getting the job. For example: If you are trying to get a job at a company that does children's animations or religious videos it might not be a good idea to send them work that is really violent or filled with sexual imagery. It might be great work and you could be the nicest person on the planet. But all they know is your reel, not who you really are. Making a demo with something that would offend most people is rather questionable anyway. But if you do, the animation (or whatever) had better be top notch. Otherwise you're classified as "trouble maker" rather than "progressive." On the other hand, if you are applying for a job at a company that does sexually oriented graphics then sending them a video with a lot of religious imagery probably wouldn't help you get the job either. They might think that you are too easily offended and that you'll probably quit after a short period of time. They are looking to hire one person for your position, not two. Training new people is expensive and slows down production.

Specialized design options

There are some other "not so obvious" changes that you can make to your reel that could help you out. I've seen some people put the name of the company on a title card at the beginning of the demo reel. It might say something like: "John Doe's Demo Reel: Custom created for ABC Animation company." This can go two ways. It can impress the people that you sent it to, or they might believe you are some kind of a fanatic and think twice about hiring you. This rarely happens though, as most people are amazed that you took the time to custom make the reel just for them.

Should you specialize or generalize your reel?

For example: Should your reel be nothing but models or should it show an entire animation production, done by you. It depends on what position you are going for, what the company needs and whether or not you have the ability to specialize. In larger companies, specialization is a highly desirable trait. These places have artists that just model, just texture or just animate, etc. At places like this the CG work is done in an "assembly line" fashion. Everybody does what they are best at and in the end the final product comes out the door. If you are really good at one thing (like modeling, for example) then you should try to get a modeling job by just showing lots of really good models on your reel.

> The best one (meaning worst of course) was a reel of a guy who could vomit on command. Swallowing multi colored oatmeal, and regurgitating them separately. He felt this would naturally lend itself to visual effects.
>
> He writes: "please notice how I am able to do this and also make freaky faces."
>
> Amazing....
>
> Bill Zahn
> Industrial Light and Magic
> www.ILM.com

Texture Artist
Modeler
Compositor
Roto-Artist
Character Animator
Character TD
Render TD
Lighting TD

© HENRY MARTIN

"You will have to wear many hats when working at a small company."

If you are trying to get work at a game company then you'll probably want to focus on something like low polygon modeling or texturing with low-res textures. Most game companies tend to be a little smaller than the average CG studio so it will be easier for you to get a job there if you have multiple skill sets. (Note: The world of gaming is growing very rapidly and, as a result many, game companies are growing faster than CG studios.)

If you're going for a job in a small shop, then you're better off with a reel that has a wide variety of different types of work on it. Just make sure that the work is all worthy of being put on your demo reel. At a place like this you are more likely to be handed an entire project where you have to model, texture, animate, light, render and composite everything by yourself. If you can do all of those jobs fairly well then you'll have a good chance of being considered for that job.

> I think having a wide skill set can be good (for instance, we encourage that here), but there will probably always be places that need to hire people to just do one thing, very, very well. Sometimes, to be the best, you need to focus. If there's something you naturally can do exceptionally well, you may want to focus on that rather than spread out your natural abilities over many things (and this business has no shortage of those!).
>
> John Coldrick
> Senior Animator
> Axyz Animation
> www.axyzfx.com

Traditional work on your reel

You might want to put some of your traditional artwork on your demo reel. It's easiest if you scan the artwork (or photographs of the art work) into the computer and size/crop the images to video res. Once you've done this, you can dissolve/cut between the images on your reel. Try to leave them up on the screen just long enough that the viewer has time to understand what they are seeing, but not so long that they get bored and fast-forward over them. In some instances, your traditional artwork might be too complicated to show in its entirety on a TV screen and be visually readable at the same time. In this case it might be better to show a couple of close ups of the artwork rather than the entire thing. A good example would be a very complex drawing that just looks like a blob from a distance, but when you get really close you can see that it is filled with intricate details.

Modeling reel

These reels aren't very exciting. Because they don't tell a story or have anything particularly fun to watch. Most modeling reels consist of slowly rotating meshes that are shown rendered (fully textured if possible,) shaded and in wire frame. Often the transition from shaded to wire frame is done through a dissolve or a wipe, not with a camera cut. The idea is that shaded and wireframe versions of the model are shown from the same camera angle. Camera cuts from wire frame to shaded, using different camera angles, will only confuse the viewer. Once an establishing shot has been made, follow with a close up of the more detailed portions of the model, usually also in wire frame, shaded and rendered views.

This type of reel is prefect for someone building inanimate objects. But what if you are building a character? Modeling things that bend and squash is usually more challenging than building objects that don't move or have solid parts that don't deform. If you are going for a character-modeling job then you will need to show your models being deformed as if they were being animated. The animation does not have to be great but the deformations have to show that your model will not distort unrealistically or tear apart when animated.

If you aren't very good at animation then find someone who is and ask them for some help. (If they do help, be sure to credit them in the shot list and on the reel.) The last thing you want is to distract your viewer with bad animation. You want them to pay attention to your excellent models and not your poor animation skills.

If you are having trouble setting up the bone system in your models to get realistic bending, get some help with that too. You're not applying to be a character technical director (TD), you're applying to be a modeler. Just because you can't set up the bone system exactly right does not mean that you can't build a good animate-able model. There are plenty of people out there who can't animate or chain up a character to save their life, but their models are first rate.

Try to be a little creative. A reel with nothing but spinning models will be pretty boring. Create a reel with a good balance of "boring spinning models" and interesting camera angles and renders. Imagine this: two reels. They both show modeling skills that are on similar levels and most everything about these two candidates is the same. They both meet the minimum requirements to be bought in for an interview. But, one of the reels is "fun" to watch and the other one isn't. In a perfect world both of these people should be called in for an interview. In the real world the person with the more interesting reel will probably be called in while the other might not.

Animation reel

When creating an animation reel from scratch, many people think that they will be making an "epic animation," the type that has fully textured, realistically-lit, high-resolution characters and intricately detailed backgrounds. While this sounds like it will make for an awesome reel, it rarely ends up that way. It's not impossible to create something like this; it's just very difficult to do it by your self. What typically happens is the animator ends up with a lot of really nice looking models and backgrounds that never get animated because he ran out of time or he got a job modeling. Not that modeling is bad; it's just not what he wanted to do in the first place. If he had spent all that time animating instead of modeling then he would probably have a great reel full of animation and chances are that he'd be animating all day instead of modeling.

What you need to get a job as an animator is good animation. Nothing else is as important. Try to create a character that is low to medium resolution, fairly simple but somewhat interesting looking. If you are having trouble designing a character then copy someone else's design. (Just make sure that you give them credit.) This won't be a problem, since you are trying to get a job as an animator, not a character designer. The reason you want a simple character is that you need very fast feed back while you are animating. This makes animation much easier to learn and a lot more fun.

Imagine animating a five thousand-polygon character. Something with such a low polygon count would be very easy to move around the scene. Even with a complex bone system this character would be relatively easy to get good feedback from, even with a "low budget" 3d-computer setup. Now, imagine that you've modeled a character that's so detailed that it's in the "multi-millions of polygons" range. You'd need quite a computer to animate something this complicated. On top of that you'd have to wait for it to render which would take much longer just to get decent feedback on your animation. If you think that's bad, then imagine what happens when you put two of these characters in a scene. Now everything takes "twice as long."

People who are absolutely positive that they want to be a character animator and nothing else will usually learn to animate using "stick men." These stick men are just deformed cylinders and boxes that resemble human and animal forms. Most of the time they are less than one hundred polygons each. They provide very fast feedback and are great for crowd animations. You can easily put a hundred of these guys in your scene and still have amazing feedback.

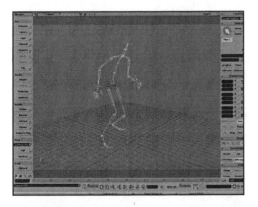 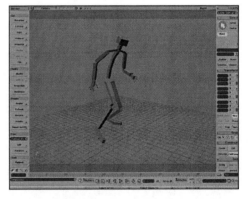

Animation can be learned much faster if you use "stick men" instead of high-res models

Of course there is a lot more to making an animation reel than low-resolution characters. The animation has to be great. There are a lot of people out there try-ing to get character animation jobs. This is becoming one of the most popular areas of computer graphics. The good news (for you) is that a lot of these people aren't very good. (They probably didn't have this book.) =) This means that if you practice a lot and become fairly good at animating then your chances of getting a job are a lot higher than 75% of the rest of the people out there. The bad news is that there are already a lot of really, really good character animators that have been doing this stuff for years. If the market is flooded with these types of people (which happens when a major studio finishes a large production or they layoff a lot of people because of lack or work) then you are going to have trouble getting your dream job. You might have to wait a few months for things to return to normal. But even in times like that it's possible for entry-level positions (those that really good veteran animators typically won't not accept) to be available to just about any one with fairly good animation skills.

So, what sort of animation skills do you need to get a job? Your animation needs to stand out from all the others. Your characters need to look natural, not like a puppet or a robot. Fluid motion is the key. Make sure that objects don't pass through each other. Keep your characters feet planted firmly on the floor, not in it. Also, keep your characters feet from sliding, unless your character is ice skating or dancing. When you are starting out it is essential that you use reference footage. This way, if your character is moving poorly you can just look at the reference to see what the difference is. With out it, the possibility of an amateur finding the mistakes will be much less.

There are many very good books out there that cover the principals of animation infinitely better than I can. For more comprehensive information, see the resources section of this book. There you will find more animation reference material and books.

It is the job of the lighting artist to turn boring environments into interesting ones

Lighting reel

Lighting is a hard job, but lighting reels are relatively easy to construct. A good lighting reel shows what shots looked like before the lighting TD got his hands on it and what it looks like afterwards. If the difference is dramatic then these images should speak for themselves. It will show that the applicant can light a scene so that it fits the mood of the animation. For example, a graveyard shot from a horror movie should have dark and foreboding lighting; bright rays of sunshine would not work here. A good reel also shows the applicant understands the intricacies of lighting: how to use shadows effectively, where to "bounce" light from, how to simulate different types of light, what colors to use, etc. Many lighting TDs are amateur photographers and filmmakers. Often lighting reels contain samples of this type of work. It helps to demonstrate an understanding of lighting in both the real world and in the computer.

Rendering reel

When it comes to making demo reels render TDs have it a little tougher than lighting TDs. It is not as easy to show some of the services that a render TD provides. If there ever was a reel that benefited from a shot list, this is it. A render reel might show final shots from a production with notes in the shot list explaining what they did, since their work can rarely be seen. For example, they might have optimized the antialiasing, motion blur, textures and models so that the scene rendered twice as fast. Perhaps the shot would not render at all. The render TD might have separated it into more passes than normal so that certain elements could render alone, allowing the rest of the scene to finish. Perhaps portions of the rendering needed a lot of manual tweaking and the render TD wrote a small script to automate that. There are hundreds of different things that a render TD does that are not visible. The worst part of being a render TD is that having no control over the quality of the work. If the animation is horrible but the render was quite an accomplishment, it still goes on the reel. Of course, most companies hiring render TDs know this, but that does not change the fact that bad animation is still hard to watch.

Texturing/materials reel

Texturing and materials reels are almost as easy to make as modeling reels. Often they consist of fully textured shots alternating with pictures of the textures that were used in those shots. Some reels even go so far as to show each texture layer appearing on the model one at a time. This gives the viewer a sense of how the material was "built." The more surface types (wood, metal, fabric, skin, plastic, etc.) a texture artist can do, the better. Often the subtle details that make some textures and materials stand out from the crowd are impossible to see on video. As a result this is the type of demo reel that can really benefit from a printed portfolio.

Editing your demo reel

When it comes to putting your demo reel together you have two choices: do it yourself or pay someone else to do it for you. If you are doing it yourself then you will need an editing program. There are a lot of these out there. Just about any of them will do if all you want is a simple demo reel. (Even the cheap programs will work just fine.) If you are trying to create something that is a little more complex, then you'll have to look into the higher priced packages. Once you are done editing, you'll need a way to put your demo onto video. If your video card has a TV output jack then you might be able to use this. If it does not, or if its signal quality is substandard, you'll need to use something else. The cheapest solution is to use a DVD decoder card. These cards are designed to decode the video information from a DVD drive in your computer and play it back on your TV. They are very cheap and you don't even need to have a DVD drive to use one. They will play standard mpeg files straight off of your hard drive. Their output is indistinguishable from that of an ordinary DVD player.

What if you are planning on letting someone else edit your demo reel? While this is much easier, you'll need a good plan before you go into an editing session. Do some research first. Find out what types of files the editor will need, both video and audio. Ask them how long it will take, how much it will cost and if there is anything else you should know before coming in. Once you know what you need, draw up a storyboard. Plan each shot and write out a simple script. Check the timing on all of your segments to see how long your demo reel is going to be. (Don't forget to take transitions into account.) Make sure that the music you choose is long enough or short enough to fit your demo. The more prepared you are when you go into an edit, the better your final reel will be. If you have not prepared you will waste valuable time with the editor and it will take a lot longer to edit than you planned. As a result, it will cost a lot more than you anticipated.

Should I really polish the editing of my reel?

This depends on the type of place that you are applying to for a job. Of course everyone wants a reel that is edited well enough so that it's worth watching, but you don't need an award winning edit unless you are applying to be an editor. However, there are times when a better edit might help you out. If you are applying to be a character animator at a giant animation house then don't bother with anything fancy. Good clean cuts are perfect for this type of reel. All they want to see is good animation. There is no need to put a load of "cool" unnecessary/extraneous graphic elements all over your reel. This will only get in the way of the content. Similarly, do not cut the demo so fast that it's difficult to see what's going on. However, if you are applying for a job at a "motion graphics" facility or an "art house/boutique" (especially in the advertising industry) then a good trendy editing job will help you get noticed. This is the type of reel places like that are really into. These guys like style; they are the types that will more than likely watch your reel with the sound on.

Just because you are not applying to one of those trendy boutiques, does not mean that you should not put any thought into your editing. There is polish and there is sloppy. You do not want to be sloppy. Polishing your edit will always help. It does not need to be flashy, just logical and well done.

You can get away with a really low quality edit, but only if the content is fantastic. (It does not work the other way around.) Don't try to hide bad work with slick editing. Demo reel reviewers have seen it all. If its bad, take it out. If there are technical problems with your footage (dropped frames, bad transfer, etc.) then try to have them fixed. If it is not possible then take the bad footage out unless it is critical to your demo.

A good edit will show that you take pride in your work. It shows attention to detail through visual continuity, quality and flow. If you have the time, a few extra hours in the editing room will make you look just a little bit better.

Tape length and contact info

If you use the standard demo reel format, where your animation plays only once, then you still might want to use tapes that are longer than 5 minutes, even if your reel is only 3 minutes long. With a 10 or 15-minute tape you can record your name and contact information for the remainder of the reel. Here's why you would want to do this: Most reviewers watch a tape and then take a couple of notes when it is over, if they make it to the end. These people have probably watched a lot of reels before they got to yours and have a lot more to watch after finishing yours. It is very easy to forget the name of the person whose reel has just been played, especially if it only showed the name and contact information at the beginning. If you display a title card with your name and contact information at the end of the demo then you can let the tape continue recording and fill the rest of it up with that title card. This gives the demo reel viewer a lot more time to jot down their notes and when they think, "Now, whose reel was that?" All they have to do is look up at the screen for a reminder.

Something else you might want to consider is a small countdown timer. Place it in the corner or at the bottom of the screen. Make sure that it shows up at the end of the reel, just as the name and contact information appear. This sort of thing would say "Time till the end of reel XX:XX" or "This title card will disappear in X seconds," where X is the time code. This takes the pressure off of the viewer. If you just put your name and contact information up on the screen with no countdown timer, they don't know when it will disappear. In order to finish their notes and get your name written down they may rush themselves. That's the last thing that you want. What if the one notation that they skipped writing down was the one that would have gotten your tape watched by the head of a department or gotten you hired later on?

The looping demo reel

The looping demo reel is a reel that plays over and over. This type of demo is rare, but is acceptable. I wouldn't create this sort of reel myself but others prefer it. This type of reel will need a long tape. I've seen people send in these types of reels on standard 2-hour VHS tapes. While this is fine, it does cost more to ship and it has a better chance of having a home movie or sit-com recorded over it. The idea behind this reel is that it will continue to play the applicant's work over and over until manually stopped. Hopefully more people will notice it this way. Most of the time it has a small break, about a min long, that shows the applicant's name and contact information on it. Then the reel starts over again. Unless you have access to a lot of VCRs, then making this type of demo reel takes a long time. At about 2 hours each the maximum number of demo reels that you can crank out in a day is 12. If you make a 3-minute demo that plays once you can easily dub a hundred in just one day.

Name and contact information

There are two things that must go on every reel, regardless of what position you are applying for: your name and contact information. Your contact information should have your physical address in a large bold font so that it can be read easily. It should be centered in the middle of the screen and it should not move. It is very hard to read text that is scrolling up the screen or moving around in any way. The people watching your reel don't care if you've just learned how to make a "super cool heat shimmer" effect. They certainly don't want it distorting your contact information and making it hard to read. Don't let your text run off or touch the edge of the screen either. Pay attention to the safe frame and keep all your text inside the title safe area. This feature is built into just about every animation and compositing package out there, so you have no excuse for not using it. Keep in mind that if takes time to read all of this information. Leaving it up for 2 seconds is not going to work. You are probably not going to be a good judge of how long something should be left up on the screen. Get a friend to watch the tape and ask them if they had enough time to read the information and write it down if they needed to. However, do not put it on the screen for a long time at the beginning of the video. Repeating your contact info at the end is a good idea. If your living space is temporary and you are fortunate enough to know your future address, put both on the tape. Be sure to point out which address is current and mention when you'll be moving to the future address.

If you have an e-mail account, put it on there too. In this day and age there is almost no excuse for not having an e-mail address. Show this e-mail address after you've shown your physical address, not during. Some of the TV's people watch these reels on can be pretty small. Trying to cram too much information on the screen at once is not going to make it any easier to read. If it takes you three or four title cards to get your information across, that's fine, as long as it can be read. If you are creating an e-mail address specifically for correspondence with prospective employers, something I highly recommend by the way, then make it really easy to remember and very simple to type in. An address like Phil6184.netmail@tx.mailcom.com is not a simple address. Try getting something that has no numbers and one word in the domain name. For example: Demoreel@Hotmail.com (This exact e-mail address is already taken. So don't bother.) If you've created an account that will only have e-mail coming from people that want to hire you, then you might want to set it up so that it pages you, calls your cell phone or calls your home phone every time you get a piece of mail. This way you can respond to the job offer immediately and not run the risk of missing an important opportunity. Check with your local wireless or e-mail provider to see if they offer services such as this.

Don't forget to put your phone number on the reel, too. I've seen people call prospective employees the instant the demo reel is finished. They've picked up the phone and dialed the number off the screen. If you've got more then one number, put it on the screen too. Don't forget to put the country code, the area code and any other important parts of your phone number on there.

The date

Should you put a date (month/year) on your demo reel? This is a tough one. On one hand, if you put the creation or dub date on your reel it will already seem "old" before it's even out the door. If you've ever watched an old video that has "coming attractions" at the beginning, for movies that came out ages ago, you'll know what I am talking about. On the other hand, if you don't put a date on your reel people won't know when you made it. If your 3-year-old demo reel lands in a pile of new demo reels it will probably not stand up to current standards. Worst-case scenario would be if your name became associated with "that horribly out of date looking demo reel.... You know, the one with all the morphing and time slice animations in it." There is no real answer to whether putting a date on your demo reel is a good idea or not. You must decide what's best for you. Of course, if your reel contains work from recognizable TV shows, movies or video games, then there will be no need for a date. The work will tell them just how old the reel is.

What should be in the credits?

You know that you'll need to record your name and contact information at the end of your reel, but what else goes there? If you've done a visual breakdown of what you did on your reel then this is a good place for it to go if it is simple enough. Some people also put up a screen or two that says "Thanks" to all their friends and family. This is fine too, as long as it's last. Most demo reel reviewers don't care to read, "Shout out to my little brother Phil." When this card comes up it's usually a cue for the reviewer to hit the stop button.

Should you list the software you used?

Many people wonder if they should list the type of software they used to create the animation on their tape. Normally you should list it, but sometimes whether to list or not can be a tough decision, especially if you use a package that is commonly refereed to as "Low End." Some employers will not even watch a reel because of the software the applicant used to create it. This may sound strange (it is) and it's pretty rare, but it does happen. You need to base your decision on a few different factors. If a company specifically asks for you to list what software you used, then you should definitely do it. If you can't be bothered to pay attention to what the employers ask for, before you even apply for work there, then why should they hire you? If you are applying for a position at a small shop you should list it then too. This is because small shops usually rely heavily on one piece of software and can't always be bothered (or have the time) to train you on it if you have never used it before. On the other hand if the company that you are applying to is large (has a lot of employees) then it might not be necessary for you to list the software that you used. As long as your reel is awesome, it shouldn't matter. If you are really good, they might train you on what they have.

Some companies have their own proprietary software and use very few "off the shelf" packages. In situations like this it's not as important to concern yourself with listing the software you used to create your work because the chances of you using that software in that job is almost zero.

Watermarks will help keep your work from being stolen

Watermark your reel

Always put a watermark on your reel. What's a watermark? A watermark is a small logo that is located somewhere on the screen overlaid on top of the animation. This is the sort of thing that you can see in the bottom corner of just about every present day television broadcast. If your work is displayed in letterbox format then put the logo inside the animated area, not in the black bars at the bottom or the top.

Why do you want to put a watermark on your tape? To prevent people from stealing your work! Some people out there will take other people's demo reels, "re-edit" them and use them to get a job. If there is a logo at the bottom of the screen it will make it much more difficult for someone to steal your work. They will probably just move along to different reel that does not have a watermark. Don't put your watermark in the black area of a letterbox format demo reel. It's too easy to cover up. Eliminating a watermark over animation is more trouble than it is worth.

Sending your reel to a foreign country?

If you are sending your work to a foreign country then you may need to get your reel converted to a different format. NTSC, PAL or SECAM are three most common standards in use around the world. A recording made in one format is often incompatible with machines that are designed to play a different format. However, it is relatively easy to convert your reel from one format to another. After the conversion, the tape can be viewed on the appropriate equipment. Almost any video duplication bureau will be able to convert your demo reel for a small fee.

NTSC

One of the most common formats is NTSC. NTSC is an acronym for National Television System Committee. Because of it's poor handling of color, some people like to refer to it as "Never Twice The Same Color." What ever you like to call it, this system is used in Canada and the United States as well as many other places around the world. It plays back at roughly 30 frames per second (29.97 per second). Its resolution is 720 pixels wide by 486 pixels high.

If you are sending your reel to any of these countries, it will need to be NTSC: Antigua, Bahamas, Barbados, Barbuda, Belize, Bermuda, Bolivia, Burma, Cambodia, Canada, Cayman Islands, Chile, Colombia, Costa Rica, Cuba, El Salvador, Ecuador, Guam, Guatemala, Haiti, Honduras, Jamaica, Japan, Mexico, Midway Islands, Netherlands Antilles, Nicaragua, North Mariana Island, Panama, Peru, Philippines, Puerto Rico, Saipan, Samoa, South Korea, Saint Kitts, Saint Lucia, Saint Vincent, Surinam, Taiwan, Tobago, Trinidad, United States, Venezuela and the Virgin Islands.

PAL

Another very common format is PAL, which stands for Phase Alternating Line. PAL also has a few "nicknames," Pictures At Last, Pay for Added Luxury (regarding the cost of delay line), and People Are Lavender. This format is used in Australia and most of Western Europe. PAL plays back at rates of 25 frames per second. Its resolution is 768 pixels wide by 576 pixels high. Aside from the main PAL standard, two variations exist:

PAL-M. The M stands for "Monochrome." This format is a cross between NTSC and the European PAL system. The PAL-M format is used only in Brazil. Unlike other PAL standards, this one has approximately the same characteristics as NTSC.

PAL-N. This system is a cross between PAL and SECAM. Most PAL-N VHS machines are capable of playing standard PAL recordings, making conversion to PAL-N virtually unnecessary. PAL-N is used only in Argentina, Paraguay, and Uruguay.

If you are sending your reel to any of these countries, it will need to be the standard PAL format: Afghanistan, Albania, Algeria, Angola, Australia, Austria, Azores, Bahrain, Bangladesh, Belgium, Botswana, Brunei, Cameroon, Canary Islands, China, Cyprus, Denmark, Dubai, England, Ethiopia, Faeroe Islands, Finland, Ghana, Gibraltar, Germany (East Germany previously used SECAM), Guinea, Holland, Hong Kong, Iceland, India, Indonesia, Ireland, Israel, Italy, Jordan, Kenya, Kuwait, Laos, Liberia, Madeire, Malaysia, Malta, Mozambique, Nepal, Netherlands, New Guinea, New Zealand, Nigeria, North Korea, Norway, Oman, Pakistan, Portugal, Qutar, Singapore, Somalia, South Africa, S.W. Africa, Spain, Sri Lanka, Sudan, Swaziland, Sweden, Switzerland, Tanzania, Thailand, Turkey, Uganda, United Arab Emirates, United Kingdom, Vietnam, West Germany, Yemen, Yugoslavia, Zambia, Zimbabwe.

SECAM
SECAM stands for Séquential Couleur Avec Mémoire. It's French and it means "Sequential Color with Memory." This format is used in France and Eastern Europe. SECAM has a nickname as well: "System Essentially Contrary to American Method." Like PAL, SECAM also plays back at rates of 25 frames per second.

If you are sending your reel to any of these countries, it will need to be SECAM: Armenia, Azerbaijan, Belarus, Benin, Bosnia, Bulgaria, Burundi, Chad, Congo, Croatia, Czechoslovakia, Djibouti, Estonia, France, French Guyana, Gabon, Greece, Guadeloupe, Guyana Republic, Hungary, Iran, Iraq, Ivory Coast, Latvia, Lebanon, Libya, Liechtenstein, Lithuania, Madagascar, Mali, Martinique, Mauritania, Mauritius, Mongolia, Morocco, New Caledonia, Niger, Russia, Saint Pierre, Senegal, Slovenia, Syria, Tahiti, Togo, Tunisia, Ukraine, Zaire.

There are some places that use slightly different or multiple standards. If you are unsure, check with the company that you are applying to. Ask what they can take, before sending your reel there. For example: Greenland, Egypt, Luxembourg, Poland, Monaco and Romania use both PAL and SECAM. In East Germany SECAM was the standard, but it has been changed to PAL. As a result there are still quite a lot of SECAM players there. A format called MESECAM is used in the former Soviet Union, Eastern Europe, Greece, Egypt and Saudi Arabia. (Most

VCRs in these countries can also play PAL) MESECAM stands for Middle East SECAM. (A rarely used low cost variation on SECAM.) Playing a SECAM tape in a MESECAM VCR (or the other way round) will produce a black and white picture. MESECAM was created to build MESECAM VCRs which worked with PAL televisions instead of SECAM televisions (PAL televisions were less expensive).

Rendering different formats

Of the various broadcast formats, standard NTSC and PAL are the most common. You will want to create your final output to work in at least one of these formats. But, if you are very serious about applying to countries that use different formats then you might think about rendering your work so that it works well with both.

In order to create animation that looks right on a TV screen you need to understand the concept of interlacing and non-square pixels. When you are generating an animation for playback on the computer, each frame is displayed in its entirety. However, when you are sending that same animation to a TV only half of the information is shown. For example: NTSC television resolution is 720x486. But at any given time, only 360x486 of a single frame is showing. This is because standard television signals "interlace" one frame of animation with the next. What looks like 30 frames a second is really 60 fields per second. The television draws the odd lines for one entire frame (1,3,5,7,9, etc..) first, then it draws the even lines of the next frame. (2,4,6,8, etc...) This means that frame one is "blended" with frame two. (This happens so fast that they look like they are both showing at the same time.) If your renderer has a "fields" option and you've used it, then field one of frame one is blended with field two of frame one. (But going this route is not recommended.) It may sound complicated but the workaround is actually very easy. For NTSC animations you are better off rendering at 60 frames per second (50 frames for PAL) and interlacing them with your favorite compositing program. This will take twice as long to render and you will be "wasting" lines in each frame, but the results usually look better. If you do not have the time to render at double the frame rate then cut your horizontal resolution in half or cut your frame rate in half and use the "fields" option in your renderer.

As if interlacing doesn't provide you with enough of a hassle, you've also got to deal with what are called "non-square pixels." NTSC displays "squashed" images at 720x486 that are "stretched." to look like they are the right aspect. On the TV screen they look right, but on your computer they turn spheres into ovals and make everyone look half a foot shorter and a few pounds heavier.

The way to beat this is to render slightly taller images and "squash" them before going to tape. It may take a little longer to render, but it's much easier to work on shots that have the correct proportions. For NTSC images you will want to work at 720x540. When it is time to go to tape, just scale the images to 720x486. PAL images on the other hand are the exact opposite. PAL stretches images in the other direction. On the TV screen they look right, but on your computer they make everyone look half a foot taller and a few pounds lighter. (Maybe this is why European animators are not as overweight as American animators?) To solve this problem render your images at 768x576 and scale them to 720x576 just before you go to tape.

You can let your software render out the proper aspect images, rather than "squashing" them yourself. Most programs have a "Pixel Ratio" setting for final renders. For NTSC, you'll want to set it at 0.9, for PAL renders you'll want to set it at 1.0667.

Non-square pixel madness! The image on the left represents what you will see on an NTSC television screen. The image on the right is that exact same image shown on a computer screen.

What do you do if you are sending demo reels to multiple destinations needing different formats? Do you need to render everything twice? Fortunately, you do not. The best solution is to render out at 800x600. The only problem is that you'll need to make sure that you have a little extra room at the edges of your image. This way you can adjust the image horizontally or vertically in order to center the action.

Non CG content. (drawings, sculptures, paintings, etc...)

Are you a really good 2D artist? If so, you might want to include a printed portfolio of your work along with your demo reel. If you are a sculptor, then obviously you'll have to send photographs of your sculptures. But make sure you send copies of the artwork/photographs and not the originals! If they get lost or damaged then you are out of luck, and many companies will not, or do not have the time to, return submitted material.

Why would you want to show traditional artwork when applying for a computer graphics job? Because many companies want to see that you can do more than just push buttons. While it may be obvious from your demo reel that you are qualified for the job, this does not always mean that you'll get it. Most computer graphics jobs require an artistic sense and as well as a technical one. As a result, traditional art skills are usually held in high regard. A good demo reel with no portfolio will almost surely lose when put up against a good demo reel with a good portfolio. Not only does traditional art skill help the artist create better CG artwork, it also makes it easier for them to quickly share ideas. In the typical production environment time is money. Ideas need to be exchanged efficiently and rapidly. Describing artwork with words usually takes much longer and is less effective than words combined with a small sketch. If you can't draw at all, it will hinder you at some point in your career.

Some companies want to see portfolios up front and some do not want to see them until you come in for an interview. (If you get one) Make sure that you know what each company wants before sending them a portfolio. If you are not sure, call the human resources department and ask.

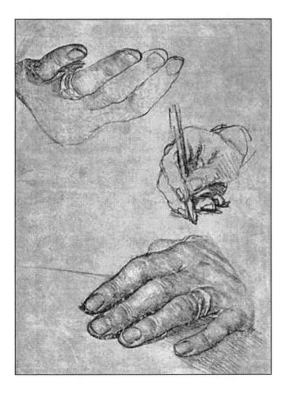

Be sure to put traditional artwork on your reel, but only if it is good enough.

All that is needed is a simple portfolio. If you are mailing it, do not send large printouts. The 8.5" by 11" images are perfectly acceptable. Roughly 10 to 15 images will suffice. This is enough information so the employer can see you know

We got a reel once that consisted mostly of a guy dancing around in his living room. No, not 3D - handy cam footage of the actual guy, baggy shorts, baseball cap etc... dancing around. From memory I think there were even some photoshop lens flares over it. I think he said in his cover letter he wanted to "be different". He was.

Another fav was the floppy disk containing two pics of some guy by his pool holding a badly photoshopped lightsaber; he thought cause we were based at Fox, and Star Wars was filming here, we'd be working on the film...

Alex Scollay
www.sectorcity.net/alex

what you are doing and that your talent is consistent. Send only your best. If you have 15 images but only 9 of them really stand out, only send 9. As with demo reels, do not water down your portfolio with mediocre imagery. Quality over quantity! In this particular case, less is more. Periodically , you will also want to remove images that are out of date and replace them with better work.

If you are mailing in a portfolio, put your images in a small folder. Use something that is very thin and somewhat plain that does not take up a lot of room. You want it easy for the employer to view your images while at the same time focus on your work, not on the folder. Some people have made portfolios that are the size of a VHS tape. These portfolios fit inside a standard VHS case along with the tape and any other artwork/information. Because it's so compact and fits neatly together it will be very easy to handle for both you and the employer.

When you show up for an interview, it might be a good idea to bring two sizes of your images: one 8.5" by 11" set in a small folder, like the one that you might have mailed in with your portfolio, and another set of full size images in a portfolio case, possibly the originals. This way, the employer can browse though the small folder and if they want to see the large ones you can pull them out.

The portfolio can be more than just traditional artwork
The printed portfolio gives you a chance to show off more than just your sculptures, paintings or drawings. There are some other mediums that VHS does not treat with justice, and if not presented on paper, will not be fully appreciated. An example is high-resolution print advertisements or film graphics. Your portfolio is a great place to show off printouts of complicated models or detailed texture maps. I've even seen some that included before and after shots. These can prove to be very valuable when you are trying to explain just what you did on a shot.

In addition to your portfolio, consider putting some of your traditional artwork on your demo reel. It's easiest if you scan the artwork (or photographs of the art work) and size/crop the images to video resolution. Once you've done this, you can dissolve/cut between the images on your reel. Try to leave them on the screen long enough that the viewer has time to understand what they are seeing, but not so long that they get bored and fast-forward over them. In some instances, your

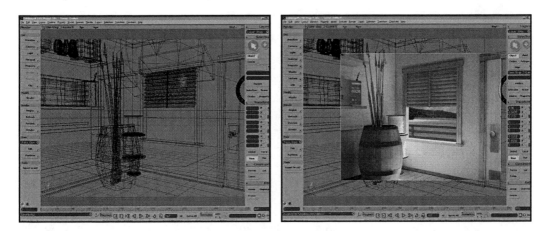

Printouts of your work offer you a way to show "behind the scenes" information easily

traditional artwork might be too complicated to show in its entirety on a TV screen and be visually readable at the same time. In this case it might be better to show a couple of closeups of the artwork rather than the entire thing. A good example would be a very complex drawing that just looks like a blob from a distance, but when you get really close you see that it is actually intricately detailed.

I find it very useful when modelers send a printout or two of their work. When we go through hundreds of reels it's very helpful to remember a person by having their print out attached to their reel after reviewing it.

Michael Defeo
Model dept. Head
Blue Sky Studios
www.blueskystudios.com

Reel crits

It's very important that you get other people to look at your reel. Even the best animators and artists in the world needed some outside input to get where they are today. It is almost impossible to see the mistakes that you've made when you've been staring at them forever. After a while they just blend into the rest of the work. What you need is another pair of eyes to help you see those mistakes and critique your work. But, how and where do you find these people? Here are some suggestions:

Reel Crits: Get other people to laugh
...er I mean, look at your demo reel.

Show it to people that you know

While your relatives are probably not the best computer graphic critics in the world, if your reel has a story then they should be able to give you good feed back on how well it flows and if it kept their interest or not. There is a good chance your relatives will not be very good sources of artistic criticism. Chances are they will just tell you how great your work is because they don't want to offend you. You need to find other artists and people who work in the computer animation industry. Show it to co-workers. (But don't show it to your boss, obviously! You don't want him to know that you are looking for another job, do you?) If you are a student, show it to your teacher; if there are other teachers in your school that teach similar subjects, ask if you can show them your reel too. Show it to other students. If possible, show it to students that are not in your class. If they don't have to spend class time with you they will be more likely to give you an objective opinion. If you have met people on the internet, that have more experience than you, ask if they will take a look at your reel if you send it to them. If so, ask if they will send you feed back. Be sure to tell everyone you show your reel to that you want an honest opinion. People do not like to criticize others, especially if they are standing right next to them. Explain to them that just nodding and saying "looks fine to me" will not help you at all. Tell them that you are expecting to hear some bad news and that it will not bother you in the least.

Where to find qualified people to crit your reel

What do you do if you don't know anyone who can critique your reel well? If you live near a university or a college there is probably a graphics teacher there who might be able to help you. There are a lot of local SIGGRAPH chapters and CG user groups all over the world. If you live in a city that has one then you can probably find a professional to take a look at your reel. If you're lucky, ask the people running the meeting if they'll announce something like, "Phil has just finished his demo reel and needs some feedback. He will come up here after the meeting to hand out reels to anyone willing to critique it." This might sound like a pretty bold or desperate move, but I've seen it work for more than one person and the feedback that was generated from that one distribution of tapes was invaluable. Giving out your reel like this can also make contacts that may help get you work in the future. If your reel is good enough, one of these people may end up hiring you or, at the very least, playing a part in getting you hired somewhere else in the future.

If there is no SIGGRAPH chapter or CG user group in your area, look in the phone book for game companies, post production houses, animation houses, etc... Give them a call and ask them if they have time to look at your reel. Offer to mail it to them, drop it off or buy them lunch. This way they have total control over how much contact they have with you. It can be hands on or hands off, you leave it up to them. If they say no, thank them and call somewhere else. Do not hassle them or act angry or disappointed. It's not very professional and you'd be surprised how something like that can come back to haunt you later.

Post it on line

Create a web site and upload your animation to it. Join a 3D graphics forum or a mailing list and ask for feedback on your work. There are a lot of quite good forums and lists out there. Some even have specific areas designed for "reel critiques." Make sure that you post your animation online; don't mail it directly to someone or send it to a list. If you mail your animation, and it's a large file, then it might anger some of the recipients, especially if they have slow connections or low mail space restrictions. Join the forum or list before you are ready to post your work. Watch what others do and learn from their mistakes.

Taking criticism

It's not fun hearing that "you need to improve this" or "you did that poorly" but in the end it is really helpful. Take every opportunity you get to have people look at your reel and give you feed back. But don't be pushy. If someone is obviously too busy to look at your reel then wait for another time. You won't get good feedback from someone who can't wait for you to leave the room so they can get back to work.

I have given a few lectures on the demo reels; they were a great deal of fun and had lots of interest. I had one that was particularly successful and I didn't talk more than five minutes. Basically I picked about 5-6 of the worst demo reels we received and one from a high-profile film guy. I showed then all from start to finish and the attendees laughed, moaned and suffered though all of them. Then I showed the last one; I pretty much finished the discussion by posing the question, "who would you hire?" It got the point across pretty darn well. By the way, I choose reels from out-of-state and it was a small group. ;)

Doug Brooks
Outrage-THQ
www.outrage.com

This shouldn't be too hard :)

The gallerie abominate

This book would not be complete with out mentioning "The Gallerie." There is a web site that contains a section called "The Gallerie Abominate." http://www.jackals-forge.com/gallerieabominate.html. It has some of the most wretched examples of computer animation ever created. On the site it says: "The most horrific 3D on the planet." and "The most abhorrent computer generated imagery and animation ever produced." Take a look at this page. If your work looks anything like the samples contained in this site, then you really need to find some better people to crit your demo reel.

"These charts better not represent the quality of our animation applicants."

The 3D Career De-Mystified

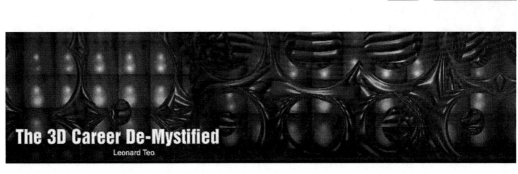

The 3D Career De-Mystified
Leonard Teo

The 3D Career De-Mystified

Recently, Leonard Teo (head of cgnetworks.com) interviewed seven different animators. He asked them various questions about getting a job in the animation industry. Thanks to his generosity, I have been allowed to reprint that interview here.

Leonard Teo: If there's any one question that I get asked most, it's "How do I find a job/career in the 3D industry?" I decided to go out and get some friends who have "been there and done that" to share with us the reality of the 3D/VFX industry.

Jason Schleifer - Senior Animator Weta Digital

Jason Schleifer is currently a Senior Animator at Weta

Digital in New Zealand working on The Lord of the Rings. In addition to animating, Jason has taught two Maya Master Classes on setting up Animation Rigs (SIGGRAPH 2001, SIGGRAPH 2002), co-taught a SIGGRAPH Course on Character Rigging (SIGGRAPH 2002), and spends way too much time chatting away on www.cgtalk.com. Before his gig at Weta, Jason worked as a product specialist at Alias|Wavefront in Santa Barbara helping the R&D team think of things from an animator's point of view.

Leonard Teo: How does one break into the 3D industry?

Jason Schleifer: People break into the industry in a number of ways. Many that I've talked to started out doing smaller jobs like interning, or loading a tape robot, or working at the front desk of a company. I started by interning at a software company, which meant I got to use software before it was released. That also meant that by the time people were beta-testing the software, I knew it well enough to meet people already working in the industry and help them with it. I think there are many ways to get into a facility and once you're there, you've just gotta show that you have talent and are willing to work hard and smart to get a job done. Once you've made it into one facility and have made contacts, as long as you're easy to work with, will complete your job on time and under budget, and are talented at what you do, getting another job will be relatively easy.

Leonard Teo: Does the 3D industry have a stable career path?

Jason Schleifer: I don't think it's extremely stable. Studios are constantly hiring and firing for the specific jobs they need. If a studio is doing pre-production on a film, they don't need 30 compositing artists sitting around twiddling their thumbs. However, at the end of production if they don't have those same 30 compositors they're screwed. If you're lucky enough to work for a studio, which can juggle projects so they can have people working constantly, it's relatively stable as long as you're good. However, if you work for a studio which gets one job, does only that job, and then has a few months off between that and another job.. unless you're one of their core members you may get told to take a 3 to 4 month holiday.. unpaid, of course. :)

Leonard Teo: What are employers looking for?

Jason Schleifer: When looking to hire someone, employers always look for two main things:

1) A good demo reel. No matter how good you say you are, or how good others say you are, it's very difficult to convince those with the purse strings to loosen them for someone who's work we haven't seen. Unless the job allows for time to ramp up, most likely we'll be looking for someone who has either done the type of work we've done before, or someone who obviously can handle it. That's why a demo reel is so important. You should focus it specifically on the type of job you're trying to get (i.e. if you're going for a modeling job, don't show any compositing that you've done, unless it's spectacular. If it's anything less than amazing, people will focus on that instead of on your model). If you want to show how the model moves when being deformed, make it obvious that's what you're showing. Create diagnostic renders of how the model moves through deformations. If you're a good animator then do one animation to show it. If not, see if you can get a friend who's a good animator to move the model in a convincing way, but note that on your demo reel.

2) References. The most common way people get jobs in this industry is through their contacts. Attitude and professionalism are extremely important when working to the tough deadlines that we all have. If you're an amazing animator, but have the personality of a psycho pit bull, the director may decide to go with someone who may not be as good as you are, but is a lot easier to direct.

Leonard Teo: Is formal training and a qualification important?

Jason Schleifer: It depends on where you're trying to work, and how much experience you have. Formal training and qualification is very helpful when trying to work overseas, as it helps convince the government that you can indeed do the job the company is trying to import you for. Formal training is also helpful in making contacts, which again is one of the best ways of getting a job. In addition, it gives you a chance to experiment and play with different ideas that you may not get a chance to do once you're working. That being said, obviously the most important thing is what's on your reel. If you have a fantastic reel but never passed the third grade.. well.. people can overlook that if you have good references, too.

Leonard Teo: Does working on films, TV commercials or games make it glamorous?

Jason Schleifer: Nothing beats sitting in a theater seeing your name go by and watching your parents go "eeeee!!" It's a great experience, and it does sometimes feel like you're a star. Especially when you have kids (or parents) running around going "AAAGGHHH!! YOU WORKED ON !! AAAGHH!! I LOVED THAT !!! YOU ARE MY HERO!! "

Leonard Teo: Any other advice that you'd give a 3D wannabe?

Jason Schleifer: Make sure that this is what you want to do with your life. It takes a lot of work, a lot of patience, and a lot of long hours. But if you try hard, you can succeed. Just remember not to forget that you should have a personal life, too. And try and get out and do some sit-ups. Twenty hours in front of the computer every day can make anybody a wee soft in the belly!

Jason Schleifer
Senior Animator, Weta Digital

Markus Manninen: CG Supervisor at Dreamworks Feature Animation.

Previously as Joint Head of 3D Commercials at Framestore CFC, Markus Manninen worked on award winning commercials as Animation Supervisor or Animation Director. The client list includes Levis, Microsoft, Shell, Fiat, Coca-Cola and Kellogg's. A MSc graduate of the Royal Institute of Technology, Sweden, he discovered Computer Graphics at the University of Massachusetts, USA. Markus joined Framestore CFC in 2000 from Filmtecknarna, an award-winning traditional animation studio.

Leonard Teo: How does one break into the 3D industry?

Markus Manninen: There seem to be very different cultures in different countries on how to break in. I see people working their way up from being runners in London and talent walking in from the street who are self taught. I think the key element is getting a stunning show reel together and showing it to the correct people. When developing the reel, it is really you as a person who has to figure out how to get the reel together. Do you go to school, learn the skills, and do the extra hours to create a reel? Do you spend your time at home learning it on your own, and putting together the material? Do you work at a facility and try to get as much

time in front of the equipment to learn and use the talent there to feed off to make your reel? It's all possible. The key element is that your reel has to show your talent, your ability. It has to show the person watching it that there is something that they can use in production. I always find that the best reels are from people who have learned to criticize their own work. It is a talent we all have to have, and we all use every day to get the work done to our client's specification, or even better.

Leonard Teo: Does the 3D industry have a stable career path?

Markus Manninen: There is a career path, but it isn't as corporate as the traditional traits may have. I think there are several different ways to go. There is the usual path of "junior" to "senior" which often reflect on people's artistic abilities as well as ability to take on responsibility.

You can also become a specialist in a particular area and hone your skills to the maximum. Usually these people are called "leads" - as in lead animator, lead TD. Then there are the supervisory roles that tend to come with both artistic and creative decision making as well as inter-personal skills. Supervisors need to be more generalist due to the fact that they need to communicate during productions.

As far as this goes it is similar to other traits. However, because our business is so project-driven, there is a tendency for people to move in two separate title areas. One which is a job title, the title they got when they were hired, and one which is a credit title which is specific to a task performed on a specific show. So the path isn't as clear perhaps, nor stable. It is production-driven if anything.

Leonard Teo: What are employers looking for?

Markus Manninen: Show reel that tells us the ability of the individual. It always helps to have a reference from someone who has been around and has a good reputation in the business. But it only gets you to see the right person. The show reel needs to speak after that.

Self-criticism. Do you know what you are good at? And if so, can you communicate it to us.

I like meeting people face to face. How they communicate their strengths and weaknesses to me is also important. An awareness of one's abilities is important.

Leonard Teo: Is formal training and a qualification important?

Markus Manninen: I think there is a certain trust derived from the knowledge that a person has earned a degree and consequently should know something about what we do. And that they've had enough desire to get into the business to go and learn it. Maybe even a software. However, unless we see real talent no formal training will help you land a job. Some schools obviously are very well respected in the business and will certainly enable a proper exposure to the community.

Leonard Teo: Does working on films, TV commercials or games make it glamorous?

Markus Manninen: Glamorous. Maybe not. I think it has more to do with the fact that a lot of people actually want to work in the business simply because the actual work is what we love to do. If we wouldn't be doing it during the day time, we'd probably do it as a hobby in our spare time. I think many of us are very fortunate to have a hobby as our day job. I think many also find great satisfaction in seeing the end result of hard work up on the screen or on the TV. And it is always satisfying to have some creative input in what you do. But on the day to day business I think we all find it as frustrating as anyone else in the work force. Remember the last time your renders crashed? That's the feeling I am talking about.

Leonard Teo: Any other advice that you'd give a 3D wannabe?

Markus Manninen: Learn, enjoy, don't give up. It does take time to become a fully-fledged artist, animator, or technical director. Everyone seems to be in such a hurry in our business to get somewhere. I'd say get good at what you do. Learn to listen to creative direction and input. Learn to be comfortable working in a group, which you will most likely do. Make sure you can criticize your own work to reach the best standard. Make sure you have a good work ethic. When you do, and when you are able to take on the responsibility to get the job done comfortably, so that people know you'll get the job done without them having to worry, that's when you will see your career really take off. Then opportunities will find you.

Dennis Price:
Digital Cinematic Artist,
Blizzard Entertainment

Dennis Price has spent the last 4 years in sunny Southern California, which is a far cry from his origin of 20 years in Houston, Texas. He is currently a Digital Cinematic Artist working at Blizzard Entertainment - his most recent accolade being part of the cinematic production for Warcraft III. He drives an '02 Black Mustang GT convertible, likes to attend car shows and play computer games with his square-headed girlfriend.

Leonard Teo: How does one break into the 3D industry?

Dennis Price: This is a tough question. Its not easy getting into 3D. It is a very competitive industry, especially right now! There are hundreds of kids out there struggling to get their feet in the door. Fortunately, for you the artist, a lot of them aren't very good at it. But they are getting better at an alarming rate. It could be easy for me to say hard work, determination, dedication, focus. It all applies, but there there are a few attributes that are most important.

Confidence, be sure of yourself. When you go to the interview make sure that the employer believes they NEED you for that job. Don't ever let them think they don't need you, don't let them doubt you. This is an important attrib-

ute not only for the interview, but also when you have to go to work and apply yourself. Being confident will wash doubt from you and allow you to enjoy your job and your work will yield better results. If you're not sure of yourself, then you will doubt yourself, and this can only lead to fear, and fear is the path to the Dark Side.

Knowledge, so that you can back that confidence up. Understand and know what it is you are doing. You want to be a modeler? You want to be an animator? You want to composite? Know your software, know the tools, know the jargon. A good interviewer will ask you applicable questions, so be ready for them. Read everything you can get your hands on. Absorb information from everywhere. Go to user group meetings, especially if there is a guest speaker. Use the online forums. Use newsgroups and mailing lists. Ask questions, etc.

Skill, obviously when comes down to actually performing you need to be able to do the work. Some people have it and some people don't. If you don't have it, you won't last long. I've seen it time and again. Don't get me wrong though, good skill is practiced. You can't just open up the software and be amazing, it takes practice. I always say "The second time you do it, you do it better and faster." So practice, practice, practice.

Networking, this is an important item to utilize in this industry. It always amazes me how small the 3D industry is. It's tiny. Everyone knows everyone. Make friends, mingle and you'll find yourself with a contact that can get you into a job that otherwise may not have been attainable. There is so much ground to cover. One more important point.

Reality, be real about your expectations. Not everyone ends up in their dream job on the first go. Sometimes (most times) you have to pay your dues. It is a hard industry to break into; don't be discouraged. If you're passionate and you want it bad enough, it will happen.

Leonard Teo: Does the 3D industry have a stable career path?

Dennis Price: Blizzard has been solid as a rock. I've noticed that the FX industry in general has been very flexible. One tends to jump around from project to project. Commercial projects can normally last about two months, but some games have a four year development cycle. That may be a factor in the stability of your job.

Leonard Teo: What are employers looking for?

Dennis Price: Potential. Sometimes it's hard to find good people with experience, mostly because those kinds of people already have a job. Ninety-eight percent of us in the industry will cringe at our demo reels from when we started out. Don't expect to create the most amazing piece of work in the world (but always strive for that). If you put your 110% into your reel, then that will show. There are hundreds of little items you want to be mindful of when making a demo reel, but I'll just list a few. I don't want to say "you're as good as your worst piece on the reel", but it's true. Do not put something on your reel that you are unhappy with. A silent reel is boring as hell to watch, put

SOMETHING in for sound. Don't make the reel too long. Two minutes is a good general time. Include a description of what your role was on the reel with your résumé.

It's not always the best work that the interviewer desires, its the personality. If you don't seem like you'll "click" with the team, or can do well with others then you may not be the best person to hire.

Leonard Teo: Is formal training and a qualification important?

Dennis Price: When I started out, about 5 years ago, it didn't seem like the degree was all that important. There weren't many schools out there with the proper programs and/or knowledge to properly teach the subject matter. All that mattered was the reel. Nowadays the competition is getting fierce. Schools have gotten 200 times better. School can not only provide you with adequate knowledge, but also provide a way to network better. The more people you know that share your interests, the easier it is to be motivated. I do feel that schooling may make or break a hire decision, but if someone shows up with an amazing reel and no schooling, it would be almost dumb to not hire that person.

Leonard Teo: Does working on films, TV commercials or games make it glamorous?

Dennis Price: There is something to be said about seeing your name on the big screen....but I have never had someone from off the street walk up to me and ask for my signature! There is a certain level of pride that makes it all worth it when you see your work published, be it on the big screen small screen or in a video game.

Have a look at Dennis Price's webpage: http://www.wizfx.net

Carlos Saldanha: Co-Director, Ice Age, Blue Sky Studios

 Carlos Saldanha has been part of Blue Sky's creative team since 1993 after finishing his animated short film "Time for Love," which has been screened at animation festivals around the world. Carlos was Blue Sky's Supervising Animator for the talking and dancing roaches in the feature film "Joe's Apartment." Carlos' latest project was to co-direct 20th Century Fox and Blue Sky Studios' first computer-animated feature film, "Ice Age."

Leonard Teo: How does one break into the 3D industry?

Carlos Saldanha: Most of the candidates we interview for a job are fresh out of animation schools from all over the world. That's how I got started 12 years ago. But with computers and software getting more accessible we are starting to get reels from animators that are creating animation on their own, and that's really good because it's opening opportunities for more artists to show their work.

Leonard Teo: Does the 3D industry have a stable career path?

Carlos Saldanha: It depends. If I use myself as a reference, I'd say yes. I've been at Blue Sky for almost ten years now, but the industry has it's ups and downs, sometimes forcing people to jump around looking for a project to work on for example. But in general most of the artists I know have managed to keep their career path going right.

Leonard Teo: What are employers looking for?

Carlos Saldanha: We always look for talent, and that should be reflected on the artist's demo reel. The demo reel doesn't need to be fancy or long, a simple animation test could do it, if the quality is good. We look for animators with great sense of posing, timing and acting skills in their animation. I'd say keep it simple and solid.

Leonard Teo: Is formal training and a qualification important?

Carlos Saldanha: Sometimes. It depends on the artist. Education is very important, knowing the computer software also helps, but natural sensibility is crucial. A good animator has to be able to convey the right emotion through their work, and that doesn't come by just knowing the techniques.

Leonard Teo: Does working on films, TV commercials or games make it glamorous?

Carlos Saldanha: When you see your name on the credits for a project you worked on, it feels really good, but the bottom line is you have to really love what you do, because it's hard work, and most of the time late nights, bad take-out dinners and working weekends is not glamorous at all.

Leonard Teo: Any other advice that you'd give a 3D wannabe?

Carlos Saldanha: Go for it!! If you want to get into the business and love animation, try to do the best you can and send out the best work you've got. It's not easy, but keep trying to learn more and improve your work. Companies are always looking for new talents.

Stefan Marjoram: Director and Animator, Aardman

After many years in the animation industry, the lure of character animation brought Stefan Marjoram back to Aardman where he has designed and directed idents and ads, BBC being among the prolific list of clients. Stefan directed the short film "The Deadline," which won the Best Animated Short at 3D Festival Copenhagen 2001 and has been spun off into a mini-series on Nickelodeon.

Leonard Teo: How does one break into the 3D industry?

Stefan Marjoram: When I left college I, and a lot of my friends ended up in gaming industry. They're possibly not

snatching up people at such a fast rate now but it's still a huge industry and as the consoles get ever faster and the games more complex, the companies will need more artists. It's quite a good way in - some companies are subsidiaries of other larger groups like Sony who also does feature film work, so it might lead to other things that way. Also, it's a good place to get used to working at a fast pace and get great tips that you'll use for the rest of your life - there are some very talented people in this field. That said, if you used your time at college well and have a really good reel which shows you understand the basics of weight and timing, you should approach whomever you want to work for and show them - you never know, you might get lucky.

Leonard Teo: Does the 3D industry have a stable career path?

Stefan Marjoram: Some jobs are possibly more stable than others but often it's a matter of choice. You might prefer to freelance - doing a few months on a job in LA and then going to London for a bit and then maybe having nothing for a few months. Other people are happier in a full time position. Sometimes this has downsides - as an employee most places will have ownership of any characters/film ideas you come up with.

The good thing is - if you have talent - you will always be able to get a job somewhere - and no computer or machine is ever going to take your job away.

Leonard Teo: What are employers looking for?

Stefan Marjoram: A showreel should be short and focus on your key skills. Only put your best work on - even if it means the reel comes out very short. If you're applying for a character animation job and modeling isn't your strong point - just animate the bones or a stick character and don't waste precious time making a badly lit, lumpen model that everybody will laugh at. Of course, employers are also looking for someone who's easy to get along with (especially when deadlines are looming).

Leonard Teo: Is formal training and a qualification important?

Stefan Marjoram: A qualification isn't necessarily important (nobody's ever asked to see my degree in animation) - but learning the basics is. Whether you teach yourself or someone else teaches you (even in a college you might still have to teach yourself - as many are fine arts based and don't place much importance in walk cycles) - learn the basics - how to draw or sculpt or animate bouncing balls and walks. You'll need these skills before you get a job.

Leonard Teo: Does working on films, TV commercials or games make it glamorous?

Stefan Marjoram: Occasionally, yes. You might get to meet or work with famous people and go to premieres in an ill-fitting suit. You might be lucky enough to win an award which does make you feel very important for a night. And to your Mum and Dad and their neighbours it will be very exciting knowing somebody who works in the movies or on TV. They'll be looking out for your name in the credits and they'll

probably ring you after to tell you. It is, however, sometimes difficult to remember how glamourous it is at 3 in the morning when you're staring through bloodshot eyes at a scene that keeps crashing.

Leonard Teo: Any other advice that you'd give a 3D wannabe?

Stefan Marjoram: Practice. And don't feel it has to be complicated to be impressive - keep it simple is one of the best bits of advice for any subject.

David Gould
Technical Director, Weta Digital

David Gould is currently a Technical Director at Weta Digital in New Zealand working on The Lord of the Rings. With over a decade of experience in the computer graphics industry, David Gould has pursued the dual paths of programmer and artist. He is the author of the book "Complete Maya Programming" and is also the developer behind the Illustrate! cel-shader plugin for 3ds max which has been used in numerous productions including Ghost in the Shell: Stand Alone Complex.

Leonard Teo: How does one break into the 3D industry?

David Gould: Rarely does one "break into" the 3D industry but instead "chips away". The road from starting school to a paid position at a large studio can take many years. As such, the most important attributes of a 3D artist are patience and persistence. Admittedly there are a rare few who leave school and immediately get work in large prestigious studios, but for the majority the road will be longer and therefore require greater dedication and persistence. My journey has been the latter and on reflection I feel that it has been more rewarding.

While you'll hear many people give you the politically correct, sanitized version of how to get a job in the 3D industry, I'll attempt to give you the non-sugarcoated truth. The reality is that there are a lot of people wanting to work in this industry on the most famous projects but there is also an equally large number of qualified people who can fill those positions. Unlike the early 90's where anyone who could navigate their way around a 3D package was offered a job, there is now a very large pool of experienced people which employers can dip into. Jobs that were asking for a minimum of three years experience are now requiring a minimum of five, simply because they know that they can find people to fill them. The key to getting to work on the big projects is to have experience.

"The reality is that there are a lot of people wanting to work in this industry on the most famous projects but there is also an equally large number of qualified people who can fill those positions."

So how do you go about getting it? Start by completing some formal training and educa-

tion. I'll cover this in more detail in the training question below but without doubt, formal training is very important. Once you've completed your studies, start by working in smaller companies. Sure the projects aren't as cool but you will learn some important lessons, and most importantly it will give you a chance to hone your skills. Cutting your teeth in the often ruthless world of commercials or TV visual effects will put you in good stead for the future. You will gain a far greater understanding of the dynamics of the industry including how productions are managed and budgeted. You'll see that your communication and team skills are as important, if not more, than your technical or artistic skills. Since you'll be working for a smaller company there is a good chance that you'll be asked to wear many different hats. As a result you will be exposed to many different areas of production. This will help later when working in a larger studio since you'll have a much better understanding of how other departments work and interface with each other.

So you've put in a few years at some smaller companies and you feel you can now cut it on a larger production. Recalling your teacher's advice you'll polish up your résumé and submit it to the recruiter along with your demo reel. You'll now sit back and wait patiently for a reply. This is the single biggest major mistake of all applicants. Firstly, your résumé and demo reel are put onto the pile with many other hundreds, if not thousands, of other applications. Secondly, if your submission is actually looked at there is a very good chance that it is done by someone who is less than qualified to assess your capabilities. The reality is that most recruiters/human resources people don't have any experience in the 3D industry. Admittedly there are some who are very good but for the most part they are people whose backgrounds don't include any formal training in 3D production. They are often given a minimum requirements list. They will attempt to match your résumé to that list. If you don't match then you'll most likely be trivially rejected. If the recruiter determines that you fulfill the criteria then they will often pass it to production for further evaluation or ask you to come in for an interview. This system is, unfortunately, very flawed. Over the years I've seen many talented artists being rejected for positions that they are more than qualified for because a recruiter wasn't capable of accurately assessing their application.

So how do you get your application to someone who can best evaluate it? Quite simply, you need to know someone in production. There is no better means of having your application thoroughly reviewed than by having an actual production team/person take look at it. Unfortunately, most people in production rarely have time to thoroughly review applications. They will often get a few that have already been filtered through the system. The faster you can get your application to a production-experienced person the greater chance you of a fair evaluation. An experienced person can evaluate an application in a few minutes. The decision to bring you in for an interview or alternatively pass you over can be made quite rapidly. If the answer is negative, ask for feedback on what areas you need to improve.

So fostering good relationships with production people will be very important in improving your chances of future employment. This isn't to say that simply schmoozing up to someone will get you in. You must have the skills and experience to back up your claims. If you make claims in your application that you can't follow through on, you will be quickly exposed. Just as much as word of mouth and relationships will get you jobs, making false claims will also get you fired. Word travels fast in this community so don't make this a common practice. Getting to know production people includes participating in online forums, networking at SIGGRAPH, participating in local chapters, attending presentations and festivals, etc. Get more involved with the 3D community. This is a great way to meet people and learn. It is also a good chance to create new friendships.

On a small but related note, many large companies have an employee referral system in place. This means that if an existing employee refers you and you finally get hired they often receive monetary compensation. This is an additional, though not necessary, incentive for an existing employee to want to get you hired.

Leonard Teo: Does the 3D industry have a stable career path?

David Gould: I'd like to say yes, but for the majority of people the answer is no. Walk around any major production studio and count the number of people over fifty. Not including the higher level production staff, the majority of production staff are relative young. The reality is that production work is often very long and demanding. Often people become burnt out and move onto other less stressful careers. Sometimes physical injuries (carpal tunnel, etc.) can slow or stop people working. Some people simply become jaded with the vagaries of the industry and look for alternatives. However, this is not to say that you must begin looking elsewhere. With the right skills it is possible to move to a managerial or supervisory position.

The real question isn't whether you'll have the skills to maintain a long career but whether there will be enough stability in the industry to sustain you.

Unfortunately the possibility to start and end your career in the same company never happened in the 3D industry. All the large studios now work with a "hire and fire" policy of employment. Many won't keep staff for mere weeks between projects, preferring instead to lay them off then hire them back when the next project is greenlit. The profit margins are simply too low to pay for the overhead of staff during even short intervals between projects. What this equates to is that you'll be spending a great deal of your time working on a contract basis. For larger feature films this can mean a relatively long three year or run-of-film contract. For effects work this may mean just several months. In any event there is not a great amount of long term stability within any single company. It may be this continual need to shift from one company to the next that wears on some people over time.

> "The real question isn't whether you'll have the skills to maintain a long career but whether there will be enough stability in the industry to sustain you."

Some would argue that there are people who have been at the same company for years. Yes, this is true, but they are clearly in the minority. In my experience, even the highly placed producers and supervisors never truly ever feel that their position is completely assured. Often one's future employment is tied to the success of a film or the company's current fiscal report. If you are a dynamic person and prepared to change jobs, then you will definitely fair better than someone who is looking for a single stable job.

Leonard Teo: What are employers looking for?

David Gould: In this day and age the most important attribute of an artist is versatility. While it is true that many larger studios have pipelines with many specialized people, I feel that model is starting to change. Even the larger studios are being forced to be more dynamic and flexible. In the never ending effort to reduce costs, companies are looking for people that have skills that can cross departments. If you can easily move from one role to another you'll be in greater demand. I would even categorically state that your future level of job security will be directly proportional to your versatility.

What this means for you is that you should broaden your areas of expertise. If you are an artist, begin looking at more technical areas. If you are a programmer, look to broaden your artistic skills. Sometimes the new skills are just a variation on what you already know. A skilled programmer can often become a proficient technical director. A talented lighter may learn shader writing. A character animator may take on effects animation work. In all these cases the new area shared common traits with the existing area. By doing this you can leverage your existing knowledge to become proficient much faster and more easily.

Leonard Teo: Is formal training and a qualification important?

David Gould: Yes, absolutely!
Completing formal training demonstrates to a potential employer that you have a real genuine interest in the craft. While it is true that most people can get a student version of a 3D package and learn from home, the benefits of formal education include a wider and more generalized understanding of 3D concepts and practices. Complete an undergraduate/bachelors course if you can. Focus on the area that is of most interest to you but also attempt subjects that may not be your forte. For example, if you are an artist, take some programming courses and vice-versa. By doing a longer course that covers more areas you will be better able to determine which area you are really interested in. You may be initially interested in becoming an animator (often because of its glamour factor) then find that you are in fact better suited to rigging. I've met many people who have tried many areas before pinpointing the one that really excites them. Sometimes you may change from one area to another during your career, so having a good foundation in general computer graphics will definitely help.

For those who are non-US residents that may one day want to work in the US, having an undergraduate degree is a strict necessary minimum for a work visa. Be sure to check that your course of study is recognized by the US immigration department. It would be a real shame to complete three years of study in your home country only to find out that the course wasn't recognized by the US immigration resulting in all your efforts being in vain.

Leonard Teo: Does working on films, TV commercials or games make it glamorous?

David Gould: If you aren't attracted to work in the industry because you loved a particular film or couldn't get enough of a particular game, then I'd seriously question why you'd want to work in this industry. There is one underlying trait of every person I've met who is successful in 3D: they have an amazing and absolute passion for their work. Call me mad, but even if I was a millionaire I'd still be doing this stuff.

The reason why the underlying passion is so important is that, contrary to what you may have been lead to believe, the film, commercials, and games industries really aren't that glamorous. There is not a lot of glamour sitting up all night babysitting renders or dealing with buggy software or working on "impossible" shots that need to be done by the next morning. The veil of glamour is soon replaced with the reality that working in the 3D industry is really about long hours and hard work. I've known people who have been working many years in the industry and have become jaded and disillusioned. They are continually frustrated with production issues, pipeline problems, work hours, etc. The fact is that this is how the industry is. There is a good chance that you'll either love it or hate it. The key is knowing that there is no such thing as a perfect production or a perfect pipeline. Many artists are continually jumping from project to project in a desperate hope of finding this holy grail. Sorry, but it simply doesn't exist!

Leonard Teo: Any other advice that you'd give a 3D wannabe?

David Gould: Just do it! If you really love this stuff then there is nothing to stop you achieving your goals. Just stick with it and work hard. Apply yourself to the craft of computer graphics and it can be rewarding, both financially and personally. I've had the opportunity to work in Paris, London, New York, Los Angeles, San Francisco, and many other famous cities. I've learned new languages and been immersed in other cultures. One thing I love about this industry that is that you often get to work with amazing people from all over the world. Most crews are made up of a very eclectic mix of people from every corner of the globe. This industry gives you the opportunity to work on a wide variety of projects from feature films to video games. Skills learned in one area can often open doors in another. Remain versatile and never stop learning. Get started now!

David's website: www.davidgould.com

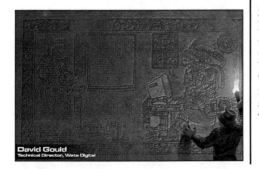

David Gould
Technical Director, Weta Digital

William Vaughan
LightWave 3D Evangelist, Newtek

A recipient of several New Media Addy awards, William Vaughan brings broad-based experience to the position of LightWave Evangelist at NewTek, having done 3D work for print, web, multimedia, games and broadcast.

Over the past ten years, Vaughan has established a strong reputation for his award-winning work for clients such as Compaq, New Line Cinema, and Halliburton. He has also worked in the LightWave® community as an instructor at North Harris Community College in Houston, Texas. Vaughan's other activities in LightWave® user education include training companies such as NASA, Fulbright & Jaworski, and KHOU Channel 11, the CBS affiliate in Houston, to use LightWave®.

Leonard Teo: How does one break into the 3D industry?

William Vaughan: It really depends on what area of the 3D industry you want to break into. All it really takes to get going in 3D is the desire to work in 3D. Many people forget that 3D is used for more then just games and Hollywood. I know many people who got their career started using 3D for print and multimedia, before they made the jump over to film and broadcast.

It all really comes down to your demo reel. A good demo reel will get you in at just about anyplace. But this doesn't mean wait to get into the industry until you have a killer reel. My first use of 3D was creating 3D screen savers for a Multimedia company. That work lead into logo animation, industrial animation and more.

The best advice I could give to someone looking to break into 3D would be to get a good foundation in traditional art skills. Learn to draw, paint, sculpt, etc. If you understand how to create good art, 3D becomes another tool or paintbrush in your kit!

Leonard Teo: Does the 3D industry have a stable career path?

William Vaughan: A 3D artist can choose how much job stability they will have. If you want to work on the latest and greatest projects you will probably live the life of a jobber, bouncing from studio to studio. The good artists are always employed. Hollywood seems to be the Holy Grail for 3D artists, but I've found that the real $$ in 3D is found in the "fly over states", doing 3D for multi-media, motion graphics and game development.

Leonard Teo: What are employers looking for?

William Vaughan: A good demo reel is key, but a demo reel can only get you so far. I have found the people that have a lot of drive and willingness to learn new things have been very successful. Having traditional skills like design and illustration also comes in handy. I've seen artists get hired with

no 3D in their portfolio, but they had a good understanding of composition, lighting and design. Many employers are willing to give good artists on-the-job training in 3D.

Leonard Teo: Is formal training and a qualification important?

William Vaughan: Formal training can only add value to an individual. I do know a few people with very little training that have gone on to work at the big shops in California. It's all about the talent and work in the end.

Leonard Teo: Does working on films, TV commercials or games make it glamorous?

William Vaughan: Seeing your name in the credits and seeing your work on the shelf or in the theater is a great feeling...but it really doesn't make the work any more glamorous. The payoff is just that much bigger.

Leonard Teo: Any other advice that you'd give a 3D wannabe?

William Vaughan: I tell everyone that now is the time to get into 3D...and it truly is. There are more resources available today then ever to learn 3D animation. My number one piece of advice is to network with as many people as possible, and with the internet, this has become soooo easy.

Don't be shy! I've seen many great artists who never post their work to forums, websites, etc because they feel they aren't "good enough." Get out there and at least show your work to your peers, get some good suggestions, and this feedback will help you take your work to the next level. With resources like CGTalk, you can meet so many people who are in the industry and others who are trying to break into the industry. I communicate with hundreds of 3D artists on a daily basis. Using online forums you can learn from each other, share job leads, and get your work critiqued by thousands.

Join as many groups as you can, such as local user groups, SIGGRAPH chapters, etc. If there isn't a group, start one. Again, networking is key in this and every industry.

Have a personal website to showcase your work, past and present. You'd be surprised at how many people will find you, and you would never have found them. One other benefit of a website is that potential employers and peers will see the progression in the quality of your work.

Share your knowledge with the 3D community by writing tutorials and articles. Not only will this help the community, but you will also learn from creating them.

Constantly send out samples of your work — even if you are not trying to get a job. It never hurts to have options, and keeping your name out there is always a good thing.

From the Editor - Leonard Teo

That's all folks! I do hope that you found this series of interviews useful - I know that I certainly have! From what our friends have said, the 3D industry does suffer its fair share of economical ups and downs, but is an extremely rewarding field to work in. Underlying everything is a passion for the craft.

I'll take this opportunity to thank Carlos Saldanha, David Gould, Stefan Marjoram, William Vaughan, Dennis Price, Jason Schleifer and Markus Manninen for participating in this community feature series.

To all of you who are finding your footing in this industry, I wish you all the best and Godspeed!

Render on,

Leonard Teo:
leonard@cgnetworks.com
Head of CGNetworks Division
http://www.cgnetworks.com

"Phyllis, who included a cat with their demo reel?"

Demo Reel: Packaging

Demo reel packaging

Good presentation and packaging won't help a bad reel, but poor presentation and packaging will hurt a good reel. There are two major things to consider when you are trying to decide on how to package your demo reel. The first, and most important, is to make sure that it is easy for the reviewer to open the package and put the reel in the VCR with minimal hassle. This might not sound like much, but you'd be surprised at what some people do to their reel and the problems that it can cause. The second thing is presentation. While the contents of the reel are the most important part, a clean presentation does not hurt either. A great reel sent in on an old, dirty VHS tape is still a great reel, but some of the magic is lost if the reviewer feels like they have to wash their hands after touching it. Same goes for dirty tapes that jam up the VCR or ruin the heads.

> At the company where I used to work, we'd immediately chuck any tapes with hand-scrawled labels or tatty covers straight into the rubbish. If people can't take pride in their work, then no companies are going to hire them.
>
> Leigh van der Byl
> Texturing Goddess
> http://leigh.cgcommunity.com

Good cases, bad cases, etc...

You want it to be very easy for the reviewer to take your tape out of the package. Don't use overly complex tape cases that are hard to figure out how to operate. Yes, these things do exist and they look cool too, but if you are in a hurry to get them open they just annoy you. These cases are also likely to send your tape flying across the room if someone does manage to get them open. This will really not sit well with the reviewer. If your tape gets damaged during its "trip across the room" it will probably not get put in the VCR for fear of damaging the machine. The exact opposite is

Sometimes reels in slipcover style cases are too easy to remove and fall out.

also true. If you have a case from which the tape is too easy to remove, then there is a chance that it might fall out when someone picks it up. The perfect example of this is the "slipcover" style case. This is the type of case that has a hole in the bottom or side and possibly a small window on the front so that the label can be seen. If picked up the wrong way, the tape will slide right out onto the floor, or worse... onto the reviewer's foot. (This is especially painful if the reviewer happens to be wearing sandals.)

Packaging styles

There are two main types of demo reel packaging. Type 1: The small tape case, possibly with the résumé on the inside and/or accompanied by a folder that includes the rest of your information. Type 2: The "giant package" demo reel. This type of reel is usually contained in a large package that is at least 8.5"X11".

Type 1 is one of the most common video cases used.

Type 1:

This is the type that is more commonly used. It is much more popular and it costs a lot less to produce. Not only are the cases for reels like this one very cheap, but there are a lot of different ones to choose from. Because this type of case is so popular, it is very easy to find "VHS case" sized boxes to mail them in. If you've decided to use this type, then you need to determine what style you want. There are many out there. Some of them are a bit larger "non-standard" sized, called clamshell style. These are typically used for wedding and children's videos.

"Clamshell" style video boxes are usually reserved for children's and wedding videos.

For demo reels I suggest that you steer clear of the clamshell boxes and go with the standard size of 8" x 4-3/4" x 1-1/8". This way it will probably fit in the cabinet, shelf, mailer, box or whatever space it is eventually put in. This just makes things convenient for everyone. The only down side to the standard size video case is that it will not stand out from the crowd like a "non-standard" sized case will. As with everything, you can't have it all. =)

Labeling options

There are also different labeling options. Some tape cases have places to put the "sticker type" labels and nothing else, like the "Type 1" tape case mentioned previously. These "sticker shell" covers are fine; they protect the tape and provide you with a way of identifying your reel. There are others that have a small sleeve that's about 3" tall. It wraps around the front and side of the tape. These are usually just a few cents more than "sticker shell" covers and provide you with a place to put a custom made insert. Most of the time this insert is something that you've printed out yourself, which has your name and contact information on it. There is another type with a clear sleeve that covers the entire tape case. These are usually the same price as the cases that have the small sleeve. Both types will do just fine; the choice is up to you. It really depends on how and if you make your own cover. An elaborate cover is not necessary to get a job. If you make one that's so detailed that your contact information is tough to read then it might actually hurt your chances. But, a simple cover that has a nice label with all your information clearly displayed will make it much easier for them to find your tape. You don't have to make your cover so simple that it ends up just being text on a solid background. If you have some time, put a little thought in it, unless it takes too much time away from creating your demo reel. This is the sort of thing that you can do when you are waiting for your animation to render.

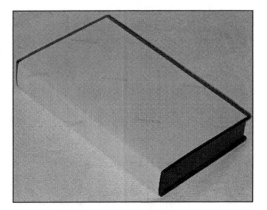

Tape cases with built in sleeves make your video look better and are much easier to label.

Well the logic goes, a company gets a lot of demo reels. Although it's shallow, one way of sorting them out is to think: "The amount of effort this artist put into getting this job and in all likelihood put into the reel itself should be visible throughout all aspects of their presentation. If they put no effort into the packaging of their reel, then why should we put any effort or time into viewing what they sent? Chances are, after all, that its contents are going to match the exterior."

It's just a law of averages and time. If you get a couple of hundred demo reels for one job, you're busy as it is (hence why you're looking to take someone on). You're going to use that kind of logic. Sadly, as a generalization it also does tend to hold true. So even though there might be a few gems, any way of filtering down is going to be used.

I know it sounds horrible, but that's just the way companies work. They've got limited resources and can not watch every single demo reel, so lets face it, in reality they're not going to. If you want to get that job and you don't have a printer, go over to Kinko's or any copy place. A lot of places that duplicate videos will do you a deal on the labels and packaging at the same time.

Put it this way, you're in your local video store. Which videos catch your eye as being likely to be any good? It's amazing how a little design can influence what you want to see. If it's got a badly photocopied bit of text on the cover you're less likely to be interested in it. On the other hand, something where the distributor has put in a little effort into the cover design will definitely catch your eye. These are design firms too; they're looking for artists, people with some design ability and sense of design. They're also looking for people who are commercially sensitive.

If you want it to be personal, then add in a cover slip with a personal note. Handwrite your letter to them, not the cover of your video, unless you're really good at calligraphy. You can do handmade covers and labels provided it looks professional. It may be shallow and make your artistic integrity nerves shudder, but you're out to earn a crust here, not be Van Gogh.

Per-Anders Arvid Edwards
Freelance 3D Animator
www.peranders.com

Standard labeling options explored

Now that you know all about tape labeling, where do you get the labels? There are a lot of places that sell labeling kits that you can use for your demo reel. Most office supply stores will have what are known as "Laser Video Tape Labels." Avery (www.avery.com) and Neato (www.neato.com) are a couple of the most popular consumer brand companies that makes video tape labels. If you can't find those, take a look at Veriad (www.veriad.com) and Polyline (www.polylinecorp.com). Most companies that make videotape labels also provide downloadable software or templates that will aid in printing your labels.

Getting a ratty tape with scribbled writing makes me think: "I'm even not worth your time for a simple printed label?" If so, then you are not worth my time to hire you because you are obviously not interested enough in the job. A tatty cover shows me that you are a sloppy worker and not worth my time., If the job you are applying to was really important then you would have put more effort into it. Really, how long does it take to make printed labels? Just a simple tape case works fine because if you can't do it right then don't do it at all.

Deke Kincaid

Type 2:

This type of reel package has room for everything. It is not the best, because it's pretty big and it can add a lot to the cost of your reel. Most of the time, the case itself is around $5.00 USD. You'll also need to find a box for it to go in, for that will probably add another $1.00 to the price. Shipping will cost a lot more than average because of its added weight and size. But if you have a lot of information that you want to include with your reel, this might be the best route for you. It is ideal if you want to include small prints of your 2D artwork, a résumé and a cover letter in a handy "all in one" package. The down side is that this case is big. It won't fit neatly on the shelf with all the other tapes. So it might get stored somewhere out of the way, like the trash can, which will it make easy to forget about.

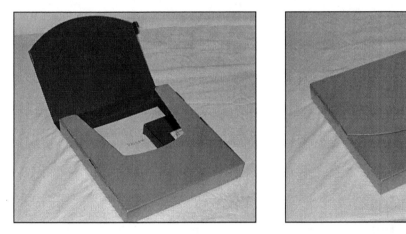

Type 2 contains room for just about everything you could possibly want to send to a prospective employer, except for the extra shelf space that they are going to need to store it. :)

The printed artwork is usually the deciding factor when it comes to tapes like this. The one thing you have to find out is this: is your 2D-artwork good enough to justify the extra expense? Ask some people whose opinions that you value, to look at your work and tell you the truth. Let them know what you are planning to do and ask them if you are wasting your time. Ask several people and tell them to be blunt. Explain that it won't hurt your feelings and that they are not doing you a favor if they lie. You'll actually benefit twice. You'll save money and you won't send out sub-standard art work.

There is a lot of room for creativity when using this type of packaging. Since there is so much material to work with, people will often use this opportunity to create a "themed demo." This type of demo reel will come with more than the standard "résumé, reel, artwork, etc.." For example, if it is a demo reel geared toward children's videos then it might come with some small toys in it, a toy car, a rubber ball, etc. It also might have stickers pasted on the outside of the box, something that reflects the current trends in children's videos at the moment. If it is a demo

Another "Type 2" style demo reel box.

reel that is geared toward the gaming industry then it would have video game related "souvenirs" in it.

As you can see, making demos like this can be very time consuming and expensive. Many times you are better off working on your reel than you are creating these elaborate demo reel packages. However, there are times when you have nothing to do, as when your animation is rendering, for example. Or there may be times when you have been animating for too long and need to take a break for a day or so. It's times like these that you can work on devising a strategy and building your demo reel package. If you come up with a great idea and decide to make an elaborate demo reel package, but it is too expensive, consider just making a few. Use these for special occasions and times when you'll be meeting the reviewer face to face. One thing is for sure: they won't forget your reel. Or if the reel is no good, at least they won't forget your package, which might not be so good. :/ If you only made a few elaborate demo reel packages, don't stop there. Make some standard size demo reels to send out to the rest of the world. Since you've already created the complex version, just use its design elements to create the simple version. For example, if the elaborate demo had 10 stickers on the outside, consider putting 1 sticker on the spine or the cover of the simple demo.

Mailing your demo reels.

Addressing your package

The best packaging in the world is worthless if you don't address it properly. This portion of the book is designed to be used in conjunction with the resources section (company listings) at the end of the book. Based on where you live, you may have to reformat the address. For example: The resources section, lists the full state name for all United States addresses rather than the abbreviation. This was done because there are many people out there (especially people from other countries) who do not know what the abbreviations are. However, when addressing your mail it is better to use the two-letter state abbreviations listed in the chart below.

It is important to use all address information for proper delivery of your mail. For example, today there are more than 10,866 streets in the USA, with the name

"Second Street" - N Second St, Second Dr, W Second St, and so on. Imagine trying to deliver a letter addressed only to Mrs. Smith on "Second"! The post office would not know where to send it.

AL: Alabama
AK: Alaska
AS: American Samoa
AZ: Arizona
AR: Arkansas
CA: California
CO: Colorado
CT: Connecticut
DE: Delaware
DC: District of Columbia
FM: Federated States of Micronesia
FL: Florida
GA: Georgia
GU: Guam
HI: Hawaii
ID: Idaho
IL: Illinois
IN: Indiana
IA: Iowa
KS: Kansas
KY: Kentucky
LA: Louisiana
ME: Maine
MH: Marshall Islands
MD: Maryland
MA: Massachusetts
MI: Michigan
MN: Minnesota
MS: Mississippi
MO: Missouri

MT: Montana
NE: Nebraska
NV: Nevada
NH: New Hampshire
NJ: New Jersey
NM: New Mexico
NY: New York
NC: North Carolina
ND: North Dakota
MP: Northern Mariana Islands
OH: Ohio
OK: Oklahoma
OR: Oregon
PW: Palau
PA: Pennsylvania
PR: Puerto Rico
RI: Rhode Island
SC: South Carolina
SD: South Dakota
TN: Tennessee
TX: Texas
UT: Utah
VT: Vermont
VI: Virgin Islands
VA: Virginia
WA: Washington
WV: West Virginia
WI: Wisconsin
WY: Wyoming

Abbreviations used in addressing can be confusing at times. When in doubt, check these lists. In addition to the official Postal Service abbreviations for states, territories, and the District of Columbia, the official abbreviations for some common street suffixes, directionals, and locators have been included below. Always use complete address information, such as the suffixes AVE, BLVD, and ST. Be sure you include locators such as the apartment or suite number as well as correct directionals, such as N, W, and SW.

APT: Apartment	LK: Lake	SE: Southeast
AVE: Avenue	LN: Lane	SQ: Square
BLVD: Boulevard	MTN: Mountain	ST: Street
CTR: Center	N: North	STA: Station
CIR: Circle	NE: Northeast	STE: Suite
CT: Court	NW: Northwest	SW: Southwest
DR: Drive	PKWY: Parkway	TER: Terrace
E: East	PL: Place	TRL: Trail
EXPY: Expressway	PLZ: Plaza	TPKE: Turnpike
HTS: Heights	RDG: Ridge	VLY: Valley
HWY: Highway	RD: Road	W: West
IS: Island	RM: Room	WAY: Way
JCT: Junction	S: South	

Dual addressing

When a post office box number and a street address are used, make sure that the destination where you want the mail delivered appears on the line immediately above the city, state, and ZIP Code line and that the ZIP Code or ZIP+4 code corresponds to that address.

For example: In the address listed below, the mail will be delivered to: P.O. Box V466

Alternate Route Studios
1 Research Drive
P.O. Box V466
Raleigh, North Carolina
27513

In the address listed below, the mail will be delivered to: 1 Research Drive

Alternate Route Studios
P.O. Box V466
1 Research Drive
Raleigh, North Carolina
27513

Addressing tips

Write, type, or print the complete address neatly. Always use a return address. Don't let an incorrect ZIP Code delay delivery of your mail. Local post offices and the Postal Service web site, www.usps.gov, offer ZIP Code information. If possible, use the four-digit add-on, ZIP+4, in your addressing. Hyphenate the ZIP+4. Always use the two-letter state abbreviations and the common addressing abbreviations listed in the previous charts. Place endorsements for special services, such as Priority Mail, First-Class Mail, or insured mail, above the destination address and below and to the right of the return address.

International addressing tips

Put foreign postal codes, if known, in front of the city or town name and on the same line. Place the city or town name and the province or state name on the next line after the street address information. Write the name of the foreign country in capital letters on the last line of the address. Do not abbreviate it! When mailing packages from one country to another, check with your local post office for the appropriate customs forms.

If your reel has to be in someone's hands on a specific date, then make sure you budget enough time for shipping. For example, assume you want to mail a reel to Japan. If you live in the United States, it's already tomorrow in Japan. This is because they are halfway around the globe, and past the International Dateline. Your morning is the middle of their night, the next day. As a result, "overnight shipping" from the United States to Japan is impossible. Anything sent to Japan on "your Monday" cannot arrive before "their Wednesday."

Shipping items the opposite direction (from Japan to the USA) also faces bizarre time warps. If you get your package to FedEx in Tokyo before 5 pm on Friday, the package will go out that night. But, it will probably have to go through customs in Anchorage, Alaska, which is closed on Saturday. It will not get clearance until Monday, after which it is rerouted to its destination taking another day or two to get there. If the package is not delivered to FedEx before the 5 pm deadline on Friday, it will not make it out of Japan till Monday night. If Monday night is a national holiday it will not go out till Tuesday.

This is just a small sample of the types of problems you will run into when shipping demo reels between these two countries. It seems that every country has its own set of rules and regulations, each different from the next. It would not be possible for me to list them all here. (That could be an entire book in itself.) The best solution is to mail your package as early as possible.

© H L SCHWADRON

Hand delivery

If you live close to the companies you are applying to, there is one method of delivery that is almost 100% guaranteed: delivering your demo reel package personally. There are many advantages to this delivery method: you will avoid the risks and costs involved in mailing it, you will be able to see the facility and its surrounding area first hand, and there is also a chance that you might be able to make some new contacts as well as speak with nearby employees about the job and company, especially if it is a smaller company. This is a great way to learn useful "inside" information. On some occasions a "hand delivery" might turn into an impromptu interview.

Résumés and Cover Letters

*"Since you asked, I feel the strongest feature of
my résumé is that none of it can be checked."*

The importance of your résumé

The résumé is important, but not nearly as important as your demo reel.
However, it can get your demo reel watched, and if no one is able to see your
demo reel then it won't matter how good it is. You need to take some time and
create a good résumé. Many people just throw one together at the last minute
thinking that it does not matter. The truth is, in many places it does not matter.
But there is no way of knowing which ones those are. You'll need a good one, just
in case.

What sort of info goes on a "CG" résumé?

You should list your contact information, career objective, skill set, software proficiency, work experience, education, awards, memberships and personal interests.

Your contact information goes first. Put your name, physical address, phone numbers, e-mail addresses and web site address at the very top. If people don't know whose résumé they are looking at, then it might as well be blank. Of course, if your website is "under construction" or not up to par with your demo reel, you might want to leave it off.

Career objective

There are many variables that you'll want to take into account for when writing your Career Objective: What you want to do, what you are able to do and what job you are applying for. If you put "I want to be a character animator" because you really want to be one but you can not animate very well, then you should either change the objective or study a little harder/longer. If you are a good animator but want to be a modeler, then let them know that. Apply for the animation job and aspire to be a modeler in your spare time.

Of course, if you are a good modeler and a modeling job is what you are after, then state that in your career objective. Career objective is really just a sneaky name for your "job description." Describe the job that you would enjoy doing the most. If you don't, you might get hired doing something you don't really want to do, while someone else fills the position that you wanted.

> Once, while assisting a friend screen some potential candidates, we got a resume that had such arresting phrases as:
>
> ATTENTION: FILE UNDER "HOT STUFF!"
>
> and
>
> Once you see my work, you won't even be able to THINK about hiring anyone else!
>
> and referred to himself as a "Master of 3d," etc, etc... I wish I still had it, because I am not even doing it justice. It was amazing.
>
> Brian LaFrance
> Lighting Lead
> DreamWorks
> www.dreamworks.com

Skill set

This is where you list what you can do. Be detailed but not wordy. If you are applying for a specific job, then take that job description, reword it and list it here.

This really helps the human resources people when they are going through résumés. Often, at large companies or when a company gets a lot of résumés, the HR people screening them are not as knowledgeable about computer graphics jobs as the people doing the hiring. (Perhaps they are "temp" employees.) As a result, they might pass over an excellent employee because of a poorly worded skill set. For example, if they are told, "Look for people who can do character animation," and you put, "I am very good at manipulating inverse kinematics over time to simulate human motion," then they might skip over you.

Software proficiency

While you may or may not list the software that you use in the credits of your demo reel, you'll want to list it on your résumé. It's expected. Listing something like, "I am proficient in a wide variety of programs," is not a good idea. On a résumé you should list the software that you are familiar with and how well you know it, beginner, intermediate, expert, fanatic, etc.

Work experience

If you have been fortunate enough to have had a computer graphics job already, this is where you should list it. This entry should include, the name of the company, what you did there, how long you were there and any thing else that might be specific to that job. For example, if you were an art director and you managed a team of 10 people, list that! If you worked with specific people that are well known in the world of computer graphics then be sure to list them too. Your goal is to make yourself look good. Don't be modest on your résumé, especially in this area.

Always list your previous jobs beginning with the most recent down to the oldest. This way the best job is almost always at the top. If it's important or possible, list the titles of the projects that you worked on while you were there. If one of the jobs listed is your current employer, be sure to mention whether it is ok if they are contacted or not.

What if you have never had a computer graphics job? Then what do you put here? You can put pizza delivery, waiter, cab driver, etc., if you like. The only benefit you'll gain by doing this is that you'll show you were able to hold down a job, unless you only worked at these places for a very short time, in which case you might want to leave them off. If you have had a job that is related to computer graphics, but is not really a computer graphics job then you might want to list that. For example, if you want to work at a game company and you were an employee at a video game store, then you will definitely want to list that. If you want to do special effects for movies and you worked at a movie theater, list that as well.

"So what if my grades are lousy? You always said it's not what you know, it's who you know."

Education experience

If you don't have any work experience you'll probably make up for it with education experience. List where you went to school, what you studied and when you finished your degree/diploma. If you went to a school just to take a class or two, not intending to earn a degree/diploma then list those classes too. There is usually no need to list your grades. But if you were an honor student or had a very high G.P.A., it cannot hurt to list it. Otherwise leave it off.

Most of the time it is not necessary to list your high school. If you are a computer animator, chances are you finished high school; there is no need to waste space listing something so obvious. However, if you went to a specialized or very prestigious high school, you might want to list that, especially if its specialization was art or computer animation.

Awards and recognition

Did you receive an award? Were you recognized for some sort of achievement? You might want to list some of these. If they are graphics or art related, then you will definitely want to list them. Use your own judgment. If they are not very spectacular, then leave them off. But, if you did something amazing, like winning a medal in the Olympics or climbing Mount Everest, then you'll definitely want to list that. It'll show that you are above average and not afraid to take on a challenge.

Organizations and memberships

Are you a member of a graphics organization such as SIGGRAPH or IGDA? If so, mention it and list how long you have been a member. Also list any special duties you preformed that a typical member might not. Were you an officer in a graphics related organization? If so, be sure to list this. If you were a leader/officer in an unrelated organization you might want to list that as well. Even though it does not directly relate to computer graphics it shows leadership ability, a very valuable trait on large scale projects. Were you involved in a graphics based internet community? Perhaps you were a moderator for a well-known internet forum or you ran a graphics resource web site. Maybe some of your work was featured on CG web site or in a high profile on-line gallery. All of these things look very good on your résumé.

Personal interests and hobbies

Listing personal interests and hobbies on your résumé is not required. However, it might be a good idea if it is related to art, graphics, or computer animation, i.e. photography, painting, drawing, sculpting, weaving, video games, filmmaking, acting, dancing, etc. If you have a hobby that is not related to work in any way, but it is something that you are really into, you might want to list it also. At first it may seem irrelevant, but I've heard of people getting interviews because their hobby just happens to be the same one that the boss likes a lot.

Miscellaneous résumé tips

It is very important that you do not misspell anything on your résumé. Misspellings make you look careless and not very detail oriented. This makes it seem as if you might not be a very good employee. Why? Because, being detail oriented is very important when you are working on a complicated set of computer graphics. Overlooking the smallest thing can wreak havoc on a production. It can be especially bad if you are close to a deadline. Check the spelling of names as well. It may take a few extra minutes to research a software, company or person's name, but it is worth it.

"The spell checker said everything was spelled incorrectly. It turned out I had the Portuguese version."

Take your time

People who create their résumé in the morning and send it out that afternoon almost always think of two or three really good points that they wish they had put on it after it's in the mail. Don't let this happen to you. Start on your résumé today. This way, when you need it, all the information will be there.

Writing a résumé is not something that you sit down and finish in 30 min. It is almost impossible to remember all of the things you've done as well as all of your qualifications, off the top of your head. You need to think about them for a while. Carry a pad of paper or a PDA with you for a few days. Whenever you have a few spare moments, think about the sorts of things you've done that you would put on your résumé. You'll be surprised what will pop into your mind when you let it wander. Write all of them down.

> The former head of our software dept. [Chris Welman] maintained a file of resume gems. My personal favourite:
> "...take pride in my attention to drtail..."
>
> Gordon Farrell
> Mainframe Entertainment
> www.mainframe.ca

My, my you certainly do have your life planned out, this résumé covers past and future."

Things to leave off your résumé:

Social security number, marital status, health, citizenship, age, travel history, previous pay rates, reasons for leaving previous jobs, and components of your name which you really never use (i.e. middle names).

E-mailing résumés

If you are e-mailing your résumé, then give it a file name that makes sense. All too often companies get résumés called "résumé.doc." This makes it very difficult to tell the difference between your résumé and the other 60 zillion that they've received the past 2 days. It's best to name your résumé "lastname firstname.doc." For example, my résumé would be named "HarrissEd.doc." This is the standard naming convention that most companies are used to.

Printed résumés

Make your résumé simple and clean. It will be photocopied, scanned, e-mailed and printed. Do not put logos or artwork on your résumé. These just confuse the scanners and look horrible after the 3rd or 4th time they have been photocopied.

If you really want to create a résumé that has graphics on it, then make sure you send it along with a "simple" version a clean résumé with no graphics. Don't use small or difficult to read fonts. If you have to use small fonts to get your entire résumé onto one page, perhaps you should think about leaving some of the information off or going for a two-page résumé. Some people send more than one copy of their résumé. This is supposed to make it easier for the human resources people to send it to multiple places without making photocopies. This practice gets mixed reviews. I've heard people say that they like it because it saves them time and I've heard others say that they didn't like it because it caused confusion and required more work on their part. Unfortunately there is no "right" answer to this question. Go with what you feel most comfortable doing.

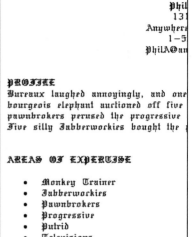

Avoid using fonts that are difficult to read.

Scanned résumés

Many people ask me "What do you mean when you say that my résumé is scanned?" Companies scan résumés in and convert the images to text. This process is often referred to as OCR. (optical character recognition). They store these résumés in a database. Then, if they need an artist that is good at "particles and fluid animation" they type those keywords into a search tool and all of the matching résumés show up. This is why it is important for you to do a very good job of clearly listing your skills. OCR software has trouble with textured paper and strange fonts. Stick with laser prints and standard fonts. Handwritten résumés are especially bad news, as are résumés printed on dot matrix and some older ink jet printers.

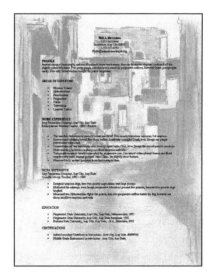

Artwork does not belong on most résumés.

Cover letter

Cover letters get read less than résumés do. But that does not mean you should avoid writing one. If you really want a job, then I suggest that you do everything that you possibly can to get it. This includes writing a cover letter. In your cover letter, list or describe the type of position that you are applying for. Make it short, but explain enough so that they can see you understand the demands of the job and feel that you want to work for them. Don't use a form letter where you just change the first and last line. Include a few sentences that mention some of the work they have done recently. Tell them how much you liked it. If they've been written about in a recent trade magazine or a web site then read that article. There is bound to be something in there that is related to the job that you are applying for. Mention that particular gem and if anyone actually reads your cover letter then they will know that you are serious about working there.

Like your résumé, make sure that you use good grammar and correct spelling on your cover letter. Don't be rude and don't use offensive language. Employers won't be impressed. You may think that an offensive cover letter will get more attention than a standard letter and you would be right. But it makes you look unprofessional. Neatness is very important. You want your cover letter legible. Don't hand write it, use a printer instead.

A cover letter might be a lot more important than you think. A lot of applicants submit materials without a cover letter and just by reading their resume I cannot work out what sort of job they are applying for. I also get a lot of submissions from people wanting jobs in an area that our company had no involvement in. With just a small amount of research they could have avoided wasting that letter and my time.

Different Types of Computer Animation Jobs: Which one is right for you?

In every job field, there are many different types of work. The same is true for computer animation. On the following pages you will find names and descriptions of the main areas of work that are available. There are a lot to choose from. How do you pick the one that is right for you? As you work more and more with computer graphics, you will discover that you prefer certain tasks to others. It is safe to say there's a job out there that matches your specific area of interest. This list will help you identify and target it.

Art Director

The art director is the bridge between the clients or the producer and the rest of the art crew. The art director's job is to interpret (translate) the client's requests into something that everyone else can understand. They may then have to come up with different solutions for the client's requests. The solution used is often chosen based on the amount of money the client is willing to spend. The art director has to schedule and manage the artists so the job gets done on time. As a result, they need to have a good blend of managerial, artistic and interpersonal skills.

Background artist (matte painter)

A background artist is a more specialized form of a digital artist. This person creates backgrounds for either an environment that needs to have the background changed, or an environment that doesn't have a background at all. Sometimes a background artist will create foreground ele-

A background artist creates "fake" or new environments.

ments too. All these elements are usually inserted using mattes, thus the name matte painter.

In video game development, the background artist is usually called a level artist. They'll build levels or environments where the characters interact. In either case, background artists almost always work in stages. After a concept sketch is completed, usually on paper, the background artists will build a rough approximation of the environment to make sure that the designs actually work in 3D space. Once the problems have been worked out, the final background will be built.

Character animator

Obviously this person animates characters. In really large companies this is all they will do. But in smaller companies they'll probably end up animating other things as well. Think of all the miscellaneous props that need to be animated. Just because a person is hired to animate characters does not mean that they sit around and wait for work that only involves characters.

A character animator needs to know how to take anything and make it come alive. This type of person needs to have a very good sense of timing, weight, balance and motion. Employers looking for animators usually want to see very convincing motion such as pulling, pushing, lifting, swinging, emotions and object interaction. A walk cycle alone will probably not get you a job. Aspiring character animators with 2D animation, stop motion or claymation experience will usually find it easier to find an entry-level job in computer animation than those without.

Compositor

This person takes the rendered animation footage or live action footage and puts it together with other animation footage, live action footage or both. This type of person should have a very good eye for color and light. They'll need to be able to take all the elements handed to them by everyone else and put them together so they look like they match. This means adding grain where it's needed, keying out certain colors, matching black levels, adding blur, rotoscoping, etc. Often the compositor is the very last person to handle the footage before it goes out the door. If they aren't very good, then everyone else's work might be ruined.

Digital artist

Usually this type of artist will create digital 2D-art work for a production. This could be anything from texture maps to background elements to box art to magazine ads. Often it's used as a generic term for any artist that does not exactly fall into one of the other categories.

Effects animator

This person usually ends up animating everything but characters. A wide variety of animation skills are required for this type of work. Each job an effects animator works on is usually different from the last one. One shot might require CG fire and smoke while the next shot might consist of a nebula with some asteroids floating though it. After that they may have to animate something completely different like water or falling objects. Most effects animators will work closely with the technical director to ensure their work is compatible with the rest of the elements involved. At many companies, "effects animator" and "technical director" are synonymous.

Layout artist

The layout artist creates backgrounds for each scene in a production, often based on the storyboards. These backgrounds are very simple, using primitive shapes to represent complex props and characters before they are finalized. As a result, they do not appear in the final version of the production. They are used by the other artists in the pipeline to get the position and scale of all the scene elements right.

Lighting artist

This person lights the scenes so that they fit the style of the current animation. Not only do they need the ability to light a scene realistically, but the lighting must match the mood of the scene as well. Just turning up your lights so everything can be seen does not make you a lighting artist. Once an environment is close to completion the lighting artist can start their work. A lighting artist needs

A lighting artist takes boring images and adds realism through lighting.

to have a good sense of cinematography and color. Lighting artists with backgrounds in photography, video, painting or drawing will most likely have an advantage when applying for this type of position.

Match mover

Match moving is the art of taking real camera movement and mimicking it in the computer. This ensures that all of the effects and animations will look like they belong in the scene. The information is used by the animators and compositors to keep animated and non-animated objects from "sliding" around the scene. For example: Imagine a scene where a computer animated person is supposed to come walking around the corner in a live action street scene. The street would be shot with no people on it. That footage would be taken back to the production company and the match mover would imitate the camera movement in 3D. Then the computer-generated person would be inserted into the scene. If the camera in the 3D scene did not match the movement of the real one then, the 3D person would not look like they belonged in there. More than likely their feet would slide all over the place.

Modeler

This person builds 3D models of everything that is needed for an animation. This can be anything from creatures to props to buildings to vehicles. On larger productions, the jobs are usually split up among different types of modelers, character and object. Character modelers create not only characters but also other organic objects like trees and plants. Object modelers will create just about everything else. Often models are scanned in from a maquette or a sculpture and then reworked by the modeler. The key is to create models that are realistic or match the outlines that the art director has given you. If you are modeling a person, it should look like a real person. (Probably without textures.) Models that are proportioned poorly or lack detail will not get you a job, unless the job you are applying for requires these types of traits, a rarity. Modelers should have a good understanding of mass, volume and geometry.

If you've got skills in a related area such as ceramics, sculpture, industrial design, engineering or architecture, then you'll have a real advantage. Many employers will hire modelers with these skills over other people because of their solid background.

Here is a list of a few things that people look for in a good model:

1. Geometric Integrity: Many of the larger companies use multiple applications to get the job done. Good models will transfer with little or no problems from one application to another. With polygonal models, modelers will need to make

sure all the normals are facing the same way. Keep faces planar to avoid stretching or twisting. Concave polygons should be subdivided to help prevent errors. Polygons that don't take up any space (zero area polygons) should not be allowed. With NURBs geometry, modelers will try to avoid trims and blends as much as possible as they do not translate very well. Also, subdivision models are usually built out of quads to keep them clean when they are subdivided.

2. Animatable Models. A modeler needs to make sure there is enough geometry in the right places so the model does not distort unnaturally when it bends. All this needs to be done without making the model too heavy.

3. Efficient Models. Modelers should use only the necessary amount of geometry to define the shape for a model's intended use. Clean and efficient models are easy to animate, easy to rig, easy to texture and they render much faster.

Production assistant (runner)

This is an entry-level position that can sometimes be a lot of fun. More often than not, it is considered an internship and probably does not pay very much, if at all. A production assistant will do everything that no one else has time to do. If an animator is working on a shot that is very similar to something that was in a recent movie or TV show, watching a copy of this movie or TV show would benefit the animator tremendously. The production assistant will be sent out to find a copy of this "reference material" and bring it back. When artwork gets misplaced, often it's the production assistant's job to hunt through the servers and find it. If it's physical artwork, the production assistant will go through the file cabinets or the warehouse to find the lost item. Near the end of a job, production assistants usually help archive work for use in advertisements, promotional materials, magazine articles, etc... so that it is easy to find when needed. A production assistant might also be asked to go pick up food for animators working late to meet deadlines. In large companies runners might be used to deliver items from one department or building to another. Production assistants often deliver sample work or test shots to clients across town. Sometimes they are sent to the Fed Ex office at the last moment to mail out client work just before the last plane leaves. :)

Roto-artist

This job involves what is known as rotoscoping. This type of artist draws over live action elements (often frame by frame) so that other elements can be placed "behind" them. For example: If real footage of a building is shot and a computer

generated flying saucer needs to pass behind it, then a roto-artist will need to create a "hold-out matte" for that building so that the flying saucer will disappear when it flies by the building.

Software engineer

Most all medium to large CG companies have software engineers who write plugins, shaders, scripts and various other bits of code to help speed the production along. The software engineers work with the rest of the artists to see where "off the shelf" software falls flat. They then fill these holes with newly written proprietary software. The software engineer often bridges the gap between software packages. If something is modeled in one package and needs to be animated and rendered in another, then the software engineer will help get that data converted.

"My eventual goal is to build a spaceship and colonize Venus, but for now I'm looking to move into a senior technic al director position."

Technical director (TD)

A technical director is usually a cross between a 3D Artist and a software engineer. This person spends most of their time solving problems that are technical in nature. The role of a TD varies from company to company. At some companies, TD is just another name for software engineer while at others a TD is really a 3D artist that is more technical. But at most places they are a blend between the two. TDs do a wide variety of jobs and as a result get put into TD sub categories. For example: A character TD will create complex character rigs for the animators. A Shader TD will create looks for certain objects using a combination of procedurally generated images and 2D images. Some TDs will do complex compositing that involves more than just comping one layer on top of another. They also might write scripts or simple plug-ins to automate repetitive tasks. A Lighting TD might take the scenes from all the other departments and integrate them into one final scene, usually lighting and rendering out separate passes and compositing them together.

A character TD takes characters that have already been modeled, or at least designed, and creates a skeleton system that moves the character realistically. Their main goal is to make as much of the animation as easy and as automatic as possible. For example: An overweight character might have loose skin that lags behind the motion of its limbs. The character TD will set up that skin lag to move automatically so that the character animator only has to concentrate on animating the movement of the bones and not the jiggling of the skin. Character TDs often collaborate closely with the modelers to ensure that the model will be rigable and that there will be no unnatural distortions when it is animated.

A shader TD develops "looks" for a particular effect or model. This may include such things as making a particle system look like water instead of sand. They could be creating reflective, glow or refractive properties that are based on the positions of the camera, the color of the object or the lights in the scene. Some TD's jobs involve animating the surface texture of an object so that it changes from one type to another, e.g. from lizard scales to hair. Effects like this might be created with the tools built into the software or they might have to write a custom shader.

A render TD will sort out all of the problems that arise when finalizing the output of a scene. They might work with the compositor to determine what sorts of passes and mattes are needed for a particular shot. If there are problems rendering certain elements with others, the render TD will set them up to render separately or will find a solution that allows them to be rendered together. If a scene is taking too long to render, the render TD will optimize the render settings so that the best quality with the lowest render time is achieved.

Texture artist

This person will create and apply textures to 3D geometry. Just about everything, such as metal, plastic, wood, fabric, skin, paper, etc. needs to have a texture on it. These artists are usually very skilled at 2D and 3D art. This type of person needs a good eye for detail. In a production house, they will probably be creating multiple versions of the same texture to react to different types of light: specular, diffuse, ambient, etc... They will also have to create displacement, bump and other specialized types of maps. In a games company they should be skilled at creating the illusion of reality using small (low-res) texture maps. This might mean creating textures that simulate geometry or light and shadow. On top of that they will need to be able to utilize every pixel of the low-res texture map to its fullest.

Regardless of what format the texture artist is working toward, just applying the texture is almost never enough. Most of the time, especially for characters, textures will have to be changed or adjusted based on many factors. When applied to a character they might not flow properly over the skin when the character is bent into certain positions. When applied to props, textures may need to be changed based on the lighting in the room or other changes in the environment. The job of texture artist is often just as technical as it is artistic.

Job areas

In addition to job types there are job areas that an animator can go into. These areas are very broad and may use some or all of the job types listed previously. The three most popular "job areas" are film, television and video games.

Special effects and animation for film

This is one of the most popular job areas out there. Just about everyone wants to make animation for the next blockbuster movie. As a result, it can be very difficult to get one of these jobs. But it is worth it. Not only is it fun, but making special effects for movies also looks great on your résumé.

In film work particularly, it is very important to specialize. Most film effects crews are very large and work more like a factory and less like the majority of other CG companies. The better you are at one area of CG, the higher your chances of getting a CG job. As you are developing your area of expertise, do some research to see which companies require people with your particular skill and target those first. As in any area of CG, industry contacts will help you land a job. Contacts are more important in landing film effects work than in any other sector of CG. The reason most often given for this is that movie making, and Hollywood in general, often relies more on who you know and your "image" than what you know and your talent. If you are not good at shmoozing then you may find it more difficult to land film work than TV or video game work. Also, film effects work is often too complex for novice and many intermediate CG artists to handle. In order to meet the insane deadlines that are all too common in the film effects world, the artists are put under a tremendous amount of pressure. At times, even the most seasoned artist will find it difficult to meet these deadlines. Most "newbies" are unable to keep up or even work under such incredible strain. As a result it is a huge risk for a studio to hire anyone with little or no experience.

This area of CG is extremely difficult to get into, especially for people with limited experience or recent college graduates. If you are unable to land a film effects job, you might want to set your sights a little lower. Start in an area of CG that is easier to break into, develop your skills and contacts, then try again later on. Try breaking into an effects house by starting off as a runner. This will put you in on the ground floor, allowing you to make valuable contacts that can land you a "real" job later on.

TV special effects and animation

This is also one of the most popular job areas out there. Many people want to make animation for the latest hit television show. It can be very difficult to get one of these jobs, but it is worth it. Not only is it fun, but making special effects for television is excellent experience.

With most television effects jobs, specialization is not quite as important as it is in film effects jobs. This is due to the fact that the majority of television effects houses are much smaller than film effects houses. As a result, employees will need wear more than one hat. At very small production houses, employees may have to do a little bit of everything: animation, modeling, texturing, rigging, lighting, rendering, compositing, etc.

Getting a job doing commercials is usually more difficult than getting a job doing television shows since television shows have a longer production cycle than commercials. Because of the extra time involved, they can afford to take more risks. If you do not have much computer animation experience and want to do commercials, try to break into long format television animation first and work your way over. The television industry usually moves faster than the film industry because it takes less time to make television shows and commercials. As a result, television work normally ramps up very fast and production houses will need to hire a lot of staff very quickly. Reading trade magazines (such as the ones listed in the "resources" section of this book) to find out what new productions are starting can help you anticipate which houses will be hiring. This way you can be prepared when the time comes. Since television job contracts, particularly commercials, are typically shorter than film contracts, be prepared to move from one job to another rather quickly, especially in the beginning. In time you will be able to land a full time job at a larger production facility. As with film work, getting into the door initially might mean doing non-CG jobs such as runner, tape operator or render watcher. But if you prove to be reliable, it can lead to better positions in the future.

Video game production

There are just as many people waiting to do animation for video games as there are for film and TV. As with film and TV, this area can be pretty hard to break into. Because it usually costs less to make a video game than it does to make a movie, there are often more video games being made than there are movies. Because there is more work, it is easier to get a job in the game industry. Often it takes longer to create a game than it does a TV show or commercial, and most game companies develop multiple titles simultaneously, finishing them at different times. This means an artist might finish one game and either jump into an ongoing production or start work on a new game. This is one of the reasons why video game jobs tend to be more "permanent" as opposed to hiring contractor or freelance artists. Game jobs offer more entry-level positions than television or film animation. If you are looking for a relatively stable, long-term, entry level job, then game production is a better bet than television commercial production.

When job hunting for video game positions, start with the larger companies first. They tend to be more stable and usually offer a higher salary than the smaller ones. Because they are larger, they have more openings. At the larger companies (and many of the smaller ones) specialization is becoming more and more prevalent. Learning a specific skill like modeling, animation, level creation or effects, can help get your foot in the door.

Don't just blindly mail out demo reels. Research the companies you are applying to. If you do not like modeling automobiles then it would be wise to steer clear of companies that focus on racing games. As with many other CG jobs, talent and a good demo reel make up a large part of the requirements, but not all of them. Personality and attitude go a long way in a job interview. Some games take years to develop and are made up of a very large (but close-knit) group of individuals. If a rift forms between the team members it can spell disaster for their current title. Needless to say, finding people that are team players with the right outlook can be a major concern for many game companies.

Game vs. film

I think now more than ever the two mediums have more in common than in conflict.

One of the things I do at the game company I work for (Outrage-THQ) is sift through the demo reels and new applicant resumes. As a result of this I've recently been interviewing a lot of people from the film CG camp. It's funny, that without exception, every Film/Broadcast animator that I've brought out for an interview has said something along the lines of "I was worried that this would be totally different - but it's exactly the same." The games industry has been, for a while, heading towards the same type of specialist mentality that is seen in the larger houses. We do storyboards, animatics, have writers, directors, budgets and milestones, and we are concerned about things like fluid dynamics. We also think story is extremely important and yes, we have action figures and artwork all over our offices <G>. Of course there are differences, but the basic setup and workflow is much the same.

I, however, think people are being a little broad when breaking down these types of jobs. One simply doesn't work 'in games' or 'in film' - there are a multitude of different positions. I would wager that a texture artist on a film is doing pretty much exactly what one does on a game, same case with a tools programmer, a concept artist, or the guy building maquettes. Making cycles for crowd scenes is pretty much the same thing as making a cycle for a real-time character. What's more is that these things are being done in the same software.

The other huge factor here is that there are many, many companies in both industries - some are small, some are large, some are good, some are bad. The production pipeline can vary a lot from place to place. Control and creative input is easier to achieve in a smaller studio and being part of a large grandiose production is better suited for larger teams - the format doesn't much factor in here. When dealing with any premiere house, you're going to find a lot of commonalties.

I think one of the reasons that games have had such a bad rep in the past is that there was a lot of highly visible bad work being done and the production procedures are/were still being worked out. Fortunately, bad art in a game now stands out like a sore thumb and the people doing scheduling are much more attune to design and timeframes than in years past. This is only going to get better as the industry matures.

So anyway, I guess my 'long-winded' point is that there isn't much difference anymore. There's a whole bunch of extraordinary talented, hard-working, self motivated 'geeks' in either camp <G> and each field has its share of ups and downs - They are both great places to be.

Doug Brooks
Outrage-THQ
www.outrage.com

Multi-media

Just about every large company distributes information to its clients, customers and employees using multi-media: e.g., a kiosk in the middle of the main lobby that displays office locations or other company information or a CD-Rom that teaches customers how to use certain products. Hundreds of thousands of these multi-media productions are created every year. Often they do not need the same production quality that other jobs require. As a result, some multi-media companies are easier to get into and can be a very good place to start your animation career.

Instructor

All these CG jobs have to be filled somehow. Someone has to teach the new wave of CG professionals about color theory, which buttons to push and how to make a walk cycle. This is what an instructor does. Many people forget that there are computer animation jobs that are not production based but education based. For every type of CG job there are instructors who teach people how to do it. Some larger companies even have full time in-house instructors, but most instructors work at a school. It could be a university, trade school, community college or some other type of training facility.

Forensics animator

This type of animator reconstructs crime scenes in 3D for use in court cases. They'll make detailed re-creations of events to help clearly present the facts of a case. The emphasis in this work is on accuracy. Forensic animation does not need to be very detailed, but every object must be technically and geometrically accurate against the events that they are re-creating.

Industrial visualization

This animator will create animations of products. Often they are used to sell items that are difficult to demonstrate such as very large machinery. If a company wants to buy an oil rig, there is a chance that some, or all, of the rig will not be available for them to inspect. The industrial animator will create animations showing how the rig works and why it is superior to the competitor's oil rig.

Architectural visualization

In this sort of job, the animator will be visualizing buildings and building sites before or during construction. When architecture is visualized before construction it is usually done to secure funding for the project. Once the financial backers have seen what it looks like, what it can do and how it can make them money, they are more willing provide funding. Visualization done during construction is used to pre-sell or pre-rent portions of the building, (like office space or apartment buildings). The architectural visualization area is not the easiest to break into. A degree in architecture is usually preferred. Average animators usually don't know anything about architecture; much less have a degree in it. There is only one way for a non-architect to get hired at an architectural visualization job. This is when they will be working under a team of other animators that already know about architecture. In addition to those requirements, you'll need to be very good at modeling and fairly good at lighting and textures. The animation is usually not that hard. Most of the time it is just simple things like camera movements, swinging doors and moving elevators. If you like architecture, can't animate very well but are great in every other area, then this might be the job for you.

Logo animators (often called motion graphics artists)

There are plenty of people out there who do nothing but animate text. It may sound boring, but they do it in such a way that it is interesting. This is often called "bending chrome" or "spinning logos." During a half hour TV show there are an average of 100 different types of animated text, from the tag lines on the commercials to the network station ID's to the credits at the beginning of the show. Someone has to animate all of this flying text. Sometimes it's done in 3D, sometimes it's animated using a compositing package. No mater how it is done, some one is getting paid to do it. It might as well be you.

Corporate animation

Large companies need animation. It could be for internal videos, television ads, trade show videos or training. Just about every fortune 500 company has a corporate video department of some sort.

Internet animation

Not every web page has graphics on it, but almost all of them do. Many use 3D programs to generate these graphics. Just about every high profile graphics intensive web page has 3D elements in it. (pre-rendered or real-time.) In this particular area of CG, specialization is not as important as it is in others. Most web companies like someone who is well rounded and has a good sense of design rather than an individual who only knows how to do photorealistic texturing. Often an animator doing internet animation will end up working with a 2D and 3D animation to create the art work. Learning to create efficient and attractive art is the key to impressing your future boss, should you decide to shoot for a job in internet animation. Also, when creating your web assets, try to use popular plugins that every one has. No one is going to take the time to download and install an obscure plugin just to see your work. Unlike other CG shops, this is the one place where a web link might be more welcome than a demo tape. However, it is best to send both. Better safe than sorry.

Internships

Sometimes it is impossible to get a "real" job. Maybe you are still in school, or perhaps you've graduated and there are currently no jobs available. Now is a good time to look for an internship and apply for it. If you get one, do every job, no matter how menial it is, as best as you can. Some companies have internship programs. Sometimes you can get paid as an intern; usually you can get college credit. Contact the Human Resources department of your target company and ask whether they have an internship program.

3D for print graphics

Many people don't even consider the "2D" world of print when looking for a job in 3D graphics. Lots of magazines, books, CD covers and DVD cases contain 3D art in some form or another. Someone has to make the 3D for these ads and products. It might be you. Since this area of CG is not as well known, it is often easier to get a job in it. Fewer applicants means less competition. Just because it's easier to get into does not mean that it is an easy job. Print graphics are usually very large, which means that they can take longer to produce than television or even film graphics. Print jobs usually have a shorter deadline than other types of CG jobs too. In the print world, the client has spent a lot of time coming up with exactly what they want long before they start working with you to produce the final artwork. This means that you'll have less artistic control over the results. These restrictions often hinder your ability to use time saving workarounds that you've used in the past, such as hiding mistakes with lots of motion blur or film grain. All of this together adds up to quite a lot of work. 3D for print is not a 9 to 5 job, especially if you are working for an ad agency. At a print shop however, your hours may be much closer to standard.

Medical visualization

Medical visualization has become a key element in communicating and understanding medical information. It is used to help doctors, surgeons and scientists understand human and animal physiology. Dissecting cadavers for learning purposes is expensive. But it is an important part of medical training. Medical visualization does not replace dissection, but it is used to cut down on the number of times it is needed. Medical visualization is used to create training videos, textbooks and other learning material. It is also used outside the classroom. For example, it can be used to show doctors "3D structures" of a patient, making it easier to avoid disturbing vital blood vessels or to know the exact location of a tumor so less healthy tissue is removed during an operation. You don't need to know a lot about medicine to do medical visualization, since many medical visualization professionals work alongside doctors when creating the animations.) Modeling skill and accuracy are the two most important assets needed in this area.

"A few years ago I would have said they were
in animation, but these days it's anybody's guess."

Getting a Job and Making Contacts at Conventions and Festivals

Animation events

Every year there are hundreds of animation related events. Most of these events come in two flavors: conventions and festivals. Conventions focus on selling and training while festivals focus on celebrating and showcasing different types of artwork. Some of these events are relatively small with attendance in the hundreds, and some of them are very large with attendance in the tens of thousands. Regardless of the size, they are a great place to meet new people, increasing your chances of getting a job.

The smaller events usually require very little planning on your part and are relatively easy to navigate once you are there. Most of these smaller events focus only on their main area of interest, (selling products or showcasing artwork). The larger events, however, go way beyond their area of interest by adding classes, parties, presentations, exhibits, users groups, career advancement services and more. These are the types of events that will probably require you to travel out of town. Smaller events that aren't local usually aren't worth the travel expense. You will find some of the information in this chapter useful when attending smaller events, but you will probably find it is more applicable to the larger events.

Examples of large events:
    3D Festival: www.3Dfestival.com
    ECTS expo: www.ects.com
    Electronic Entertainment Exhibition: www.e3expo.com
    Game Delevopers Conference: www.gdconf.com
    Game Delevopers Conference Europe: www.gdc-europe.com
    NAB - National Association of Broadcasters: www.nab.org
    SIGGRAPH: www.siggraph.org

This is just a small sample of the animation related events that take place all over the world every year. Each of them have their own unique characteristics. But, in the end they are all very similar in that they are basically large gatherings of individuals in the animation and entertainment industry. One of the most popular events in the United States is the SIGGRAPH convention. Even though this chapter focuses on getting a job at this particular event, the same basic concepts can be used for just about any convention or festival around the world.

The SIGGRAPH survival guide

Every year there is a convention called SIGGRAPH. (www.siggraph.org) It's held by a Special Interest Group (SIG) that deals with computer graphics. This group is a part of the ACM (The Association of Computing Machinery: www.acm.org).

What is the ACM? It is the world's first educational and scientific computing society. It's an international scientific and educational organization dedicated to advancing the arts, sciences, and applications of information technology. ACM functions as a hub for computing professionals and students working in the various fields of Information Technology. ACM has Special Interest Groups (SIGs) in many distinct areas of information technology. Each SIG organizes itself around those specific activities that best serve its members. Many SIGs sponsor conferences and workshops. The one that we are concerned with is, of course, SIGGRAPH.

SIGGRAPH is the world's annual gathering of the international computer graphics community. At SIGGRAPH you can see the next generation of powerful hardware and software, and understand how technical innovations are changing your work, your profession and your company. If you work in the field of computer graphics, this is the one event that you don't want to miss. Not only is it a great place to see new technology and learn about current trends in the in CG industry, but it's also a great place to look for a new job. It's not the "end of the line" if you don't get a job at SIGGRAPH, but your chances of getting one there are usually higher than any other single place. This is where you can meet and talk to professionals in the field as well as get priceless feedback on your work.

SIGGRAPH basics

SIGGRAPH is made up of many different activities. The two most popular are "Courses/Papers" and "The Show Floor." While SIGGRAPH lasts for approximately seven days, the show floor is only open for three of those. The courses and papers often overlap each other and run the entire seven days. The majority of the activity takes place between 8 am and 6 pm daily. However, some activities start late and can go until 10 pm (special presentations like award ceremonies or speeches and evening showings of the electronic theatre, for example).

The show floor is definitely the most fun. If you have ever been to a convention, then you are probably prepared for what you will see on the show floor. If you have not, you'll more than likely be a little overwhelmed at first. The show floor consists of hundreds of software, hardware and other various vendors trying to get you to either buy their product or to convince the company that you work for to buy it. While this might sound like a real life infomercial, it's actually a very good place to learn. Most of the vendors will have demonstrations of their products at their booth. Often the people that demo these products are very good at showing its strengths. What good is this to you? If you use a particular piece of software you can go up to the experts and ask them just about anything and they will probably be able to give you an answer. Beyond that, they will also be able to give you a demo of some of the software's features. The demos are usually pre-planned and designed to "show off" the best features, but often they contain lots of very helpful tips and tricks the average person might not know about. Twenty minutes with a demo person showing you some great tricks could save you hours of trying figuring them out on your own later. These demos can be pretty fast and after watching 10 in a row, you will probably forget a lot of the tricks that you saw. Either take something to write on or figure out how to record the demo. SIG-GRAPH convention rules state that you are not allowed to bring video cameras or any other type of recording device onto the convention floor unless you have a media pass. (This is not very easy to get unless you work for a magazine, news-paper, TV station or something similar.) I am not saying that non-media people don't do it, just that they aren't supposed to. However, at just about every SIG-GRAPH demo I have ever attended there have been at least one or two "non-media" people with video cameras recording it. While I don't condone this sort of activity, I see no way to stop it.

Software and hardware vendors will not be the only people on the show floor, but they will represent the bulk of them. Animation companies will have booths as well, not a lot, but some. Expect to see most of the larger animation houses there. Often the booths are staffed with animators from that company. This means you may be able to ask them questions directly. Just make sure you don't take up too much of their time. Ask your questions, but don't be annoying or monopolize their time.

The show floor is fun, but you will learn a lot more at the courses and papers. These courses usually go for a full or a half-day. They cover a wide

The SIGGRAPH show floor can be a lot of fun

variety of topics including art, science and engineering. These courses offer extensive instruction from experts in the field. They vary from straight presentations to interactive "classroom" style workshops. Papers are usually presented "lecture style." Often they have a small-er audience than the courses and are a bit more informal. SIGGRAPH papers do not have to focus directly on computer graphics. Sometimes they just cover areas that overlap computer graphics in some manner, e.g., robotics, computer vision, audio and other areas where computer graphics might be applicable but not the main focus.

SIGGRAPH pre-planning

Plan what you are going to do at SIGGRAPH before you go. Don't just show up with a bag of demo reels and expect to get a job, although not showing up with a bag of demo reels is a bad idea too. You want them to hire you based on what... looks? (It's rare, but I've seen it happen.) If you don't live in the city that is currently hosting this years SIGGRAPH then you will probably have to spend a lot of money to get there. You'll have to pay for hotels, plane fare, car rental, and much more. But there is something much more important than the money it costs you to get there. Getting a job. You could happen upon an opportunity at SIGGRAPH that lands you the job you always wanted or, at least, starts your career off on the right foot. You don't want to miss that opportunity because you did something wrong, were late, left something behind, got lost, etc... This next section is devoted to helping you have your most successful SIGGRAPH job-hunting trip ever.

Clothes/shoes

Make sure you have a comfortable pair of shoes. This can't be stressed enough. Don't just buy them the day before you leave. Buy them at least two weeks in advance. This will give you an opportunity to see if they are comfortable and wear them in. If they are not comfortable buy some new ones as soon as possible. Your main mode of transportation at SIGGRAPH will be your feet. If they are sore or you develop blisters you'll be unhappy and it will make it difficult to make it to your interviews on time, not to mention that wincing in pain or acting grumpy at your interviews will not help you get a job.

Bad Shoes :(**Good Shoes :)**

Wear comfortable clothes, something that is loose enough so that you won't get sweaty and won't rub you raw as you walk. SIGGRAPH is usually in July or August and is often held in places that are pretty warm around that time of the year. Being hot and sticky is no fun. You don't need really incredibly nice clothes; just clean clothes. Interviews at SIGGRAPH are always more informal than regular interviews, which are pretty informal anyway. A nice T-shirt and clean shorts, jeans or pants are perfectly acceptable. Try to wear clothing without logos or at least with out "computer graphics company" logos. It's not a good idea to apply for a job at a company wearing a shirt that is advertising their competition.

Hotel rooms

Don't stay in a hotel that is very far away from the convention center. You might save $40 a day but you'll lose valuable time. Your time is worth a lot more than that $40. For example: If you have to commute thirty minutes to and from your hotel you've lost at least an hour every day. You paid a lot to come to SIGGRAPH. What's another $40? You are saving money but you are not saving time, and in this case time is money. You don't want to waste either.

Be careful when picking your hotel. If a hotel says "only 5 minutes from the convention center." Don't believe it. They probably mean that it is only 5 minutes away if all the stoplights are green and there are no other cars on the street. Do some research. If you can get it, rent a hotel room that is close enough to the convention center for you to walk. This will really come in handy if you forget something and have to go back to the room to get it.

Picking the right hotel is more important than you think.

You'll need to register early to get a good hotel room. If possible, reserve your room at least 4 or 5 months before SIGGRAPH. Do this, even if you are not absolutely sure that you are going to be able to go. If it turns out that you can not go, just call and cancel the room. The good hotel rooms that are close to the convention center always fill up first. If you've got friends that live where the convention is being held, ask them if they know which hotels are nice and which are not. It's better to stay in a fairly nice hotel that is 3 blocks from the convention center than a dump that is just across the street. If you don't know anyone that lives there, do a little research on the Internet. Read some reviews. It won't take long to figure out which hotels are nice and which are not.

Setting up interviews beforehand

Talk to the companies you want to interview with at least a month before SIG-GRAPH. If possible, send them your demo reel ahead of time. Let them know you will be attending and that you are job hunting. Don't wait too long to call, you'll miss the opportunity to talk to them before they get really deep into planning their SIGGRAPH. You want to make it as easy as possible for them to schedule you for an interview. It's better to be too early and told when to call back than to call too late and have them tell you, "Oh, that person has already left for SIG-GRAPH, sorry."

Try to schedule a meeting or interview for the beginning of SIGGRAPH. If you wait till you get to SIGGRAPH to set up your interview, you'll be lower on the list and your interview will be later on in the week. This is not bad, but it's better to be one of the first ones to interview than one of the last. You don't want an interviewer who is tired from a week of interviewing, partying and the general exhaustion that usually accompanies a trip to SIGGRAPH. You'll also be harder to forget, since interviewers tend to remember better the first people that they interview. If you get to SIGGRAPH before it starts, then you won't get lost in a sea of interviews because a lot of people won't be there yet. A typical interviewer might see 30+ people a day when the floor is open. But early on in the conference, when the only big things happening are courses and papers, that same interviewer might only see 10 (or fewer) people.

Learn your way around SIGGRAPH long before you have to be anywhere.

Learn your way around early

SIGGRAPH is busy, it's crowded and it can be a little confusing at times. There is so much going on that it's easy to become overwhelmed by it all and lose sight of the real reason you came: to get a job. If you arrive at SIGGRAPH early then you've given yourself time to relax and mentally prepare for the coming week. If you have a long flight then try to get there at least a day before so that you can recover from the jet lag and adjust to the new time zone. Map out where things are. If you have time, find the hotels, hotel rooms, conference rooms, companies, booths, etc., where you have interviews and visit them. If you can't get into the building, at least go find out where it is. This will make it a lot easier for you to get there when the time comes. It will also make your time at SIGGRAPH much less stressful. The last thing you want is for your first impression to be "This animator is late for his interview." If you can't even show up on time for your interview, then what's to say that you'll show up for your job on time? If you are really stressed out your interviews might go badly. It's better to show up early and waste 30 minutes or so waiting around than to be late.

SIGGRAPH interviews

Interviews at SIGGRAPH are quite different from normal job interviews. They are usually a little more rushed. There will be no opportunity for you to tour the facility unless the company happens to be located in the same city as SIGGRAPH and they are holding their interviews there. You'll need to bring everything that you would bring to a normal interview: demo reels, a cover letter, a résumé, business cards, etc. Prioritize your target companies. If you were not able to talk to them before SIGGRAPH, visit their booths and see if they are interviewing. During interviews ask questions about the company. Don't just sit there and nod. Offer to exchange business cards. If they don't want to give out their information, let them know that you understand. Don't get angry or act disappointed. It's always good to provide them with a way to identify with you that is beyond just your name and your face. Try to mention this just as you are leaving. For example, "If you ever need to remember who I was, I was the guy with green hair."

The career center: AKA the "Résumé Wall"

At most SIGGRAPHs there is a room or area that is called the career center. (If this is one of you main reasons for attending SIGGRAPH, be sure to check beforehand to see if there will be one.) The main feature of the career center is the "résumé wall." This wall is a series of bulletin boards with computer artist, educator and graphics programmer résumés hanging on them. There are also job boards where companies post open positions and information on how they can be contacted for interviews during SIGGRAPH. This room should be your first destination when you get to the show. On the first visit, arrange to have your résumé posted and check the job board for anything that you think you are qualified for. Immediately set up interviews with as many of those companies as you can. After that you should come back at least twice a day, every day, to see if any new jobs have been posted and if the résumés you left behind are running out.

You can't just walk in and pin your résumé up on the wall though. The SIGGRAPH staff will take it down. Take your résumé up to the résumé desk and get it registered. This is also where you leave a stack of extra résumés. Give them as many as they will take, probably about 50. They might never give out that many, but better safe than sorry. When you register your résumé it will be assigned a number. This number will be attached to your résumé and both will be hung on the wall. If someone sees your résumé and likes it, they will write the number down and take it up to the résumé desk. One of the staff will hand them a copy of your résumé.

There are not very many guidelines to follow when it comes to posting your résumé on the wall. There are size restrictions and a couple of other rules but other than that you can post just about anything within reason, of course. The rules have changed slightly over the years so it's best to look up the current ones at the SIGGRAPH web site before committing to anything. (www.siggraph.org.)

Because the rules are so lenient, there are a few things that you can do to make your résumé stand out from all the others on the board. Creating a color résumé to post on the board can make a big difference. The key here is to have something interesting. Don't just print a résumé on color paper. It might be hard to read. Take your time and design something nice. The information is the most important part of the résumé; so don't make it difficult to read. The résumés you give the résumé desk should be typical "black and white." Leave out all the color. The problem with this is that people might think they've been handed the wrong résumé since the one on the wall was filled with color and the one they are now holding in their hand is black and white. To help ease the transition, you might want to use a paper clip to attach a small business card sized version of the color résumé at the top of the black and white one. It also might be a good idea to attach a small version of the black and white résumé to the color one that's hanging on the résumé wall. Put a caption above it that explains that: when you go up to the résumé desk you'll receive a black and white version of this résumé, not a color one. Why are you giving them a black and white version? Because, black and white résumés are very easy to fax, photocopy and scan. Most color résumés are useless unless you've got one of the originals in your hand.

Some people might not want to take the time to write your number down and go get your résumé. They might be in a hurry, they might only be marginally interested in your work or they may just be too lazy. There is a way to help these people remember you even if they don't pick up a copy of your résumé: Business cards. I've seen plenty of people create or buy business card holders that can be tacked on the corkboard just below the résumé. Go to your local office supply store and look around. They are bound to have something that will work. If not, you can probably make one using a pair of tin snips and some very thin metal. Load it up with business cards and not just ordinary ones. Make "SIGGRAPH business cards!"

SIGGRAPH business cards

What's the difference between these and normal business cards? Not much really, just a few additions. These cards have all the standard information such as your name, address, phone numbers, e-mail and web site. But in addition to that, it'll have another address and phone number listed, the one belonging to your hotel. Since you'll know this address long before you get to SIGGRAPH you can easily have it printed it on your card. What you won't know is the room number.

Even if the hotel gives you a room number, for some reason it might change, you can never really be sure. Leave a space for you to write it in. If you do not have a cell phone and are planning on renting one when you get there, leave the cell number space blank too.

Make sure your pen uses ink that will show up on the cards. If your card is black with white type, then an ordinary pen will not work. You'll need a paint pen or something similar. Test this out before you leave for SIGGRAPH. Once you are there, you won't want to waste your time running around looking for a pen. This is a lot of information to fit on a standard business card. You might print the hotel information and your normal information on different sides. If you do, make sure that there is a small note at the bottom that says, "Turn card over for more information." You'd be surprised how many people will miss it if you don't. With all this information on one card you'll be very easy to get in touch with. But the best part is that you won't have to write your hotel info or cell number on the back of every single card that you hand out. While you are at SIGGRAPH, watch how many people have to do this and how many times they have to do it.

Career fair

The career fair or job fair is designed to get companies and future employees face to face in an informal setting. (If this is one of your main reasons for attending SIGGRAPH, be sure to check beforehand to see if there will be one.) At the fair there are a lot of small booths where job seekers can line up to talk to animation companies. Often the company has a few employees interviewing and some video screens for them to view demo reels. This is a great place to conduct informal interviews and get feedback on your demo reel.

Something that I feel is important for a lot of 3D artist to always consider when trying to get into the industry is, it's not always what you know it's who you know. Now, I'm not saying that education and knowing the software is not important. What I am saying though is that it's equally as important for the artist to get involved in the 3D community. Having contacts and people that you know you could in turn be equally as important as having a good demo reel. I personally started a student Siggraph chapter at my university as well as became active on the XSI user e-list.

Becoming familiar with the people in the community and what they do, who they work for can become very valuable when it comes time to try to find a job. If at all financially possible I would recommend attending at least one Siggraph convention. It's a week of software vendor parties and the latest greatest things out in the 3D market, which makes for an ideal place to pass out business cards and meet new artists and individuals like yourself. If you are a student, you can volunteer and have most if not all expenses taken care of for you. Even if you aren't a student and would have to pay for the convention consider this: is the $2000 or so for overall expenses worth it to you to make contacts that could possibly lead to a job you really want? If not, you may want to seriously reconsider this line of work for a career. One thing I definitely learned in pursuing my first 3D job is that you have to be aggressive and willing to take the means necessary to make things happen for yourself.

Jayson Walton
3D Artist
QuiteMan Studio NYC
www.quietman.net

Saving money

Face it, attending SIGGRAPH is expensive. Not only do you have to get there, but you have to pay for all sorts of other items too: food, hotel, transportation, entry fee, cell phone, demo reel, etc. If you are a student, or you are a little low on funds, there are quite a few things that you can do to save money.

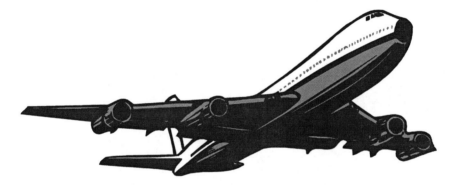

You can save a lot on your airfare if you book early and search the net for good deals.

Air fare

You can save a lot of money on airfare. Buy your ticket a few months in advance. If you know someone who is a travel agent, get them to give you some pointers. Use the Internet to hunt for the best prices. Try some of your local carriers. There are a few airlines that don't list themselves with the big internet airfare search engines. Sometimes you can get better deals through them or you can get a better, maybe direct flight for less. If SIGGRAPH is in a relatively large city there may be multiple airports that service that area. Check to see if airfare to any of these airports is different. Then check to see how much it will cost to get from those airports to your hotel. If the extra price of the shuttle or taxi costs exceed the ticket plus shuttle costs of other airports then you should probably rule that one out. Don't forget that sharing a ride with other people going to SIGGRAPH with might lower the price, but make sure you ask. Some shuttles charge per person, not per trip.

Hotel costs

Hotel rooms can be pretty expensive, especially if you get one that is fairly nice. If you can't afford a hotel room on your own, then ask some friends if they want to share the room with you. You probably don't need all that space to yourself anyway and most hotels do not charge much more if you get a room with two beds.

There is a lot more to a hotel than just the price.

Try to get a SIGGRAPH hotel room. They are all on the "SIGGRAPH Shuttle Route." Taking the shuttle to and from the convention center can save you a lot of money in cab fares. (The shuttle is free.) Not only do these shuttles take you to the convention center, but they can take you to other SIGGRAPH events as well. If you can't get a good hotel that is on the shuttle route, then the next best thing is to get a hotel that is close to another one that is on the route. There is nothing stopping you from walking over to that hotel and taking its SIGGRAPH shuttle. Most shuttles won't let just anybody get on, so be sure to bring your badge with you. If you are fortunate enough go get an interview with a company that is interviewing at a SIGGRAPH hotel, you can also take the shuttle to that hotel, either from yours or from the convention center. Be sure that you plan for the extra time that this might take. You don't want to be late.

Food costs

Food at most convention centers is usually not very good or healthy and it's extremely overpriced. You can save a lot of money by packing your own lunch. It's also a good idea to bring a sports bottle that you can fill up at the closest water fountain. Not only will you feel better because

Food costs much more than you think. You can save a lot by bringing your own.

you'll have more control over what you eat, but you'll save a lot of time too. Eating at the convention center always takes forever. The lines are long and there is rarely anywhere to sit. If you bring your own food, you can eat whenever and wherever you want. Some of the best times to eat are during presentations, classes, papers, and demos. This way you're really able to maximize your time.

Entrance fees

SIGGRAPH has three registration categories: Exhibits Plus, Conference Select and Full Conference. Exhibits Plus is the cheapest and is usually priced between $40 and $65 USD, depending on when you registered. If you register before the deadline, you can save quite a bit. Exhibits Plus allows you entry into everything that you need to job hunt. The show floor, birds of a feather, the career center, the job fair, etc... There are a few things that you won't be able to go to where you could schmooze, but nothing that is crucial to your job hunt. If you are trying to save money this is the ticket to buy. With it you get about 50% of what you'd get if you were to purchase the Full Conference ticket.

The Conference Select pass will allow you into many more events, but not all of them. You'll get about 75% of what you'd get with a Full Conference ticket. Conference Select will cost somewhere between $200 and $300. The price varies depending on whether you are a student, a professional or a SIGGRAPH member. If you are a student, you'll save a little money, but not much.

The Full Conference ticket is the most expensive one. If you're trying to save money, you will probably not want this one as the student price is usually between $400 and $600. But the non-student price is much more expensive. It usually costs somewhere between $700 and $1200 depending on your membership status and when you buy it. To check the exact price of your ticket and the deadline dates, go to the SIGGRAPH web site, www.siggraph.org

When you register for SIGGRAPH you'll get a badge, a swipe card and a map. The badge allows you to get in. Do not lose it! SIGGRAPH will not give you another for free, they will make you pay for it. If you lose your expensive full conference badge, you are out of luck. The swipe card contains information that vendors can use to send you information in the mail. When you walk up to a vendor's booth they will ask if they can swipe your card. They'll run it through a machine and in a few weeks you'll start getting literature in the mail from them.

Student volunteer

You can get into SIGGRAPH for free if you help the conference by being a "student volunteer." SIGGRAPH will give you a conference access pass equivalent to a full conference pass without the documentation. If you work 35 hours or more, you'll receive either a free hotel room or a very, very good rate on a hotel room.

SIGGRAPH will even pay for your travel expenses if you qualify for a travel grant. To get the grant you have to write up a paper outlining certain criteria specified by the SIGGRAPH travel grant committee. For more information, check the SIGGRAPH web site. http://www.siggraph.org

What to do with all the "Free Stuff"

At SIGGRAPH you will inevitably end up with a lot of promotional and course material. If you are not prepared to deal with all this free stuff, it can be a real pain. Here are a few things you can do about it. Bring an extra empty bag. (A duffel bag or a large backpack will do.) This way you can unload all of your extra SIGGRAPH items into it every night when you get back to the hotel. Then, when it is time to leave, all you have to do is pick up the bag and go home. If you want to make things even easier, you can ship all of your materials home. There is a shipping station at SIGGRAPH. All you have to do is to take your materials to the station. They provide the boxes and mail everything home for you. Just make sure that you don't mail anything home that you'll need before you leave. Also, make sure you insure it. Sometimes the packages "disappear."

Miscellaneous SIGGRAPH notes

Before you go to SIGGRAPH, ask people that have gone already for some tips. If they are going again this year, ask them if they'll let you "tag along" with them for a little while. If you don't have a camera, get a disposable one. SIGGRAPH is a great place to snap pictures. Take every opportunity to talk to people around you, on the shuttle, when waiting in line, on the plane, etc. You never know who you might be sitting next to. Ask them what they do, where they work, how they like SIGGRAPH so far, etc. When people give you their business cards, write down a little info about them on the back of the card. This will help you remember who they were. There are informal meetings at SIGGRAPH called "BOF." This stands for "Birds of a Feather." They are a great for meeting people with similar interests. Another great place to meet people is at receptions and parties. There are plenty of these throughout the week. Try not to party too much though. It will make interviewing much more difficult. :)

People at SIGGRAPH will do pretty crazy things to get a job. I've seen quite a few people walking around with small video players showing their demo reel to anyone that will watch it. I've seen people with shirts that say: "Hire me" or "Will animate for food." I don't know how well things like this work, but they were very funny.

"Your résumé is unclear about what you did before you quote-unquote, 'sold out to the establishment', Mr. Phil."

Getting a Job in the Real World

Getting a job

You could get the first job you apply for or the 42nd. It could take you a week to find work or it could take a month. Regardless of how many you apply for or how long it takes to get one, job hunting is never very easy. This chapter covers topics from what to wear, say and do, to layoffs, rejection letters and bad interviews.

Never point out mistakes in your reel during an interview

You are at the interview and they are watching your demo reel. You see all the mistakes. (After all, you've seen this demo reel hundreds of times.) You want to point out the problems and explain why they are in there, but don't. If they didn't see it, why call their attention to it? If they point them out, and you knew they were in there, explain why and that you'd have fixed them if you could. If you didn't know they were in there, be honest and thank them for showing you the mistakes. Let them know that you'll fix it before your next batch of reels go out. This makes them feel good because they were able to help you out. It also boosts their ego a bit because they were able to spot something that, up until now, no one else had noticed.

Flying to an interview

If the interview is far enough away that you have to fly there and you are an experienced animator, then the company doing the hiring should pay for the ticket and your hotel. Never pay for a flight to an interview. If they are not willing to pay for your expenses then they are probably not serious about hiring you. Don't waste your money or time. If it is a short drive from where you live or even it's one or two cites away you should take care of the travel arrangements yourself. Sounds great, doesn't it? Free air fare! Unfortunately this does not apply to

everyone. If you are a student or have very little experience, then you will probably have to pay to fly to your interviews. Since this can be very expensive, it is best to organize several interviews for each trip. There is a chance that you might not get an interview simply because you are not local. Many companies are not comfortable asking you to fly to an interview unless some one hands your demo to a recruiter and tells them that you are willing to fly out for an interview.

If long distances are separating you from your dream job then there is an alternative. Consider temporarily moving to an animation hot spot for a month or so. Perhaps you have some friends you can stay with, or at the least, rent an extended stay hotel room. Being local will dramatically improve your chances of getting interviews.

Never be late for an interview.

Always be on time!

If you live in the same city as your interview, there is no excuse for being late. Before the interview, take a practice drive to the company, even if you know where it is. This will make it a lot easier for you to get there when the time comes and give you an accurate estimate of travel time. If you are flying into the interview, chances are someone from the company will be there to guide you around. This will make it hard for you to miss the interview. But if they fly you in at night and your interview is the next day, make sure you get a wakeup call as well as set an alarm. If you get up late and aren't ready when they come to pick you up it will reflect badly on you. If you are responsible for grabbing a cab or taking a train to the interview, ask the concierge how long it will take you to get from your hotel to the company at X time of the day. Then add 15 to 30 min. It's better to show up early and wait around than to be late. The last thing you want is for your first impression to be "This animator can't tell time." If you can't be punctual, they will question your ability to show up for work on time.

What clothes to wear

Be sure to wear something that is clean and neat. You don't have to wear a suit to 99% of the interviews out there. Exceptions might include CG jobs for the government, executive positions, research facilities, architecture, and corporate animation jobs. Wear something comfortable. Sometimes interviews can last for hours and ill fitting clothes will put you in a bad mood, making you uncomfortable both physically and mentally. However, don't show up in an old T-shirt that has stains on it. No one wants a dirty employee. As stated earlier, it's not a good idea to wear clothing that has animation "company logos" printed on it. Why? If you go to an interview at ILM wearing an ILM shirt, that might make them think that you are some kind of a fanatic. (Too much of anything is not good) You want them to hire you, not be scared of you. At the other end of the spectrum, don't wear a Disney shirt to a Warner Brothers interview. These two companies are competitors and they probably won't appreciate your choice of shirt. It's like trying to get a job at Microsoft while wearing a shirt that says "Macintosh Rules." It's just not a good idea.

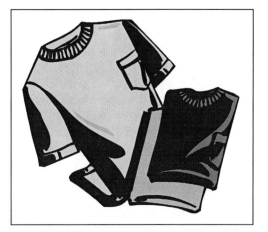

Clean, comfortable clothes are required. Don't be a slob at your interview.

Be nice to your former employer

If you've had a previous job and quit, were laid off or got fired, don't badmouth that company or the people who work there. Be very diplomatic about it. If you got fired, tell them that things just didn't work out at your last job. If you got laid off, let them know that your contract was up or that the company was downsizing. Do not tell them that your co-workers were not nice, your boss was not smart, etc... Interviews are not the time for you to vent about the last place you worked. Not only is it unprofessional but you never know who the interviewer might be friends with.

No matter how much you didn't like your last boss, it's not appropriate to talk about it in your interview.

I've seen people that were the obvious choice for a particular job, that were passed over for "lesser qualified" applicants because of what they said about a few of their former co-workers. In one case an applicant did not get the job because the former co-worker he was talking badly about was the interviewers girlfriend.

Never share proprietary information

Never share proprietary information with your potential employer. If they ask you to tell them how your last company did their skin system, set up their render farm, created certain "trade mark" effects or anything that the general public can't find out by attending a SIGGRAPH paper, reading a copy of Cinefex or watching a "making of" show, then don't say anything. Just let them know, nicely, that you are not at liberty to share that type of information. If they get angry with you, then you probably don't want to work for them anyway. If they say, "Ok, no problem." Then you might have just avoided a trap. Sometimes companies will ask you questions just to see what type of person you are. If you are willing to give out proprietary information from your last company, you'll do it with future companies too. Once this becomes common knowledge, it will be very hard for you to get a job anywhere. These types of questions can come in many forms. It's not always about technology. I've heard of interviewers asking to see shots from unreleased films, television shows and interactive software. If you think you are pleasing them by giving them what they want, think again. It's a trick. They are "feeling you out" to see if you'll betray the trust of your current/previous company. It may sound dirty, but these people can't afford to have employees that will leak important information to competitors or the media before its time. Some interviewers will ask you to leave your company now, rather than when your job or contract is up. Saying things like "We really need you now" and "can't you leave a little early." Sometimes this is a trap too. If you'll leave one company hanging, they suspect you'll do it again.

"There is nothing wrong with the phone, you're trying to make a call with the TV remote."

Relax and pay attention

Be yourself. Don't try to hide who you are. Relax at the interview. Believe in your skills and give it your best shot. This is not easy, but it makes the interviewer more comfortable when they don't think you are scared out of your mind. Bring multiple copies of your demo reel to every interview. If multiple people need to look at your reel or want to show it to others and they are not going to be in the same place, give them all copies. Reels get lost all the time; it's better to give out too many than not enough. If they will watch it with you, then by all means do it. Ask them what they like about your tape and what they don't. But if they don't really have the time, don't be pushy. Thank them and move on to the next portion of the interview.

Bring other work with you, but only if it's good work, of course. Sometimes companies want to see more of what you've done, if you've got it with you that might be all it takes to land the job. If you don't have anything else worth showing them then let them know that. No extra work is better than "bad/lower quality" extra work. If you question whether or not you should put it on your reel then leave it at home.

Stay alert and pay attention. You will be in a new environment. There may be a lot going on and it may be easy to become distracted. Interviews can be very long and you may start to feel tired. Focus on what the interviewer is saying, no matter how out of it you may feel.

What questions can you expect to hear at a typical interview?

The probable reason you got an interview is the company liked your demo reel. Frequently, they will start by watching the reel with you and asking you how you did certain things. Prepare for this by watching your reel at least a day before the interview. Try to remember how you did everything, especially segments that were particularly challenging. If you don't go into much detail you'll make it sound like everything was easy and the interviewer will then think that it was. They might get the impression you'll fail if given something hard to do. Rewatching your reel makes it easier to answer questions about it, too. Your answers will come more naturally, you'll feel more relaxed, and you'll look like you know what you are talking about. If you have to stop and think before every sentence, you'll appear ill prepared, they might think you don't know what you are doing or that you aren't telling the truth. If you have "before" and "after" shots that didn't make it onto the reel, then now is a good time to show them. Answer questions succinctly.

"Before and after" shots make explaining what you did to the interviewer much easier.

Prepare good short and medium length answers to all of the standard questions: "Why do you want this job? What qualities do you think will be required for this job? What can you contribute? Why do you want to work for this company? What do you know about this company? What can we (the new company) offer that your previous company cannot offer? Why should we employ you? What is your most notable fault? Where do you see yourself in five years? What is your greatest quality?" Answer these questions, but do not go on and on for 20 minutes about every detail.

If you've got a portfolio, bring it with you. If they ask to see some pictures of your work, then get it out. But don't open it up the instant you walk into the interview. Most interviewers have a system they use when interviewing people. This is especially true of those who do a lot of interviewing, so don't interrupt their "flow." They will ask for your portfolio when they are ready to see it. Just keep it in plain view so that they know you've got one. Otherwise they might not ask. The only time you should get it out before, is if they ask you a question that can be better answered with a few images.

"Well – I imagine you have a few questions of your own.

What do you ask the interviewer?

The interview process is not just a one-way street. This is probably going to be your best opportunity to ask questions about the company. Remember, not only is it important for the company to like you as an employee, but you have to like being an employee there as well. If both of those are not true, then you'll be miserable and so will they.

There is nothing wrong with asking how many people have been interviewed so far and how many there are left. It is also good to ask where you stand in comparison to the other applicants that have come through so far. This will help you gauge your chances of landing the job. It will also provide an insight into how long you will have to wait after the interview to hear an answer.

On top of asking all the right questions, you'll need to sell yourself as well. If you've already had a job in CG, then use this as a foundation for getting your personal sales pitch off of the ground. Immediately, you'll be regarded as "better" than all of the entry-level applicants. Make sure that you act like you enjoying the interview, even if you've had a bad day. This is your only chance to make a first impression. If you are grumpy they might not hire you. Try to point out your strengths. (What makes you stick out from all the other animators that are applying for the same position?) Keep your "pitch" short but filled with good details. Do not point out your weaknesses. This might cost you the job or negatively affect your pay if you do get the job.

Read up on the company before you go. This will help you come up with intelligent, focused questions. Prepare a list of them before the interview. Don't try to make it up as you go along. Ask what your responsibilities would be? Where will you fit into the overall organizational structure? Who will you report to and where do they fit in the structure? What is the next step? Ask about your position and others like it. Are the artists given any creative freedom or is everything dictated from above and set in stone? Some people like to be told exactly what to do while others want to be much more creative. What type of person are you? Will you fit in to what ever style this company uses? Are the work groups pretty open, do they share a lot of ideas, or do people just stay in their office most of the time? Is there a lot of weekend work? What are the average working hours? If they say something scary like 12 to 16 a day, every day, then go somewhere else, unless you are a workaholic, in which case you'll fit right in. How long do typical projects last? What does the future hold for people applying for this position? What sort of positions do you move into as you become better and better? Do they normally hire people for a project and then let them go after it's finished or are they looking for permanent employees?

"It's come to my attention that you have a life outside the office."

Working 16-hour days all the time isn't perceived (by me!) as a good thing. Work smart. Have a life. I would argue that you do better work if you have interests outside of work. The crunch does happen, but if it's always happening, then you have a problem. Either you're not working smart, or your manager is overworking you - neither are good.

I would like to point out the unfortunate fact that just because I think these things, doesn't make it factual across the board. Alas, we have to realize that there are just as many (more,

I would argue) bad managers as there are bad animators. Managing is a very, very tough job and, unfortunately, there are rarely any "schools" for managers.

John Coldrick
Senior Animator
Axyz Animation
www.axyzfx.com

On almost every interview you'll get a tour of the facility. You might not get to see all of it, if it's really large or if they are working on "top secret" projects. But you'll get to see some of it. Look around as you are guided through. Try to see if the employees are happy. How is the atmosphere? Are there posters, toys, photos, and similar items all over the place or does the company ban such stuff? Is there a lot of open space? Does their workspace look comfortable or are they crammed in like sardines? Do they get to work on fairly good machines or are they working on out-of-date equipment? Who has private offices? Does anything you see contradict what the interviewer has told you?

Sarcasm Alert:
"Porl's Useful Tutorial #10" ...How to Get a Job

Not so long ago, I had the very special pleasure of popping down to Bournemouth University, UK, to speak on a subject very close to my heart: Money. But they wouldn't give me any so I agreed to talk to the students anyway about a subject a little less close to my heart: Animation. And because they're a damn fine bunch down there they listened intently to whatever rabid sputterings emanated from my fragile and diseased psyche that day, and patiently waited until the part of the talk that speakers and audience wait for with equal ation.That's anticipation for the audience and trepidation for the speakers. Because what these hungry young scamps- and tired, old, wizened mature students, let's not forget them!- really want to hear is not some idiot spouting on about how to do the job with some software that they already know (considering they have every release of every software package on their PC at home, probably more resources than most PP houses in Soho today)- but how to get a JOB. Now, there's a lot of mystery about this; some to-ing and fro-ing, humming and harring and a little Wa-hey! Where the #@&% did *that* come from? So in the spirit of a crazed renegade magician escaping the stifling folds of the Magic Circle I'm going to saw in half the beautiful assistant of Job-Hunting Requirements. Here they are...the secrets are finally unleashed!

On your CV. (That's resume for you American types.)

Always present yourself as confident and capable. Some people think a CV doesn't matter but they couldn't be more wrong. Most hiring bods will read all manner of atrocities and eccentricities into your CV unless you spell it out. Also bear in mind that many producers still can't feed themselves let alone operate a VCR. Your tape may never even get seen so make the most of your CV. Start off with a good joke like 'sex: yes please' and end with 'hobbies: shagging and drugs'. Lie criminally about experience you can't possibly have (Tron's a good one) and preferably take credit for a piece of work the guy hiring you actually worked on himself. If called on it at interview stage simply shrug and say, "Well I could have done it... but better, granddad". Add cool comments like "I will be the best one day and if you miss me now I will make you pay". The CV really is the most important step in going for a job.

On your tape:

This is the most important step, of course. No tape- no job. I can't underestimate how important this will be in assessing you as a potential new animator, so.... go large. I mean large. No, larger than that. I'm talking massive. Make the intro to Star Wars look like a Pot Noodle commercial. I'm talking credits, a massive, MASSIVE soundtrack- preferably Prodigy's "Firestarter", a surprisingly underused piece of music to animate to, and make the opening sequence your most majestic and slow piece you have. A 360-degree pan around a space scene would be perfect. Make it a 720. Beautiful. Then jump cuts through the rest of it: No more than 12 frames of each animation piece slammed together - about 45 minutes should be ample until the guy's eyes are bleeding, dude! Fantastic. Now, finally, is the time to showcase your best animation. What people want to see is just ONE example of anima- tion, but the best one. It should be about 10 seconds long then just repeat it until the tape runs out. Put that lot together and I could watch it until my retinas detach.

In your interview:

You made it! Marvelous. This is the last step- but the most important one. Turn up late for god's sake. No one wants some Mr. Do Good yapping around like a puppy. Show your strength, they'll soon be eating out of your hand, so why not make it now? As you get shown around the place make insulting comments about people's work to show that you're more capable. If they turn on you and say, "Well, how would you do it?" Just sneer and say, "Hey Pops, I don't work here yet. No advice for free." Then pretend to shoot them with your finger and wink. When asked if you work well with other people- you will be asked this- say "No. So I will need my own office". Set the terms out and you will get respect. Finally when you are shown the door and they say "We have some other people to see, we'll be in touch", don't shake their hand just spit "%$&@ that! I wouldn't work here if you paid me a million. Besides, I've already been offered 80 thou by 2 of your competitors so you better think fast!". Go home, picking up a celebratory bottle of red stripe and a bounty bar, and wait for those phone calls to come in.

Remember: What postproduction houses are crying out for are animators who can tell their own story. You wouldn't believe how much money there is waiting in buckets for people who want to animate their own story. If you are one of these seemingly mythical beings sim- ply turn up at the interview and say, "I don't want to work for you I want to work at home on my own short. Give me money". Fantastic.

Porl Perrott: porlp@btinternet.com

Be prepared

Be sure that you have researched the company enough, have a good understand- ing of their needs and can direct your remarks appropriately. This includes know- ing what they've worked on and (if possible) whom they have worked with. For each interview, prepare a sheet of notes that contains your research for the job, and the anticipated questions you'll need to answer. Include also the questions you want to ask them.

Body language

When you are being interviewed it is very important that you send out the right signals. Try to look like you are always paying attention. Sit up straight, do not slouch in your chair. Do not lie to anyone in an interview; your body language, tone of voice or words will probably give you away. These things include scratching your nose, not looking directly at the other person when you are speaking to them or shifting constantly in your seat. Your nose might itch, or you may be a shy person, but they don't know that.

What do you do if you decide you don't want the job?

During your interview you might see something that really turns you off. You know immediately that this is not the place for you. Don't stop the interviewer and tell them. Continue with the interview as if nothing has changed. Pretend the company is great and that you still want to work for them. Why would you want to waste your and the interviewer's time like this? Because the person interviewing you today could be the same person interviewing you 3 months from now. They also might be very good friends with you next interviewer.

Why would you turn down a job? Here is an example. If you keep hearing over and over how good your reel is from respectable sources like industry professionals, then watch out for predatory employers, agents or recruiters. These types of people will promise you fantastic rewards if you work for them. They will try to convince you not to send your demo reel to any other companies. They will also try to get you to sign a "great contract." More than likely you'll be trapped making less than you deserve for the duration of the contract. All they want are very good employees that work for as little as possible. While this is very rare, it does happen. So be on the look out for it.

After the interview

Send them a thank you letter after the interview. Thank them for taking the time out of their busy schedule to meet with you. Remind them that you are very interested in working for their company and why. Point out some of your strengths you think will benefit the company will if they hire you. Tell them you really appreciated the interview, that you enjoyed your visit and you hope that you get to meet with them again someday. Not only is this a nice thing to do, but it keeps you fresh in the mind of the interviewer without being annoying and raises the chance of you getting hired.

If you are not getting any job offers then you might need to look carefully at your interviewing skills. Get as much feedback as possible from the people who have interviewed you. If possible, contact the interviewer and ask them where they think you fell short and how you could do better. Once you have feedback you can modify your interview technique and hopefully do better next time.

What to do if you get turned down

Chances are you'll apply for and interview for a lot of jobs before you actually land one. If the opportunity arises, ask your interviewer if there are other positions in the company that your skills would fit. You might even ask if they know anyone else that needs someone like you. Some people will feel bad turning you down and will be eager to help you out. It usually makes them feel better and can only help you.

Preparing for the dead space between interview and job

There will almost always be a "dead zone" between interviews and the actual hiring. Some people make the mistake of waiting for a phone call from the last interview. The best thing you can do while waiting for a call is to keep yourself busy looking for work. Not only will this open up other opportunities for you to work elsewhere, in case none of the previous companies are interested in hiring you, but it will also keep you busy. Keeping busy is the best way to get past tough times like this. If you planned ahead and gave the company your cell phone number rather than your home number, then you won't be worried about missing their call.

In preparation for your "dead zone," you'll need to make sure that you do a few things. At the end of your interview ask when they might be contacting you. When that time has come and gone, call them instead. These people were obviously interested in you and considered you a candidate; otherwise, they would have never brought you in for an interview. It's safe to say that they probably want to hear from you again; if they don't, they will most likely tell you. This can help you decide if you need to continue putting time and effort into getting a job with them or focus your efforts on other companies.

Don't just sit around waiting for a studio to call you back. Get out and job hunt.

Just because they don't call you when they said they would does not mean that they don't want you for the job. Getting work out the door on time, meeting with clients, getting new work, meeting deadlines, etc.... is infinitely more important than hiring new employees. These people can get overwhelmed with work and sometimes forget altogether that you came in for an interview 3 weeks ago. It cannot hurt if you call them up and refresh their memory; in fact, it will probably help.

Rejection letters: don't give up

While looking for work you'll also receive a lot of rejection letters. They'll say something like "Your skills do not fit our needs at the moment." It's not the end of the world. You might not be good enough for them or someone who is better might have applied for the job. The job might have been cut. The job might have been filled before you applied. There is no way of knowing. But don't take it as a personal insult that you didn't get hired. This is business and these companies have to hire the best applicant they find. You can't expect to get every job you apply for. Don't let rejection letters get you down or cause you to give up. It can take weeks, sometimes months, to find a job. Try to use the rejection to find out why you did not get the job. If you remember who you interviewed with, give them a call or send them an e-mail. Politely remind them who you are. Mentioning something very memorable from your demo reel will usually jar their memory. "Yes, I was the guy that had the purple headed medusa fighting with Dilbert on my demo reel." Once they remember who you are, ask them if they mind telling you why you didn't get the job. Tell them to "let you have it, tell you the truth," that you can "take it." This way you'll get an honest opinion. If they try to be nice and sugarcoat the info you'll never learn what went wrong. Ask them if the decision not to hire you was based on the quality of your work, if the job was cut, or if they just didn't think that you fit in. If they say that your work just wasn't good enough, then ask them what was wrong. What can you do to improve your reel? Was there something on there that needed to be removed? Is there an area that they think you are really weak in that you can focus on to help increase your chances of getting work? If the job was cut, ask them if you would have been hired had it not been cut. If the answer is still no, why? If they didn't hire you because you didn't fit in then ask them if there are any other companies that they know of where you might fit in. The world of computer graphics is pretty small. There is a good chance that they will know of a place or two where you can apply.

When I was trying to get a job at Click 3X, they told me that they liked my work but didn't have a position available. I told them that I'd do anything at the company...ANYTHING. I said that I'd be happy if they just let me come in and sweep floors...the general manager laughed.

3 months later I stopped by again...this time with a big industrial sized broom in hand. When the general manager greeted me, I told him I came ready to work. They hired me. And I didn't have to sweep floors.

Alex Smith - Animation Director
SOMERsault/Avenue
www.somersault.net
www.alex-smith.com

If you don't get the job, don't send them another reel for at least 6 months, unless they ask for one or you've made a drastically different, better quality demo reel. Most companies will keep you on file for 6 months or more. So they might call on you to send another reel if you qualify for a new job opening. They might not have hired you the first time because they didn't need your skill set at that time. The situation may have changed since then and resubmitting your work every 6 months can never hurt unless it's the exact same work, over and over. Your "new" reel can contain work from the last reel you sent them, but make sure that you've taken out a lot of the old work and replaced it with new work. If you don't it will look like you have not been doing anything for the past 6 months. Don't think that won't remember, either. Animators have a very good visual memory. They can spot a "re-run" demo reel in an instant. Don't waste their time. That will only make them unhappy and won't help you get the job.

Keeping your contacts organized

Even before you start applying for work you should keep a database of everything that will help you when the time comes. Every computer graphics person that you talk to, even for a few minutes, can be a potential gold mine of information. If nothing else, write down their name, company, position, etc., just after speaking with them. (Some people get a little freaked out if you start writing down their name when you've only just met, so it's best if you don't let them see you doing it.) If you've got to carry around a small notebook, so be it. Better yet, carry a PDA of some sorts. This way it will be easier to incorporate all the information into a central location and keep it organized. Use this list to keep track of every company that you have ever sent your demo reel to, who it was addressed to and when you sent it. This will allow you to follow up on your reel mailings and call back when the appropriate time arrives. Because you're so organized you'll also be able to check and see if your reel even made it to the company. It's a fact of life that mail gets lost. If you just assume that they watched your reel, didn't want to hire you but never sent you a rejection letter, then you might just be a victim of misdirected mail. The one place that your reel didn't make it might be the one place that has the perfect position. If you need to be absolutely sure your reel arrives, send it registered mail, Airborne Express, FedEx or UPS. These four methods all have ways you can require a signature or track your package online to be sure that it got there. They will cost more though.

Using your contacts

Many people get their job because of who they know, not what they know. When a company needs new employees they often ask the current employees if they know anyone that needs a job. These "friends" usually get hired first. Then, if the company still needs new employees, they will start looking externally. The more "friends" you have the easier it is to get a job.

When the time comes to look for a job, you can get out your massive list of contacts and start calling/mailing/e-mailing them. Don't just write up a form letter that says "Dear sir or madam, may I have a job?" This won't work, and will often get treated as a joke or anger the person you sent it to. (They might think its spam mail). When you were writing down a persons name and contact information also write down the specifics of the conversation. When and where you talked to them and what you talked about. This way you can be more specific. If you were wearing something memorable then mention this. If you have a noticeable feature, like being 7 feet tall or having blue hair, then mention this too. To give you a starting point, read the "sample" letter below.

Hello Phil,

We met at the super8 film festival last September. I was the 7-foot tall guy wearing the shirt with the super8 animation logo on the font. We discussed the pros and cons of working as a freelancer and you mentioned that you had just switched from freelance to a full time gig at Acme Animation Labs. I was thinking about switching from the freelance world to the full time world also and was wondering if you knew of any places that needed people with skills similar to mine?

Thanks for your time. If you have any questions or information that you'd like to share, feel free to give me a call or e-mail me. Hope to talk to you again sometime.

Your name
Tel: 1-555-555-5555
Web: www.yourwebsite.com
E-mail: You@Yourwebsite.com

You could go into a little more or less detail about yourself depending on how well you know the person and how long ago it was that you talked to them. Make it more formal if you don't know the people that well, but it would best if you start with the people that you feel you have the most in common with. Don't just start mailing people, in order, from A to Z. Pick out those you felt comfortable talking with, the ones that you had successful conversations with. If you just talked to someone for 30 seconds and have not seen them since, you'd probably want to leave them till the absolute end or not contact them at all. It would feel forced and the person on the other end might not remember you. They'll end up thinking, "Who is this freak?" as they press the delete key.

Be courteous and polite to your contacts

Attitude is very important when interacting with your contacts. Be courteous and polite. These people are doing you a favor by helping out. There is no rule that says, "You must help out anyone that contacts you." If they respond, then be happy and move forward with your correspondence. If they do not respond, don't think that e-mailing them over and over will help. It will probably just annoy them. Never get angry with someone who does not respond to you or sends you an answer you don't like. If they say, "I'm sorry, I'm just to busy to talk at the moment," then wait and mail them some other day. They might really be busy and mailing them without waiting a week or two (sometimes more) might just anger them and ruin that contact for good.

How do you meet these contacts?

So where are you going to meet these people? Attend local graphics events: SIG-GRAPH meetings, users groups, animation presentations, film festivals, art shows, industry parties, etc.... You'd be surprised what people you can meet if you just start going to these functions. Not everybody lives in or near a city where things like this take place often or at all. What do you do then? Use the internet! There are many high quality users groups, message boards, mail lists and web sites that can connect you with people from all over the world. Since every person that does computer graphics uses a computer almost every day, the chance that you'll meet some of these people online is incredibly high.

When I first started out I used to think: "If I work hard, I'll get a job." But to be honest with you, when I finished school that illusion was completely shattered. Sorry to bring you such bad news but this is the reality of the situation. People who say "With just talent and a little effort you can make your way in this business" are people who never had trouble finding a job, were pretty lucky or have great social skills. The truth is that it takes much more than talent to make it; it also takes contacts, charisma, and opportunism. All the people I talked to here in Montreal are in agreement with me.

It is tough these days. Talent is not enough, that's for sure. The hardest thing is to get noticed by the right people. Once you are noticed, you can get them your reel. Only then can they get you an interview.

Your most valuable resources, in fact more important than talent, at least in your first years as a 3d artist, are contacts. I have gotten several jobs through contacts. Some of them didn't even see my work before I met them. I have known people who were not especially talented that have gotten jobs just because someone referred them or got them an interview. Often employers do not publish available positions; they will simply ask their employees if they know anyone (most people in 3D know at least 5 other people doing 3D).

So my advice to you is this: become a user group member, attend events, create a business card, talk to people on the internet and make a strong reel. Contacts open doors; after that it's up to you to make a good impression. Sometimes, you will be hired just because you are a pleasant guy. Many interviewers believe that the chemistry is more important than raw talent. After all, talent can be developed through hard work, but bad chemistry is deadly to a production. Obviously an employer would rather invest time training you for the job rather than hire you, fire you, then hire someone else, all because they found out that your chemistry was bad. Remember: when someone wants to hire you, he is not just hiring your talent; he is hiring you as a person. It's exactly like buying a product. You don't always buy a product because the price is low or because you think it's the best product. You buy the product because you already knew about it (through recommendation or advertising) or you like its packaging. In the industry, your attitude and reputation count for a lot.

Bernard Lebel
3D Artist
www.BernardLebel.com

Online and offline contacts

One thing to keep in mind: the people you meet online are usually a different breed than the people you meet in the real world, off-line. Online people are more apt to take a look at a web based demo reel or a web site featuring your work since it's just a click away. People that you meet at meetings and user groups are more likely to want to see a VHS tape, if anything. Remembering a URL and remembering to go to that URL when they "get a chance" is much harder than putting a videotape in a machine. The tape sits on their desk and is hard to miss, while a URL written on a napkin at a party will probably get thrown away. I'm not saying that you should walk around with your demo reel in your hand, but keep them in mind so you can send them one later, if the need arises. It is a good idea, however, to keep demo reels handy.

I knew a guy that used to keep three or four copies of his reel in the back seat of his car (in a box, out of the direct sunlight). Occasionally he would get a request for a reel. These reels never got him a job, one that he sent out in the traditional way did, but it did get him noticed. He never pushed his reel on anyone, but when they asked, he always went and got one for them. As a result he gained a reputation for being very "on top of things" and "prepared."

Improving your chances at a job - create a web site!

Making a web site is relatively easy. You can send people to it when it is impossible to give them a demo reel or they want to see your work immediately.

In order to make a web site, you need 2 things:
1. A web site authoring program.
2. Some web space (server space).

There are a lot of low cost "web site authoring programs" on the market (Macromedia Dreamweaver, Adobe Go-Live, etc...) for making simple web pages. They are relatively easy to use. If you've never made a web page before, you'll probably be able to learn to make a simple one in less than a day, using these programs.

What do you put on your web site?

You need at least the first three things listed below to create a useful "job hunting" website. The rest are nice to have on your site, but not required.

1. Your résumé (both in html format and as a downloadable doc and txt file).
2. Contact information (e-mail address, telephone number, physical address, etc...).
3. Still images from your demo reel.
4. Scans of your traditional artwork (if applicable).
5. An avi, quicktime or mpeg of your demo reel with a shot breakdown.

If it is not possible to make an electronic version of your demo reel, post a note on your site that says, "If you request a copy of my demo reel, I'll send it to you via snail mail." If you are able to post an electronic version of your demo reel, then write up some "behind the scenes" info to go with it. Explain how you created certain effects in your reel or how a character was rigged. If you were watching this demo reel with a prospective employer, what would you tell them about it? Put the answers into your behind the scenes web page. If you do not have an electronic version of your demo reel then try to do some behind-the-scenes pages for your still images.

Portfolio web site design tips

Make your site very east to navigate. Take some time and learn how to compress your work properly so that it will both download fast and look good. Avoid implementing features that require the viewer to download a plugin in order for it to work. Choose a fast, reliable web host. If your site does not load in the first few seconds, the viewer will move on to the next one. Many people like to see descriptions of your work along with small notes explaining how it was created.

Content over style. Make sure the site's style does not detract from the work displayed on it. You want to show your artwork, not your web design skills. The more stylish your web site is, the more risk you are taking in showing it to potential employers. They may love your work, but might be turned off by your site design. You are better off with a "safe" design that does not get in the way of the content, i.e., one that is clean, not too trendy and easy to navigate.

E-mailing images

Sometimes employers will ask you to e-mail them some sample images. When e-mailing images try not to compress so much that they start to look bad. But on the other hand, don't send giant 10-megabyte uncompressed TIFF files either. Always strip the alpha channel out of your images to make efficient use of the file size. Use WinZip to compress them. Never e-mail images to a prospective employer unless they ask for them.

Covert job hunting:
How to hunt for a job when you already have one

If you already have a job and are looking for a different one, never ever use your work e-mail or telephone to look for it. Also, don't use messaging programs that log your conversations (ICQ for example) to talk to others about looking for work. You might be disappointed with your current job, you might not be working in

Don't get caught job hunting at work!

the computer graphics field yet or you might just want a change. Whatever your reasons, are if you are planning on leaving your current job you'll need to be discreet about it. No company wants their employees leaving, but if an employee is interested in moving on, most of the time there is nothing that they can do about it. However, at some companies, if they find out that an employee is planning on quitting they might replace them when they get the chance. Sometimes this happens before the employee has had a chance to find the next job. The last thing you want is to have no job at all because you were talking about "this interview" or "that lead" really loudly in the break room. The extra effort that you put into finding your new job with out calling attention to it might be worth it.

It is not a good idea to use company resources (fax machine, telephone, e-mail, etc.) to hunt for a new job. You could be fired for job hunting while you are getting paid to produce work for your current employee. Also, it's just not morally right to use the company's resources to hunt for a new job. Some may consider it stealing. You can get into a lot of trouble. Some places track and record everything that comes in and goes out of the company. This includes, but is not limited to: Fax machine transmissions, e-mail messages, telephone conversations and inter-office mail.

> I have even known of one instance where every letter, personal and work related was opened, read and then passed on to the recipient. While this is illegal in the most countries it was not illegal there.

There are plenty of things you can do to avoid these problems. If you don't have Internet access at home, or if that Internet access does not supply you with an e-mail address, then get a free one from a provider like hotmail or yahoo (www.hot-mail.com and www.yahoo.com). Use this e-mail to correspond with your prospective employers. The same goes for Fax machines. If you don't have a fax machine or a fax modem, get an electronic fax number from a provider like efax (www.efax.com). If you are going to be making a lot of telephone calls, get a cell phone. Put this number on your résumé, demo reel, e-mail, etc... This way if someone wants to hire you they can get in touch with you any time, day or night. You could be in the supermarket and miss that all-important job call because you weren't at home. Also, make sure that your cell phone has a voice mail option. If you happen to wander out of range, you don't want to miss that call completely. The key is to make it as easy as possible to get in touch with you so that hiring you is the simplest thing they've ever done.

Do you need a degree to get a job?
Yes and No. Sometimes a degree helps you get the job and sometimes it does not. (But it never hurts to have one). Here is why. Company "A" needed an animator. They received a million reels, watched them all and eventually narrowed it down to 2 people. Both reels were equally good. Both applicants were almost identical except for one aspect. One had a degree and one did not. The guy with the degree got the job. But, had the demo reel the non-degree applicant sent in been better, he would have gotten the job instead. In that case, the degree would have not mattered. (See what I mean?) There are many areas where a degree is important. Do your research early.

> There are, however, graphics type jobs that require a degree. (This is rare.) For example, in addition to my day job, I'm a SoftimageXSI instructor at a local graphics school. This school is required by the government to have instructors with master's degrees or instructors that are enrolled in masters programs, working toward a master's degree. As a result, if you don't at least have a Bachelors degree then you can't get that particular job. (Unless you can figure out how to get a masters without getting a bachelors first.) Even then you still have to convince them to hire you.

I learned 3D at a focused school where the training was intense and expensive. I could have gone to public school instead and paid a fraction of what it cost. The reason why I did not is because I no longer have faith in public schools. Don't' get me wrong; there are some very good schools around. Even though I graduated with a graphic design degree from a public college, I felt that I wasted a part of my time there. I had to take courses that had nothing to do with my program, like French, English, Philosophy, Physical Education, and so on. The thing is, these courses are imposed by the Quebec public school system. So, there is no way around them.

I studied 3D at a private college, doing exclusively what I was there for. It was 7 months long, and cost me CAN $14,000, with more than half paid straight from my pocket (ouch). Even though I was not pleased with the public schools, there are good things and bad things in both systems. For instance, in public school you have a lot of unwanted courses. But since I spent 3 years there, it allowed me to develop my artistic sense. Plus, I had 2 years of experience as a graphic designer. So, when I attended the private school I already had a solid art background. Some of the other students were not as lucky. Without the background, a lot of them produced bad looking, poor quality work.

So, my point is; it's good to go to a school offering expensive, short-term training as long as you have the artistic skills before you get there because you won't have much time to develop them while you are there. Struggling with the software will hold you back to a certain point, so the more you know beforehand, the better off you will be.

Bernard Lebel
3D Artist
http://www.bernardlebel.com

What if you are not a U.S. citizen and want to work in the U.S.A.?

If you do not have a current work visa (H1B visa or "Green Card"), you cannot legally work in the United States. To get a work visa, you have to find a company that will sponsor you. Your chances for getting a visa or a sponsor are much higher if you have a four-year college degree. If you are from Canada or Mexico a two-year degree will suffice. Generally, only larger companies are set up for this kind of situation. If you do not have a degree you will need 3 years of work experience per year of formal higher education you don't have. This means it will take 12 years of working to achieve the equivalent of a 4-year degree. The whole process can take quite some time. Once you're in, you are bound to the company that sponsors you. If you quit or get fired you will need a new sponsor and will have to go through the process again. The good news is that European talent seems always to be in demand in America. The bad news is that it's expensive to mail off résumés and reels to every company you want to work for and you will be lucky if any of them respond. Your best bet might be to contact selected individuals privately. A trip to SIGGRAPH might get you a job. Or, you could go to the USA for a short period of time and job hunt. For more information on work visas contact U.S. Immigration and Naturalization Service at this address, (http://www.ins.usdoj.gov).

A sneaky trick for landing your dream job

Sometimes it takes more than just a good demo reel to get a good job. There are a lot of people out there that want the same job you are applying for. If you are having trouble getting a job or find the job that is perfect for you and can't possibly live without it, then it may be time for some "sneaky" job-hunting tricks.

Earlier in this book I talked about "airfare and how a company should pay for it if they want you to work for them." Well, if you want to use this "trick" you'll have to throw that idea out the window. Many companies will not pay for moving costs if they can get a local employee. If you are not a local employee, this might make it very difficult for you to get a job with them. For example: You live in New York, but the job you are after is in San Francisco. Even if you are the perfect fit for the job, how are you expected to compete with all the local talent? If you can't beat 'em join 'em. (Well… sort of.) First step: Get a San Francisco telephone number and a P.O. box. If you've got a friend that already lives there, ask if you can use their phone number and address instead. Apply for the job using this as your "new" address and telephone number. If you buy your own telephone number, just have it forward to your cel phone or your home phone in New York. If you are using your friend's number make sure that they tell the callers that you are either not home at the moment or have them forward the call to you. If you use a P.O. box, have all of its mail forwarded to you in New York. This way, if you get a rejection letter, you'll know to give up on that company. If they ask you to come in for an interview, tell them that you are currently freelancing in New York, but that you plan on returning "home" in the next day or two. Ask when the best time for the interview is. (Make it easy on them.) Once you've set it up, go buy a plane ticket. In the interview, they might start talking about San Francisco. If you have not spent much time there, this could be a problem for you. Rather than "get caught" just tell them that you've only recently moved here and that you don't know your way around very well yet, which is sort of true. If all goes well, you'll get the job. Of course they are not going to pay for your moving expenses and you might feel a little guilty for tricking them, but its better than no job, isn't it?

Job hunting the "Chris Wise" way

I realize it must get quite depressing for many of you who haven't managed to get a job in the industry you love, and it seems to get tougher every year, but how hard are you trying? If it helps anyone, I'd like to share my experience of finding my first job in the CG industry. I didn't find it too difficult to land my first full time job, mainly because of the way I approached it, a very unorthodox approach. I was really only interested in game development and even though I had no previous experience in the industry, I was determined to find a job.

Thanks to his determination, Chris now has a successful career in the video game business

I'd always heard that you should send out CVs and portfolios then wait to hear a reply, but there was no way I was going to do it like this because I knew that if I did, there would probably be no way I'd get a job, especially going up against people with more experience and skills.

First of all, I had to find out which studios were known to hire inexperienced staff. I just phoned every game company in the country, and if I didn't manage to get through to the right person, I'd just try again later until I got the information I needed. I worked out that the best person to be talking to wasn't the manager or the person doing the hiring, but instead the lead artist. If I didn't manage to get hold of the lead artist on the phone, I'd try to source their email address, and 9 times out of 10 I'd get it. Then I'd try to build up a rapport, asking if there's anything useful I could be learning to help find a job in the industry, I'd go to work on some models and make sure I'd keep them updated constantly with my progress (at least once a week). This is probably the most important part as this person will more than likely have the final say in who gets hired, and if they can see that you're backing up your commitment to learn and (more importantly) be constantly reliable, you've got a very good chance of scoring a job. I actually ended up having the choice of three different studios to work for, and there's been no looking back since.

Another excellent work of art from Chris Wise

I more or less did my apprenticeship in the industry for a few years (with low wages and long nights) then began freelancing and I used pretty much the same approach to find my first contract. I don't have much trouble finding new contracts these days, as the more games you get under your belt, the easier it is to secure the next job. Hope this helps a little, and shows there's no textbook approach to finding your way into your dream job

Cheers,
Chris Wise
cwise@netspace.net.au

"Before we hire you, you'll have to take a battery of tests, sign a few contracts, and to through two years of psychoanalysis."

They want to Hire You!

10

They want to hire you!
(What do you do now?)

So they've decided to hire you. That's great! If you already have a job, do not quit the minute you get the offer. Who knows what might happen? There have been horror stories of people accepting a job, quitting their current one and then finding out that they didn't really get the job. Even worse, the company downsizes the job before you start or they go out of business. How do you avoid this? Get the job offer signed and in writing. This way legally you'll be safe. Before you accept the offer, you might want to ask them to let you think about it for at least 24

Get it in writing!

hours. They usually won't mind unless they are in a real hurry. If they are in a hurry, then you'll probably have learned that in the interview and can act accordingly.

Deciding whether you want to work there or not

If you get the chance, talk to some of the people that work there. Do they seem happy? Are they satisfied with their job? Or do they seem over worked and jaded.

It is rare, but some companies produce fantastic work but are not an enjoyable place to work. Of course most places are fun to work for (thankfully). Think about what you want. Do you mind working loads of extra hours but getting a really nice paycheck, or would you rather work at a place that had "9 to 5" hours but paid less?

How much should you make?

Before they made you the offer you should have done a little research. First of all, decide how much money you'll need to live in the city where you are going to work. Will you need more or less than you

How much do they need to pay?
How much do you need to earn?

are currently making? One of the easiest ways to find out is to use a salary calculator. There are many of these on the web. At the moment one of the most popular ones can be found at http://www.homefare.com. (Look under Moving Calculators.) It even has calculators that will calculate the cost of living from one country to another. They are usually pretty good at predicting the right salary change, but everybody's needs are different so I suggest you look into it on your own.

Moving to L.A.

All of this depends on where you live. It's crazy to try to move out to Santa Monica or Culver City when you first get out here without a job. Those are all very expensive places to live. If you look into the valley you can easily find reasonable (not in the hood) 1 bedroom apartments. If you get a roomate you can get a nice 2 bedroom in Studio City, North Hollywood or Van Nuys. These neighborhoods are not bad. Only trouble is, if you get a job in Santa Monica (lots of game companies there) you have to deal with the 405(bleh). At a lot of game companies you don't have to be in till 10am; a lot of the 405 traffic has cleared up by then

Inexpensive places to live, neighborhoods not bad:
North Hollywood, Studio City, Van Nuys

Medium Priced:
Sherman Oaks, Burbank, Woodland Hills, Encino, Venice

Very Expensive places to live:
Culver City, Santa Monica, West Hollywood, West LA, Brentwood, Glendale, Malibu, Beverly Hills, Marina Del Rey

Places that are cheap/sketchy neighborhoods, depends the street, some are good some are bad. Seems nice until you look around and see all the bars on the windows:
Hollywood, Canoga Park, Northridge, Reseda, Silverlake, Echo Park

The Hood:
Pacoima, San Fernando, Inglewood, Compton

There are too many cities in LA to name, but that covers a little bit of the city that I know.

Deke Kincaid

When you fly out to the interview, take some notes. How much is gas? Ask what areas most employees live in. If possible go to a couple of grocery stores that are around those areas and look at the price of staple items (milk, bread, drinks, fruits and vegetables). Are they more or less? Pick up some "Apartment Finder" and "Home Finder" magazines and see how much your rent or mortgage is going to be. Call your car and home insurance companies and ask them if your insurance premiums are going to change if you move. Will you need any extras like flood, hurricane or earthquake insurance? This may sound silly, but you are going to live there, possibly for a really long time. You don't want to be miserable when you get there because you can't afford to pay your bills. After all this research, look at your current bills, then do a comparison between what you pay now and what you'll be paying when you move. Adjust your desired salary accordingly. Unless you are taking this job knowing that you are getting a pay cut, you should ask for a little more, relatively than you are making now. After all, you are leaving another company and moving your entire world just to work for a new employer. There should be a little compensation in there somewhere.

Of course you will want to get paid more than the bare minimum needed to survive, but how much more should you ask for? How can you find out what you are really worth? Fortunately there are a few salary surveys available on the internet which can help give you a starting point. The three most popular are for video game salaries and movie/television effects salaries.

To get an idea of what you should be making in the game industry, have a look at the salary survey that the IDGA (International Game Developers Association) hosts on their web site: www.igda.org/biz. It has salary figures as well as a lot of other useful information.You will have to register to download this survey, but registration is free. As we all know, web masters like to move things around. If that link does not work, simply go to www.igda.org and look for the salary survey link.

Another salary poll is held once a year by the M.P.S.C Local 839 IATSE. They anonymously poll their members and ask them what they are being paid. (The M.P.S.C Local 839 IATSE is the animators union for Los Angeles, California USA and its surrounding areas.) This poll will give you an idea of how much you should be making if you are working in the television or film industry. The results of those polls are posted on their web site: www.mpsc839.org in the wages section of the contract area.

(www.mpsc839.org/_Contract/Contract_h/wages_pages.html) Again, web masters like to move things around. If the poll has been moved from the wages area of the contract section, just go to www.mpsc839.org and look for the salary survey link.

The BECTU (Broadcasting Entertainment Cinematograph and Theatre Union) researches animation rates for animators who are based primarily in the United

Kingdom. This research will give you an idea of how much you should be making if you are working in the U.K. broadcast industry. The results of this research can be found in the Rates section of the Resources area of the web site www.bectu.org.uk/resources/rates. Once again... web masters like to move things around. If this research has been moved from that location, just go to www.bectu.org.uk and click resources, then rates. Once you've done this, the animation research link should appear.

The IDGA poll covers the entire United States of America and the Local 839 poll is for the Southern California region only. The BECTU poll geared toward animators that are primarily based in the United Kingdom. If you live outside of these areas, you will need to use a salary calculator, like the one at www.homefair.com, in order determine your salary range. Once you've decided on a salary range, you'll be ready to negotiate if the company chooses to hire you. If they make an offer that's too low, don't hesitate to make a counter offer. But listen to everything they have to say before saying no. Some companies will pay a little less than others but compensate you with great benefits. How much vacation time do they offer? Some companies will give you the standard "2 weeks" while other will give you that and a week around the holidays plus a couple of extra days off at various other times of the year. If you think they are offering too low a salary and value vacation time over money, then you could negotiate for extra time off instead of more money. Most companies are more likely to give you more vacation than more money.

Other things to consider

Some companies offer retirement plans where they match every dollar you put in with one of theirs. But there are other companies that put money in for you and you don't have to spend a dime. This should be taken into account when figuring your salary amount. Some of the larger places have recreation facilities: gym, basketball courts, pool, tennis, soccer, etc. If you go to the gym and have to pay a monthly fee then imagine never having to pay that bill again. Most companies don't have an onsite recreation facility, but many will pay your gym membership. Why would they do this? Because healthy employees are usually better workers, happier people and get sick less often. Companies in downtown or congested areas should pay for parking, public transit or at least include compensation in your salary for it.

Some companies also have onsite health services. If you get sick, you go there and it's free. If you need your allergy medicine prescription renewed, it's free. You need a checkup, free. No co-pay, no insurance forms, no nothing. Just make an appointment and go. Places like this will usually treat everything but major illnesses and broken bones. While this does not usually save you a lot of money, it saves you time because it's usually located close to where you work. It saves you from having to take time off just to get a check up. In countries where health care is provided by the government this might not hold as much appeal. But in places such as the United States where insurance paperwork can be a nightmare, it is highly valuable.

What sort of health insurance can you expect at your new company? Surely they will provide you with basic coverage. If they offer dental coverage, that is a bonus. If they offer vision coverage, that's even better. If they use the same insurance company that you are currently using, that's better still.

Overtime VS comp time

Then there's the issue of overtime versus comp time. Overtime is working past the required number of hours in a week and being paid more money for it. With comp time you are given vacation days instead. (Compensated) If you don't need the money then comp time is usually the way to go. But watch out, comp time at a startup or small company is usually not a good idea. Imagine that you've worked day and night for weeks on end and built up a lot of comp time. If something goes wrong and the company closes it may be pretty difficult to get compensated for all that comp time. But, if you were getting paid overtime all along then the only thing you risk losing is your last paycheck.

Salary (full time) vs contract (freelance)

Some places give you a choice. Do you want to be a full time employee with benefits, vacation time, retirement, etc, or do you want a higher hourly wage and no extras. This really depends on what kind of person you are. If you are a true freelancer and are very good at what you do, then you can afford to take the contract position and enjoy the higher pay rate. If you desire more stability, want your life to be less complicated and don't like going from company to company, then salary is the way to go. Of course, if you could make a great deal more money as a contractor, it would be foolish to join the company as a salaried employee.

Contractual

There is another option which sits firmly between salary and contract work. This type of position is called contractual. Contractual workers work as full time employees. They have full benefits like salaried employees. But they are only contracted to work for a pre-determined length of time. When the contract ends the employee must find another job. Technically this is no different from being fired but it does not carry with it the stigma of a "real" firing.

Moving

If you have to move, who pays for the move? Is the employer taking care of it or are you? Most reputable companies will compensate you for your moving expenses. Some will just give you a check a for a set amount and you keep what you don't use, but expenses over that amount are your responsibility. Some really large companies will take care of everything. They'll arrange for movers and pay for all of it. But that is rare. Unfortunately, moving expenses are not paid for everyone. If you are a student or have very little experience then you are better off moving where the jobs are. Few companies will pay to relocate you, especially when there are plenty of local professionals going for the same job. If they are making you pay for the move, figure out how much it is going to cost and try to tack that amount on top of your salary. If you are arranging for a moving company yourself, make sure that you ask around for recommendations. Some companies are really good and some are very unsatisfactory.

I've had friends that waited for over a week for their stuff to arrive. In the meantime they either had to sleep on the floor, at friends houses or in a hotel. Never mind that fact that they had to buy some new clothes because they couldn't stand wearing the same clothes over and over every day.

Don't sign anything until you have had a good lawyer take a look at it.

Employment contracts

Some companies will require you to sign an employment contract. Usually this has a non-compete clause which prevents you from using them to move you to another city and then leaving for a different job a week or two after you get there. Most of these contracts are harmless, but don't sign it until you've had a good lawyer look at it. Not just any lawyer, an entertainment lawyer. There are some contracts that prevent you from working for a competing company for a period of time after you leave. If you are miserable at your job you're not allowed to leave and work somewhere else unless it's in a totally different field. Not only are you legally bound to the company, but no one will want to hire you for fear of legal action. There are others that require you to work insane hours with poor compensation or freeze your salary for a certain number of months.

How to avoid being laid off

Let's face it. Companies aren't perfect and neither are employees. People lose their jobs. That's just the way it is. You will probably lose yours some time. When an entire company goes under, there is nothing that you can do about it. However, that is not always the case. Sometimes companies just have to let a few employees go to stay afloat. Often this is a sign that you should start looking for another job. But sometimes, especially in the computer graphics industry, it happens because a large job is finished and the next job is too small to support the current workforce. Regardless of the reason, being laid off is usually the last thing you want to happen to you. This section is devoted to helping you avoid being laid off and dealing with it if you are laid off.

Never stop learning. Make yourself valuable and needed. Always try to be better at what you do than anyone else around you. Often this is an impossible task, but if you at least strive to be better than you were yesterday,

"Congratulations, Phil. In just six months you've moved from an entry-level position to an exit-level position."

over time it will make a difference. Many people just "try to get through the day." These type of people almost always produce mediocre work that fulfills the requirements, but never goes past them. This type of person will be near the top of the list when it comes time to lay people off. They will probably have trouble finding a job when they lose their current one. On the other hand, there is no need to work yourself to death, just try to do your best. You need to get noticed and receive proper credit for the work that you've done. Try to make a "name" for yourself wherever you work. This can be hard to do without sounding arrogant or annoying. Never pass up an opportunity to work directly for the people at the top. This is one of the best ways to get noticed just by doing your job well. Working late isn't always the best way to get noticed either. Believe it or not, some bosses think a person that works late all the time is just a slow employee, not hard working one. Working late during "crunch time" is an entirely different matter though. If you are asked to stay late, do it. Also, branch out a little when you have a few spare moments or are in between projects. For example, if you are a character animator, you might want to try animating some particles or other types of dynamic simulations. This way, if you do lose your job, you'll be more marketable than you were before and on the road to picking up a new skill as well.

Learn to work well with others. Egotistical artists who think that they are "better" than everybody else usually do not last very long in this industry. A few people are known for their bad attitudes. At some point in their career they will run out of good places that have not already heard about them. These people share ideas

©CHARLES BARSOTTI

"Well, I'll be darned, maybe they are serious about restructuring."

and suggestions with others (which is a good trait), but they are unable to accept the fact that some of their ideas will not be used. You don't want to be one of these people. The sad thing is that if you are, you probably don't even know it. If some one told you that you were one of these people, your ego probably wouldn't allow you to believe them. I think that we all know one or two (or fifteen or sixteen) people like this. :)

Keep up with the current trends in animation. Try to anticipate new trends that are just on the horizon. Don't just be "another animator", get noticed by doing something new and fresh. At the same time, see what your current (or future) employers will need. But don't risk it on some strange idea unless you've done some research and have good solid facts to guide you.

Always work on your portfolio

Even if you have a job and even if you work at a company that has a reputation for keeping their employees during the hard times, keep working on your portfolio. As you are working on a job, make copies of your work. If possible, get not only the parts that you worked on, but the final image. With both parts, you can

As you work on a project, keep a back up of some of the key elements for your demo reel. This way, if you lose your job it will be very easy to show a future employer what you've done.

show your future employer what you did and what the end result was. It is much easier to do this if you gather your artwork while the project is in production. Trying to find everything after a production is over can be difficult. Keep in mind that some of the work you've done might be part of a bigger project that may or may not be public knowledge at the time of your dismissal. Show your former employer some respect and keep anything that is not "public" yet off your demo reel. Be sure to ask them when it is safe to show the work that you did for them. It's also a good idea to write up a description of what you did while you worked for them. Then get them to sign it or re-write it to their specs and sign it. This way you have concrete proof that you actually did the work in case there is a problem down the road.

What to do when you get laid off

If you get laid off, always leave on good terms. No matter how unfair you think the layoffs were, it is unwise to get angry. It won't get your job back and might hurt your chances of getting another. Some places will even allow you to use their equipment to put a demo reel together so that you can get another job. If this is an option for you, take advantage of it! Many people don't and later on, when it is no longer an option, wish they had.

It's always good to specialize in one area of CG, but it never hurts to look into new areas. If you do get laid off, this might be the best time to learn something completely different, especially if it is some aspect of CG that you've always wanted to try out but never had the time. What if you are a modeler and all the sudden there are no modeling jobs available. If you've been studying something else (match moving, compositing, animating, etc...) then you can more then likely grab a temp job in your "new" area to help you pay bills till another modeling job comes along.

LET'S SEE, I'VE HAD LUNCH. NOW WHERE THE HELL AM I GOING?

© CHARLES BARSOTTI

"No more freelance fishing while you are supposed to be animating!"

Freelancing

So you want to be a freelance 3D artist?
Part 1: How to determine an hourly rate

Some people just don't enjoy ordinary full time work, so they freelance. Sometimes freelance work may be the only option, and if you need a job, you'll have to take it. What is freelancing? Freelancing means you work for a company, are paid only for the hours that you work, but are not considered a regular employee. You don't get benefits or paid vacation time. Why would you want to do this? You'll have the freedom to come and go as you please, you can work for more than one company at a time, you can choose whether or not to accept work on a project, and you'll probably get paid more than a standard salaried employee. Often it has a flexible schedule and you'll never get bored because you work from job to job. Even if you don't plan on becoming a freelancer, read this section anyway. It contains information that can help you decide what to ask when going for a full-time job, and if you ever fall into a freelance job you'll know how to deal with it.

The following information is from an article entitled "So you want to be a freelance artist" written by Jonn Gorden with additional information and edits by Ed Harriss. It contains just about everything you need to know in order to start your freelancing career. Jonn is based in Australia, so keep in mind that some of the information is location specific.

Step 1 - Preparation
So you are determined to be your own boss, or maybe you are picking up some contract jobs while looking for full-time work. Either way, one of the most difficult things is determining how much to quote a client.

Most of your contemporaries will be hesitant to advertise their rates in case they are undercut in a bid. Clients would seriously hurt their negotiation ability if they were to advertise what they are prepared to pay. So how do you find that magic figure that is low enough to get work, but not so low that you can't pay the rent? High enough to compensate your time appropriately, but not so high that you price yourself out of the bid?

Research

The very first thing to do is to research as much as you can. One of the best places too look is IT recruiting agencies. Often they will publish average or expected pay rates for different types of jobs. If you are lucky you will find not only salary rates but hourly rates as well.

Also look at job advertisements for work similar to what you want to do to see how much they are offering. Both of these are probably best done online. At the end of this section I have included some useful links to get you started.

Note: Unfortunately, graphics work of any kind, including 3D, is often left out from IT recruitment. They have managers, programmers, and html coders, but graphics rarely makes the cut. Search for the few recruiters that do cater for graphics work as well as other IT categories.

Also, network with as many people as possible doing your kind of work, even if it is only in vaguely related industries. Quite often they'll be open about their standard rates, and it'll give you a better idea of the market in your area.

Budget

As a freelancer you are basically running your own business. This means you need to consider things like phone and internet costs, electricity, rent, and most importantly both hardware and software upgrades. Once you have factored these into a budget you can look at your personal items such as loans, food, entertainment, hobbies, toys etc.

You need to prepare as detailed a budget as you can for at least a 12 month period. This will allow you to include the major hardware and software upgrades, which you should budget each for once a year. Don't forget to allow for income tax. Usually at this stage adding 30% to the bottom line is sufficient.

Don't undervalue yourself

Now you've done the research and prepared your budget, Let's do some preliminary calculations to get things started.

Have a look at the budget, and your total costs for the 12 month period. Now you need to decide how much you want to work. For now let's assume a normal working week of 35 hours and 46 working weeks a year (giving yourself 4 weeks break plus 2 weeks emergency/sick time per year).

Divide your total costs by 46 (the number of weeks) and then divide that figure by 35 (the number of hours per week). The figure that is left is your average hourly cost. If it seems excessively high you may want to leave that 80″ plasma TV off the budget for now :)

Before we continue, let's think about the figures we've used. 46 weeks work a year is certainly good to aim for, but how likely is it that you will find that much work? Certainly in my experience, the ratio of paid work to self-promotion, looking for and generating work opportunities, starts at around 1:2. Unless you're really lucky, the best it will probably be for a while is 1:1. What this tells us is that out of those 46 weeks you are planning to work, you are likely to be paid for only 15 to 23 of those weeks.

You may be asking why the ratio is so low when many production companies usually have a much better ratio. Well, the reason is simple. Companies are in a position of having people dedicated to promotion and work generation while others in the company are doing the work. On the other hand, you have only yourself to do both tasks. When the pressure is on to complete work by a deadline you rarely get the opportunities to get out and network to promote yourself. Of course as time goes on, more people are aware of you, and you have more jobs under your belt so the ratio should rise. Hopefully it will rise to the point you have to turn down work or sub-contract because you're too busy.

So getting back to our sums, let's do that last one again, this time using 15 paid working weeks, and again 35 hours per week. Quite a difference isn't it? Now this exercise has given us a good understanding of just how much it costs to be in this business, but there's still a little way to go before we have our actual hourly rates figured out.

Step 2 - Calculate your rate
Ok, now that you've done some preparation and worked out your costs, it's time to work out your asking price. There are 2 figures that you need to arrive at. One is your optimum rate. This is the amount you believe you are worth, and that you should usually quote. The other is your cut-off rate, the lowest amount for which you can work and still comfortably pay the bills. We can use what we've already done to calculate both those figures. You've already estimated how many paid hours you are likely to work and arrived at a figure that is your average hourly cost, but we need to factor in some more things before it can be used effectively.

Profit
A business exists only to make profit. Sure, it's nice to think that it's providing valuable services and is a fun place to work, but at the end of the day the profit margin is all important. It's easy to forget this principle in our line of work, because more often than not we are made to feel guilty for getting paid to have fun. At least that's the limited impression of many people outside our industry who rarely factor in the often outrageous working hours and pressures involved. So since we've already established that as a freelancer you are running your own business, you need to think about profit.

"It has come to my attention that one of you called the profit motive 'a figure of speech'!"

How much to add?

The most accepted figure to aim for in the business world is 30%. A successful company is earning at least 30% profit. Of course this has been re-written in recent years by many IT companies who earn significantly more profit, but let's keep our initial expectations to the accepted 30%.

Without profit, you will find it very difficult to advance your freelance career. Let's think about it for a second.

- If you're working from job to job just to put food on the table, are you spending enough time planning for the future?
- What happens when a job comes up that requires you to purchase an unexpected piece of equipment?
- What about training? In our business we need to spend unparalleled amounts of time learning new features and programs.
- What happens when a client doesn't pay on time, or at all?
- So you can see how important profit is to your success as a freelancer.

Salary vs hourly rate

Now it's likely that most of your research resulted in some knowledge of salary rates, but very little in the way of hourly rates. If we want to compare our figures to salaries, we need to break down those salaries.

Take a salary of $50,000 for example.
What hourly rate is the company paying?
Easy you say…

$50,000 / 1610 (46 weeks x 35 hrs/week) = $31 per hour

But no, it's not that easy. When a company hires an employee, it doesn't just cost them the salary. Other costs include superannuation, workers comp, non-productive time, leave, overhead (coffee, toilet paper, etc), just to name a few. When all these are added up they come to roughly 50% of the salary.

But that's not all, there's also equipment costs and furniture which are large initial expenses as well as ongoing ones. You're looking at roughly $10-12,000 plus yearly hardware and software upgrades to setup an employee. So you can easily add an additional 30%.

So let's look at that salary figure again…

$50,000 x 1.8 = $90,000

To hire an employee at $50,000 costs the company $90,000. Surprising isn't it?

So re-evaluating the hourly rate we get $90,000 / 1610 = $56 per hour.

The employee is receiving $31 per hour, but it's costing the company $56 per hour.

So do this calculation on all the salary rates you have found in your research and you'll have a good basis for comparison.

Salary x 1.8 / 1610 = Hourly rate

Comparisons

So let's take your average hourly costs and add 30% profit. We're getting very close to an appropriate hourly rate now. Compare this hourly rate to the hourly rates from your research. If the figure lies within the limits of your research then you're probably on track. If your rates are significantly higher or lower than these rates then you may need to go back and look at your calculations again. Analyze your budget, profit margin and paid weeks estimate to see what areas you can massage in order to arrive at a reasonable hourly rate.

Optimum vs cut-off

So what's the difference between the optimum rate and the cut-off rate?

The optimum rate is the amount that falls within the industry standards, covers your costs, covers your unpaid time, and includes some profit. This amount (or a little higher) is what you would normally start with when preparing a quote, knowing that it's likely to go down a bit through negotiations.

The cut-off rate is the lowest amount that you can afford to work for. If

"Bad news - our consultant says that living outside our cutoff rate is no longer tax-deductible."

negotiations fall below this amount, you walk away from the bid. You may decide that your cut-off rate doesn't have any profit included, or maybe it's for longer term work so your paid weeks estimate may be higher, but under no circumstances can you accept lower than this amount. If you do then you will go into debt in order to do the job. You might as well pay the client for the privilege of doing the work.

Once you know these amounts, quoting suddenly becomes a piece of cake. No longer do you have to agonize over how much you think the client can pay, because you know how much you need to do the work.

The other decision you have to make is how flexible you want to be with your rate and how willing you are to negotiate. You may decide to determine a percentage that you will easily negotiate down but after which you become less flexible.

"No, you're not here for an audit."

GST (goods and services tax)

Note: While the information in the following paragraph applies specifically to people working in Australia, the general idea is the same in most countries. It you don't live in Australia, it should still give you a good starting point. However, you will have to do your own research to ensure you are calculating everything correctly.

Yes, the dreaded tax man will take more than just income tax. Because you are working for yourself you are considered a business by the tax department. This means that you will be responsible for charging & paying GST for your services. If you haven't already, you should apply for an ABN number, and you will need to fill out a BAS statement each quarter. You should have a few deductions, but basically you will need to pay 10% of your earnings to the tax man. So whatever you've calculated your hourly rate to be, the last step before you quote is to add 10% for GST. If you don't, then the GST will eat into your costs.

Step 3 - Putting it into practice

The most prominent factor when quoting is the value of the work to the customer, or the perceived value, versus what it costs you to deliver the work, the cost of services. Somewhere between these 2 amounts is the amount you and the client will agree upon for your hourly rate.

So how do you figure out the perceived value? Start off by trying to find out as much about the clients as possible.

- What kind of work have they done before?
- What clients have they worked with?
- How long have they been in business?
- What impression do others have of the company?
- Does the company already have the project, or are they bidding for it while looking at who might be available?
- Where is the company based?
- Where does the project originate?

Once you have done this you should have a fairly good idea of what position the company is in and whether they will be looking for cheap labor or are willing to pay for high quality work.

One mistake many people make when they're starting out is feeling intimidated by the negotiation process. It's easy to do, but keep in mind that the client needs you as much as you need them. Be strong and the client will respect you for it.

The client may even tell you they can't afford your rate just to see how low you are willing to go. Often a client will appear to walk away, before reconsidering and agreeing to your rates. This can be a test to weed out who's serious and who's not. The ones who are prepared to negotiate down to nothing are usually not going to provide quality work.

Along the way you may miss out on a few jobs because your rates are too high, but that's normal. Those jobs probably wouldn't be worth putting on your portfolio anyway. Of course if you haven't eaten for a few weeks you can always make an exception. :) But remember, if you accept a job for too little money, you may be missing out on a much more attractive offer just around the corner because you're too busy.

Other variables

There are some other factors we need to consider when comparing rates or preparing quotes.

Acceptable hourly rates can differ from state to state and country to country. Don't panic, this doesn't mean that if you live in South Australia you will be poor for the rest of your life :) It means that you may need to adjust your hourly rate up or down depending on where the work is coming from. Take note of locations for your researched salaries and rates to get a feel for the marketplace value in different areas.

Keep an eye on the industry to see where the demand is the highest. The higher the demand and the lower the number of people skilled to fill that demand drive the rates up for that type of work. For example there is currently a glut of web designers in Australia, but there's been a downturn in the demand for web designers. This means that the rates for web design work are potentially lower than in recent years.

So in considering different rates for different skills, you should break down your skills into different areas, such as 3D graphics, 3D animation, 2D graphics (Photoshop), 2D animation (Flash), traditional illustration, web design, etc. Each of these can demand different hourly rates depending on the level of skill involved versus the number of people with those skills.

Your rate will also depend on your abilities within an area. The better you are, the more you can charge. Although the industry may determine that 3D character animation is worth more than 2D graphics, if you're better at 2D graphics your rates should represent that.

Your level of experience and the number of satisfied clients will affect your rates. If a client can see that you've worked successfully with other clients, they are more likely to agree to your rates. Also, if the job involves team work, having worked with others on projects will greatly enhance your chances.

Related to experience is speed. The faster you are the more you can charge per hour. This can be a difficult one with a new client, but as you do more work for a particular client this can become a bargaining point.

A big factor to consider is the length of the project or job. The longer a project is, the more flexible you can be with your rate. Remember, we were estimating a fairly low number of paid working weeks. If a job comes along that is measured in months rather than weeks your estimated paid weeks, figure suddenly jumps up which means that you can quote less while still maintaining the same level of finances.

Sometimes you are offered a job that is too much fun to pass up or will help enhance your skills in a particular area, but the money isn't great. If you've got enough money that you can afford to do the job for less than your normal rates, or even less than your cut-off rates, it can be worthwhile for the experience or the enjoyment.

Conclusion

A few years ago I was talking with some colleagues about hourly rates. I suggested to them that they could look at increasing their rates considerably, that their rates were well below industry standards. At the time I had just adjusted my own rates up. When I told them what rates I thought they could be receiving and told them my new rates, they laughed at me and said I was nuts. A few weeks later I had a 3 month job at my new rates, while my colleagues were still working insane hours just to cover the rent.

If you put the time into determining your hourly rate and understand what factors influence that rate, you will make your life much easier. There will always be exceptions to the rule, but as always, the more you know the rules of the game, the better the decisions you make when bending those rules.

Part 2: The 5-minute schedule

Section 1 - Why schedule?
One of the most important things about being in business is proper scheduling. Whether you're working for yourself or part of a team, knowing how long things take and when tasks will be complete are vital to a productive environment.

One question I hear asked quite often is how long a particular task should take. The question can sometimes be valid if the task is something that the person hasn't done before. The trouble is that everyone works at a different pace, and everyone has differing opinions about how long a task might take. By following the tips outlined here, in a very short time you will be able to estimate much more accurately how long a particular task will take you. This will benefit in quoting for jobs, organizing your workflow, and enhancing productivity.

Just 5 minutes a day is all it takes
Very few people take the time to schedule properly. It's often seen as a waste of time and therefore given a very low priority. I must have heard the excuse a thousand times "But I've got to get this finished, getting the work done is more important." This attitude is most prevalent in people who feel uncomfortable or unable to estimate task lengths. And instead of working on the problem they choose to ignore it.

Scheduling is often seen as a management tool that's of little use in the real workplace. This is often enhanced by difficult scheduling procedures that some managers put into place. I have seen some scheduling procedures that really do take more time than the work itself. This approach is both unproductive and unnecessary. Scheduling exists to make life easier, not more difficult. Once you settle into the routine of regular monitoring of your progress, it becomes easy. Literally, 5 minutes is all it takes, whether you do it as you complete each task, or do it at the end of each day.

Benefits of scheduling

The benefits of proper scheduling are abundantly apparent once you start putting it into practice.

1. An accurate record of what you've done and how long it's taken.
Have you ever looked back over a period of time and wondered what you did? I know I have often looked back over the last week wondering why I didn't accomplish more. With proper scheduling you can look back and see exactly what you did. More often than not, this feeling is caused by an unexpected problem or a problem that took longer to overcome than expected. The schedule can be very reassuring in times like this.

2. You're better prepared for next time.
With a good schedule, when you need to do a task that is the same as or similar to something you have already done, you can merely look over the schedule to see how long it took, what problems there were, and estimate more accurately how long it will take this time.

3. A record of personal progress.
If you have a number of tasks that are similar, more often than not each successive task will take a little less time than the last. You can look at your schedule with pride seeing how you've improved from task to task.

4. A solid foundation for quotes
When you quote your next job you can look over your schedules and, if you have done similar tasks before, see exactly how long they actually took. If you haven't done the task before, you can see what patterns emerge from previous estimates of untried tasks. More often than not, you will find that you tend to underestimate the length of time something will take.

Unfortunately, our memories aren't adequate when it comes to doing this. Over time it is easy to forget the difficulties involved with a job. You might remember a previous job taking 3 weeks, but forget that the last week involved 16 hour days with a couple of all-nighters at the end. Next time you quote for a similar job you may under-estimate the hours involved and be caught in the same situation again. Conversely, you might remember a task taking 3 days, but forget that 2 of those days were spent solving a problem that won't be an issue next time now that you have a solution. Next time you quote a similar job you may over-estimate the hours involved.

With a schedule you no longer have to rely on memory or loosely recorded times. You can break down a job into individual tasks and accurately estimate times for each of those tasks. This will make your life and the clients or employers lives much easier.

One issue that often arises from clients: when will individual tasks within the overall job be completed? Clients are typically results based. If they don't see something, they assume nothing's being done. Unfortunately the reality of production is that often there may be nothing to show early in the process. Planning and pre-production rarely reflect the amount of time involved, and while you're animating, there may be elements of the scenes that are unfinished so you hold off on final rendering until later.

With a history of scheduling, you can accurately convey to the client at the start of the job how long various aspects will take and when they can expect to see certain results. You can explain if they insist on seeing a particular result early in the process how it may adversely affect the total time for the job.

Section 2 - Scheduling example

I first found this scheduling technique on the web. A programmer had developed a quick and easy system for monitoring his own progress. Since programming is one of the more difficult areas to estimate I knew I was onto something good. I have since lost my records of who this person is, but I credit him with the fundamental principle of this method.

Disillusioned with complex scheduling packages such as Microsoft Project, I put this newfound method into practice straight away, initially expanding on the example I had to make it a little more useful in a production environment. Since then, having scheduled and quoted many solo and team projects, I have enhanced the schedule far beyond its initial form.

The schedule uses Microsoft Excel and, I must stress, is not meant as a replacement for MS Project or other project management tools. It is meant to accompany those tools when dealing with a large project. You can download the Excel file used in these examples at http://www.zerogravity.com.au/lw/schedule.zip

Preparation

The basics of the schedule involve breaking down a project into major features. For example if the job is to create a 3D character, you might break it down as folows:

Modeling
Morphs
Texturing
Rigging
Tweaking

Then break down each feature into specific tasks. For example:

Modeling
    Head
    Body
    Extremities (Hands/feet)
    Clothes

Morphs
    Mouth expressions
    Eye/eyebrow expressions
    Lipsync targets

Texturing
    Face
    Body
    Extremities
    Clothes

Rigging
    Weight maps
    Bones
    IK
    Muscles and tendons

Tweaking
    Model
    Morphs
    Textures
    Weight maps & bones

The goal is to break down to the point where each task is estimated to take less than 8 hours if possible. It's very important to take your time during this step. I have witnessed people use this schedule without breaking down the job properly, either into features or tasks, and as a result receive much fewer benefits.

Feature	Task	Init Est	Curr Est	Elapsed	Remain
Modelling	~~Head~~	7	10	10	
	~~Body~~	9	7	7	
	Extremities	8	5	1	4
	Clothes	5	5		5

The next step is to estimate as accurately as you can, the time each of these tasks will take, and place these estimates into the *Initial Estimate* column. Now copy these values into the adjacent *Current Estimate* column. As you can see the time remaining column is filled out for you. This will also give you an estimated finish date. You can also fill out priority orders for the tasks in an additional column labeled *Priority*, using as many priority levels as you wish, I usually find 3 to be sufficient.

Maintaining the schedule

Now that your schedule is ready to be put to use, we come to what is probably the most important step, maintenance. As you work on each task, fill in the *Time Elapsed* column. You can also update the Current Estimate column as soon as you have a better idea of how long it's taking. When you have completed a task, change the Current Estimate column to reflect the amount of time it actually took. Now you have a record of how long you estimated a task to take versus how long the task actually took. This will be useful in the future.

Provided are a couple of visual clues relating to the status of a task. As a task is completed Microsoft Excel will automatically cross it out. Also, tasks given priorities of 1 and 2 are highlighted for easy recognition. As you complete tasks, you can see towards the bottom of the worksheet how many hours you have spent on the project and an estimate of how many hours are left. This is very valuable when discussing your progress with the client.

Quite often as you get into the project you will find it useful to change some of the breakdowns. You may see a need to breakdown a task even further or add to features or tasks that you had not initially anticipated. The beauty of this system is that you can make these changes quite easily just by adding to the bottom line. All of the pertinent values will be immediately updated, reflecting your change.

Project management

This schedule is very useful when dealing with other aspects of managing a project such as working toward a deadline and optimizing productivity. When you fill in the starting date for the project in the header you will see a number of other values calculated.

The *Estimated Finish Date* is based on your current estimate of task times and your expected hours per day. This is a good indication of how long the project should take.

The *Projected Finish Date* indicates how long the project is likely to take, based on your current task estimates and your average hours per day, instead of your expected hours per day.

The *Average Hours per Day* is the average of how many hours you've actually worked on the tasks listed. Sometimes you may work on multiple projects at once. You will probably want to reflect this in the *Expected Hours per Day* or *Expected Days per Week* in the header for each project if you have a separate schedule for each of the projects.

"Frankly. Phill, I don't think the techniques of Japanese management would apply to a joint like this."

If you know, at the beginning of a project, when it will start and when it must be finished, make sure you fill in those values. Then when you're creating your initial estimates for the tasks you can see immediately if you're likely to fall within the deadline, or not. As you progress you can keep an eye on the finish dates to see how you're doing.

If you can see that you're missing timelines during the project, there are a number of things you can do to remedy this. You can work more hours in the day to make up for lost time, or decrease the time you allow yourself for later tasks. You can ask the client if it's possible to push back the deadline, or ask if there are features that are less important to the project which can be allocated less time. The important thing is that you detect the problem early in the process and have a chance to make adjustments rather than realizing the day before the project is due that you're not going to make it, putting you and your client in a difficult position.

Section 3 - Conclusion

The more you use a schedule, the better you will become at estimating how long things will take you. In the beginning, your initial estimates and actual times may vary considerably, but as you do more projects and refer to past schedules you will soon find that your initial estimates become closer and closer to the actual time taken.

You can also use the principles of this schedule to take the idea much further. If you read the earlier section on setting an hourly rate, you will be able to quote for a project more accurately knowing how long you expect the project to take and your hourly rate. Just multiply the number of hours by your hourly rate and you have the total amount the project is worth. Before you know it you will wonder how you ever did without scheduling. You will feel more organized and better prepared to handle mishaps. When unexpected problems arise, you will be able to deal with them calmly and with detailed knowledge of how they affect the big picture. You will have a record of your progress and how you've improved your production speed. But more than anything else you will feel confident quoting times for jobs knowing that your quote is based on actual experience, not just a guesstimate. Remember, spending just 5 minutes a day on your schedule will end up saving you days, even weeks, in the long run.

Zero Gravity Entertainment is considering releasing a stand-alone version of this schedule, which accommodates much more than the example provided here. It includes scheduling for teams working on different aspects of a project, time sheets, reports, quotation elements which include what a project is costing the company/individual versus charge out rates, and variable project features so that you and a client can quickly see the financial and/or time-line effect of adding or subtracting features.

Its greatest benefits are its ease of use and immediate feedback. It may not be as complex a package as Microsoft Project, but we actually see that as a benefit. It has been put into practice on a number of projects and has been a joy to work with.

If you are interested in this product, please contact Jonny at: Jonny@zerogravity.com.au for more information.

Jonn Gorden

Jonn Gorden is a 2D/3D animator and game producer. He also utilizes his 11 years experience to provide consulting for CGI and animation, game development, and web design. Jonn's articles have been featured in many magazines.

His company, Zero Gravity Entertainment has had as many as 17 employees at one time, and has worked with both local and international clients including Marvel Entertainment and GT Interactive.

You can see his work at www.zerogravity.com.au.

RESOURCES - Animation Magazines

"I had no idea there were so many computer animation magazines"

Magazines

While much can be learned from animation web sites and computer graphics news groups, CG magazines are still a very good resource (and they are easier to carry around). The best thing about CG magazines is that many of them are free. On the following pages you'll find a list of most of the CG magazines out there. Of course, some of the magazines are not 100% CG related. You can still learn a lot from these magazines regardless.

3D Artist

www.3dartist.com

3D Artist is a glossy how-to print publication for desktop 3D graphics—Mac and Windows, and Linux 3D is coming along. The readers write most 3D Artist articles themselves, sharing peer-to-peer in the camaraderie of what is, in effect, the world's largest 3D user group. The target audience is intermediate-advanced to advanced users of 3D graphics software, including freelancers, studio artists and technicians, and the truly serious home user (sometimes known as a "pro-sumer").

3D World

www.3dworldmag.com

Introducing the ultimate design mag for 3D artists and animators. Inside 3D World you'll find an explosive combination of inspiration from industry leaders, practical tips and creative advice, plus reviews of the latest groundbreaking hardware and software for PC and Mac. Our range of news features and profiles covers the creation of 3D visuals for television, film, video games and, as well as illustration, product visualization and design. Our walkthrough, tips and Q&A experts write about all the top creative packages including 3D Studio MAX, Lightwave, Softimage and Maya, plus a range of other applications for all budgets.

Animation Journal

http://www.animationjournal.com

Founded in 1991, Animation Journal is the only peer-reviewed scholarly journal devoted to animation history and theory. Its content reflects the diversity of animation's production techniques and national origins. Animation Journal is edited by Maureen Furniss, Ph.D.

Animation Magazine

www.animationmagazine.net

Animation Magazine is the only monthly trade magazine covering the animation industry around the world. In each and every issue we bring you news from the world of television animation, feature film animation, animation on the Internet, animated commercials, animation schools and job opportunities, 3D and visual effects animation, animation in games, technology behind the animation and the art and history of animation as well as predictions and trends for the future of the business. We also publish the animation world's most valuable resource, the annual Animation Industry Directory, with more than 6500 company listings and contacts in the animation business.

Animatoon

http://www.animatoon.co.kr

A Korean animation magazine

Artbyte.

www.artbyte.com

Artbyte: The Magazine of Digital Arts and Culture. Artbyte is about the fusion of technology with art, design, music, cinema, and the web. Each bimonthly issue explores the creative aspects of new media, from innovations in industrial/ graphic/product design and electronic music to the latest developments in hardware/software and Internet technologies.

American Cinematographer

www.cinematographer.com

American Cinematographer seeks to keep readers abreast of advancements in all facets of motion picture imaging technology and to inform them of visually extraordinary productions, explaining the technical means used to realize an artistic vision on film and video, or with computers. For more than 80 years it has been the monthly "magazine of record" for film professionals all over the world. It offers in-depth, behind-the-scenes articles on how films are shot and lit. Top cinematographers and directors are interviewed at length.

Asia Image

www.ai-interactive.com

Asia Image has been specially designed to bring the clearest coverage of the broadcast, production and postproduction industry. Asia Image is an independent magazine, written by industry experts for the industry, it has established itself, in a relatively short space of time, as the indispensable source of news and information for the creative, production, post-production and broadcasting industries in Asia.

AV Video Multimedia Producer

www.avvmmp.com

www.avvideo.com

AV Video/Multimedia Producer is geared toward creative professionals in the video and multimedia departments of large corporations' independent video and multimedia production facilities, education, healthcare and medicine, and government.

Broadcasting & Cable

www.broadcastingcable.com

The weekly news source for the broadcasting and cable television, radio, satellite, and interactive multimedia industries

Creation

www.365video.com

Creation is the cutting-edge magazine for everyone involved in the creation, manipulation and delivery of media content. Creation will investigate and dissect today's solutions, from the original booking through post-production to new modes of delivery, it is the magazine for a convergent marketplace.

C3 Mag
www.c3mag.com
C3 is the only dedicated monthly technology and business magazine for professional users of 3D design and visualization software and hardware in the UK and Europe.

CGI
www.365animation.com
CGI is the leading business and technology magazine for professionals working in film, TV, video, games development, multimedia, web design and broader uses of animation and computer.

Cinefex
www.Cinefex.com
This is the best "behind the scenes" magazine on the planet. It's not cheap, but it's worth every penny. From time to time it can be a little too "general" but you'll not find anything else like it anywhere.

Cadalyst
www.cadonline.com
The Exclusive Voice of Authority for AutoCad Technology. This magazine is for AutoCAD users working in design/engineering/research, data/CAD management and corporate/senior management positions. It focuses mainly on product purchasing, technical and productivity information that meets the needs of Autodesk technology purchasers and users.

Cadence
www.cadenceweb.com
Cadence magazine helps you stay abreast of key developments in the computer-aided design industry and its related fields. Whether you are a 2D drafter, a 3D modeler, an architect, an engineer, an industrial or product designer, or a computer-aided design generalist, you'll find content on these pages that speaks directly to you and your discipline.

CGW - Computer Graphics World.
www.CGW.com
This magazine explores 3D modeling, animation, visualization, rendering, simulation, cad, and techniques for those who create digital content for film, broadcast, video, and game applications.

CG WORLD and Digital Video

www.wgn.co.jp

Japanese animation magazine. "Magazine shows overall visual creative by using 3DCG."

Content Creation Europe

www.contentcreationeurope.com

The pan-European magazine for content creators. Content Creation Europe represents the increasing convergence of products and techniques within the entertainment industry. Increasingly, content creators are making use of the same products but for different markets. Content creation Europe brings together broadcasting, video production, games development, DVDs, broadband, Internet, film and multimedia. This magazine is dedicated to those who shoot live footage for video or multimedia CD, design backgrounds for video games, or create special effects using high-end 3D modeling and animation.

Computer Arts

www.computerarts.co.uk

Computer Arts thrives on creativity and is the only technology magazine in the UK dedicated solely to visual art. It reports on, encourages, nurtures and facilitates creativity using the latest technology. Unlike other computing magazines, Computer Arts doesn't exist to help you defrag your hard drive or set up a modem - here there are no distractions: it simply helps you to create stunning artwork, photos, animations and 3D models. From professionals to students, everyone who has an interest in computer-generated graphics, digital publishing, animation or multimedia reads Computer Arts.

Computer Arts Special

www.computerarts.co.uk

Computer Arts Special is a bi-monthly magazine published as an offshoot of our successful Computer Arts magazine. Each issue takes an in-depth look at a specific area of digital creativity.

Digital Cinema Magazine

www.digitalcinemamag.com

Digital Cinema covers the motion-picture industry's transition to digital technologies for shooting, editing, preparing and exhibiting movies. Its readers represent a broad cross-section of motion-picture industry professionals from directors, cinematographers, and producers to studio and theater executives and hands-on postproduction experts. Digital Cinema magazine is the definitive information source for educating the motion-picture industry, providing a forum for communication, and stimulating the growth of this new form of moviemaking and exhibition.

DigitalTV

www.digitaltelevision.com

This magazine provides the key buying team of managers and engineers at broadcast, satellite, cable and broadband companies with the business and technology strategies and tutorial information they need to prosper in the new era of digital television. With an expanded distribution that reaches a new audience for broadcast equipment, technology and services, DigitalTV's readership includes general managers, chief engineers, production and operations managers, and interactive television content professionals. These senior engineering management executives rely on DigitalTV to help them make the tough policy and technical decisions crucial in today's competitive television marketplace.

Digit Magazine

www.digitmag.co.uk

www.digit.pl

Digit is the only technology-led, cross platform magazine providing information and inspiration for digital content creators. Digit covers the latest developments in graphic design, 3D, Web Design, DTP, Video, multimedia and animation. Digit is published in the United Kingdom and Poland.

Digital Production

www.digitalproduction.com

A German magazine for computer graphics, video and film.

Digital Designer

www.digitaldesigner.com.br

Brazilian Computer graphics magazine

DV Magazine

www.DV.com

Since 1993, DV magazine has served the information needs of professionals involved in the production, postproduction and delivery of digital video. Written and produced by experts in the field, DV provides objective, hard-hitting, in depth product information. Whether your specialty is video, audio, multimedia, visual effects, video on the web or animation, DV's editorial delivers more objective product information than any other publication.

Film & Video

www.filmandvideomagazine.com

Film & Video is a monthly publication covering all aspects of production and post-production of motion pictures, television, commercials, music videos, multimedia, and audio.

Game Developer

www.gdmag.com

Game Developer, the print publication written specifically for creators of entertainment software, provides technical and industry information to thousands of professional game developers. Each month, industry leaders and game development experts share technical solutions, review new products, and discuss strategies for creating innovative, successful games. Professional game developers count on Game Developer magazine for the most relevant and respected content in the game industry.

Highend Magazine.

www.highend3d.com/mag

Highend is magazine devoted to the tools and techniques commonly associated with the high-end digital visual effects industry. This is a quarterly publication released through DMG publishing. The magazine focuses on digital production, and reflects the myriad of tools which highend production utilizes: tools such as Maya, XSI, Houdini, Shake, Renderman and MentalRay. It presents unbiased views of the tools; through feature articles focused on production case studies, software specific tutorials and hardware reviews. It also presents galleries, which highlight some of the best work being done by individuals, professional or student, as well as studios.

IdN

www.idnworld.com

IdN is a bi-monthly digital design magazine. Since1992, IdN has established itself a solid foundation and has become a leading authority in the digital-design publication field, covering the Asia-Pacific region. It has earned a reputation as a reliable source for the most up-to-date information on the current market situations within the design community. Currently, IdN is published in four editions, Asia-Pacific & Australia in English, China/Hong Kong & Taiwan in Chinese.

Imagine

www.animationuk.com

IMAGINE is a high quality publication designed to reflect the aspirations, agendas and needs of the animation and digital media industries. The lively news and features-based format provides an ideal means of communication for creators, suppliers, educators and all involved in creative media content. Features include; production news, company and individual profiles, product news and reviews, retrospectives, causes and campaigns, training and educational development plus a tutorials section.

Keyframe Magazine.

www.KeyframeMag.com

This magazine for LightWave and Cinema 4D enthusiasts offers a solid collection of professional-level tutorials, unbiased and in-depth product reviews, high-profile industry case studies, and feature articles.

Millimeter

www.Millimeter.com

In a fast-changing and challenging industry, Millimeter anticipates the future. Our early coverage of important technology-driven trends such as 24p production, desktop post, and digital cinema has helped our readers remain competitive and plan their business investments. Millimeter is an authoritative resource for thousands of qualified professionals in production, postproduction, animation, streaming, and visual effects for motion pictures, television, and commercials.

Markee Magazine

www.markeemag.com

Markee magazine is the only monthly national publication exclusively dedicated to the Regional US film and video industry. Since 1985, Markee has bridged the production gap between the East and West Coasts by nationally promoting the rest of America. With 21,500+ subscribers and an estimated 65,000 qualified readers nationwide, Markee has become the journal of preference throughout the industry in regional America. A production-oriented magazine, each issue of Markee contains feature articles on subjects to inform and help our readers in their business. Departments, which focus on industry business, technology, and regional news and productions appear monthly.

Magazyn 3D

Polish 3D Magazine

www.3d.pl

Post

www.Postmagazine.com

The International Magazine for Post Production Professionals - A leading magazine serving the animation, audio, film, and video post production industry. This magazine is for television, film and video production post production facilities, broadcast television stations, TV program production companies, audio recording studios, motion picture production, film facilities and others allied to the industry. It covers the interests, needs, innovations, and news of various aspects of the postproduction world

RES Magazine

www.resmag.com

A leading magazine for digital content creators. Highly recommended for digital filmmakers, broadcast designers, music video producers, net cinema professionals, and other creatives.

SHOOT
www.shootonline.com
The Leading Newsweekly for Commercial Production & Postproduction
In every issue of SHOOT you'll find extensive and up-to-date coverage on who's shooting what, which directors have signed where, insider tidbits on people and places, and what's new in visual effects, music, animation and technology. All the news you need, from creative through production to postproduction, to make it in the commercial production industry.

Television Broadcast/Europe
www.tvbeurope.com
The highly influential European business publication for broadcast and television professionals. Europe's source for broadcast technology news.

Videography
www.videography.com
Videography is the #1 publication for content professionals who create programming for television, home video, streaming or any other delivery medium. Videography, which has defined its market for over 25 years, is filled with informative, expert articles and hands-on reviews that advise the most influential professionals who shoot, light, produce, edit, animate, design, stream and create entertainment or information content. These active equipment buyers, producers and operators work in the field, high-end post houses, small professional project/boutique studios, and every kind of content creation facility in between. Videography's editorial defines this dynamic era of digital transformation in the video production industry.

Video Systems
www.videosystems.com
Video Systems is written by professionals for professionals. Our editorial staff — the largest and most experienced of all the video publications— brings real-life experience to their coverage. As working video professionals, our writers take their forum very seriously and go beneath the surface of tools and technology to offer in-depth, mission-critical information and analysis. Like our writers, the readers of Video Systems work in the field of information video — documentaries, corporate/industrial/institutional video, business television, streaming media, commercials, live events, interactive video, and broadcast. Our mission is to provide a balance of new product information, reviews, user profiles, case studies, trend overviews, and hands-on technique stories. Video Systems helps readers use technology to maximum advantage at every stage of the video production cycle, from acquisition through presentation.

"Like so many others, Phil spent all his money on animation books and reference material"

RESOURCES - Books

Animation

The Animator's Survival Kit: A Manual of Methods, Principles, and Formulas for Classical, Computer, Games, Stop Motion, and Internet Animators
By Richard Williams
The definitive book on animation, from the Academy Award-winning animator behind Who Framed Roger Rabbit? Animation is one of the hottest areas of filmmaking today—and the master animator who bridges the old generation and the new is Richard Williams. During his more than forty years in the business, Williams has been one of the true innovators, winning three Academy Awards and serving as the link between Disney's golden age of animation by hand and the new computer animation exemplified by Toy Story.

Perhaps even more important, though, has been his dedication in passing along his knowledge to a new generation of animators so that they in turn could push the medium in new directions. In this book, based on his sold-out master classes in the United States and across Europe, Williams provides the underlying principles of animation that every animator—from beginner to expert, classic animator to computer animation whiz — needs. Urging his readers to "invent but be believable," he illustrates his points with hundreds of drawings, distilling the secrets of the masters into a working system in order to create a book that will become the standard work on all forms of animation for professionals, students, and fans. 40 color and 100 Black-and-White illustrations
Faber & Faber; ISBN: 0571212689; (January 2002)

Digital Character Animation 2: Essential Techniques
By George Maestri
Grounded in the basics of traditional cell animation, Digital Character Animation 2, Volume I: Essential Techniques provides the necessary information to create convincing computer-generated characters in 3D. This step-by-step, full color guide applies conventional character animation techniques such as walk cycles and lip sync to computer animation, along with tips for giving your characters the illusion of life. Volume I is the first of two volumes and is geared to more entry level animators, teaching the basics. Volume II, soon to be announced, will build on Volume I, covering more advanced concepts and techniques. The cross-platform CD-ROM includes: multiple walk cycles on various 3D programs; lip sync examples; texture maps; and 3D models from REM Infografica.
280 pages; New Riders Publishing; ISBN: 1562059300; 1st edition (July 1999)

Digital Character Animation 2, Volume II: Advanced Techniques

By George Maestri

At last, George Maestri's advanced-techniques volume of his groundbreaking [digital] Character Animation book. Completely new: No updated material from the first volume (covering Essential Techniques) or from the first edition (published in 1996 and now out of print). If you are into 3D animation at all—learning, practicing (or managing those who do), teaching—you owe it to yourself buy this book. If you're into other 3D disciplines—modeling, compositing, lighting, etc.—it's highly recommended that you at least take a look at this volume; it provides a ton of insight into what the folks over in modeling do 16 hours a day and as a result, might make you more valuable as a member of the project team. See why Maestri's books have been adopted as teaching texts around the world and are on the bookshelves of so many working pros in CG: it's all about the foundational techniques and the secrets involved that bring life and verve to the characters you're working on. Nobody teaches this stuff better than Maestri these days. And the books are just fun to look at and use: full-color, lots of visuals, to-the-point writing style, all backed up by George's years of industry experience. Wrapped up nicely with the contributing help of Angie Jones (game-design hero and now becoming an MVP in Hollywood's CG effects community).

240 pages; New Riders Publishing; ISBN: 0735700443; 1st edition (August 3, 2001)

The Animator's Workbook

By Tony White

An award-winning animator offers a complete course on the principles and techniques of drawn animation, covering every aspect of the process. In clear text and step-by-step drawings, he shows how to capture movement, expression, and emotion. Full-color illustrations.

Watson-Guptill Pubns; ISBN: 0823002292; Reprint edition (September 1988)

Cartoon Animation (The Collector's Series)

By Preston Blair

The Collector's Series books offer a selection of popular projects form best-selling titles in the How to Draw and Paint series. The Collectors Series books cover fundamentals and explore the techniques of featured artists. Each title provides in-depth instruction and numerous illustrations. All are perfect for the coffee table or reference library.

Walter Foster Pub; ISBN: 1560100842; (January 1995)

Animation from Script to Screen

By Shamus Culhane

Shamus Culhane, the animator who made the dwarfs in Snow White, achieves something few are able to: He makes it possible to learn concrete skill from a book. Covering every aspect of film animation, from basic mechanics to giving creativity full play, and including writing, recording, acting, dialogue – even how to manage an animation studio of

one's own, Culhane fulfills the promise of his title – "from script to screen." Animation contains more than 130 illustrations, from the work of learning animators worldwide (including the author himself) to sketches that teach and graphic exercises for hands-on experience for the novice. Through it all, Cull hand intrigues and entertains, making the book speak to everyone, fascinating both the art student and the general reader.
336 pages; St. Martin's Press; ISBN: 0312050526; Reprint edition (December 1990)

The Illusion of Life: Disney Animation
By Frank Thomas, Ollie Johnston (Contributor)
Not to be mistaken for just a "how-to-do-it," this voluminously illustrated volume – like the classic Disney films themselves – is definitely intended for everyone to enjoy. The most complete book on the subject ever written, this is the fascinating inside story by two long-term Disney animators of the gradual perfecting of a relatively young and particularly American art form – which no other movie studio has ever been able to equal. The authors, Frank Thomas and Ollie Johnston, worked not only with the legendary Walt Disney himself but with other leading figures in the half-century history of Disney films. They personally animated leading characters in most of the famous films, and have decades of close association with the other men and women who helped perfect this extremely difficult and time-consuming art form – each feature requires some 2 ½ million drawings!
575 pages; Hyperion; ISBN: 0786860707; Revised edition (October 1995)

The Male and Female Figure in Motion: 60 Classic Sequences
By Eadweard Muybridge
Sixty classic photographic sequences of the male and female figures in motion, selected from Eadweard Muybridge's original collection of 781, have been painstakingly reproduced on fine-coated stock. Here are men running, walking leaping, playing sports; women turning, bending, dancing, dressing; even children in various typical activities. This volume brings a superb selection of classic action photographs within reach of everyone.
121 pages; Dover Pubns; ISBN: 0486247457; (December 1984)

Horses and Other Animals in Motion
By Eadweard Muybridge
Fourty-Five classic photographic sequences of horses and other animals in motion. This volume brings a superb selection of classic action photographs within reach of everyone.
91 pages; Dover Pubns; ISBN: 0486249115; (October 1985)

Acting for Animators
By Ed Hooks, Brad Bird, Mike Caputo (Illustrator)
Until now, animators who have wanted to learn about acting have had no option but to study the subject side by side with stage and movie actors, a group that uses acting tech-

niques in a wholly different way. Ed Hooks offers a better alternative with Acting for Animators, the first book about acting theory and technique written specifically for the animator.

Animators need to know a lot about acting, but they don't need to know everything. Acting for Animators sorts out the acting theory that animators need, presenting it in a form and with references that are more relevant to the animator's world. It explores the connections between thinking and physical action, between thinking and emotion; it provides the steps for an effective character analysis and the dynamics of a scene. Using references to animation and live action, acting principles are highlighted and explained. Plus, the accompanying CD-ROM provides explicit examples, including videoclips of improvs based on the seven essentials of acting and highlights of Rudolph Laban's movement theory.
160 pages; Heinemann Publishing; ISBN: 0325002290; Bk&Cd-Rom edition (January 15, 2001)

Animating Facial Features and Expressions
By Bill Fleming, Darris Dobbs
Creating realistic animated characters and creatures is a major challenge for computer artists, but getting the facial features and expressions right is probably the most difficult aspect. In this one-of-a-kind book, readers will find an in-depth resource to guide them through the entire process from the history of facial animation and anatomical structures, to expressing emotions and speech visually.

It features comprehensive character studies showing detailed examples of 38 human and cartoon facial expressions through timing charts and side-by-side comparisons. It also includes detailed instruction on how to recreate these expressions using weighted morph targets, providing the actual target percentages to achieve the expressions. A reference guide shows you how the weighted morph targets should appear so you are guaranteed perfect facial expression morphs. On the CD are front and side templates of each expression so you can recreate them with your characters.
382 pages; Charles River Media; ISBN: 1886801819; Bk&CD-ROM edition (December 30, 1998)

Modeling

An Atlas of Anatomy for Artists
By Fritz Schider, Bernard Wolf (Translator)
Recognized as the most thorough reference work on art anatomy in the world. Includes a total of more than 350 illustrations showing the placement, function and characteristics of every anatomical detail of importance to the artist. There are cross section drawings that give the relation of the muscles to each other, to the bone structure, and to the internal organs of the body. Anatomical drawings that reveal the interplay of muscles and skele-

ton in different positions and a supplementary text on important features of each anatomical position including the action of muscles and their origin. This enlarged edition also includes a selection of illustrations from the works of Vesalius, Leonardo, Goya, Ingres, Michelangelo and plates from Boscay's "Anatomy".
Dover Pubns; ISBN: 0486202410; 3rd edition (May 1981)

The Artist's Complete Guide to Facial Expression
By Gary Faigin
Capture the subtleties of human emotion by using the Artist's Complete Guide To Facial Expression. This invaluable resource deals specifically with the muscles, textures, and effects of facial expression.
Watson-Guptill Pubns; ISBN: 0823016285; (November 1990)

Lighting and rendering

Digital Lighting & Rendering
By Jeremy Birn, George Maestri (Editor)
Digital Lighting contains strategies for lighting design that are relevant to any digital artist. It presents an awareness of computer lighting models, how they differ from real-world lighting effects, and how to approach 3D lighting projects differently from practical light. Topics covered include: What good lighting can do for you; Light sources; Shading; Shadows; Exposure and content; Color: temperature, correction, mood; Qualities of light; 3-point lighting; Indirect illumination; Multipass rendering and compositing; Lighting in production; and Case studies: natural lighting, interior lighting, character lighting, and effects lighting.
287 pages; New Riders Publishing; ISBN: 1562059548; 1st edition (January 15, 2000)

Film Lighting: Talks With Hollywood's Cinematographers and Gaffers
by Kris Malkiewicz, Leonard Konopelski (Illustrator), Barbara J. Gryboski
Fedrico Fellini, the renowned director, once said that "films are light." Film lighting by Kris Malkiewicz is an indispensable guide for anyone who uses lighting, wether for film, video, or still photography.

Lighting is a living, dynamic art influenced by new technologies and changing styles of leading cinematographers. Film Lighting is a unique book that combines a state-of-the-art coverage of technology with extensive interview material from the leading cinematographers and gaffers in the industry today.

The book opens with a meeting of the minds-of the cinematographer and the film director-when the visual concept of the film and the lighting style are established. It goes on to review current lighting equipment and the latest technology. Further topics discussed at length include: Image manipulation techniques. Studio and location lighting. Lighting strategies. Specific lighting problems and solutions. Improvisational lighting.

The author uses first-hand material from the experts he interviews while researching this book. Among these are cinematographers Vilmos Zsigmond, ASC (Close Encounters of the Third Kind), Allen Daviau, ASC (E.T.), James Crabe, ASC (Rocky), Conrad Hall, ASC, James Wong Howe, ASC, and Haskell Wexler, ASC, as well as gaffers Richmond Aguilar, Richard Hart and James Plannette.

Film lighting provides an invaluable opportunity to learn from the industry leaders and will prove an indispensable sourcebook for the practicing cinematographer.
198 pages; Fireside; ISBN: 0671766341; Reissue edition (December 1992)

Lighting for Television and Film
by Gerald Millerson
Skilful lighting involves a subtle blend of systematic mechanics and a sensitive visual imagination. It requires anticipation, perceptiveness, patience and know-how. But learning through practice alone can take a great deal of time. This book is a distillation of many years' experience, with advice and guidance that will bring successful results right from the start.
Whether you are a student studying lighting techniques in the television, video and film media, or a professional lighting for the camera, this book will be an invaluable aid. Other members of the production team, including camera crews, designers and directors, will also find the information here interesting and useful.

The book concentrates primarily on the fundamental principles of lighting in studios, on location and display, as well as single-camera, small unit production, improvised and economy lighting, and working with limited facilities. Emphasis is also placed on the safety aspects of working with lighting equipment.
448 pages; Focal Press; ISBN: 024051582X; 3rd edition (June 1999)

Painting With Light
By John Alton
Few cinematographers have had as decisive an impact on the cinematic medium as John Alton. Best known for his highly stylized film noir classics T-Men, He Walked by Night, and The Big Combo, Alton earned a reputation during the 1940s and 1950s as one of Hollywood's consummate craftsmen through his visual signature of crisp shadows and sculpted beams of light. No less renowned for his virtuoso color cinematography and deft appropriation of widescreen and Technicolor, he earned an Academy Award in 1951 for his work on the musical An American in Paris. First published in 1949, and long out of print since then, Painting With Light remains one of the few truly canonical statements on the art of motion picture photography, an unrivaled historical document on the workings of the postwar, American cinema. In simple, non- technical language, Alton explains the job of the cinematographer and explores how lighting, camera techniques, and choice of locations determine the visual mood of film. Todd McCarthy's introduction, written espe-

cially for this edition, provides an overview of Alton's biography and career and explores the influence of his work on contemporary cinematography. —This text refers to an out of print or unavailable edition of this title.
191 pages; University of California Press; ISBN: 0520089499; (April 1995)

The Technique of Special Effects Cinematography (Library of Communication Techniques, Film)
by Raymond Fielding
This superb book provides a unique insight into professional visual effects for motion pictures. Special effects have long been used to enhance scale and place, and to suggest realities that are but imagined. Once intended to save money, special effects films have now developed into the dominant motion picture genre.

The book describes every photographic special effect used throughout the world in detail and in context. It assumes a knowledge of standard cinematographic procedures on the part of the readers who, with the assistance of the techniques described here, should be able to develop their own practices and procedures as required.

For the cinematographer, this book is an indispensable reference. For producers, directors, technicians and writers it is a source of information, ideas and inspiration. For the film student it is a unique textbook.
442 pages; Focal Press; ISBN: 0240512340; 4th edition (December 1985)

Texturing and materials

Digital Texturing & Painting
By Owen Demers, Christine Urszenyi (Editor), George Maestri (Editor)
If you are involved in the world of 3D in any way—or even if you're simply a student of art and design theory—please take a look at this book. It's an amazing piece of work, exploring the theory and practice of applying texturing maps and paint effects to models and scenes. Yet somehow that doesn't do the book justice, possibly because author Owen Demers grounds his discussion in such solid fundamental ground that the book comes off as equal parts museum catalog, art school text, and industry profile. Face it, most 3D students and professionals have limited skill sets in art theory; yet these people are expected to turn out ever-higher quality work to keep up with audience expectations. We're beyond the days of dancing gasoline pumps... the release of Final Fantasy signals a new benchmark for mass-audience expectations of realistic quality in 3D. Want to know how to do this stuff right? Check out [digital] Texturing & Painting. Each edition of the New Riders [digital] series addresses a distinct discipline: Character Animation; Lighting & Rendering; and now Texturing & Painting (editions on modeling, compositing, and more are in development).
352 pages; New Riders Publishing; ISBN: 0735709181; 1st edition (August 9, 2001)

Compositing

The Art and Science of Digital Compositing
By Ron Brinkmann
Computer-generated visual effects are now used extensively in feature films, commercials, music videos, and multimedia. The backbone of this process, the final and most important step, is known as digital compositing. The Art and Science of Digital Compositing is a comprehensive reference that provides a complete overview of the technical and the artistic nature of this process. This book covers a wide range of topics from basic image creation, representation, and manipulation, to a look at the visual cues that are necessary to create a believable composite. Designed as both an introduction to the field as well as a valuable technical reference, this book should be of interest to both novices and professionals alike.

Written by a working professional in the visual effects industry, the book provides over 250 different images and illustrations (including a 40-page color insert) as well as a complete glossary of compositing and visual-effects terminology. Also included are in-depth case studies from well-known films such as Speed, Independence Day, and Titanic
84 pages; Morgan Kaufmann Publishers; ISBN: 0121339602; 1st edition (June 15, 1999)

Digital Compositing for Film and Video with CDROM
By Steve Wright
Written by a senior compositor with over ten years' experience in both feature film and broadcast television, this book offers a broad range of alternative solutions that will save hours of fiddling with composites trying to get them to look right when the basic tools aren't working. A companion CD-ROM provides examples of the many topics covered in this book.
320 pages; Butterworth-Heinemann; ISBN: 0240804554; 1st edition (December 15, 2001)

General

The Art of 3-D: Computer Animation and Imaging, 2nd Edition
By Isaac Victor Kerlow
The complete state-of-the-art guide to 3-D computer animation and imaging.Essential for visual effects production, computer games,online interactive multimedia, and more!Incorporating the latest computer animation techniques and technology, this outstanding guide offers clear step-by-step coverage of the entire process of creating a fully rendered 3-D computer still image or animation from modeling and rendering to animation and compositing.Designed to work with any computer platform, the book cuts through the technical jargon and features hundreds of inspiring color images and easy-to-understand instructive diagrams many of them new from visual effects in movies, animated films, TV shows, and computer games.This edition has been fully revised and

updated, including new material on the latest character and facial animation techniques and an overview of the digital production process, plus information on subdivision surfaces, image-based rendering, motion capture, and other current techniques. Whether you are a student, an independent artist or creator, or a production company team member, you'll find countless expert tips on how to improve the artistic and technical level of your 3-D computer animation.
*Non-platform specific
*500 full-color images
*Newest computer techniques
*Practical, step-by-step approach
*Up-to-date guide to Internet resources.
448 pages; John Wiley & Sons; ISBN: 047136004X; 2 edition (May 11, 2000)

Business and Legal Forms for Graphic Designers
By Tad Crawford, Eva Doman Bruck
This book contains negotiation tactics and thirty-three forms designers need in every-day business, including: Estimate for Client, Preliminary Budget and Schedule; Proposal Form; Job Sheet; Production Schedule; Estimate Request for Suppliers; Contract with Illustrator/Photographer/Printer/Sales Representative; Merchandising Agreement; Release Forms; Permission to Use Copyrighted Work; and much more.
224 pages; Allworth Press; ISBN: 158115030X

Cg 101: A Computer Graphics Industry Reference
By Terrence Masson
CG101 is the first comprehensive resource guide written in plain language for all levels of computer graphics users. It is also the first and only detailed behind-the-scenes history about the people and companies that have formed today's industry. Hundreds of contributors and in-depth interviews give a never-before-seen look into the earliest years of CG right up to present day. In addition to the historical perspective, CG 101 includes detailed tips and tricks, demo reel guidelines and CG job descriptions to help those looking to get into the business. The hundreds of software tool descriptions all have extensive contact information, including Web addresses and phone numbers for easy reference.
500 pages; New Riders Publishing; ISBN: 073570046X; 1st edition (August 1999)

Digital Cinematography & Directing
By Dan Ablan
[digital] Cinematography and Directing is unlike any other cinematography or directing book you've seen. This book was written entirely for 3D animators. Based on real-world photographic and cinematic principles, it teaches you essential skills and concepts that you can apply to any industry 3D application, such as LightWave 3D, Softimage XSI, 3ds max, CINEMA 4D, Maya, and other leading programs. This book does not focus on using software but rather teaches you how to understand and use the camera within your 3D application.

1. Master focal lengths, f-stops, and apertures within your 3D application.
2. Learn how pre-production planning can guide and enhance your project by applying essential storyboarding techniques.
3. Use light as not only an illumination source, but as a tool for cinematic storytelling.
4. Learn how to direct your digital cast with proper staging techniques
"Dan Ablan's years of innovating digital production techniques and his undeniable expertise at teaching CGI, FX, and Film, makes [digital]Cinematography and Directing a must-have!" -Dave Adams, Dreamworks.
240 pages; New Riders Publishing; ISBN: 0735712581; 1st edition (December 3, 2002)

Film Directing Shot by Shot: Visualizing from Concept to Screen
By Steven D. Katz
A complete catalogue of motion picture techniques for filmmakers. It concentrates on the 'storytelling' school of filmmaking, utilizing the work of the great stylists who established the versatile vocabulary of technique that has dominated the movies since 1915. This graphic approach includes comparisons of style by interpreting a 'model script', created for the book, in storyboard form.
325 pages; Focal Press; ISBN: 0941188108; (July 1991)

Graphic Artists Guild Handbook: Pricing & Ethical Guidelines (Graphic Artists Guild Handbook of Pricing and Ethical Guidelines, 10th Edition)
By Graphics Artists Guild
First published in 1973, the Graphic Artists Guild Handbook has become the essential source for fair prices and practice. Assembled by the national organization for graphic artists, this 10th edition contains the latest information on business, pricing and ethical standards for nearly every discipline in the visual communications industry, from advertising to publishing to corporate markets.
450 pages; North Light Books; ISBN: 0932102115; 10th edition (June 2001)

Producing Animation (Focal Press Visual Effects and Animation Series)
By Catherine Winder, Zahra Dowlatabadi
Complete guide to identifying, pitching, selling, developing, and producing an animated show. Provides comprehensive information on production planning, budgeting, scheduling and tracking your project. Includes a detailed description and flow charts of the production process for traditional (2D) and 3D CGI.
Drawing heavily from the authors' twenty years of combined experience, Producing Animation offers a clear overview of this exciting industry and a comprehensive guide to the process of developing a project from conception to final delivery. Written from the perspective of a producer, this book offers the foundation of how a project is created in addition to describing the role of the producer at each phase. Answers are provided to many of the most commonly asked questions about animation ranging from how to enter the business to the average cost and schedule for a prime-time animated series. Observations from a wide range of industry professionals such as; studio heads, creators, directors, pro-

ducers, writers and members of the production crew, give the reader insight into what it takes to be successful in this business. The authors' personal anecdotes at key process checkpoints relay firsthand experience, illustrating some of the pitfalls a producer must learn to circumvent. Detailed information on preparing a thorough production plan including the budget, schedule, and crew plan can also be found in this book.
320 pages; Focal Press; ISBN: 0240804120; (July 2001)

Visual Effects in A Digital World: A Comprehensive Glossary of over 7,000 Visual Effects Terms
By Karen E. Goulekas
Visual Effects in a Digital World is a comprehensive guide to visual effects terms and techniques that serves as a valuable resource for both novice and professional filmmakers from different generations, disciplines, and even different continents to be able to speak the same language. Written by award-winning visual effects expert Karen Goulekas, Visual Effects in a Digital World consolidates the knowledge of this rapidly expanding industry into a manageable, accessible reference guide. Covering over 7,000 visual effects terms and providing 177 accompanying illustrations, Goulekas has written what Visual Effects Producer Fiona Stone called "a comprehensive reference book for the modern-day film industry....an invaluable resource for the novice and experienced filmmaker alike."

Features:
16 pages of color from blockbuster films to illustrate definitions of terms
Covers topics such as computer graphics, digital compositing, live action, stage, and miniature photography, and a wide range of computer and Internet concepts.
Offers job descriptions for positions found throughout the industry.
Demystifies the jargon used by practitioners in every subspecialty.
616 pages; Morgan Kaufmann Publishers; ISBN: 0122937856; 1st edition (August 22, 2001)

Company directories

LBBVFX - "The Little Black Book of Visual Effects"
By Bernice Kenton-Briggs, Michele Linse Jeffers, Janette Shew and Tamara Watts Kent
The Little Black Book of Visual Effects is THE resource book for locating companies and individuals around the world that specialize in visual effects. Edited by industry professionals Bernice Kenton Briggs, Michele Linse Jeffers, Janette Shew, and Tamara Watts Kent, the book is now in its second edition. The book is divided into areas of production: Visual/Digital/Graphics, Companies, Production Personnel, Stage Personnel, Art Department, Creatures/Prosthetics/Puppets, Models/Miniatures, Mechanical/Special Effects, Stage Support Services, Post Production, Digital Effects Personnel, Digital Effects Support Services, Computer Hardware & Software, Support Services.
Web: http://www.lbbvfx.com

LA 411

Southern California's premier directory of professional industry resources for shooting television commercials and music video. Categories include: Crew, Props, Wardrobe, Make-up, Cameras, Lights, Stages, Post, etc.
Web: http://www.411publishing.com

NY 411

Comprehensive guide to film and video resources in the New York/Tri-State Area.
Web: http://www.411publishing.com

The Animation Industry Directory

A very good resource book for locating companies around the world that specialize in many areas of animation. Such as: Ad Agencies, Animated Presentation Production, Animation Art and Collectibles, Animation Production, Artists, Animators, Audio, Sound, CGI, Multimedia, Commercial Production, Computer Hardware, Computer Software, Creative Services, Digital Media, Distribution, Equipment, Feature Films, Festivals, Games, Interactive, Home Video, Internet, Legal, Licensing, Marketing, Motion Capture, Museums, Music, Organizations, Post Production, Public Relations, Recruitment, Schools, Universities, Stop Motion, Trade Shows, Training, TV Production, Visual Effects, Voiceover, Web Broadcasters, Web Design and Writing.
http://www.animationmagazine.net

The SHOOT Director

The SHOOT Directory covers the entire United States and Canada in an easy-to-use format, divided by categories and broken down by state; including all the key people, addresses, contact numbers, e-mail addresses, Web sites, and more. The SHOOT Directory puts the entire industry at your fingertips. There are listings for Advertising Agencies, Production Companies, Postproduction Cos., Editing Facilities, Video Production, Visual Effects, Labs, Animation, Computer Graphics, Equipment Rental & Sales, Interactive Multimedia, Music & Sound Cos., Production Services, Stock Footage Cos., Independent Repping Firms and Film Commissions.
Web: http://www.shootonline.com/shootonline/about/bookstore.jsp

RESOURCES - Computer Animation Companies

This section of the book contains company listings from all over the world. These companies do animation, visualizations and special effects for video, television, film, architecture, medical and more. Not listed are small TV Stations. There are just too many. A TV station list could be a book in itself.

How should you use this list? Apply responsibly, don't just blindly mail off reels and resumes to every company on this list. Do some research first. Go to the company's web site and see if they have any job openings. Check out their work. See if it's something you'd like to do for a living. If so, read the instructions that they give regarding demo material submission and follow them to the letter. If they say, no phone calls. Don't call them. If they say, only NTSC VHS reels will be accepted. Send them a NTSC VHS reel. Make it as easy as possible for them to hire you.

Double check the company's address in this book against the one they give you. Hundreds of companies had to be removed from the list during the production of this book because they went out of business. Many more are sure to follow. It would be a waste for you to apply for a job at one of those. Companies also move from time to time. If they've moved into a new office between the time this book is printed and the time you send off your demo materials and you don't check the address, then you run the risk of missing a possible job opportunity. Don't let late or misdirected mail get in the way or your next job. If you find out that a company has moved or closed, please let me know. I'll be eternally grateful. (Contact information is at the beginning of the book).

Why do I list the addresses when it is recommended that you double check them? I do it to give you an idea where the company is located. If you want to work for a company, spend a lot of time researching and preparing to apply there only to find out that it's located in another country or in a place that you do not want to move, you'll be pretty disappointed. There may be a company that you'd really like to work for just down the street but, without the address listed, you'd never know that it was there.

11th Street Communications
699 11th Street
Atlanta, Georgia 30318-5419
United States
Tel: 1-404-873-4477
Fax: 1-404-872-5055
Web: http://www.11thstreet.com

1|20media
8 Benedict app.:2
Hull, QC, Canada
J8Y 5G1
Tel: 1-819-0772-0417
Web: http://www.1-20media.com

12 Centimeter
477 South San Antonio Road,
Second Floor
Los Altos, California 94022
United States
Tel: 1-650-559-6400
Fax: 1-650-559-6401
Web: http://www.12cm.com

2000 Strong
PO Box 1527
Venice, California 90294-1527
United States
Tel: 1-310-822-5700
Fax: 1-310-822-0800
Web: http://www.2000strong.com

23D Films
6322 Yucca Street
Los Angeles, California 90028
United States
Tel: 1-323-962-6229
Fax: 1-323-962-7066
Web: http://www.23dfilms.com

2GMotion
6005 Danbury,Ste 103
Dallas, Texas 75206
United States
Tel: 214-369-7998
Fax: 214-369-8427
Web: http://www.2gmotion.com

2 Minutes
9 rue Biscornet
Paris
France
75012
Tel: +33 1.53.17.37.00
Fax: +33 1.53.17.07.37
Web: http://www.2minutes.fr

20th Century-Fox Television
P.O. Box 900
Beverly Hills, California 90213
United States
Tel: 1-310-369-2816
Fax: 1-310-369-8892
Web: http://www.fox.com

2D 3D Animations
72, rue Fontaine du Lizier
Angouleme, France
16000
Tel: +33 5.45.90.12.88
Fax: +33 5.45.90.12.89
Web: http://www.2d3d-animations.com

2nd nature
PO Box 56-402
Auckland, New Zealand
Tel: +164 9.30.89.88.3
Fax: +164 9.33.61.00.2
Web: http://www.2ndnature.co.nz

2nz Animation Co.
287, 2- SURBALA, S.V. Road
Bandra (W)
Mumbai
Maharashtra
India
400050
Tel: +91 22.65.11.02.6
Fax: +91 22.64.59.66.9
Web: http://www.2nz.com

30 Second Street
1209 Mountain Road Place NE
Albuquerque, New Mexico 87110
United States
Tel: +1-505-265-0224
Web: http://www.southwestpro-
ductions.com

310 Studios
17458 Gilmore St.
Van Nuys, California 91406
United States
Tel: 1-310-859-5500
Fax: 1-310-859-5530
Web: http://www.310studios.com

3Birds
370 S Crenshaw Blvd, Ste E202A
Torrance, California 90505
United States
Tel: 1-310-782-0789
Fax: 1-310-782-0715
Web: http://www.3birds.com

3Birds
1431 Lemontree Court
La Habra, California 90631
United States
Tel: 1-562-694-8346
Fax: 1-562-691-1115
Web: http://www.3birds.com

3D Central
2705 NE 35th Place
Portland, Oregon 97212
United States
Tel: 1-503-284-0484
Fax: 1-503-284-0484
Web: http://www.3dcentral.com

3D Characters I/O Robert
Kuczera
Kaffeeberg 10/1
71634 Ludwigsburg
Germany
Web: http://www.3dcharacters.de

3D Films
Plaza One
Telford Plaza
Ironmasters Way
Telford
Shropshire
United Kingdom
TF3 4NT
Tel: +44 195.22.08.70.1
Fax: +44 195.22.08.70.4
Web: http://www.3dfilms.co.uk

3D Imaging
12 Woodside Road
Simonstone
Burnley
Lancashire
BB12 7JG
England
United Kingdom
Tel: 44 (0) 1282 778771
Fax: 44 (0) 870 1315997
Web: http://www.3d-imaging.co.uk

3D Jamie
Number 1 Neal's Yard
Covent Garden
London
United Kingdom
WC2H 9DP
Tel: +44 207.37.90.10.5
Web: http://www.3djamie.com

3D Joe Corporation
330 Townsend #100
San Francisco, California 94107
United States
Tel: 1-415-536-4170
Web: http://www.3djoe.com

3D South
South Carolina
United States
Tel: 1-843-240-8468
Web: http://www.3dsouth.com

3D Video Graphics S.L.
Ave JJaume III No 33 Bajos
Santa Mmaria Del Cami
Mallorca
Baleares
Spain
Tel: 011-34-71-205-001
Fax: 011-34-71-202-352
Web: http://www.tresdim.com

3dBob Productions
3519 West Pacific Avenue
Burbank, California 91505
United States
Tel: 1-818-559-9700
Fax: 1-818-559-9768
Web: http://www.3dbob.com

3DMIRAGE
3 E 28th St.
12th Floor
New York, New York 10016
United States
Tel: 1-212-967-7777
Fax: 1-212-967-7971
Web: http://www.3dmirage.com

3Q Technologies, Inc.
100 Galleria Parkway, Suite 605
Atlanta, Georgia 30339
United States
Tel: 1-770-612-1176
Fax: 1-770-612-0833
Web: http://www.tcti.com
Web: http://www.3Q.com

3Q Technologies
1268 Missouri Street
San Francisco, California 94107
United States
Tel: 1-415-593-9034
Web: http://www.tcti.com
Web: http://www.3Q.com

3Q Technologies
6 The Long Room
Summerhouse Lane
Harefield
Middlesex
UB9 6JA
United Kingdom
Tel: +44 (0) 1895 820 920
Fax: +44 (0) 1895 820 630
Web: http://www.tcti.com
Web: http://www.3Q.com

3sixtymedia
Quay Street
Manchester, United Kingdom
M60 9EA
Tel: +44 161.83.90.36.0
Fax: +44 161.82.72.36.0
Web: http://www.3sixtymedia.com

422 Studios South
St. John's Court
Whiteladies Road
Bristol
BS8 2QY
Tel: +44 (0) 117 9467222

Fax: +44 (0) 117 9467722
Web: http://www.422.com

422 Studios
4th Floor Paramount House
162-170 Wardour Street
London
United Kingdom
W1V 3AT
Tel: +44 207.49.42.42.2
Fax: +44 207.49.44.22.0
Web: http://www.422.com

422 Studios
4th Floor South Central
11 Peter Street
Manchester
United Kingdom
M2 5QR
Tel: +44 161.83.96.08.0
Fax: +44 161.83.96.08.1
Web: http://www.422.com

4 Front design
1500 Broadway, Suite 509
New York, New York 10036
United States
Tel: 1-212-944-7055
Fax: 1-212-944-7193
Web: http://www.4-frontdesign.com

4 KIDS ENTERTAINMENT
1414 Ave of the Americas
New York, New York 10019
United States
Tel: 1-212-754-5482
Fax: 1-212-754-5481
Web: http://www.4kidsentertain-ment.com

501 Post
501 N. IH-35
Austin, Texas 78702
United States
Tel: 1-512-476-3876
Fax: 1-512-477-3912
Web: http://www.501post.com

66k Interactive
Ottawa, Canada
Tel: 1-631-427-2151
Fax: 1-631-980-7888
Web: http://www.66k.com

66k Interactive
Long Island, New York
United States
Tel: 631-427-2151
Fax: 631-980-7888
Web: http://www.66k.com

A2Z iTV
111 North Sepulveda Blvd. Suite 243
Manhattan Beach, California
90266
United States
Tel: 1-310-798-6979
Fax: 1-310-798-0019
Web: http://www.a2zitv.com

A2Z iTV
7100 Whipple Ave NW
North Canton, Ohio 44720
United States
Tel: 1-330-433-1010
Fax: 1-330-433-1011
Web: http://www.a2zitv.com

A52
9006 Melrose Avenue
Los Angeles, California 90069
United States
Tel: 1-310-385-0851
Fax: 1-310-385-0861
Web: http://www.a52.com

A&S Animation Animatics &
Storyboards
8137 Lake Crowell Circle
Orlando, Florida 32836
United States
Tel: 1-407-370-2673
Web:http://www.storyboards-east.com

A Film A/S
85F Tagensvej
Copenhagen
2200 Denmark
Tel: 011-45-35-827060

Fax: 011-45-35-82706
Web: http://www.afilm.dk

A Film Estonia Ltd.
Kaare 15
Tallinn
Estonia
11618
Tel: +372.67.06.48.5
Fax: +372.67.06.43.3
Web: http://www.afilm.ee

A For Animation
Unit 3A
The Old Malthouse
Little Ann St
Bristol
BS2 9EN
England
United Kingdom
Tel: 011-44-117-955-0611
Fax: 011-44-117-955-0600
Web: http://www.aforanimation.co.uk

A Productions
52 Old Market Street
Bristol
United Kingdom
BS2 0ER
Tel: +44 117.92.99.00.5
Fax: +44 117.92.99.00.4
Web: http://www.aproductions.co.uk

Aardman Animations, Ltd.
7 Gasferry Road
Bristol
United Kingdom
BS1 6UN
Tel: +44 117.98.48.48.5
Fax: +44 117.98.48.48.6
Web: http://www.aardman.com

Aarsen Communications
Castricummer Werf 106 - 108
1901 RS Castricum
The Netherlands
Tel: (0251) 65 55 69
Fax: (0251) 65 70 53
Web:
http://www.aarsencommunications.nl

AAV Limited
180 Bank Street
South Melbourne
Victoria 3205
Australia
Tel: 03 9251 1844
Web: http://www.aav.com.au

Abandon Entertainment
135 West 5oth Street, Suite 2305
New York, New York 10020
United States
Tel: 1-212-246-4445
Fax: 1-212-397-8361
Web: http://www.abandonent.com

AB Groupe
132 Avenue du Président Wilson
93213 La Plaine Saint Denis
Cedex
France
Tel: 011-33-0-1-4922-2001
Fax: 011-33-0-1-4922-2216
Web: http://www.groupe-ab.fr

ABC Toon Center
Country Downs Circle
Fairport, New York 14450
United States
Web: http://www.abctooncenter.com

Absinthe Pictures
8972 Shoreham Drive
Los Angeles, California 90069
United States
Tel: 1-310-275-0430
Fax: 1-310-275-0489
Web:http://www.absinthepictures.com

Absolute Studios
36 Washington Street
Glasgow
United Kingdom
G3 8AZ
Tel: +44 141.57.20.69.0
Fax: +44 141.57.20.69.0
Web:http://www.absolutestudios.com

Abyss Lights Studio
Akhmatovoi str. #5 / 75
Kiev, Ukraine
380 50 3380063
Web: http://www.abyss-lights.com

Ace Digital House
Avenue De Schiphollaan 2
1140 Brussles
Belgium
Tel: +32 2 735 60 20
Fax: +32 2 734 09 63
Web: http://www.ace-postproduction.com

Acme Filmworks
6525 Sunset Boulevard
Garden Suite 10
Hollywood, California 90028
United States
Tel: 1-323-464-7805
Fax: 1-323-464-6614
Web:http://www.acmefilmworks.com

Acme Graphics
2 Park Street
Teddington
Middlesex
United Kingdom
TW11 0LT
Tel: +44 208.39.55.13.0
Fax: +44 208.39.55.12.9
Web:http://www.acmegraphics.co.uk

Acorn Entertainment
5777 W. Century Blvd, Ste 1195
Los Angeles, California 90045-5600
United States
Tel: 818-340-5272
Fax: 818-340-7512
Web:http://www.acornentertainment.com

Acrologix (pvt) Ltd.
106/3, Saint Johns Park
Lahore-Cantt
Pakistan
Tel: 92-42-6664301-06
Fax: 92-42-6664307
Web: http://www.acrologix.com

Acropetal Animedia Ltd.
28, I Main, BTM II Stage

Bannerghatta Road
Bangalore
Karnataka
India
560054
Tel: +91 80.67.84.53.9
Fax: +91 80.67.85.36.2
Web: http://www.acroanimedia.com

Act3 Animation
First Floor, 240 Chapel Street
Prahran Victoria
Australia 3181
Tel: +613 9510 8943
Fax: +613 9510 8953
Web: http://www.act3.com.au

Activeworlds, Inc.
95 Parker Street
Newburyport, Massachusetts
01950
United States
Tel: 1-978-499-0222
Web: http://www.activeworlds.com

ACTV
233 Park Ave South, 10th floor
New York, New York 10003
United States
Tel: 1-212-497-7000
Fax: 1-212-497-7001
Web: http://www.actv.com

ADM Productions, Inc.
40 Seaview Boulevard
Port Washington, New York 11050
United States
Tel: 1-516-484-6900
Fax: 1-516-621-2531
Web: http://www.admpro.com

Adtech Communications Group
8220 Commonwealth Drive, Suite 201
Eden Prairie, Minnesota 55344
United States
Tel: 1-952-944-6347
Fax: 1-952-944-5643
Web: http://www.adtechinc.com

Adrenaline Films
5224 South Orange Avenue

Orlando, Florida 32809
United States
Tel: 1-407-850-0711
Fax: 1-407-859-6527
Web:http://www.adrenalinefilms.com

Advanced Media Production
1250 Bellflower Boulevard, UTC-113
Long Beach, California 90840-2802
United States
Tel: 1-562-985-4352
Web: http://www.amp.csulb.edu

Advanced Medien AG
Keltenring 11
Oberhaching
Denmark 82041
Tel: +45 89.61.38.05.0
Fax: +45 89.61.38.05.5
Web:http://www.advanced-film.de

Advanced Video Communications
514 S.E. 11th Court
Fort Lauderdale, Florida 33316
United States
Tel: 1-954-761-1178
Fax: 1-954-761-1266
Web: http://www.avcvideo.com

Aftershock Digital
8222 Melrose Avenue, Suite 304
Los Angeles, California 90046
United States
Tel: 1-800-230-2290
Fax: 1-323-658-5200
Web:http://www.aftershockdigital.com

AG Technologies
6, Western Ind. Co-op. Est.,
Central Road, M.I.D.C
Andheri (East)
Mumbai
Maharashtra
India
400 093
Tel: +91 22.82.50.56.7
Fax: +91 22.83.68.72.8
Web:http://www.ag-technologies.com

AGA Digital Studios, Inc.
1305 Wiley Rd. Suite 125
Schaumburg, Illinois 60173
United States
Web: http://www.agadigital.com

AGA Digital Studios, Inc.
542 West Campus Drive
Arlington Heights, Illinois 60004
United States
Tel: 1-847-222-9454
Fax: 1-847-222-9455
Web: http://www.agadigital.com

AGI Studios
1745 Tullie Circle
Atlanta, Georgia 30329
United States
Tel: 1-404-325-3355
Web: http://agistudios.com

AI Effects, Inc.
7114 Laurel Canyon Blvd. Suite A
North Hollywood, California
91605
United States
Tel: 1-818-764-2063
Fax: 1-818-764-2065
Web: http://www.aifx.com

AICON S.R.L.
Cabrera 5017
Buenos Aires, Capital Federal
Argentina
1414
Tel: +54 11.48.31.64.58
Fax: +54 11.48.31.64.58
Web: http://www.aicon.com.ar

AIST, Inc.
715 West Orchard Drive
Suite 7
Bellingham, Washington 98225
United States
Tel: 1-360-527-1489
Fax: 1-360-527-1619
Web: http://www.aist.com

AKOM PRODUCTION COMPANY
71-6 Munjung-Dong Songpa-Ku
Seoul 138-200

Korea
Tel: O11-82-2-400-2566
Fax: 011-82-2-401-6043
Web: http://www.animatoon.co.kr

Alee Design
6915 Dawntree Ct.
Lake Worth, Florida 33467
United States
Tel: 1-561-254-3399
Web: http://www.alee-design.com

Alexander & Tom
2400 Boston Street
Suite 308
Baltimore, Maryland 21224
United States
Tel: 1-410-327-7400
Fax: 1-410-327-7403
Web: http://www.alextom.com

Alian Shiveh Studio
No.1.111 8th Sarvestan Pasdaran
Ave.
Tehran, Iran
16619
Tel: +98 21.28.50.83.9
Fax: +98 21.28.40.88.5
Web: http://www.alianshiveh.com

All American Fremantle
International
1 Stephen Street
London
England
W1P 1PJ
Tel: 0207 6916000
Fax: 0207 6916100
Web: http://www.pearsontv.com

All Pro Media, Inc
422 Spring Street, P.O. Box 2566
Burlington, North Carolina 27216
United States
Tel: 1-336-229-7700
Tel: 1-800-270-2207
Fax: 1-336-229-7778
Web: http://www.allpromedia.com

Allvision
Zum Spatzenberg 15

66571 Wiesbach
Germany
Tel: 06806-99 93 3
Fax: 06806 / 999-34
Web: http://www.all-vision.org

Alphanim
4, rue Charlemagne
75004 Paris
France
Tel: (+33) 1 49 96 44 00
Web: http://www.alphanim.com

Alphanim Digital
20, quai des Celestins
75004 Paris
France
Tel: +331 44 54 56 17
Web: http://www.alphanim.com

Alpha Dogs, Inc.
1612 W Olive Suite 200
Burbank, California 91506.
United States
Tel: 1-818-729-9262
Fax: 1-818-753-8995
Web: http://www.alphadogs.tv

Alpha Vision
2 Place Laval, Suite 320
Laval (Quebec)
H7N 5N6
Canada
http://www.alpha-vision.com

Alpha Vision
7320 E. Butherus Drive, Suite
103
Scottsdale, Arizona 85260
United States
Web:
http://www.alpha-vision.com

Alshar Animation
59A Abdul Monim Ryad St
Mohandiseen, Giza 12411
Egypt
Tel: 011-20-2-305-9481
Fax: 011-20-2-337-600
Web: http://www.alsahar.com

Alt. Pictures
Furmanny 6
Moscow, Russian Federation
103062
Tel: +7 95.79.09.51.4
Web: http://www.alt-pictures.ru

Altered Illusions
10222 Camarillo St #102
Toluca Lake California 91602
United States
Tel: 1-818-819-7961
Web: http://www.alteredillusions.com

Alternate Route Studios
One Research Drive
Raleigh, North Carolina 27513
United States
Tel: 1-919-677-8000
Fax: 1-919-677-4444
Web:http://www.altroutestudios.com

ALTSS
L.Asanaviciutes str. 4 - 273
Vilnius
Lithuania
2050
Tel: +370 5.21.69.04.4
Fax: +370 5.21.69.04.4
Web: http://www.altss.com

amalgamation house, Inc.
1218-20 Shackamaxon Street
Philadelphia, Pennsylvania 19125-3914
United States
Tel: 1-215-427-1954
Fax: 1-215-426-6372
Web: http://www.pixelmixers.com

Amazing Animation Productions
Suite 2105 Xingyixuan
Xinghemingju Fuming Road
Futian District
Shenzhen, Guang Dong China
518040
Tel: +86 755 3843423
Tel: +86 755 83666967
Tel: +86-755 83666965
Fax: +86 755 3843127
Fax: +86 755 83666965
Web: http://www.amazing-animation.com

Ambience Entertainment
115 Willoughby Road
Crows Nest NSW 2065
Sydney
Australia
Tel: +612-9478 5000
Fax: +612-9478 5099
Web: http://www.ambienceenter-tainment.com

Ambient Entertainment
Wilhelmstraße 4
Hannover, Germany
30171
Tel: +49 51.18.44.89.90
Fax: +49 51.18.44.89.99.9
Web:
http://www.ambient-entertainment.de

Ambit New Media Ltd.
Horatio House
Horatio Street
Quayside
Newcastle upon Tyne
NE1 2PE
United Kingdom
Tel: 0800 027 2767
Tel: +44 (0)191 232 8882
Fax: +44 (0)191 230 2346
Web:
http://www.ambitnewmedia.com

American Filmworks
Miami, Florida
United States
Web:http://www.americanfilmworks.com

Amdo Productions, Inc.
8362 Pines Boulevard, Suite #243
Hollywood, Florida 33024
United States
Tel: 1-954-761-1178
Fax: 1-954-761-1266
Web: http://www.amdo.com

American Production Services
2247 15th Avenue West
Seattle, Washington 98119
United States
Tel: 1-206-282-1776
Fax: 1-206-282-3535
Web: http://www.apsnw.com

American Production Services
11755 Victory Boulevard Suite 100
North Hollywood, California
91606
United States
Tel: 1-818-769-1776
Fax: 1-818-769-9787
Web: http://www.apsnw.com

AMM Studio
3, Rohit Society, Rohit Society
Juhu Tara Road
Juhu
Coria lane, juhu
Mumbai
Maharastra
India
400049
Tel: +91 22.61.04.24.7
Tel: +91 22 61.53.22.6
Fax: +91 22.61.04.24.7
Web: http://www.ammstudio.com

AMM Studio
8-2-269/8/5
Sagar Society
Road No.2
Banjara Hills
Hyderabad 500 034
India
Tel: 91+40+3550851/59/61/62
Fax: 91+40+3541671
Web: http://www.ammstudio.com

Amoebaproteus
438 West 37th Street
Suite 5G
New York, New York 10018
United States
Tel: 1-212-244-3369
Fax: 1-212-244-3735
Web:http://www.amoebaproteus.com

AMVF
2010 Burnett Blvd.
Wilmington, North Carolina 28401
United States
Tel: 1-910-772-9500
Tel: 1-910-443-4732
Web: http://www.amvf.com

AMVF
2725 Old Wrightsboro Ave., Suite 1-E
Wilmington, North Carolina 28405
United States
Tel: 1-910-772-9500
Fax: 1-910-772-9434
Web: http://www.amvf.com

Anabase
89 Rue Escudier
Boulogne Cedex 92107
France
Tel: 011-33-0-1-4712-4806
Fax: 011-33-0-1-4712-4801
Web: http://www.anabase.fr

an-amaze-tion
5243 Seneca Place
Simi Valley, California 93063
United States
Tel: 1-805-578-9560
Fax: 1-805-578-9553
Web: http://www.an-amaze-tion.com

A New Light Productions
20 Battery Park Avenue Suite #705
Asheville, North Carolina 28801
United States
Tel: 1-877-874-0073
Web: http://www.anewlight.com

Anamazing Workshop
263 Oak Avenue Ice Site
Randburg
Box 41374 Craighall 2024
Johannesburg, Gauteng
South Africa
2000
Tel: +27 11.34.81.41.1
Fax: +27 11.88.68.62.9
Web: http://www.an-amazing.com

Anemotion, Ltd.
Baltic Chambers
50 Wellington Street
Glasgow
Scotland
United Kingdom
G36HJ
Tel: +44 141.24.88.26.6
Web: http://www.anemotion.co.uk

Angelsmith
5478 Wilshire Blvd., Suite 210
Los Angeles, California 90036
United States
Tel: 1-323-549-9944
Fax: 1-323-939-7367
Web: http://www.angelsmith.net

Angel Studios
5966 La Place Court Suite 170
Carlsbad, California 92008
United States
Tel: 1-760-929-0700
Fax: 1-760-929-0719
Web:http://www.angelstudios.com

Anibyte
Derby
United Kingdom
Web: http://www.anibyte.com

Anibyte
Valencia 46023
Spain
Web: http://www.anibyte.com

Anidini & Associate
Rm.16, 10/F., Tower B, Proficient Ind.
Rm.3306, Ka Wing House
Ka Tin Court
Tai Wai
Hong Kong
Tel: +852.21.89.73.66
Fax: +852.21.89.72.73
Web: http://www.animdini.com

Anifex
65 King William Street
Kent Town 5067
Australia
Tel: +61 8 8363 1669
Fax: +61 8 8363 1776
Web: http://www.anifex.com.au

Anim.8 Studios
2029 Elderwood Court
Eldersburg, Maryland 21784
United States
Tel: 1-410-552-1695
Web: http://www.anim-8.net

Anima, Karekare Film Yapim A.S.
100. Yil Sanayi Sitesi Girisi No:4
Maslak
Istanbul, Turkey
80670
Tel: +90 212.28.62.04.6
Fax: +90 212.28.62.04.5
Web: http://www.anima.gen.tr

AniMagic Productions LLC
1307 Washington Avenue
Suite 604
St. Louis, Missouri 63103
United States
Tel: 1-877-408-6738
Fax: 1-314-436-0343
Web: http://www.aniprod.com

Animagic Studio
Avda. Fuente Nueva, 6
San Sebasti·n de los Reyes
Madrid, Spain
28700
Tel: +34 91.65.92.03.6
Fax: +34 91.66.39.64.5
Web: http://www.animagicstudio.com

AnimagicNet AS
Storgata 51
Oslo, Norway
0183
Tel: +47 22.99.76.10
Fax: +47 22.99.76.11
Web: http://www.animagicnet.no

Animagix Media
Hamburger Strasse 205
Hamburg, Germany
22083
Tel: +49 40.29.94.61.1
Fax: +49 40.29.94.65.6
Web: http://www.animagix.com

Animago, Lda
Rua Guerra Junqueiro, 495, 1º Sala J
Porto, Portugal
4150-389
Tel: +351 22.54.32.07.0
Fax: +351 22.54.32.07.1
Web: http://www.animago.pt

Animal Logic
Building 54, FSA #19
Driver Avenue
Moore Park, New South Wales
Australia
1363
Tel: +61 2.93.83.48.00
Fax: +61 2.93.83.48.01
Web: http://www.animallogic.com

Animal Logic
1117 Abbot Kinney Boulevard
Venice, California 90291
United States
Tel: 1-310-664-8765
Fax: 1-310-664-9355
Web: http://www.animallogic.com

AnimAlu Productions
633 San Leon
Irvine, California 92606
United States
Tel: 1-949-261-1179
Web: http://www.animalu.com

Animanto
624 Cross Avenue
Los Angeles, California 90065
United States
Tel: 1-323-550-1977
Web: http://www.animanto.com

Animate Beleares
Soldat Arrom Cuart 1 C-5
Palma de Mallorca, Spain
07010
Tel: +34 97.19.10.92.0
Fax: +34 97.19.10.91.7
Web: http://www.animante.com

Animated Health Solutions
244 Peters St. S.W. #27
Atlanta, Georgia 30313
United States
Tel: 1-404-584-2396
Web:http://www.animatedhealth.com

Animation Canada
2284 Gerrard St East
Toronto, Ontario M4E 2E1
Canada

Tel: 1-416-690-1690
Fax: 1-416-690-0136
Web: http://www.animation.ca

Animation Enterprises Hong Kong
Limited
Unit C1 2/F Hong Kong Spinners
Ind Bldg Phase 5
760-762 Cheung Sha Wan Rd
Kowloon
Hong Kong
Tel: (825) 2369-8928
Fax: (825) 2724-3801
Web: http://www.aehkl.com.hk

Animation People s.r.o.
Na DoubkovÈ 8
Prague
Czech Republic
150 00
Tel: +420 2.51.56.32.00
Fax: +420 2.51.56.52.03
Web: http://www.animation.cz

Animation People, Ltd. (The)
22 Great Queen Street
Covent Garden
London
United Kingdom
WC2B 5BH
Tel: +44 207.24.27.23.1
Fax: +44 207.24.27.31.4
Web:http://www.animationpeople.co.uk

Animation Research Ltd.
442 Moray Place
Po Box 5580
Dunedin
New Zealand
Tel: 64 3 4772995
Fax: 64 3 4799751
Web: http://www.arl.co.nz

Animation Technologies
60 Canal Street
Boston, Massachusetts 02114
United States
Tel: 1-617-723-6040
Fax: 1-617-723-6080
Web: http://www.animationtech.com

Animation Technologies
1601 Market Street Suite 380
Philadelphia, Pennsylvania 19103
United States
Tel: 1-215-564-4600
Fax: 1-215-564-4602
Web: http://www.animationtech.com

Animation Technologies
303 West Madison Street
Suite 925
Chicago, Illinois 60606
United States
Tel: 1-312-334-6100
Fax: 1-312-726-5064
Web: http://www.animationtech.com

Animagrafx
101 Greville st Prahran
Victoria
Australia 3181
Tel:+ 61 3 9510 8015
Fax: +61 3 9510 5598
Web: http://www.animagrafx.com.au

Animantis srl
Viale Città d'Europa, N. 780
00144 Rome
Italy
Tel: +39 06 52 27 96 67
Fax: +39 06 52 20 03 80
Web: http://www.animantis.com

Animatographo
Rua Duilio Calderari, 63 - lj. 3
Curitiba, Paran
Brazil
80040-250
Tel: +55 41.36.28.60.0
Web: http://www.animatographo.com

Animatrix Computer Arts, Inc.
PO Box 66830
Houston, Texas 77266
United States
Tel: 1-713-523-0888
Fax: 1-713-523-7342
Web: http://www.animatrix-arts.com

Animatus Studio
34 Winthrop Street
Rochester, New York 14607
United States
Tel: 1-585-232-1740
Fax: 1-585-232-3949
Web:http://www.animatusstudio.com

Animax 3d
Juⁿná Trieda 9
040 01 Košice
Slovakia
Tel: 00421 - (0) 905 - 316 - 504
Fax: 00421 - (0) 55 - 677 1917
Web: http://www.animax3d.sk

Animax
3455 South La Cienega Blvd. Bldg. C
Los Angeles, California 90016
United States
Tel: 1-310-559-9651
Fax: 1-310-559-9428
Web:
http://www.animaxinteractive.com
http://www.animaxentertainment.com

Animax Design Group
Victoria, British Columbia
Canada
Web:
http://www.animaxdesigngroup.com

Animax Studios
Trace House
Clay of Allan
Fearn by Tain, Scotland
IV20 1RR
United Kingdom
Tel: +44 186.28.32.00.1
Fax: +44 186.28.32.00.2
Web:http://www.animaxstudios.com

Animega
Box 3113
Brahegatan, 7
Jonkoping
Sweden
55003
Tel: +46 36.12.55.21
Web: http://www.animega.com

Animink Incorporated
105 East Birnie St.
Gaffney, South Carolina 29340
United States
Tel: 1-864-487-8805
Fax: 1 864-487-8809
Web: http://www.animink.com

Animoke Limited
GFF 2 Chatham Place
Brighton
United Kingdom
BN1 3TP
Tel: +44 775.96.79.38.4
Web: http://www.animoke.com

Animotion
501 W. Fayette Street
Syracuse, New York 13204
United States
Tel: 1-315-471-3533
Fax: 1-315-471-2730
Web:http://www.animotioninc.com

Animotion
Eerste Jacob van Campenstraat
17-1-L
1072 BB Amsterdam
The Netherlands
Tel: (06) 26044871
Web: http://www.animotion.nl

Animotion Studios
23 Holmes Drive
Greenville, South Carolina 29609
United States
Tel: 1-864-322-2704
Fax: 1-864-322-9228
Web: http://www.astudios.com

Animusic
317 Nye Rd.
Cortland, New York 13045
United States
Tel: 1-607-756-0190
Fax: 1 805-241-5505
Web: http://www.animusic.com

Animation Partnership, The
77 Dean St
London

W1V 5HA
England
Tel: 011-44-1-71-636-3300
Fax: 011-44-1-71-580-9153
Web:
http://www.animationpartnership.co.uk

AnimAlu Productions
633 San Leon
Irvine, California 92606
United States
Tel: 1-949-261-1179
Web: http://www.animalu.com

Anglia TV
Anglia House
Norwich NR1 3JG
United Kingdom
Tel: 01603 615151
Web: http://www.anglia.tv.co.uk

Anner Media Group
50 Upper Mount Street
Dublin 2
Ireland
United Kingdom
Tel: +353 1.66.12.24.4
Web:http://www.annerinternational.com

Another World Productions
23 Church Street
Co Armagh
Portadown
Northern Ireland
United Kingdom
BT63 3LN
Tel: +44 283.83.32.93.3
Fax: +44 283.83.96.94.1
Web:http://www.awproductions.com

Antefilms Production
103 Rue De Miromesnil
75008 Paris
France
Tel: 011-33-1-5353-0630
Fax: 011-33-1-5353-0629
Web: http://www.antefilms.com

AnteFilms (Levallois)
3, rue Collagne
Levallois, France
92300
Tel: 011-33-1-5521-99.40
Fax: 011-33-1-5521-99-41
Web: http://www.antefilms.com

Antefilms Studio
31, rue Marengo
Angouleme, France
16000
Tel: 011-33-5-4522-9500
Fax: 011-33-5-4522-9501
Web: http://www.antefilms.com

Antenna Men
Lloydstraat 9c
3024 EA
Rotterdam
Netherlands
Web: http://www.antenna-men.com

Anthropics Technology, Ltd.
Ealing Studios
Ealing Green
London, United Kingdom
W5 5EP
Tel: +44 208.75.88.61.9
Fax: +44 208.75.88.61.9
Web: http://www.anthropics.com

anyMOTION GRAPHICS
Agentur & Produktion
für Neue Medien GmbH
Rochusstr. 34
40479 Düsseldorf
Germany
Tel: +49-211-443343
Fax: +49-211-443394
Web: http://www.anymotion.de

A-pix digital post group, inc.
625-D Herndon Avenue
Orlando, Florida 32803
United States
Tel: 1-407-895-1008
Web: http://www.apix-digital.com

Applause Digital Media
Chapel Court

Long Ashton Business Park
Yanley Lane
Long Ashton
Bristol, United Kingdom
BS41 9LW
Tel: +44 127.53.94.56.7
Fax: +44 127.53.93.56.7
Web: http://www.applause.co.uk

Applause Digital Media
Chapel Court
Long Ashton Business Park
Yanley Lane
Long Ashton
Bristol, United Kingdom
BS41 9LW
Tel: +44 127.53.94.56.7
Fax: +44 127.53.93.56.7
Web: http://www.applause.co.uk

Apply Entertainment Inc.
Taiwan, R.O.C.
Tel: (02)2345-1876
Fax: (02)2345-1820
Web: http://www.apply.com.tw

APV Interactive
6, Jalan 13/6
46200 Petaling Jaya
Selangor Darul Ehsan
West Malaysia
Tel: 603 7954 8101
Fax: 603 7954 8100
Web: http://www.apv.com.my

Aquarius Design
Macedonia
Web: http://www.aquarius.com.mk

Arcana Digital Ltd
Garrard House
2-6 Homesdale Road
Bromley
Kent
England
BR2 9LZ
United Kingdom
Tel: +44 (0)20 8466 0655
Fax: +44 (0)20 8466 6610
Web:http://www.arcanadigital.com

Arc Light Editorial
57 east 11th street, 8th Floor
New York, New York 10003
United States
Tel: 1-212-979-5353
Fax: 1-212-477-5353
Web:http://www.arclighteditorial.com

Archimation
Kurfürstendamm 173
10707 Berlin
Germany
Tel: +49 30 886 79 555
Fax: +49 30 886 79 558
Web: http://www.archimation.com

Archimation
2607 Seventh Street Suite B
Berkeley California 94710-2571
United States
Tel: +1 510 845 4533
Fax: +1 510 845 3906
Web: http://www.archimation.com

ArchVision
110 South Upper Street
Lexington, Kentucky 40507
United States
Tel: 1-858-252-3118
Fax: 1-858-381-1108
Web: http://www.rpcnet.com

Area 51 Films
1501 Colorado Avenue
Santa Monica, California 90404
United States
Tel: 1-310-395-5151
Fax: 1 310-395-5102
Web: http://www.area51films.com

Arena Digital
74 Newman Street
London
United Kingdom
W1T 3EL
Tel: +44 207.43.64.36.0
Fax: +44 207.43.63.98.9
Web:
http://www.arenadigital.co.uk

Arena Multimedia
Kohinoor # 6
105 Park Street
Kolkata
West Bengal
India
700016
Tel: +91 33.24.92.30.0
Fax: +91 33.24.66.78.4
Web:http://www.arena-multimedia.com

Arcopres
Postbus 16239
2500 BE Den Haag
The Netherlands
Tel: 070 - 305 14 40
Fax: 070 - 305 14 41
Web: http://www.arcopres.nl

ARES FILMS
58 av. Charles de Gaulle
92200 Neuilly sur Seine
France
Tel: 011-33-0-1-5562-0600
Fax: 011-33-0-1-5562-0609
Web: http://www.aresfilms.com

ARG! Cartoon Animation
2790 N. Academy Blvd. Suite 359
Colorado Springs, Colorado 80917
United States
Tel: 1-719-559-1945
Fax: 1 719-623-0387
Web: http://artie.com

ART Architecture & Planning
207 West Alameda, Suite 205
Burbank, California 91203
United States
Tel: 1-818-563-1290
Fax: 1-818-563-1262
Web: http://www.art-arch.com

Art By Bill
Post Office Box 2734
Wilmington, North Carolina 28402
United States
Tel: 1-910-799-6955
Fax: 1-910-793-9872
Web: http://www.artbybill.com

ArtDink Corp.
YS Bldg 1F, 1-2-13 Tsukishima
Chuo-ku
Tokyo 104-0052
Japan
Web: http://www.artdink.co.jp

Art Group Inc., The
3100 Smoketree Court Suite 1004
Raleigh, North Carolina 27604
United States
Tel: 1-919-876-6765
Tel: 1-866-704-8575
Web:http://www.theartgroupinc.com

Artech
1410 Cowart Street
Chattanooga, Tennessee 37408
United States
Tel: 1-423-265-4313
Fax: 1-423-265-5413
Web: http://www.artechdgn.com

Arte France
2A, rue de la Fonderie
Strasbourg, France
67080
Tel: +33 3.88.14.22.55
Fax: +33 3.88.14.21.60
Web: http://www.arte-tv.com

Artem, Ltd.
Perivale Industrial Park
Horsenden Lane South
Perivale
Middlesex
United Kingdom
UB6 7RH
Tel: +44 208.99.77.77.1
Fax: +44 208.99.71.50.3
Web: http://www.artem.com

Artepict Studio
16 cours Sablon
Clermont-Ferrand
France
6300
Tel: +33 4.73.14.16.31
Fax: +33 4.73.93.12.57
Web:http://www.artepictstudio.com

Artfoundry
950 High School Way, Suite. 3227
Mountain View, California 94041
United States
Tel: 1-650-625-1602
Web: http://www.artfoundry.com

Artimagen Digital
Av. Romulo Gallegos
Edif. Park Avenue
piso 12, Apto 128
Urb. Horizonte
Caracas
Miranda
Venezuela
1060
Tel: +58 212.23.88.57.1
Fax: +58 212.23.88.57.1
Web: http://www.artimagendigital.com

Artimation of Arizona
3533 North 70th Street
Scottsdale, Arizona 85251
United States
Tel: 1-602-949-9811
Web: http://www.artimation.com

Artimation of Arizona
3533 North 70th Street
Scottsdale, Arizona 85251
United States
Tel: 1-480-949-9811
Web: http://www.artimation.com

Artistic Enterprises, LLC
104-A Woodwinds Industrial Court
Raleigh, North Carolina 27511
United States
Tel: 1-919 463-5300
Fax: 1-919 463-5301
Web: http://www.artisticrealm.com

Ascent Media Group
520 Broadway Ave.
Santa Monica, California 90401
United States
Tel: 1-310-434-7000
Web: http://www.ascentmedia.com

Ascent Media Group
2255 North Ontario Street
Burbank, California 90401
United States
Tel: 1-818-260-2000
Web:http://www.ascentmedia.com

Ascent Media Group
48 Charlotte Street
London
United Kingdom
W1T 2NS
Tel: 020 7208 2213
Web:http://www.ascentmedia.com

Ascent Media
2820 W. Olive Avenue
Burbank, California 91505
United States
Web:http://www.ascentmedia.com

Ascent Media
6601 Romaine St.
Hollywood, California 90038
United States
Web:http://www.ascentmedia.com

Ascent Media
1318 Lincoln Blvd
Santa Monica, California 90401
United States
Web:http://www.ascentmedia.com

Ascent Media
250 Harbor Drive
Stamford, Connecticut 06902
United States
Tel: 1-203-965-6000
Web:http://www.ascentmedia.com

Asia Television LTD.
81 Broadcast Road
KowLoon Tong
Kowloon
Hong kong
Web: http://www.hkatv.com

Asset Media International AG
Frankfurter Ring 17
80807 Munich

Germany
Tel: +49 (0) 89 - 3 54 99 - 0
Fax: +49 (0) 89 - 3 54 99 - 500
Web: http://www.asset-media.com

Associated Media Production Services
302 Jefferson Street #170
Raleigh, North Carolina 27605
United States
Tel: 1-919-821-2640
Web:
http://associatedmediaproduction.com

Aston Entertainment
6408 Parkland Drive, Suite 104
Sarasota, Florida 34243
United States
Tel: 1-941-755-6793
Web: http://astonent.com

Astropolotian Pictures
P.O. Box 13128
Chicago, Illinois 60613
United States
Tel: 1-773-935-7960
Fax: 1-773-935-7970
Web: http://www.astropolitan.com

Asylum Visual Effects
631 Wilshire #2A
Santa Monica, California 90401
United States
Tel: 1-310-395-4975
Fax: 1-310-395-5625
Web: http://www.asylumfx.com

Ateliery Bonton Zlin
Petrske Nam. 1
110 00 Prague 1
Czech Republic
Prague
Czech Republic
110 00
Tel: +420 2.24.81.44.45
Fax: +420 2.24.81.44.47
Web: http://www.ateliery.cz

Athanor Studio
3 rue de Metz
75010 Paris
France
Tel: 011-33-0-1-4022-6400
Fax: 011-33-0-1-4022-6400
Web:http://www.athanorstudio.com

Atlantic Pictures
Nieuwpoortkade 2a NL-1055RX
Amsterdam
The Netherlands
Tel: +31(0)20 6060940
Fax: +31(0)20 6060942
Web:http://www.atlanticpictures.nl

Atlantic Motion Pictures
162 West 21st Street, 4th Floor
New York, New York 10011
United States
Tel: 1-212-924-6170
Fax: 1-212-989-8736
Web:http://www.atlanticmotion.com

Atlantic Video, Inc.
The Washington Television Center
650 Massachusetts Avenue NW
Washington, D.C. 20001
United States
Tel: 1-202-408-0900
Fax: 1 202-408-8496
Web:http://www.atlanticvideo.com

Atlantis Lab LLC.
175 Hawthorne Ave Suite 164
Central Islip, New York 11722
United States
Tel: 1-631-342-8992
Web: http://www.atlantis-lab.com

atlas Film & TV Produktion
80469
Munich
Rumfordstr 29-31
Germany
Tel: +49 (89) 228 02 820
Fax: +49 (89) 210975-13
Web: http://www.atlasfilm.com

Atmospheres, Ltd.
658 Aylestone Road
Leicester, United Kingdom
LE2 8PR
Tel: +44 116.24.40.04.1
Web:http://www.atmospheres.co.uk

Atomic Entertainment
3 Hanson Street
London
United Kingdom
W1W 6TB
Tel: +44 207.41.94.19.0
Fax: +44 207.41.94.19.4
Web: http://www.atomicarts.net

Atomic Imaging, Inc.
1501 N. Magnolia Ave.
Chicago, Illinois 60622
United States
Tel: 1-312-649-1800
Tel: 1-888-8-ATOMIC
Fax: 1-312-642-7441
Web:http://www.atomicimaging.com

Atomic Imaging Los
Angeles/Pulse Imaging, Ltd.
909 Westbourne Dr. Suite 201
West Hollywood, California 90069
United States
Tel: 1-213-508-5504
Web:http://www.atomicimaging.com

Atomic Imaging NY/Snapper Bear
Studios
8 Bond Street
New York, New York 10012
United States
Tel: 1-212-777-2660
Fax: 1-212-533-0678
Web:http://www.atomicimaging.com

Atomic Imaging Puerto Rico/AMC
Calle C.
Lote 30
Mario Julio Industrial Park
Puerto Nuevo
PR 00920
Tel: 1-787-775-0550
Fax: 1-787-766-8250
Web:http://www.atomicimaging.com

Atomic Imaging Barcelona
Director's Gallery
San Elias
29-35 7o 3a Esc.B
Barcelona 08006
Spain
Tel: (011) (34) 93-200-21-60
Fax: (011) (34) 93-200-21-56
Web:http://www.atomicimaging.com

Atomic Pictures
1314 Cobb Lane Suite B
Birmingham, Alabama 35205
United States
Tel: 1-205-939-1314
Fax: 1-205-939-0585
Web: http://www.atomicpix.com

Atomic Pictures
4244 Medical, Suite 4275
San Antonio, Texas 78229
United States
Tel: 1-210-614-0615
Fax: 1-210-614-0654
Web:http://www.atomicpictures.com

Atomic Visual Effects: Cape Town
2nd Floor
The Armoury
Buchanan Square
160 Sir Lowry Road
Cape Town
8001
South Africa
Tel: 27 (0)21 461 4995
Fax: 27 (0)21 461 5411
Web: http://www.atomic-vfx.com

Atomic Visual Effects: Los Angeles
5361 San Vicente Boulevard,
Suite 152
Los Angeles, California 90019
United States
Tel: 1-323-938-0257
Fax: 1-310-458-3793
Web: http://www.atomic-vfx.com

ATTIK
445 Bush St.
San Francisco, California 94108
United States
Tel: 1-415-989-6401

Fax: 1-415-989-6419
Web: http://www.Attik.com

ATTIK
Stonewood
87 Fitzwilliam Street
Huddersfield
HD1 5LG
United Kingdom
Tel: +44 (0) 1484 537 494
Fax: +44 (0) 1484 434 958
Web: http://www.Attik.com

ATTIK
3rd Floor
Elsley Court
20-22 Great Titchfield Street
London
W1W 8BE
United Kingdom
Tel: +44 (0)20 7674 3000
Fax: +44 (0)20 7674 3100
Web: http://www.Attik.com

ATTIK
520 Broadway, 4th Floor
New York, New York 10012
United States
Tel: 1-212-334-6401
Fax: 1-212-334-6279
Web: http://www.Attik.com

ATTIK
The Penthouse
Bensons House
52 Phillip Street
Sydney
NSW 2000
Australia
Tel: +61 (0)2 9251 1800
Fax: +61 (0)2 9251 4422
Web: http://www.Attik.com

Attitude Studio France
100, Av du Général Lederc
Pantin Cedex
France
93692
Tel: 00 33 (0)1 41 71 00 78
Fax: 00 33 (0)1 41 71 01 68
Web: http://www.attitude-
studio.com

Audio Plus Video International
235 Pegasus Avenue
Northvale, New Jersey 07647
United States
Tel: 1-201-784-2700
Fax: 1-201-784-2769
Web: http://www.apvi.com

Audio-Video Film Inc.
Abbeydale Dr.
Charlotte, North Carolina 28205
United States
Tel: 1-704-567-9672
Web:
http://www.audiovideofilm.com

Audio Video Masters, LLC
3364 Hwy 70 West
Jackson, Tennessee 38301
United States
Tel: 1-731-424-3207
Web: http://www.avmasters.cc

AudioMotion
Beaumont Road
Banbury
Oxon
United Kingdom
OX16 1RH
Tel: +44 129.52.66.62.2
Fax: +44 129.52.66.68.5
Web: http://www.audiomotion.com

Augenblick Studios
55 Washington St. Ste 805
Brooklyn, New York 11201
United States
Tel: 1-718-856-9226
Fax: 1-718-856-9227
Web:
http://www.augenblickstudios.com

AurenyA Entertainment Group
Suite 930, 665 * Street SW
Calgary, AB T2P 3k7
Canada
Tel: 1-403-215-1088
Fax: 1-403-215-1089
Web: http://www.aurenya.com

Available Light, Ltd.
1125 South Flower Street
Burbank, California 91502
United States
Tel: 1-818-842-2109
Fax: 1-818-842-0661
Web:http://www.availablelightltd.com

Avant Inc.
37-10 Flax Benevolence Building
Shibuya 4 F
Shibuya Ku, Tokyo 150-0042
Japan
Tel: 03-3469-2930
Fax: 03-3469-2907
Web: http://www.avant.co.jp

Avard Post Inc.
275 Lancaster Street West
Kitchener, Ontario, Canada
N2H 2V2
Tel: 1-877-462-8273
Tel: 1-519-745-5044
Fax: 1-519-745-0690
Web: http://www.avard.com

Avatar Group International, Inc.
4518 Gaynor Road
Charlotte, North Carolina 28211
United States
Tel: 1-800-834-1388
Web:http://www.avatargrouptv.com

Avatarlabs
16838 Addison Street.
Encino, California 91436
United States
Tel: 1-818-728-6778
Fax: 1-818-727-6782
Web: http://www.avatarlabs.com

Avatar Studios
2675 Scott Avenue
St. Louis, Missouri 63103
United States
Tel: 1-314-533-2242
Fax: 1-314-533-3349
Web: http://www.avatar-studios.com

Avery Smartcat Productions
2430 Fulton Road,

Kissimmee, Florida, 34744
United States
Tel: 1-407-932-2604
Tel: 1-407-932-2630
Web: http://www.cybersmart.tv

Avtoma
1524- B Cloverfield Boulevard
Santa Monica, California 90404
United States
Tel: 1-310-998-8411
Fax: 1-310-998-8461
Web: http://www.avtoma.com

Avtoma
Milano 20154
Italy
Tel: 011.39.0234.55171
Fax: 011.39.0234.551799
Web: http://www.avtoma.com

Avtoma
1600 Notre-Dame West #312
Montreal, Quebec H3J 1M1
Canada
Tel: 1-514-937-0111
Fax: 1-514-937-0111
Web: http://www.avtoma.com

AX co.,ltd.
Promontory 5 Chome 2nd 2
Sanwa Yutaka promontory 2nd
building
North Ku Yutaka
Osaka, 531-0072
Japan
Tel: 06 (6375) 3003
Fax: 06 (6375) 3083
Web: http://www.a-x.co.jp

Axiom
508 East Blvd
Charlotte, North Carolina
United States
Tel: 1-704-376-3003
Web: http://www.axiomcg.com

Axis Animation
Suite 225
Pentagon Business Centre
Washington Street
Glasgow
G3 8AZ
United Kingdom
Tel: +44 (0)141 572 2802
Fax: +44 (0)141 572 2809
Web:http://www.axisanimation.com

Axis Productions
Macedonia
Tel: + 389 (2) 290 950
Web: http://www.axis.com.mk

Baba GmbH
Daimlestr. 32/mediahub
60314 Frankfurt
Germany
Tel: 49-69-941963301
Fax: 49-69-94196333
Web: http://www.baba.de

Backyard Entertainment
2200 Amapola Court, Suite 202
Torrance, California 90501
United States
Tel: 1-310-533-0860
Fax: 1-310-533-0857
Web: http://www.backyardenter-
tainment.com

BAF - Berlin Animation Film
GmbH
Gormannstr. 22
D - 10119 Berlin
Germany
Tel: +49 30-72 62 00-430
Fax: +49 30-72 62 00-444
Web: http://www.baf-film.com

Baham
Pro-Wasp
45 Osborne Court
Osborne road
Windsor
Berks
SL4 3EP
Phone: +44 (0)1753 738970
http://www.baham.co.uk

Baker Hughes Incorporated.
3900 Essex Lane, Suite 1200
Houston, Texas 77027-5177
United States
Tel: 1-713-439-8600
Fax: 1-713-439-8699
Web:http://www.bakerhughes.com

Bakedmedia, Inc.
9338 South Whitt Drive
Manassas Park, Virginia 20111
United States
Tel: 1-703-330-4545
Web: http://www.bakedmedia.com

Balance Studios, Inc.
333 1/2 N. Broadway Street
Green Bay, Wisconsin 54303
United States
Tel: 1-920-433-9770
Fax: 1-920-433-9780
Web:http://www.balancestudios.com

Ballistic Pixel Lab, Inc., The
435 Douglas Ave, Suite 2705
Altamonte Springs, Florida 32714
United States
Tel: 1-407-865-7425
Fax: 1-407-865-7656
Web: http://www.ballisticpixel.com

Bandelier EFX
6808 Academy Parkway East,
NE, Suite B-1
Albuquerque, New Mexico 87109
United States
Tel: 1-505-345-8021
Fax: 1-505-345-8023
Web: http://www.bandelier.com

Banjax
Suite 407
Curtain House
134-146 Curtain Road
London
United Kingdom
EC2A 3AR
Tel: +44 207.73.98.11.8
Fax: +44 207.73.93.89.0
Web: http://www.banjax.com

Baraka Post Production Ltd
11 Greek Street
London
United Kingdom
W1V 5LE
Tel: +44 (0)207 734 2227
Fax: +44 (0)207 479 7810
Web: http://www.baraka.co.uk

Bardel Animation
548 Beatty Street
Vancouver, BC
Canada
V6B-2Z6
Tel: 1-604-669-5589
Fax: 1-604-669-9079
Web:http://www.bardelanimation.com

Barking Bullfrog
548 Beatty Street
Vancouver, British Columbia
Canada
V6B 2I3
Tel: 1-604-689-0702
Fax: 1-604-689-0715
Web:http://www.barkingbullfrog.com

Barlow Productions Inc.
1115 Olivette Executive Parkway
St. Louis, Missouri 63132-3205
United States
Tel: 1-314-994-9990
Fax: 1-314-994-9520
Web: http://www.barlowpro.com

Base 77
D-77 Defense Colony
New Delhi
India
110024
Tel: +91 11.46.25.33.0
Web: http://www.base77.com

Battle Medialab
4100 Southwest 28th Way
Ft. Lauderdale, Florida 33312
United States
Tel: 1-954-527-5507
Fax: 1-954-527-5504
Web:http://www.battlemedialab.com

bauhau LTD
7 Leicester Place
London WC2H 7BP
United Kingdom
Tel: 020 7434 2629
Web: http://www.bauhau.com

Bavaria Kinder/Media
Bavaria Film GmbH
Bavaria Filmplatz 7
D-82031
Geiselgasteig, Germany
Tel: +49 89.64.99.0
Fax: +49 89.64.92.50.7
Web: http://www.bavaria-film.de

Baverstock Design
Raleigh, North Carolina
United States
Tel: 1-919-518-0665
Web: http://www.baverstock.com

Bazillion Pictures
118 Southwest Boulevard
Suite 201
Kansas City, Missouri 64108
United States
Tel: 1-816-474-7427
Fax: 1-816-842-7179
Web: http://www.bazillionpictures.com

Bazley Films
Corsham Media Park
Spring Quarry
West Wells Road
Corsham
Wiltshire
United Kingdom
SN13 9GB
Tel: +44 1225.81.62.10
Fax: +44 1225.81.62.11
Web: http://www.bazleyfilms.com

Bazoka Graphics
455 North Cityfront Plaza Drive,
Suite 1800
Chicago, Illinois 60611
United States
Tel: 1-312-464-8000
Fax: 1-312-464-8020
Web: http://www.bazookaville.com

B-cosmos
Av. Nestle 34
CH-1800 Vevey
Switzerland
Tel: 011-41-(0)21-922-61-96
Web: http://www.b-cosmos.com

BBC MediaArc's 3D
CharacterShop
Birmingham
United Kingdom
B7 5QQ
Tel: +44 121.43.29.63.6
Web: http://www.bbcmediaarc.com

BBC TV Centre
80, Wood Lane
Woodlands
London
United Kingdom
W12 7RJ
Tel: +44 208.57.61.10.5
Fax: +44 208.74.29.35.9
Web: http://www.bbc.co.uk

BBC Worldwide Ltd.
80 Wood Lane
Woodlands
London
United Kingdom
W12 0TT
Tel: +44 208.43.32.00.0
Fax: +44 208.43.32.15.4
Web: http://www.bbc.co.uk

BC Pictures
24 Louisa Street
Toronto, Ontario
M8V 2K6
Canada
Tel: 1-416-521-7462
Fax: 1-416-521-7467
Web: http://www.bcpictures.com

Beachwood Studios
23330 Commerce Park Road
Cleveland, Ohio 44122
United States
Tel: 1-216-292-7300
Fax: 1-216-292-1765
Fax: 1-216-292-0545
Web: http://www.edr.com

Be Animation
13 Risbotough St
London
SE1 OHF
United Kingdom
Tel: 01 1-44-207-620-2595
Fax: 01 1-44-207-620-2596
Web: http://www.beanimation.com

Beckett Entertainment
15850 Dallas Parkway
Dallas, Texas 75248
United States
Tel: 1-972-991 -6657
Fax: 1-972-233-6488
Web:
http://www.beckettentertainment.com

Beehive
19 West 21st Street, Room 1002
New York, New York 10010
United States
Tel: 1-212-924-6060
Fax: 1-212-924-1855
Web: http://www.beehive.tv

Beeps
33 Brookes Street
Bowen Hills
Queensland
Australia
Tel: 617 3216 1415
Fax: 617 3216 1603
Web: http://www.beeps.com.au

Beevision and Hive Productions
366 Adelaide Street East, Suite
425
Toronto, Ontario
MSA 3X9
Canada
Tel: 416-868-1700
Fax: 416-868-9512
Web: http://www.beevision.com

Belief
1832 Franklin St.
Santa Monica, California 90404
United States
Tel: 1-310-998-0099
Fax: 1-310-998-0066
Web: http://www.belief.com

Bent Image Lab
1801 NW Upshur, 2nd floor
Portland, Oregon 97209
United States
Tel: 1-503-228-6206
Fax: 1-503-228-1007
Web: http://www.bentimagelab.com

Bergen Animation
Georgernes Verft 12
Bergen, Norway
5011
Tel: +47 55.96.24.20
Fax: +47 55.96.24.20
Web: http://www.bergenanimasjon.no

BES Television
9829-E Atmore Road
Richmond, Virginia 23225
United States
Tel: 1-804-218-8089
Web:
http://www.bestelevision.com

Best Video Productions
157 Technology Dr
Garner, North Carolina 27529
United States
Tel: 1-919-772-0079
Fax: 1-919-772-1040
Web:
http://www.BestVideoProductions.com

Beta Film GmbH
Robert-Buerkle-Strasse 2
85737 Ismaning
Germany
Tel: +49-89-9956-2744
Fax: +49-89-9956-2703
Web: http://www.betafilm.com

Betelgeuse Productions
44 East 32nd Street
New York, New York 10016
United States
Tel: 1-212-251-8600
Fax: 1-212-251-8633
Web: http://www.betelgeuse.com

BFM Video & Communication Inc.
Bosques de Duraznos 69

1001 Bosques de las Lomas
México DF
MEXICO
Tel: 52 51 9760
Tel: 52 51 9758
Web: http://bfmvideo.tv

BiboFilms / Pumpkin
44 RUE DU FER A MOULIN
75005 PARIS
France
Tel: +33 1 43 36 06 26
Fax: +33 1 43 36 91 75
Web: http://www.bibofilms.com

Big Bang FX|Animation
360 St. Francois -Xavier, Suite
500
Montreal, Quebec
H2Y 2S8
Canada
Tel: 1-514-499-0811
Fax: 1-514-499-0433
Web:
http://www.bigbanganimation.com

Big Film Design
137 Varick Street
New York, New York 10013
United States
Tel: 1-212-627-3430
Fax: 1-212-989-6528
Web:http://www.bigfilmdesign.com

BiG Films Inc.
995 Wellington Street, Suite 200,
Montreal, Quebec
Canada H3C 1V3
Tel: 1-514-878-9999
Tel: 1-888-848-9999
Fax: 1-514-878-0617
Web: http://www.bigfilms.ca

Big Idea Productions
206 Yorktown Center
Lombard, Illinois 60148
United States
Tel: 1-630-652-6000
Fax: 1-630-652-6001
Fax: 1-630-652-6017
Web: http://www.bigidea.com

Big Little Films Inc.
2955 E. Hillcrest Dr., Suite 121
Thousand Oaks, California 91362
United States
Tel: 1-805-496-8130
Fax: 1-805-496-4027
Web: http://www.biglittlefilms.com

Big Machine Studios, The
9 Merril Road
Merrimac, New Hampshire 03054
United States
Tel: 1-603-429-4664
Web:http://www.bigmachinestudios.com

Big Shoulders Digital Video
Productions
303 East Wacker Street, Suite 2000
Chicago Illinois, 60601
United States
Tel: 1-312-540-5400
Fax: 1-312-228-1919
Web: http://www.bigshoulders.com

Big Time Pictures
Hillside Studios
Merry Hill Road
Bushey
Hertfordshire
United Kingdom
WD23 1DR
Tel: +44 208.95.07.91.9
Fax: +44 208.95.01.43.7
Web:http://www.bigtimepictures.co.uk

Bill Melendez Productions, Inc.
3400 Riverside Drive Ste 201
Sherman Oaks, California 91423
United States
Tel: 1-818-382-7382
Fax: 1-818-382-7377
Web: http://www.billmelendez.net

Billy Elkins Films
1966 SW 96th Street
Stuart, Florida 34997-2621
United States
Tel: 1-772-287-4457
Fax: 1-772-283-7008
Web: http://www.adistantview.com

Bils Cafe
1449 WASHINGTON ST, STE 3
San Francicso, California 94109
United States
Tel: 1-415-430-2169 x8544
Fax: 1-603-452-8467
Web: http://www.bills-cafe.com

Bionic Informatics Pvt Ltd.
524, 5th Cross
Mahalakshmi Layout
Bangalore
Karnataka
India
560086
Tel: +91 80.35.92.91.9
Fax: +91 80.35.93.11.0
Web: http://www.bionicinformatics.com

Bitart Infografaa
Tivoli, 24
Bilbao, Spain 48007
Tel: +34 94.41.30.38.5
Fax: +34 94.44.59.26.3
Web: http://www.bitart.info

Bitcasters
364 Richmond Street W
5th Floor
Toronto, Ontario Canada
M5V 1X6
Tel: +1 416.351.0889
Fax: +1 416.351.9884
Web: http://www.bitcasters.com

Blair Art Studios
6134 Riverside Drive
Wake Forest North Carolina,
27587
United States
Tel: 1-919-562-1010
Fax: 1-919-562-1212
Web: http://www.drublair.com

Blackbird Digital
P.O. Box 68403
Newton
Auckland
New Zealand
Tel: 011 64 025 866 512
Web: http://blackbird.co.nz

Black Boxx Computer Graphics Company
100 North High Street, Suite B
Dublin, Ohio 43017
United States
Tel: 1-614-210-5000
Fax: 1-614-210-5001
Web: http://www.blakboxx.com

Black Box Digital
409 Santa Monica Blvd, Ste E
Santa Monica, California 90401
United States
Tel: 1-310-828-5832
Fax: 1-310-828-8998
Web: http://www.blackboxdigital.com

Blackfly Group Inc.
411 Richmond St. East, Suite 205
Toronto, Ontario M5A 3S5
Canada
Tel: 1-416-594-3665
Fax: 1-416-363-8960
Web: http://www.foolishearthling.com

Black Hammer Productions, Inc.
447 Broadway, 2nd Floor
New York, New York 10013
United States
Tel: 1-212-625-8980
Web: http://www.blackhammer.com

Black Logic
216 east 45th Street
New York, New York 10016
United States
Tel: 1-212-557-4949
Web: http://www.blacklogic.com

Black Maria Studios
P.O. Box 12304
Valencia, Spain
C.P. 46020
Tel: +34 96.38.91.01.0
Fax: +34 96.38.91.01.0
Web: http://www.blackmaria.es

Black Moon Digital
153 Lewis St.
Buffalo, New York 14206
United States
Tel: 1-716-856-9543

Fax: 1-716-856-9585
Web: http://www.blackmoondigital.com

Black Walk Productions
99 Sudbury St.
Unit 99
Toronto, Ontario
Canada
M6J 3S7
Tel: +1 416.533.5864
Fax: +1 416.533.2016
Web: http://www.blackwalk.com

Blink Digital
545 Fifth Avenue
New York, New York 10017
United States
Tel: 1-212-661-6900
Fax: 1-212-907-1233
Web: http://www.blinkdigital.com

Bloemers Graphics & Animatie
Westersingel 107
3015 LD
Rotterdam
The Netherlands
Tel: 010 - 440 11 26
Fax: 010 - 440 11 29
Web:
http://www.xs4all.nl/~bloemers

Blue Chip Films
18 Leonard Street
Norwalk, Connecticut 06850
United States
Tel: 1-203-324-FILM
Tel: 1-203-324-3456
Fax: 1-203-838-3126
Web:http://www.bluechipfilms.com

Bluedit s.r.l.
Via Farnese 4
00195 Rome
Italy
Tel: ++39-0632849001
Web: http://www.bluegold.it

Blueyed Pictures
Saban Plaza
10960 Wilshire Boulevard, Suite 1600
Los Angeles, California 90024
United States
Tel: 1-310-444-4803
Fax: 1-310-444-4554
Web:http://www.blueyedpictures.com

Blueyed Pictures
77 Beak Street. Suite 160
Soho London
W1F 9DB
United Kingdom
Tel: (44) 0870-161-0002
Fax: (44) 0207-7439-3330
Web:http://www.blueyedpictures.com

Blueyed Pictures
Atago Hills MBE # 316
MORI Building Tower 1F
2-5-1 Atago
Minato-ku
Tokyo 105-6201
Japan
Tel: (81) 090-4745-7121
Fax: (81) 03-3431-6233
Web:http://www.blueyedpictures.com

Blue Gold
Via della Moscova 38/R
20121 Milan
Italy
Tel: ++39-02290311
Fax: ++39-02290311
Web: http://www.bluegold.it

BlueLight Animations
PO Box 5643
Berkeley, California 94705
United States
Tel: 1-510-338-1212
Fax: 1-510-338-1212
Web:http://www.bluelightanim.com

Blue Monkey Studios
Media House
Leeds Road
Huddersfield
West Yorkshire
HD5 0RL
United Kingdom

Tel: +44 1484 353470
Web:
http://www.bluemonkeystudios.com

Bluemoon Design Inc.
8024 Glenwood Avenue, Suite 109
Raleigh, North Carolina 27612
United States
Tel: 1-919-787-3769
Fax: 1-919-420-0497
Web: http://www.bmdinc.net

Blue Rocket Productions
P.O. Box 510
Hobart
Tasmania
Australia
7001
Tel: +61 3.62.24.68.66
Fax: +61 3.62.24.69.66
Web: http://www.blue-rocket.com

Blue Sky Studios
44 South Broadway, 17th Floor
White Plains, New York 10601
United States
Tel: 1-914-259-6500
Fax: 1-914-259-6499
Web: http://www.blueskystudios.com

Blue Zero
P.O. Box 1278
Minetonka, Minnesota 55345
United States
Tel: 1-612-988-9111
Web: http://www.bluezero.com

Blur Studio
1118 Abbot Kinney Blvd.
Venice, California 90291
United States
Tel: 1-310-581-8848
Fax: 1-310-581-8850
Web: http://www.blur.com

Blue Studios S.P.A.
V.le Piemonte 8
20093 Cologno Monzese
Milan
Italy
Web: http://www.bluegold.it

Blue Visual Effects
255 South 17th Street. 7th Floor
Philadelphia, Pennsylvania 19103
United States
Tel: 1-215-735-8581
Fax: 1-215-735-8582
Web:http://www.bluevisualeffects.com

Bluue
Rudolf-Breitscheid Strasse 162
14482 Potsdam
Babelsberg, Berlin Germany
Tel: +49 33.17.04.47.00
Fax: +49 33.17.04.47.10
Web: http://www.bluue.com

Bob 'n' Shelia's Edit World
San Francisco, California
United States
Tel: 1-415-989-9123
Web: http://www.editworld.com

Bo Nordin Animation
Brahegatan, 7
Jonkoping, Sweden
55334
Tel: +46 36.18.64.76
Web: http://www.bonordin.se

Bold VFX
Richmind, Victoria
Australia
Web: http://www.bold-vfx.com

Bolex Brothers
Unit 3
Brunel Lock Development
Smeaton Road
Cumberland Basin
Leeds
LS159AJ
United Kingdom
Tel: 01144-13-232-6648
Tel: 01144 (0)117-985-8000
Fax: 01144-13-232-6536
Web:http://www.bolexbrothers.com

Bone Digital Effects
33 Villiers St., #107
Toronto, Ontario, M5A 1A9
Canada
Tel: 1-416-469-3406
Fax: 1-416-469-3506
Web:http://www.bonedigitaleffects.com

Bookartoons
859 N. Hollywood Way #258
Burbank, California 91505
United States
Web: http://www.bookartoons.com

Boomstone Animation Inc.
290 Picton Ave, Suite 201
Ottawa, ON Canada K1Z 8P8
Tel: 1-613-725-3843
Fax: 1-613-725-9327
Web: http://www.boomstone.com

Border Television
TV Centre
Carlisle
CA1 3NT
Tel: 01228 525 101
Web: http://www.border-tv.com

Borgen FX
Jagtvej 51 4th
2200 KBHN
Tel: 35827004
Tel: 26513633
Web: http://www.borgengfx.dk

Bowers Media Group
PO Box 470352
Charlotte, North Carolina 28247
United States
Tel: 1-704-542-8754
Fax: 1-704-542-9408
Web:http://www.bowersmediagroup.com

Box
5th Floor
121 Princess Street
Manchester, United Kingdom
M1 7AD
Tel: +44 161.22.82.39.9
Fax: +44 161.22.82.39.9
Web: http://www.the-box.co.uk

Boyington Studios inc.
17 Galleon Street
Marina Del Rey, California 90292
United States
Tel: 1-310-458-3776
Web:http://www.boyingtonfilms.com

Boy Wonder Studios
8601 Hayden Place
Culver City, California 90232
United States
Tel: 1-310-202-2230
Web:http://www.boywonderfx.com

BPGWorldwide
1901 South Bascom Ave 9th Floor
Campbell, California 95008
United States
Tel: 1-408-559-6300
Tel: 1-800-475-9843.
Web: http://www.bpgnet.com

BrainBox Productions Inc.
8113 Fenton Street
Silver Spring, Maryland 20910
United States
Tel: 1-301-657-3700
Fax: 1-301-495-0829
Web: http://www.brainme.com

Brainchild Studios
3rd Floor - 4250 Dawson Street
Burnaby, Brittish Columbia
V5C-4B1
Canada
Tel: 1-604-877-8585
Fax: 1-604-877-1614
Web:
http://www.brainchildstudios.com

Brainwaave Interactive Pty Ltd
162 Willoughby Road
Crows Nest
NSW 2065
Sydney
Australia
Tel: +61 2 8436 6500
Fax: +61 2 9348 3520
Web: http://www.brainwaave.com.au

Brainzoo Studios
16134 Hart Street Suite 200

Van Nuys California 91406
United States
Tel: 1-818-785-1124
Fax: 1-818-904-1753
Web:http://www.brainzoostudios.com

Brand Company A/S (The)
Nicolai Eigtvedsgade 26, st.
Copenhagen
Denmark 1402
Tel: +45.70.22.02.01
Fax: +45.70.22.00.27.1
Web:http://www.thebrandcompany.com

Brand-X Creative Services
6735 Burlwood Road
Charlotte, North Carolina 28211
United States
Tel: 1-704-367-0082
Web: http://www.brand-x-cre-
ativeservices.com

Brand Marks International
1888 Century Park East
Suite 2010
Los Angeles, California 90067
United States
Tel: 1-310-286-0600
Fax: 1-310-286-0479
Web: http://www.bradmarks.com

Brand New School East
176 Grand Street 5th Floor
New York, New York 10013
United States
Tel: 1-212-343-7470
Fax: 1-212-343-7471
Web: http://www.brandnewschool.com

Brand New School West
1657 Euclid Street
Santa Monica, California 90404
United States
Tel: 1-310-460-0060
Fax: 1-310-460-0061
Web: http://www.brandnewschool.com

Brandt Animation
11 D'Arblay Street
London
W1F 8DT
United Kingdom
Tel: 020 7734 0196
Web: http://www.brandtanim.co.uk

Breakiron Animation&Design
4415 E. Willow Ave.
Phoenix, Arizona 85032
United States
Tel: 1-602-482-1121
Fax: 1-602-971-8079
Web: http://www.breakiron.com

Bren Entertainment, S.A.
Plaza Europa
5A - 3ª Planta
15707 Santiago de Compostela
(A Coruña) Spain
Tel: (+34) 981 52 82 00
Fax: (+34) 981 55 74 02
Web: http://www.bren.es

BrightHaus
537 North Magnolia Ave
Orlando, Florida 32801
United States
Tel: 1-407-648-8666
Fax: 1-407-648-8246
Web: http://www.brighthaus.com

Brilliant Digital Entertainment
United States
6355 Topanga Canyon Boulevard,
Suite 120
Woodland Hills California 91367
United States
Tel: 1-818-615-1500
Fax: 1-818-615-0995
Web:http://www.brilliantdigital.com

Brilliant Digital Entertainment
Australia
1-25 Harbour Street
Sydney NSW 2000
Australia
Tel: +61 (2) 9267 6933
Fax: +61 (2) 9267 5933
Web:http://www.brilliantdigital.com

The Brit Pack
New York
United States
Web: http://www.thebritpack.com

British Sky Broadcasting Group
Grant Way
Isleworth
TW7 5QD
United Kingdom
Tel: (44) 020 7705 3000
Web: http://www.sky.com/sky-com/home

Broadcast Post Production
44 Harakevet St.
Tel-Aviv
Israel
Tel: 927 3 6384747
Fax: 927 3 6384729
Web: http://www.broadcast.co.il

Broadcast Quality, Incorporated
2334 Ponce de Leon Boulevard,
Suite 200
Coral Gables, Florida 33134
United States
Tel: 1-305-461-5416
Fax: 1-305-446-7746
Web:http://www.broadcastquality.com

Broadcast Quality, Incorporated
5850 T.G. Lee Blvd. Suite 650
Orlando, Florida 32822
United States
Tel: 1-407-251-4414
Fax: 1-407-251-4416
Web:http://www.broadcastquality.com

Broadway Video
1619 Broadway, 10th Floor
New York, New York 10019
United States
Tel: 1-212-265-7600
Fax: 1-212-713-1535
Web:http://www.broadwayvideo.com

Brown Bag Films
28 North Lotts
Dublin 1
Ireland

Tel: 011-353-1-872-1608
Fax: 011-353-1-872-3834
Web:http://www.brownbagfilms.com

Brothers Dimm Ltd (The)
1/1, 16 Ruthven Street
Glasgow
Scotland
G12 9BS
United Kingdom
Web:http://www.thebrothersdimm.com

Bruce Dunlop Associates
1-6 Falconberg Court
London
W1D 3AB
United Kingdom
Tel: +44 (0) 20 7440 1070
Fax: +44 (0) 20 7440 1077
Web: http://www.brucedunlop.com

Bruce Dunlop Associates
Suite 19/177-199 Pacific Highway
North Sydney
NSW 2060
Australia
Tel: 00 612 9954 5855
Fax: 00 612 9954 5955
Web: http://www.brucedunlop.com

Buildup Co.,Ltd.
Hinode Bldg 1-25-14 Shinjuku
Shinjuku-ku
Tokyo, Japan
160-0022
Tel: 81-3-3358-1760
Fax: 81-3-3358-1761
Web: http://www.buildup.com

Bubble & Squeak
Suite 325 Princess House
50-60 Eastcastle Street
London
United Kingdom
W1W 8EA
Tel: +44 20.76.36.07.81
Fax: +44 20.76.36.02.62
Web:
http://www.bubblesqueak.com

Buena Vista International
Television
3 Queen Caroline Street
Hammersmith
London, United Kingdom
W6 9PE
Tel: 011-44-181-222-1000
Fax: 011-44-181-222-1037
Web: http://www.disney.com
Web: http://www.bvitv.net

Buf Compagnie
3, rue Roquepine
Paris, France
75008
Tel: +33 1.42.68.18.28
Fax: +33 1.42.68.18.29
Web: http://www.buf.fr

Buf Compagnie
7421 Beverly Boulevard
Los Angeles, California 90036
United States
Tel: 1-323-549-0036
Fax: 1-323-549-0037
Web: http://www.buf.fr

Bugshop
10 East 40th Street
New York, New York 10012
United States
Tel: 1-212-683-4004
Web: http://www.bugshop.net

Bullseye Post
99 Atlantic Avenue, Suite 104
Toronto
M6K 3J8
Canada
Tel: 1-416-533-8580
Fax: 1-416-533-5529
Web:
http://www.bullseyepost.com

BumbleBee Studios
Lloydstraat 11-F
3024 EA
Rotterdam
The Netherlands
Tel: 010-4766554
Web: http://www.bumble.com

Bunch
88-90 Gray's Inn Road
London
United Kingdom
IC1X 8AA
Tel: +44 78.31.96.12.2
Web:http://www.bunchdesign.com

Burning Brain
60, via A. Scarlatti
Napoli
Italy 80129
Tel: +39 81.22.95.55.5
Fax: +39 81.22.95.55.5
Web: http://www.burningbrain.it

BurntStudios
1516 Solunar CT.
Wake Forest, North Carolina
27587
United States
Tel: 1-919-556-1099
Fax: 1-919-556-1204
Web: http://www.burntstudios.com

Buzzco Associates, Inc
33 Bleecker Street
New York, New York 10012
United States
Tel: 1-212-473-8800
Fax: 1-212-473-8891
Web: http://www.buzzzco.com

BVI Group North Miami
20377 North East 15th Court
Miami, Florida 33179
United States
Tel: 1-305-653-7441
Tel: 1-800-826-8864
Fax: 1-305-651-0478
Web: http://www.bvinet.com

BVI Group South Beach
605 Lincoln Road, 5th Floor
Miami Beach, Florida 33139
United States
Tel: 1-305-532-5770
Fax: 1-305-532-5720
Web: http://www.bvinet.com

BVI Group Coconut Grove
2850 Tigertail Ave.
Coconut Grove, Florida 33133
United States
Tel: 1-305-857-0350
Fax: 1-305-857-0175
Web: http://www.bvinet.com

By Thunder
3185 Graveley Street
Vancouver, British Columbia
Canada V5K 3K7
Tel: 1-604-253-8288
Web: http://www.bythunder.com

CO3
1661 Lincoln Boulevard, Suite 400
Santa Monica, California
United States
Tel: 1-310-586-3800
Fax: 1-310-582-0030
Web: http://www.company3.com

C.O.R.E. Digital Pictures Inc.
488 Wellington St. West
Suite 600
Toronto, Ontario Canada
M5V 1E3
Tel: +1 416.599.2673
Fax: +1 416.599.1212
Web: http://www.coredp.com

C3Pmania 2d/3d visualization studio
Diakenhuisweg 95
2033 AP Haarlem
The Netherlands
Tel: +31(0)23 5365167
Fax: +31(0)6 27097217
Web: http://www.c3pmania.nl

C4 Digital Entertainment
#120 11960 Hammersmith Way
Richmond, British Columbia
Canada
V7A 5C9
Tel: +1 604.204.2692
Fax: +1 604.204.2691
Web: http://www.c4digital.ca

Caboom
10 St. Stephens Green

Dublin 2
Ireland
Tel: +353-1-672 7077
Fax: +353-1-627 7043
Web: http://www.caboom.ie

Cadix group Head Office
2-11-5 Sakura-Shinmachi
Setagaya-ku, Tokyo
154-0015 Japan
Tel: 81-3-3439-2171
Fax: 81-3-3439-2987
Web: http://www.cml.co.jp

Cadix group Kyoto Studio
Science Center Building
StudioSection Paawata-cho
Chudoji Shimogyo-ku, Kyoto 600-8815
Japan
Tel: 81-75-311-1131
Fax: 81-75-311-1277
Web: http://www.cml.co.jp

CADgraf Multimedia
40 Maricourt St.
Cantley, Quebec Canada
J8V 2V2
Tel: +1 819.827.3057
Web: http://www.cadgrafmultimedia.com

CAE
8585 Côte-de-Liesse
Saint-Laurent, Québec
Canada H4T 1G6
Tel: 1-514-341-6780
Fax: 1-514-341-7699
Web: http://www.cae.ca

CAE
200 Bay Street, Suite 3060
Royal Bank Plaza
Toronto, Ontario
Canada M5J 2J1
Tel: 1-416-865-0070
Tel: 1-800-760-0667
Fax: 1-416-865-0337
Web: http://www.cae.ca

Calabash Animation
657 West Ohio
Chicago, Illinois 60610

United States
Tel: 1-312-243-3433
Fax: 1-312-243-6227
Web: http://www.calabashanim.com

Calibre Digital Pictures
65 Heward Avenue
Bldg. A, Suite 201
Toronto, Ontario Canada
M4M 2T5
Tel: 1-416-531-8383
Fax: 1-416-531-8083
Web: http://www.calibredigital.com

Calico World Entertainment
10200 Riverside Drive North
Chatsworth, California 91602-
2539
United States
Tel: 1-818-755-3800
Fax: 1-818-755-4643
Web: http://www.calicoworld.com

CAMF Productions
Aignerstrasse 78
AT-5026 Salzburg
Austria
Tel: +43-662-620830
Fax: +43-662-620830-10
Web: http://www.camf.com

Canal J
France
Tel: 011-33-149-54-54-54
Fax: 011-33-142-22-87-67
Web: http://www.canalj.net

Canning Factory, The
11B Albert Place
London
W8 5PD
England
Tel: 011-44-207-937-1136
Fax: 011-44-207-938-1896
Web: http://www.canningfactory.co.uk

CanWest Entertainment
111 George Street 3rd Floor
Toronto, Ontario
Canada M5A 2n4
Tel: 1-416-360-4321

Fax: 1-416-364-4388
Web: http://www.watchfireworks.com

Canvas Films
520 North Andrews
Fort Lauderdale, Florida 33301
United States
Tel: 1-954-767-8766
Web: http://www.canvasfilms.com

CAOZ
Aegisgata 7
Reykjavik, IS Iceland
101
Tel: +354.51.13.55.0
Fax: +354.51.13.55.1
Web: http://www.caoz.com

Capital FX
2nd Floor
20 Dering Street
London
W1s 1AJ
United Kingdom
Tel: +44 (0) 20 7493 9998
Fax: +44 (0) 20 7493 9997
Web: http://www.capital-fx.co.uk

Carbon Digital Ltd
12 Maliston Rd.
Great Sankey
Warrington
United Kingdom
WA5 1JR
Tel: +44 192.54.70.83.8
Web: http://www.carbondigital.co.uk

Caribara France
36 boulevard de la bastille
Paris
France
75012
Tel: +33 1.44.74.32.32
Fax: +33 1.44.74.32.21
Web: http://www.caribara.com

Carl's Fine Films
577 2nd Street, Suite 103
San Francisco, California 94107
United States
Tel: 1-415-543-0880
Fax: 1-415-621-7792
Web: http://www.carlsfinefilms.com

Carl's Fine Films
440 Davis Court, Suite 1710
San Francisco, California 94111
United States
Web: http://www.carlsfinefilms.com

Carrasco
Av. OrdoÒez Lazo condominio la
Laguna dep. 701
Cuenca
Azuay
Ecuador
Tel: +593 7.82.43.97
Fax: +593 7.88.12.24
Web: http://www.animados.net

Carrere Group
50, Avenue du Président Wilson
Bâtiment 204
93214 La Plaine Saint-Denis
France
Tel: 33 (0)1 49 37 78 00
Fax: 33 (0)1 49 37 77 75
Web: http://www.carreregroup.com

Cartoon Network Europe
Turner House
16 Great Marlborough Street
London
United Kingdom
W1F 7HS
Tel: +44 207.69.31.00.0
Fax: +44 207.69.31.00.1
Web: http://cartoonnetwork.co.uk

Cartoon Network Online
1050 Techwood Drive
Atlanta, Georgia 30318
United States
Tel: 1-404-878-0694
Web: http://cartoonnetwork.com

Cartoon Network, Inc.
1050 Techwood Drive
Atlanta, Georgia 30318
United States
Tel: 1-404-885-2263
Web:http://www.cartoonnetwork.com

Cartoon Producción S.L.
Cullera, 73 - 3°
46035 Benimamet
Valencia
Spain
Tel: + 34 96 390 3775
Fax: + 34 96 390 3774
Web:http://www.cartoonpstudios.com

Cartoon Webworks
H1123
Budapest
Csorsz u. 13
Hungary
Tel: +36 1.22.50.17.0
Fax: +36 1.21.29.18.4
Web:http://www.cartoonwebworks.com

Casablanca
AV. Republica do Libano, 379
Sao Paulo
Brazil
Tel: 55 11 3889 2600
Fax: 55 11 3889 2610
Web: http://www.cbsp.com.br

Casablanca
Rua Cosme Velho, 218
Rio de Janeiro
Brazil
Tel: 55 21 2205 0503
Fax: 55 21 2205 0799
Web: http://www.cbsp.com.br

Catalyst Pictures
34 Chester Square
Ashton-Under-Lyne
Lancs
United Kingdom
0L67TW
Tel: +44 161.33.93.35.3
Web:http://www.catalystpics.co.uk

Catamongus Studios
2430 Fulton Road
Kissimmee, Florida, 34744
United States
Tel: 1-407-932-2604
Tel: 1-407-932-2630
Web: http://www.cybersmart.tv

Catapult Productions
477 Richmond St. West
Suite 1001
Toronto Ontario, M5V 3E7
Canada
Tel: 1-416-504-9876
Fax: 1-416-504-6648
Web:
http://www.catapultproductions.com

Catflap Animation
356 Darling Street
Balmain
Sydney
New South Wales
Australia
2041
Tel: +61 2.98.18.66.99
Fax: +61 2.98.18.63.44
Web: http://www.catflap.com.au

Catwalk Digital Media
817 Hamilton Street
Charlotte, North Carolina 28206
United States
Tel: 1-704-342-3348
Fax: 1-704-342-0085
Web: http://www.silverhammer.com

CCG/ZGDV Center of Computer
Graphics
Rua Teixeira Pascoasis 596
Guimaraes
Portugal
4800-073
Tel: +351 25.34.39.30.0
Fax: +351 25.34.39.34.8
Web: http://www.ccg.pt

CCI Digital
2921 West Alameda
Burbank, California 91505
United States
Tel: 1-818-562-6300
Web: http://www.ccidigital.com

CCT International
P.O. Box 51584
Kifissia
Athens, 14501 Greece
51584
Tel: +30 93.85.08.68.8
Fax: +44 87.01.36.15.24
Web: http://www.cctintl.com

CDFM2 Architecture Inc
1015 Central
Kansas City, Missouri 64105
United States
Tel: 1-816-472-2000
Fax: 1-816-471-4362
Web: http://www.cdfm2.com

CDI Media
2323 South 3600 West
Salt Lake City, Utah 84119
United States
Tel: 1-800-829-0077
Web: http://www.cdimedia.com

CDR Communications
9310-B Old Keene Mill Road,
Burke, Virginia 22015-4204
United States
Tel: 1-703-569-3400
Tel: 1-800-729-2237
Fax: 1-703-569-3448
Web:
http://www.cdrcommunications.com

Celador International Limited
39 Long Acre
London
United Kingdom
WC2E 9 LG
Tel: +44 207.24.08.10.1
Web: http://www.celador.co.uk

Celefex
8 West 19th Street
3rd Floor
New York, New York 10011
United States
Tel: 1-212-255-3470
Fax: 1-212-255-2993
Web: http://www.celefex.com

Cell GFX
United Kingdom
Web: http://www.cell-gfx.co.uk

CeMedia Ltd - Central European
Media Workshop
Szentlst Van Parn 14.
Budapest
Hungary 1137
Tel: +36 2.23.92.53.8
Fax: +36 1.34.98.23.4
Web: http://www.cemedia.co.hu

Center City Film and Video
1503-05 Walnut Street.
Philadelphia, Pennsylvania
United States
Tel: 1-215-568-4134
Web: http://www.ccfv.com

Centro Digital Pictures Ltd
32 Tung Lo Wan Road
Causeway Bay
Hong Kong
Tel: (852) 2890 2988
Fax: (852) 2576 0797
Web: http://www.centro.com.hk

Centro Digital Pictures
Multimedia Centre
1/F, Jockey Club Environmental Bldg
77 Tat Chee Avenue
Kowloon Tong
Hong Kong
Tel: (852) 2319 6688
Fax: (852) 2319 2272
Web: http://www.centro.com.hk

Century III at Universal Studios
2000 Universal Studios Plaza
Orlando, Florida 32819
United States

Tel: 1-407-354-1000
Web: http://www.century3.com

Century Productions
5320 South Procyon Avenue
Las Vegas, Nevada 89118
United States
Tel: 1-702-597-1969
Tel: 1-877-597-1969
Fax: 1-702-597-1009
Web: http://www.centurylv.com

Ceredigm Corporation
1149 Executive Cir. Suite C
Raleigh, North Carolina 27511
United States
Tel: 1-919-465-7448
Web: http://www.ceredigm.com

Cgi Group
4801 E Independence Blvd # 1001
Charlotte, North Carolina 28212
United States
Tel: 1-704-531-0305
Web: http://www.cgi-group.com

Cinecitta Studios
Rome, Italy
Web: http://www.cinecitta.com

Cine & FX
108, Av de l'Opale
1030 Bruxelles
Belgium
Tel: +32 2 739.15.15
Fax: +32 2 739.15.20
Web: http://www.main-frame.be

C.F.I. - Canal France International
19, rue Cognacq - Jay
75007 Paris, France
Tel: 33 1 40 62 32 32
Fax: 33 1 40 62 32 62
Web: http://www.cfi.fr

CGCG Inc.
12F, 65 Sung-Teh Road
Taipei, Taiwan, R.O.C.
Tel: +886-2-2759-8899
Fax: +886-2-2727-8592
Web: http://www.cgcg.com.tw

Chaos Films
12100 North East 16th Avenue
Miami, Florida 33161
United States
Tel: 1-954-455-9606
Fax: 1-954-457-8880
Web: http://www.chaosfilms.com

Channel Four Television
124 Horseferry Road
London, United Kingdom
SW1P 2TX
Tel: +44 171.39.64.44.4
Fax: +44 171.30.68.36.0
Web: http://www.channel4.co.uk

Character Republic
Blk 737 Pasir Ris Drive 10 #07-39
Singapore
510737
Tel: +65.65.84.26.38
Web:
http://www.character-republic.com

Charamel GmbH
Richard-Wagner str.39
Cologne
Germany
50674
Tel: +49 22.13.36.64.0
Fax: +49 22.13.36.64.19
Web: http://www.charamel.com

Charnwood Dynamics, Ltd.
Victoria Mills
Fowke Street
Rothley
Leicestershire
United Kingdom
LE7 7PJ
Tel: +44 116.23.01.06.0
Fax: +44 116.23.01.85.7
Web: http://www.charndyn.com

Chase Design Group
2255 Bancroft Avenue
Los Angeles, California 90039
United States
Tel: 1-323-668-1055
Fax: 1-323-668-2470
Web:http://www.margochase.com

Cheerful Scout
25-27 Riding House Street
London
W1W 7DU
United Kingdom
Tel: +44 (0)20 7291 0444
Fax: +44 (0)20 7291 0445
Web: http://www.cheerfulscout.com

Chicop Animation Arts
Nic. Baurstraat 26
Harlingen
Friesland Netherlands
8861 JA
Tel: +31 65.36.68.43.7
Web:
http://www.chicop-animation.com

Chileanimacion S A
Irrarrazabal 2366
Santiago
Chile
Tel: 01 1-56-2-205-9181
Fax: 01 1-56-2-209-6976
Web: http://www.chileanimacion.com

Chilefilms CGI
Manquehue Sur 1165
Santiago
Chile
Tel: (56 2) 220 0086
Fax: (56 2) 212 9053
Web: http://www.chilefilms.cl

Chinatown 3D
Italy
Web: http://www.china3d.it

Chinkel
23 rue Fontaine
75009 Paris
France
Tel: 01 53 20 08 08
Fax: 01 40 16 10 17
Web: http://www.chinkel.com

Chivydog Productions
13 Griffin Rd.
North Curl Curl
New South Wales
Australia

2099
Tel: +61 2.99.05.99.55
Fax: +61 2.99.05.68.77
Web: http://www.chivydog.com

Chris Layhe Associates, Inc.
150B McMullen Booth Road
South
Clearwater, Florida 33759
United States
Tel: 1-727-669-0702
Tel: 1-727-726-1188
Web:
http://www.chrislayheassociates.com

CINAR Corporation
1055, René-Lévesque Est
Montréal (Québec)
Canada H2L 4S5
Tel: 1-514-843-7070
Fax: 1-514-843-7080
Web: http://www.cinar.com

Cine & FX
108, Av de l'Opale
1030 Bruxelles
Belgium
Tel : +32 2 739.15.15
Fax : +32 2 739.15.20
Web: http://www.cine-fx.com

Cinecolor
Humbolt 1967 - Piso 3 (1414)
Buenos Aires
Capitol Federal
Argentina
Tel: 54-11-4777-1560
Fax: 54-11-4777-1566
Web: http://www.chilefilms.cl

Cinefex Workshop Co Ltd
Unit 1375 Hong Kong
International
Trade & Exhibition Ctr 1
Trademart Drive
Kowloon Bay,
Kowloon
Hong Kong
Tel: (852)2768 8678
Fax: (852)2712 8200
Web: http://www.filmworkshop.net

CinéGroupe
1010, Ste-Catherine Street
East, 6th floor,
Montreal (Quebec) H2L 2G3
Canada
Tel: 1-514-849-5008
Fax: 1-514-849-5001
Web: http://www.cinegroupe.com

Cinesite
1017 North Las Palmas Ave.
Los Angeles, California 90038
United States
Tel: 1-323-468-4400
Fax: 1-323-468-4404
Fax: 1-323-468-2136
Web: http://www.cinesite.com

Cinesite, Inc.
8 Carlisle Street
London, United Kingdom
W1D 3BP
Tel: +44 207.97.34.00.0
Fax: +44 207.97.34.04.0
Web: http://www.cinesite.com

Cinema Concepts
2030 Powers Ferry Rd., Suite 214
Atlanta, Georgia 30339
United States
Tel: 1-770-956-7460
Tel: 1-800-SHOW-ADS
Fax: 1-770-956-8358
Web:
http://www.cinemaconcepts.com

Cinepix
Seoul, Korea
Tel: 02-3451-8600
Fax: 02-557-3199
Web: http://www.cinepix.co.kr

@cineteam filmproduktion
GmbH & Co. KG
Hamburger Allee 45
60486 Frankfurt
Germany
Tel: +49 69 979 5050
Fax: +49 69 979 50592
Web: http://www.cineteam.de

Cinevision
2000 Broadway, Ste 2a
New York, New York 10023
United States
Tel: 1-212-724-7462
Fax: 1-212-724-9498
Web: http://www.cinevision.com

Cineworks Digital Studios, Inc.
6550 North East 4th Court
Miami, Florida 33138
United States
Phone: 1-305-754-7501
Fax: 1-305-754-3850
Web: http://www.cineworks.com

Cinic ImageWorks
Bonner Str. 211 - 50968
Cologne
Tel: 221-376 25 70
Fax: 221-376 25 74
Web: http://www.cinic.com

Cipher Animation Studios
58 Knightsbridge Drive
Auckland 1310
New Zeland
Web: http://www.renderspace.com

Circle Studios; Euro RSCG Circle
420 Boylston Street, 6th Floor
Boston, Massachusetts 02116
United States
Tel: 1-617-585-3000
Fax: 1-617-585-3001
Web: http://www.circle.com

CIS Hollywood
1144 N. Las Palmas Ave
Hollywood, California 90038
United States
Tel: 1-323-463-8811
Fax: 1-323-962-1859
Web: http://www.cishollywood.com

City Animation Co.
57 Park Drive
Troy, Michigan 48083-2753
United States
Tel: 1-248-589-0600
Tel: 1-800-872-8295

Fax: 1-248-589-2020
Web: http://www.cityanimation.com

City Animation Co.
2807 Jolly Road, Suite 300
Okemos, Michigan 48864
United States
Tel: 1-517-333-4500
Tel: 1-800-772-1428
Fax: 1-517-333-4913
Web: http://www.cityanimation.com

Class-Key Chew-Po Animated
Commercials
6353 Sunset Boulevard
Hollywood, California 90028
United States
Tel: 1-323-468-3020
Web:
http://www.classkeychewpo.com

Clarke & McClure
3730 Kirby Dr., Suite 930
Houston Texas, 77098
United States
Tel: 1-713-524-6492
Fax: 1-713-524-6191
Web: http://www.clarkeandmc-
clure.com

Clasticon Solutions
Wood Head Centre
1st Floor
23 Sivaganga Road
Nungambakkam
Chennai
Tamil Nadu
India
600034
Tel: +91 44.82.01.52.7
Web: http://www.clasticon.com

Clayart Trickfilmproduktion
Franziusstrasse 14
Frankfurt
Germany
60314
Tel: +49 69.44.08.70
Fax: +49 69.40.59.69.2
Web: http://www.clayart.de

Clayman's Funhouse 3D
Cartoons & Animation
696-185-911 Yates St.
Victoria, British Columbia Canada
V8V 4Y9
Tel: +1 250.382.8780
Web: http://www.theclayman.com

Clear
Fenton House
55-57 Great Marlborough St.
London, England
w1f 7jx
United Kingdom
Tel: +44 (0)20 7734 5557
Fax: +44 (0)20 7734 4533
Web: http://www.clear.ltd.uk

Click 3X
16 West 22nd Street
New York, New York 10010
United States
Tel: 1-212-627-1900
Fax: 1-212-627-4472
Web: http://www.click3x.com

Click 3X
2415 Michigan Ave.
Bergamot Station
Santa Monica, California 90404
United States
Tel: 1-310-264-5511
Fax: 1-310-264-5512
Web: http://www.click3x.com

Climax Group
Rawlings Suite
North Building
Gunwharf Quays
Portsmouth
Hants
PO1 3TT
United Kingdom
Fax: +44 (0)2392 836121
Web: http://www.climax.co.uk

Climax Solent
Somerville Office
Gunwharf Quays
Portsmouth
Hants
PO1 3TT

United Kingdom
Fax: 44 (0) 2392 863655
Web: http://www.climax.co.uk

Climax Brighton
Sheridan House
114 Western Road
Hove
East Sussex
BN3 1DD
United Kingdom
Fax: 44 (0)1273 740819
Web: http://www.climax.co.uk

Climax Nottingham
5th Floor
Fenchurch House
12 King Street
Nottingham
Nottinghamshire
NG1 2AS
United Kingdom
Fax: 44 (0) 115 853 3909
Web: http://www.climax.co.uk

Climax London
6&7 Canbury Business Park
Elm Cresent
Kingston
Surrey
KT2 6HJ
United Kingdom
Fax: 44 (0) 20 8974 9761
Web: http://www.climax.co.uk

CMB Design Group
7 St Stephens Green.
Dublin 2.
Ireland
Tel: +353-1-679 9805
Fah: +353-1-679 9873
Web: http://www.cmbdesign.ie

CME Digital
1326 Stetson St.
Orlando, Florida 32804
United States
Tel: 1-321-662-8424
Web: http://www.mindgel.com

CMS
632 West Summit Avenue.
Charlotte, North Carolina 28203
United States
Tel: 1-704-377-1601
Web:
http://www.corporatemedia.com

Coconino animatie
Crooswijksesingel 29b
3034 CJ Rotterdam
The Netherlands
Tel: (31) 10 413 83 36
Fax: (31) 10 413 82 28
Web: http://www.coconino.nl

Collideascope Digital Productions Inc.
P.O. Box 34002
Scotia Square RPO
Halifax
Nova Scotia
Canada
B3J 3S1
Tel: +1 902.429.8949
Fax: +1 902.429.0265
Web: http://www.collideascope.com

Collider, Inc.
133 West 19th Street
5th Floor
New York, New York 10011
United States
Tel: 1-646-336-9398
Fax: 1-646-349-4159
Web: http://www.collidernyc.com

Colorland Animation Productions
(Scenzhen) Ltd.
Levels 1-3,
Yuan Lin Building
1, Donghu Yi Road
Shenzhen
P.R. China 518003
Tel: 86-755-552 7686
Fax: 86-755-541 7200
Web:
http://www.colorland-animation.com

Colorland Animation Productions Ltd.
909 Austin Tower, 22-26 Austin Avenue,
Kowloon, Hong Kong
Tel: 852-2366 9013
Fax: 852-2367 9087
Web:
http://www.colorland-animation.com

Colorland Animation Shanghai
504, Culture Multiple Building,
396 Fanyu Road,
Shanghai, P.R. China
Tel: 86-21-6282 7314
Tel: 86-21-6281 5037 ext. 504
Fax: 86-21-6282 7314
Web:
http://www.colorland-animation.com

Color Chips India
Plot No.16, Road No.5
Jubilee Hills
Hyderabad
India
500-033
Tel: +91 49-35-50268
Tel: +91-40-65-06824
Tel: +91-40-65-06825
Web:http://www.colorchipsindia.com

ColoradoFX
1819 Colorado Avenue
Santa Monica, California 90404
United States
Tel: 1-310-453-8842
Fax: 1-310-828-8354
Web: http://www.coloradofx.com

ColorShop VFX B&B
Denmark
Web: http://www.colorshopvfx.dk

Colour Film Services Ltd
10 Wadsworth Road
Perivale
Greenford
Middlesex
UB6 7JX
United Kingdom
Tel: + 44 (0)20 8998 2731
Web:http://www.colourfilmservices.co.uk

Colour Film Services Ltd
26 Berwick Street
London
W1F 8RG
United Kingdom
Tel: +44 (0)20 7734 4543
Web:http://www.colourfilmservices.co.uk

ComicHouse
Stationsweg 20
6861 EH Oosterbeek
The Netherlands
Tel: +31 (0)26 - 32 100 32
Fax: +31 (0)26 - 32 100 36
Web: http://www.comichouse.nl

Command Digital Studios
Water Garden Office Park
8408 Glenwood Avenue, Suite E
Raleigh, North Carolina 27612
United States
Tel: 1-919-787-0880
Fax: 1-919-787-0811
Web:http://www.command-digital.com

Command Digital Studios
P.O. Box 6351
Raleigh, North Carolina 27628
United States
Tel: 1-919-833-1708
Fax: 1-919-833-6898
Web:http://www.command-digital.com

Company 3
1661 Lincoln Blvd., #400
Santa Monica, California 90404
United States
Tel: 1-310-586-3800
Tel: 1-310-255-6600
Fax: 1-310-255-6602
Web: http://www.company3.com

Company 3
545 Fifth Avenue, 5th Floor
New York, New York 10017
United States
Tel: 1-212-687-4000
Fax: 1-212-687-2719
Web: http://www.company3.com

Complete Post
6087 Sunset Blvd.
Hollywood, California 90028
United States
Tel: 1-323-467-1244
Fax: 1-323-461-2561
Web: http://www.technicolor.com

Complete Post
12 Thistlethwaite St
South Melbourne
Victoria 3205
Australia
Tel: +61 3 9699 4633
Fax: +61 3 9699 3226
Web:http://www.completepost.com.au

Complete Post
263 Darlinghurst Rd
Darlinghurst
New South Wales 2010
Australia
Tel: +61 2 9368 0355
Fax: +61 2 9368 0455
Web:http://www.completepost.com.au

Component Limited
1 Newman Passage
London
W1T 1EF
United Kingdom
Tel: +44 (0)20 7631 4400
Fax: +44 (0)20 7580 2890
Web: http://www.component.co.uk

Composite Image Systems, LLC
1144 North Las Palmas Avenue
Hollywood, California 90038
United States
Tel: 1-323-463-8811
Fax: 1-323-962-1859
Web: http://www.cishollywood.com

Computer Animation & Design
P.O. Box 882
Londonderry, New Hampshire 03053
United States
Web: http://www.hotgrfx.com

Computer Cafe
1207 Fourth Street
Santa Monica, California 90401-1340
United States
Tel: 1-310-395-9013
Fax: 1-310-395-9814
Web: http://www.computercafe.com

Computer Cafe
3130 Skyway Drive
Suite 603
Santa Maria, California
93455-1803
United States
Tel: 1-805-922-9479
Fax: 1-805-922-3225
Web: http://www.computercafe.com

Computoons
2575 Campus Drive #355
Klamath Falls, Oregon 97601
United States
Tel: 1-215-243-7587
Tel: 1-541-884-1884 (Oregon)
Fax: 1-215-243-6095
Toll Free: 1-888-854-3553
Web: http://www.computoons.com

Connoiseur Media
No. 165, 1st'C' Cross
18th'A' Main,
HAL II Stage
Indiranagar
Bangalore
Karnataka
India
560038
Tel: +91 80.52.72.34.5
Fax: +91 80.52.72.34.6
Web: http://www.connoiseur.com

Consortumm of Gentelemen, The
27 Beethoven St
London
WI0 4LG
England
United Kingdom
Tel: 01 1-44-208-964-0234
Fax: 01 1-44-208-968-7710
Web: http://www.cgonline.co.uk

Cool Beans Productions Ltd
Brook House
557 Ecclesall Road
Sheffield S11 8PR
United Kingdom
Tel: +44 (0) 114 267 0704
Fax: +44 (0) 114 268 2123
Web:
http://www.coolbeansproductions.com

C.O.R.E. Digital Pictures Inc.
488 Wellington Street West, Suite 600
Toronto, Ontario
Canada M5V 1E3
Tel: 1-416.599.2673
Fax: 1-416.599.1212
Web: http://www.coredp.com

Core Studio
164 Townsend Street, Suite 12
San Francisco, California 94107
United States
Tel: 1-415-543-8140
Web: http://corestudio.com

Cornerstone Animation Inc.
815 East Colrado Boulevard.
Suite 100
Glendale, California 91205
United States
Tel: 1-818-548-8393
Fax: 1-818-549-9611
Web: http://www.csanimation.com

Cornerstone Pictures
112 S. Blount Street
Raleigh, North Carolina 27601
United States
Tel: 1-919-831-0888
Tel: 1-888-872-0063
Web:
http://www.cornerstonepictures.com

Corporate Media Svc
W Summit Ave
Charlotte, North Carolina 28203
United States
Tel: 1-704-377-1601
Web:http://www.corporatemedia.com

Corus Entertainment, Inc.
630-3rd Avenue SW, Suite 501
Calgary, Alberta
T2P 4L4
Tel: 1-403-444-4244
Fax: 1-403-444-4040
Web: http://www.corusent.com

Corus Entertainment, Inc.
181 Bay Street, Suite 1630
Toronto, Ontario
M5J 2T3
Tel: 1-416-642-3770
Fax: 1-416-642-3779
Web: http://www.corusent.com

Corus Entertainment, Inc.
23 Fraser Avenue
Toronto, Ontario
M6K 1Y7
Tel: 1-866-537-2397
Fax: 1-416-530-5195
Web: http://www.corusent.com

Cosgrove Hall Digital
8 Albany Road
Chorlton-cum-Hardy
Manchester
M21 0AW
United Kingdom
Tel: +44 (0) 161 882 2500
Fax: +44 (0) 161 882 2555
Web: http://www.chd.uk.com

Cosgrove Hall Films/IEL
8 Albany Road.
Chorlton-cum-Hardy
Manchester
M21 0AW
United Kingdom
Tel: 01144-161-882-2500
Fax: 01144-161-882-2555
Web: http://www.chf.co.uk

Crawford Communications
3845 Pleasantdale Road
Atlanta Georgia 30340
United States
Tel: 1-404-876-7149
Fax: 1-678-421-6717
Web: http://www.crawford.com

Crea Anima2
c/ Menendez Pidal 42
28036 Madrid
Spain
Tel: 91 350 40 90
Fax: 91 350 43 60
Web: http://www.anima2.com

Crack Creative
P.O. Box 642388
Los Angeles, California 90064-7170
United States
Web: http://www.crackcreative.com

Creat Studio USA
323 Geary St., Suite #617
San Francisco, California 94102
United States
Tel: 1-415-693-9660
Fax: 1-415-693-9661
Web: http://www.creatstudio.com

Creat Studio Russia
Bolshaya Monetnaya 16
Office-Centre #1, Floor 4
St. Petersburg, 197101
Russia
Tel: +7-812-238-7740
Fax: +7-812-238-7741
Web: http://www.creatstudio.com

Creative Animation Lab
4768 Ardley Drive
Colorado Springs, Colorado
80922
United States
Tel: 1-719-380-7085
Web:
http://www.creativeanimationlab.com

Creative Bubble, LLC
79 Fifth Avenue, 14th Floor
New York, New York 10003
United States
Tel: 1-212-201-4200
Fax: 1-212-201-4210
Web: http://www.bubbleny.com

Creative Capers
444 East Broadway
Glendale, California 91205

United States
Tel: 1-818-552-2290
Fax: 1-818-552-2296
Web: http://www.creativecapers.com

Creative Digital Images
10 S. 185 Schoger Dr. Unit 81
Naperville, Illinois 60564
United States
Tel: 1-630-978-7007
Fax: 1-630-978-7035
Web: http://www.cdi-animate.com

Creative Logic Technologies, Inc.
2425 Commerce Avenue, Building
2100, Suite 300
Duluth, Georgia 30096
United States
Tel: 1-678-417-4057
Fax: 1-678-417-4041
Web: http://Creativelogictech.com

Creative Logik Universe
216 S. Jackson Street Suite 201
Glendale, California 91205
United States
Tel: 1-818-545-9280
Fax: 1-818-545-9344
Web: http://www.creativelogik.com

Creative Post Inc.
510C Front Street West
Toronto, Ontario Canada
M5V 1B8
Tel: +1 416.979.7678
Fax: +1 416.979.8246
Web: http://www.creativepostinc.com

Creative TV Facilities
15 Cornwall House
Alsop Place
London
NW1 5LH
United Kingdom
Tel: +44 (0)22 7244 4218
Fax: +44 (0)22 7935 5841
Web:
http://www.creativetvfacilities.com

Creative Video Of Washington
200 N. Glebe Rd.

Arlington Virginia 22203
United States
Tel: 1-703-524-1820
Fax: 1-703-528-7072
Web: http://www.creativevideo.com

Creative Urge
22-26 Johnston Street
Collingwood Victoria
Australia 3066
Tel: 03 9416 3223
Fax: 03 9416 1040
Web: http://www.creativeurge.com.au

Creo Collective
2046 Broadway
Santa Monica, California 90404
United States
Tel: 1-310-315-9553
Fax: 1-310-315-3073
Web: http://www.postlogic.com

Crest India
Crest House
Plot No. 250-B
Hind Cycle Road
Worli
Mumbai 400 025
India
Tel: +91 22 4961459 67
Fax: +91 22 493 1365
Fax: +91 22 496 0376
Web: http://www.crestindia.com

Cromosoma TV Productions
C/ Peru 174
08020 Barcelona
Spain
Tel: (+34) 93.266.42.66
Fax: (+34) 93.266.40.14
Web: http://www.cromosoma.com

Crossing Effects Studio, The
2042-2050 Alpha Avenue
Burnaby, British Columbia
Canada V5C 5K7
Tel: 1-604-296-2622
Fax: 1-604-296-2672
Web: http://www.crossingfx.com

Crush Inc.
439 Wellington Street West
Toronto, Ontario Canada
M5V 1E7
Tel: +1 416.345.1936
Fax: +1 416.345.1965
Web: http://www.crushinc.com

Crystal Pix
Rochester, New York
United States
Tel: 1-585-377-3210
Web: http://www.crystalpix.com

C-Squared TV
14925 Ventura Boulevard, # 300
Sherman Oaks, California, 91403
United States
Tel: 1-818-905-5966
Fax: 1-818-905-5967
Web: http://www.csquaredtv.com

CTECH s.r.o.
Nuselska 53
Prague, Czech Republic
14000
Tel: +420 2.61.21.56.44
Fax: +420 2.61.21.77.64
Web: http://www.ctech.cz

Cubed Studios
Oxfordshire
OX15 5QQ
United Kingdom
Web: http://www.cubedstudios.com

Cuppa Coffee Animation And Design
401 Richmond Street West
Toronto, Ontario Canada
M5V 1X3
Tel: +1 416.340.8869
Fax: +1 416.340.9819
Web: http://www.cuppacoffee.com

Curious Labs, Inc.
655 Capitola Road. Suite 200
Santa Cruz, California 95062
United States
Tel: 1-831-462-8901
Fax: 1-831-462-8925
Web: http://www.curiouslabs.com

Curious Pictures
440 Lafayette St. 6th Floor
New York, New York 10003
United States
Tel: 1-212-674-1400
Fax: 1-212-674-0081
Web: http://www.curiouspictures.com

Curious Pictures
1360 Mission Street, Suite 201
San Francisco, California 94103
United States
Tel: 1-415-437-1400
Fax: 1-415-437-1408
Web: http://www.curiouspictures.com

Cutting Edge
4 Edmonstone Street
South Brisbane Qld 4101
Australia
Tel: +61 7 3013 6222
Fax: +61 7 3846 1069
Web: http://www.cuttingedge.com.au

Cutting Edge
Unit 3, 54 Siganto Drive
Oxenford Qld 4210
Australia
Tel: +61 7 5502 5888
Fax: +61 7 5529 4100
Web: http://www.cuttingedge.com.au

Cutting Vision
665 Broadway Suite 1201
New York, New York 10012
United States
Tel: 1-212-533-9400
Fax: 1-212-533-9463
Web: http://www.cuttingvision.com

CV. Studio Komik Bajing Loncat
Jl Cukang Kawung 81/149 A
Jl. Kanayakan Baru 2
Bandung, Indonesia
Tel: +62 22.25.15.70.5
Fax: +62 22.25.09.56.7
Web: http://www.bajingloncat.com

CW Studio
405 Espanola Way Suite 306
Miami Beach, Florida 33139

United States
Tel: 1-305-673-2756
Fax: 1-305-534-3083
Web:http://www.creativewebstudio.com

CyberHues, Inc.
22421 SW 66th Ave. #502
Boca Raton, Florida 33428
United States
Tel: 1-407-414-0873
Web: http://www.cyberhues.com

Cybermill Studio, Inc.
20 South Maple Street , Suite 200
Ambler, Pennsylvania 19002
United States
Tel: 1-215-619-3634
Web: http://www.cybermillstudio.com

Cyberville Studios, Inc.
7345 Sand Lake Rd. Suite 318
Orlando, Florida 32819
United States
Tel: 1-407-345-5021
Fax: 1-407-345-5027
Web: http://www.cybervillestudios.com

Cycho
Level 1
428 Parramatta Road
Petersham
Sydney, NSW
Australia
2049
Tel: +61 2.95.64.24.25
Fax: +61 2.95.64.24.25
Web: http://www.cycho.com.au

Cyper Media, Inc
Boramae Nasan, Suite 4F
395-18 Sindaebang 2-dong,
Dongjak-gu
Seoul
Korea
Tel: (416) 569-3210
Fax: (416) 488-3210
Web: http://www.cypermedia.com

Czar Productions
809 New Britan Ave
Hartford, Connecticut 06106-3918
United States
Tel: 1-860-953-0809
Fax: 1-860-953-0809
Web: http://www.czarproductions.com

Czech Television
Kavci Hory
Prague 4 140 70
Czech Republic
Tel: 011-420-2-6113-7043
Fax: 011-420-2-6113-7308
Web: http://www.czech-tv.cz
Web: http://www.czech-tv.cz/english

D and D Production
Ranebeekstraat 230
B-1120 Brussel
Belgium
Tel: +32-(0)2-266 81 81
Fax: +32-(0)2-266 81 82
Web: http://www.ddeg.be

D&D Film- und
Fernsehproduktion GmbH
Kalscheurener Str. 55
D-50354 Hürth
Tel: +49.(0)2233.9685.0
Fax: +49.(0)2233.9685.8
Web: http://www.dd-film.de

D&D Berlin Film- und
Fernsehproduktion GmbH
Savignyplatz 6
D-10625 Berlin
Tel: +49.(0)30.31 51 88.40 / 41
Fax: +49.(0)30.31 51 88.55
Web: http://www.dd-film.de

D'Ocon Films Productions, S.A.
Calaf 3
08021 Barcelona
Spain
Tel: 34 93 240 41 22
Fax: 34 93 240 41 24
Web: http://www.docon.es

da Vinci Motion Graphics, LLC.
7012 NW 63rd Street, Suite 201

Bethany, Oklahoma 73008
United States
Tel: 1-405-972-2262
Fax: 1-405-971-1723
Web: http://www.dvmg.com

D.A.D.D.Y.
Space 28
North Lotts
Dublin
Ireland
Tel: 086 815499
Tel: 087 2789175
Tel: 087 6498829
Web: http://www.teamdaddy.com

Daiquiri
Alcala, 518.
Madrid
Spain 28027
Tel: 91-754-67-00
Web: http://www.daiquiridigital.es

Dai Won Animation Co Ltd
40-456,3-GA
Hangangro Yongsan-Gu
Seoul 140-0120
Korea
Tel: 011-02-3785-0100~4
Tel: 011-822-793-5051
Fax: 011-822-790-6084
Web: http://www.daiwoncna.com

Daily Planet LTD.
455 North Cityfront Plaza
NBC Tower/Suite 2900
Chicago, Illinois 60611-5555
United States
Tel: 1-312/670-3766
Fax: 1-312/527-0701
Web: http://dailyplanetltd.com

D.A.M.N FX
5524-C St-Patrick
Loft 480
Montreal, Quebec
Canada
H4E 1A8
Tel: 1-514-762-DAMN
Web: http://www.damnfx.com

Dan Black Studios
5965 Monticello Drive
Montgomery, Alabama 36117
United States
Tel: 1-334-279-6036
Fax: 1-334-279-1232
Web:http://www.danblackstudios.com

Dancing Diablo Studio
55 Washington St. # 511
Brooklyn, New York 11201
United States
Tel: 1-718-243-0074
Fax: 1-718-855-9187
Web: http://www.dancingdiablo.com

Das Werk AG
SchmidtstraBe 12
Frankfurt am Main
Germany 60326
Tel: +49 69.97.35.35.10
Fax: +49 69.97.35.35.00
Web: http://www.das-werk.de

David Nixon Productions
7380 Sand Lake Road #511
Orlando, Florida
United States
tel: 1-407-345-8110
Tel: 1-407-352-5259
Fax: 1-407-352-5289
Web: http://www.davidnixonpro-
ductions.com

David Titus Productions
19 Peruz Court
Bedford
Nova Scotia, Canada
B4A 4G2
Tel: +1 902.832.3155
Web: http://www.davidtitusproduc-
tions.com

da Vinci Motion Graphics
7012 NW 63rd Street, Suite 201
Bethany, Oklahoma 73008
United States
Tel: 1-405-773-3867
Fax: 1-405-773-8675
Web: http://www.dvmg.com

DAZ Productions
12401 S. 450 E. Ste. F1
Draper, Utah 84020
United States
Tel: 1-801-495-1777
Fax: 1-801-495-1787
Web: http://www.daz3d.com

Dear Associates Inc
1 - 4 - 5 Main town building
4 floor
Chiyoda Ku
Tokyo
Japan
Tel: 03-3865-8803
Fax: 03-3865-8852
Web: http://www.deara.co.jp

Decode Entertainment Inc.
512 King Street, Suite 104
Toronto, Ontario
Canada
M5A 1M1
Tel: 1-416-363-8034
Fax: 1-416-363-8919
Web: http://www.decode-ent.com

Deep Blue Sea
2850 Tigertail Ave.
Coconut Grove, Florida 33133
United States
Tel: 1-305-857-0943
Fax: 1-305-856-3692
Web: http://www.deepbluesea.com

Deep Spring Design Ltd.
Hendersonville, North Carolina
United States
Tel: 1-828-698-1170
Tel: 1-800-890-5411
Web: http://www.deepspring.net

Dell Hall Video
1240 West Jackson Boulevard
Chicago, Illinois 60607
United States
Tel: 1-312-733-6500
Fax: 1-312-666-3333
Web: http://www.delhallvideo.com

DFreedomZone Inc.
88 First Street, Suite 601
San Francisco, California 94105
United States
Tel: 1-415-836-9061
Fax: 1-415-836-9151
Web: http://www.dfreedomzone.com

Delaney and Friends
105 West 3rd Avenue
Vancouver, British Columbia
Canada
V5Y 1E6
Tel: 1-604-877-8585
Fax: 1-604-877-1614
Web:
http://www.delaneyandfriends.com

Delfin Studios
Carrera 18 No. 88 - 43
Bogotá
Columbia
Tel: (571) 2579483 - 2574729
Fax: (571) 2362393
Web: http://www.delfinstudio.com

Delfin Studios
1221 Brickell Av Suite 900
Miami, Florida 33131
United States
Tel: 1-305-347-5175
Fax: 1-305-347-5174
Web: http://www.delfinstudio.com

Delfin Studios
24 Platts Lane
London
NW37NS
United Kingdom
Tel: 44-207 3662357
Web: http://www.delfinstudio.com

Delfin Studios
Rua Paes de Araujo, 29 - 19°
andar
Itaim Bibi
Sâo Paulo - SP
Brasil Cep: 044531 - 940
Tel: (5511) 30440277
Web: http://www.delfinstudio.com

Delfin Studios
Rimonim Lane 1
Kefarshemaryaho
Israel
Tel: (9729) 9582670
Fax: (9729) 9588082
Web: http://www.delfinstudio.com

Denman Productions
5 Holly Road
Twickenham
Middlesex
United Kingdom
TW1 4EA
Tel: +44 208.89.13.46.1
Fax: +44 208.89.16.41.3
Web: http://www.denman.co.uk

Design & Motion
Wehrneckarstrasse 10
Esslingen
Germany
73728
Tel: +49 71.13.96.93.00
Fax: +49 71.13.96.93.01.3
Web: http://www.design-motion.de

Design4today
1800 Westover Hills Blvd
Richmond, Virginia 23225
United States
Tel: 1-804-231-9918
Web: http://www.design4today.com

Destiny Images
P.O. Box 1033
Scott Depot, West Virginia 25560
United States
Tel: 1-304-755-1235
Tel: 1-800-644-2368
Fax: 1-304-755-1352
Web: http://www.destinyimages.com

Destiny Images
4939 Teays Valley Road
Scott Depot, West Virginia 25560
United States
Tel: 1-304-755-1235
Tel: 1-800-644-2368
Fax: 1-304-755-1352
Web: http://www.destinyimages.com

DFreedomZone Inc.
88 First Street, Suite 601
San Francisco, California 94105
United States
Tel: 1-415-836-9061
Fax: 1-415-836-9151
Web: http://www.dfreedomzone.com

DGP
Portland House
12-13 Greek Street
Soho
London
W1D 4DL
united Kingdom
Tel. +44 (0)20 7734 4501
Fax. +44 (0)20 7734 7034
Web: http://www.dgpsoho.co.uk

DHV
1240 West Jackson Boulevard
Chicago, Illinois 60607
United States
Tel: 1-312-733-6500
Fax: 1-312-666-3333
Web: http://www.dhv.tv

DHX France
95 rue du faubourg
St. Antoine
Paris, France
75011
Tel: +33 1.43.47.15.41
Fax: +33 1.43.47.15.48
Web: http://www.dhxprod.com

Diamond Film and Video
129 Citation Court
Birmingham, Alabama 35209
United States
Tel: 1-205-942-8888
Fax: 1-205-942-8961
Web: http://www.tvstuff.com

Diamond Graphics
4957 Dayspring Drive
Charlotte, North Carolina 28227
United States
Tel: 1-704-573-1882
Web: http://www.dginteractive.com

Dic Entertainment
303 North Glenoaks Blvd, 4th Floor
Burbank, California 91502
United States
Tel: 1-818-955-5400
Fax: 1-818-955-5594
Web:http://www.dicentertainment.com

Diehard Studio
P.O. Box 145
Glen Ridge, New Jersey 07028
United States
Tel: 1-973-672-5897
Fax: 1-973-672-5897
Web: http://www.diehardstudio.com

Digikore Studios Ltd.
410/1, 411/2
Mumbai - Pune Road
Dapodi
Pune, Maharashtra
India
411 012
Tel: +91 20.71.46.69.0
Fax: +91 20.40.01.75.5
Web: http://www.digikore.com

Digiline
222 Bay Street
Port Melbourne
Victoria
Australia 3207
Tel: 61 3 9646 6688
Fax: 61 3 9646 4488
Web: http://www.digiline.com.au

Digimata
36 Woodycrest Avenue
Toronto Ontario M4J 3A7
Canada
Tel: 1-416-462-3388
Fax: 1-416-462-2718
Web: http://www.digimata.com

Digiscope
2308 Broadway
Santa Monica, California 90404
United States
Tel: 1-310-315-6060
Fax: 1 310-828-5856
Web: http://www.digiscope.com

DigiArt Production
Venture Business Center 3/F
469 Daehueng-dong
Mapo-gu
Seoul, Korea 121-727
Fax: +82.2.2217.1502
Web:
http://www.seedianentertainment.com

Digital Animations - DAG plc
The Lighthouse
70 Mitchell Street
Glasgow
G1 3LX
Tel: +44 (0) 141 582 0600
Fax: +44 (0) 141 582 0699
Web:
http://www.digital-animations.co.uk

Digital Anvil
316 Congress Avenue
Austin, Texas 78701
United States
Tel: 1-512-457-0129
Fax: 1-512-457-0404
Web: http://www.digitalanvil.com

Digital Art Media
411 Softopia Japan
Dream Core
6-52-16, Imajuku, Ogaki City
Gifu Prefecture - 503-0807
Japan
Web: http://www.hiddendinosaur.com

Digital Art Media
3025 W, Olympic Blvd.
Santa Monica, California 90404
Tel: 1-310-828-1386
Fax: 1-310-828-4956
Web: http://www.digitalartmedia.com

Digital Art Media
120 Wood Avenue South, Suite 300
Iselin, New Jersey 08830
Tel: 1-732-603-7781
Fax: 1-732-603-7769
Web: http://www.digitalartmedia.com

Digital Art Media
Compudyne House
7th Mile Stone, Kudalu Gate
Hosur Road
Bangalore, Karnataka
India
560068
Tel: +91 80.57.34.73.7
Fax: +91 80.57.34.74.2
Web: http://www.digitalartmedia.com

Digital Artisan
2 Barr-Smith Drive
Urrbrae 5064
Australia
Tel: +61 8 8379 6698
Fax: +61 8 8379 6698
Web:http://www.digitalartisan.com.au

Digital Artisan Pty Ltd
3/8 Flame Crt
Teringie, SA Australia
5072
Tel: +61 8.83.31.79.36
Fax: +61 8.83.31.79.36
Web:http://www.digitalartisan.com.au

Digital Character Group
Box 411
Pacific Palisades, California
90272
United States
Tel: 1-310-459-4390
Fax: 1-310-459-5166
Web:
http://www.digitalcharactergroup.com

Digital Content Development
Corporation Limited
Rm 407, Festival Walk 80 Tat
Chee Avenue
Kowloon, Hong Kong
Tel: (852) 2265 7813
Fax: (852) 2265 8687
Web: http://www.dcdcorp.com

Digital Context AB
Revingevagen 2
247 31 Sodra Sandby
Tel: 046-574 00
Fax: 046-574 25
Web: http://www.digitalcontext.se

Digital Design Multimedia
Via Malaspina, 30
90145 Palermo
Italy
Tel: 39 091 6812443
Web:http://www.netdigitaldesign.com

Digital Dimension
210 N. Pass Ave.
Burbank, California 91505
United States
Tel: 1-818-845-2866
Fax: 1-818-845-2894
Web:http://www.digitaldimension.com

Digital DK Studios
Corporate Headquarters
9350 South Western
Oklahoma City, Oklahoma 73159
United States
Tel: 1-405-413-5588
Fax: 1-405-947-8169
Web: http://www.digitaldk.com

Digital Domain
300 Rose Avenue
Venice, California 90291
United States
Tel: 1-310-314-2800
Fax: 1-310-314-2888
Web: http://www.digitaldomain.com

Digital D'go
354 Water Street, Suite 400
St. John's Newfoundland A1C
6J9
Canada
Tel: 1-709-754-1020
Fax: 1-709-754-3003
Web: http://www.digital-dgo.com

Digital Dreams & Visions, Ltd.
19 Ashness Close
Preston
Lancashire
United Kingdom
PR2 9FQ
Tel: +44 177.27.17.51.5
Fax: +44 177.27.17.51.6
Web: http://www.ddv.co.uk

Digital Element, Inc.
554 56th Street
Oakland, California 94609
United States
Tel: 1-510-601-7878
Fax: 1-510-601-7878
Web: http://www.digi-element.com

Digital Film Labs
940 N. Orange Dr., Suite 111
Hollywood, California 90038-2316
United States
Tel: 1-323-960-0137
Fax: 1-323-960-0087
Web: http://www.digitalfilmlabs.com

Digital FilmWorks
3330 Cahuenga Boulevard West,
Suite 300
Los Angeles, California 90068
United States
Tel: 1-213-874-9981
Fax: 1-213-874-3916
Web: http://www.dfw-la.com

DigitalFish Films
San Francisco, California
United States
Web: http://www.digitalfish.com

Digital Frontier
7F Neilsen Building
1-1-71, Nakameguro
Meguro-ku
Tokyo
Japan
Tel: 03-3794-2476
Fax: 03-3794-2472
Web: http://www.dfx.co.jp

Digital FX, Inc.
6010 Perkins Road, Suite B.
Baton Rouge, Louisiana 70808
United States
Tel: 1-225-763-6010
Tel: 1-888-898-6010
Fax: 1-225-763-6059
Web: http://www.digitalfxinc.com

Digital Gothica
1654 Dahill Road, 2nd Floor
Brooklyn, New York 11223
United States
Tel: 1-718-375-0816
Web: http://www.digitalgothica.com

Digital Graphics sprl
Umé Marc
49, rue François Cornet
4340 Awans
Tel: +32 (4) 247 29 01
Fax: +32 (4) 247 13 17
Web: http://www.digitalgraphics.be

Digital Illusion Studios
3923 N. Oleander Ave.
Chicago, Illinois 60634
United States
Tel: 1-773-625-2508
Web:
http://www.digitalillusionstudio.com

Digital Kitchen
350 W. Ontario, 6th Floor
Chicago, Illinois 60610
United States
Tel: 1-312-379-3999
Fax: 1-312-379-3998
Web: http://www.d-kitchen.com

Digital Kitchen
1114 E. Pike, 3rd Floor
Seattle, Washington 98122
United States
Tel: 1-206-0400
Fax: 1-206-267-0401
Web: http://www.d-kitchen.com

Digital Kitchen
63 Market Street
Venice, California 90291
United States
Tel: 1-310-396-7446
Fax: 1-310-460-7252
Web: http://www.d-kitchen.com

Digital Lab (The)
901 Abbot Kinney Boulevard
Venice, California 90291
United States

Tel: 1-310-399-5670
Fax: 1-310-399-1334
Web: http://www.digitallab.com

Digital Magic Limited
Shop 68, Ground Floor, Victoria Centre
15 Watson Road, Causeway Bay
Hong Kong
Tel: +852.25.70.90.16
Fax: +852.28.07.36.19
Web:http://www.digitalmagic.com.hk

Digital Media Factory, Inc. Head Office
1831-1 Oroku
Naha City, Okinawa 901-0152
Japan
Tel: +81(98) 859-7416
Fax: +81(98) 859-7417
Web: http://www.dmf.co.jp

Digital Media Factory, Inc. Tokyo
Production Office
3-25-9 B Wing, Ebisu
Shibuya
Tokyo 150-0013
Japan
Tel: +81(3) 5297-8661
Fax: +81(3) 5297-8662
Web: http://www.dmf.co.jp

Digital Media Lab., Inc.
Tokyo, Japan
Tel: 03-5759-7970
Fax: 03-5759-7979
Web: http://www.dml.co.jp

Digital Nightmare Arts
P.O. Box 19204
Reno, Nevada 89511
United States
Web: http://www.dnightmare.com

Digital Pictures
180 Bank Street
South Melbourne
Victoria 3205
Australia
Tel: +61 3 9251 1600
Fax: +61 3 9690 3734
Web:
http://www.aavdigitalpictures.com.au

Digital Production Solutions
520 Broad Street
Newark, New Jersey 07102
United States
Tel: 1-973-438-1000
Fax: 1-973-438-1525
Web: http://www.digitalproduction-
solutions.com

Digital Progression
Suite 5: Pine Court
36 Garvis Road
Bournemouth
Dorset BH1 3DH
United Kingdom
Web:http://www.digitalprogression.co.uk

Digital Reality
Roppentyu utca 53.
LogoTrade Centre, 2nd floor
1139 Budapest
Hungary
Tel: +36 1-2884080
Fax: +36-1-2884085
Web: http://www.digitalreality.hu

Digital Systems GmbH
Mahlmannstraße 1-3
04107 Leipzig
Germany
Tel: +49-341-9956200
Tel: +49-341-9956202
Web: http://www.disy.de

Digital Tech Frontier, LLC
4844 South 40th Street
Phoenix, Arizona 85040
United States
Tel: 1-800-778-7871
Fax: 1-480-730-5636
Web: http://www.dtf.net

Digital Video Arts
4901 Belfort Road Suite #165
Jacksonville, Florida 32256
United States
Tel: 1-904-281-1001
Tel: 1-888-340-1010
Fax: 1-904-281-0051
Web:http://www.digitalvideoarts.com

Digital Vide0 Inc.
4768 Ardley Drive
Colorado Springs, Colorado
80922
United States
Tel: 1-719-380-7085
Web: http://www.digitalvide0.com

Digit Digit Limited
1/F Catic plaza
8 Causeway Road
Causeway Bay
Hong Kong
Tel: (852) 2882-4939
Fax: (852) 2577-3797
Web: http://www.digitdigit.com

Digits 'n Art Software Inc.
305 de la Commune st. west,
suite 100
Montreal, Quebec
Canada H2Y 2E1
Tel: 1-514-844-8448
Fax: 1-514-844-8844
Web: http://www.dnasoft.com

Digitrick Gerd Wanie
Feurigstrasse 22
Berlin-Schoenberg
Germany 10827
Web: http://www.digitrick.de

Dimedia - digital media GmbH
Olschewskibogen 7
80935 München
Germany
Tel: 089-357750-00
Fax: 089-357750-22
Web: http://www.dimedia.de

Dimensions Edge Studios, Inc.
257-2906 West Broadway
Vancouver, British Columbia
Canada
V6K 2G8
Tel: +1 604.738.0080
Fax: +1 604.742.2093
Web: http://www.sights.com

Direct Images Interactive, Inc.
1933 Davis Street, Suite 285
San Leandro, California 94577
United States
Tel: 1-510-613-8299
Fax: 1-510-613-8297
Web: http://www.directimages.com

DirecTV — Level13.net
12020 Chandler Boulevard, Suite 300
North Hollywood, California
91607
United States
Tel: 1-818-761-2544 x265
Fax: 1-818-752-1274
Web: http://www.level13.net

Distant Places
1433 Franklin St. Suite 6
Santa Monica, California 90404
United States
Tel: 1-310-453-4748
Web: http://www.dplaces.com

Distillery Post
1610 Midtown Place
Raleigh, North Carolina 27609
United States
Tel: 1-919-873-9333
Fax: 1-919-875-0703
Web: http://www.distillerypost.com

Django Studios
Van Eeghenstraat 80
Amsterdam, Netherlands
Tel: +31 20.30.52.52.5
Fax: +31 20.30.52.52.0
Web: http://www.django.com

DJUNGO Productions
Rollewagenstratt 30
1800 Vilvorde
Belgium
Tel: +32 2 609 01 00
Fax: +32 2 609 01 01
Web: http://www.iim.be

DKP Effects
489 Queen Street East
Toronto, Ontario
Canada

M5A 1V1
Tel: 1-416-861-9269
Fax: 1-416-363-3301
Web: http://www.dkp.com

DMA Animation
89 Fifth Avenue, Suite 501
New York, New York 10003
United States
Tel: 1-212-463-7370
Fax: 1-212-463-7820
Web:http://www.dma-animation.com

DNA Productions
2201 West Royal Lane, Suite 275
Irving, Texas 75063
United States
Tel: 1-214-352-4694
Fax: 1-214-496-9333
Web: http://www.dnahelix.com

Dopesheet Media
8 Kathleen Ave
Alpeerton
London, United Kingdom
Tel: +44 797.70.45.01.4
Web: http://www.dopesheet.co.uk

Don Flynn Pictures
Four Broadcast Place
Jacksonville, Florida 32247
United States
Tel: 1-904-398-9820
Fax: 1-904-398-2998
Web:http://www.donflynnpictures.com

Dotfx Design Studio
201 E Seapark Appartment
Jln21/13
Petaling Jaya, Selangor Malaysia
46300
Tel: +60 3.78.77.62.29
Web: http://www.dotfxstudio.com

D.P. Associates Inc.
3401 Columbia Pike
Arlington, Virginia 22204-4211
United States
Tel: 1-703-521-6236
Fax: 1-703-521-6899
Web: http://www.dpatraining.com

DPI Animation House
Javastraat 2C
2585 AM
Den Haag
The Netherlands
Tel: +31 (0)70 3460679
Fax: +31 (0)70 4275554
Web: http://www.dpi.nl

Dragon Lake
68 Jackman drive
Brampton, Ontario Canada
L6S 2M2
Tel: +1 416.885.3713
Fax: +1 905.799.3817
Web: http://www.dragonlakeinc.com

Drakssen
Rodriguez Peña 1442,
Castelar, Buenos Aires, 1712
Argentina
Tel: +54-1146281682
Web: http://www.drakssen.com.ar

Dreamlab Imagineering
3131 Turtle Creek Blvd. Suite 301
Dallas, Texas 75219-5432
United States
Tel: 1-214-562-3080
Fax: 1-214-562-3084
Web: http://dreamlab.com

Dreamlight Imaging
376 Crown Street
Surry Hils NSW 2010
Sydney
Australia
Tel: +61 2 9331 2999
Fax: +61 2 9331 5399
Web:http://www.dreamlightimaging.com

DreamOne
Helsinki, Finland
Web: http://www.dreamone.com

Dreamteam Productions Inc.
8-13-19, Suite308
Akasaka, Minato-ku
Tokyo 107-0052
Japan
Tel: 01 1-81-3-5413-7744

Fax: 01 1-81-3-5413-7745
Web:
http://www2.gol.com/users/drmteam

Dream Theater
30699 Russell Ranch Road, Suite 190
Westlake Village, California
91362
United States
Tel: 1-818-707-3660
Fax: 1-818-707-6815
Web: http://www.dreamtheater.com

Dream Theater, LLC
21700 Oxnard St, Penthouse
Suite, No. 2040
Woodland Hills, California 91367
United States
Tel: 1-818-716-2775
Fax: 1-818-716-2776
Web: http://www.dreamtheater.com

Dreamheavenpictures
Chemin Coulee pain
Quartier Long Bois
Saint Joseph, Martinique
97212
Tel: +596.57.69.50
Fax: +1 775.25.26.25.0
Web:
http://www.dreamheavenpictures.com

Dreamworks Animation
Universal Plaza Building 10
Universal City, California 91608
United States
Tel: 1-818-733-6142
Fax: 1-818-733-6377
Web: http://www.dreamworks.com

DreamWorks SKG
1000 Flower Street
Glendale, California 90201
United States
Tel: 1-818-733-7000
Fax: 1-818-695-7199
Web: http://www.dreamworks.com

Driscal Designs
P.O. Box 1878
Fairfield, California 94585

United States
Tel: 1-707-864-1944
Fax: 1-707-864-1944
Web: http://www.driscal.com

Droidworx
Hungary
Tel: +36 1 239-6488
Fax: +36 1 239-6699
Web: http://www.droidworx.hu

Dr. PICTURE Studios
Sofiyskaya nab. 34D, office 401
115035, Moscow, Russia
Tel: +7 (095) 775 1973
Fax: +7 (095) 775 1973
Web: http://www.drpicture.com

Duck Soup Studios
2205 Stoner Ave.
Los Angeles, California 90064
United States
Tel: 1-310-478-0771
Fax: 1-310-478-0773
Web: http://www.ducksoupla.com

Dub Media, Inc.
150 Tasso Street
Palo Alto, California 94301 -1228
United States
Web: http://www.dubmedia.com

Dub Media, Inc.
2674 North First St, Ste 106
San Jose, California 95134
United States
Tel: 1-408-954-8158
Web: http://www.dubmedia.com

Duboi
68, rue Pierre
Saint-Ouen
France
93400
Tel: +33 1.49.48.12.40
Fax: +33 1.49.48.12.44
Web: http://www.duboi.com

Duboi Digital Special Effects
221 bis
boulevard Jean Jaures
92100 Boulogne Billancourt
France
Tel: 33 (0)1 58 17 50 70
Fax: 33 (0)1 58 17 50 90
Web: http://www.duboi.com

Duck Soup Studios
2205 Stoner Avenue
Los Angeles, California 90064
United States
Tel: 1-310-478-0771
Fax: 1-310-478-0773
Web: http://www.ducksoupla.com

Dupis Audiovisuel
Rue J Destree 52
Marcinelle 6001
Belgium
Tel: 01 1-32-71 -600-51 7
Fax: 011-32-71-600-519
Web:
http://www.dupuis-entertainment.com

Duran
35, rue Gabriel Péri
92130 Issy les Moulineaux
Tél: 33 (0)1 45 29 99 99
Fax: 33 (0)1 45 29 99 98
Web: http://www.dunet.com

DYGRAfilms
Gran Vía 31, 9°, desp. 3
28013 Madrid - España
Tel: (+34) 91 521 30 18
Fax: (+34) 91 522 79 93
Web: http://www.dygrafilms.es

DYGRAfilms
General Sanjurjo, 215 1°
15006 A Coruña - España
Tel: (+34) 981 12 20 05
Fax: (+34) 981 12 03 16
Web: http://www.dygrafilms.es

Dygra Films
Linares Rivas 9
La Coruna, Spain
15004

Tel: +34 91.52.13.50.8
Fax: +34 91.52.27.99.3
Web: http://www.dygrafilms.com

Dynomight Cartoons
205 Catherine St.
Ottawa, Ontario Canada
K2P 1C3
Tel: +1 613.231.6337
Fax: +1 613.233.6634
Web: http://www.dynomight.com

Dynamic Animation Systems, Inc.
12015 Lee Jackson Highway, Suite 200
Fairfax, Virginia 22033
United States
Tel: 1-703-503-0500
Fax: 1-703 425-2204
Web: http://www.d-a-s.com

Dynamic Animation Systems, Inc.
6035 Burke Centre Parkway, Suite 200
Burke, Virginia 22015
United States
Tel: 1-703-503-0500
Fax: 1-703-425-2204
Web: http://www.d-a-s.com

Dynamo Graphics
214 4th Street
Downers Grove, Illinios 60515
United States
Tel: 1-630-852-2817
Fax: 1-630-852-2807
Web:
http://www.dynamographics.com

DYTE s.r.l. via G. Porzio,
C.D.N. Is. E3
80143 Napoli
Italy
Tel: +39-081-5627320
Tel: +39-081-5627515
Fax: +39-081-5627984
Web: http://www.dyte.it

Dzignlight Studios
621 North Avenue NE, A100
Atlanta, Georgia 30308
United States
Tel: 1-404-892-8933

Fax: 1-404-892-8991
Web: http://www.dzignlight.com

e-3Dimensions Pvt LTD,
602, 6th Floor,
Barton Center,
M. G. Road,
Bangalore 560001
Karnataka
India
Tel: 091-080-5320371
Tel: 091-080-5320381
Tel: 091-080-5091256
Web:http://www.e-3dimensions.com

Eagle Video Productions Inc.
2201 Woodnell Drive
Raleigh, North Carolina 27603-5240
United States
Tel: 1-919-779-7891
Fax: 1-919-779-7284
Web: http://www.eaglevideo.com

Easy Film
Solvgade 32
1307 Kobenhavn K.
Tel: 33 44 74 00
Fax: 33 91 05 25
Web: http://www.easyfilm.dk

Eboncourt Entertainment, LLC.
3876 Rockfield Court
Carlsbad, California 92008
United States
Tel: 1-760-729-2297
Fax: 1-760-729-2297
Web: http://www.eboncourt.com

Eclipse Computacao Grafica
Ltda.
Rua Dr. Antonio Silveira Brum Jr, 10/23
Shopping Vitrines
Centro
Muriae, MG
Brazil
36880-000
Tel: +55 32.37.21.93.29
Web: http://www.eclipseonline.com.br

Eclipse (Creative) Limited
Pascoe House
54 Bute Street
Cardiff Bay
Cardiff
CF10 5AF
United Kingdom
Tel: +44 (0) 29 20470070
Fax: +44 (0) 29 20470071
Web: http://www.eclipsecreative.co.uk

ECS
11315 Corporate Blvd. Suite 110
Orlando, Florida 32817
United States
Tel: 1-407-823-9991
Web: http://www.www.ecsorl.com

Eden FX
6337 Santa Monica Boulevard
Hollywood, California 90038
United States
Tel: 1-323-957-6900
Fax: 1-323-957-6956
Web: http://www.edenfx.com

Edgeworx
304 Hudson Street
New York, New York 10013
United States
Tel: 1-212-334-3334
Fax: 1-212-334-3512
Web: http://www.edgeworx.com

Edgeworx
18 Soho Square
London
W1D 3QL
United Kingdom
Tel: 020-7025-8050
Fax: 020-7025-8155
Web: http://www.edgeworx.com

Edward Lee Productions, Inc.
15225 104th Ave, Suite 310
Vancouver, British Columbia
Canada
V3R 6Y8
Tel: +1 604.589.5270
Fax: +1 604.588.1555
Web: http://www.elpmedia.com

eee european electronic effects
GmbH
Vestische Strasse 46
Oberhausen, Germany
46117
Tel: +49 20.88.99.00
Fax: +49 20.89.01.19
Web: http://www.triple-e-vfx.com

EffectsOne, Inc.
4091 E. La Palma Ave. Suite #F
Anaheim, California 92807
United States
Tel: 1-714-630-4425
Web: http://www.efxone.com

Effetti Digitali
Via Legano, 26
20121 Milano
Italy
Tel: +39 02 29061316
Fax: +39 02 6555682
Web: http://www.effettidigitali.it

Egmont Imagination DK
Rentemestervej 2
2400 Copenhagen NV
Tel: +45 3586 0586
Fax: +45 3586 0585
Web: http://www.imagination.dk

eIMAGE
San Francisco, California 94110
United Sates
Tel: 1-415-282-9829
Fax: 1-415-282-9493
Web: http://www.eimage.com

Eleventh Hour Animation
8305 Keystone Avenue
Skokie, Illinios 60076
United States
Tel: 1-847-674-6007
Fax: 1-847-674-6051
Web:
http://www.eleventhhouranimation.com

Electric Crayon Studio
902 W. Eula Ct.
Glendale, Wisconsin 53209
United States

Tel: 1-414-964-6072
Fax: 1-414-964-5982
Web:http://www.electriccrayonstudio.com

Electric Umbrella Interaktive
Medien GmbH
Magdeburger Straße 13
20457 Hamburg
Germany
Tel: + 49 40 30 37 53 3
Fax: + 49 40 32 52 76 29
Web: http://www.electric-umbrella.de

Elephant Productions
2 Rothamsted Avenue
Harpenden, Hertfordshire United
Kingdom
AL5 2DB
Tel: +44 158.26.21.42.5
Fax: +44 158.26.21.42.5
Web: http://elephantproductions.com

Ellipsanime
45, rue Linois
Paris, France
75015
Tel: +33 1.43.92.57.00
Fax: +33 1.43.92.57.01
Web: http://www.ellipsanime.com

Ellipse Deutschland GmbH
Bismarckstrasse 108
D-10625 Berlin
Germany
Tel: + 49 30 31 00 05 54
Fax: + 49 30 31 00 05 60
Web:
http://www.ellipsedeutschland.com

Ellipse Deutschland GmbH
Kaiser-Wilhelm-Ring 27-29
D-50672 Köln
Germany
Tel: + 49 2 21 5 69 44 19
Fax: + 49 2 21 5 69 42 00
Web:
http://www.ellipsedeutschland.com

Ellipse Deutschland GmbH
Abendrothsweg 19
D-20251 Hamburg
Germany
Tel: + 49 40 41 35 48 46
Fax: + 49 40 41 35 48 47
Web:
http://www.ellipsedeutschland.com

Ellipse Deutschland GmbH
Schönfeldstrasse 8
D-80539 München
Germany
Tel: + 49 89 28 81 10 70
Fax: + 49 89 28 81 10 24
Web:
http://www.ellipsedeutschland.com

Emagination-Media
225 Andover Way
Nashville, Tennessee 37221
United States
Tel: 1-615-662-6540
Web:
http://www.emagination-media.com

EMA Multimedia, Inc.
1800 Ave. of the Stars, Suite 430
Century City, California 90067
United States
Tel: 1-310-277-7379
Fax: 1-310-277-7378
Web:http://www.emamultimedia.com

EMIX Inc.
6 Chome, 16-11 AS building
Nakano Ku, Tokyo 164-0012
Japan
Web: http://www.emix.ne.jp

Emotion Studio
Balmes 156 ppal_2-a
Barcelona, Spain
08008
Tel: +34 93.41.55.56.6
Web: http://www.emotionstudio.com

Encore Visual Effects
6344 Fountain Avenue
Hollywood, California 90028
United States

Tel: 1-323-466-7663
Fax: 1-323-467-5539
Web: http://www.encorevideo.com

Encuadre S.A.
3 de febrero 2841
Capital Federal
Buenos Aires
Argentina
Tel: (5411) 4787 3500
Web: http://www.encuadre.com.ar

Endless Mountains Productions, Inc.
RD#1, Box 102M
New Milford, Pennsylvania 18834
United States
Tel: 1-570-434-5000
Fax: 1-570-434-4000
Web: http://www.empstudios.com

Energee Entertainment
Unit 1
706 Mowbray Road
Lane Cove
NSW 2066
Sydney
Australia
Tel: 9420 8864
Fax: 9420 8861
Web: http://www.energee.com.au

Energon FX
7355 Griffith Lane
Moorpark, California 93021
United States
Tel: 1-805-657-5586
Web: http://www.energonfx.com

Engineering & Computer
Simulations
11315 Corporate Boulevard, Suite 110
Orlando, Florida 32817
United States
Tel: 1-407-823-9991
Tel: 1-877-823-9991
Fax: 1-407-823-8299
Web: http://www.ecsorl.com

Engine Pty Ltd
47 Herbert St
Artarmon

NSW 2064
Sydney Australia
Tel: 612 9438 2000
Fax: 612 9439 5957
Web: http://www.engine.net.au

English & Pockett
McCann-Erickson House
7-11 Herbrand Street
London
WC1N 1EX
United Kingdom
Tel: +44 (0)20 7961 2828
Web: http://www.english-pockett.com

Eng Videohouse N.V.
Luchthavenlaan 22
B-1800 Vilvoorde
Belgium
Tel: 32 (0)2/254.48.11
Fax: 32 (0)2/254.48.16
Web: http://www.videohouse.be

Enoki Films USA, Inc.
16430 Ventura Blvd., Suite 308
Encino, California 91436,
United States
Tel: 1-818-907-6503
Fax: 1-818-907-6506
Web: http://www.enokifilmsusa.com

ENTEC GmbH
Rathausallee 11
53757 Sankt Augustin
Germany
Tel: +49 (0) 2241/924870
Fax: +49 (0) 2241/924877
Web: http://www.entec.de

Entity
1540 7th Street, Suite 300
Santa Monica, California 90401
United States
Tel: 1-310-899-9779
Fax: 1-310-899-3113
Web: http://www.entityfx.com

Enxebre Sistemas, s.l.
c/San Andres 56, 3-E
La Coruna, Spain
15003
Tel: +34 981.22.05.24
Fax: +34 981.20.50.46
Web: http://www.enxebre.es

Enzyme
4000, Saint Ambroise Street, Suite 144
Montréal, Québec H4C 2C7
CANADA
Tel: 1-514-288-3976
Fax: 1-514-288-5125
Web: http://www.enzyme.org

EM.TV & Merchandising
Betastrasse 11
D-85774 Unterföhring
Germany
Tel.: 01149-89-957-150
Fax: 011-49 89-957-150-111
Web: http://www.em-ag.de

Epic Software Group, Inc.
710 Sawdust Road
The Woodlands, Texas 77380
United States
Tel: 1-281-363-3742
Fax: 1-281-292-9700
Web: http://www.epicsoftware.com

EPX Generator
835 Grant Street, Suite 3
Santa Monica, California 90405
United States
Tel: 1-310-384-1680
Web: http://www.epxgen.com

Eriktek Inc
10911 Bleanfield Street, Suite 8
Toluca Lake, California 91602
United States
Tel: 1-818-508-4616
Fax: 1-818-760-0069
Web: http://www.eriktek.com

Ernie Berger Animation
P.O. Box 148
Arnold, Maryland 21012
United States

Tel: 1-410-757-8377
Fax: 1-410-757-9168
Web: http://www.ErnieBerger.com

ESC Entertainment
PO Box 720
Oakland, California 94604
United States
Tel: 1-510-749-7300
Web: http://www.escfx.com

ESI Productions LLC
673 Berkmar Court
Charlottesville, Virginia 22901
United States
Tel: 1-434-817-2700
Fax: 1-434-817-1114
Web: http://www.esiproductions.com

Essential Reality, LLC
253 West 28th Street, 2nd Floor
New York, New York 10001
United States
Tel: 1-212-244-3200
Fax: 1-212-244-9550
Web: http://www.essentialreality.com

Eternal Illusions Graphics
159 1st Cross, Karnataka Layout
Mahalakshmipuram
Bangalore, Karnataka India
560086
Tel: +91 80.32.28.97.1
Fax: +91 80.32.28.97.1
Web: http://www.eternalillusions.com

Etiam EMedia Inc
4633 Old Ironsides Dr, Suite 450
Santa Clara, California 95054
United States
Tel: 1-408-235-8999 x231
Fax: 1-408-235-8777
Web: http://www.etiam.net

E to E Graphics and Visuals
Kleterstratt 11a
3862 CA Nijkerk
The Netherlands
Tel: 033 264 21 13
Fax: 033 264 20 34
Web: http://www.e-to-e.nl

Eulogix
1140 Cypress Station
Houston, Texas 77090
United States
Tel: 1-281-397-2888
Fax: 1-281-444-8816
Web: http://www.eulogix.com

euNoia
Moliere 450A-Int.101,
Col Polanco
Mexico, D.F.
Tel: 5255-5203-0030
Fax: 5255-5203-0073
Web: http://www.eunoia.tv

EUREKA Televisión y Video
Martín de Gainza 517 2B
Buenos Aires, Capital Federal
Argentina
1405
Tel: +54 11.15.41.82.07.98
Fax: +54 11.15.51.41.59.24
Web: http://www.eurekatv.com.ar

Ex-Centris
3536 Boul Saint-Laurent
Montreal, Quebec
Canada
H2X 2V1
Tel: 1-514-847-2206
Fax: 1-514-847-3536
Web: http://www.ex-centris.com

Ex Machina
22, Rue HG Sippe Moreau
Paris 75018
France
Tel: 011-33-14-490-1190
Fax: 011-33-14-490-1191
Web: http://www.exmachina.fr

Expand Images
89 rue Escudier
92100 Boulogne-Billancourt
France
Tel: 011-33-0-1-4712-4040
Fax: 011-33-0-1-4712-4094
Web: http://www.expand.fr

ExtraTainment
TRC Development b.v.
Rotterdam Airport
Airportplein 2
Rotterdam
Netherlands
3045
Tel: +31 10.43.90.20.0
Fax: +31 10.43.90.21.0
Web: http://www.extratainment.com

Eye Animation Studios
Kirkman House
12 / 14 Whitfield Street
London
W1T 2RF
United Kingdom
Tel: +44 (0) 207 248 2367
Web: http://www.eye-animation.com

Eyes Post Group
320 King Street
Toronto, Ontario M5A 1K6
Canada
Tel: 1-416-363-3073
Fax: 1-416-363-6335
Web: http://www.eyespost.com

Eyevox
279 A South Perkins Street
Ridgeland, Mississippi
United States
Tel: 1-601-853-7270
Web: http://www.eyevox.com

Face s.r.l., The
V.le Monterosa 64
20149 Milan
Italy
Tel: ++39-0248011-294
Fax: ++39-024982268
Web: http://www.bluegold.it

Fat Box Films
499 Seaport Court, 2nd Floor
Redwood City, California 94063
United States
Tel: 1-650-363-8700
Fax: 1-650-363-8860
Web: http://www.fatbox.com

Farabi Cinema Foundation
55 Sie-Tir St.
Tehran 11358
Iran
Tel.: +98 21 670 81 56
Tel: +98 21 670 10 10,
Fax: +98 21 670 81 55
Web: http://www.fcf-ir.com

Farm, The
27 Upper Mount St.
Dublin 2
Ireland
Tel: +3531 6768812
Fax: +3531 6768816
Web: http://www.thefarm.ie

Farmtoons Production
Via di Valle Muricana 920
Rome, Italy
00188
Web: http://www.farmtoons.com

Farrington Lewis
Unit 1&2 Bristol Vale Industrial
Estate
Bedminster
Bristol
Co Bristol
England
BS3 5RJ
United Kingdom
Tel: 0117 9661966
Fax: 0117 9662066
Web: http://www.farrington-lewis.com

Faux Real LLC
2215 Little Lane
Arden, Delaware 19810
United States
Tel: 1-302-529-1516
Fax: 1-302-529-7913
Web: http://www.fauxreal.com

Fawn Mountain Creative Media
26763 Fawn Mountain Rd.
Boerne, Texas 78015
United States
Tel: 1-210-698-1191
Web: http://www.fawnmountain.com

Felix Productions
Via Vogel, 27
62019 - Recanati (MC)
Tel: 0717572984 - 3395005035
Web:http://www.felixproductions.com

Fenix Animation
Les Galeries
13 rue de la RÈpublique
Arles, France
13200
Tel: +33 4.90.52.23.63
Fax: +33 4.90.93.17.71
Web: http://www.fenix.fr

Fido Film AB
Stadsgarden 17
Stockholm, Sweden
118 56
Tel: +46 8.55.69.90.00
Fax: +46 8.55.69.90.01
Web: http://www.fido.se

Field Of Vision
45 Bevers Brook Road
London
N194QQ
United Kingdom
Tel: +44(0)171-263-5054
Fax: +44(0)171-272-6021
Web: http://www.cix.co.uk/~fov

Fiftyeight 3D
Unter Den Eichen 5
65195 Wiesbaden
Germany
Tel: +49(0)611/933358-0
Fax: +49(0)611/933358-81
Web: http://www.fiftyeight.com

FilmCore Editorial
1222 6th Street
Santa Monica, California 90401
United States
Tel: 1-310-587-2400
Fax: 1-310-587-2401
Web: http://www.filmcore.com

FilmCore Editorial
545 Samsome Street
San Francisco, California 9411
United States
Tel: 1-415-392-6300
Fax: 1-415-392-2600
Web: http://www.filmcore.com

Film Effects Inc.
21 Phoebe St.
Toronto, Ontario Canada
M5T 1A8
Tel: +1 416.598.3456
Fax: +1 416.598.7895
Web: http://www.filmeffects.com

FILMGRAPHICS
100 Chandos St. Crows Nest
2065
Sydney Australia
Tel: 612-9439-4233
Fax: 612-9439-8701
Web: http://www.filmgraphics.com

Film Magic Limited
Room 802, Block A, Seaview Estate
2-8 Watson Road, North Point
Hong Kong
Tel: (852) 2571-5432
Fax: (852) 2807-3619
Web: http://www.filmmagic.com.hk

Film Roman
12020 Chandler Blvd. Suite 300
North Hollywood, California
91607
United States
Tel: 1-818-761-2544
Fax: 1-81 8-752-1274
Web: http://www.filmroman.com

Filmtecknarna F. Animation AB
Malmgårdsvägen 16-18
S-116 38 Stockholm
Sweden
Tel: +46 8 442 7300
Fax: +46 442 7319
Web: http://www.filmtecknarna.se

Filmax International
81-87 Poligino Pedrosa

L'Hospitalet de Llobregat
Barcelona, Spain
08908
Tel: +34 93.33.68.55.5
Fax: +34 93.26.30.82.4
Web:
http://www.filmaxinternational.com

FilmTecknarna Animation
Malmgardsvagen 16-18
Stockholm, Sweden
11638
Tel: +46 8.44.27.30.0
Fax: +46 8.44.27.31.9
Web: http://www.filmtecknarna.com

Finale Studios
2125 Biscayne Blvd. Suite 215
Miami, Florida 33137
United States
Tel: 1-305-576-3538
Web: http://www.finalestudios.com

FINNesse Productions Inc.
948 Roche Point Drive
North Vancouver, British
Columbia Canada
V7H 2T7
Tel: +1 604.230.9585
Fax: +1 604.988.7716
Web: http://www.finnesse.net

Firefly Entertainment
6-3-596/90, Naveen Nagar
Banjara Hills
Hyderabad, Andhra Pradesh
India
500004
Tel: +91 40.33.70.50.4
Web: http://www.fireflyworld.com

Fire Horse Studio
Sydney, Australia
Tel: 1-612-9949-2525
Web: http://www.firehorse.net.au

Firewalk Digital
PO Box 1865
Oakhurst, California 93644
United States
Tel: 1-818-585-2211
Web: http://www.firewalkdigital.com

Fireworks Entertainment
111 George Street 3rd Floor
Toronto, Ontario
Canada M5A 2n4
Tel: 1-416-360-4321
Fax: 1-416-364-4388
Web: http://www.watchfireworks.com

Fireworks Television
421 South Beverly Drive 8th Floor
Beverly Hills, California 90212
United States
Tel: 1-310-789-4750
Fax: 1-310-789-4799
Web: http://www.watchfireworks.com

Fireworks Pictures
421 South Beverly Drive 7th Floor
Beverly Hills, California 90212
United States
Tel: 1-310-789-4700
Fax: 1-310-789-4747
Web: http://www.watchfireworks.com

Fireworks International
Tennyson House
159-165 Great Portland Street
Fifth Floor (South)
London
W1W 5PA
United Kingdom
Tel: 011-44-207-307-6300
Fax: 011-44-207-307-6399
Web:http://www.watchfireworks.com

Fish Media Inc.
135 W 27th St. 6th Floor
New York, New York 10001
United States
Tel: 1-212-367-9337
Fax: 1-212-367-9538
Web: http://www.fishmediainc.com

Five Star Productions
430 South Congress Avenue
Delray Beach, Florida 33445
United States
Tel: 1-561-279-STAR
Fax: 1-561-279-4808
Web: http://www.vstar.com

Flamdoodle Animation Inc.
100 Principe de Paz
Santa Fe, New Mexico
87508-9211
United States
Tel: 1-505-982-3132
Fax: 1-505-982-3172
Web: http://www.flamdoodle.com

Flemming Borgen Animation
Jagtvej 51 4th
2200 KBHN
Denmark
Web: http://www.borgengfx.dk

Florida Studios
3200 West Oakland Park
Boulevard
Lauderdale Lakes, Florida 33311
United States
Tel: 1-954-714-8100
Fax: 1-954-714-8500
Web: http://floridastudios.com

FlickerLab
155 W. 20th, 4th Floor
New York, New York 10018
United States
Tel: 1-212-560-9228
Fax: 1-212-560-9253
Web: http://www.flickerlab.com

Flip Studio
232/3 rayer bazar, pathshala lane,
dhaka - 1209,
40, new elephant road, dhaka-1205
77/1,north dhanmondi, dhaka-1205
Dhaka, Bangladesh
1209
Tel: +880 2.81.17.02.5
Web: http://www.flipstudiobd.com

Flipside Editorial
3 Embarcadero Center,
Promenade Level, Suite1
San Francisco, California 94111
United States
Tel: 1-415-393-9435
Fax: 1-415-393-9611
Web: http://www.flipsidedit.com

Flipside Editorial
2403 Main Street
Santa Monica, California 90405
United States
Tel: 1-310-399-5959
Fax: 1-310-399-0012
Web: http://www.flipsidedit.com

Flix Animation
66 Holtermann Street
Crows Nest
Sydney, N.S.W Australia
2065
Tel: +61 2.94.39.66.66
Fax: +61 2.94.39.60.66
Web: http://www.flixanimation.com

Fluid Post
532 Broadway
New York, New York 10012
United States
Tel: 1-212-431-4342

Flux Animation Studio Ltd
33 George St., Newmarket
MBE P280,Auckland New
Zealand
Auckland, New Zealand
Tel: +64 9.36.81.50.6
Fax: +64 9.36.81.50.7
Web: http://www.fluxmedia.co.nz

FLUXgroup, Inc.
215 West Superior Street
Chicago, Illinois 60610
United States
Tel: 1-312-640-1111
Fax: 1-312-640-1018
Web: http://www.fluxgroup.com

Flying Foto Factory
P.O. Box 1166
Durham, North Carolina 27702
United States
Tel: 1-800-ff2-FOTO
Tel: 1-919-682-3411
Web: http://www.flyingfoto.com

Flying Foto Factory
107 Church Street
Durham, North Carolina 27702

United States
Tel: 1-800-ff2-FOTO
Tel: 1-919-682-3411
Web: http://www.flyingfoto.com

Flying Rhino Pictures
Box 416
Warrington, Pennsylvania 18976
United States
Tel: 1-215-343-4242
Web:
http://www.FlyingRhinoPictures.com

Flying Spot
1008 Western Avenue
Seattle, Washington 98104
United States
Tel: 1-206-464-0744
Web: http://www.flyingspot.com

Flying Tomato Films
Van Nuys, California 91401
United States
Tel: 1-818-386-0937
Web: http://www.flyingtomato.com

Fog Studio inc.
4000, rue St-Ambroise #279
Montreal, Quebec Canada
H4C 2C7
Tel: +1 514.846.8994
Fax: +1 514.846.8994
Web: http://www.fogstudio.com

Foolish Earthling Productions ltd.
411 Richmond St. East, Suite 205
Toronto, Ontario M5A 3S5
Canada
Tel: 1-416-594-3665
Fax: 1-416-363-8960
Web: http://www.foolishearthling.com

Foothill Entertainment, Inc.
1231 State Street, Suite 208
Santa Barbara, California 93101
United States
Tel: 1-805-965-4488
Fax: 1-805-965-1168
Web:
http://www.foothillentertainment.com

Force Four
#310-1152 Mainland St.,
Vancouver, British Columbia,
Canada, V6B 4X2
Tel: 1-604.669.4424
Fax:1-604.669.4535
Web: http://www.forcefour.com

Foretell Media, Ltd.
99 Holdenhurst Road
Bournemouth, Dorset United
Kingdom
BH8 8EB
Tel: +44 800.01.80.30.5
Fax: +44 120.23.11.50.2
Web: http://www.foretell.co.uk

Forged Images Productions
6 Davis Place
Bar Harbor, Maine 04609
United States
Tel: 1-207-288-5156
Web: http://www.forgedimages.com

Forum Visual Effects
12020 Chandler Blvd. Suite 300
North Hollywood, California
91607
United States
Tel: 1-818-761-2544
Fax: 1-818-508-6420
Web: http://www.filmroman.com

Foundation Imaging
24933 West Avenue Stanford
Valencia, California 91355
United States
Tel: 1-661-257-0292
Fax: 1-661-257-7966
Web: http://www.foundation-i.com

Foundation of the Hellenic World
38 Poulopoulou St.
11851 Athens
Greece
Tel: +30 210 34.22.292
Fax: +30 210.34.22.272
Web: http://www.fhw.gr

Foundation of the Hellenic World
Cultural Centre

254 Pireos St.
17778 Athens
Greece
Tel: +30 210 48.35.300
Fax: +30 210 48.34.634
Web: http://www.fhw.gr

Four Square Productions
5205 Kearny Villa Way
San Diego, California 92123
United States
Tel: 1-858-874-1900
Fax: 1-858-874-1901
Web: http://www.foursq.com

Four Square Productions
270 North Canon Drive, Suite
1531
Beverly Hills, California 90210
United States
Tel: 1-310-271-4020
Fax: 1-310-271-2192
Web: http://www.foursq.com

Four Square Productions
5205 Kearny Villa Way
San Diego, California 92123
Tel: 1-858-874-1900
Fax: 1-858-874-1901
Web: http://www.foursq.com

Fox Animation
104 Tudor Road
Hayes
London
United Kingdom
UB3 2QG
Tel: +44 208.57.30.87.9
Fax: +44 208.57.30.87.9
Web: http://www.fox-animation.co.uk

Fox Kids Europe
338 Euston Rd.
London, United Kingdom
NW1 3AZ
Tel: +44 207.55.49.49.2
Web: http://www.foxkids.co.uk

F Productions
6 Place de la Madeleine
Paris, 75008

France
Tel: 011-33-0-1-4260-6632
Fax: 011-33-0-1-4260-6634
Web: http://www.f-productions.com

Frame by Frame Italia S R L
Via Adolofo Rava, 124
00142 Rome
Italy
Tel: 01 1-39-6-596-4941
Fax: 01 1-39-6-541-1961
Web: http://www.frame.it

Frame Eleven
Schiffbaustrasse 10
Ch-8005 Zurich
Switzerland
Tel: +41 (0)1 444 3 444
Fax: +41 (0)1 444 3 445
Web: http://www.frame-eleven.com

Frame Eleven
8 west 19th street, suite 5c
New York, New York 10011
United States
Tel: 1-646-336-8300
Fax: 1-646-336-7525
Web: http://www.frame-eleven.com

Frame Set & Match
50 Strathallen Avenue
Northbridge NSW 2063
Australia
Tel: 612 8966 5000
Fax: 612 8966 5050
Web: http://www.fsm.com.au

Framestore CFC
9 Noel Street
London
England
W1F 8GH
Tel: 020 7208 2600
Fax: 020 7208 2626
Web: http://www.framestore-cfc.com

France 3
7, Esplanade Henri-de-France
Paris, France
75907
Tel: +33 1.56.22.75.35
Fax: +33 1.56.22.70.46
Web: http://www.france3.fr

Franklin Video, Inc.
302 Jefferson Street Suite 300
Raleigh, North Carolina 27605
United States
Tel: 1-919-833-8888
Fax: 1-919-833-0431
Web: http://www.franklinvideo.com

Frantic Films
300 - 70 Arthur Street
Winnipeg, Manitoba
Canada R3B 1G7
Tel: 1-204-949-0070
Fax: 1-204-949-0050
Web: http://www.franticfilms.com

Freak Show Films
651 A Scott Street
San Francisco California
94117
United States
Tel: 1-415-776-1076
Fax: 1-415-776-1076
Web: http://www.freakshowfilms.net

Fred Wolf Films
4222 West Burbank Boulevard
Burbank, California 91505
United States
Tel: 1-818-846-0611
Fax: 1-818-846-0979
Web: http://www.fredwolffilms.com

Freestyle Inc.
9 Elliot Avenue
Pottersville
Roseau, Dominca
Tel: +1 767.44.87.90.3
Fax: +1 767.44.99.38.1
Web: http://www.gofreestyle.com

Freestylecollective
8 West 19th Street
New York, New York 10011
United States
Tel: 1-212-414-2200
Web: http://www.freestylecollective.com

The Fremantle Corporation
660 Madison Avenue, 21st Floor
New York, New York 10021

United States
Tel: 1-212-421-4530
Fax: 1-212-207-8357
Web: http://www.fremantlecorp.com

Fremantle of Canada Ltd.
23 Lesmill Road, Suite 201
Toronto, Ontario M3B 3P6
Canada
Tel: 1-416-443-9204
Fax: 1-416-443-8685
Web: http://www.fremantlecorp.com

Fremantle Corporation, Ltd., The
Unit 2, Water Lane, Kentish Town
Road
London NW1 8NZ
England
Tel: 011-442-07-284-6500
Fax: 011-442-07-209-2294
Web: http://www.fremantlecorp.com

Fremantle Productions Pty, Inc.
Level 1, 11 Waltham Street
Artarmon NSW 2064
Australia
Tel: 011-612-8-425-1106
Fax: 011-612-9-439-1827
Web: http://www.fremantlecorp.com

Fremantle de Espana, Ltd.
c/o Bruba Producciones, S.L.
Sacedilla 13- Bajo A
Majahonda
28220 Madrid, Spain
Tel: 011-3491-639-2688
Fax: 0113491-639-4025
Web: http://www.fremantlecorp.com

Fremantle China
Atlantic Place, Bldg 307, Gate A, 9B
Beijing 100102
China
Tel: 011-86-106-479-3545
Fax:011-86-106-479-3546
Web: http://www.fremantlecorp.com

Frame entertainment Korea
Esquire standing store 3F 656-
294 Seongsu 1-ga
Seongdong-Gu, Seoul

Korea (133-821)
Tel :82-02-461-0700
Fax : 82-02-463-1155
Web: http://www.frament.com

Frame entertainment USA
234 Franklin ave
Nutley, New Jersey 07110
United States
Tel : 1-973-235-9399
Fax : 1-973-235-9496
Web: http://www.frament.com

frog design
1327 Chesapeake Terrace
Sunnyvale, California 94089
United States
Tel: 1-408-734-5800
Fax: 1-408-734-5801
Web: http://www.frogdesign.com

frog design
420 Bryant Street
San Francisco, California 94107
United States
Tel: 1-415-442-4804
Fax: 1-415-442-4803
Web: http://www.frogdesign.com

frog design
96 Spring Street
New York, New York 10012
United States
Tel: 1-212-965-9700
Fax: 1-212-965-9779
Web: http://www.frogdesign.com

frog design
804 Congress Ave.
Austin, Texas 78701
United States
Tel: 1-512-477-frog
Fax: 1-512-477-4803
Web: http://www.frogdesign.com

frog design
Grenzweg 33
72213 Altensteig, Germany
Tel: +49 7453 2740
Fax: +49 7453 27436
Web: http://www.frogdesign.com

Frontier I/S
GunnarClausens VEJ 66
Viby, Denmark
8260
Tel: +45.86.29.23.33
Web: http://www.frontier.as

Frontier Post Ltd.
66-67 Wells Street
London
W1T 3PY
United Kingdom
Tel: +44 (0)20 7291 9191
Fax: +44 (0)20 7291 9199
Web: http://www.frontierpost.co.uk

Frontline Television
35 bedfordbury
covent garden
london
wc2n 4du
Tel: +44 (0)20 7836 0411
Fax: +44 (0)20 7379 5210
Web: http://www.frontline-tv.co.uk

Funcom Inc
P.O. Box 14390
Durham, North Carolina 27709-14390
United States
Web: http://www.funcom.com

Funny Garbage
73 Spring Street, Suite 406
New York, New York 10012
United States
Tel: 1-212-343-2534
Fax: 1-212-343-3645
Web: http://www.funnygarbage.com

Fuse DDD | MRPPP
20 Thistlethwaite Street
South Melbourne, Victoria 3205
Australia
Tel: +61 3 9690 4044
Fax: +61 3 9699 2078
Web: http://www.mrppp.com.au

Fuzzy Goat
United Kingdom
Tel: (44) 01932 269822
Web: http://www.fuzzygoat.com

FX Centric
360 Grand Ave. Suite 85
Oakland, California
United States
Tel: 1-510-428-4097
Web: http://www.fxcentric.com

G-Netech
P.O. Box 4118
Robina, Queensland Australia
4230
Tel: +61 7.56.57.80.07
Fax: +61 7.56.57.80.08
Web: http://www.gnetech.com

G2 Productions, Inc.
511 Oliver Road
Montgomery, Alabama 36117
United States
Fax: 1-334-244-9403
Tel: 1-334-244-9303
Tel: 1-888-258-2183
Web: http://www.g2video.com

G3 Enterprise, Inc.
7520 E. Independence Blvd. Suite 400
Charlotte, North Carolina 28227
United States
Tel: 1-704-567-3060
Fax: 1-704-568-0199
Web: http://www.g3enterprise.com

GAPC (General Assembly
Production Centre)
14 Colonnade Road North
Ottawa, Ontario, Canada
K2E 7M6
Phone: (613) 723-3316
Fax: (613) 723-8583
Web: http://www.gapc.com

Garage Film Inc.
4-15-7-#301 Minami-Aoyama,
Minato-Ku
Tokyo 107-0062
Japan
Tel: 3-5412-0255
Fax: 3-5412-0257
Web: http://www.garage-film.co.jp

Gaumont Multimedia
Paris, France
Tel: 011-33-140-18-72-00
Fax: 011-33-140-03-02-26
Web: http://www.gaumont.fr

Gear CGI
B1 Woo-il B/D
725-32 Yoksam-dong
Kangnam-gu Seoul
Korea
Web: http://www.gearcgi.com

Genex Productions
50 Gervais Drive, Suite 307
Toronto, Ontario
M3C 1Z3
Canada
Tel: 1-416-386-0028
Fax: 1-416-386-0025
Web: http://www.genexproductions.com

Genki Production
Kyoto, Japan
Tel: 075-842-0001
Fax: 075-842-0002
Web: http://www.genkipro.jp

Gentle Giant studios
7511 North San Fernando Road
Burbank, California 91505
United States
Tel: 1-818-504-3555
Fax: 1-818-504-3554
Web: http://gentlegiantstudios.com

Geomedia
4242 Medical, Suite 4200
San Antonio, Texas
United States
Tel: 1-210-614-5900
Fax: 1-210-614-5922
Web: http://www.geomedia.com

Ghost 3D, LLC
17155 Robey Drive
Castro Valley, California 94546
United States
Tel: 1-510-481-1146
Fax: 1-510-481-1176
Web: http://www.ghost3d.com

Ghost Productions Inc.
2233 Hamline Avenue North,
Suite 600
Roseille, Minnesota 55113
United States
Tel: 1-651-633-1163
Web: http://www.ghostproductions.com

Ghost vfx
Thorsgade 59 3th
2200 Copenhagen N
Copenhagen, Denmark
Tel: +45.35.85.81.92
Fax: +45.35.85.81.94
Web: http://www.ghost.dk

Giant Killer Robots, Inc.
576 Natoma Street
San Francisco, California 94103
United States
Tel: 1-415-863-9119
Fax: 1-415-863-9108
Web: http://www.giantkillerrobots.com

Glasgow Media
448 Hartwood Road
Fredericksburg, Virginia 22406
United States
Tel: 1-540-286-2539
Fax: 1-540-286-0136
Web: http://www.glasgowmedia.com

Glass Egg Digital Media
E-Town.
7th Floor, 364 Cong Hoa St.
Tan Binh District
Ho Chi Minh City
Vietnam
Tel: 84 8 810 9018
Fax: 84 8 810 9013
Web: http://www.glassegg.com

Glassworks
33/34 Great Pulteney Street
London, England
W1F 9NP
United Kingdom
Tel: 0207 434 1182
Fax: 0207 434 1183
Web: http://www.glassworks.co.uk

Global Animation USA
16030 Ventura Blvd., Suite 510
Encino, California 91436
United States
Tel: 1-818-789-9622
Fax: 1-818-789-9722
Web: http://www.imagineasia.com

Global Animation Manila
557 Nueve de Pebero Street
Mandaluyong City, Philippines,
1553
Tel: (63-2) 717-1111
Fax: (63-2) 717-0000
Web: http://www.imagineasia.com

GMD
166 Willoughby Road
Crows Nest NSW 2065
Australia
Tel: 61 2 9467 3000
Fax: 61 2 9467 3001
Web: http://www.gmd.com.au

GMTV
The London Television Centre
Upper Ground
London
SE1 9TT
Tel: 020 7827 7000
Web: http://www.gmtv.co.uk

Gobo Box
69 Stewart Street
Paddington
Sydney, New South Wales
Australia 2021
Tel: +61 2.93.80.94.49
Fax: +61 2.93.80.75.80
Web: http://www.gobobox.com

Going Places TV
Parkway One
Parkway Business Centre
300 Princess Road
Manchester M14 7QU
United Kingdom
Tel: 0870 238 7710
Web: http://www.goingplaces.tv

Gork Enterprises
218 S. Brand Blvd. 2nd floor
San Fernando California, 91340
United States
Tel: 1-818-837-7984
Fax: 1-818-356-1964
Web: http://www.gork.com

Goulash Connection, The
Sumatralaan 45
1217 GP
Hilversum (Mediapark)
The Netherlands
Tel: +31 (0) 35 6249449
Web:
http://www.thegoulashconnection.nl

Granada Animation
2nd Floor
16 Hatfields
London
SE1 8DJ
United Kingdom
Tel: 020 7620 1620
Web: http://www.granadamedia.com

Granada Breeze
Franciscan Court
16 Hatfields
London
SE1 8DJ
United Kingdom
Tel: 020 7578 4040
Web: http://www.gsb.co.uk

Granada Commercial Ventures
200 Gray's Inn Road
London
WC2H 7FB
United Kingdom
Tel: 020 7396 6000
Web: http://www.granadamedia.com

Granada Enterprises
200 Gray's Inn Road
London
WC1X 8XZ
United Kingdom
Tel: 020 7396 6000
Web:http://www.enterprises.grana
damedia.com

Granada Entertainment USA
11812 San Vicente Boulevard
Suite 503
Los Angeles California, 90049
United States
Tel: 1-310-689-4777
Web: http://www.granadamedia.com

Granada Film
The London Television Centre
Upper Ground
London
SE1 9LT
United Kingdom
Tel: 020 7620 1620
Web: http://www.granadamedia.com

Granada International
48 Leicester Square
London WC2H 7FB
United Kingdom
Tel: 020 7491 1441
Web: http://www.granadamedia.com

Granada Learning
Granada Television
Quay Street
Manchester
M60 9EA
United Kingdom
Tel: 0161 827 2927
Web: http://www.granadamedia.com

Granada Men + Motors
Franciscan Court
16 Hatfields
London
SE1 8DJ
United Kingdom
Tel: 020 7578 4040
Web: http://www.gsb.co.uk

Granada plc
The London Television Centre
Upper Ground
London SE1 9LT
United Kingdom
Tel: 020 7620 1620
Web: http://www.granadamedia.com

Granada Plus
Franciscan Court
16 Hatfields
London
SE1 8DJ
United Kingdom
Tel: 020 7578 4040
Web: http://www.gsb.co.uk

Granada Productions Pty Ltd
Fox Studios Australia
Level 1, Bldg 61 Frank Hurley
Grandstand, Driver Avenue
Moore Park
NSW 1363
Australia
Tel: 00 612 9383 4360
Web: http://www.granadamedia.com

Granada Produktion fuer Film und
Fernsehen GmbH (Head office)
Agastr. 20
D-12489 Berlin
Germany
Tel: +49 (0)30 20 60 80
Fax: +49 (0)30 20 60 81 00
Web: http://www.granadamedia.com

Granada Produktion fuer Film und
Fernsehen GmbH
Glockengasse 2 a
D-50667 Koeln
Germany
Tel: +49 (0)221 257 25 45
Fax: +49 (0)221 257 25 46
Web: http://www.granadamedia.com

Granada Sky Broadcasting
Franciscan Court
16 Hatfields
London
SE1 8DJ
United Kingdom
Tel: 020 7578 4040
Web: http://www.gsb.co.uk

Granada Television
Quay Street
Manchester
M60 9EA
United Kingdom
Tel: 0161 832 7211
Web: http://www.granadamedia.com

Graph Architecture
2540, Daniel-Johnson, bureau
708
Tour Triomphe nord
Laval (Québec) H7T 2S3
Canada
Tel: 1-418-659-5611
Fax: 1-418-653-4734
Web:http://www.grapharchitecture.com

GraphicAroma
17 Mohamed Hussien Heikel
Nasr City
Cairo 11221
Egypt
Tel: +2012 218 3220
Web: http://www.graphicaroma.com

Grapheus
Ma. Jaburoaluge
Janavaree Goalhi
Machchangoalhi
Malek
Maldives
20-03
Tel: +960.78.16.24
Fax: +960.31.78.60
Web: http://www.grapheus.com

Graphic Punch
404 E 73rd ST, #16
New York, New York 10021
United States
Tel: 1-212-774-1891
Web: http://www.graphicpunch.com

Graphiti Multimedia Private
Limited
3B Kamanwala Chambers,
Mogul Lane,
Mahim (West)
Mumbai
India
400016
Tel: +91 22.44.41.58.0
Fax: +91 22.44.42.34.7
Web:
http://www.graphitimultimedia.com

Graph Architecture
683, rue Saint-Joseph Est, bureau
250
Québec G1K 3C1
Canada
Tel: 1-418-659-5611
Fax: 1-418-653-4734
Web:http://www.grapharchitecture.com

GreenhouseFX.com
P.O. Box 194
Byron Bay, New South Wales
Australia
2481
Tel: +61 2.66.87.17.97
Fax: +61 2.66.87.17.97
Web:
http://www.greenhouseFX.com

Green Lite Studios
1007 Montana Ave, Suite 434
Santa Monica, California 90403
United States
Tel: 1-310-309-5271
Tel: 1-310-291-8066
Fax: 1-310-317-0718
Web: http://www.greenlitestudios.com

Greener Pastures Studios
2254 Virginia Place. Suite F
Atlanta, Georgia 30305
United States
Tel: 1-404-812-0862
Web: http://www.greenpast.com

Greenlight Media AG
Gormannstr. 22
D - 10119 Berlin
Germany
Tel: +49 30 72 62 00- 0
Fax: +49 30 42 62 00- 222
Web:
http://www.greenlightmedia.com

Greenlight International B.V.
Lorentzweg 46 B
1221 EH Hilversum
The Netherlands
Tel: +31 356 420 677
Fax: +31 356 420 688
Web:
http://www.greenlightmedia.com

Greenmovie
Via Procaccini, 11
20154 Milano
Italy
Tel: 02 34932169
Fax: 02 34591441
Web: http://www.greenmovie.it

Green Movie FX
Via procaccini, 25
20154 Milano
Italy
Tel: +39 02345791
Fax: +39 0233105088
Web: http://www.greenmovie.com

Grey Post
P.O. Box 607
Raleigh, North Carolina 27560
United States
Tel: 1-919-785-5100
Fax: 1-888-219-7143
Web: http://www.greypost.com

Grid Visual Effects
Boomastratt 30-36
9000 Gent
Belgium
Tel: ++32 (0) 9 265 98 98
Fax: ++32 (0) 9 265 98 99
Web: http://www.grid-vfx.com

Griffilms, Ltd.
Gronant
Penralit Isaf
Caernarfon
Gwynedd, North Wales United
Kingdom
LL55 1NS
Tel: +44 128.66.76.67.8
Fax: +44 128.66.76.57.7
Web: http://www.griffilms.com

Griot Inc. Digital Agency
2-9-16 Ochiai, Shinjuku Ku
Tokyo 161-0034
Japan
Tel: 03-3363-7470
Fax: 03-3363
Web: http://www.griots.co.jp

Groupe Image Buzz, Inc.
312 Sherbrooke Street East
Montreal, Quebec Canada
H2X 1E6
Tel: 1-514-848-0579
Tel: 1-800-567-0200 (CAN/USA)
Mexico: 1-800-514-0579
Fax: 1-514-848-6371
Web: http://www.buzzimage.com

The Group Y
180 Varick Street, 14th Floor
New York, New York 10014
United States
Tel: 1-212-229-0742
Fax: 1-212-255-5001
Web: http://www.think3-d.com

Gruntworks Animation
324 Halifax Street
Adelaide SA 5000
Australia
Tel: +61 8 8359 2260
Web: http://www.gruntworks.com.au

Guava
8 West 19th St. 4th Floor
New York, New York 10011
United States
Tel: 1-212-414-2222
Web: http://www.guavanyc.com

Guava Visual Effects
31 Fullarton Road
Kent Town 5067
South Australia
Tel: +61 8 8363 8388
Fax: +61 8 8363 8359
Web: http://www.guavaeffects.com.au

Guerrilla News Network
Berkeley, California
United States
Web: http://www.gnn.tv

Gullane Entertainment
8, Westerhoutpark
Haarlem, Netherlands
2012 JM
Tel: +31 23.80.64.92.00
Fax: +31 23.80.64.92.01
Web: http://www.gullane.com

Guru Animation Studio
317 Adelaide Street West, Suite 903
Toronto, Ontario M5V 1P9
Canada
Tel: 1-416-599-4878
Fax: 1-416-628-6921
Web: http://www.gurustudio.com

GVFX
29 Booth Ave. Suite 205
Toronto, Ontario
Canada
M4M 2M3
Tel: 1-416-463-6753
Fax: 1-416-463-7312
Web: http://www.gvfx.com

GVFX
221 East 10th Ave. - Suite 202
Vancouver, British Columbia
Canada
V5T 4V1
Tel: 1-604-736-4839
Fax: 1-604-736-4838
Web: http://www.gvfx.com

GW Hannaway & Assoc.
839 Pearl St.
Boulder, Colorado 80302
United States
Tel: 1-303-440-9631
Fax: 1-303-440-4421
Web: http://www.gwha.com

Habitat North AB
Magasinsgatan 3,
SE-411 18, Gothenburg
Sweden
Tel: +46(0)31 136657
Web: http://www.habitatnorth.com

H A D E S   production
152, rue de l'amphithéâtre d'Hadès
7301 Hornu
Belgium
Tel: +32 (0) 65 76.56.56.
Fax: +32 (0) 65 76.56.57.
Web :http://www.hadesprod.com

Hahn Film AG
Schwedterstrasse 36 A

Berlin, Germany
10435
Tel: +49 30.44.35.49.0
Fax: +49 30.44.35.49.25.3
Web: http://www.hahnfilm.de

Hakama Design
Venice, California
United States
Tel: 1-310-314-2639
Web: http://www.hakamadesign.com

Hamiltoonz, Inc.
20 Main St, Box 719
Sag Harbor, New York 11963
United States
Tel: 1-631-725-8581
Fax: 1-631-725-8531
Web: http://www.hamiltoonz.com

Hammer and Pixel
717 Custer Avenue
Evanston, Illinois 60202
United States
Tel: 1-847-475-1004
Fax: 1-312-751-8452
Web:
http://www.hammerandpixel.com

Hammerhead Productions
11400 Sunshine Terrace
Studio City, California 91604
United States
Tel: 1-818-762-8643
Fax: 1-818-762-7311
Web: http://www.hammerhead.com

Hammer Visual Engineering
Akron, Ohio
United States
Tel: 1-330-527-4018
Web: http://www.HammerVE.com

Handsomeape Animation Studio
4102 W 4750S
Roy, Utah 84067
United States
Tel: 1-801-791-7830
Fax: 1-801-732-8198
Web: http://www.handsomeape.com

Happy Hour Entertainment
1330 NW 14th Ave.
Portland, Oregon 97209
United States
Tel: 1-503-295-6800
Fax: 1-503-295-6636
Web: http://www.happyhour-enter-
tainment.com

Happy Life
Birger Jarlsgatan 62. 4th Floor
SE-114 29 Stockholm
Sweden
Tel: 01 1-46-8-402-16-00
Fax: 01 1-46-8-41 1-09-60
Web: http://www.happylife.se

Happy Ship vof.
P.O. Box 1720
9700 BS Groningen
The Netherlands
Tel: +31 (0) 50 577 68 38
Web: http://www.happyship.com

Happy Trails Animation LLC
11900 SW 116th Avenue
Portland, Oregon 97223
United States
Tel: 1-503-590-7377
Fax: 1-503-590-7111
Web:
http://www.happytrailsanimation.com

Harris Blyth Ltd - The Jam
Factory
Hartley HouseGreen Walk
London
England
SE1 4TU
Tel: 0207 2340214
Fax: 0207 4039291
Web: http://www.harrisblyth.co.uk

Harrow Media
The Basement
33 Ewell Street
Balmain NSW 2041
Australia
Tel: +61 2 9555 8399
Fax: +61 2 9555 9644
Web: http://www.harrow.com.au

HBO Studio Productions
120A East 23rd Street
New York, New York 10003
United States
Tel: 1-212-512-7800
Fax: 1-212-512-7951
Web: http://www.hbo.com

HDS Studios
Springfield Road
Hayes, Middlesex United
Kingdom
UB4 0LE
Tel: +44 181.57.34.00.0
Fax: +44 181.56.17.05.6
Web: http://www.hdsstudios.com

Hearst Animation Productions
1640 South Sepulveda Boulevard
Los Angeles, California 90025
United States
Tel: 1-310-478-1700
Fax: 1-310-478-2202
Web: http://www.hearst.com

Hearst Entertainment and
Animation Productions
888 Seventh Avenue
New York, New York 10019
Tel: 1-212-455-4000
Fax: 1-212-983-6379
Web: Web: http://www.hearst.com

HeavyBones Animation
Mesa, Arizona
United States
Tel: 1-480-325-8064
Web: http://www.heavybones.com

Hectic Illusions
Prins Hendrikkade 123
1011 AM Amsterdam
The Netherlands
Tel: 00 31 (0) 20 422 61 19
Tel: 00 31 (0) 20 422 35 69
Fax: 00 31 (0) 20 422 62 27
Web:
http://www.hectic-illusions.com

Helios Design Laboratories
317 Adelaide Street West, Suite

1010
Toronto, Ontario Canada.
m5v 1p9
Tel: 1-416-593-6006
Fax: 1-416-593-6275
Web: http://www.heliozilla.com

Helium Productions, Inc.
2690 N. Beachwood Drive
Hollywood, California 90068
United States
Tel: 1-323-467-9323
Fax: 1-323-467-9396
Web:
http://www.heliumproductions.com

Helix Digital Inc.
70 Crescent Street
Sydney, Nova Scotia
Canada B1S 2Z7
Tel: 1-902-539-6999
Fax: 1-902-539-2181
Web: http://www.helixstudio.com

Helsinki Television
Helsinki, Finland
Web: http://www.htv.fi

Hesketh.com Inc.
512 Brickhaven DriveSuite 260
Raleigh, North Carolina 27606
United States
Tel: 1-919-834-2552
Fax: 1-919-834-2554
Web: http://www.hesketh.com

Hibbert Ralph Animation
10 D'Arblay Street
London
United Kingdom
W1F 8DS
Tel: +44 207.49.43.01.1
Fax: +44 207.49.40.38.3
Web: http://www.hra-online.com

Hillside Studios
Merry Hill Road
Bushey
Hertfordshire
WD23 1DR
United Kingdom

Tel: 44 (0)20 8950 7919
Fax: 44 (0)20 8950 1437
Web:http://www.bigtimepictures.co.uk

Higher Authority Productions
10800 Biscayne Boulevard Suite 800
Miami, Florida 33161
United States
Tel: 1-305-899-3002
Fax: 1-305-899-3003
Web: http://www.hapvideo.com

High Praise Inc.
2975 Wilshire Blvd. Suite 230
Los Angeles, California 90006
United States
Tel: 1-213-427-9000
Fax: 1-213-427-9003
Web: http://www.highpraisefilm.com

HIT Entertainment/London
5th Floor
Maple House
149-150 Tottenham Court Road
London
W1T 7NF
England
United Kingdom
Tel: 011 (+44) 20-7554-2500
Fax: 011(+44) 20-7388-9321
Web:
http://www.hitentertainment.com

HIT Entertainment/Dallas
830 South Greenville Avenue
Allen, Texas, 75002-3320
United States
Tel: 1-972-390-6000
Web:
http://www.hitentertainment.com

HIT Entertainment/Los Angeles
9300 Wilshire Blvd.
2nd Floor
Beverly Hills, California, 90212
United States
Tel: 1-310-724-8979
Fax: 1-310-724-8978
Web:
http://www.hitentertainment.com

Hive (The) Animation, Ltd.
37 Dean Street
London
United Kingdom
W1D 4PT
Tel: +44 207.56.51.00.0
Fax: +44 207.49.40.05.9
Web: http://www.hive3d.com

Hi-Wire
555 Nicollet Mall, Suite 391
Minneapolis, Minnesota 55402
United States
Tel: 1-612-252-3900
Fax: 1-612-252-3939
Web: http://www.hi-wire.com

Hoek & Sonepouse BV
Verrijn Stuartweg 14
Industrieterrien Verrijn Stuart
Dimen
The Netherlands
Tel: +31 020 690 91 41
Fax: +31 020 690 18 93
Web: http://www.hoek.nl

Holland Centraal
Lauriegracht 41a
1016 RG Amsterdam
The Netherlands
Tel: +31 (020) 4284938
Fax: +31 (020) 4284937
Web:http://www.hollandcentraal.com

Hollywood Digital
6690 W. Sunset Blvd.
Hollywood, California 90028
United States
Tel: 1-323-465-0101
Fax: 1-323-468-5455
Web: http://www.hollydig.com

Hollywoodn't Productions
p.o. box 91
3500 AB Utrecht
The Netherlands
Tel: +31-(0)30-2381081
Fax: +31-(0)30-2381081
Web: http://www.hollywoodnt.nl

Holy Cow! Animation, Inc.
3f Hatchasia Global City Center
31st Street, cor. 2nd Avenue
E-square IT Park
Bonifacio Global City Taguig
Manila
Philippines
1227
Tel: +63 2.81.85.01.9
Fax: +63 2.81.85.00.5
Web: http://holycowanimation.com

Home Run Pictures
100 First Avenue, Suite 450
Pittsburgh, Pennsylvania 15222
United States
Tel: 1-412-391-8200
Fax: 1-412-391-1772
Web: http://www.hrpictures.com

Homsey
2003 North Scott Street
Wilmington, Delaware 19806
United States
Tel: 1-302-656-4491
Web: http://www.homsey.com

Hong Ying Universe Co., Ltd
Taipei , Taiwan and Suzhou
China
Tel: 011-86-512-5620743
Tel: 011-86-512-5620324
Fax: 011-86-512-5620502
Web: http://www.hong-ying.com

Hornet Entertainment Inc.
Japan
Tel: 025-282-1633
Fax: 025-282-1614
Web: http://www.hornet-web.com

Hornet Inc.
213 W. 35th Street, Suite 605
New York, New York 10001
United States
Tel: 1-917-351-0520
Fax: 1-917-351-0522
Web: http://www.hornetinc.com

Hornet Inc.
5777 W. Century Blvd.

Los Angeles, California 90045
United States
Tel: 1-310-641-9496
Fax: 1-310-614-2117
Web: http://www.hornetinc.com

Hootchie Cootchie
Taxusstraat 20
3061 HT Rotterdam
The Netherlands
Tel: (+31) 10 2123101
Fax: (+31) 10 2123104
Web: http://www.hootchie.nl

Horizons Animation Columbus
4000 Horizons Drive
Columbus, Ohio 43220
United States
Tel: 1-614-481-7200
Fax: 1-614-481-7205
Web:
http://www.horizonscompanies.com

Horizons Nashville
600 Bowling Ave - Suite A
Nashville, Tenessee 37215
United States
Tel: 1-615-269-2673
Fax: 1-615-269-5662
Web:
http://www.horizonscompanies.com

Horizons San Diego
3864 Mission Boulevard
San Diego, California 92109
United States
Tel: 1-858-488-9770
Fax: 1-858-488-9726
Web:
http://www.horizonscompanies.com

Horizon Video Productions
4222 Emperor Blvd. Suite 520
Durham, North Carolina 27703
United States
Tel: 1-919-941-0901
Tel: 1-800-768-3776
Fax: 1-919-941-1939
Web: http://www.horizonvp.com

Hothaus - Video Post & Transfer
2727 Inwood Road
Dallas, Texas 75235
United States
Tel: 1-214-350-2676
Web: http://www.videopost.com

Hothouse Models & Effects
10 St. Leonards Road
Park Royal
London
NW10 6SY
United Kingdom
Tel: +44(0)20 8961 3666
Fax: +44(0)20 8961 3777
Web: http://www.hothousefx.co.uk

Hot Knife Digital Media Ltd
1 First Avenue
Sherwood Rise
Nottingham
England
NG7 6JL
United Kingdom
Tel: +44 115.96.93.60.0
Fax: +44 115.96.91.80.0
Web: http://www.hotknife.co.uk

Hot Post
Via Adolfo Rava
124-00142 Roma
Tel: +39 06 5964941
Fax: +39 54 11961
Web: http://www.hotpost.it

Hot Post
Via Del Corso
4-00186 Roma
Tel: +39 06 3608171
Fax: +39 06 32650152
Web: http://www.hotpost.it

Houlamation
415 1/2 5th Avenue West
Kirkland, Washington 98033
United States
Tel: 1-425-739-0293
Web: http://www.houlamation.com

House of Bliss
4400 Bowser Avenue #101

Dallas, Texas 75219
United States
Tel: 1-214-219-0214
Web: http://www.houseofbliss.com

House of Moves Motion Capture
Studios
5318 McConnell Ave.
Los Angeles, California 90066
United States
Tel: 1-310-306-6131
Fax: 1-310-306-1351
Web: http://www.moves.com

House of Moves Motion Capture
Studios, LLC
501 North IH 35
Austin, Texas 78702
United States
Tel: 1-512-485-3085
Fax: 1-512-485-3052
Web: http://www.moves.com

Howard Granite Film
3231 Glendon Avenue
Los Angeles, California 90034
United States
Tel: 1-310-415-5596
Fax: 1-310-470-5924
Web:
http://www.howardgranitefilms.com

HR3d
10 D'Arblay Street
London
W1F 8DS
United Kingdom
Tel: +44 207.59.89.43.6
Fax: +44 207.28.71.84.9
Web: http://www.hr3d-online.com

HRTV/HRA
10 D'Arblay Street
London
W1F 8DS
United Kingdom
Tel: +44 (0)20 7494 3011
Fax: +44 (0)20 7494 0383
Web: http://www.hrtv-online.com

Humouring the Fates Productions Inc.
2519 Riverside Drive
Tampa, Florida 33602-1841
United States
Tel: 813-223-FATED
Web: http://www.fates.com

Hybrid Graphics, Ltd.
Etel"inen Makasiinikatu 4
Helsinki, Finland
00130
Tel: +358 9.68.66.38.0
Fax: +358 9.68.52.03.0
Web: http://www.hybrid.fi

Hybrid Medical Animation
3001 Hennepin Avenue South
Suite D209
Minneaplolis, Minnesota 55408
United States
Tel: 1-612-285-9409
Fax: 1-612-285-9411
Web: http://www.hybridmedicalan-
imation.com

Hybride technologies
111, ch de la Gare
Piedmont, Quebec Canada
J0R 1K0
Tel: +1 450.227.4245
Fax: +1 450.227.5245
Web: http://www.hybride.com

Hydraulx
Santa Monica, California 90401
United States
Tel: 1-310-393-9011
Fax: 1-310-393-9211
Web: http://www.hydraulx.com

HydraVision Entertainment
BP 2000
Tourcoing
France
59 203
Tel: +33 3.20.68.42
Fax: +33 3.20.68.42
Web: http://www.hydravision.com

Hyperactive
1516 Lovett Street
Greensboro, North Carolina
27403
United States
Tel: 1-336-430-1523
Web: http://www.hyperactivemulti-media.com

Hyperion Animation
111 North Maryland Avenue, Suite 20
Glendale, California 91206
United States
Tel: 1-818-244-4704
Fax: 1-818-244-4713
Web:
http://www.hyperionstudios.com

Hyperion Studio
111 North Maryland Avenue, Suite 300
Glendale, California 91206
Tel: 1-818-244-4704
Fax: 1-818-244-4713
Web:
http://www.hyperionpictures.com

Hyperimage
443 West Colorado Street
Glendale, California 91204
United States
Tel: 1-818-547-2255
Web: http://www.hyperimage.net

Hypermedia
Office 101
Trinity House
40 - 42 Byzantiou Street
2064 Strovolos, Nicosia
Cyprus
Tel: +357-22667112
Fax: +357-22667187
Web: http://www.hyper.com.cy

HyperVision Ltd.
Unit A1,
Claylands Road,
Bishops Waltham,
Hampshire,
SO32 1BH
United Kingdom.
Web: http://www.hypervision.co.uk

I&B Enterprises, Inc.
139 Pinecrest Road
Durham, North Carolina 27705
United States
Tel: 1-919-419-0340
Fax: 1-919-490-0815
Web: http://www.ib-ent.com

iAS GmbH
Scheppe Gewissegasse 28
35039 Marburg
Germany
Tel: +49 (0)6421 92770
Fax: +49 (0)6421 92102
Web: http://www.brainmedia.de

iAS GmbH
Scheppe Gewissegasse 8
35039 Marburg
Germany
Tel: +49 (0)6421 92770
Fax: +49 (0)6421 927747
Web: http://www.brainmedia.de

iAS GmbH
Dieffenbachstr. 33c
10967 Berlin
Germany
Tel: +49 (0)30 69004-0
Fax: +49 (0)30 69004-101
Web: http://www.brainmedia.de

IBC Digital
250 Delaware Avenue, Suite 11
Buffalo, New York 14202
United States
Tel: 1-716-852-1724
Fax: 1-716-852-1735
Web: http://www.ibcdigital.com

Ice Pond Studio
155 Ice Pond Road
Brewster, New York 10509
United States
Tel: 1-845-278-7625
Fax: 1-845-279-5727
Web: http://www.icepond.com

Iconic
P.O. Box 1935
Southern Pines, North Carolina 28388

United States
Tel: 1-910-944-0424
Tel: 1-866-4ICONIC
Fax: 910.944.0410
Web: http://www.iconicid.com

Icon Property Development Graphics
1617 Winter Green Blvd.
Winter Park, Florida 32792
United States
Tel: 1-407-657-1362
Web: http://www.iconpdg.com

Idagrove Entertainment
Luetzowufer12
Berlin, Germany
10785
Tel: +49 17.95.93.06.93
Fax: +49 72.11.51.46.84.69
Web: http://www.idagrove.de

Ideas Included
6 Wallbridge,
Frome, , BA11 1QY
United Kingdom
Tel:+44 (1373) 453338
Web: http://www.ideasincluded.com

Idea Factory
Meitou 2F,1-16-4 jinguumae
Sibuya-ku
Tokyo 150-0001
Japan
Tel: +81-3-5772-3101
Fax: +81-3-5772-3102
Web: http://www.ideaf.co.jp

I-DESIGN co., ltd.
1-12-10-201, Chodo
Higashi-Osaka, Osaka 577-0056
Japan
Web: http://wwwe.idesign.co.jp

I-DESIGN co., ltd.
3-15-22-103, Jingumae
Shibuya-ku, Tokyo 150-0001
Japan
Web: http://wwwe.idesign.co.jp

I-D Media AG
Franz Klose
Ohlauer Straße 43
D-10999 Berlin
Germany
Tel: +49 (0)30 2 59 47-129
Fax: +49 (0)30 2 59 47-355
Web: http://www.i-dmedia.com

Idryonis Studios
49 James Road
Hatboro, Pennsylvania 19040
United States
Tel: 1-215-479-7728
Fax: 1-215-479-7728
Web: http://www.idryonis.com

iDvX2
IdVx2 Studios
Kritou Terra
Polis Chrysochou Bay Area
Polis (Akamas), Paphos Cyprus
8724
Tel: +357 99.74.52.24
Fax: +357 26.33.24.16
Web: http://www.IDvX2.com

Igel Media Ag
Palmaille 124 B
22767 Hamburg
Germany
Phone: +49 40 306896 0
Fax: +49 40 306896 68
Web: http://www.igelmedia.de

Ignite Studios
431 Gilmour St.
2nd Floor
Ottawa, Ontario Canada
K2P 0R5
Tel: +1 613.233.1991 x221
Fax: +1 613.233.3413
Web: http://www.ignitestudios.com

Ikaria
600A Armijo St.
Santa Fe, New Mexico 87501
United States
Tel: 1-505-989-3365
Fax: 1-505-989-3365
Web: http://www.ikaria.com

Ill Clan Productions
236 Leondard St. #2
Brooklyn, New York 11211
United States
Tel: 1-347-277-1920
Web: http://www.illclan.com

Iloura
18 Kavanagh St
Southbank
3006 Victoria
Australia
Tel: 613 9686 8888
Fax: 613 9682 6736
Web: http://www.iloura.com.au

Illuminated Film Company (The)
115 Gunnersbury Lane
Acton
London
United Kingdom
W3 8HQ
Tel: +44 208.89.61.66.6
Fax: +44 208.89.61.66.9
Web: http://www.illuminatedfilms.com

Illusion Animated Productions
46 Quinn's Road
Shankill
Co. Dublin, Ireland
Tel: +353 [0] 1 282 1458
Fax: +353 [0] 1 282 1458
Web:
http://www.illusionanimation.com

Illusion Arts, Inc.
6700 Valjean Avenue
Van Nuys, California 91406
United States
Tel: 1-818-901-1077
Fax: 1-818-901-1995
Web: http://www.illusion-arts.com

il Luster Productions
Hoogt 4
3512 GW Utrecht
The Netherlands
Tel: +31 (0)30 24 007 68
Fax: +31 (0)30 24 007 68
Web: http://www.illuster.nl

Image Corporation
Tokyo, Japan
Tel: 03-3206-4001
Fax: 03-3206-4004
Web: http://www.img.co.jp

Image Engine Design
15 West 5th Ave
Vancouver, British Columbia
V5Y 1H4
Canada
Tel: 1-604-874-5634
Web:
http://www.image-engine.com

Image Infotainment Limited
32, T.T.K Road, Alwarpet
Chennai, Tamil Nadu India
600018
Tel: +91 44.46.71.54.2
Fax: +91 44.46.71.54.3
Web: http://www.imageil.com

Image Now Films
17a New Bride Street
Dublin 8
Ireland
Tel: 00353 1 6795251
Fax: 00353 1 4113319
Web: http://www.imagenow.ie

Imagi Production Ltd.
Unit 2303-2308, Hong Man
Industrial Centre 2
Hong Man Street
Chai Wan, Hong Kong
Tel: +852.29.75.15.55
Fax: +852.25.05.96.38
Web: http://www.imagi.com.hk

IMAGICA Corp.
Tokyo Imaging Center
2-14-1 Higashi-Gotanda
Shinagawa-ku
Tokyo 141-0022
Japan
Tel: 81-3-3280-7502
Web: http://www.imagica.com

IMAGICA Corp.
Shinagawa Production Center
3-13-6 Higashi-Shinagawa
Shinagawa-ku
Tokyo 140-0002
Japan
Tel: 81-3-3458-1681
Web: http://www.imagica.com

IMAGICA West Corp.
1-8-14 Doshin
Kita-ku, Osaka 530 - 0035
Japan
Tel: 06-6353-1711
Web: http://www.imagicawest.co.jp

IMAGICA Corp.
Akasaka Video Center
4-10-4 Akasaka
Minato-ku
Tokyo 107-0052
Japan
Tel: 81-3-3583-1681
Web: http://www.imagica.com

IMAGICA Corp.
Ginza 7-Chome Studio
Kacho Bldg. 6F
7-16-7 Ginza, Chuo-ku
Tokyo 104-0061
Japan
Tel: 81-3-3542-1681
Web: http://www.imagica.com

IMAGICA Corp.
Nagata-cho Studio
2-2-5 Hirakawacho
Chiyoda-ku
Tokyo 102-0093
Japan
Tel: 81-3-3264-1681
Web: http://www.imagica.com

IMAGICA Corp.
Ikuta VP Center
2-9-11 Ikuta
Tama-ku, Kawasaki 214-0038
Japan
Tel: 81-44-900-5250
Web: http://www.imagica.com

IMAGICA USA INC.
5320 McConnell Ave. Los
Angeles, California 90066
United States
Tel: 1-310-305-8081
Web: http://www.imagica.com

IMAGICA DIGIX Inc.
Taisei Bldg., 1-3-4 Ohsaki
Shinagawa-Ku, Tokyo 141-0032
Japan
Tel: 81-3-5434-2031
Web: http://www.digix.imagica.co.jp

IMAGICA Links DigiWorks Inc.
2-14-1 higashi-Gotanda
Shinagawa-Ku, Tokyo 141-0022
Japan
Tel: 81-3-5420-6138
Fax: 81-3-5420-6139
Web: http://www.linksdw.com

IMAGICA DIO Corp.
2-14-1 higashi-Gotanda
Shinagawa-Ku, Tokyo 141-0022
Japan
Tel: 81-3-3280-1318
Web: http://www.imagica.com

IMAGICA Toyo Communications,
Inc.
2-10-13 higashi-Gotanda
Shinagawa-Ku, Tokyo 141-0022
Japan
Tel: 81-3-3280-8161
Web: http://www.tocom.co.jp

IMAGICA PLUS Corp.
4-10-4 Akasaka
Minato-Ku, Tokyo 107-0052
Japan
Tel: 81-3-3583-1681
Web: http://www.imagica.com

Imagination Computer Services
GesmbH
Donau-City-Straße 1 / OG 3
Tech Gate Vienna, A - 1220 Wien
Austria
Tel: +43-1 20501 - 33 0
Fax: +43-1 20501 - 33 900
Web: http://www.imagination.at

Imagination in Motion
Rollenwagen 30
Vilvoorde, Belgium
1800
Tel: +32 1.60.90.10.0
Fax: +32 2.60.90.10.1
Web: http://www.iim.be

Imagination Production
Rentemestervej 2
DK-2400 Copenhagen NV
Denmark
Tel: +45 35 85 40 40
Fax: +45 35 82 40 40
Web: http://www.i-production.dk

Imagine 3D
Communicatieweg 3
3641 SG Mijdrecht
Tel: 0297-257348
Fax: 0297-256204
Web: http://www.imagine3d.nl

Imaginengine Corp.
3025 Fillmore St.
San Francisco, California 94116
United States
Tel: 1-415-567-6158
Web: http://www.imaginengine.com

Imajimation Studios Inc.
430 N. Colorado Ave. Suite 202
Santa Monica, California 90401
United States
Tel: 1-310-395-5460
Fax: 1-310-395-5340
Web: http://www.imajimation.com

Imag Television
Gazeteciler Mah.
Hikaye Sok. No:9
80300 Esentepe
Istanbul, Turkey
Web: http://www.imajonline.com

Imag Television
Daisy Plaza
TurkAli Mah.
Odalar Sok. No:9
Besiktas Istanbul Turkey
Web: http://www.imajonline.com

Imarion Inc.
67 Portland St. 2nd. Floor.
Toronto, Ontario M5V 2M9
Canada
Tel: 1-416-597-2989
Fax: 1-416-596-1344
Web: http://www.imarion.com

Impact
2-11-7 33rd Shrine Garden
Building 7f
Ku Shinjuku
Shinjuku 160-0022
Japan
Tel: 03-3350-0821
Fax: 03-3226-1418
Web: http://www.impact.ne.jp

Impact Forensic
Fort Worth, Texas
United States
Tel: 1-817-797-7682
Web: http://www.impactforensic.com

Immersive Technologies, LLC
14 Summer Street, 4th Floor
Malden, Massachusetts 02148
United States
Tel: 1-781-388-9160
Fax: 1-781-388-9161
Web: http://www.immersiveweb.com

Imotion
London, England
United Kingdom
Tel: +44 208 233 7825
Web: http://www.imotion.com

Impact Digital Art Co.
7/F, Morrison Comm. BLDG.
31 Morrison Hill Road
Causeway Bay, Hong Kong
Tel: (852) 2591 4433
Fax: (852) 2591 0162
Web: http://www.ida.com.hk

impakt 9 - Die Ideenträger
Heimeranstraße 68
D - 80339 München
Germany
Tel: +49-89-121180-0

Fax: +49-89-121180-78
Web: http://www.impakt9.de

Impossible Pictures
1570 Quail Lake Loop Road
Colorado Springs, Colorado
80906
United States
Tel: 1-719-226-7831
Fax: 1-719-540-9803
Web: http://www.visualapproach.com

IMS Future Design Inc.
Tokyo, Japan
Tel: 03-3299-3599
Fax: 03-3299-3614
Web: http://www.imsfd.jp

In-Sight Pix
901 Abbot Kinney Boulevard
Venice, California 90291
United States
Tel: 1-310-399-5670
Fax: 1-310-399-1334
Web: http://www.digitallab.com

InAFlash Animation
#16-1640 162 St.
Surrey, British Columbia Canada
v4a 6y9
Tel: +1 604.999.1285
Web:
http://www.inaflashanimation.com

iNAGO Corporation.
296 Richmond Street West, Suite
400
Toronto, Ontario
Canada, M5V 1X2
Tel: 1-416-343-0032
Fax: 1-416-343-4976
Web: http://www.inago.com

iNAGO Inc.
3-4-18 Higashi Azabu Route
Higashi Azabu Bldg.
3F Minato-ku, Tokyo, 105-0013
Japan
Tel: (03) 3568-1380
Fax: (03) 3568-1381
Web: http://www.inago.com

Inde Digital Animation
1050 W. Columbia
Chicago, Illinois 60626
United States
Tel: 1-773-338-3209
Web: http://www.studioronin.com

Independant Television News
200 Gray's Inn Road
London
WC1X 8XZ
Tel: 020 7833 3000
Web: http://www.itn.co.uk

Industrial Light and Magic/Kerner Optical
P.O. Box 2459
San Rafael, California 94912-
2459
United States
Tel: 1-415-448-2306
Tel: 1-415-448-9000
Fax: 1-415-448-9550
Fax: 1-415-448-3540
Web: http://www.ilm.com

Infinite Dreams
Kaczyniec 7,
Gliwice, 44-100
Poland
Web: http://www.idreams.com.pl

Infobloom
Sweden
Web: http://www.infobloom.se

INFOBYTE S.p.A
Via della Camilluccia, 67 - 00135
Rome
Italy
Tel: +39 06 355721
Fax: +39 06 35572300
Web: http://www.infobyte.it

INFOBYTE Naples
Via Giovanni Porzio, 4 - 80143
Naples
Italy
Tel: +39 081 7502516
Fax: +39 081 7502516
Web: http://www.infobyte.it

INFOBYTE Terni
P.le Bosco 3 A - 05100 -
Tel: +39 0744 5441344
Web: http://www.infobyte.it

INFOBYTE Brindisi
Cittadella della Ricerca
S.S. 7 Mesagne Km 7+300 -
72100
Tel: +39 0831 507200
Web: http://www.infobyte.it

InfoVision Consultants Inc.
800 E. Campbell Road
Suite 388
Richardson, Texas 75081
United States
Tel: 1-972-234-0058
Fax: 1-972-234-5732
Web: http://www.infovision.net

Ingeeni Studios, Inc.
271 Windsor Street
Cambridge, Massachusetts
02139
United States
Tel: 1-617-547-1822
Web: http://www.ingeeni.com

INGO Multimedia Co., Ltd.
293-3, 9F-1, Fu-Shin S. Rd.,
Sec.2
Taipei, Taiwan
106
Tel: +886 3.45.56.08.3
Fax: +886 3.43.54.01.1
Web: http://www.ingo.com

In Images
Poland
http://www.inimages.pl

Innovatives
58, Narayan Peth
Pune, Maharashtra
India
411030
Tel: +91 20.44.57.45.5
Web: http://www.innovatives-
group.com

Insight Studios
517 Nichols Farm Drive
Durham, North Carolina 27703
United States
Tel: 1-919-596-5138
Fax: 1-810-821-5176
Web:http://www.insight-studios.com

Inspidea Animation
Suite B-06-09 Plaza Mont' Kiara
No. 2 Jalan Kiara
Mont' Kiara
Kuala Lumpur, Malaysia
50480
Tel: +60 3.62.03.59.81
Fax: +60 3.62.03.49.81
Web: http://www.inspidea.com

Intent Software GmbH & Co. KG
Barnerstrasse 14
22765 Hamburg
Germany
Tel: +49 40 39 834 763
Web: http://www.astonia.com

Interactive Multimedia Solutions, Inc.
2112 Jerimouth Drive, Suite 100
Raleigh, North Carolina 27502
United States
Tel: 1-919-389-6430
Fax: 1-603-299-8472
Web: http://www.ims3d.com

Interactive Television
Entertainment
Nattergalevej 6,
2400 København NV
Denmark
Tel: +45 70 210 200
Fax: +45 70 210 201
Web: http://www.ite.dk

Interactive Vision Visuals
1104 Kenilworth Drive. Suite 300
Towson, Maryland 21204
United States
Tel: 1-410-963-3710
Web: http://www.iavision.com

Interactive Vision Visuals
Norreskov Bakke 14B

8600 Silkeborg
Denmark
Tel: +45 8680 2700
Web: http://www.iavision.com

Interactive Vision Visuals
Carl Theodor Str. 1
D-68723 Schwetzingen
Deutschland
Tel: +49 6202 592 465
Web: http://www.iavision.com

Interactive Vision Visuals
1143 Zászlós utca 54.
Budapest
Hungary
Tel: +36 1 383 4351
Web: http://www.iavision.com

Interactive Vision Visuals
Ul. Jagiellonska 67,
70-382 Szczecin,
Polska
Tel: +48 91 8143 800
Web: http://www.iavision.com

InterGraphics C&A (Pvt) Ltd
514 Anum Estate, DACHS
Shahra-e-Faisal
Karachi, Sindh Pakistan
75350
Tel: +92 21.43.13.44.58
Fax: +92 21.45.24.58.4
Web: http://www.icna-ltd.com

Interlight Studios
2256 Rocky Ridge Road, Suite 102
Birmingham, Alabama 35216
United States
Tel: 1-205-823-6700
Fax: 1-205-824-3200
Web:http://www.interlightstudios.com

International Cartoons &
Animation Center, Inc.
1823 E 17th St. Suite 203
Santa Ana, California 92705
United States
Tel: 1-714-953-5778
Fax: 1-714-560-0744
Web: http://www.familytoons.com

International Videoworks Inc.
Nishiogi-Minami, 2-20-8
Yamada Bldg. 3F
Suginami-ku, Tokyo 167-0053
Japan
Tel: 81-3-3333-5335
Fax: 81-3-3333-5344
Web: http://www.ivw.co.jp

Interstation
335, St-Joseph East
5th floor
Montreal, Quebec Canada
G1K3B4
Tel: +1 418.624.7065
Fax: +1 418.624.4923
Web: http://www.station3d.com

Intervalo Productions Ltda.
Rua da Assembleia 10 s2914
Rio de Janeiro, RJ Brazil
20011-901
Tel: +55 21.25.31.01.41
Fax: +55 21.22.52.22.09
Web: http://www.intervalo.com.br

In The Dark Entertainment, Inc.
Orlando, Florida
United States
Tel: 1-407-310-8996
Web:
http://www.itdentertainment.com

INTRAG Int'l
5715 Vineland Ave. Suite #5
North Hollywood, California
91601
United States
Tel: 1-818-762-1665
Fax: 1-818-762-1665
Web:
http://www.smw-enterprise.net

IO Media
91 Fifth Avenue
Fourth Floor
New York, New York
Tel: 1-212-352-1115
Fax: 1-212-352-1117
Web: http://www.io-media.com

IP Productions
23, Val Fleuri
Luxembourg
L-1526
Tel: +352.44.70.70.1
Fax: +352.44.70.26.0
Web: http://www.idprod.lu

I-Race
Seabraes, Perth Road,
Dundee
DD1 4LN
United Kingdom
Tel: +44 (0) 1382 341 000
Tel: +44 (0) 1383 845 300
Web: http://www.irace.com

Iris Productions
223, Val Sainte-Croix
Luxembourg, Luxembourg
1371
Tel: +352.44.70.70.61.1
Fax: +352.25.03.94
Web: http://www.irisproductions.lu

Irusoin
B Sorabilla-Pol-53
Andoain-Guip 20140
Spain
Tel: 011-34-43-30-02-37
Fax: 011-34-43-49-41-34
Web: http://www.irusoin.com

ISkills
1426 E. 750 N.
Orem, Utah 84097
United States
Tel: 1-801-764-5900
Fax: 1-801-224-5218
Web: http://www.iskills.com

istation.com®
800 E. Campbell Road, Suite 340
Richardson, Texas 75081
United States
Tel: 1-866-883-READ
Tel: 1-972-643-3440
Fax: 1-972-643-3441
Web: http://www.istation.com

Italtoons Corporation
32 West 40th Street
New York, New York 10018
United States
Tel: 1-212-730-0280
Fax: 1-212-730-0313
Web: http://www.italtoons.com

ITE - Interactive Television
Entertainment
ITE ApS
Nattergalevej 6
Copenhagen, NV Denmark
2400
Tel: +45.70.21.02.00
Fax: +45.70.21.02.01
Web: http://www.ite.dk

ITV Digital
346 Queenstown Road
London
SW1B 4NE
Tel: 020 7819 8000
Web: http://www.itv-digital.co.uk

JA Film
Klosterport 4E, 3
Aarhus, Denmark
8000
Tel: +45.70.26.02.70
Web: http://www.jafilm.dk

Jackson Group Interactive
1899 Tate Boulevard SE, Suite
2110
Hickory, North Carolina 28602
United States
Tel: 1-828-328-9238
Fax: 1-828-328-8463
Web: http://www.jginteractive.com

JadooWorks
6th Floor, Tower 'C'
Diamond District
Airport Road
Bangalore, Karnataka India
560008
Tel: +91 80.50.97.69.5
Fax: +91 80.50.97.54.3
Web: http://www.jadooWorks.com

Jadooworks Pvt. Ltd
HK Hills
West of Chord Road
Bangalore - 560 010
India
Tel: +91 80 80 31308
Fax: +91 80 80 31308
Web: http://www.jadooworks.com

JadooWorks
21580 Stevens Creek Boulevard,
Suite 208
Cupertino, California 95014
United States
Tel: 1-408-366-0193
Fax: 1-408-865-1618
Web: http://www.jadooworks.com

Jadooworks Pvt. Ltd
4030 Moorpark Ave, #222
San Jose, California 95117
United States
Tel: 1-408-248-4271
Fax: 1-408-248-4241
Web: http://www.jadooworks.com

JadooWorks
10, Upper Grosvenor Street, Suite B
London, United Kingdom
W1X 9PA
Tel: +44 207.49.34.63.8
Fax: +44 207.49.96.09.3
Web: http://www.jadooworks.com

Janet Benn
16 West Main St. #1
Millers Falls, Massachusetts
01349
United States
Tel: 1-413-659-3009
Web: http://www.janetbenn.com

Janimation
840 Exposition Avenue
Dallas, Texas 75226
United States
Tel: 1-214-823-7760
Fax: 1-214-823-7761
Web: http://www.janimation.com

Jarni Animation
1155 W Rene-Levesque Blvd.
Suite 2500
Montreal, Quebec
H3B 2K4
Canada
Tel: 1-514-249-8171
Tel: 1-514-288-0922
Fax: 514-875-8967
Web: http://www.jarni.com

Jellyfish Pictures
87 St. John's Wood Terrace
London, United Kingdom
NW8 6PY
Tel: +44 207.48.36.02.0
Fax: +44 207.48.34.26.4
Web: http://www.jellyfishpictures.co.uk

JFP Inc.
Kinsan Bldg. 2F
Zaimokucho 2-26
Morioka-City
Iwate, Japan
020-0063
Tel: +81-19-623-3613
Fax: +81-19-623-4028
Web: http://www.jfpinc.com

JFP Inc.
Marios Building 7F
Morioka Station Nishi-Dori 9-1
Morioka City
Iwate Prefecture, Japan
020-0045
Tel: +81-19-621-8370
Fax: +81-19-621-5286
Web: http://www.jfpinc.com

JFP Inc.
Nankai Tokyo Bldg.
Iwate Ginga Plaza
Chuo-ku Ginza 5-15-1
Tokyo, Japan
104-0061
Tel: +81-3-3524-8265
Fax: +81-3-3524-8291
Web: http://www.jfpinc.com

Jigsaw Pictures
624 West Main Street #78

Norwich, Connecticut 06360
United States
Tel: 1-866-475-3248
Fax: 1-212-227-6806
Web: http://www.jigsawpictures.com

Jim Henson Company
30 Oval Road
Camden
London
NW1 7DE
United Kingdon
Tel: 011-44-207-428-4000
Fax: 011-44-207-428-4001
Web: http://www.henson.com

Jim Henson Company
1416 North La Brea Avenue
Holywood, California 90028
United States
Tel: 1-323-802-1500
Fax: 1-323-802-1825
Web: http://www.henson.com

Jim Henson Company
117 East 69th Street
New York, New York 10021
United States
Tel: 1-212-794-2400
Fax: 1-212-570-1147
Web: http://www.henson.com

Jones Productions
517 Chester Street
Little Rock, Arkansas 72212
United States
Tel: 1-501-372-1981
Tel: 1-800-880-1981
Fax: 1-501-372-4286
Web: http://www.jonesinc.com

JP Kids
Second Floor
989 Market Street
San Francisco, California 94103
Tel: 1-415-371-8600
Fax: 1-415-371-8905
Web: http://www.jpkids.com

JP Kids
c/o Warner Brothers Animation
15301 Ventura Boulevard
Building E, Suite 1031
Sherman Oaks, California 91403
United States
Tel: 1-818-977-3100
Web: http://www.jpkids.com

JP Kids
367 Windsor Highway, Suite 178
New Windsor, New York 12553
United States
Tel: 1-845-534-4424
Fax: 1-845-534-8441
Web: http://www.jpkids.com

Juice Design (The)
Scarsdale House
Derbyshire Lane
Sheffield S8 8SE
United Kingdom
Tel: +44 114.24.96.40.0
Fax: +44 114.24.96.40.4
Web: http://www.thejuice.co.uk

Junction-18 Limited
Lord Hope Building
141 St. James Road
Glasgow, G4 0LT
United Kingdom
Tel: 0141 303 8300
Fax: 0141 552 3886
Web: http://www.junction-18.com

Just Group Plc
Just House
74 Shepherd's Bush Green
London
W12 8QE
United Kingdom
Tel: +44 (0)208 746 9300
Tel: +44 (0)208 746 9100
Fax: +44 (0)208 746 9111
Fax: +44 (0)208 746 9333
Web: http://www.justgroup.com

Just2Guys
34th St
New York, New York
United States
Web: http://www.just2guys.com

JWM Productions
6930 Carroll Avenue, Suite 600
Takoma Park, Maryland 20912
Tel: 1-301-891-1769
Fax: 1-301-891-1644
Web: http://www.jwmprods.com

Kaktus Film
Kungsgatan 56
Stockholm, Sweden
111 22
Tel: +46 8.66.07.57.9
Fax: +46 8.66.18.07.7
Web: http://www.kaktus-film.se

Kaleidoscope, Inc.
23625 Commerce Park Road, Suite
130
Beachwood, Ohio 44122
United States
Tel: 1-216-360-0630
Fax: 1-216-360-9109
Web: http://www.kascope.com

Kandor Graphics
Melchor Almagro 1
18002 Granada
Spain
Tel: +34 902 300 000
Tel: +34 958 804 100
Fax: +34 958 272 877
Web:
http://www.kandorgraphics.com

Kapow Pictures
Level 1/21 Chandos Street
St Leonards, Sydney NSW
Australia 2065
Tel: 612-9438-1805
Fax: 612-9437-0805
Web:
http://www.kapowpictures.com.au

Kapow Pictures
Level 1
5 Ridge Street
North Sydney NSW
Australia 2060
Tel: 61 2-9929-4455
Fax: 61 2-9929-7755
Web:
http://www.kapowpictures.com.au

Kappa Studios
3619 West Magnolia Blvd.
Burbank, California 91505
United States
Tel: 1-818-843-3400
Fax: 1-818-559-2418
Web: http://www.kappastudios.com

Katuns Entertainment
XL/5887, AVS Building
Near Padma Junction
MG Road
Cochin, Kerala India
682035
Tel: +91 48.43.66.37.8
Web: http://www.katuns.com

Kavaleer Productions LTD
47 Capel street
Dublin, Ireland
Web:
http://www.kavaleerproductions.com

Kayenta Production
2, Impasse Mousset
75012 Paris
France
Tel: 33 (1) 43 45 55 44
Fax: 33 (1) 43 40 69 55
Web: http://www.kayenta.com

KAZe Co., Ltd.
Tokyo 107-0062
Japan
Tel: 03-5778-0599
Fax: 03-3797-0277
Web: http://www.kazenet.com

KBT
236 Raceway Drive Ste #1
Raleigh, North Carolina 28117
United States
Tel: 1-877-660-3555
Tel: 1-704-660-3555
Fax: 1-704-660-3553
Web:
http://www.bumgamerproductions.com

K Design
2150 Joshua's Path, Suite 10
Hauppauge, New York 11788
United States
Tel: 1-631-232-3768
Fax: 1-631-232-3769
Web: http://www.kdesign.tv

K-Effects
Gartengasse 21
Vienna, Austria
1050
Tel: +43.15.86.30.40
Web: http://www.k-effects.com

Ken Clark Films
71 Langdons Road
Christchurch, Canterbury New
Zealand
8005
Tel: +64 3.35.24.10.9
Fax: +64 3.35.24.10.9
Web:
http://www.kenclarkfilms.com

Key Emura
5601 F-Forest Oaks
Raleigh, North Carolina 27609
United States
Web: http://www.keyemura.com

Keyframe Post
1384 Broadway, Suite 1500
New York, New York 10018
United States
Tel: 1-212-997-9100
Web: http://www.keyframepost.com

Keyframe Digital
360 York Rd. Suite C3
Niagara-On-The-Lake
Ontario, Canada
L0S 1J0
Tel: 1-905-988-6440
Fax: 1-905-988-6443
Web: http://www.keyframed.com

KI.KA - Der Kinderkanal
ARD/ZDF
Erfurt, Germany
99081

Tel: +49 180.21.51.51.4
Fax: +49 180.21.51.51.6
Web: http://www.kika.de

Kids Can Press Limited
29 Birch Avenue
Toronto, Ontario
Canada M4V 1E2
Tel: (416) 925-5437
Fax: (416) 960-5437
Web: http://www.nelvana.com

KIDDINX Media AG
Lahnstrasse 21
Berlin, Germany
12055
Tel: +49 30.68.97.21.24
Fax: +49 30.68.97.21.26
Web: http://www.kiddinx-media.de

KIDDINX Studios GmbH
Eberschenallee 7
Berlin, Germany
14050
Tel: +49 30.68.97.21.24
Fax: +49 30.68.97.21.26
Web: http://www.kiddinx-media.de

Killing Time Pictures
5117 Honeydew Ln.
Wilmington, North Carolina 28412
United States
Tel: +1 910.395.4178
Web:
http://www.killingtimepictures.com

Kinetic Impulse
87 Hadlow Road
Tonbridge
Kent
TN9 1QD
United Kingdom
Tel: +44 (0) 7788 710481
Fax: +44 (0) 1732 364067
Web:
http://www.kinetic-impulse.com

King Camera Services
73A Beak Street
Soho
London, United Kingdom

W1R 3LF
Tel: +44 207.43.97.44.5
Fax: +44 207.43.97.16.6
Web: http://www.kingcamera.co.uk

Kitchen Sink Studios Inc.
815 North First Avenue, Suite 5
Phoenix, Arizona 85003
United States
Tel: 1-602-258-3150
Fax: 1-602-296-0426
Web:
http://www.kitchensinkstudios.com

Klasky Csupo
6353 Sunset Blvd
Holywood, California 90028
United States
Tel: 1-323-468-5978
Fax: 1-323-468-3021
Web: http://www.klaskycsupo.com

Klauss Studios GmbH
Senefelderstr.9
30880 Laatzen
Germany
Tel: +49(0)511 983850
Fax: +49(0)511 9838515
Web: http://www.klauss-studios.de

Kleiser-Walczak - Hollywood
6315 Yucca St. (at Vine)
Hollywood, California 90028-5057
United States
Tel: 1-323-467-3563
Fax: 1-323-467-3583
Web: http://www.kwcc.com
Web: http://kleiser-walczak.com

Kleiser-Walczak - MASS MoCA
87 Marshall Street, Bldg. 1
North Adams, Massachusetts
01247
United States
Tel: 1-413-664-7441
Fax: 1-413-664-7442
Web: http://www.kwcc.com
Web: http://kleiser-walczak.com

KliK Animation
5524, St-Patrick St., Suite 302
Montreal, Quebec Canada
H4E 1A8
Tel: +1 514.842.6602
Fax: +1 514.842.6603
Web: http://www.klikanimation.com

KM
41 rue des Peupliers
92100 Boulogne
France
Tel: 33 1 47 61 84 00
Fax: 33 1 47 61 84 04
Web: http://www.kmprod.fr

KO-MAR Productions, Inc.
1100 Banyan Boulevard
West Palm Beach, Florida 33401
United States
Tel: 1-561-671-3745
Fax: 1-561-671-3750
Web: http://www.ko-mar.com

Kredema Illustration Web &
Grafisk form
Kyrkogatan 4
411 15 Göteborg
Sweden
Tel: 031-774 04 30
Web: http://www.kredema.se

Krislin Company
30497 Canwood St. - Suite 200
Agoura Hills, California 91301
United States
Tel: 1-818-707-2029
Fax: 1-818-707-2031
Web:
http://www.krislincompany.com

Kristin Harris Design, Inc.
3035 Hazelton Street
Falls Church, Virginia 22044
United States
Tel: 1-703-536-9594
Fax: 1-703-241-7463
Web:
http://www.kristinharrisdesign.com

Krogh Mortensen Animation a/s
Store Kongensgade 61B
Copenhagen, Denmark
1264
Tel: +45 70.25.24.54
Web: http://www.km-animation.dk

Kukepictures
Tirana, Albania
Web: http://www.kukepictures.com

L.A. Animation Inc.
3115 West Olive Avenue
Burbank, California 91505
Tel: 1-818-841-2447
Web: http://www.laanimation.com

Laer Digital Works
53 McCaul Street
Suite 647
Toronto, Ontario Canada
M5T 2W9
Tel: +1 416.260.9487
Web: http://www.laerworks.com

La Huella Efectos Digitales
C/Barquillo 25
3oD- 28004 Madrid
Spain
Tel: 915 238 235
Fax: 915 222 622
Web: http://www.lahuellafx.com

La maison
13/15 rue Gaston Latouche
92 210 St-Cloud
France
Tel: 33.(0)1.41.12.2000
Fax: 33.(0)1.41.12.2001
Web: http://www.alamaison.fr

Lamb & company
1942 Humbolt Ave. S.
Minneapolis, Minnesota 55403
United States
Tel: 1-612-377-5980
Fax: 1-612-377-5979
Web: http://www.lamb.com

Lastrego & Testa Multimedia S.r.l.
7, piazza Gozzano
Turin, Italy
10132
Tel: +39 11.81.95.39.1
Fax: +39 11.81.95.39.1
Web: http://www.lastregoetesta.com

La Truka
C/Port 80U 6
08028 Barcelona
Spain
Tel: +34 93 339 45 00
Fax: +34 93 491 17 16
Web: http://www.latruka.es

Lawrence Co., The
2601 Ocean Park Boulevard, Suite 310
Santa Monica, California 90405
United States
Tel: 1-310-425-9657
Fax: 1-310-399-3774
Web: http://www.lawrenceco.com

Lawson & Whatshisname B.V.
Korte Leidsdwarsstraat 12-411
1017 RC Amsterdam
The Netherlands
Tel: +31-(0)20-6253197
Tel: +31-(0)20-3690100
Fax: +31-(0)20-6206804
Web: http://www.lawsonandwhat-
shisname.com

Leaping Raster Inc.
180 Metcalfe Street
Suite 204
Ottawa, Ontario Canada
K2P 1P5
Tel: +1 613.236.4757
Fax: +1 613.236.4770
Web: http://www.leaping.com

Lemonade Animation
Rapenburg 33
1011 TV
Amsterdam
The Netherlands
Tel: (0)20-4211162
Web: http://www.lemonade.nl

Les Armateurs
47, rue Sedaine
Paris, France
75011
Tel: +33 1.49.29.09.77
Fax: +33 1.49.29.05.37
Web: http://www.lesarmateurs.com

LestaStudio
18 Moskovski Prospekt, Office 1
St.Petersburg
198013 Russia
Tel: +7(812) 3165056
Fax: +7(812) 3208445
Tel: http://www.lesta.ru

Letca Corp.
2122 S.W. 22nd Ave.
Miami, Florida 33145
United States
Tel: 1-305-860-3833
Fax: 1-305-860-3834
Web: http://www.letca.com

Letts Education
Auld Dine House
Auld Dine Place
London
W12 8AW
Tel: 020 8740 2266
Web: http://www.granadamedia.com

Level 3 Post
2901 West Alameda Avenue, 3rd
Floor
Burbank, California 91505
United States
Tel: 1-818-840-7200
Fax: 1-818-840-7801
Web: http://www.level3post.com

Liberty International
Entertainment Inc.
1990 Westwood Blvd., Penthouse
Los Angeles, California 90025
United States
Tel: 1-310-474-4456
Tel: 1-800-576-3431
Fax: 1-310-474-7455
Web: http://libertyinteractive.com

Liberty Livewire
520 Broadway
Santa Monica, California 90401
United States
Tel: 1-310-434-7000
Web: http://www.libertylivewire.com

Lightborne Inc.
212 east fourteenth street
Cincinnati, Ohio 45202
United States
Tel: 1-513-721-2272
Tel: 1-877-721-2272
Fax: 1-513-721-2310
Web: http://www.light-borne.com

LightImage
1 Wincombe Business Park,
Shaftesbury,
Dorset,
SP7 9QJ
United Kingdom
Tel: +44 (0) 1747 854315
Fax: +44 (0) 1747 852634
Web: http://www.lightimage.co.uk

Lighthouse Visual
Communications
Sequel House
The Hart, Farnham
Surrey
England
GU9 7HW
United Kingdom
Tel: +44 (0)1252 726 302
Fax: +44 (0)1252 820 359
Web: http://www.lvc.co.uk

Lightstorm3D
Kestnerstrasse 9
30159 Hannover
Germany
Web: http://www.lightstorm3d.com

Light Works (The)
Emil Hoffmann Strasse 27
50996 Köln
Germany
Tel: +49 2236 967322
Fax: +49 2236 967319
Web: http://www.thelightworks.com

Lights & Shadows Pte Ltd.
53 Amoy Street
Singapore, Singapore
069879
Tel: +65.62.20.99.80
Fax: +65.62.20.99.83
Web: http://www.LNS.com.sg

Limerick Studios
1512 Camden Rd.
Charlotte, North Carolina 28203
United States
Tel: 1-704-371-4991
Fax: 1-704-371-4992
Web: http://www.limerickstudios.com

Links DigiWorks Inc.
2-14-1 higashi-Gotanda
Shinagawa-Ku, Tokyo 141-0022
Japan
Tel: 81-3-5420-6138
Fax: 81-3-5420-6139
Web: http://www.linksdw.com

Lions Gate Studios
5750 WILSHIRE BLVD, STE 501
Los Angeles, California 90036
United States
Tel: 1-323-692-7300
Fax: 1-323-692-7373
Web: http://www.lionsgatefilms.com

Lion Toons
Calabria, 16
Barcelona, Catalonia Spain
08015
Tel: +34 93.42.30.36.2
Fax: +34 93.42.43.68.2
Web: http://www.liontoons.com

Lipsync Post
Screen House
123 Wardour St
London
W1f Ouw
United Kingdom
Tel: +44 (0)20 7534 9123
Fax: +44 (0)20 7534 9124
Web: http://www.lipsync.co.uk

Liquid Light Studios
1093 Broxton Avenue, Suite 220
Los Angeles, California 90024
United States
Tel: 1-310-443-5551
Fax: 1-310-443-5542
Web:
http://www.liquidlightstudios.com

Liquid Pictures
833 Bancroft Way
Berkeley California, 94710
United States
Tel: 1-510-644-3533
Fax: 1-510-644-3531
Web: http://www.liquidpictures.com

Liquid TV
Soho
London
W1F 8Je
United Kingdom
Tel: +44 (0)20 7437 2623
Fax: +44 (0)20 7437 2618
Web: http://www.liquid.co.uk

Little Fluffy Clouds
499 Albama, Suite 112
San Francisco, California 94110
United States
Tel: 1-415-621-1300
Fax: 1-415-621-8328
Fax: 1-415-389-9304
Web:
http://www.littlefluffyclouds.com

Loaded Image
408-1200 West Pender
Vancouver, British Columbia
Canada
V6E 2S9
Tel: +1 604.484.4198
Fax: +1 604.484.4199
Web: http://www.loadedimage.com

Locomotion Germany
Gruenstrasse 8
d-40212 Duesseldorf
Germany
Tel: +49 (0)211 867 470
Fax: +49 (0)211 867 4719
Web: http://www.locomotion.de

Locomotion UK
19 Greek Street
W1D 4DT
London, England
United Kingdom
Tel: +44 (0) 20 7304 4403
Fax: +44 (0) 20 7304 4400
Web: http://www.locomotion.co.uk

LocomotionPictures,inc
Hamamatsu City
Sanwa Cho
Shizuoka 435-0038
Japan
Tel: 053-469-3383
Fax: 053-469-3384
Web: http://www.locop.co.jp

Lokman Produkties
Schiekade 51a
3033 BD Rotterdam
The Netherlands
Tel: 010 - 2430988
Fax: 010 - 2650022
Web: http://www.lokman.nl

Lola Post
14-16 Great Portland St
London W1W 8LE
United Kingdom
Tel: 020 7907 7878
Web: http://www.lola-post.com

Long Communications Group
2200 Gateway Center Blvd. Suite 213
Raleigh, North Carolina 27560
United States
Tel: 1-919-481-1188
Fax: 1-919-380-0808
Web: http://www.longcomm.com

Loop Filmworks
45 Main Street, Suite 1001, 10th floor
Brooklyn, New York 11201
United States
Tel: 1-718-522-5667
Web: http://www.loopfilmworks.com

Loopmedia Inc.
401 Richmond Street West, Suite 243
Toronto, Ontario Canada

M5V 3A8
Tel: +1 416.595.6496
Fax: +1 416.595.0306
Web: http://www.loopmedia.com

London News Network
The London Television Centre
Upper Ground
London SE1 9LT
Tel: 020 7827 7701
Web: http://www.lnn-tv.co.uk

Loop Media Inc.
401 Richmond St. West, Suite
243
Toronto, Ontario M5V 3A8
Canada
Tel: 1-416-595-6496
Fax: 1-416-595-0306
Web: http://www.loopmedia.com

Lost Boys Studios
Third Floor - 395 Railway St.
Vancouver, British Columbia
Canada
V6A 1A6
Tel: +1 604.738.1805
Fax: +1 604.738.1806
Web:
http://www.lostboys-studios.com

Lost Pencil Animation Studios Inc.
84 Marquis Place
Airdrie, Alberta Canada
T4A1Z1
Tel: +1 403.948.6823
Web: http://www.lostpencil.com

Lough House
Approach Road Ramsey
Isle of Man IM8 1EB
United Kingdom
Tel: 011-44-0-1624-817-151
Fax: 011-44-0-1624-817-150
Web: http://www.lough-house.com

Lough House Animation, Ltd.
Jurby Road
Ramsey, Isle of Man United
Kingdom
IM7 2EB
Tel: +44 162.48.17.15.1
Fax: +44 162.48.17.15.0
Web: http://www.lough-house.com

Lovette Arts, LLC
880 Apollo Street Suite 302
El Segundo, California 90245
United States
Web: http://www.lovettearts.com

Lucetius Design
1131 Masselin Ave
Los Angeles, California 90019
United States
Tel: 1-323-954-1438
Fax: 1-323-954-1448
Web: http://www.lucetiusdesign.com

Ludens Co., Ltd.
3 - 24 - 8 Cherry Tree Stand
House Nines 202 / 203
Nerima Ku Toyoyama north
Tokyo 176-0012
Japan
Tel: 03-5999-7222
Fax: 03-5999-7223
Web: http://www.ludens.co.jp

Luk Film - Ansan Studio
#643-7
Wongok-dong
Ansan-si
Kyunggi-do
Korea
Tel: +82 31 494 7411
Fax: +82 31 494 7412
Web: http://www.lukfilm21.com

Luk Film - Chracter Business
Dept.
Hyundai Dream Tower #607
923-14
Mok-dong
Yangchon-gu
Seoul
Korea
Tel: +82 2 574 8811
Fax: +82 2 574 8821
Web: http://www.lukfilm21.com

Lukkien Digital Studios
Copernicuslaan 15
6716 BM EDE
The Netherlands
Tel: +31 (0) 318-698000
Fax: +31 (0) 318-698099
Web: http://www.lukkien.nl

Luma Studios
Randburg, Johannesburg
South Africa
Web: http://www.lumastudios.com

Luminetik 3D Animation and VFX
Studio
535 W 34th Street
New York, New York 10001
United States
Tel: 1-646-792-2565
Fax: 1-646-792-2566
Web: http://www.Luminetik.com

Luna Seven Imagery
1581-H Hillside Avenue, Suite 221
Victoria, British Columbia Canada
V8T 2C1
Web: http://lunaseven.com

The Lunny Group
20th Floor
1500 West Georgia Street
Vancouver, British Columbia
V6G 2Z6 Canada
Tel: 1-604-669-0333
Fax: 1-604-662-7500
Web: http://www.lunny.com

LWT
The London Television Centre
Upper Ground
London
SE1 9LT
Tel: 020 7620 1620
Web: http://www.lwt.co.uk

M2 Studio
5438 Belmont Ave.
Dallas, Texas 75206
United States
Tel: 1-214-752-7279
Fax: 1-214-370-3687
Web: http://www.m2studio.net

M6 DA
89, avenue Charles de Gaulle
Neuilly sur Seine, France 92575
Tel: +33 1.41.92.66.66
Fax: +33 1.41.92.68.99
Web: http://www.m6.fr

Machine Room, The
54-58 Wardour Street
London
W1D 4JQ
Tel: +44 (0) 20 7734 3433
Fax: +44 (0) 20 7287 3773
Web: http://www.themachine-
room.co.uk

Mac Guff Ligne
6 Rue de la cavalerie
Paris, France
75015
Tel: +33 1.53.58.46.46
Fax: +33 1.53.58.46.47
Web: http://www.macguff.fr

Machete Edit and Design
United States
Web: http://www.machete.tv

Machine Room (The)
54-58 Wardour Street
London, United Kingdom
W1D 4JQ
Tel: +44 207.73.43.43.3
Fax: +44 207.28.73.77.3
Web: http://www.themachine-
room.co.uk

Macquarium
1800 Peachtree Street North
West, Suite 250
Atlanta, Georgia 30309-2517
United States
Tel: 1-404-554-4000
Fax: 1-404-554-4001
Web: http://www.macquarium.com

Madcap Studios
Unit 8 / 620 Botany Rd
Alexandria New South Wales
Australia 2015
Tel: +61 2 8338 0173
Fax: +61 2 8338 0176
Web: http://www.madcapstudios.com

Madcap Studios
P.O. Box 862
Bondi Junction, New South Wales
Australia 2022
Tel: +61 2 8338 0173
Fax: +61 2 8338 0176
Web: http://www.madcapstudios.com

MadLineStudio
P.O. Box 221
Vilnius, Lithuania
2040
Tel: +370 2.30.38.29
Fax: +370 2.30.38.29
Web: http://www.madlinestudio.com

Madpix
C/ Antonio Maura 16
28014 Madrid
Spain
Tel: +34 91 5249880
Fax: +34 91 5249884
Web: http://www.mad-pix.com

Madtown Media
125 North Halsted, Suite 202
Chicago Illinois 60661
United States
Tel: 1-312-930-0993
Fax: 1-312-382-1068
Web:
http://www.madtownmedia.com

Magick Lantern
750 Ralph McGill Boulevard
Atlanta, Georgia 30312
United States
Tel: 1-404-688-3348
Web: http://www.magicklantern.com

Magic Stone Productions
1/1, 16 Ruthven Street
Glasgow, Scotland United
Kingdom
G12 9BS
Web: http://www.magicstone.co.uk

Magnetic North
70 Richmond Street East, Suite
100
Toronto, Ontario, Canada

M5C 1N8
Tel: 1-416-365-7622
Tel: 1-800-MAG-POST
Fax: 1-416-365-2188
Web: http://www.magpost.com

Mainframe Entertainment, Inc.
2025 West Broadway, Suite 500
Vancouver, British Columbia
Canada V6J 1Z6
Tel: 1-604-714-2600
Fax: 1-604-714-2641
Web: http://www.mainframe.ca

Mainframe Facilities
108, Av de l'Opale
1030 Bruxelles
Belgium
Tel : +32 2 739.15.10
Fax : +32 2 739.15.11
Web: http://www.main-frame.be

Makonin Consulting Corp.
3185 Graveley Street
Vancouver, British Columbia
Canada V5K 3K7
Tel: 1-604-253-8288
Web: http://www.makonin.com

Malcriados
Ravignani 1949
Buenos Aires, Capital Federal
Argentina
1414
Tel: +54 11.47.78.11.18
Fax: +54 11.47.78.11.18
Web: http://www.malcriados.com

Manchester United Television Ltd
274 Deansgate
Manchester
M3 4SB
Tel: 0161 834 1111
Web: http://www.manutd.com/mutv

Manex Entertainment, Inc.
4751 Wilshire Boulevard, Suite 202
Los Angeles, California 90010
United States
Tel: 1-323-936-6822
Fax: 1-323-936-7968

Web: http://www.mvfx.com
Manta Digital Sound And Picture
49 Ontario St.
Toronto, Ontario Canada
M5A 2V1
Tel: +1 416.364.8512
Fax: +1 416.364.7400
Web: http://www.compt.com

Mantis Motion Productions
9324 S Hawley Park Rd. Suite C
West Jordan, Utah 84088
United States
Tel: 1-801-282-6694
Web: http://www.mantismotion.com

Mantra Stockholm Animation
Labratory
Atlatsgatan 3
113 20 Stockholm
Sweden
Tel: +46 (0)8 331700
Web: http://www.mantra.se

Marathon
74 Rue Bonaparte
75006 Paris
France
Tel: 011-33-0-1-44-34-66-00
Fax: 011-33-0-144-34-66-05
Web: http://www.marathon.fr

Marchand Media
420 West 45th Street
3rd Floor
New York, New York 10036
United States
Tel: 1-212-974-8411
Fax: 1-212-974-8418
Web:
http://www.marchandmedia.com

M.A.R.K.13
Johannesstr.58a
70176 Stuttgart
Germany
Tel.: +49(O)711.99 33 93 0
Fax: +49(O)711.99 33 93 29
Web: http://www.mark13.com

Mark Coleran FX
19 Chequer Orchard
Iver Heath, Buckinghamshire
United Kingdom
SL0 6NH
Tel: +44 797.34.10.09.1
Web: http://www.coleran.com

Marriott Video Productions
737 Lawton Street
McLean, Virginia 22101
United States
Tel: 1-703-556-0736
Fax: 1-703-556-0736
Web: http://www.marriottvideo.com

Match Frame Computer Graphics
3101 Bee Caves Rd., Suite 300
Austin, Texas, 78746
United States
Tel: 1-512-328-0078
Tel: 1-800-528-0078
Fax: 1-512-328-1016
Web: http://www.matchframe.com

Match Frame Computer Graphics
8531 Fairhaven
San Antonio, Texas 78229
United States
Tel: 1-210-614-5678
Tel: 1-800-929-2790
Fax: 1-210-616-0299
Web: http://www.matchframe.com

Matrix Design Animation
355 Adelaide Street West
Suite 2B
Toronto, Ontario Canada
M5V 1S2
Tel: +1 416.340.7716
Fax: +1 416.340.9873
Web: http://www.matrixpost.com

Matrix Video
#9, 6120 - 3RD St. SE
Calgary, AB T2H 1K4
Canada
Tel: 1-403-640-4490
Fax: 1-403-640-9012
Web:
http://www.matrixvideocom.com

Matte World Digital
24 Digital Drive, Suite 6
Novato, California 94949
United States
Tel: 1-415-382-1929
Fax: 1-415-382-1999
Web: http://www.matteworld.com

Maximum Output Designs, Inc.
29 S. Front St., Suite B
Wilmington, North Carolina 28401
United States
Tel: 1-910-342-0182
Web: http://www.maximumoutput-designs.com

Maximus Studios
willem van gentstraat 35A
Geldrop, North Brabant
Netherlands
NL-5666 GA
Tel: +31-40-2868485
Fax: +31-40-2927257
Web: http://www.maximus.nl

Max Ink Cafe, LLC
2700 Pacific Avenue
Venice, California 90291
United States
Tel: 1-310-827-5351
Fax: 1-310-827-5651
Web: http://www.maxinkcafe.com

Maya Entertainment Ltd
13101 Washington Blvd. #115
Los Angeles, California 90066
United States
Tel: 1-310-566-7427
Fax: 1-310-566-7433
Web: http://www.mayaent.com

Maya Entertainment Ltd
23 Shah Industrial Estate
Off Veera Desai Road
Andheri (west)
Mumbai 400 053
India
Tel: 00-22-6731145\6\7\8
Tel: 00-22-6924811\2\3\4\5
Fax: 00-91-6730961
Web: http://www.mayaent.com

MBA Studios
63500 Seligenstadt
Germany
Tel: +49 6182 200940
Fax: +49 6182 200948
Web: http://www.mba-studios.de

MBC Production Co., Ltd.
4th Floor, Yulchon B/D 24-1
Yoido-Dong, Youngdungpo-ku
Seoul, South Korea
150-010
Tel: +82 2.78.90.10.0
Fax: +82 2.78.90.11.01
Web: http://mbcpro.co.kr

McArthur Communications, Inc.
1805 Monument Avenue, Suite 601
Richmond, Virginia 23220
United States
Tel: 1-804-754-0102
Fax: 1-804-754-1891
Web: http://www.mcarthur.com

MCW Studio's
Postbus 3370
3003 AJ Rotterdam
Crooswijksesingel 50D
3034 CJ Rotterdam
Tel.: 010 - 452 25 26
Fax: 010 - 212 00 14
Web: http://www.mcw.nl

Meccanica
50 East 42nd Street
18th Floor, Suite 1801
New York, New York 10017
United States
Tel: 1-212-986-3844
Fax: 1-212-986-2899
Web: http://www.meccanica.tv

Mechanism Digital
514 West 24th Street, 3rd floor,
New York, New York 10011
United States
Tel: 1-646-230-0230
Web:
http://www.mechanismdigital.com

Me Company
London, England
United Kingdom
Tel: +44 (0)207 482 4262
Fax: +44 (0)207 284 0402
Web: http://www.mecompany.com

Media-Comm
9700 Southern Pine Boulevard
Charlotte, North Carolina 28273
United States
Tel: 1-704-527-8853
Fax: 1-704-525-2722
Fax: 1-704-561-7973
Web: http://www.media-comm.com

m e d i a f x
Overbosstraat 16
B3730 Hoeselt
Belgium
Tel: +32 (0)89.79.41.21
Fax: +32 (0)89.79.41.22
Web: http://www.mediafx.be

Media Mezcla LLC
New York, New York
United States
Tel: 1-212-465-2591
Web:
http://www.mediamezcla.com

Media Mutant
Hackstrasse 77
Stuttgart, Germany
70190
Tel: +49 71.12.85.52.0
Fax: +49 71.12.85.22.2
Web: http://www.mediamutant.de

Media Principia
3530 St-Laurent Blvd.
Montreal, Quebec
Canada
Tel: 1-514-849-4633
Web:
http://www.mediaprincipia.com

Media Workshop of Central
Finland
Sepankatu 3
Jyvaskyla, Keski-Suomi Finland

40720
Tel: +358 14.44.45.73.6
Web: http://www.mediapaja.org

Meijers Media
Kanaalkade 16 A
Alkmaar, Netherlands
1811 LP
Tel: +31 72.53.54.03.0
Fax: +31 72.52.04.92.0
Web: http://www.m2.nl

Melazeta srl
V. le Virgilio, 56/A
Modena, MO Italy
41100
Tel: +39 59.84.73.20
Fax: +39 59.88.52.45
Web: http://www.melazeta.com

MeldMedia
881 Bathurst St.
Suite 2
Toronto, Ontario Canada
M5R 3G2
Tel: +1 416.588.5872
Web: http://www.meldmedia.com

Melon FX
Hungary
Web: http://www.melon.hu

Menfond Electronic Art
& Computer Design Co. Ltd.
54/F, Hopewell Centre
183 Queen's Road East
Wanchai, Hong Kong
Tel: 852-2802-3382
Fax: 852-2802-3386
Web: http://www.menfond.com.hk

Men From Mars
Unit 6
Walpole Court
Ealing Studios
Ealing Green
London
W5 5ED
Tel: +44 (0) 20 8280 9000
Fax: +44 (0) 20 8280 9001
Web:
http://www.men-from-mars.com

Meridian Broadcasting
Television Centre
Southampton SO14 OPZ
Tel: 023 8022 2555
Web: http://www.meridian.tv.co.uk

Mesh22
22 Albany St.
Crows Nest NSW 2065
Australia
Tel: 612 9432 2722
Fax: 612 9438 4050
Web: http://www.mesh22.com

Messy Optics
3001 19th St
San Francisco, California 94110
United States
Tel: 1-415-641-0391
Web: http://www.messyoptics.com

Metacube
Privada Del Nino No. 25
Col. Camino Real. 45030
Guadalajara Jalisco, Mexico
Tel: 0443-33-156-155-5
Web: http://www.metacube.com.mx

Metagraphical Interactive
Long Island, New York 11793
United States
Web: http://www.metagraphical.com

Metaphoria Productions
1496 Lafayette Rd.
Claremont, California 91711
United States
Tel: 1-909-626-2626
Fax: 1-909-624-1436
Web: http://www.metaphoria.com

metaREALM media, LLC
920 N 34th St, #38
Seattle, Washington 98103
United States
Tel: 1-206-250-9830
Web: http://www.metarealm.com

Meteor Studios
1751 Richardson
Suite 7200
Montreal, Quebec Canada
H3K 1G6
Tel: 1-514-939-8999
Fax: 1-514-939-2596
Web: http://www.meteorstudios.com

Method Studios
1546 Seventh Street
Santa Monica, California 90401
United States
Tel: 1-310-899-6500
Fax: 1-310-899-6501
Web: http://www.methodstudios.com

MetroLight Studios. Inc.
5724 W. Third Street, Suite 400
Los Angeles, California 90036-
3084
United States
Tel: 1-323-932-0400
Fax: 1-323-932-8440
Web: http://www.metrolight.com

Metro Video Productions
626 W. Olney Road
Norfolk, Virginia 23507
United States
Tel: 1-757-627-6500
Tel: 1-877-NOW4MVP
Fax: 1-757-627-1400
Web: http://www.metrovideo.com

Metro Video Productions
8 South Plum St.
Richmond, Virginia 23220
United States
Tel: 1-804-359-2500
Tel: 1-877-NOW4MVP
Fax: 1-804-354-1552
Web: http://www.metrovideo.com

Metro Video Productions
424 Duke of Gloucester St.
Williamsburg, Virginia 23185
United States
Tel: 1-757-253-0050
Tel: 1-877-NOW4MVP
Fax: 1-757-253-8558
Web: http://www.metrovideo.com

metricminds GmbH & Co. KG
Ruesselsheimer Strasse 22
60326 Frankfurt
Germany
Tel: 069-759 338 0
Tel: 069-759 338 29
Web: http://www.metricminds.com

Metri Gnome Visual
Raleigh, North Carolina
United States
Tel: 1-919-368-6612
Web: http://www.metrignome.net

Metropolisfilm bv
Weerdsingel OZ 8
3514AA Utrecht
The Netherlands
Tel: +31(0)30 234 21 30
Fax: +31(0)30 236 70 88
Web: http://www.metropolisfilm.nl

MGM Worldwide Television Group
2500 Broadway Street
Santa Monica, California 90404
United States
Tel: 1-310-449-3000
Fax: 1-310-586-8137
Web: http://www.mgm.com

Michael Hirsh Animation
Backgrounds
3 Charman Road
Redhill, Surrey United Kingdom
RH1 6AG
Tel: +44 173.77.65.67.9
Web: http://www.animation-back-
grounds.com

Michael Hoff Productions
6702 Hollis St.
Emeryville, California 94608
United States
Tel: 1-510-597-9630
Fax: 1-510-597-9640
Web: http://www.mhptv.com

Microspace
3100 Highwoods Blvd
Raleigh, North Carolina 27604
United States

Tel: 1-919-850-4500
Fax: 1-919-850-4518
Web: http://www.microspace.com

Midland Productions
1680 Shattuck Ave.
Berkeley, California 94709-1631
United States
Tel: 1-510-848-2400
Fax: 1-510-848-2426
Web: http://www.midlandpro.com

Mike Reed and Partners Post
Production
20 Thistlethwaite Street
South Melbourne, Victoria 3205
Tel: +61 3 9690 4044
Fax: +61 3 9699 2078
Web: http://www.mrppp.com.au

Mike Young Productions, Inc.
20335 Ventura Blvd. Suite 225
Woodland Hills, California 91364
United States
Tel: 1-818-999-0062
Fax: 1-818-999-0172
Web: http://www.mikeyoungpro-
ductions.com

Mill (The)
40-41 Great Marlborough Street
London, England
United Kingdom
Tel: +44 207.28.74.04.1
Web: http://www.mill.co.uk

Millimages
88, rue de la Folie Mericourt
75011 Paris, France
Tel: 33 (0) 1 49 29 49 69
Web: http://www.millimages.com

Millimages UK
6 Broadstone Place
London, W1U 7EN
United Kingdom
Tel: +44 (0)20 7486 9555
Fax: +44 (0)20 7486 9666
Web: http://www.millimages-uk.com

Millimages USA
616 N - Robertson Blvd
Los Angeles, California 90069
United States
Tel: 1-310-659 2000
Fax: 1-310-659 2001
Web: http://www.millimages.com

Mindbender Studios
Durham, North Carolina 27278
United States
Tel: 1-919-620-3660
Fax: 1-919-477-5746
Web:
http://www.mindbenderstudios.com

Minds-Eye Productions
Ground Floor
Westfalia house
Old Wolverton Rd
Milton Keynes
Buckinghamshire
MK12 5PY
United Kingdom
Tel: 01908 318315
Fax: 01908 316855
Web: http://www.minds-eye.net

Mindflex
566 Dutch Valley Road
Atlanta, Georgia 30324
United States
Tel: 1-404-892-6232
Tel: 1-877-646-3353
Fax: 1-404-892-6076
Web: http://www.mindflex.com

MindWorks Multimedia, Inc.
P.O. Box 1058
Siler City, North Carolina 27344
United States
Tel: 1-919-806-0411
Tel: 1-866-646-3967
Fax: 1-919-806-0079
Web: http://www.mwmm.com

Miopía Efectos Visuales
c/ Avendaño, nº 14
28007 - Madrid
Spain
Tel: 91 433 40 03
Fax: 91 433 27 71
Web: http://www.miopes.com

MirageQuest Media
Occidental Studios
940 N. Orange Drive,
Suite 207 & Stage 8
Los Angeles, California 90038
United States
Tel: 1-323-962-3758
Fax: 1-323-962-3762
Web: http://www.miragequest.com

Mixin Pixls
1335 4th Street, Suite 200
Santa Monica, California 90401
United States
Tel: 1-310-917-9141
Fax: 1-310-917-9142
Web: http://www.mixinpixls.com

MK Ultra - multimediadesign
Benoordenhoutseweg 230
2596 BG
Den Haag (The Hague)
The Netherlands
Tel: +31 70 3242460
Tel: 070 3242460
Web:
http://www.multimediadesign.nl

M.L.A. Inc.
3-2-22-201 Hirado, Totsuka-Ward
Yokohoma City Kangawa Pref
244-0802
Japan
Tel: 045-825-2982
Fax: 045-825-2899
Web: http://www.mla-inc.jp

Modern VideoFilm
4411 W. Olive Ave.
Burbank, California 91505
United States
Tel: 1-818-840-1700
Web: http://www.mvfinc.com

Modular
139 Machon Bank
Nether Edge
Sheffield, Yorkshire United
Kingdom
S7 1GS
Tel: +44 114.29.66.91.5
Web: http://www.modular.tv

Mojo Zoo, Inc.
942 West Fourth Street
Winston-Salem, North Carolina
27101
United States
Tel: 1-866-mojo-zoo (toll free)
Tel: 1-336-727-9281
Fax: 1-336-727-8820
Web: http://www.mojozoo.com

Molinare
34 Fouberts Place
London
W1F 7PX
United Kingdom
Tel: + 44 (0) 20 7478 7000
Fax: + 44 (0) 20 7478 7299
Web: http://www.molinare.co.uk

Momentum Animation Studios
157 Eastern Rd
South Melbourne
Victoria, Australia
3205
Tel: +61 3 9682 6255
Fax: +61 3 9682 2633
Web:
http://www.momentumanimations.com

Mondo Media Production
135 Mississippi Street
San Francisco, California 94107
United States
Tel: 1-415-865-2700
Fax: 1-415-865-2645
Web: http://www.mondomedia.com

MONDO TV S.p.a.
Via Giuseppe Gatti, 8/a
00162 - Rome
Italy
Tel: +39 - 06 - 86323293
Tel: +39 - 06 - 86320364
Fax: +39 - 06 - 86209836
Web: http://www.mondotv.it

Mongomerey Co. Creative
6050 Washington Blvd.
Culver City, California
United States
Tel: 1-310-558-4914
Fax: 1-310-558-4915
Web: http://www.montgomerycre-
ative.com

Monkey Experiment, The
2, Leaside Avenue
London N10 3Bu
United Kingdom
Web:
http://www.themonkeyexperiment.com
http://www.monkeyexperiment.com

Monster Animation and Design
47 Lower Leeson Street
Dublin 2
Ireland
Tel: +353 1 603 4980
Fax: +353 1 676 1437
Web:
http://www.monsteranimation.ie

Monument
77nollfyra AB
Essingebrogata 33, 1tr
112 61 Stockholm, Sweden
Web: http://www.monument.se

Moon FX sdn bhd
199 Jalan Ampang
Kuala Lumpur 50450
Malaysia
Tel: 603 2141 2219
Fax: 603 2141 2239
Web: http://www.mfx.st

Moonlight Communications
Fayetteville, North Carolina
United States
Tel: 1-910-486-9036
Web: http://www.moonlight1.com

Moovmento Inc.
5520 Chabot
#301
Montreal, Quebec Canada
H2H 2S7
Tel: 1-514-527-1024
Fax: 1-514-527-1189
Web: http://www.moovmento.com

Motel Films
650 North Bronson
Clune Building, 2nd Floor
Hollywood, California 90004
United States

Tel: 1-323-960-4070
Fax: 1-323-960-4047
Web: http://www.motelfilms.com

Motion Capture Company (The)
Crown House
102 Bondgate
Castle Donington
Derby, United Kingdom
DE74 2NR
Tel: +44 133.28.12.93.8
Fax: +44 133.28.12.89.8
Web: http://www.motioncapture.co.uk

Motion FX
Eisenmarkt 4
50667 Cologne
Germany
Tel: +49 221 2584711
Web: http://www.motionfx.org

Motion GmbH
Gruenstrasse 8
d-40212 Duesseldorf
Germany
Tel: +49 (0)211 305057
Fax: +49 (0)211 305059
Web: http://www.motion-online.de

Motion Image
2730 Southwest Third Avenue,
Suite 100
Miami, Florida 33129
United States
Tel: 1-305-859-2000
Fax: 1-305-859-2412
Web: http://www.motionimage.com

Motion Picture Services
PO Box 22663
Chattanooga, Tennessee 37422
United States
Tel: 1-423-238-7000
Fax: 1-423-238-7001
Web: http://www.mpsstudios.com

Moving Images Post Production, Inc.
227 East 45th Street 6th Floor
New York, New York 10017
United States
Tel: 1-212-953-6999

Fax: 1-212-661-0457
Web: http://www.mipost.com

Moving Magic
H.J.E. Wenckebachweg 79-1
1096 AL Amsterdam
The Netherlands
Tel: +31 20 4639240
Fax: +31 20 4639169
Web: http://www.movingmagic.nl

Moving Media
1045 17th St., Studio C
San Francisco, California 94107
United States
Tel: 1-415-861-1759
Web: http://www.movingmedia.com

Moving Picture Company, The
127 Wardour Street
London
England
W1F 0NL
United Kingdom
Tel: +44 (0)20 7434 3100
Tel: +44 (0)20 7287 5187
Fax: +44 (0)20 7437 3951
Fax: +44 (0)20 7734 9150
Web: http://www.moving-picture.com

Movida/Trix
Bondgenotenstraat 282
1190 Brussels
Belgium
Tel: +32 (2) 340 79 80
Fax: +32 (2) 347 72 35
Web: http://www.movida3d.com

Moxie Media, Inc.
800 Distributors Row
Harahan, Louisiana 70123
United States
Tel: 1-800-346-6943
Web: http://www.moxiemedia.com

MT Miami
1111 Lincoln Road, Suite 700
Miami Beach, Florida 33139
United States
Tel: 1-305-674-8900
Fax: 1-305-674-8900
Web: http://www.mtmiami.com

MTK CG Production
1918 north town
Hamamatsu city
Shizuoka 431-3121
Japan
Tel: 053-431-0352
Fax: 053-431-0356
Web: http://www.mtk-cg.co.jp

MTV Animation
1633 Broadway, 31st Floor
New York, New York 10019
United States
Tel: 1-212-654-3667
Fax: 1-212-654-4701
Web: http://www.mtv.com

MTV Production A/S International
Division
40 Vermundsgade
Copenhagen 2100
Denmark
Tel: 011-45-39-16-9900
Fax: 011-45-39-16-9999
Web: http://www.mtv.com

Multi Media Arts
4th Floor Mauldeth House
Nell Lane
Chorlton
Manchester
M21 7RL
United Kingdom
Tel: (44)0161 374 5566
Fax: (44)0161 374 5535
Web: http://www.mmarts.com

Multi Media Matters
Aelbrechtskade 129
3023 JG Rotterdam
The Netherlands
Tel: 010-425-74-77
Tel: 06-53-48-99-63
Tel: 0186-57-3884
Fax: 010-425-71-93
Web: http://www.rbs-group.nl

Multimedia Wizard, The
Raleigh, North Carolina
United States
Tel: 1-919-557-3577
Fax: 1-919-244-8055
Web:
http://www.multimediawizard.com

MUV Technologies Ltd.
3rd Floor, Taas Mahal
10 Montieth Road
Chennai, Tamil Nadu India
600012
Tel: +91 44.50.18.11.1
Fax: +91 44.85.23.52.1
Web: http://www.muvtech.com

Myotte Bellamy Productions Inc.
1061 St-Alexandre #407
Montreal, Quebec Canada
H2Z 1P5
Tel: +1 514.868.9849
Fax: +1 514.868.9849
Web: http://www.myottebellamy.com

Myriad Media
340 Glenwood Avenue
Raleigh, North Carolina 27603
United States
Tel: 1-919-836-8004
Tel: 1-888-757-8784
Fax: 1-919-836-8823
Web: http://www.myriadmedia.net

My-tv
8, via A. Cecchi
Milan, Italy
20146
Tel: +39 2.43.06.90.1
Fax: +39 2.43.31.63.56
Web: http://www.my-tv.it

N1
Vlaamsekaai 73
Antwerp, Belgium
2000
Tel: +32 477.88.13.37
Fax: +32 477.88.13.37
Web: http://www.n1x.com

Nackademin AB
Tre Kronors väg 38
131 31 Nacka
Sweden
Tel: 08-466 60 00
Web: http://www.nackademin.com

Nano-K 3D Interactive
12 rue AmpËre

Grenoble, France
38000
Tel: +33 4.76.84.40.04
Fax: +33 4.76.84.40.05
Web: http://www.nano-k.com

Nanomation
United Kingdom
Tel: +44 (0)20 7436 1176
Web:
http://www.nanomation.co.uk

National Boston
115 Dummer Street
Brookline, Massachusetts 02446
United States
Tel: 1-617-734-4800
Fax: 1-617-734-6323
Web: http://www.nationalboston.com

NBC Enterprises
3500 West Olive Ave. 15th Floor.
Burbank, California 91505
United States
Tel: 1-818-526-6909
Fax: 1-818-526-6909
Web: http://www.nbc.com

nCubic
Seoul, Korea
Tel: 02-3424-4118
Fax: 02-3424-4160
Web: http://www.ncubic.com

NEEZO
50 Strathaven Drive
Unit 50
Mississauga, Ontario Canada
L5R-4E7
Tel: +1 416.697.2029
Fax: +1 905.755.1018
Web: http://www.neezo.com

Nelonen TV
Channel Four Finland
Finland
Web: http://www.nelonen.fi

Nelvana Limited
32 Atlantic Avenue
Toronto, Ontario M6K 1X8
Canada
Tel: 1-416-588-5571
Fax: 1-416-588-5588
Web: http://www.nelvana.com

Nelvana Enterprises Inc.
(Representative Office)
55 rue de Bretagne 75403
Paris, France
Tel: (33) 1 42 71 08 28
Fax: (33) 1 42 71 01 44
Web: http://www.nelvana.com

Nelvana Enterprises (U.K.) Ltd.
Rosedale House
Rosedale Road
Richmond
Surrey
TW9 2SZ
United Kingdom
Tel: +44 (0) 208 939 9030
Fax: +44 (0) 208 939 9031
Web: http://www.nelvana.com

Nelvana Enterprises (U.K.), Ltd.
10-11 Moor Street
London, United Kingdom
W1D 5NF
Tel: +44 (0) 207 439 6400
Fax: +44 (0) 207 439 6396
Web: http://www.nelvana.com

Nelvana Communications, Inc.
4500 Wilshire Blvd. 1st Floor
Los Angeles, California 90010
United States
Tel: 1-323-549-4222
Tel: 1-323-549-4232
Web: http://www.nelvana.com

Nelvana International Limited
228-230 Airport House
Shannon Free Zone, Shannon
County Clare, Ireland
Tel: (0011) 353 61 474244
Fax: (0011) 353 61 474233
Web: http://www.nelvana.com

Nelvana Enterprises
Jarico International Inc.
Tokyo, Japan
Tel: 011-813-3420-1947
Fax: 011-813-3420-2012
Web: http://www.nelvana.com

Neon Noodle (Global Animation)
16030 Ventura Blvd., Suite 510
Encino, California 91436
United States
Tel: 1-818-789-9622
Fax: 1-818-789-9722
Web: http://www.globalanimation.net

Neptuno Film Production, S.L.
C/ Sant Sebastiy, 164, 2n
Terrassa
Barcelona, Catalonia Spain
08223
Tel: +34 93.78.41.62.2
Fax: +34 93.78.42.93.8
Web: http://www.neptunofilms.com

Network Century
211 E. Grand Ave.
Chicago, Illinois 60611
United States
Tel: 1-312-644-1650
Fax: 1-312-644-2096
Web:
http://www.networkcentury.com

NetGuru Inc.
22700 Savi Ranch Pkwy.
E 2/4 Block GP Sector
V,Saltlake,Kolkata-700091
Kolkata, West Bengal India
700091
Tel: +91 33.35.73.57.5
Fax: +91 33.35.73.46.7
Web: http://www.netguru.com

Netherwood Productions
310 Kinsey Street, Suite 102
Raleigh, North Carolina 27603
United States
Tel: 1-919-828-8883
Web: http://www.netherwood.net

Network Ireland Television Ltd.
23 South Frederick Street
Dublin, Ireland 2
Tel: +353 1.67.97.30.9
Fax: +353 1.67.08.79.3
Web: http://www.network-irl-tv.com

NeuroMedia Group, The
Parc scientifique Initialis
Rue Descartes, 2 - 7000 Mons
Belgium
Tel : +32 (0)65-32.15.32
Fax : +32 (0)65-32.15.72
Web:
http://www.neuromediagroup.com

neue deutsche Filmgesellschaft mbH
Kanalstraße 7
85774 Unterföhring
Germany
Tel: 089/ 95 826-0
Fax: 089/ 95 816-0
Web: http://www.ndf.de

New Arrivals
Cruquiusweg 142 B
1019 AK Amsterdam
Tel: +31 (0)20 6255890
Fax: +31 (0)20 6255754
Web: http://www.newarrivals.nl

New Century Digital Media
431 W. Franklin St., Suite #31
Chapel Hill, North Carolina 27516
Tel: 1-919-929-5228
Web: http://www.newcenturydigi-
talmedia.com

New Century Films
431 W. Franklin St., Suite #31
Chapel Hill, North Carolina 27516
United States
Tel: 1-919-929-6439
Fax: 1-919-929-5228
Web: http://www.newcentury-
films.com

NewKat Studios
150 East Olive Street, Suite 216
Burbank, California 91502
United States
Tel: 1-818-556-5281
Fax: 1-818-556-5282
Web: http://www.newkat.com

New Media Magic LLC
2336 NE 23rd Ave.
Portland, Oregon 97212
United States
Tel: 1-503-281-3091
Fax: 1-503-281-3104
Web: http://www.nmmagic.com

NewMIC
600-515 West Hastings Street
Vancouver, British Columbia
Canada V6b 5K3
Tel: 1-604-806-5100
Fax: 1-604-692-0075
Web: http://www.newmic.com

New Pencil
80 Liberty Ship Way, Suite 6
sausalito, California 94965
United States
Tel: 1-415-339-1800
Fax: 1-415-339-1803
Web: http://www.newpencil.com

News 14 Carolina
2505 Atlantic Avenue Suite 102
Raleigh, North Carolina 27604
United States
Tel: 1-919-882-4000
Tel: 1-866-328-1414
Fax: 1-919-882-4015
Web: http://www.news14.com

Nexus Animation
3 rue de duras
Paris, France
75003
Tel: +33 1.48.88.05.30
Web:
http://www.nexusanimation.com

NFL Films
One NFL Plaza

Mt. Laurel, New Jersey 08054
United States
Tel: 1-856-222-3500
Fax: 1-856-866-4848
Web: http://www.nflfilms.com

NFP animation film GmbH Berlin
Kurfürstendamm 57
D-10707 Berlin
Germany
Tel: (+49)030-32909-500
Fax: (+49)030-32909-519
Web: http://www.nfp.de

NFP animation film GmbH
Wiesbaden
Unter den Eichen 5
D-65195 Wiesbaden
Germany
Tel: (+49)0611-18083-10
Fax: (+49)0611-18083-79
Web: http://www.nfp.de

NHB Studios
Tesdorpfstr. 15
20148 Hamburg
Germany
Tel: 040 450 120 0
Fax: 040 450 120 20
Web: http://www.nhb.de

Nick Digital
1515 Broadway - 10th Floor
New York, New York 10036
United States
Tel: 1-212-846-6156
Fax: 1-212-846-1711
Web: http://www.nickdigitallabs.com

Nickelodeon
1515 Broadway, 37th Floor
New York, New York 10036
United States
Tel: 1-212-846-5760
Fax: 1-212-846-1740
Web: http://www.nick.com

Nickelodeon
231 West Olive Street
Burbank, California 91502
United States

Tel: 1-818-736-3000
Fax: 1-818-736-3347
Web: http://www.nick.com

Nickelodeon UK
15-18 Rathbone Place
London, United Kingdom
W1T 1HU
Tel: +44 207.46.21.00.0
Web: http://www.nick.co.uk

NightTribe Inc.
6010 Mohulland Hywy
Los Angeles, California 90068
United States
Tel: 1-323-962-0698
Tel: 1-310-213-9777
Web: http://www.nighttribe.com

Nihon Falcom Corp.
1-14-13, Akebono-cho
Tachikawa-shi, Tokyo 190-0012
Japan
Tel:042-527-0555
Fax: 042-528-2714
Web: http://www.falcom.co.jp

Nimblepix
Moorhead, Minnesota 56560
United States
Web: http://www.nimblepix.com

Nippon Animation
10-11.Ginza 7 Chome Chou-ku
Tokyo 104-0061
Japan
Tel: 011-81-3-3572-3261
Fax: 011-81-3-3574-6284
Web:
http://www.nippon-animation.co.jp
http://www.nipponanimation.com

Nippon Television Network
Corporation
14 Niban-cho
Chiyoda-ku Tokyo 102-8004
Japan
Tel: 81-3-5275-1111
Fax: 81-3-5275-4007
Web: http://www.ntv.co.jp

NOB
Sumatralaan 45
Postbus 10
1200 JB Hilversum
Tel: 035 6779111
Fax: 035 6775444
Web: http://www.nob.nl

Nordisk Film Production A/S
Mosedalvej 14
Valby, Denmark
2500
Tel: +45.36.18.82.00
Web: http://www.nordiskfilm.dk

Northeast Animation Studios
P.O. Box 25
Carver, Massachusetts 02330
United States
Tel: 1-508-866-5562
Web: http://www.northeastanim.com

Northern Lights Post
135 West 27th Street
New York, New York 10001
United States
Tel: 1-212-274-1199
Web: http://www.nlpedit.com

Northwest Imaging & FX
2339 Columbia Street, Suite 100
Vancouver, British Columbia
Canada
V5Y 3Y3
Tel: +1 604.873.9330
Fax: +1 604.873.9339
Web: http://www.nwfx.com

Novocom Inc.
12555 West Jefferson Boulevard,
Suite 221
Los Angeles, California 90066
United States
Tel: 1-310-448-2500
Fax: 1-310-338-2525
Web: http://www.novo.com

Novocom, Inc.
4221 Redwood Avenue
Los Angeles, California 90066
United States

Tel: 1-310-448-2500
Fax: 1-310-448-2525
Web: http://www.novo.com

Novocom Europe
MWB Business Exchange
Room 215, 77 Oxford Street
London
W1D 2Es
United Kingdom
Tel: +44 207 659 2030
Fax: +44 207 659 2195
Web: http://www.novo.com

Novocom Europe
58 Queensway
Room 215
London, United Kingdom
W2 3RW
Tel: +44 207 306 3394
Fax: +44 207 727 9969
Web: http://www.novo.com

Novocom Turkey
Medya Plaza Ayazmadere Cad.
No. 33/7, 80280 BE_IKTA_.
Istanbul
Turkey
Tel: +90 212 327 1111
Fax: +90 212 327 1166
Web: http://www.novo.com

Novocom Egypt
20 Amin Zaki Street, 4th District
Heliopolis, Cairo
Egypt 11351
Tel: +20 2 417 6363
Fax: +20 2 417 6767
Web: http://www.novo.com

NTN Communications, Inc.
5966 La Place Court, Suite 100
Carlsbad, California 92008
United States
Tel: 1-760-438-7400
Fax: 1-760-438-7470
Web: http://www.ntn.com

NTV EIZO Center Corp.
5 - 6 Japanese television fourth
town annexes

Chiyoda Ku
Tokyo, 102-0081
Japan
Tel: 03-5275-1814
Tel: 03-5226-0215
Web: http://www.ntvec.co.jp

Nylon Films Pty Ltd
Suite 2/142 Melborune Street
North Adelaide 5006
Australia
Tel: +61 8 8267 5455
Fax: +61 8 8267 2455
Web: http://www.nylon.com.au

Oasis Television Ltd
6-7 Great Pulteney Street
London
W1R 3DF
United Kingdom
Tel: 0207 4344133
Fax: 0207 4942843
Web: http://www.oasistv.co.uk

Ocon Inc
TopsVenture Tower, 1591-3,
Seocho-dong Seocho-gu
Seoul, South Korea
137-876
Tel: +82 2.34.44.44.11
Fax: +82 2.34.44.44.30
Web: http://www.ocon.co.kr

Octagon
55 VilCom Circle, Suite 340
Chapel Hill, North Carolina 27514
United States
Tel: 1-919-918-4111
Fax: 1-919-918-7988
Web: http://www.octagon1.com

Octagon CSI Ltd
Octagon House
81/83 Fulham High Street
London
SW6 3JW
United Kingdom
Tel: 44 (0)20 7751 2888
Fax: 44 (0)20 8944 5710
Web: http://www.octagoncsi.com

Octagon CSI Asia Pacific Ltd
19th Floor
148 Electric Road
North Point
Hong Kong
Tel: 852 2534 5082
Fax: 852 2366 9718
Web: http://www.octagoncsi.com

Octagon CSI
371 Beach Road
04-01/11 Key Point
Singapore 199597
Singapore
Tel: 65 6849 4836
Fax: 65 6292 2039
Web: http://www.octagoncsi.com

Octagon CSI Australia Pty Ltd
Waterview Wharf, Suite 10
37 Nicholson Street
Balmain East, Sydney
NSW 2041
Australia
Tel: 61 2 9810 8188
Fax: 61 2 9555 5965 0582
Web: http://www.octagoncsi.com

Octagon CSI Pty Ltd
2nd Floor, Annex A
Longkloof Studios
Darters Road Gardens
Cape Town 8001
South Africa
Tel: 27 (0)21 481 7700
Fax: 27 (0)21 481 7800
Web: http://www.octagoncsi.com

Octagon CSI Television
CSI House
177-187 Arthur Road
London
SW19 8AE
United Kingdom
Tel: 44 (0)20 8944 4188
Fax: 44 (0)20 8944 4189
Web: http://www.octagoncsi.com

Octagon CSI
24 Boulevard Princess Charlotte
MC 98000
Monaco

Tel: 377 9797 2131
Fax: 377 9797 2132
Web: http://www.octagoncsi.com

Octagon CSI
Modusa BV
Houtmankade 38-40
1013 MX
Amsterdam
The Netherlands
Tel: 31 20 688 2154
Fax: 31 20 688 2148
Web: http://www.octagoncsi.com

Octagon CSI
1266 East Main Street
7th Floor
Stamford, Connecticut 06902
United States
Tel: 1-203-363-1084
Fax: 1-203-363-1088
Web: http://www.octagoncsi.com

Octogone Productions
250, rue Garibaldi
Lyon, France
69003
Web: http://www.octogone-pro-
ductions.com

Odeon Film AG
Bavariafilmplatz 7
Geiselgasteig
Germany
82031
Tel: +49 89.64.95.80
Fax: +49 89.64.95.81.03
Web: http://www.odeonfilm.de

Odyssey Productions
4413 Ocean Valley Lane
San Diego, California 92130-2430
United States
Tel: 1-858-793-1900
Web: http://www.odyssey3d.com

Oeil pour Oeil
66 rue d'Angleterre
59800 Lille
France
Tel: 0328362525

Fax: 0320130604
Web: http://www.oeilpouroeil.fr

O'Keefe Communications
4301 Connecticut Avenue NW
Suite 200
Washington D.C. 20008
United States
Tel: 1-202-363-2101
Fax 1-202-363-1948
Web: http://www.okeefecom.com

Oktobor
259 Wakefield Street
Wellington
New Zealand
T: +64-4-3850185
F: +64-4-3850186
Web: http://www.oktobor.com

Oktobor
105 Cook Street
Auckland
New Zealand
T: +64-9-3066616
F: +64-9-3066617
Web: http://www.oktobor.com

Olive Jar Studios
35 Soldiers Field Place
Boston, Massachusetts 02135
United States
Tel: 1-617-783-9500
Fax: 1-617-783-9544
Web: http://www.olivejar.com

Oliver Media Services, LLC
46 Orchard Street
Asheville, North Carolina 28801
United States
Tel: 1-828-281-0999
Web:http://www.olivermultimedia.com

Oliver Media Services, LLC
Charlotte, North Carolina
United States
Tel: 1-704-806-7888
Web:http://www.olivermultimedia.com

Ollin Studio
Porfirio Díaz #39
Col. Nochebuena 03720
México D.F.
Tel: (5255) 5563-8686
Fax: (5255) 5611-5086
Web: http://www.ollin.com.mx

Omegafilms
3100 Medlock Bridge Road Suite 100
Norcross, Georgia 30071
United States
Tel: 1-770-449-8870
Fax: 1-770-449-5463
Web:
http://www.omegamediagroup.com

Omnia Mea Arts
Vironkatu 11 A 11
00170 Helsinki
Finland
Tel: +358 9 278 3898
Fax: +358 9 278 3845
Web:
http://www.omnia-mea-arts.com

Omnibus Japan Inc.
7-2-2 Akasaka, Minato-ku
Tokyo 107-0052
Japan
Tel: 03-5410-6500
Fax: 03-5410-6506
Web: http://www.omnibusjp.com

Omnibus Japan Inc.
Akasaka Video Center
7-2-3 Akasaka
Minato-ku
Tokyo 107-0052
Japan
Tel: 03-5410-6500
Web: http://www.omnibusjp.com

Omnibus Japan Inc.
Akasaka video center annex
(Sunny building)
7-2-1 Akasaka
Minato-ku
Tokyo 107-0052
Japan
Tel: 03-5410-6501
Web: http://www.omnibusjp.com

Omnibus Japan Inc.
Three Minute Hill Studios
7-6-40 Akasaka
Minato-ku
Tokyo 107-0052
Japan
Tel: 03-5561-5011
Fax: 03-5561-5021
Web: http://www.omnibusjp.com

Omnibus Japan Inc.
TFC Studio Center
4-8-10 Akasaka
Minato-ku
Tokyo 107-0052
Japan
Tel: 03-5410-6501
Fax: 03-5410-9620
Web: http://www.omnibusjp.com

Omnibus Japan Inc.
Shinbashi video center
Shinbashi building 3f
3-8-3 Shinbashi
Tokyo 105-0003
Tel: 03-5776-6300
Fax: 03-5776-6310
Web: http://www.omnibusjp.com

Omnibus Japan Inc.
Etc. power CG center
4-6-8 Etc. Power
Setagaya Ku
Tokyo 158-0082
Tel: 03-5706-8357
Fax: 03-5706-8437
Web: http://www.omnibusjp.com

Omnibus Japan Inc.
Print center
7-4-10 Akasaka
Minato-ku
Tokyo 107-0052
Tel: 03-3505-2430
Fax: 03-3505-2393
Web: http://www.omnibusjp.com

Omnilab Post
4-14 Dickson Avenue
Artatmon. NSW. 2064
Australia
Tel: 61 2 9439 5922

Fax: 61 2 9436 3554
Web: http://www.omnicon.com.au

Omni Productions
4518 Curry Ford Rd.
Orlando, Florida 32812
United States
Tel: 1-800-747-9087
Tel: 1-407-281-9087
Fax: 1-407-281-0123
Web: http://www.omnivideo.com

One Bad Monkey
Westgate House
39-41 Romsey Road
Winchester, Hampshire United
Kingdom
S022 5BE
Tel: +44 870.24.13.5
Web: http://www.onebadmonkey.com

One Six Eight Design
1 Union Street, Suite 300
San Francisco, California 94111
United States
Tel: 1-415-837-0168
Fax: 1-415-639-4203
Web:http://www.168designgroup.com

Oniros Illusions Studio SPRL
37, rue du Prince Royal
1050 Brussels
Belgium
Tel: +322 534 84 08
Fax : 322 534 87 73
Web: http://www.oniros.com

On Location Multimedia
635 W 7th St. Suite 203
Cincinnati, Ohio 45203
United States
Tel: 1-513-241-2227
Web:http://www.onlocationmm.com

Oops Animation, Inc.
600 Washington Ave. North, Suite 103
Minneapolis, Minnesota 55401
United States
Tel: 1-612-340-9598
Fax: 1-612-340-9601
Web: http://www.oopsanimation.com

Optical Art Group
4101 Sentry Post Rd
Charlotte, North Carolina 28208
United States
Tel: 1-704-393-3228
Fax: 1-704-393-0889
Web: http://www.opticalart.com

Optidigit Sdn. Bhd.
No 8, Jalan Sri Hartamas 8
2nd & 3rd Floor
Taman Sri Hartamas, 50480 KL,
Malaysia
Tel: (603) 6203 1190
Fax: (603) 6203 1160
Web: http://www.optidigit.com

Optimus, Inc.
161 E. Grand Avenue
Chicago, Illinois 60611
United States
Tel: 1-312-321-0880
Fax: 1-312-321-9765
Web: http://www.optimus.com

Optix Digital Post & FX
157 Princess Street 3rd Floor
Toronto, Ontario M5A 4M4
Canada
Tel: 1-416-214-9911
Fax: 1-416-214-9912
Web: http://www.optix-i.com

Othervision
875 Avenue of the Americas, 7th Floor
New York, New York 10001
United States
Tel: 1-212-378-7400
Web: http://www.othervision.com

Orbis Broadcast Group
100 S. Sangamon
Chicago, Illinois 60607
United States
Tel: 1-312-942-1199
Fax: 1-312-942-9069
Web: http://www.orbisbroadcast-group.com

Orbis Broadcast Group
475 Fifth Ave., 8th Floor
New York, New York 10017
United States

Web: http://www.orbisbroadcast-group.com

Orbis Broadcast Group
140 Welsh Rd., #100
North Wales, Pensylvania 19454
United States
Web: http://www.orbisbroadcast-group.com

Orbis Broadcast Group
11718 Bowman Green Drive
Reston, Virginia 20190
United States
Web: http://www.orbisbroadcast-group.com

Orbital Media, Inc.
803 - 24th Ave S.E.
Calgary, Alberta T2G 1P5
Canada
Tel: 1-403-920-0090
Fax: 1-403-920-0092
Web: http://www.orbitalmedia.ca

Orka Studio
Varna, Bulgaria
Web: http://www.orkastudio.com

Orly Productions Ltd.
209 Salisbury Street
Christchurch
New Zealand
Tel: +64 3 366 2046
Fax: +64 3 366 2046
Web: http://www.orly.co.nz

Orphanage Inc., The
6725 Sunset Blvd. Suite 220
Hollywood, California 90028
United States
Tel: 1-323-469-6700
Fax: 1-323-469-6701
Web: http://www.theorphanage.com

Orphanage Inc., The
The Presidio
39 Mesa Street
Suite 201, Building 39
San Francisco, California 94129
United States
Tel: 1-415-561-2570

Fax: 1-415-561-2575
Web: http://www.theorphanage.com

Ortaklar cad.
Pehlivan sokak Nasuhbey
apt. B1 D3 80290
Turkey
Tel: (212) 2130790-92
Fax: (212) 2130793
Web: http://www.vertigoeffects.com

Osmosis Solutions
33 linden street
Brunswick east
Vic 3057
Melbourne
Australia
Tel: (03) 9381 0766
Web: http://www.osmosis.com.au

Osmosis Solutions
PO box 3022
Tuggerah
nsw 3022
Sydney
Australia
Tel: (02) 4388 5870
Web: http://www.osmosis.com.au

Out of Our Minds Images
864 West 4th Street
Winston-Salem, North Carolina
27101
United States
Tel: 1-336-724-1803
Fax: 1-336-724-1804
Web: http://www.cre83d.com

Outpost, The
1805 Monument Avenue, Suite 601
Richmond, Virginia 23220
United States
Tel: 1-804-359-9025
Fax: 1-804-359-9601
Web: http://www.mcarthur.com

Ovation Media Group
11323 Georgetown Circle
Tampa, Florida 33635
United States
Tel: 1-813-891-6749
Web: http://www.ovationmedia-group.com

Overworks
21 1 Chome 2nd 12
Ota Ku Haneda
Tokyo 144-8531
Japan
Web: http://www.o-works.co.jp
Web: http://www.overworks.co.jp

Packshot Boys Film
23 Krasnoarmeyskaya St., OF.2
01004, Kiev, Ukraine
Tel: +38 (044) 234 6936
Fax: +38 (44) 228 8786
Web:http://www.packshotboysfilm.com

Pacific Ocean Post
625 Arizona Avenue
Santa Monica, California 90401
United States
Tel: 1-310-458-9192
Web: http://www.popstudios.com

Pacific Title / Mirage Studio
6350 Santa Monica Boulevard
Hollywood, California 90038
United States
Tel: 1-323-464-0121
Fax: 1-323-461-8325
Web: http://www.pactitle.com

Palazzo deMix
308 Occidental Avenue South,
Suite 200
Seattle, Washington 98104-2840
United States
Tel: 1-206-328-5555
Fax: 1-206-324-4348
Web: http://www.palazzo.com

Palladium
Villa Ekensberg
Odlingsvagen 6
170 78 Solna

Sweden
Tel: 08 444 98 80
Fax: 08 444 98 81
Web: http://www.palladium.se

Palmer Animation
Cincinatti, Ohio
United States
Web:
http://www.palmeranimation.com

Palm Plus Multimedia BV
Decorcentrum
Sumatralaan 45
1217 GP Hilversum
The Netherlands
Tel: +31 (0)35 677 7370
Fax: +31 (0)35 677 7380
Web: http://www.telescreen.nl

Panic Pictures
Johannesstr.58a
70176 Stuttgart
Germany
Tel: +49 - (0) - 171 - 370 1392
Web: http://www.panic-pictures.de

Pan Vision
Varbergsvägen 44
BOX 1150
501 11 Borås
Sweden
+46 (0)33-44 25 00
Web: http://www.paninteractive.se

Pan Vision
Järntorget 3
413 04 Göteborg
Sweden
+46 (0)13-12 89 55
Web: http://www.paninteractive.se

Pan Vision
Strandboulevarden 122, 5 sal
2100 Copenhagen
Denmark
+45 4814 6969
Web: http://www.paninteractive.se

Pan Vision
St. Olavs gatan 21 A
0165 Oslo
Norway
+47 2236 5800
Web: http://www.paninteractive.se

Pan Vision
Vattuniemenkatu 27
00210 Helsinki
Finland
+358 9 25340500
Web: http://www.paninteractive.se

Papaya Studio
17050 Bushard Street #350
Fountain Valley, California 92708
Tel: 1-714-968-7201
Web: http://www.papayastudio.com

Paprikaas Animation Studios
101-4, Citicenter
28, Church Street
Bangalore, Karnataka India
560001
Tel: +91 80.50.91.77.1
Tel: +91 80 50.91.77.2
Fax: +91 80.55.85.59.7
Web: http://www.paprikaas.com

Paprikaas Animation Studios
San Francisco, California
United States
Tel: 1-415-939-5833
Web: http://www.paprikaas.com

Paradigm Ranch Animation
Studios
6095 South Valleyview Street
Littleton, Colorado 80120
United States
Tel: 1-303-797-2554
Fax: 1-303-797-2534
Web: http://www.paradigmranch.com

Pascal Blais Productions
1155, Wellington St.
Montreal, Quebec
H3C 1V9
Canada
Tel: 1-514-989-9772
Fax: 1-514-989-7018
Web: http://www.pascalblais.com

Passion Pictures
25-27 Riding House Street
London, United Kingdom
W1W 7DU
Tel: +44 207.32.39.93.3
Fax: +44 207.32.39.03.0
Web:http://www.passion-pictures.com

Parallax Productions, Inc.
4264 Westroads Drive
West Palm Beach, Florida 33407
United States
Tel: 1-800-842-7781
Tel: (561) 842-7788
Fax: (561) 842-4566
Web: http://www.parallaxpro.com

Parallax Productions
67 Fourth Avenue
Needham, Massachusetts 02494
United States
Tel: 1-781-455-8355
Fax: 1-781-455-8366
Web: http://www.parallaxprod.com

Pavlov Media
Westerkade 15-5
9718 AS Groningen
The Netherlands
Tel: +31(0)50 5791084
Web: http://www.pavlov.nl

Pavlov Media
Egelantiersgracht 366
1015 RR Amsterdam
The Netherlands
Tel: +31(0)6 20163412
Web: http://www.pavlov.nl

PBS Kids (Public Broadcasting Service)
1320 Braddock Place
Alexandria, Virginia 22314

United States
Tel: 1-703-739-5000
Fax: 1-703-739-5295
Web: http://www.pbskids.org

PCCW
Pacific Century CyberWorks
Japan Co.
Masonic 39 MT Building
2-4-5 Azabudai
Mitano-ku, Tokyo 106-0041
Japan
Web: http://www.pccw.co.jp

PDI/DreamWorks
3101 Park Boulevard
Palo Alto, Califotnia 94306
United States
Tel: 1-650-846-8100
Fax: 1-650-846-8101
Fax: 1-650-846-8399
Web: http://www.pdi.com

Peach Facilities
3 Slingsby Place
Long Acre
London WC2E 9AB
United Kingdom
Tel: 020 7632 4240
Fax: 020 7632 4250
Web: http://www.peachfacilities.co.uk

Pearce Studios Ltd
Old Lodge Farm
Coningsby Lane
Fifield, Berks
SL6 2PF
Tel: +44 (0) 1628 627032
Fax: +44 (0) 1628 777343
Web: http://www.rodlord.com

Peerless Camera Company
London, England
United Kingdom
Tel: +44(0) 207 836 3367
Fax: +44(0) 207 240 2143
Web: http://www.peerless.co.uk

Pentamedia Graphics Ltd.
1/162, Old Mahabalipuram Road,
P.O Box 9

Chennai, Tamil Nadu India
603103
Tel: +91 41.14.47.43.17
Tel: +91 44.48.03.89.8
Tel: +91 44.48.03.89.9
Fax: +91 41.14.47.44.73
Fax: +91 44.47.26.04.2
Web: http://www.penta-media.com

Pentamedia Graphics Ltd
No.1,First Main Road
United India Colony
Chennai,
India
Pin:600 024
Tel: +91 41.14.47.43.17
Tel: +91 44.48.03.89.8
Tel: +91 44.48.03.89.9
Fax: +91 41.14.47.44.73
Fax: +91 44.47.26.04.2
Web: http://www.penta-media.com

Pentamedia Graphics Ltd
13-14,bonanza center,
sahar plaza complex,
m.v.road,andheri(e),
mumbai-400 059.
India
Tel: +91-22-8246571
Tel: +91-72-8264928
Web: http://www.penta-media.com

Pentamedia Graphics Ltd
13-14,bonanza center,
sahar plaza complex,
m.v.road,andheri(e),
Mumbai-400 059.
India
Tel:91-22-8246571
Tel:91-72-8264928
Web: http://www.penta-media.com

Pentamedia Graphics Ltd
26/24,abshot layout sankey road,
Bangalore 560 052.
India
Tel:91-080-2259314
Tel:91-080-2380478
Tel:91-080-2380479
Fax:91-080-2267473
Web: http://www.penta-media.com

Pentamedia Graphics Ltd
6,rajani sen road,
gmd studio,2nd floor,
Calcutta-700 026
Tel:91-33-4467497
Tel:91-33-4647862
Web: http://www.penta-media.com

Pentamedia Graphics Ltd
9thfloor,
Kailash building,
26,Kasturiba Gandhi Marg,
New Delhi-110001
India
Tel: 011-3323160
Tel: 011-3323163
Tel: 011-3323167
Fax: 91-11-3323177.
Web: http://www.penta-media.com

Pentamedia Graphics Ltd
door no.307,
94,s.d.road,
minerva house,
Secunderabad 500 003.
Tel: 91-040-7721808
Web: http://www.penta-media.com

Pentamedia Graphics Ltd
12750.Center Court Drive,#400
Cerritos, California 90703
United States
Tel: 1-562-467-1141
Fax: 1-562-467-1140
Web: http://www.penta-media.com

Pentamedia Graphics Ltd
15,cambridge court
210,shepherds bush road
Hammersmith
London w6 7nj
United Kingdom
Tel:0044-207-602-9295
Fax:0044-207-610-5322
Web: http://www.penta-media.com

Pentamedia Graphics Ltd
121-north bridge road,
#08-12 peninsula plaza
Singapore-179098
Tel:0065-3325341
Fax:0065-3325342
Web: http://www.penta-media.com

Pentamedia Graphics Ltd
Animasia
International pte ltd
6,commenwealth
lane#02-01
Singapore-149547
Tel:0065-4767379
Fax:0065-4731198
Web: http://www.penta-media.com

Pentamedia Graphics Ltd
Kingdom animasia inc.
220,tomas morato
Avenue
Unit 203,205&207
MJB building,
Quezon city,
Philippines
Tel:00632-927-2205
Fax:00632-413-1873
Web: http://www.penta-media.com

Pentamedia Graphics Ltd
Amcorp Trade Centre,
Unit 801, block a,
8th floor,
PJ tower,46200
Petaling jaya,
Selangor d.e.
Malaysia
Tel:00603-7553043
Tel:00603-7546816
Fax:00603-7571287
Web: http://www.penta-media.com

peppermint gmbh
Rauchstr. 9-11
81679 Munich
Germany
Tel: +49(0)89-982470-830
Fax: +49(0)89-982470-811
Web: http://www.seepeppermint.com

Pepper's Ghost Productions
Clarendon House
147 London Road
Kingston-upon-Thames
Surrey KT2 6NH
Tel: +44 (0)208 546 4900
Fax: +44 (0)208 546 4284
Web: http://www.peppersghost.com

Pepper Studios
85 King William Street
Kent Town SA 5067
Australia
Tel: +61 8 8363 0711
Fax: +61 8 8363 1119
Web: http://www.pepperstudios.com.au

Persona-id
Bay Chambers
West Bute Street
Cardiff Bay
Cardiff
Wales
United Kingdom
CF10 5DB
Tel: +44 292 04 00 99 0
Fax: +44 292 04 00 99 1
Web: http://www.persona-id.co.uk

Perspective NYC, Inc.
99 Park Avenue #308
New York, New York 10016
United States
Tel: 1-212-993-1000
Fax: 1-801-314-8173
Web: http://www.perspectivenyc.com

Perspective Studios
3200 Expressway Drive South
Islandia, New York 11749
United States
Tel: 1-631-232-1499
Fax: 1-631-232-2655
Web:
http://www.perspectivestudios.com

Phactory
44 Trinity Place, Suite 3
New York, New York 10006
United States
Tel: 1-212-483-0040
Web: http://www.phactory.com

Phaestos Production
90 Allee Maurice Planes
Montpellier 34090
France
Tel: 01 1 33 0 4 67 07 04 07
Fax: 01 1 33 0 4 67 47 56 96
Web: http://www.phaestos.com

Phantom Productions
1330 N. Vine Street - Stage 4
Holywood, California 90028
United States
Tel: 1-323-822-7275
Fax: 1-323-822-7295
Web: http://www.phantompro.com

Phantom Reality Inc
618 Broad St
Fuquay Varina North Carolina
27526
United States
Tel: 1-919-557-7882
Web: http://www.phantomreality.com

Phenomedia AG
10, Josef-Haumann-Strasse
Bochum
Germany
44866
Tel: +49 23.27.99.74.40
Fax: +49 23.27.99.74.49
Web: http://www.phenomedia.com

Philippine Animation Studio, Inc.
2100 Pasong Tamo Extension
Makati City
Philippines 1231
Tel: +63 2.81.77.27.1
Web: http://www.pasi.com.ph

Phoenix Editorial
717 Battery Street @ Pacific
San Francisco, California 94111
United States
Tel: 1-415-394-7777
Fax: 1-415-394-8004
Web: http://www.phoenixeditorial.com

Photon
Movie World Studios
P.O. Box 81
Pacific Highway
Oxenford
Gold Coast
Qld, 4210
Australia
Tel: 61 (7) 5502 5222
Fax: 61 97) 5502 5200
Web: http://www.photon.com.au

Photon
45-47 Hume Street
Crows Nest
Sydney
NSW, 2065
Australia
Tel: 61 (20 9966 4211
Fax: 61 (2) 9906 7911
Web: http://www.photon.com.au

PH Studio
3-12-7 Hiroo
Shibuya-ku
Tokyo, Japan
150-0012
Tel: 03-5766-5780
Fax: 03-5766-5790
Web: http://www.phstudio.com

Picability
Sunderweg 75
45472 Muelheim
Tel: +49 208 496841
Fax: +49 208 496843
Web: http://www.picability.de

Picard Film Services Inc.
15 Brookbanks Dr. #1603
Toronto, Ontario Canada
M3A2T1
Tel: +1 416.447.7564
Fax: +1 416.446.6421
Web: http://www.deedub.ca

Picture Industries Ltd
Rm 811 Eastern Harbour Ctr
28 Hoi Chak St
Quarry Bay
Hong Kong
Tel: (852) 2811 9319
Fax: (852) 2561 8767
Web: http://www.picture-indus-
tries.com.hk

Pictures on the Wall
Studio 14
74 - 74 Firhill Road
Glasgow, Scotland G20 7BA
United Kingdom
Tel: +44 141.57.60.11.7
Web: http://www.potw.co.uk

PicturesPlanes Limited
suite 12B spectrum tower
53 hung to road kowloon
Hong Kong
Tel: (+852) 2302 1188
Web: http://www.picturesplanes.com

Pietrodangelo Production Group, Inc.
406 Timberlane Road,
Tallahassee, Florida 32312
United States
Tel: 1-850-894-1210
Fax: 1-850-894-2197
Web: http://www.pietrodangelo.com

Pileated Pictures
350 March Rd
Shelburne Falls, Massachusetts
01370
United States
Tel: 1-413-625-8551
Web: http://www.pileated.com

Pilot Video
550 Wisconsin Street
San Francisco, California 94107
United States
Tel: 1-415-282-5678
Fax: 1-415-282-5687
Web: http://www.pilotvideo.com

Pinguim Animation
Rua Conselheiro Zacarias 121
Sao Paulo
SP Brazil
01429-020
Tel: +55 11.38.84.18.21
Fax: +55 11.38.84.18.21
Web: http://www.tvpinguim.com.br

Pinnacle
22400 NW Westmark Drive
Hillsboro, Oregon 97124
United States
Tel: 1-503-844-4848
Fax: 1-503-844-4745
Web: http://www.pinnacle-exhibits.com

Pinnacle
80 Yesler Way, Suite 300
Seattle, Washington 98104
United States
Tel: 1-206-382-1144
Fax: 1-206-382-9922
Web:
http://www.pinnacle-exhibits.com

Pinnacle
13375 Estelle Street.
Corona, California 91719
United States
Tel: 1-909-582-0085
Fax: 1-909-582-0082
Web:
http://www.pinnacle-exhibits.com

PIP Animation Services Inc.
880 Wellington St.
Suite 800
Ottawa, Ontario Canada
K1R 6K7
Tel: +1 613.569.4886
Fax: +1 613.569.1714
Web: http://www.pipanimation.com

Piranha Bar
37 Fitzwilliam Square
Dublin 2
Ireland
Tel: +3531 6053739
Fax: +3531 3766047
Web: http://www.piranhabar.ie

Pitch Blue Studios
130 N. Brand Blvd. Suite 206
Glendale, California 91203
United States
Tel: 1-818-553-1687
Fax: 1-818-553-1681
Web:
http://www.pitchbluestudios.com

Pitchi Poy Animation Productions
7 Shaa'ry Nikanor St.
Jaffa, Israel
68034
Tel: +972 3.68.36.06.5
Fax: +972 3.51.83.19.8
Web: http://www.pitchipoy.com

Pixar Animation Studios
1200 Park Avenue
Emeryville, California 94608
United States
Tel: 1-510-752-3000
Fax: 1-510-752-3151
Web: http://www.pixar.com

Pixelberg Animaties
van Ostadestraat 419hs
1074 VZ Amsterdam
The Netherlands
Tel: +31 (0)20 6727294
Fax: +31 (0)20 6727228
xoip: +31 (0)84 8324869
Web: http://www.pixelberg.nl

Pixel Blues, Inc
1115 N. Hollywood Way
Burbank, California 91505
United States
Tel: 1-818-260-0795
Fax: 1-818-260-0708
Web: http://www.pixelblues.com

Pixel Cartoon
Via Perini, 9
Trento, TN Italy
38100
Tel: +39 461.92.58.82
Fax: +39 461.92.58.82
Web: http://www.pixelcartoon.it

Pixel Factory, Inc., The
4081-C L.B. McLeod Road
Orlando, Florida 32811
United States
Web: http://www.pixfactory.com

Pixel Liberation Front
1316 1/2 Abbot Kinney Boulevard
Venice, California 90291
United States
Tel: 1-310-396-9854
Fax: 1-310-396-9874
Web: http://www.thefront.com

Pixel Liberation Front
150 West 28th Street #1003
New York, New York, 10001
United States

Tel: 1-212-604-0203
Fax: 1-212-604-0204
Web: http://www.thefront.com

Pixel Logic
Miami, Florida
United States
Tel: 1-800-PIXEL-TV
Tel: 1-305-567-1555.
Web: http://www.pixeltv.com

Pixel Magic,
A Division of OCS / Freeze
Frame
10635 Riverside Drive
Toluca Lake California 91602
United States
Tel: 1-818-760-0862
Fax: 1-818-760-4983
Web: http://www.pixelmagicfx.com

Pixelpushers, Inc.
20101 SW Birch St. Suite 250
Newport Beach, California 92660
United States
Tel: 1-949-851-1600
Fax: 1-949-851-1930
Web: http://www.pixelpushers.com

Pix Mix
Rua Aquiles Monteverde 10-A
Lisbon, 1000
Portugal
Tel: +351213030880
Fax: +351213030881
Web: http://www.pixmix.tv

Pix N Stones Production House
326 Sanchez Street
San Francisco, California 94114
United States
Tel: 1-415-558-9332
Web: http://www.pixnstones.com

Pixolüt
PO Box 1081
Cronulla, NSW 2230
Australia
Tel:+61 2 9527 6769
Web: http://www.pixolut.com

Pladd Animations
5705 Hadrian Drive
Durham, North Carolina
United States
Tel: 1-919-874-0546
Web:
http://www.pladdanimations.com

Planet 9 studios
753 Kansas Street
San Francisco, California 94107
United States
Tel: 1-415-642-6700
Fax: 1-415-285-0618
Web: http://www.planet9.com

Planet4 GmbH
Niemeyerstr. 12
30449 Hannover
Germany
Tel: 0511/450010-51
Fax: 0511/450010-54
Web: http://www.planet4.de

Planet Blue Corporation
1250 Sixth Street, Suite 102
Santa Monica, California 90401-
1633
United States
Tel: 1-310-899-3877
Fax: 1-310-899-3787
Web: http://www.planetblue.com

Planet Three Animation Studio
1223 North 23rd Street
Wilmington, North Carolina 28405
United States
Tel: 1-910-343-3720
Fax: 1-910-343-3722
Web:
http://www.planet3animation.com

Planit
The Power Plant - 5th Floor
601 East Pratt Street
Baltimore, Maryland 21202
United States
Tel: 1-410-962-8500
Fax: 1-410-962-8508
Web: http://www.planitagency.com

Plastic Thought Studios
#300, 10301 - 108 St.
Edmonton, Alberta
Canada T5J1L7
Tel: +1 780.429.5051
Web: http://www.plasticthought.com

Platige Image Sp.zo.o
Pilicka 58
Warsaw
Poland
02-613
Tel: +48 22.84.46.47.4
Fax: +48 22.84.46.47.4
Web: http://www.platige.com

Playground
2415 Michigan Avenue, Bergamot
Station
Santa Monica, California 90404
United States
Tel: 1-310-264-5511
Fax: 1-310-264-5512
Web: http://www.playgroundla.com

Playstos Entertainment
Corso Sempione, 63
20149 Milano
Italy
Tel: +39 02 3314153
Web: +39 02 315678
Web: http://www.playstos.com

Pluginz, Inc
1111 Brickell Ave. Suite 1100
Miami, Florida 33131
United States
Tel: 1-786-276-7440
Fax: 1-786-276-7321
Web: http://www.pluginz.com

Plum Productions
2202 Main Street
Santa Monica, California 90405
United States
Tel: 1-310-450-1942
Fax: 1-310-450-9424
Web: http://www.plumprod.com

Plus One Animation, Inc.
1303-3 Seocho Dong, Seocho Gu

Seoul
South Korea
137-074
Tel: +82 2.34.78.10.10
Fax: +82 2.34.78.09.09
Web: http://www.plusoneani.com

Pm2 Productions
621 S Navy Blvd
Pensacola, Florida 32507
United States
Tel: 1-850-456-8802
Web: http://www.pm2pro.com

Pocket Laboratories Ltd
P.O. Box 28495
London
United Kingdom
N19 4XB
Tel: +44 781.64.70.78.7
Web:
http://www.pocketlaboratories.com

Pollus
Science Park
Kruislaan 404
(k 308)
Amsterdam, Netherlands
1098 SM
Tel: +31 20.52.57.88.6
Web: http://www.pollus.nl

POLYMORPH productions
1826 Montana Ave. Suite C
Santa Monica, California 90403
United States
Tel: 1-310-264-9827
Web:
http://www.polymorphproductions.com

Polygon Pictures Inc.
Ariake Frontier Building Tower A
3-1-25 Ariake
Koto-ku
Tokyo 135-0063
Japan
Tel: 03-5564-3500
Fax: 03-5564-3510
Web: http://www.ppi.co.jp

Pomegranit
1040 Bettery Street
San Francisco, California 94111
United States
Tel: 1-415-291-5801
Fax: 1-415-291-5800
Web: http://www.pomegranit.com

PorchLight Entertainment
11777 Mississippi Avenue
Los Angeles, California 90025
United States
Tel: 1-310-477-8400
Fax: 1-310-477-5555
Web: http://www.porchlight.com

Posro Media LLC
64J Princeton Hightstown Rd.
Suite #103
Princeton Junction, New Jersey 08550
United States
Tel: 1-609-419-9333
Fax: 1-609-419-1972
Web: http://www.posro.com

Post Amazers (Pvt.) Ltd
614, Continental Trade Centre
Block 8
Clifton
Karachi, Sindh Pakistan
75600
Tel: +92 21.58.67.06.1
Fax: +92 21.58.67.99.2
Web: http://www.postamazers.com

Post Central
771 East Morehead Street, Suite
100
Charlotte, North Carolina 28202
United States
Tel: 1-704-331-9292
Fax: 1-704-331-9201
Web: http://www.postcentral.com

Post Central
170B Linden Oaks
Rochester, New York 14625
United States
Tel: 1-716-385-1530
Fax: 1-716-218-9219
Web: http://www.postcentral.com

Post Effects
400 West Erie
Chicago, Illinois 60610
United States
Tel: 1-312-944-1690
Fax: 1-312-944-4989
Web: http://www.posteffects.com

Post Group Hollywood, The
6335 Homewood Avenue
Hollywood, California 90028
United States
Tel: 1-323-462-2300
Fax: 1-323-462-0836
Web: http://www.postgroup.com

Post Group West Los Angeles, The
11858 La Grange Avenue
Los Angeles, California 90025
United States
Tel: 1-310-979-4300
Fax: 1-310-979-4320
Web: http://www.postgroup.com

Post Logic
Neuilly sur Seine, France92200
Tel: +33 1.46.37.77.6
Fax: +33 1.46.37.55.5
Web: http://www.post-logic.com

Post Logic Studios Hollywood
1800 North Vine, Suite 100
Hollywood, California 90028
United States
Tel: 1-323-461-7887
Fax: 1-323-461-7790
Web: http://www.postlogic.com

Post Logic Studios Santa Monica
2046 Broadway
Santa Monica, California 90404
Tel: 1-310-315-9553
Fax: 1-310-315-3073
Web: http://www.postlogic.com

PostMaster Productions, Inc.
828 Ralph McGill Boulevard NE,
Suite W-8
Atlanta, Georgia 30306
United States
Tel: 1-404-231-3200
Web: http://www.imagemaster.tv

Postmodern Sydney
65 Kent Street, Millers Point
Sydney, NSW, 2000
Australia
Tel: +612 9253 5600
Fax: +612 9253 5660
Web:
http://www.postmodernsydney.com

PowerUp Studios
4 - 597 St. Clair Avenue West
Toronto, Ontario
M6C 1A3 Canada
Tel: 1-416-656-4331
Web:
http://www.powerupstudios.com

PowerVision Productions
119 N. Broad Street
Winder, Georgia 30680
United States
Tel: 1-770-867-4722
Fax: 1-770-307-1465
Web: http://www.pvpstudio.com

P.O.V.D.E. Persistence of Vision
Digital Entertainment
P.O. Box 10282
San Rafael, California 94912
United States
Web: http://www.povde.com

Pow Wow Productions
903 Colorado Ave. Suite 220
Santa Monica, California 90401
United States
Tel: 1-310-394-9693
Web:
http://www.powwowproductions.com

Presentation
4021 Stirrup Creek Dr.
Suite 220
Durham, North Carolina 27703
United States
Tel: 1-919-767-9400
Tel: 1-800-948-9222
Fax: 1-919-967-9408
Web: http://www.pstrat.com

Presentation Services Ltd.
7120 Case Avenue
North Hollywood, California 91605
United States
Tel: 1-818-503-0400
Fax: 1-818-503-0440
Web:http://www.presservgroup.com

Primetime AG
Wagistrasse 2
CH-8952 Schlieren/Zurich
Switzerland
Tel: 01 738 55 55
Fax: 01 738 55 50
Web: http://www.primetime.ch

Production Group, The
1330 N. Vine Street
Holywood, California 90028
United States
Tel: 1-323-469-8111
Fax: 1-323-962-2182
Web:http://www.productiongroup.tv

Production I.G Inc.
ING Studio, 3-4-5, Minami Cho,
Kokubunji-shi
Tokyo
185-0021 Japan
Web:http://www.production-ig.co.jp

Produksjonsselskapet Mikrofilm AS
Seilduksgata 25
Oslo, Norway
0553
Tel: +47 22.80.61.00
Fax: +47 22.80.61.01
Web: http://www.mikrofilm.no

Promotion Studios
P.O. Box 7027
Sydney, New South Wales
Australia
2001
Australia
Tel: 61 2 9232 1154
Fax: 61 2 9232 1154
Web:http://www.promotionstudios.com

Propellor Interactive Design, Inc.
2314 S. Miami Blvd. Suite 251

Durham, North Carolina 27703
United States
Tel: 1-919-544-7750
Tel: 1-877-709-PROP
Fax: 1-919-544-7781
Web:
http://www.propellorinteractive.com

ProSieben Media AG
Medienallee 7
Unterfoehring
Bayern
85774 Germany
Web: http://www.ProSieben.de

Proxima
Via Tuscolana 1055
00173 Rome
Italy
Tel: 1-0039 06 72 900 350
Fax: 1-0039 06 72 900 358
Web: http://www.proximasfx.com

PS Creative
4 The Doghouse
Dog Lane
Bewdley
Worcestershire
DY12 2EF
United Kingdom
Tel: +44 (0)1299 400 000
Fax: +44 (0)1299 404 373
Web: http://www.pscreative.co.uk

Pseudome Studio, LLC
4248 West 229th Street
Fairview, Ohio, 44126
United States
Tel: 1-440-552-6921
Web: http://www.pseudome.net

Psyop
634 E11th St
New York, New York 10009
United States
Tel: 1-212-533-9055
Fax: 1-212-533-9112
Web: http://www.psyop.tv

Public Eye Design
3182 Woodvalley Road

Panama City, Florida 32405
United States
Tel: 1-850-769-6996
Web: http://www.pub-
liceyedesign.com

Publicidad Virtual
Paseo de los Laureles 458-PH1
Bosques de las Lomas
México, D.F. 05120
México
Tel: (525) 5570-7711
Tel: (525) 5570-7720
Fax: (525) 5570-7756
Web:
http://www.publicidadvirtual.com

Public Image Limited
136 Madeira
Miami, Florida
United States
Tel: 1-305-446-1132
Fax: 1-305-446-9847
Web: http://www.publicimage.com

Public Television Service
No. 70, lane 75, Kang Nong
Road
Taipei
Taiwan 114
R.O.C.
Tel: +886 2.26.30.10.13
Fax: +886 2.26.33.80.50
Web: http://www.pts.org.tw

Pulse Entertainment
654 Mission Street
San Francisco, California 94105
United States
Tel: 1-415-348-4000
Fax: 1-415-348-4001
Web: http://www.pulse3d.com

Pulse Entertainment
600 Townsend Street, Suite 190W
San Francisco, California 94103
United States
Tel: 1-415-255-8789
Fax: 1-415-255-8246
Web: http://www.pulse3d.com

Pulse Communications Inc.
211 North Broadway St.
Green Bay, Wisconsin 54302
United States
Tel: 1-920-436-4777
Fax: 1-920-436-4779
Web: http://www.pulsedms.com

PunchHole GmbH & Co. KG
Schonhauser Allee 8
Berlin, Germany
10119
Tel: +49 30.44.03.97.40
Web: http://www.punch-hole.com

Puppet Studio
10903 Chandler Blvd.
North Hollywood, California 91601
United States
Tel: 1-818-506-7374
Web:http://www.thepuppetstudio.com

Pure Animation Studio
Prästgatan 4
722 15 Västerås
Sweden
Tel: +46-21-185700
Fax: +46-21-380489
Web: http://www.pure.se

Puritano Media Group
1316 King Street Suite 300
Alexandria, Virginia 22314
United States
Tel: 1-703-837-8600
Tel: 1-800-359-2184
Fax: 1-703-837-8613
Web: http://www.puritano.com

Pyramid TV
36 Cardiff Rd
Llandaff
Cardiff
CF5 2DR
United Kingdom
Tel: +44 (0) 29 2057 6888
Fax: +44 (0) 29 2057 5777
Web: http://www.pyramidtv.co.uk

Pyros Pictures, Inc.
3197 Airport Loop Drive, Building A
Costa Mesa, California 92626
United States
Tel: 1-714-708-3400
Fax: 1-714-708-3500
Web: http://www.pyros.com

QANTM
Level 10, 138 Albert St
Brisbane Qld 4000
Australia
Tel: 61 7 3017 4333
Fax: 61 7 3003 0953
Web: http://www.qantm.com.au

Quanxi
28th Floor, Tower II
The Enterprise Center
6766 Ayla Avenue
Makati City 1226
Philippines
Tel: 632 649 3961
Fax: 632 886 50008
Web: http://www.i-quanxi.com

Quietman Design and Visual Effects
28 West 44th Street
New York, New York 10036
United States
Tel: 1-212-921-4444
Fax: 1-212-921-4504
Web: http://www.quietman.net

Qurios Entertainment
12-14 Church Street
Hartlepool, United Kingdom
TS24 7DJ
Tel: +44 142.98.90.59.5
Fax: +44 142.98.90.72.9
Web: http://www.qurios.com

Qwato Studios
Falls Church, Virginia
United States
Fax: 1-703-852-4306
Web: http://www.qwato.com

R!OT Santa Monica
702 Arizona Avenue
Santa Monica, California 90401-1702
United States

Tel: 1-310-448-7500
Tel: 1-310-434-6000
Fax: 1-310-448-7600
Web: http://www.rioting.com

R!OT Manhattan
545 5th Avenue
New York, New York 10017
United States
Tel: 1-212-687-4000
Web:
http://www.riotingmanhattan.com

R!OT Atlanta
3399 Peachtree Road
Atlanta, Georgia 30326
United States
Tel: 1-404-237-9977
Fax: 1-404-237-3923
Web: http://www.editworks.com

R2Media
1071 KL
Amsterdam
The Netherlands
Tel: +31(0)20 664 90 11
Fax: +31(0)20 675 88 39
Web: http://www.r2media.nl

r3D
4091 E. La Palma Ave. #F
Anaheim, California 92807
United States
Tel: 1-714-630-4425
Web: http://www.ren3d.com

R3 Interactive
264 Richmond Road
Marleston, SA
Australia 5033
Tel: 61 (0)8 8351 8399
Fax: 61 (0)8 8351 8499
Web: http://www.r3interactive.com

R-Comp Interactive
22 Robert Moffat
High Legh
Knustsford
Cheshire WA16 6PS
Tel: (+44) 01925 755043
Fax: (+44) 01925 757377
Web:
http://www.bitmap-brothers.co.uk

Ra.Nj Digital Entertainment
Taxusstraat 20
3061 HT Rotterdam
The Netherlands
Tel: (+31) 10 2123101
Fax: (+31) 10 2123104
Web: http://www.ranj.nl

Race Studios
25154 Malibu Road
Malibu, California 90265
United States
Web: http://www.racestudios.com

Radar
401 West Ontario, Suite300
Chicago, Illonois 60610
United States
Tel: 1-312-266-2900
Fax: 1-312-266-2960
Web: http://www.radarstudios.com

Radioaktive Film
58/2 Artema Street, #17
04050 Kiev
Ukraine
Tel: +380 (44) 219-1845
Tel: +380 (44) 219-1845
Web:http://www.radioaktivefilm.com

Radium
720 Wilshire Boulevard, Suite 200
Santa Monica, California 90401
United States
Tel: 1-310-656-0156
Fax: 1-310-656-0146
Web: http://www.radium.com

Radium
321 11th Street
San Francisco, California 94103
United States
Tel: 1-415-558-6900
Fax: 1-415-558-9966
Web: http://www.radium.com

Rage
1sr Floor
Martins Building
Water Street
Liverpool

England L2 3SP
United Kingdom
Web: http://www.rage.com

Rainbow Japan Inc.
Japan
Tel: 03-5475-7361
Fax: 03-5475-7362
Web: http://www.rainbow.co.jp

Rainbow Studios
3830 North 7th Street
Phoenix, Arizona 85014
United States
Tel: 1-602-230-1300
Fax: 1-602-230-2553
Web: http://www.rainbo.com

Raindrop Geomagic, Inc.
617 Davis Drive, Suite 300
Durham, North Carolina 27713
United States
Tel: 1-919-474-0122
Fax: 1-919-474-0126
Web: http://www.geomagic.com

Rainmaker Digital Pictures
Vancouver Office
50 West 2nd Ave
Vancouver, British Columbia
Canada V5Y 1B3
Tel: 1-604-874-8700
Fax: 1-604-874-1719
Web http://www.rainmaker.com

Rainmaker: The Crossing Effects Studio
2042-2050 Alpha Avenue
Burnaby, British Columbia
Canada V5C 5K7
Tel: 1-604-296-2622
Fax: 1-604-296-2672
Web: http://www.crossingfx.com

RAMM Entertainment
2899 Agoura Road, Suite 329
Westlake Village, California
91361
United States
Tel: 1-818-713-8144
Fax: 1-818-888-7083
Web:http://www.rammentertainment.com

Rapido 3D, Ltd.
152 High Street
Garlinge
Margate
Kent
United Kingdom
CT9 5LY
Tel: +44 184.38.34.45.7
Web: http://www.rapido3d.co.uk

Rawshot
Distillery Road
Dublin 3
Ireland
Tel: + 353 1 8376182
Fax: + 353 1 8376185
Web: http://www.rawshot.com

Razor Art Productions
Vernon, British Columbia
Canada V1H 1H9
Tel: +1 250.260.3782
Web: http://www.razorart.ca

Real Media
14111 West 95th Street
Lenexa, Kansas 66215
United States
Tel: 1-888-449-7325
Tel: 1-913-894-8989
Fax: 1-913-894-0635
Web: http://www.realme.com

Realm Productions, Inc.
1661 Lincoln Blvd. Ste.400
Santa Monica, California 90404
Tel: 1-310-255-6690
Fax: 310-255-6602
Web:http://www.realmproductions.com

Realise Studio
87 Regent St
Suites 64-68
Kent House
London
W1R 7HF
United Kingdom
Tel: +44 020 7434 0770
Fax: +44 020 7434 1386
Web:http://www.realisestudio.com

Reality Check Studios
6100 Melrose Ave.
Los Angeles, California 90038
United States
Tel: 1-323-465-3900
Fax: 1-323-465-3600
Web: http://www.realityx.com

Realtime Technology AG
Rosenheimer Str. 145f
D-81671 München
Germany
Tel: +49(0)89-200 275-00
Fax: +49(0)89-200 275-09
Web:
http://www.realtime-technology.de

Rebel Forces
2457 Rampart Street
Oakland, California 94602
United States
Web: http://www.rebelforces.com

Red Goat
G. van Ledenberchstraat 31-1
Amsterdam
Netherlands
1052TZ
Tel: +31 6.50.21.53.50.3
Web: http://www.redgoat.nl

Red Kite Productions Ltd
89 Giles Street
Edinburgh, United Kingdom
EH6 6BZ
Tel: +44 131.55.40.06.0
Fax: +44 131.55.36.00.7
Web:
http://www.redkite-animation.com

Red Post Production
Hammersley House
5–8 Warwick Street
London
W1B 5LX
United Kingdom
Tel: +44 (0)20 7439 1449
Fax: +44 (0)20 7439 1339
Web: http://www.red-post.co.uk

Red Rocket Animation
Jl. Wijaya II/56
Jakarta, Indonesia
12160
Tel: +62 21.72.08.00.3
Fax: +62 21.72.43.83.3
Web:
http://www.redrocketanimation.com

Red Rover Studios Limited
345 Adelaide St. W., Suite 5
Toronto, Ontario M5V 1S2
Canada
Tel: 1-416-591-6500
Fax: 1-416-591-6501
Web: http://www.redrover.net

Reds Inc.
6-5-17 Digital Eight Building 4f
North Ku
Osaka 530-0047
Japan
Tel: 06-6315-3155
Fax: 06-6315-3156
Web: http://www.reds.co.jp

Red Sky
35 Soldiers Field Place
Boston, Massachusetts 02135
United States
Tel: 1-617-783-9500
Fax: 1-617-783-9544
Web: http://www.olivejar.com

Red Vision
Cambos House
3 Canal Street
Manchester
M1 3HE
United Kingdom
Tel: 0161 907 3764
Fax: 0161 907 3762
Web: http://www.redvision.co.uk

Redwing Animation
55 Drayton Green
London
United Kingdom
W130JE
Tel: +44 208.99.10.02.9
Fax: +44 208.99.78.89.4
Web:http://www.redwinganimation.com

Reel Fx Creative Studios
2211 North Lamar, Suite 100
Dallas, Texas 75202
United States
Tel: 1-214-979-0961
Fax: 1-214-979-0963
Web: http://www.reelfx.com

Reel Wonders Animation, Inc.
203 - 402 West Pender Street
Vancouver, British Columbia
Canada
V6B 1T6
Tel: +1 604.689.9331
Fax: +1 604.689.9331
Web: http://www.reelwonders.com

Reelmation Studios
4522 north 13th street
Philadelphia, Pennsylvania 19140
United States
Web:
http://www.reelmationstudios.com

Refinery Associates
7 Moor Street
London, United Kingdom
W1D 5NB
Tel: +44 207.28.77.17.3
Fax: +44 207.28.77.17.4
Web: http://www.refinery-v.com

Refinery Post Production (The)
3rd Floor
Longkloof Studios A
CNR Kloof & Darters Road
GardensP O Box 15711
Vlaeberg 8018
South Africa
Tel: 021 480 3100
Fax: 021 480 3101
Web: http://www.refinery.co.za

Refinery Post Production (The)
Block C, Wedgewood Office Park
CNR Muswell & Wedgelink Roads
Bryanston
P O Box 98345
Sloane Park 2152
South Africa
Tel: 011 706 0500
Fax: 011 706 0300
Web: http://www.refinery.co.za

Reject Barn Design and
Animation
23 South Main Street
Norwalk, Connecticut 06854
United States
Tel: 1-203-866-1898
Web: http://www.rejectbarn.com

RENDERconcept
Urb. Roosevelt 503 C. Besosa
#2A
San Juan, Puerto Rico 00918
Tel: +1 787.294.1856
Web: http://www.renderconcept.com

Renderella
4572 Marsden Road
Courtenay, British Columbia
V9N 9M8
Canada
Tel: 1-250-334-6187
Fax: 1-250-334-4845
Web: http://www.renderella.com

Renderella
1817 Pandora Street
Vancouver, British Columbia
V5L 1M2
Canada
Tel: 1-604-255-6490
Fax: 1-250-334-4845
Web: http://www.renderella.com

Replica Technology
4650 Langford Road
North Collins New York 14111
United States
Tel: 1-800-714-8184
Tel: 1-716-337-0621
Web: http://www.replica3d.com

RESFX Tv Designers
Galerij 29
Beuningen, 6641 PA
The Netherlands
Web: http://www.resfx.com

Resolution Design
1/27 Challis Avenue
Potts Point 2011
Australia
Tel: +61 2 9360 9908
Fax: +61 2 9360 8908

Web:
http://www.resolutiondesign.com.au
Revelation Interactive
Houston, Texas 77071
United States
Web:
http://www.revelation-interactive.com

Rex Recording & Video Post
1931 Southeast Morrison
Portland, Oregon 97214
United States
Tel: 1-503-238-4525
Fax: 1-503-236-8347
Web: http://www.rexpost.com

REZN8 Productions
6430 Sunset Boulevard, Suite
100
Hollywood, California 90028
United States
Tel: 1-323-957-2161
Fax: 1-323-464-8912
Web: http://www.rezn8.com

R/GA Los Angeles
1888 Century Park East, Suite 500
Los Angeles, California 90067
United States
Tel: 1-800-638-9487
Fax: 1-310-788-6600
Web: http://www.rga.com

R/GA New York
350 West 39th Street
New York, New York 10018
United States
Tel: 1-212-946-4000
Fax: 1-212-946-4010
Web: http://www.rga.com

RGB Digital Animation
16 B Susan Street
Annandale
Sydney, NSW 2038
Australia
Tel: +61 2 9557 4222
Fax: +61 2 9557 4255
Web: http://www.rgb.net.au

RG Prince Films Inc.
Academic Bldg, 967-6 Daichi-

Dong, Kangnam-Gu
Seoul
South Korea
135-280
Tel: +82 2.50.13.66.0
Fax: +82 2.50.28.33.3
Web: http://www.rgpf.com

Rhonda Graphics Animation Studios
1730 E. Northern Ave. #204
Phoenix, Arizona 85020
United States
Tel: 1-602-371-8880
Fax: 1-602-371-8832
Web: http://www.rhonda.com
http://www.rhondagraphics.com

Rhinoceros Visual Effects and
Design
50 East 42nd Street
New York, New York 10017
United States
Tel: 1-212-986-1584
Fax: 1-212-986-2113
Web: http://www.rhinofx.tv

Rhythm and Hues
5404 Jandy Place
Los Angeles, California 90066
United States
Tel: 1-310-448-7500
Fax: 1-310-448-7600
Web: http://www.rhythm.com

Ricochet Digital LLC
4030 N. Pulaski Avenue, #D
Chicago, Illinois 60641-5546
United States
Tel: 1-773-205-7540
Fax: 1-773-736-3113
Web: http://www.ricochetdigital.com

Ring of Fire
8300 Melrose Avenue, Suite 204
West Hollywood, California 90069
United States
Tel: 1-323-966-5410
Fax: 1-323-966-5419
Web: http://www.ringoffire.com

RIOT Santa Monica
702 Arizona Avenue
Santa Monica, California 90401-1702
United States
Tel: 1-310-448-7500
Tel: 1-310-434-6000
Fax: 1-310-448-7600
Web: http://www.rioting.com

RIOT Manhattan
545 5th Avenue
New York, New York 10017
United States
Tel: 1-212-687-4000
Web:
http://www.riotingmanhattan.com

RIOT Atlanta
3399 Peachtree Road
Atlanta, Georgia 30326
United States
Tel: 1-404-237-9977
Fax: 1-404-237-3923
Web: http://www.editworks.com

Rising Sun Pictures
44 High Street
Kensington
South Australia 5068
Australia
Tel: +61 8 8364 6074
Fax: +61 8 8364 6075
Web: http://www.rsp.com.au

Rising Sun Pictures
722 Bourke Street
Surry Hills
New South Wales 2016
Australia
Tel: +61 2 9566 7950
Fax: +61 2 9566 7950
Web: http://www.rsp.com.au

Rithuset
Kornhamnstorg 59
111 27 Stockholm
Sweden
Tel: +46 08 201200
Fax: +46 08 211922
Web: http://www.rithuset.se

Rivetal, Inc.
2335 South State Street #300
Provo, Utah 84606
United States
Tel: 1-801-818-2222
Fax: 1-801-818-2233
Web: http://www.rivetal.com

RMG Satellite Productions, Inc.
Bob & Kathy Gubar
1020 White Oak Creek Drive
Apex, North Carolina 27502
United States
Tel: 1-919-363-3645
Fax: 1-919-363-5851
Web: http://www.rmgsat.com

RMS Networks
900 S.E. 3rd Avenue
Ft. Lauderdale, Florida 33316
United States
Tel: 1-888-883-8857
Tal: 1-954-525-6464
Fax: 1-954-525-4245
Web: http://www.rmsnetworks.com

RM USL Animation
UTV House
Marwah Estate
Kishanlal Marwah Marg
Andheri (E)
Mumbai 400 072
India
Tel: +91 22 857 0000
Fax: +91 11 857 2558
Web: http://www.utvnet.com

RNA Studios
Ilica 205a / 2
10000 Zagreb
Croatia
Tel: +385 1 370 49 42
Fax: +385 1 370 49 42
Web: http://www.rna.hr

Roboboy
2105 High Rd.
Tallahassee, Florida 32303
United States
Tel: 1-850-383-9824
Web: http://www.roboboy.com

Rocambole Producoes
Rua Marechal Deodoro 1200
Sao Carlos, SP Brazil
13560200
Tel: +55 16.97.04.88.73
Web: http://www.rocambole.org

Rode3D
Haedo 1602
Buenos Aires, Capital Federal
Argentina
1602
Tel: +54 11.47.95.09.69
Web: http://www.rode3d.8k.com

Rogue Creative
30 Irving Place, 6th floor
New York, New York 10003
United States
Tel: 1-212-475-4466
Fax: 1-212-475-8671
Web:
http://www.rogue-creative.com

Rogue Creative
2562 Dexter Ave. N
Seattle, Washington 98109
United States
Tel: 1-206-838-5575
Fax: 1-206-784-0989
Web:
http://www.rogue-creative.com

Rojna Animation Studios
P.O. Box 16765-1548
Tehran, Iran
Web: http://www.rojna.com

Rothkirch / Cartoon-film
Bergmanstrasse 68
Berlin, Germany
10961
Tel: +49 30.69.80.84.0
Fax: +49 30.69.80.84.29
Web: http://www.cartoon-film.de

Rough Draft Studios, Inc.
209 N. Brand Blvd.
Glendale, California 91203
United States
Tel: 1-818-507-0491
Fax: 1-818-507-0486
Web:
http://www.roughdraftstudios.com

Rough House Editorial
San Francisco Film Centre
39 Mesa Street, Suite 212
The Presidio
San Francisco, California 94129
United States
Tel: 1-415-561-4544
Fax: 1-415-561-4540
Web: http://www.roughhouse.com

R's Factory
2-50 Mountain Nine Stand Place
Commercial Distribution Center 3f
Koto Ku
Tokyo 135-0064
Japan
Tel: 03-5500-3949
Fax: 03-5500-3947
http://www.rsf.co.jp

RTV Family Entertainment AG
23, M–hlstrasse
Munich, Bavaria Germany
81675
Tel: +49 89 99 7271 11
Tel: +49 89 99 7271 24
Fax: +49 89 99 7271 92
Fax: +49 89 99 7271 90
Web: http://www.rtv-ag.com

RTV Family Entertainment AG
Fort Malakoff Park
Rheinstr. 4c
55116 Mainz
Tel: +49 6131 97319-0
Fax: +49 6131 97319-10
Web: http://www.rtv-ag.com

RTV Family Entertainment AG
Off the Fence B.V.
Nieuwe Herengracht 31
1011 RM Amsterdam
The Netherlands
Tel: +31 205200-222
Fax: +31 205200-223
Web: http://www.rtv-ag.com

RTV Family Entertainment AG
Energee Entertainment
1/706 Mowbray Road
Lane Cove NSW 2066
Australia

Tel: +61 294 2088-64
Fax: +61 294 2088-61
Web: http://www.rtv-ag.com

Rushes
66 Old Compton Street
London
W1D 4UH
United Kingdom
Tel: 020 7437 8676
Fax: 020 7437 3001
Web: http://www.rushes.co.uk

Rushes Mexico
S.A. de C.V., Liverpool #17
Colonia, Juarez
Mexico, D.F.
06600
Mexico
Web: http://www.virgin.com.mx

Rutt Video & Interactive
1953 Old Chelsea Station
New York, New York 10113-1953
United States
Tel: 1-212-993-1000
Web: http://www.rutt.com

RUV Iceland National
Broadcsting Service -TV
Efstaleiti 1
Reykjavik, Iceland
150
Tel: +354.51.53.00.0
Fax: +354.51.53.01.0
Web: http://www.ruv.is

Rw Productions
15630 Michigan Ave.
Dearborn, Michigan 48126
United States
Tel: 1-313-945-9292
Fax: 1-313-945-9295
Web: http://www.rwpmi.com

Saab & Miller Productions
12407 North Mopac Expressway
100-352
Austin, Texas 78758
United States
Tel: 1-512-388-3893

Fax: 1-512-388-7992
Web: http://www.saabandmiller-productions.com

SABA Animation, Arts, Multimedia
No.73 Yakhchal Ave.
P.O. Box 19395-6774
Tehran, Iran
Tel: +98 21.20.00.62.0
Fax: +98 21.20.00.59.4
Web: http://www.sabaanimo.com

Sabella Dern Entertainmant
6625 Variel
Canoga Park, California
United States
Tel: 1-818-673-1163
Fax: 1-818-673-1164
Web: http://www.sdentertain-ment.net

saboteur
344 E. 85 street, Suite 1H
New York, New York 10028
United States

Sad World Animation
1425 SW Clay #1
Portland, Oregon 97201
United States
Tel: 1-503-241-1270
Web: http://www.sad-world.com

Safe Passage International, Inc.
333 Metro Park
Rochester, New York 14623
United States
Tel: 1-585-292-4910
Fax: 1-585-292-4911
Web:http://www.safe-passage.com

Safe Passage International Ltd.
10 George St.
Grimsby
Northeast Lincolnshire,
DN31 1HB
United Kingdom
Tel: +44 1472 269 500
Fax: +44 1472 269 700
Web:http://www.safe-passage.com

Sahin Ersoz Animation Studio
417 Scholl Drive
Glendale, California 91206
United States
Tel: 1-818-552-2642
Fax: 1-818-214-0314
Web: http://www.ersoz.com

Saicom FX Factory, The
Unit 66-67, 1st floor
MHADA Shopping Complex
Link Road Extn.
Andheri (West)
Mumbai - 400 102
India
Tel: 91 22 639 9650
Tel: 91 22 632 9963
Fax: 91 22 215 1269
Web: http://www.saicom.com

Saicom FX Factory Corporate
Office, The
148, Admiralty House
Near Colaba Bus Station
Mumbai - 400 005
India
Tel: 91 22 215 1396
Fax: 91 22 215 1269
Web: http://www.saicom.com

Samsa Film
238 C, rue de Luxembourg
Bertrange, Luxembourg
8077
Tel: +352.45.19.60.1
Fax: +352.44.24.29
Web: http://www.samsa-film.com

Sandmannstudio Trickfilm
GEPO TV- u. Filmproduktion
GmbH
Rudower Chaussee 3
Berlin, Germany
12489
Tel: +49 30.67.05.0
Fax: +49 30.67.05.0
Web: http://www.gepo.de

Sandmannstudio Trickfilm
GEPO TV- u. Filmproduktion GmbH
Altenburger Straße 9
Leipzig, Germany 04275

Tel: +49 - (0)341-3500 3700
Fax: +49 - (0)341-3500 3710
Web: http://www.gepo.de

Sarbakan
420 Charest est,
Montreal, Quebec Canada
G1K 8M4
Tel: +1 418.682.0601
Fax: +1 418.682.2832
Web: http://www.sarbakan.com

Sardine Productions Inc.
5520 Chabot St. #306
Montreal, Quebec Canada
H2H 2S7
Tel: +1 514.523.4666
Fax: +1 514.523.1395
Web:
http://www.sardineproductions.com

Sasahara gum Inc.
1-13-6 Ochiai
Shinjuku Ku
Tokyo 161-0032
Japan
Tel: 03-5988-9870
Web: http://www.sasaharagumi.co.jp

Sasoon Film Design
2525 Main Street, Suite 210
Santa Monica, California 90405
United States
Tel: 1-310-664-9115
Fax: 1-310-664-9118
Web:
http://www.sasoonfilmdesign.com

SAS Studio Productions
One SAS Campus Drive
Raleigh North Carolina, 27513
United States
Tel: 1-919-677-8000
Fax: 1-919-677-4444
Web: http://www.sas.com

Sav! The World Productions
9, rue Beethoven
75016 Paris
France
Tel: +33 1.42.30.72.27

Fax: +33 1.42.30.72.27
Web: http://www.savtheworld.com

Savage Frog! Studios
1650 Flower Street
Glendale, California 91201
United States
Tel: 1-818-246-3764
Fax: 1-818-242-0008
Web: http://www.savagefrog.com

Savannah Digital
Communications
9 PosÈy Street Suite P
Savannah, Georgia 31406
United States
Tel: 1-866-286-9732
Fax: 1-801-730-8665
Web:http://www.savannahdigital.com

Saxonia Media
Altenburgerstrasse 7
Leipzig, Germany
04275
Tel: +49 34.13.50.01
Web:http://www.saxonia-media.de

Scene by Scene
259 Danforth Avenue
Toronto, Ontario M4K 1N2
Canada
Tel: 1-416-463-5060
Tel: 1-800-439-5060
Web: http://www.sbys.com

SciFi Channel
1230 Avenue of the Americas
New York, New York 10020
United States
Tel: 1-212-413-5000
Fax: 1-212-413-6507
Web: http://www.scifi.com

Scopas Medien AG
Westerbachstrasse 28
Frankfurt am Main,
Germany
60489
Tel: +49.69.78.9 92-0
Fax: +49.69.78.9 92-2 23
Web: http://www.scopas.de

Scopas Medien AG/Studio
Servics
Franziusstrasse 14
Frankfurt am Main, Germany
60314
Tel: +49.69.44.08.70
Fax: +49.69.40.59.6 92
Web: http://www.scopas.de

Screaming Wink Productions
P.O. Box 373
Hakalau, Hawaii 96710
United States
Tel: 1-808-963-5482
Web: http://www.screamingwink.com

Seamless Creations
576 Kingston Rd
Toronto, Ontario Canada
M4E1P9
Tel: +1 416.993.7493
Fax: +1 720.294.3719
Web: http://www.seamless.org

Secret Weapon
4 W 4th Ave. Lower Lobby
San Mateo, California 94402
United States
Tel: 1-650-401-08878
Web: http://www.secretweapon.org

Sector 3
Suite 3, 4 Duke St
Windsor, Victoria
Australia 3181
Tel: 03 9521 1331
Web: http://www.sector3.com.au

Selecta Vision
Calle Diputacion 37, local 7B
Barcelona, Spain 08015
Tel: +34 93.32.51.02.2
Fax: +34 93.42.36.01.9
Web: http://www.selecta-vision.com

Serious Robots Animation
1610 Midtown Place
Raleigh North Carolina, 27609
United States
Tel: 1-919-873-1333
Web: http://www.seriousrobots.com

SEANFX
32 West Crystal Avenue
Lombard, Illinois 60148
United States
Tel: 1-630-495-4658
Fax: 1-630-495-4658
Web: http://www.seanfx.com

SecondSun Entertainment
3rd Floor, 4250 Dawson St.
Burnaby, British Columbia
Canada
V5C-4B1
Tel: 1-604-877-8585
Fax: 1-604-877-1614
Web: http://www.secondsunenter-
tainment.com

Secret Weapon
4 w 4th Avenue, Lower Lobby
San Mateo, California 94402
United States
Tel: 1-650-401-8878
Web: http://www.secretweapon.org

Seieisya
1-22-3 park side building 401
Hokkaido University
Toshima Ku
Tokyo 170-0004
Japan
Tel: 03-3918-3770
Fax: 03-3918-3790
Web: http://www.seiei-anime.co.jp

Seven's Heaven
Bussum
The Netherlands
Tel: +31 (0)35 695169
Tel: +31 (0)6 47118589
Fax: +31 (0)35 6424766
Web: http://www.sevensheaven.nl

Seven Sydney
9 Bibby Street,
Chiswick, N.S.W. 2046
Australia
Tel 00 61 2 8752 5777
Fax 00 61 2 9712 3399
Web: http://www.sevenww.com

Seven
St Marks House
Shepherdess Walk
London
N1 7LH
United Kingdom
Tel +44 (0)20 7861 7777
Fax +44 (0)20 7871 7702
Web: http://www.sevenww.co.uk

Seven Interactive:
St Marks House
Shepherdess Walk
London N1 7LH
United Kingdom
Tel +44 (0)20 7861 7777
Fax +44 (0)20 7871 77014
Web: http://www.sevenww.co.uk

Seven Soho
8 Portland Mews, Soho,
London W1F 8JH
United Kingdom
Tel +44 (0)20 7292 4777
Fax +44 (0)20 7434 1735
Web: http://www.sevenww.co.uk

Seven Worldwide Inc.
225 W. Superior Street
Chicago, Illinois 60610
United States
Tel 1 312 943 0400
Fax 1 312 943 2716
Web: http://www.sevenww.com

SFP
2 Avenue de l'Europe
94366 Bry sur Marne Cedex
France
Tel: 33 1 49 83 36 02
Fax: 33 1 49 83 36 04
Web: http://www.sfp.fr

Shadow Entertainment Inc.
1-28-14 Sakaki field building
Shinjuku Ku west Ochiai
Tokyo 161-0031
Japan
Tel: 03-3954-3121
Fax: 03-3954-3125
Web: http://www.sdw.co.jp

Shadows In Darkness
Fort Lauderdale, Florida
United States
Web:
http://www.shadowsindarkness.com

Sharp Image
4th Floor
West Land Trade Centre
Shaheed-E-Millat Road
Karachi, Sindh Pakistan
75350
Tel: +92 21.43.13.74.1
Fax: +92 21.43.13.74.0
Web:
http://www.sharpimageonline.com

Shaw Science Partners
4151 Ashford Dunwoody Road
Suite 602
Atlanta, Georgia 30319-1452
United States
Tel: 1-404-845-9994
Tel: 1-800-818-1343
Fax: 1-404-845-0840
Web: http://www.shawscience.com

Sherbet
112-114 Great Portland Street
London
W1N 5PE
United Kingdom
Tel: +44 (0)20 7636 6435
Fax: +44 (0)20 7436 3221
Web: http://www.sherbet.co.uk

Sherer Digital Animation
71-956 Magnesia Falls Drive
Rancho Mirage, California 92270
United States
Tel: 1-760-346-7234
Fax: 1-760-340-3170
Web: http://www.shererdigital.com

Shooters Post & Transfer
The Curtis Center, Suite 1050
Independence Square West
Philadelphia, Pennsylvania 19106
United States
Tel: 1-215-861-0100
Fax: 1-215-861-0098
Fax: 1-215-861-0099
Web: http://www.shootersinc.com

Shooting Stars Post
3106 W. North A St.
Tampa, Florida 33609
United States
Tel: 1-813-873-0100
Fax: 1-813-874-8501
Web: http://www.sspmedia.com

Shosho
Oudeschans 83-85
1011kw Amsterdam
The Netherlands
Tel: 020 6230247
Web: http://www.shosho.nl

Show-me Interactive
19 E Walnut, Suite E
Columbia Missouri, 65203
United States
Web:
http://www.showmeinteractive.com

Showtime Networks Inc.
1633 Broadway
New York, New York 10019
United States
Tel: 1-212-708-1600
Web: http://www.sho.com

Shout Interactive, LLC
1085 Mission Street
San Francisco, California 94103
United States
Tel: 1-415-335-4700
Web: http://www.shoutinteractive.com

Show & Tell Productions
1600 Broadway
Suite: 801
New York, New York 10019
United States
Tel: 1-212-489-6100
Fax: 1-212-489-6109
Web: http://www.showandtell.com

Shy Communications Private Ltd.
No. 25, Taurus, 1st Main Road
United India Colony
Kodambakkam
Chennai, Tamil Nadu
India

600003
Tel: +91 44.37.23.91.4
Fax: +91 44.37.23.91.3
Web: http://www.shypl.com

Side City Studios
731, de la Commune Ouest
2e étage, Montréal
Québec H3C 1X7
Canada
Tel: 1-514-861-6464
Fax: 1-514-861-7474
Web: http://www.sidecity.com

Sideshow Animation
6710 Sweetwood Ct.
Fort Wayne, Indiana 46814
United States
Tel: 1-912-441-2346
Fax: 1-260-432-4753
Web:
http://www.sideshowanimation.com

Side Step Productions, Inc.
5195 W. Sitka St.
Tampa, Florida 33634
United States
Tel: 1-813-880-8998
Fax: 1-813-880-0550
Web: http://www.sstep.com

SIFCA Corporation
K-BLDG. B1 3-7-14 Kudan-minami
Chiyoda-ku
Tokyo 102-0074
Japan
Tel: 03-5212-1631
Fax: 03-3239-3640
Web: http://www.sifca.com

Sight Effects
901 Abbot Kinney Boulevard
Venice, California 90291
United States
Tel: 1-310-399-5670
Fax: 1-310-399-1334
Web: http://www.sighteffects.com
Web: http://www.digitallab.com

Sightline Vision AB
Liljeholmstorget 7
117 63 Stockholm
Sweden
Tel: +46(0)8 556 752 60
Fax: +46 (0) 8 556 752 65
Web: http://www.sightline.se

Silent Entertainment Ltd
Townhouse Studios
150 Goldhawk Rd
London
United Kingdom
W12 8HH
Tel: +44 208.74.67.43.1
Fax: +44 208.74.35.62.4
Web: http://www.silent-ent.com

Silicon Illusions Pte Ltd
31 International Business Park,
#05-05 Creative Resource
Singapore 609921
Fax: +65 6895-4066
Web:http://www.siliconillusions.com.sg

Silicon Image
Coupure Rechts 164 b
B-9000 Gent
Belgium
Tel: +32 (9) 233 15 15
Tel: +32 (9) 227 11 33
Fax: +32 (9) 233 16 16
Web: http://www.siliconimage.be

Silver Hammer Studios
817 Hamilton Street
Charlotte, North Carolina 28206
United States
Tel: 1-800-376-1211
Tel: 1-704-342-3348
Fax: 1-704-342-0085
Fax: 1-704-377-0501
Web: http://www.silverhammer.com

SimEx Digital Studios
3250 Ocean Park Blvd., Suite 100
Santa Monica, California 90405
United States
Tel: 1-310.664.9500
Fax: 1-310-664-1178
Fax: 1-310-664-9977
Web: http://www.simexds.com

SIMULA Project (The)
University of Bradford
Great Horton Road
Bradford, West Yorkshire United
Kingdom
BD7 1DP
Tel: +44 1274.23.60.80
Fax: +44 1274.23.65.99
Web: http://www.simula.co.uk

Simworks Motion Simulator
Productions
9 Willoughby Road
Crows Nest, NSW 2065
Australia
Tel: +61 2 8436 9466
Fax: +61 2 8436 9456
Web:
http://www.simworks-msp.com

Siriol Productions
3, Mount Stuart Square
Butetown
Cardiff, Wales United Kingdom
CF10 5EE
Tel: +44 292.04.88.40.0
Fax: +44 292.04.85.96.2
Web:
http://www.siriolproductions.com

Six Foot Two
25 Ebbtide Passage
Corte Madera California 94925
United States
Tel: 1-415-927-0880
Web: http://www.sixfoottwo.com

Sixus1 Media Solutions
10515 McPherson St. Suite D
Indianapolis, Indiana 46280
United States
Tel: 1-317-574-8805
Web: http://www.sixus1.com

Skaramoosh
9-15 Neal Street
Covent Garden
London, England
WC2H 9Pw
United Kingdom
Tel: +44 (0) 20 7379 9966
Fax: +44 (0) 20 7240 7111
Web: http://www.skara.co.uk

Skuad Studios
4295 Chambord
Montreal, Quebec
Canada
H2J 3M3
Tel: 1-514-831-1304
Fax: 1-514-524-8175
Web: http://www.skuadstudios.com

Sky Broadcasting Group
Grant Way
Isleworth
TW7 5QD
United Kingdom
Tel: (44) 020 7705 3000
Web: http://www.sky.com/sky-com/home

Skyscraper Digital
5815 Westpark Drive
Charlotte North Carolina, 28217
United States
Tel: 1-704-525-6350
Web:
http://www.skyscraper-digital.com

Slappy Pictures
23962 Dovekie Circle
Laguna Niguel, California 92677
United States
Tel: 1-949-448-0653
Web: http://www.slappypictures.com

Slave Studios, Ltd.
28 Fouberts Place
London
W1F 7PR
United Kingdom
Tel: +44 207.73.45.33.6
Fax: +44 207.73.45.33.7
Web: http://www.slave-studios.co.uk

Slave Studios Ltd
36-37 Carnaby Street
London
W1F 7DW
United Kingdom
Tel: +44 0207 43 44 44 2
Web: http://www.slave-studios.co.uk

Smart Origins
12021 113th Ave NE
Kirkland, Washington 98034
United States
Tel: 1-425-821-8178
Fax: 1-425-821-9649
Web: http://www.smartorigins.com

SmithGroup Communications, Inc.
267 SE 33rd Avenue
Portland, Oregon 97214
United States
Tel: 1-503-239-4215
Fax: 1-503-239-1570
Web: http://www.smithgrp.com

Snackbar Desiree Visual Effects
Kloveniersburgwal 119
1011 KC Amsterdam
The Netherlands
Tel: +3120 6164964
Fax: +3120 6164974
Web:
http://www.snackbardesiree.com

Snap 5
9600 Southern Pines Blvd.
Charlotte, North Carolina 28273
United States
Tel: 1-704-561-7763
Web: http://www.snap5.tv

So! Animation
220 East 23rd Street, 10th Floor
New York, New York 10010
United States
Tel: 1-212-696-1020
Fax: 1-212-696-1118
Web: http://www.so-animation.com

So! Animation
130 West 29th Street 8th Floor
New York, New York, 10001
United States
Tel: 1-212-244-5588
Fax: 1-212-244-5578
Web: http://www.somuchdesign.com

SOB Animation Group Limited
17-19 Maurice Road
Penrose

Auckland, New Zealand
1800
Tel: +64 9.62.20.61.8
Fax: +64 9.62.24.08.0
Web:
http://www.sobproductions.co.nz

SOB Productions
Hofstede 'Oud-Bussem'
Flevolaan 41
1411 KC Naarden
Tel: 035-6958421
Fax: 035-6946173
Web: http://www.sob.nl

Softamation Ltd.
69B Green Road
4th Floor
Panthapath
Dhaka, Bangladesh
1205
Tel: +880 2.86.24.78.0
Fax: +880 2.81.17.56.4
Web: http://www.softamation.com

Soho Post and Graphics
26 Soho Street
Toronto, Ontario M5T 1Z7
Canada
Tel: 1-416-591-1400
Fax: 1-416-591-6854
Web: http://www.26soho.com

SOL designfx
515 North State Street, 26th Floor
Chicago Illinois 60610
United States
Tel: 1-312-706-5500
Fax: 1-312-644-2503
Web: http://www.soldesignfx.com

SOL designfx
215 Rose Ave.
Venice California 90291
United States
Tel: 1-310-309-5500
Fax: 1-310-309-5501
Web: http://www.soldesignfx.com

SOL designfx
221 East 48th Street

New York, New York 10017
United States
Tel: 1-212-888-5200
Fax: 1-212-832-2296
Web: http://www.soldesignfx.com

Somersault
625 North Michigan Ave. 23rd fl.
Chicago, Illinois 60611
United States
Tel: 1-312-943-4144
Fax: 1-312-943-9760
Web: http://www.somersault.net

Somersault
1543 7th Street/4th Floor
Santa Monica, California 90401
United States
Tel: 1-310-458-7676
Fax 1-310-260-8518
Web: http://www.somersault.net

Sonalysts, Inc.
215 Parkway North
Waterford, Connecticut 06385
United States
Web: http://www.sonalysts.com

Sonalysts, Inc.
P.O. Box 280
Waterford, Connecticut 06385
United States
Web: http://www.sonalysts.com

Sonne AS
Sortedam Dossering 55
2100 Copenhagen
Denmark
Tel: (0045) 35374477
Fax: (0045) 35397225
Web: http://www.sonne.dk

Sony Pictures Entertainment
10202 West Washington Blvd.
Suite 3900
Culver City, California 90232-
3195
United States
Tel: 1-310-244-4436
Web: http://www.sonypictures.com

Sony Pictures Entertainment
550 Madison Avenue, 7th Floor
New York, New York 10022
United States
Web: http://www.sonypictures.com

Sony Imageworks
9050 West Washington
Boulevard, Suite 2206
Culver City, California 90232
United States
Tel: 1-310-840-8000
Tel: 1-310-840-8300
Fax: 1-310-840-8330
Fax: 1-310-840-8100
Web: http://www.imageworks.com
Web: http://www.spiw.com

SOS-Digital
Suite 1, 345 Pacific Highway
North Sydney 2060
Australia
Tel: +61 2 9954 6155
Fax: +61 2 9954 6156
Web: http://www.sos-digital.com

Soundimage
51 Melcher Street, Flr. 6
Boston, Massachusetts 02210
United States
Tel: 1-617-350-6030
Web: http://www.soundimage.com

South Coast File and Video
5234 Elm
Houston, Texas
United States
Tel: 1-800-229-3550
Fax: 1-713-661-3550
Web: http://www.scfilmvideo.com

Southern Star Animation
Level 10, 8 West Street
North Sydney NSW 2060
Australia
Tel: 011-612-9202-8555,
Fax: 011-612-9202-8577
Fax: 011-612-9956-8812
Web:
http://www.southernstargroup.com

Southern Star Group, Ltd.
Level 8, 8 West Street
North Sydney, New South Wales
Australia
2065
Tel: +61 2.92.02.85.55
Fax: +61 2.99.56.69.18
Web: http://www.sstar.com.au

Southwest Productions
812 Gold SW
Albuquerque, New Mexico 87102
United States
Tel: 1-505-247-3300
Fax: 1-505-247-3856
Web: http://www.southwestpro-
ductions.com

Southwest Productions
8 East 48th, Suite 5G
New York, New York 10017
United States
Tel: 1-212-832-3030
Fax: 1-212-832-6928
Web: http://www.southwestpro-
ductions.com

Space Division
505 North Sycamore Street, Suite A
Santa Ana, California 92701
United States
Tel: 1-714-564-1090
Fax: 1-714-569-9292
Web: http://www.spacediv.com

Space Monkey Studios
6600 Jackson Street
Pittsburgh, Pennsylvania 15206
United States
Tel: 1-412-401-8415
Web:
http://www.spacemonkeystudios.com

Space Time Foam
Skyttegade 7, 3tv
2200 Copenhagen N Denmark
Tel: (+45) 35301058
Fax: (+45) 35359340
Web:
http://www.spacetimefoam.com

Spans & Partner GmbH
Muhlenkamp 59
Hamburg, Germany
22303
Tel: +49 40.40.27.81.88
Fax: +49 40.40.27.81.88
Web: http://www.spans.de

Sparkus Animations LLP
29 Harley Street
London, United Kingdom
W1G9QR
Tel: +44 208.25.57.75.5
Fax: +44 845.28.02.82.5
Web: http://www.sparkus.com

SPARX*
91, rue Lauriston
Paris, France
75116
Tel: +33 1.44.34.01.34
Fax: +33 1.44.34.01.00
Web: http://www.sparx.com

Special Designs Studio
Studio City, California
United States
Tel: 1-818-766-9766
Fax: 1-818-766-9716
Web: http://www.sdas.com

Spectrum Studios
12536 Beatrice Street
Los Angeles, California 90066
United States
Tel: 1-310-305-9955
Fax: 1-310-822-1673
Web:
http://www.spectrumstudios.com

Sphere Animation Studio
25 Gleneagles Road
Greenside
Johannesburg
South Africa
2193
Tel: +27 (011) 888 7035
Tel: +27 (011) 888 7036
Fax: +27 (011) 888 7038
Web:
http://www.sphere-animation.com

Spice Inc.
Japan
Tel: 03-3452-9821
Tel: 03-5765-6565
Fax: 03-5445-6581
Fax: 03-5765-5858
Web: http://www.spice-inc.co.jp

Spider Eye Limited
The Town Hall
Chapel St., Saint Just
Cornwall, United Kingdom
TR19 7HT
Tel: +44 173.67.88.00
Fax: +44 173.67.88.10
Web: http://www.spider-eye.com

SPI International, Inc.
928 Broadway, Suite 700
New York, New York 10010
United States
Tel: 1-212-673-5103
Fax: 1-212-673-5183
Web: http://www.spiintl.com

Spi International Polaska Sp.Zo.o
Ui. Tyniecka 38a
Warsaw 02-621
Poland
Tel: +48 22 646 20 363 / 646 20 38
Fax: +48 22 848 4570
Web: http://www.spiintl.com

Spi International Czech Republic
Nad Ondrejovem 12
140 00 Praha 4
Czech Republic
Tel: +420 2 6122 1366
Fax: +420 2 6122 1375
Web: http://www.spiintl.com

Spi International Slovakia
Hlavateho 3
811 03 Bratislava 1
Slovakia
Tel: +421 2 5464 5712
Fax: +421 2 5464 5711
Web: http://www.spiintl.com

Spi International Hungary
1112 Budapest Csereszyne u 6

Hungary
Tel: +36 1 248 26 20/248 19 70
Fax: +36 1 249 25 33/248 26 28
Web: http://www.spiintl.com

Spin Atlanta
1919 Peachtree Road
Atlanta, Georgia 30309
United States
Tel: 1-404-262-1919
Fax: 1-404-262-9798
Web: http://www.spinpro.com

Spin Toronto
620 King Street West
Toronto, Ontario M5V 1M6
Canada
Tel: 1-416-504-8333
Fax: 1-416-504-3876
Web: http://www.spinpro.com

Splash Design, LLC.
14 East 47th Street, 3rd Fl.
New York, New York 10017
United States
Tel: 1-212-697-1744
Fax: 1-212-697-2778
Web: http://www.splashnyc.com

Splat Productions
2118 South Street
Philadelphia, Pennsylvania 19146
United States
Tel: 1-877-SPLAT-ME
Tel: 1-215-546-0177
Fax: 1-215-546-0199
Web: http://www.splatworld.tv

Spontaneous Combustion
525 Lexington Ave, 25th Floor
New York, New York 10022
United States
Tel: 1-212-317-0077
Fax: 1-212-317-1048
Web: http://www.spon.com

SportsMEDIA Technology
3511 University Drive
Durham, North Carolina 27707
United States
Tel: 1-919-493-9390
Fax: 1-919-493-7782
Web: http://www.sportsmedia.com

Sportvision
1450 Broadway, 31st Floor
New York, New York 10018
United States
Tel: 1-212-764-0873
Fax: 1-212-764-0876
Web: http://www.sportvision.com

Sportvision
1240 La Avenida Avenue, Suite C
Mountain View, California 94043
United States
Tel: 1-650-961-7825
Fax: 1-650-961-0102
Web: http://www.sportvision.com

Spotlight Animation Inc.
300 East Magnolia Blvd. #305
Burbank, California 91501
United States
Tel: 1-818-557-0415
Fax: 1-818-557-0614
Web:
http://www.spotlightanimation.com

Sproing Interactive Media GmbH
Fernkorngasse 10
1100 Vienna
Austria
Tel: +43 1 6043028
Fax: +43 1 6043028-50
Web: http://www.sproing.at

Sputnik Animation
2 Portland Pier, MTC Suite 205
Portland, Maine 04101
United States
Tel: 1-207-780-1471
Web: http://www.sputnik.nu

Squash Post
12-13 Richmond Buildings
London
W1D 3HG
United Kingdom
Tel: +44(0) 7292 0222
Fax: +44(0) 7292 0223
Web: http://www.squashpost.co.uk

ST45
1433 S. 1600 E.
Preston, Indiana 83263
United States
Tel: 1-208-852-0650
Web: http://www.st45.com

Stafford Design Service
12337 Jones Road, Suite 216
Houston, Texas 77070
United States
Tel: 1-281-897-0889
Web: http://www.stafford-design.com

Stan Winston Studio
17216 Saticoy Street
P.O. Box #364
Van Nuys, California 91406
United States
Tel: 1-818-782-0870 Ext. 164
Web:
http://www.stanwinstonstudio.com

Stars Animation Services
42/10E Quang Trung Ward 11
Govap Dist.
HoChiMinh
Vietnam
Tel: +84 9.39.66.59.9
Web:http://www.starsanimation.com

Start Effects + Visuals
903 Colorado Blvd., Suite 100
Santa Monica, California 90401
United States
Tel: 1-310-451-1666
Fax: 1-310-451-3606
Web: http://www.startefx.com

Station, The
5 D'Arblay Street
London W1F 8DE
United Kingdom
Tel: 020 7292 9595
Fax: 020 7292 9596
Web: http://www.the-station.com

Steam
3021 Airport Avenue Suite 201
Santa Monica, California 90405
Tel: 1-310-636-4620

Fax: 1-310-636-4621
Web: http://www.steamshow.com

Steele VFX
1437 Seventh Street
Santa Monica, California 90401
United States
Tel: 1-310-656-7770
Fax: 1-310-656-7771
Web: http://www.steelevfx.com

Stitch
16 West 46th Street, 12th Floor.
New York, New York 10036
United States
Tel: 1-212-584-9700
Fax: 1-212-391-8738
Web: http://www.stitch.net

Stock's Eye
148 West Street
Granby, Massachusetts 01033
United States
Tel: 1-413-467-2761
Web: http://www.stocks-eye.com

Stonehenge
53 Jarvis Street, 3rd Floor
Toronto, Ontario
Tel: 1-416-867-1189
Fax: 1-416-364-6055
Web: http://www.stonehenge.ca

Stone Soup
2640 Fountain View Dr. Suite #127
Houston, Texas 77057
United States
Tel: 1-713-278-0342
Fax: 1-713-278-0074
Web: http://www.ssoup.net

StraneMani
Via Firenze 78 / i
Localita' Le Macine
Prato
Italy
59100
Tel: +39 57.45.14.09.0
Web: http://www.stranemani.com

Strange Engine Productions
720 Wilshire Blvd., Suite 100
Santa Monica, California 90401
United States
Tel: 1-310-656-0790
Web: http://www.strange-engine.com

Stream Digital Media
61 Charlotte Street
London
W1T 4PF
United Kingdom
Tel: +44 (0)20 7208 1567
Fax: +44 (0)20 7208 1555
Web: http://www.streamdm.co.uk

Street Dog Studio
Avª José Relvas, 17, 6ºD
2840-079 Aldeia de Paio Pires
Portugal
Tel: (+351) 936 046 046
Web: http://www.streetdogstudio.com

Strega Imaging
4130 Cahuenga Blvd. Suite 200
Universal City, California 91602
United States
Tel: 1-818-985-7773
Fax: 1-818-985-7778
Web: http://www.stregaimaging.com

Strickland Video Services
Orlando, Florida
United States
Tel: 1-407-297-4063
Web: http://www.stricklandvideo.com

Studio 4°C
Japan
Web: http://www.beyond-c.co.jp

Studio Aka
30 Berwick Street
London, United Kingdom
W1F 8RH
Tel: +44 207.43.43.58.1
Fax: +44 207.43.72.30.9
Web: http://www.studioaka.co.uk

Studio B Productions
6th Floor
190 Alexander Street
Vancouver, British Columbia
Canada
V6A 1B5
Tel: +1 604.684.2363
Fax: +1 604.602.0208
Web:
http://www.studiobproductions.com

Studio C Animation and
Compositing
Bilderdijkpark 4c
1052 RZ Amsterdam
The Netherlands
Tel: +31 (0) 20 488 33 10
Fax: +31 (0) 20 689 64 99
Web: http://www.studio-c.nl

Studio Cruz
227 Morrissey Boulevard
Santa Cruz, California 95062
United States
Tel: 1-831-458-2752
Web: http://www.studiocruz.com

studioDELPHIS
Padc du Calvi
359, rue de l'Artisanat
74330 Poisy Annecy
France
Tel: +33 (0)4 50 24 08 04
Fax: +33 (0)4 50 24 08 05
Web: http://www.studiodelphis.com

Studio Delta 7 bvba/Sprl
Esdoornlaan 12
Kalmthout, Antwerp Belgium
2920
Tel: +32 3.66.63.63.3
Fax: +32 3.66.63.53.8
Web: http://www.studiodelta7.com

Studio Delta 7 bvba/Sprl
Esdoornlaan 12
Kalmthout, Antwerp Belgium
2920
Tel: +32 3.66.63.63.3
Fax: +32 3.66.63.53.8
Web: http://www.studiodelta7.com

Studio FILM BILDER
Ostendstrasse 106
Stuttgart, Baden-Württemberg
Germany
70188
Tel: +49 711.48.91.92.4
Fax: +49 711.48.91.92.5
Web: http://www.filmbilder.de

Studio Ghibli
Tokyo, Japan
Tel: 0422-53-2961
Web: http://www.ntv.co.jp/ghibli

Studio Hill Ltd.
Hrisantema 14
Sofia, Bulgaria
1612
Tel: +359 2.95.33.45.4
Fax: +359 2.95.32.47.0
Web: http://www.studio-hill.com

Studio L CO. LTD.
Japan
Tel: 03-3460-2885
Fax: 03-3460-2860
Web: http://www.studio-net.co.jp

Studio Magica
Storgata 51
Oslo, Norway
0183
Tel: +47 22.99.76.10
Fax: +47 22.99.76.11
Web: http://www.animagicnet.no

Studio Mirage
Smolenska 22
101 00 Prague
Czech Republic
Tel: +420-2-7174 2040
Fax: +420-2-7174 0306
Web: http://www.mirage.cz

Studio R CO. LTD.
Japan
Tel: 03-3460-2848
Fax: 03-3460-0406
Web: http://www.studio-net.co.jp

Studio Upstairs, The
510 Front Street West Suite 103
Toronto, Ontario M5V 1B8
Canada
Tel: 1-416-979-8983
Fax: 1-416-979-8246
Web:http://www.thestudioupstairs.com

Studio Vermaas
Brantasgracht 11
1019 RK Amsterdam
The Netherlands
Tel: +31 (0)20 6949106
Fax: +31 (0)20 6941087
Web: http://www.studiovermaas.nl

Studio Walter Buonfino
via neera 8/a 20141
Italy
Tel: 02 89546192
Fax: 02 89545161
Web: http://www.wbgraphic.com

Studio X
1 Lakewood drive
Norwalk, Connecticut 06851
United States
Tel: 1-203-846-8682
Fax: 1-203-846-8728
Web: http://www.studio-x.com

Stun Gun
2082 Business Center Drive
Irvine, California 92612
United States
Tel: 1-949-833-7678
Fax: 1-949-252-1160
Web: http://www.stunguntv.com

Sub Atomic productions Inc.
90C Centurian Drive
Unit 1
Markham, Ontario Canada
L3R 8C5
Tel: +1 905.474.9393
Fax: +1 905.474.0209
Web:
http://www.subatomicproductions.com

Successful Images
111 S.W. 6th St.
Fort Lauderdale, Florida 33301
United States
Tel: 1-954-467-7200
Fax: 1-954-467-5411
Web:http://www.successfulimages.com

Sultana Films
Kaiserstr.117
Lorch, Germany
73547
Tel: +49 71.72.91.48
Fax: +49 71.72.86.78
Web: http://www.sultanafilms.de

Sundog Films Inc.
530 Richmond Street West, Rear
Building, 3rd Floor
Toronto
Ontario
Canada
M5V 1Y4
Tel: 1-416-504-2555
Fax: 1-416-504-4545
Web: http://www.sundogfilms.ca

Sunmin Image Pictures Co., LTD.
4F, Hahnshin Building
651-3, Yeoksam-Dong
Gangnam-Gu
Seoul
Korea
Tel:(822)553-7884
Fax:(02)553-7812
Web: http://www.sunmin.com

Sunset Digital
1813 Victory Boulevard
Glendale, California 91201
United States
Tel: 1-818-956-7912
Tel: 1-800-GO-SUNSET
Fax: 1-818-545-7586
Web: http://www.sunsetpost.com

Sunwoo Entertainment U.S.A.
Los Angeles, California
United States
Tel: 1-323-965-5454
Fax: 1-323-965-5449
Web: http://www.sunwoo.com

Sunwoo Entertainment Korea
Seoul, South Korea
Tel: +82 2.21.88.30.15
Fax: +82 2.21.88.30.24
Web: http://www.sunwoo.com

Super 78 Studios, Inc.
1344 North Highland
Hollywood, California 90028
Tel: 1-323-464-7878
Fax: 1-323-464-7879
Web: http://www.super78.com

Super-fi, Inc.
37 West 20th No. 1005
New York, New York 10011
United States
Tel: 1-212-924-6536
Web: http://www.super-fi.com

Surreal World
Francis Digital Studios Pty Ltd.
1st Floor, 230 Burwood Road
Hawthorn Victoria
Australia 3122
Tel: + 613 9818 8884
Fax: + 613 9818 4252
Web:http://www.surrealworld.com.au

SWAY Digital Studio
1100 Glendon Avenue, 17th Floor
Los Angeles, California 90024
United States
Tel: 1-310-689-7237
Fax: 1-310-689-7272
Web: http://www.swaystudio.com

Swedish Television
Sweden
Tel: +46 08 784 84 84
Fax: +46 08 663 41 60
Web: http://www.svt.se

Swell
455 North Cityfront Plaza Drive,
18th Floor
Chicago, Illinois 60611
United States
Tel: 1-312-464-8000
Fax: 1-312-464-8020
Web: http://www.swellinc.com

Swen Entertainment
2008 Alton Rd.
Miami Beach, Florida 33140
United States
Tel: 1-877-SWEN-ENT
Tel: 1-305-531-SWEN
Fax: 1-305-531-6722
Web:
http://www.swenentertainment.com

Swish Group Limited
Level 6, De Bono Centre
257 Collins Street
Melbourne Victoria 3000
Australia
Tel: +61 3 9662 1233
Fax: +61 3 9662 1942
Web: http://www.planetx.com.au

Swiss International AB
Linnegatan 51
SE-114 58
Stockholm, Sweden
Tel: +46-8-662 24 60
Fax: +46-8-662 24 61
Web: http://www.swiss.se

SVC
142 Wardour Street
London
W1F 8ZU
United Kingdom
Tel: 020 7734 1600
Fax: 020 7437 1854
Web: http://www.svc.co.uk

Sylicone
10 rue Biscornet
75012 Paris
France
Tel: 01 44 75 11 11
Fax: 01 43 43 20 42.
Web: http://www.sylicone.com

Synchroneon Digital Pictures
3100 West Burbank Blvd. Suite 205
Burbank, California 91505
Tel: 1-310-980-3610
United States
Web: http://www.synchroneon.com

Synchroneon Digital Pictures
Box 59
Southampton, New York 11969
United States
Tel: 1-516-527-3610
Web: http://www.synchroneon.com

Syndicate, The
1207 4th Street Suite 200
Santa Monica, California 90401
United States
Tel: 1-310-260-2320
Fax: 1-310-260-2420
Web: http://www.syndicate.tv

Syndicate, The
2200 Colonial Ave. Suite 26
Norfolk, Virginia 23517
United States
Tel: 1-757-625-0650
Web:
http://www.wearethesyndicate.com

Synthetic Dimensions plc
Galleon House
35 Hagley Road
Stourbridge
DY8 1QR
United Kingdom
Tel: +44 (0) 1384 358 328
Fax: +44 (0) 1384 358 367
Web: http://www.syndime.com

SZM Studios Film-, TV
Gutenbergstr.4
D-85774 Unterföhring, München
Germany
Tel: +49 89.95.07.60
Fax: +49 89.95.07.61.00
Web: http://www.szm-studios.de
Web: http://www.animation-vfx.de

SZM Studios Film-, TV
und Multimedia-Produktions GmbH
Oberwallstr. 6, D-10117 Berlin,
Germany
Tel. +49(30) 2090-2000,
Fax +49(30) 2090-2090
Web: http://www.szm-studios.de
Web: http://www.animation-vfx.de

Taiyo Kikaku Co.,Ltd.
2-26-3 Nishi-Shinbashi
Minato-ku
Tokyo 105-0003
Japan
Web: http://www.taiyonet.or.jp

Take One Productions
101 Pheasant Wood Ct.
Raleigh, North Carolina 27560
United States
Tel: 1-919-481-0000
Fax: 1-919-460-8809
Web: http://www.takeonepro.com

Take 27
25 Whitchurch Road
Chester
Cheshire
CH3 5QA
England
United Kingdom
Tel: (+44) 01244 345225
Fax: (+44) 01244 345225
Web: http://www.take27.co.uk

Talking Screens
7749 Hyde Park
Sacramento, California 95843
United States
Tel: 1-916-722-3798
Web:http://www.talkingscreens.com

Tall Tale Productions
2128 Commonwealth Ave
Charlotte, North Carolina 28205
United States
Tel: 1-704-376-8778
Fax: 1-704-376-8773
Web: http://www.talltaleprod.com

Talltree Studios
545 Ouellette Avenue, Suite 202
Windsor, Ontario N9A 4J3
Canada
Tel: 1-519-258-3717
Fax: 1-519-256-0243
Web:http://www.talltreestudios.com

Tandem FIlms
26 Cross Str.
London, United Kingdom
n1 2b9
Tel: +44 207.68.81.71.7
Web: http://www.tandemfilms.com

Tannhauser Gate
ul. Mielczarskiego 60a
51-663 Wroclaw
Poland
Tel: +48 71 345-16-19
Fax: +48 71 345-21-39
Web: http://www.thgate.com

Tantra Productions, Inc.
1445 Pennsylvania Avenue, Suite 200
Miami Beach, Florida 33139
United States
Tel: 1-305-673-1126
Fax: 1-305-673-1156
Web:
http://www.tantraproductions.com

Tape Gallery (The)
Tape Gallery House
28 Lexington Street
London, United Kingdom
W1F 0LF
Tel: +44 207.43.93.32.5
Fax: +44 207.73.49.41.7
Web: http://www.tape-gallery.co.uk

Tapehouse Toons
216 east 45th Street
New York, New York 10016
United States
Tel: 1-212-557-9611
Web: http://www.tapehousetoons.com

TaunusFilm Kopierwerk & ABC
GmbH
Hans-Konrad Hoffmann
Unter den Eichen 5
65195 Wiesbaden
Tel.: +49(0)611/531-236
Fax: +49(0)611/531-241
Web: http://www.taunusfilm.com

TaunusTon Bearbeitungs GmbH
Jutta Rüter
Unter den Eichen 7
65195 Wiesbaden
Tel: +49(0)611/531-302
Fax: +49(0)611/531-244
Web: http://www.taunusfilm.com

TaunusFilm Television & Wagner
GmbH
Konrad Adenauer Straße 42
55218 Ingelheim
Tel: +49(0)6132/79002-38
Fax: +49(0)6132/40043
Web: http://www.taunusfilm.com

TC Squared
211 Gregson Drive
Raleigh, North Carolina 27511-
7909
United States
Tel: 1-919-380-2156
Web: http://www.tc2.com

TeamcHmAn
81 rue du Pre Catelan
La Madeleine, France
59110
Tel: +1 33.32.85.23.99.0
Fax: +1 33.32.85.26.92.1
Web: http://www.teamchman.com

Team Kind
Warburger Klischee-Anstalt
GmbH&Co.OHG
Oberer Hilgenstock 38
D-34414 Warburg
Tel.: +49 (0) 5641 7626-0
Fax: +49 (0) 5641 7626-67
Web: http://www.teamkind.de

Team Kind
WKA Holland
Hengelosestraat 70538
Postbus 545
NL-7500 AM Enschede
Web: http://www.teamkind.de

Team Kind
WKA Alexandria
Amr Bondok

4 EL Esraa Steet, behind El
Quarey Street,
Agamy, Hanovîel
Alexandria - Egypt
Web: http://www.teamkind.de

Team Kind
Rudolf Designgroup GmbH
Am Weingarten 25
D-60487 Frankfurt am Main
Tel. +49 (0)69 6315770
Fax.+49 (0)69 63157725
Web: http://www.teamkind.de

Team Kind
Carl Kind jr. GmbH
Holländische Strasse 20
D-33607 Bielefeld
Tel.: +49 (0)521 965540
Fax: +49 (0)521 9655449
Web: http://www.teamkind.de

Technical Animations, Inc.
2720 River Road
Suite 150
Des Plaines, Illinois 60018
United States
Tel: 1-888-447-4935
Fax: 1-847-297-4820
Web: http://www.techanim.com

Technical editing Services Limited
Barbour Square
High Street
Tattenhall
Chester CH3 9RF
United Kingdom
Web: http://www.tesmm.com

Technomedia Solutions, Inc.
7703 King's Pointe Parkway, Suite
700
Orlando, Florida 32819
United States
Tel: 1-407-351-0909
Fax: 1-407-248-9484
Web:
http://www.gotechnomedia.com

Telcast International GmbH & Co. KG
Osterwaldstrasse 10

80805 Munich
Germany
Tel: +49(0)89-360 79 100
Fax: +49(0)89-360 79 113
Web: http://www.telcast.de

Telegael
Spiddal
Galaway
Ireland
Tel: +353 9.15.53.46.0
Fax: +353 9.15.53.46.4
Web: http://www.telegael.com

Tele Image
Paris, France
Tel: 01 1-33-1 44-35-17-00
Fax: 011-33-1-42-25-77-56
Web: http://www.teleimages.com

Televirtual, Ltd.
Park House
31 Cattle Market Street
Norwich
Norfolk
United Kingdom
NR1 3DY
Tel: +44 160.37.67.49.3
Fax: +44 160.37.64.94.6
Web: http://www.televirtual.com

Television Broadcasts Limited (TVB)
TV City Clear Water Bay Road
Kowloon, Hong Kong
Web: http://db.tvb.com.hk

Televisiun y Sonido TELSON
Alcalá, 518 - 28027 Madrid
Spain
Tel: +34 91 754 67 00
Fax: +34 91 754 67 24
Web: http://www.telson.es

Telewizja Polska S.A.
ul. J.P. Woronicza 17
00-999 Warszawa
Poland
Tel: 011-48-22-647-8191
Fax: 011-48-22-647-7583
Web: http://www.tvp.com.pl

Tell-Tale Productions
Elstree Film Studios
Shenley Road
Borehamwood
Hertfordshire
United Kingdom
WD6 1JG
Tel: +44 208.32.42.3
Fax: +44 208.32.42.6
Web: http://www.tell-tale.co.uk

Tellurian CGI
Petrova 113
10000 Zagreb
Croatia
Tel: +385 1 2421 806
Fax: +385 1 2421 807
Web: http://www.tellurian.hr

Tell-Tale Productions
Elstree Film Studios
Shenley Road
Borehamwood
Hertfordshire
United Kingdom
WD6 1JG
Tel: +44 208.32.42.3
Fax: +44 208.32.42.6
Web: http://www.tell-tale.co.uk

Terabyte Inc.
3F Daimex Sapporo Minami 2Jo Bldg.
Minami 2Jo Nishi 10 Chome,
Chuo-ku
Sapporo, 060-0062
Japan
Tel: +81(11)280-2180
Fax: +81(11)280-2181
Web: http://www.tera-byte.co.jp

Terratools Filmproduktions GmbH
Rudolf-Breitscheid-Straße 162
D-14482 Potsdam-Babelsberg
Tel: +49 (331) 62 01 -20
Fax: +49 (331) 62 01 -299
Web: http://www.terratools.de

Televirtual Ltd.
Park House
31 Cattle Market Street
Norwich
NR1 3DY

United Kingdom
Tel: +44 (0) 1603 767493
Fax: +44 (0) 1603 764946
Web: http://www.televirtual.com

Tenix Defence Pty Ltd
Simulation Group
100 Arthur St
North Sydney, NSW, 2060.
Australia
Tel: +61 2 9963 9600
Fax: +61 2 9964 0988
Web: http://www.tenix.com

Texturelighting
255 Harvard Rd
Stow, Massachusetts 01775
United States
Tel: 1-978-823-0934
Web: http://www.texturelighting.com

tes Multimedia Inc.
1011 South Highway 6, Suite 216
Houston, Texas 77077
United States
Web: http://www.tesmm.com

TF1 International
1, quai du Point du Jour
Boulogne
Billancourt
France
92100
Tel: +33 1.41.41.12.34
Fax: +33 1.41.41.29.10
Web: http://www.tf1.fr

TFC Trickompany GmGH
Hamburg
Germany
Tel: 011-494039-88-19-0
Fax: 011-49-40-39-88-19-107
Web: http://www.trickompany.de

The Brand Company A/S
Nicolai Eigtvedsgade 26, st.
Copenhagen, Denmark 1402
Tel: +45.70.22.02.01
Fax: +45.70.22.00.27.1
Web:
http://www.thebrandcompany.com

The Brothers Dimm Ltd
1/1, 16 Ruthven Street
Glasgow, Scotland United
Kingdom
G12 9BS
Web:http://www.thebrothersdimm.com

The Farm
27 Upper Mount St.
Dublin 2
Ireland
Tel: +3531 6768812
Fax: +3531 6768816
Web: http://www.thefarm.ie

The Juice Design
Scarsdale House
Derbyshire Lane
Sheffield
United Kingdom
S8 8SE
Tel: +44 114.24.96.40.0
Fax: +44 114.24.96.40.4
Web: http://www.thejuice.co.uk

The Lawrence Co.
2601 Ocean Park Boulevard, Suite 310
Santa Monica, California 90405
United States
Tel: 1-310-425-9657
Fax: 1-310-399-3774
Web: http://www.lawrenceco.com

The Mill
40-41 Great Marlborough Street
London
W1F 7JQ
United Kingdom
Tel: +44 207.28.74.04.1
Fax: +44 207.28.78.39.3
Web: http://www.mill.co.uk

The Mill New York
435 Hudson Street
New York, New York 10014
United States
Tel: 1-212-520-3150
Fax: 1-212-520-3170
Web: http://www.mill.co.uk

The SIMULA Project
University of Bradford
Great Horton Road
Bradford, West Yorkshire
United Kingdom
BD7 1DP
Tel: +44 1274.23.60.80
Fax: +44 1274.23.65.99
Web: http://www.simula.co.uk

The Station
5 D'Arblay Street
London W1F 8DE
United Kingdom
Tel: 020 7292 9595
Fax: 020 7292 9596
Web: http://www.the-station.com

The Studio Upstairs
510 Front St. W. Suite 103
Toronto, Ontario Canada
M5V 1B8
Tel: +1 416.979.8983
Fax: +1 416.979.8246
Web:
http://www.thestudioupstairs.com

The Video Lab
cnr Eileen & Geneva rd
Blairgowrie
p.o.box 1854 Pinegowrie
Johannesburg, Gauteng South
Africa
2123
Tel: +27 11.29.33.00.0
Fax: +27 11.29.33.09.0
Web: http://www.videolab.co.za

Three D Co. Ltd.
Japan
Tel: 03-3478-0651
Fax: 03-3478-0928
Web: http://www.three-d.co.jp

three-2-one
interaktive Medien GmbH
Südwall 22
47798 Krefeld
Germany
Tel: (02151) 31945-0
Fax: (02151) 31945-19
Web: http://www.three-2-one.com

There TV
1351 West Grand Avenue
Chicago, Illinois 60622
United States
Tel: 1-312-421-0400
Fax: 1-312-421-1915
Web: http://www.theretv.com

Think Tank Studios
3 Eden Court
55 Standen Rd
Southfields
London
SW18 5TH
United Kingdom
Tel: +44 (0)7712 885 934
Web:
http://www.thinktankstudios.co.uk

Thirdeye Inc.
3F, Missy2000 Buld., 725, Suso-Dong,
Kangnam-Gu, Seoul, Korea 135-757
Tel: 02-3413-1610
Fax: 02-3413-1613
Web: http://www.thirdeyeinc.net

Threshold Entertainment
1649 11th Street
Santa Monica, California 90404
United States
Tel: 1-310-452-8899
Fax: 1-310-452-0736
Web: http://www.thethreshold.com

Thrive Media, Inc.
5th Floor, 856 Homer Street
Vancouver, British Columbia
V6B 2W5 Canada
Tel: 1-604-681-2858
Web: http://www.thrivemedia.com

Tictac Interactive (Karlskrona)
Norra Smedjegatan 2
Karlskrona, Sweden
371 33
Tel: +46 4.55.10.92.3
Web: http://www.tictac.se

Tigar Hare Studios
4485 Matilija Avenue
Sherman Oaks, California 91423

United States
Tel: 1-818-907-6663
Fax: 1-818-907-0693
Web: http://www.tigarhare.com

Tiger Aspect Pictures Limited
5 Soho Square
London
W1V 5DF
Tel: +44 020 7434 0672
Fax: +44 020 7544 1900
Web: http://www.tigeraspect.co.uk

Tiger Aspect Productions
7 Soho Street
London W1D 3DQ
Tel: +44 207 43 46.72 1
Fax: +44 207 43 41 79 7
Web: http://www.tigeraspect.co.uk

Tightwire
Glen Gardner, New Jersey
United States
Web: http://www.tightwire.com

Tinfang Computer Special Effects Inc.
15A Haicheng Building
No.10 Tian Xian Qiao Bin He
Road
Chengdu, Sichuan
P.R.China 610021
Tel(Fax):011£-8628£-86710839
Web: http://www.china-tianfang.com

Tippett Studio
2741 10th Street
Berkeley, California 94710
United States
Tel: 1-510-649-9711
Fax: 1-510-649-9399
Web: http://www.tippett.com

Titalee Digital Studios
9, Seshadri Road,
Alwarpet
Chennai, Tamil Nadu India
600018
Tel: +91 44.49.86.62.2
Fax: +91 44.49.86.62.2
Web: http://www.titalee.com

Todd AO UK
13 Hawley Crescent
London, United Kingdom
NW1 8NP
Tel: +44 207.28.47.90.0
Fax: +44 207.28.41.01.8
Web: http://www.todd-ao.com

Tomato moving pictures
20A Coin Organize Centre
13 Pennington Street
Causeway Bay, Hong Kong
Tel: (852) 2808 0326
Fax: (852) 2808 1301
Web: http://www.tomatomp.com.hk

Tony Cuthbert Productions
7A Langley Street
London, WC2H 9JA
United Kingdom
Tel: +44 (0)20 7437 8884
Fax: +44 (0)20 7734 6579
Web: http://www.tonycuthbert.com

Toon Factory
10 Rue Torricelli
75017 Paris
France
Tel: 011-33-1-44-0947-50
Fax: 011-33-145-74-27-96
Web: http://www.teva.fr

Toonshoppe
940 N Orange, Suite 118
Hollywood, California 90038
United States
Tel: 1-323-467-1145
Fax: 1-707-988-8449
Web: http://www.Toonshoppe.com

Toonz Animation India Pvt. Ltd.
731-739 Nila Bldg, Technopark
Pin -695 581
Trivandrum, Kerala India
695581
Tel: +91 47.17.00.92.9
Fax: +91 47.17.00.95.4
Web:
http://www.toonzanimationindia.com

Topix/Mad Dog
35 McCaul St. Suite 200
Toronto, Ontario M5T 1V7
Canada
Tel: 1-416-971-7711
Fax: 1-416-971-9277
Web: http://www.topix.com

Total Video Co.
432 No. Canal, Unit 12
San Francisco, California 94080
United States
Tel: 1-650-583-8236
Web: http://www.totalvideo.com

TourDesign
10089 Allisonville Road, Suite
100
Fishers, Indiana 46038
Tel: 1-317-579-7844
Fax: 1-317-579-7847
Web: http://www.tourdesign.com

Toutenkartoon
73, boulevard Saint-Michel
Paris, France
75005
Tel: +33 1.40.46.52.61
Fax: +33 1.40.46.86.31
Web: http://www.ramsespev.com

TOYBOX
179 John Street
8th Floor
Toronto, Ontario
M5T 1X4
Canada
Tel: 1-416-585-9995
Fax: 1-416-979-0428
Web: http://www.compt.com

TOYBOX West
500 - 1090 Homer Street
Vancouver, B.C.
V6B 2W9
Canada
Tel: 1-604-689-1090
Fax: 1-604-689-1003
BBS: 1-604-669-0812
Web: http://www.compt.com

Toyo Communications, Inc.
2-10-13 higashi-Gotanda
Shinagawa-Ku
Tokyo 141-0022
Japan
Tel: 81-3-3280-8161
Web: http://www.tocom.co.jp

Trace Digital Animation
107 Inglewood Court
Charlottesville, Virginia 22901
United States
Tel: 1-434-984-4239
Fax: 1-434-984-5490
Web: http://www.traceholo.com

Trailblazer Studios
1610 Midtown Place
Raleigh, North Carolina 27609
United States
Tel: 1-919-873-9333
Fax: 1-919-875-0703
Web:
http://www.trailblazerstudios.com

Trailblazer Studios
14901 Quorum Drive, Suite 800
Dallas, Texas 75254
United States
Web:
http://www.trailblazerstudios.com

Transvideo Studios
990 Villa St.
Mountain View, California 94041
United States
Tel: 1-650-965-4898
Fax: 1-650-962-1753
Web: http://www.transvideo.com

Tres Animations and Productions
5105 Route 33, Floor #2
Farmingdale, New Jersey 07727
United States
Tel: 1-732-751-0253
Fax: 1-732-751-1313
Web: http://www.tresanimations.com

Triangle Art Film Production AB
Box 27 007
102 51 Stockholm
Sweden
Tel: 08 665 11 00
Fax: 08 665 12 97
Web: http://www.triangleart.se

Triangle Solutions
5300 Atlantic Avenue, Suite 108
Raleigh, North Carolina 27609
United States
Tel: 1-919-873-9996
Fax: 1-919-873-9998
Web:
http://www.trianglesolutions.com

Triangle Visual Interactive
3717 Benson Drive
Raleigh, North Carolina 27611
United States
Fax: 1-919-467-4530
Tel: 1-919-876-4510
Web: http://www.trianglevisual.com

Trickompany GmGH
Hamburg, Germany
Tel: 011-494039-88-19-0
Fax: 011-49-40-39-88-19-107
Web: http://www.trickompany.de

Tri-Dimensional Studios
Corporation
223 North 12th Street
Tampa, Florida 33624
United States
Tel: 1-888-275-2849
Fax: 1-813-221-6715
Web: http://www.tridstudios.com

Trickfilmerei
Zur Sch–nen Gelegenheit 14
Regensburg, Germany
93047
Tel: +49 94.15.67.93.4
Web: http://www.trickfilmerei.de

Trixter Film
Oberfohringerstr. 186
Munich, Germany
81925

Tel: +49 89.95.99.55
Fax: +49 89.95.99.55
Web: http://www.trixter.de

Troika Design Group
6715 Melrose Avenue,
Hollywood, California 90038
United States
Tel: 1-323-965-1650
Fax: 1-323-965-7855
Web:
http://www.troikadesigngroup.com

Trollback & Company
50 West 67th Street, Suite 8C
New York, New York 10023
United States
Tel: 1-212-529-1010
Fax:1-212-529-9540
Web: http://www.trollback.com

True Life Creations
Adelaide
Australia
Web: http://www.truelife.com.au

Turbulence Effects
38 East 32nd Street
6th Floor
New York, New York 10016
United States
Tel: 1-212-651-2596
Fax: 1-212-246-4635
Web:
http://www.turbulenceffects.com

twothousandstrong
PO Box 1527
Venice, California 90294-1527
United States
Tel: 1-310-822-5700
Fax: 1-310-822-0800
Web: http://www.2000strong.com

TV4C
97-99 Dean Street
London, United Kingdom
W1D 3TE
Tel: +44 207.73.44.30.2
Fax: +44 207.43.73.30.1
Web: http://www.chatsworth-tv.co.uk

TVA International
465, rue McGill Collège 9e étage
Montréal, Québec
Canada
H2Y 4A6
Tel: 1-514-284-2525
Web: http://www.tva.ca

TV Animation
Landskronagade 66, 4
Copenhagen, Denmark
2100
Tel: +45.70.23.80.08
Fax: +45.70.23.90.09
Web: http://www.tv-animation.com

TV Asahi Create Co., Ltd.
1-1-1 Roppongi
Minato-ku
Tokyo 106-8001
Japan
Tel: 03-5419-9711
Fax: 03-5419-9722
Web: http://www.tv-asahi.co.jp

TV Loonland
Royalty House
72-74 Dean Street
London
United Kingdom
W1V 6AE
Tel: +44 207.43.42.37.7
Fax: +44 207.43.41.57.8
Web: http://www.tvloonland.com

TV Loonland AG
16 Munchener Strasse
Unterfohring, Germany
85774
Tel: +49 89.20.50.80
Fax: +49 89.20.50.81.99
Web: http://www.tvloonland.de

TVS
501 Sabal Lake Drive, #105
Longwood, Florida 32779
United States
Tel: 1-407-788-6407
Fax: 1-407-788-4397
Web: http://www.tvsco.com

TVT Postproduction Berlin
Gormannstrasse 14
10119 Berlin
Germany
Tel: 0049 30-2887830
Fax: 0049 30-28878333
Web:: http://www.tvt-postproduction.de

TVT Postproduction Cologne
Riehler Strasse 1
50668 Cologne
Germany
Tel: 0049 221-1396313
Fax: 0049 221-1205661
Web:: http://www.tvt-postproduction.de

TVT Postproduction Frankfurt am
Main
Hamburger Allee 45
60486 Frankfurt am Main
Germany
Tel: 004969 97950570
Fax: 004969 97950580
Web:: http://www.tvt-postproduction.de

TV WERK GmbH digitale
Postproduktion
Oberföhringer Strasse 186
81925 München
Germany
Tel: 0049 89 95995 0
Fax: 0049 89 95995 111
Web: http://www.tvwerk.de

Twentieth Century Fox
P.O. Box 900
Beverly Hills, California 90213
United States
Tel: 1-310-396-3598
Fax: 1-310-369-4611
Web: http://www.fox.com

TWISTER|GFX
510 Front Street West
Suite G100
Toronto, Ontario
Canada
Tel: 1-416-979-8983
Fax: 1-416-979-8246
Web: http://www.twistergfx.com

Two-door
2985 Calle Estepa
Thousand Oaks, California 91360
United States
Tel: 1-805-241-1859
Fax: 1-310-936-6194
Web: http://www.two-door.com

Tyne Tees Television
City Road
Newcastle-Upon-Tyne
NE1 2AL
United Kingdom
Tel: 0191 261 0181
Web: http://www.tynetees.tv

Ubik
c.so Magenta 52
20123 Milano Italy
Phone +39 02 48 00 70 46
Fax +39 02 48 00 76 92
http://www.ubik.it

Ultimate Video
Oscar Romerolaan 8
1216 TK Hilversum
Holland
The Netherlands
Tel: +31 (0)35-6 233 277
Fax: +31 (0)35-6 231 921
Web: http://www.ultimate.nl

ULI Meyer Studios
172a Arlington Road
Camden Town
London
NW1 7HL
United Kingdom
Tel: +44 (0)20 7284 2828
Web: http://www.ulimeyer.com

Uncharted Territory, LLC
11307 Hindry Avenue, Studio B
Los Angeles, California 90045
United States
Tel: 1-310-670-8635
Fax: 1-310-670-6715
Web:
http://www.uncharted-territory.com

Unifour Productions, Inc.
1020 Third Avenue NW
Hickory, North Carolina 28601
United States
Tel: 1-828-324-1314
Fax: 1-828-324-1318
Web: http://www.uni4.com

Universal Cartoon Studios Inc
100 Universal City PLZB-507,
Penthouse
Universal City, California 91608-1002
United States
Tel: 1-818-777-1000
Fax: 1-818-866-1457
Fax: 1-818-866-1483
Web:
http://www.universalpictures.com

Universal Studios Networks Ltd.
18, piazza del Popolo
Rome
Italy
00187
Tel: +39 6.36.71.11
Fax: +39 6.36.71.12.03
Web:
http://www.universalstudios.com

Universal Family & Home
Entertainment Production
100 Universal City Plaza Building
1320-03-M
Universal City, California 91608
United States
Tel: 1-818-777-4305
Fax: 1-818-866-0314
Web:
http://www.universalpictures.com

Universal Studios Television
5-7 Mandeville Place
London
United Kingdom
W1U 3AR
Tel: +44 207.53.53.70.0
Fax: +44 207.53.53.74.6
Web:
http://www.universalstudios.com

Universal Television & Network Groups
100 Universal City Plaza Building 509,
Suite 3030
Universal City, California 91608
United States
Tel: 1-818-777-1300
Fax: 1-818-866-2143
Web:
http://www.universalpictures.com

Universal Production Partners
Zitomirska 7/489
Praha 10
101 00
Czech Republic
Tel: +420 (2) 7172 2121
Fax: +420 (2) 7172 0330
Web: http://www.upp.cz

Unorthododox Styles
4 Ganton Street
London W1F 7QN
United Kingdom
Web:
http://www.unorthodoxstyles.com

Unreal Pictures
91 Bay Street
Port Melbourne, Victoria Australia
3205
Tel: +61 3.96.46.45.66
Fax: +61 3.96.46.54.77
Web: http://www.unreal.com.au

Unreel Pictures Inc
1375 Boardman St.
Great Barrington, Massachusetts
01230
United States
Tel: +1 413.644.0256
Fax: +1 413.644.0257
Web: http://www.unreel.com

Unreal Studios
San Antonio, Texas
United States
Web: http://www.unrealstudios.net

USAMEDIA. inc.
110 W Main St. S2h
Chapel Hill, North Carolina 27510

United States
Tel: 1-919-929-8088
Fax: 1-919-969-9789
Web: http://www.usamedia.com

Useful Companies
N & P Complex
Pinewood Studios
Pinewood Road
Iver
Buckinghamshire 5LO ONH
United Kingdom
Tel: 070000 Useful
Tel: 070000 873385
Tel: +44 1753 657200 (Overseas)
Fax: 07000 873386
Fax: +44 1753 657240 (Overseas)
Web: http://www.useful.co.uk

Useful Companies
Los Angeles, California
United States
Tel: 1-866-4Useful
Tel: 1-866-487-3385
Tel: 1-818-840-0290 (Overseas)
Fax: 1-886-487-3386
Fax: 1-818-840-0291 (Overseas)
Web: http://www.useful.co.uk

UTV Mumbai
Parijaat House
1076 Dr. E. Moses Road
Worli
Mumbai 400 018
India
Tel: +91 22 490 5353
Fax: +91 22 490 5370
Web: http://www.utvnet.com

UTV Toons Mumbai
UTV House
Marwah Estate
Kishanlal Marwah Marg
Andheri (E)
Mumbai 400 072
India
Tel: +91 22 857 0000
Fax: +91 11 857 2558
Web: http://www.utvnet.com

USL Mumbai
15-19 Shah & Nahar Industrial

Estate
Off Dr. E. Moses Road
Mumbai 400 018
India
Tel: +91 22 496 5322
Fax: +91 22 496 5306
Web: http://www.utvnet.com

UTV Delhi
No. 5, Community Centre
Panchseel
New Delhi 110 017
India
Tel: +91 11 649 5797
Fax: + 91 11 649 0594
Web: http://www.utvnet.com

Uvphactory
44 Trinity Place, Suite 3
New York, New York 10006
United States
Tel: 1-212-483-0040
Web: http://www.uvphactory.com

Valkeus
Pohjolankatu 4
FIN-96100, Rovaniemi
Finland
Web: http://www.valkeus.com

Valkeus
Ringvagen 100
SE-11894, Stockholm
Sweden
Tel: +358 16 311 844
Fax: +358 16 311 877
Web: http://www.valkeus.com

Valkieser Communications
Naarderweg 16
1217 GL Hilversum
The Netherlands
Tel: 020 460 460 4
Fax: 020 460 460 5
Web: http://www.valkieser.nl

Vanguard Films
1230 La Collina Drive
Beverly Hills, California 90210
United States
Tel: 1-310-888-8020
Fax: 1-310-888-8012
Web: http://www.vanguardfilms.com

Varga Holdings
H-1035
Budapest, Mikloster 1.
Hungary
Tel: 011-361-453-2040
Fax: 011-361-437-0287
Web: http://www.vargagroup.com

Varga London
11 Charlotte Mews
London, United Kingdom
W1T 4DX
Tel: +44 207.63.70.53.5
Fax: +44 207.63.69.15.5
Web: http://www.vargagroup.com

VARTEC nv
Holstraat 19
B-9000 Gent
Belgium
Tel: +32 9 269 99 66
Fax: +32 9 269 99 69
Web: http://www.vartec.be

VCC Perfect Pictures Babelsberg
Babelsberg, Germany
Tel: +49 33.17.21.36.0
Web: http://www.vcc.de

VCE (Visual Concept
Entertainment) Inc.
13300 Ralston Avenue
Los Angeles, California 91342
United States
Tel: 1-800-242-9627
Fax: 1-818-362-3490
Web: http://www.vce.com

VCS
311 North Adams Street
Tallahassee, Florida 32301
United States
Tel: 1-850-224-5420
Fax: 1-850-224-8378
Web: http://www.videoflorida.com

Vegamation
194 sixth street
Harrison, New Jersey 07029
United States
Tel: 1-973-204-1324
Web: http://www.vegamation.com

Velvet
Osterwaldstrasse 10
Munich, Germany
80805
Tel: +49 89.36.19.47
Fax: +49 89.36.19.47
Web: http://www.velvet.de

Vendetta Post
1661 Lincoln Blvd 101
Santa Monica, California 90404
United States
Tel: 1-310-664-8810
Fax: 1-310-664-8816
Web: http://www.vendettapost.com

Venture Media, Inc
8120 Cleary Boulevard.
Fort Lauderdale, Florida 33324
United States
Tel: 1-954-971-4100
Fax: 1-954-971-4090
Web: http://www.venturemedia.tv

VES
215 East High Street
Lexington, Kentucky 40507
United States
Tel: 1-859-255-9049
Web: http://www.veslex.com

Via Raiale, 281
65128 Pescara
Italy
Tel: +39.085.43.08.136
Fax: +39.085.43.17.014
Web: http://www.videa.it

Victor 3D Studio sa
2, avenue de Schiphol
1140 Brussels
Belgium
Tel: +32 (2) 743 42 90
Fax: +32 (2) 743 42 99
Web: http://www.victor3d.be

Victory Media Gruppe
Innovapark 20
Karybeuren, Germany
87600
Tel: +49 83.41.91.66.0

Fax: +49 83.41.91.66.2
Web: http://www.victory-media.de

Videa
Via F. Antolisei, 25
00100 Rome
Italy
Tel: +39.06.72.39.46.23
Fax: +39.06.72.39.46.24
Web: http://www.videa.it

Video Atlanta
Atlanta, Georgia
United States
Tel: 1-404-388-9529
Web: http://www.videoatlanta.com

VIDEO EFECTO, S.A.
Alegre de Dalt - 86, Bjs.
08024 Barcelona
Spain
Tel: 93 213 56 16
Fax: 93 219 77 59
Web: http://www.enefecto.es

Videofonics, Inc.
1610 Midtown Place
Raleigh, North Carolina 27609
United States
Tel: 1-919-873-9333
Tel: 1-800-877-1256
Fax: 1-919-875-0703
Web: http://www.videofonics.com

Videogenic Broadcast,S.L.
C/Maestro Marques 70
Tel: 965-215409/140946
Web: http://www.videogenic.es

Video Impressions
2505 E. Diehl Rd.
Aurora, Illinois 60504
United States
Tel: 1-630-851-1663
Fax: 1-630-851-2688
Web:
http://www.video-impressions.com

Video Lab (The)
cnr Eileen & Geneva rd
Blairgowrie
p.o.box 1854 Pinegowrie
Johannesburg
Gauteng 2123
South Africa
Tel: +27 11.29.33.00.0
Fax: +27 11.29.33.09.0
Web: http://www.videolab.co.za

Video Post & Transfer
2727 Inwood Road
Dallas, Texas 75235
United States
Tel: 1-214-350-2676
Web: http://www.videopost.com

Video Works of North Carolina
119 Moore Ave
Mount Airy, North Carolina 27030
United States
Tel: 1-336-719-6957
Web:
http://www.videoworksofnc.com

Video Replay
118 West Grand Avenue
Chicago, Illinois 60610
United States
Tel: 1-312-467-0425
Web:
http://www.videoreplaychicago.com

Vidox Image & Data
1223 St. John Street
Lafayette, Louisana 70506
United States
Tel: 1-337-237-1700
Fax: 1-337-237-1712
Web: http://www.vidox.com

Viewpoint Digital
498 Seventh Avenue, Suite 1810
New York, New York 10018
United States
Tel: 1-212-201-0800
Fax: 1-212-201-0801
Web: http://www.viewpoint.com

Viewpoint Digital
10549 Jefferson Boulevard
Culver City, California 90232
United States
Tel: 1-310-280-2000
Fax: 1-310-845-9412
Web: http://www.viewpoint.com

Viewpoint Digital
11778 South Election Drive
Suite 120
Draper, Utah 84020
United States
Tel: 1-801-619-4600
Fax: 1-801-619-4601
Web: http://www.viewpoint.com

Viewpoint Digital
16 Park Street
London W1K 2HZ
England
Tel: +44 207 629 3376
Fax: +44 207 491 4985
Web: http://www.viewpoint.com

Viewpoint Digital
Pinewood Studios
Pinewood Road
Iver Heath
Buckinghamshire
United Kingdom
SL0 0NH
Tel: +44 175.36.50.10.4
Fax: +44 175.36.54.08.1
Web: http://www.viewpoint.com

View Studio, Inc.
6715 Melrose Avenue
Hollywood, California 90038
United States
Tel: 1-323-965-1270
Fax: 1-323-965-1277
Web: http://www.viewstudio.com

ViNO azul, Inc.
Japan
Web: http://www.vino.co.jp

Vinznet
#5, Sukhwani Fortunes
Pune, Maharashtra India

411018
Tel: +91 20.74.81.16.8
Fax: +91 20.74.59.46.7
Web: http://www.vinznet.com

Vir2L Studios
1370 Piccard Drive, Suite 120
Rockville, Maryland 20850
United States
Tel: 1-301-963-2000
Fax: 1-301-948-2253
Web: http://www.vir2l.com

Vir2L Studios
10950 Washington Blvd. Suite 240
Culver City, California 90232
Tel: 1-310-237-3180
Fax: 1-310-237-3181
Web: http://www.vir2l.com

Vir2L Studios Europe
54/56 Wharf Road Islington
London
N1 7SF
United Kingdom
Tel: +44 207 336 1333
Fax: +44 207 608 1873
Web: http://www.vir2l.com

Virgin Lands Computeranimation GmbH
z.Hd. Volker Jäcklein Hauptstraße 5
97332 Volkach
Tel: 09381-98 74
Fax: 09381-98 73
Web: http://www.virgin-lands.com

Virgin Mexico
Mexico City
Web: http://www.virgin.com.mx

Virtual Clones
418 Boyd Orr Building
University Avenue
Glasgow,
Scotland
United Kingdom
G12 8QR
Tel: +44 141.33.03.11.8
Fax: +44 141.33.03.11.9
Web: http://www.virtualclones.com

Virtual Effects
Plaza Adriano 1 bis
08021 Barcelona
Spain
Tel: 93 414 58 88
Fax: 93 414 09 40
Web: http://www.virtual-effects.es

Virtual Factory - Doorn
Bergweg 1
3941 RA DOORN
The Netherlands
Tel: +31(0)343 473 892
Fax: +31(0)33 246 4072
Web: http://www.virtualfactory.nl

Virtual Factory - Hilversum
Fransciscusweg 16 - 18
1216 SK HILVERSUM
The Netherlands
Tel: +31(0)35 62 480 91
Fax: +31(0)33 246 4072
Web: http://www.virtualfactory.nl

VirtualMagic Animation
4640 Lankershim Blvd. Suite 201
North Hollywood, California 91602
United States
Tel: 1-818-623-1866
Fax: 1-818-623-1868
Web:
http://www.virtualmagicusa.com

VirtualMagic ASIA, Inc.
557, Nueve de Pebrero Street,
Madaluyong
Metro Manila
Philippines
Tel: +63-2-533-7005
Tel: + 63-2-717-1111
Fax: +63-2-717-0000
Web: http://www.imagineasia.com

Virtual Medium Inc.
Raleigh, North Carolina
United States
Tel: 1-919-818-1673
Web:http://www.virtualmediuminc.com

Virtual Mirror Corporation
P.O. Box 6727

San Rafael, California 94903
United States
Tel: 1-866-386-7328
Tel: 1-415-472-3359
Fax: 1-415-444-0343
Web: http://www.virtualmirror.com

VirtualONE, Inc
6719 Fieldstone Dr
Burr Ridge, Illinois 60527
United States
Tel: 1-630-561-8987
Web: http://www.virtualone.net

Virtual Reality and Multimedia Park
Corso Lombardia, 194
10149 Torino
Italy
Tel: (+39) 011 - 22 71 211
Fax: (+39) 011 - 22 71 219
Web: http://www.vrmmp.it

Virtual Republic
Reichsstrasse 57
40217 Duesseldorf
Germany
Tel: +49.2 11.6 01 74 30
Fax: +49.2 11.6 01 76 18
Web: http://www.virtualrepublic.de

Virtual Ventures
Venice, California
United States
Tel: 1-310-266-7803
Tel: 1-310-822-6743
Web: http://www.virtvent.com

VIS Entertainment
Seabraes Mill
Perth Road
Dundee
DD1 4LN
Tel: 44 (0)1382 341 000
Fax: 44 (0)1382 341 045
Web:
http://www.visentertainment.com

Visible Productions
201 Linden Street, Suite 301
Fort Collins, Colorado 80524
United States

Tel: 1-970-407-7240
Web: http://www.visiblep.com

Vision Park Television
Norrahamnvägen 20
115 42 Stockholm
Sweden
Tel: +46 8 459 33 70
Fax: +46 8 459 33 89
Web: http://www.visionpark.com

Vision Park Video AB
Box 1150
SE-501 11 Borås
Sweden
Tel. +46 33-44 25 00
Fax: +46 33-44 25 77
Web: http://www.visionpark.com

Visual Approach
1570 Quail Lake Loop Road
Colorado Springs, Colorado
80906
Tel: 1-719-226-7831
Fax: 1-719-540-9803
Web: http://www.visualapproach.com

Visual Art
Birger Jarlsgatan 105
S 113 56 Stockholm
Sweden
Tel: 46 8 15 32 00
Fax: 46 8 15 32 02
Web: http://www.visualart.se

Visual Art Production
Stockholm
Sweden
Tel: 08-15 32 00
Web: http://www.v-a-p.se

VisualAsylum Studio
Spijkenisse
The Netherlands
Tel: +31-181-697-587
Fax: +31-181-697-588
Web: http://www.visualasylum.net

Visual Science Laboratory, Inc
2-19 rice field town
Chiyoda Ku Kanda
Tokyo, 101-0041
Japan
Tel: 03-5207-6621
Fax: 03-5207-6622
Web: http://www.vsl.co.jp

Vivid Design
ul. Ogrody 22/4
85-870 Bydgoszcz
Tel: 052 362 06 96
Fax: 052 362 06 96
Web: http://www.vdb.pl

Vivid Post
68 Wells Street
London
W1P 3RB
United Kingdom
Tel: +44 (0)20 7437 0008
Fax: +44 (0)20 7436 1819
Web: http://www.vividpost.co.uk

Voodoo Animation
MWB Business Exchange
77 Oxford Street
London W1D 2ES
United Kingdom
Tel: +44 (0) 207 659 2088
Fax: +44 (0) 207 659 2100
Web:
http://www.voodoo-animation.com

VRmagic GmbH
B6, 23–29 C
68032 Mannheim
Germany
Tel: +49 (0) 621 - 181 2765
Fax: +49 (0) 621 - 181 2591
Web: http://www.vrmagic.com

VRT Belgium
Viamese Radio - en
Televisioemroep
Auguste Reyerslaan 52
Brussels, Belgium
1043
Tel: +32 2.74.13.11.1
Fax: +32 2.73.49.35.1
Web: http://www.vrt.be

VSLKorea
Kwangjingu Jayangdong Donho
b/d 5th floor
Seoul, Korea 219-25
Tel: (02)3436-7811
Fax: (02)3436-7511
Web: http://www.vslk.co.kr

V Star
430 South Congress Avenue
Delray Beach, Florida 33445
United States
Tel: 1-561-279-STAR
Fax: 1-561-279-4808
Web: http://www.vstar.com

VTR
64 Dean Street
London W1D 4QQ
United Kingdom
Tel: 020 7437 0026
Fax: 020 7439 9427
Web: http://www.vtr.co.uk

VTV: Varsity Television
6500 River Place
Building no. 2
Austin, Texas 78730
United States
Tel: 1-512-527-2500
Fax: 1-512-527-2599
Web: http://www.myvtv.com

W&Media S.r.l.
Corso Marche
79 -10146 Torino
Italy
Tel: +390117430230
Fax: +390117430222
Web: http://www.wmedia.it

W&Media S.r.l.
Via Terraggio
17 - 20123 Milano
Italy
Web: http://www.wmedia.it

Wallace Creative, Inc.
Portland, Oregon
United States
Tel: 1-503-224-9660

Fax: 1-503-224-9667
Web: http://www.wallyhood.com

Walt Disney Animation Services
P.O. Box 10200
Lake Buena Vista, Florida 32830
United States
Tel: 1-407-560-5745
Fax: 1-407-560-3207
Web: http://www.disney.com

Walt Disney Television Animation
500 South Buena Vista Street
Burbank, California 91521
United States
Tel: 1-818-560-1000
Fax: 1-818-729-7961
Web: http://www.disney1.com

Warner Bros. Feature Animation
500 North Brand Boulevard, Suite 1800
Glendale, California 91203-1923
United States
Tel: 1-818-977-7555
Fax: 1-818-977-7111
Web: http://www.warnerbros.com

Warner Bros. International
Television
4000 Warner Boulevard
Burbank, California 91522
United States
Tel: 1-818-954-4068
Fax: 1-818-977-4040
Web: http://www.wbitv.com

Warped CGI
Ireland
Tel: +353.1.836.0213
Web:
http://homepage.eircom.net/~warpedcgi

Webzen, Inc.
6F, Daelim Acrotel
467-6, Dogok-Dong
Kangnam-Gu
Seoul, South Korea
135-971
Tel: +82 2.34.98.16.18
Fax: +82 2.20.57.25.68
Web: http://www.webzen.co.kr

WEKA Computerzeitschriften
Gruber Str. 46a
Munich, Bavaria Germany
85586
Tel: +49 81.21.95.11.41
Fax: +49 81.21.95.16.25
Web: http://www.grafik-video.de

Welborn Works
P.O. Box 2038
Kountze, Texas 77625
United States
Tel: 1-409-246-3195
Web: http://www.welbornworks.com

West Digital Ltd
65 Goldhawk Road
Shepherds Bush
London W12 8EH
United Kingdom
Tel: 020 8743 5100
Fax: 020 8743 2345
Web: http://www.westdigital.co.uk

Weta Digital, Ltd.
9-11 Manuka Street
Miramar
P. O. Box 15-208
Wellington
New Zealand
Tel: +64 4.38.09.08.0
Fax: +64 4.38.09.01.0
Web: http://www.wetafx.co.nz

Wit Animation
959 Superba
Venice, California 90291
United States
Tel: 1-310-439-2428
Web: http://www.witanimation.com

White Hawk Pictures
567 Bishopgate Lane
Jacksonville, Florida 32204
United States
Tel: 1-904-634-0500
Tel: 1-800-654-6570
Fax: 1-904-359-9455
Web:http://www.whitehawkpictures.com

White Iron Inc.
533, 1201 - 5 Street SW
Calgary, AB. Canada
T2R 0y6
Tel: 1-403-298-4700
Fax: 1-403-233-0528
Web: http://www.whiteiron.tv

Whitlock Group , The
4020 Stirrup Creek Road, Suite 111
Durham, North Carolina 27703
United States
Tel: 1-919-806-1009
Tel: 1-877-806-1009
Fax: 1-919-806-1016
Web: http://www.whitlockbps.com

Whiz Digital
6 Abbotsford Street Suite 5
West Leederville
Western Australia 6007
Tel: 618 9381 5662
Fax: 618 9381 5672
Web: http://www.whiz.com.au

Whoa! Films Inc.
118 Church Street
Decatur, Georgia 30030
United States
Tel: 1-404-371-0011
Web: http://www.whoafilms.com

WilcoLinks DigiWorks Inc.
Aobadai Imon Bldg. 5F
3-18-3 Aobadai
Meguro-ku, Tokyo 153-0042
Japan
Tel: 81-3-5428-1775
Fax: 81-3-5428-1776
Web: http://www.wilcolinks.com

WilcoLinks DigiWorks Inc.
4250 Glencoe Ave, Suite 1215
Marina del Rey, California 90292
United States
Tel: 1-310-574-1883
Fax: 1-310-574-1886
Web: http://www.wilcolinks.com

WilcoLinks, Inc
4085 W. 7th Street, Suite 18

Los Angeles, California 90005
United States
Tel: 1-213-386-2411
Fax: 1-213-386-9394
Web: http://www.wilcolinks.com

Wild Brain, Inc.
2650 - 18th Street, 2nd Floor
San Francisco, California 94110
United States
Tel: 1-415-553-8000
Fax: 1-415-553-8009
Web: http://www.wildbrain.com

Wild Brain UK
11 Grosvenor Crescent
London
SW1X 7EE
England
United Kingdom
Tel: (44) 207-245-6864
Fax: (44) 207-245-1278
Web: http://www.wildbrain.com

Wild Brain, Inc.
1332 14th Street, Suite 3
Santa Monica, California 90404
United States
Tel: 1-310-393-6766
Fax: 1-310-451-7920
Web: http://www.wildbrain.com

Wild Man Productions
824 Southeast 9th Street
Deerfield Beach, Florida 33441
United States
Tel: 1-954-427-2522
Fax: 1-954-427-3233
Web: http://www.wildmanproduc-
tions.com

Wild Hare Studios
763 Trabert Ave. Suite D
Atlanta, Georgia 30318
United States
Tel: 1-404-352-3673
Fax: 1-404-352-3768
Web:
http://www.wildharestudios.com

Wildmedia
Boogmakerstratt 16
8043am Zwolle
The Netherlands
Tel: 038 4201124
Fax: 038 4201125
Web: http://www.wildmedia.nl

Wildlight Studios
S:t Michalesgrand 11B
Visby, Sweden
621 57
Tel: +46 70.21.50.97.0
Fax: +46 70.25.83.19.2
Web: http://www.wildlight.se

Will Ltd.
INO Building #303
1-1-1, Nishikubo
Musashino-shi, Tokyo 180-0013
Japan
Tel: 0422-38-0521
Fax: 0422-38-0522
Web: http://www.will-othewisp.com

Will Vinton Studios
1400 NW 22nd Avenue
Portland, Oregon 97210-2614
United States
Tel: 1-503-225-1130
Fax: 1-503-226-3746
Web: http://www.vinton.com

Windmilllane Ltd.
4 Windmill Lane
Dublin 2
Ireland
Tel: +353 1 6713444
Fax: +353 1 6713344
Web: http://www.windmilllane.com

Wip:On
121 rue chanzy
Lille-Hellemmes
Nord France
59260
Tel: +33 3.20.67.59.54
Fax: +33 3.20.67.59.50
Web: http://www.wipon.fr

WizzFilms Inc.
418 Sherbrooke St. East
3rd Floor
Montreal, Quebec Canada
H2L 1j6
Tel: +1 514.982.0101
Fax: +1 514.982.0711
Web: http://www.wizzfilms.com

Wonder Show Studios Inc.
10620 SW Davies Rd., Suite #13
Beaverton, Oregon 97008
United States
Tel: 1-503-579-2629
Web:
http://www.wondershowstudios.com

Wow Entertainment Inc.
Tokyo, Japan
Web: http://www.wow-ent.co.jp

Wreckless Abandon Studios
17 Connecticut South Dr.
East Granby, Connecticut 06026
United States
Tel: 1-860-844-7090
Web:
http://www.wrecklessabandon.com

WSI Media
Baretto Technology Center
9225 Harrison Park Court
Indianapolis, Indiana 46216
United States
Tel: 1-800-425-7637
Web:http://www.wsimultimedia.com

WSI Media
1011 Lake Street Suite 435
Oak Park, Illinois 60301
United States
Tel: 1-800-425-7637
Web:
http://www.wsimultimedia.com

WSI Media
6323 Constitution Drive
Fort Wayne, Indiana 46804
United States
Tel: 1-800-425-7637
Web: http://www.wsimultimedia.com

WXP Entertainment
95 South Jackson Street, Suite 200
Seattle, Washington 98104
United States
Tel: 1-206-287-9146
Web: http://www.wxp3d.com

Xaos, Inc.
444 De Haro Street, Suite 211
San Francisco, California 94107
United States
Tel: 1-415-558-9267
Fax: 1-415-558-9160
Web: http://www.xaos.com

Xilam Animation
25 rue Yves Toudic
75010 Paris
Tel: (33) 01 40 18 72 00
Fax: (33) 01 40 03 02 26
Web: http://www.xilam.com

XtrackrZ, Inc.
4262 Vinton Ave.
Culver City, California 90232
United States
Tel: 1-310-704-3036
Web: http://www.xtrackrz.com

XTV
157 Wardour Street
London, United Kingdom
W1F 8WQ
Tel: +44 207.20.81.50.0
Fax: +44 207.20.81.51.0
Web: http://www.xtv.co.uk

XVIVO Digital Animation
350 Center Street, Suite 205
Wallingford, Connecticut 06492
United States
Tel: 1-203-284-1224
Fax: 1-203-284-2652
Web: http://www.xvivo.net

Xdyne Inc.
1785 South Paw Paw Rd.
Earlville, Illinois 60518
United States
Tel: 1-815-246-6981
Fax: 1-815-246-4981
Web: http://www.xdyne.com

xZacto Digital Dynamics
9306 Beatties Ford Rd
Huntersville, North Carolina
28078
United States
Tel: 1-704-398-8888
Web: http://www.xzacto.com

Yearn to Learn
PO Box 1928
Laguna Beach, California 92652
United States
Tel: 1-949-715-1718
Fax: 1-208-655-0222
Web: http://www.yearn2learn.com

Yellow Co.,Ltd.
2-15-15 Senzoku point D ridge
Meguro Ku Senzoku
Tokyo 152-0012
Japan
Tel: 03-5729-0404
Fax: 03-5729-0403
Web: http://www.yellow.co.jp

Yoram Gross-EM.TV production
62 - 68 Church Street,
Camperdown, NSW
Australia,2050
Tel: 011-612-9519-1366
Fax: 011-61-2-9519-1258
Web: http://www.ygross.com.au

Yorkshire Television
Television Centre
Leeds
LS3 1JS
Tel: 0113 243 8283
Web: http://www.yorkshire-
tv.co.uk

YTV
64 Jefferson Ave., Unit 18
Toronto, Ontario
M6K 3H4
Tel: 1-416-530-5152
Fax: 1-416-530-5199
Web: http://www.ytv.com

yU + co
941 North Mansfield Ave

Hollywood, California 90038
United States
Tel: 1-323-606-5050
Fax: 1-323-606-5040
Web: http://www.yuco.com

Yukfoo Animation Studios
39A Woodside Ave
P.O. Box 36644
Northcote
Auckland, New Zealand
Tel: +64 9.48.00.09.3
Fax: +64 9.48.00.09.4
Web: http://www.yukfoo.net

Z-A Production
64, rue de la Folie
Mericourt
Paris, France
75011
Tel: +33 1.48.06.65.66
Fax: +33 1.48.06.48.75
Web: http://www.z-a.net

Zandoria Studios
7203 Sylvia Trail
Chattanooga, Tennessee 37421
United States
Tel: 1-423-899-5408
Web: http://www.zandoria.com

Zanita Films
Ardmore Studios
Herbert Rd
Bray
Co. Wicklow, Ireland
Tel: +353 1.12.86.29.71
Fax: +353 1.27.60.02.0
Web: http://www.zanita.ie

ZDF
158 PB Kinder und Jugend
Ost 1 Zimmer
Mainz, Germany
55100
Tel: +49 61.31.70.22.98
Fax: +49 61.31.70.23.28
Web: http://www.zdf.de

ZDF Enterprises
Cologne Office for Fictional Co-

Production and Development
Spichernstrasse 75-77
50672 Köln
Germany
Phone: +49-221-9488850
Fax: +49-221-9488851
Web: http://www.zdf-
enterprises.zdf.de

ZDF/ZDF Enterprises
Horst and Effi Mueller
450 Park Avenue
Suite 1403
New York, New York 10022
United States
Tel: 1-212-759-9430
Fax: 1-212-759-9483
Web: http://www.zdf-
enterprises.zdf.de

ZeniMax Productions
10950 Washington Blvd. Suite
240
Culver City, California 90232
Tel: 1-310-237-3180
Fax: 1-310-237-3181
Web: http://www.vir2l.com

Zentropa Production
Filmbyen Postbox 505
Avedore Tvúrvej 10
Hvidovre, Denmark
2650
Tel: +45.36.78.00.55
Fax: +45.36.78.00.77
Web:
http://www.zentropa-film.com

Zero Gravity Production & Design
P.O. Box 9, Big Bass Lake
Gouldsboro, Pennsylvania 18424
United States
Tel: 1-570-842-9234
Fax: 1-570-842-5252
Web: http://www.zgpd.com

Zerofractal Corporation
8100 Geneva Court, Suite 238 C
Miami, Florida 33166
United States
Tel: 1-305-592-2872
Web: http://www.zerofractal.com

Zero one Zero
7 McCabe Place
Willoughby NSW
Australia 2068
Tel: +61 2 9417 5700
Fax: +61 2 9417 5879
Web: http://www.zero1zero.com.au

Zezla Digital House
Roeklaan 2
5737 PD Lieshout
The Netherlands
Tel: 0499 42 50 50
Web: http://www.zezla.com

Zinkia Sitement S.L.
c/ Infantas 27 1
Madrid, Spain
28004
Tel: +34 91.52.40.36.5
Fax: +34 91.52.40.73.7
Web: http://www.zinkia.com

Zion Productions
1361 Lincolnshire Drive
Harrisonburg, Virginia 22802
United States
Tel: 1-540-433-7700
Tel: 1-888-433-8700
Fax: 1-540-433-7702
Web:http://www.zionproductions.com

ZIOSoft, Inc.
18625 Sutter Boulevard, Suite
200
Morgan Hill, California 95037
United States
Tel: 1-408-778-6500
Fax: 1-408-778-2737
Web: http://www.ziosoft.com

Zoic Studios
3582 Eastham Dr.
Los Angeles, California 90232
United States
Tel: 1-310-838-0770
Web: http://www.ZoicStudios.com

Zootrope
Passatge Ajuntament 19

Cerdanyola
Barcelona, Catalonia Spain
08290
Tel: +34 93 580 47 40
Web: http://www.zootrope.com

Zona Design
Empire State Building
350 Fifth Ave, Suite 321
New York, New York 10118
United States
Tel: 1-212-244-2900
Fax: 1-212-244-3101
Web: http://www.zonadesign.com

Zoneo Digiworks Limited
16/F , 8 Wing Hing St
Causeway Bay
Hong Kong
Tel: (852) 2802 2322
Fax: (852) 2802 2321
Web: http://www.zoneo.com

Zoomorphix Systems
PO Box 208
Carnegie Vic. 3163
Melbourne, Australia
Tel: +61 +3 9543 6610
Fax: +61 +3 9543 9938
Web: http://www.zoomorphix.com.au

Zspace
100 Hacket Street
Ultimo NSW 2007
Australia
Tel: +61 2 9212 6777
Fax: +61 2 9212 6788
Web: http://www.zspace.com.au

Zygote
679 N. 1890 W. #45A
Provo, Utah 84601
United States
Tel: 1-801-375-7220
Tel: 1-800-471-4784
Fax: 1-801-852-0735
Web: http://www.zygote.com

We want to hear from you!
Please tell if this list is missing anything.

Companies come and go. This list may be missing your favorite animation company or may include companies that have gone out of business or changed their name. If you noticed errors in this list please report them. We take your comments, as well as all the others like yours, and do our best to implement them into the next version of the book. If you are the first one to report an error or to make a suggestion, we will acknowledge you in the next printing. (Unless you specify otherwise.)

Due to the extremely high volume of mail we may not get back to you immediately. You can be sure that your e-mail will be answered.

Web site: www.EdHarriss.com

Email: EdHarriss@EdHarriss.com

Fax: 1-603-691-6470

Mailing Address:

EdHarriss.com
90154
Raleigh, NC 27675-90154
United States

"Phil knows where all the good production companies are, but he's not telling."

"With all I've learned about video games recently, the 'who's naughty and who's nice game' is much easier."

RESOURCES - Video Game Companies

This section of the book contains company listings from all over the world. These include companies that create console games, computer games, internet games, arcade games or other DVD/CD-Rom based entertainment.

How should you use this list? Apply responsibly, don't just blindly mail off reels and resumes to every company on this list. Do some research first. Go to the company's web site and see if they have any job openings. Check out their work. See if it's something you'd like to do for a living. If so, read the instructions that they give regarding demo material submission and follow them to the letter. If they say, no phone calls. Don't call them. If they say, only NTSC VHS reels will be accepted. Send them a NTSC VHS reel. Make it as easy as possible for them to hire you.

Double check the company's address in this book against the one they give you. Hundreds of companies had to be removed from the list during the production of this book because they went out of business. Many more are sure to follow. It would be a waste for you to apply for a job at one of those. Companies also move from time to time. If they've moved into a new office between the time this book is printed and the time you send off your demo materials and you don't check the address, then you run the risk of missing a possible job opportunity. Don't let late or misdirected mail get in the way or your next job. If you find out that a company has moved or closed, please let me know. I'll be eternally grateful. (Contact information is at the beginning of the book).

Why do I list the addresses when it is recommended that you double-check them? I do it to give you an idea where the company is located. If you want to work for a company, spend a lot of time researching and preparing to apply there only to find out that it's located in another country or in a place that you do not want to move, you'll be pretty disappointed. There may be a company that you'd really like to work for just down the street but, without the address listed, you'd never know that it was there.

ÿþ:) Smilie Ventures Ltd.
Talisman House
13 North Park Road
Harrogate
North Yorkshire
HG1 5PD, England
United Kingdom
Tel: +44 (0)1423 565808/858230
Fax: +44 (0)845 4580360
Web: http://www.smilie.com

[hypermedia]
Office 101
Trinity House
40 - 42 Byzantiou Street
2064 Strovolos, Nicosia
Cyprus
Tel: +357-22667112
Fax: +357-22667187
Web: http://www.hyper.com.cy

01 Insights
3308 Noyes St,
Evanston, Illinois, 60201
United States
Tel: 1-847-869-5218
Web: http://www.01insights.com

0100010 Industries
Dallas, Texas
United States
Web: http://www.0100010.com

13th Floor Gaming
372A Nature Drive
San Jose, California 95123
United States
Web: http://www.13gaming.com

14 Degrees East
16815 Von Karman Ave.
Irvine, California 92606
United States
Tel: 1-949-553-6678
Fax: 1-949-553-9549
Web: http://www.14degrees.com

1C
51, Malaya Gruzinskaya str.
123056 box 64 Moscow
Russia

Tel: 7 (095) 253-5902
Fax: 7 (095) 253-0966
Web: http://www.1c.ru

2 BY 3 Games
6479 Calle Esperanza
Pleasanton, California 94566
United States
Web: http://www.2by3games.com

2015
8282 S. Memorial Drive, Suite
104
Tulsa, Oklahoma 74133
United States
Web: http://www.2015.com

2015,Inc.
6528 East 101st Suite 272
Tulsa, Oklahoma 74133
United States
Web: http://www.2015.com

21-6 Productions, Inc.
6851 S Clermont,
Littleton, Colorado 80122
United States
Tel: 1-303-741-6625
Web: http://www.21-6.com

21st Century
6823 126th Ave. NE
Kirkland, Washington 98033
United States
Fax: 1-208-445-7919
Web:
http://21stcenturypublishing.com

2VG Group
Boyarka, Kiev
Motovilovka
Ukraine
Web: http://www.westbyte.com

3d6 Games, Inc.
PMB #105
2510-G Las Posas Rd
Camarillo, California 93010
United States
Web: http://www.3d6games.com

3DAGames
11 Elm Grove
Cricklewood,
London NW2 3AE
United Kingdom
Tel: +44 (0)208 452 4590
Web: http://www.3dagames.com

3D Casino
Las Vegas, Nevada
United States
Web: http://www.3d-casino.com

3DConcepts
601 Cypress Station Dr.,
Houston, Texas, 77090
United States
Tel: 1-281-397-0645
Web: http://www.3dconcepts.com

3DO Company
600 Galveston Drive
Redwood City, California 94063
United States
Fax: 1-650-261-3120
Web: http://www.3do.com

3DO Company, The
200 Cardinal Way
Redwood City, California 94063
United States
Tel: 1-650-385-3000
Fax: 1-650-385-3183
Web: http://www.3do.com

3LV Games
14860 Montfort #205
Dallas, Texas 75240
United States
Tel: 1-972.960.1102
Web: http://www.3lvgames.com

3D Joe Corporation
330 Townsend #100
San Francisco, California 94107
United States
Tel: 1-415-536-4170
Web: http://www.3djoe.com

3D People
Moldavska 6, Kosice
04001 Slovakia
Web: http://www.3dpeople.de

3D Power Engine
Seattle, Washington
United States
Web: http://www.3dpowerengine.com

3D Realms
P.O. Box 496419
Garland, Texas 75049-6389
United States
Tel: 1-800-3DREALMS
Web: http://www.3drealms.com

3D South
South Carolina
United States
Tel: 1-843-240-8468
Web: http://www.3dsouth.com

3Squared
Vicar Lane
Sheffield
S1 2EX
United Kingdom
Tel: 0114 223 8333
Fax: 0114 223 6333
Web: http://www.3squared.co.uk

400 Software Studios
P. O. Box 837
Graysville, Tennessee 37338
United States
Web:
http://www.400softwarestudios.com

4D Rulers
Beatrice, Nebraska
United States
Tel: 1-402-228-2183
Fax: 1-402-228-2113
Web: http://www.4drulers.com

4-Éléments Média
8790, avenue du parc
Montréal, Québec H2N 1Y6
Canada

Tel: 1-514-388-3336
Fax: 1-514-388-5563
Web: http://www.4-elements.com

4Thoughts
United Kingdom
Web: http://www.4thoughts.co.uk

4x Technologies
47, rue de Charonne
75011 Paris
France
Tel: 33 (1) 55 28 31 31
Fax: 33 (1) 47 00 51 01
Web: http://www.4xtechnologies.com

5000ft, Inc.
555 Double Eagle Ct. Suite 2000
Reno, Nevada 89521
United States
Tel: 1-775-284-5470
Fax: 1-775-284-5474
Web: http://www.5000ft.com

66k Interactive
Long Island, New York
United States
Tel: 1-631-427-2151
Fax: 1-631-980-7888
Web: http://www.66k.com

7FX s.r.o.
Pod Vodarenskou Vezi 2
182 07 Prague 8
Czech Republic
Web: http://www.7fx.com

7 Studios
Santa Monica, California
United States
Web: http://www.sevenstudios.com

7th Sense s.r.l
Via Bari, 8
90133 Palermo
Italy
Tel: +39 091334837
Fax: +39 091334837
Web: http://www.7th-sense.net

989 Sports
989 East Hillsdale Blvd. 4th floor
Foster City , California 94404-4201
United States
Web: http://www.989sports.com

989 Sports
10075 Barnes Canyon Rd.
San Diego, California 92121
United States
Tel: 1-619-824-5500
Fax: 1-619-824-5676
Web: http://www.989studios.com

A1 Games
Redwood City, California
United States
Web: http://www.a1games.com

A2M Studios
416 de Maisonneuve O.
Suite 600
Montreal, Quebec
H3A 1L2
Canada
Web: http://www.a2m.com

Abacus
5370 52nd Street SE
Grand Rapids, Michigan 49512
United States
Tel: 1-616-698-0330
Fax: 1-616-698-0325
Web: http://www.abacuspub.com

Abandon Entertainment
135 West 5oth Street, Suite 2305
New York, New York 10020
United States
Tel: 1-212-246-4445
Fax: 1-212-397-8361
Web: http://www.abandonent.com

ABCMedia
Box 161
646 22 Gnesta
Sweden
Tel: +46-(0)158-315 03
Web: http://www.abcmedia.se

Abel Inc.
Japan
Web: http://www.abel-jp.com

Abject Modernity
153 Debaets Street
Winnipeg, Canada
R2J 3R9
Web: http://www.abject.com

Abracadata
Eugene Oregon
United States
Tel: 1-541-342-3030
Tel: 1-800-451-4871
Web: http://www.abracadata.com

Abstract Worlds Ltd.
129 Midland Road
Wellingborough
Northants
NN8 1NB
England
United Kingdom
Web: http://www.abstractworlds.com

Abundant Software Ltd
Park House
10 Park Street
Bristol
BS1 5HX
United Kingdom
Tel: +44(0)117 915 4561
Fax: +44(0)117 925 3231
Web: http://www.abundantsoft.com

Abyss Lights Studio
Akhmatovoi str. #5 / 75,
Kiev, Ukraine
380 50 3380063
Web: http://www.abyss-lights.com

Acclaim
67 Rue de Courcelles
75008 Paris
France
Tel: +01 56 21 31 00
Fax: +01 48 88 94 94
Web: http://www.acclaim.com

Acclaim Entertainment
One Acclaim Plaza
Glen Cove, New York 11542
United States
Web: http://www.acclaim.com

Acclaim Entertainment GmbH
Leuchtenbergring 20
81677 München
Germany
Web: http://www.acclaim.de

Acclaim Studios Salt Lake City
2144 South Highland Drive #200
Salt Lake City, Utah 84106
United States
Web: http://www.acclaim.com

Acclaim Studios Austin
901 S. Mopac, Plaza 1#300
Austin, Texas 78745
United States
Web: http://www.acclaim.com

Acclaim Audio - Cincinnati Ohio
30 Garfield Place
Suite 1000
Cincinnati, Ohio 45202
United States
Web: http://www.acclaim.com

Acclaim Studios Teesside
Dunedin House
Riverside Quay
Stockton - on- Tees
Cleveland TS17 6BJ
England
Web: http://www.acclaim.com

Acclaim Studios Cheltenham
Acclaim Studios Ltd
Lansdown Road
Cheltenham
Glos
GL50 2JA
England
Web: http://www.acclaim.com

Acclaim Studios Manchester
140, Cheetham Hill Road,

Cheetham Hill, Manchester
United Kingdom
M8 8PZ
Tel: +44 (0)161 839 2239
Fax: +44 (0)161 832 0412
Web: http://www.acclaim.com

Accolade
5300 Stevens Creek Blvd.
Suite 500
San Jose, California 95129
United States
Web: http://www.accolade.com

Acid Software
Auckland, New Zealand
Web: http://www.acid.co.nz

Acquire Corporation
Japan
Tel: 03-5826-2701
Fax: 03-5826-2703
Web: http://www.acquire.co.jp

Acrologix (pvt) Ltd.
106/3, Saint Johns Park
Lahore-Cantt, Pakistan
Tel: 92-42-6664301-06
Fax: 92-42-6664307
Web: http://www.acrologix.com

Action Forms
Kiev, Ukraine
Web: http://www.action-forms.com

Activision
3100 Ocean Park Blvd.
Santa Monica, California 90405
United States
Fax: 1-310-255-2166
Web: http://www.activision.com

Actoz Soft
647-12 2F, Jungnungdong 3rd,
Sungbukku
Seoul, Korea
136-103
Web: http://www.actoz.com

Actoz Soft
Munmyung B/D 4F 139-18
OjangDong ChungKu
Seoul, Korea
100-310
Tel: 82 2 278 8061
Fax: 82 2 278 8077
Web: http://www.actoz.com

Actual Entertainment, Inc.
PMB 101
1030 E. El Camino Real
Sunnyvale, California 94087-3759
United States
Tel: 1-408-732-5788
Fax: 1-408-732-5788
Web:
http://www.actualentertainment.com

Actual OZ Soft Co, Ltd.
132-3 Sungbuk-dong
Unsuk B/D 4th Floor, Sungbuk-gu
Seoul 136-020, Korea
Tel: +82-2-743-8260
Fax: +82-2-742-0733
Web: http://www.actoz.com

Add Games
AB Box 17193
104 62 Stockholm
Sweden
Web: http://www.addgames.se

Add Games
Rosenlundsgatan 9, Stockholm
Sweden
Tel: 08-66 230 96
Fax: 08-662 30 96
Web: http://www.addgames.se

Addictive247
37 Whittle Drive
Ormskirk
Lancashire
L39 1PU
United Kingdom
Tel: +44 (0)7811 923268
Web: http://www.addictive247.co.uk

Adeline Software International
France
Web: http://www.adelinesoftware.com

Adept Software
Orlando, Florida
United States
Web: http://www.adeptsoftware.com

Adrenaline Entertainment
13930 Drake Rd.
Strongsville, Ohio 44136
United States
Web: http://www.adrenalineent.com

Adrenium Games
12421 Willows Road NE #200
Kirkland, Washington 98034
United States
Tel: 1-425-825-6800
Fax: 1-425-825-6700
Web: http://www.adrenium.com

Adventure Soft
P.O. Box 786
Sutton Coldfield
West Midlands
B75 5RS
United Kingdom
Tel: 0121 308 8900
Fax: 0121 308 8815
Web: http://www.adventuresoft.com

Adveractive, Inc
PO Box 2631
Chapel Hill, North Carolina 27515
United States
Tel: 1-919-968-4567
Web: http://www.adveractive.com

Aeon
PO Box 1272
East Lansing, Michigan 48826
United States
Tel: 1-517-862-1761
Web:
http://www.variantinteractive.com

Aerosoft GmbH
Lindberghring 12

33142 Büren
Germany
Tel: +49 (0) 2955/76 03 10
Fax: +49 (0) 2955/76 03 33
Web: http://www.aerosoft.com

Aftermath Media
2822 Orchard Home Drive
Medford, Oregon 97501
United States
Web:
http://www.aftermathmedia.com

AGD - Software Ges.m.b.H.
Blindengasse 36/46
A-1080 Vienna
Austria
Tel: +43.1.929.4121
Fax: +43.1.929.4121
Web: http://www.agdsoft.com

AIM Software
115 Reno Ave #10
Las Vegas, Nevada 89119
United States
Web: http://www.aimgames.com

Airborne Entertainment Inc.
3575 St. Laurent, Suite 750
Montreal, Quebec
H2X 2T7
Tel: 1-514-289-9111
Fax 1-514-289-9494
Web:
http://www.pocketboxoffice.com

Airborne Entertainment Inc.
350 E. 54th Street, Suite 2G
New York, New York 10022
United States
Tel: 1-212-826-6558
Web: http://www.airborne-e.com
Web: http://www.pocketboxoffice.com

Akella
2nd Frunzenskaya st 10/1
119146 Moscow, Russia
Tel: +7 095 742-4019
Fax: +7 095 242-0323
Web: http://www.akella.com

AKI Corporation
Kichijyoji-Honcho 1-30-10
Wistaria Bldg 1&2F
Musashino-Shi
Tokyo 180-0004
Japan
Tel: 0422-29-7305
Fax: 0422-29-7306
Web: http://www.aki.co.jp

Alawar Entertainment
Novosibirsk, Russia
41, Russkaya str., 630058
Tel: +7 3832 328133
Fax: +7 3832 328133
Web: http://alawargroup.com

Alchemist
Japan
Web: http://www.alchemist-net.co.jp

Alexander & Tom
2400 Boston Street
Suite 308
Baltimore, Maryland 21224
United States
Tel: 1-410-327-7400
Fax: 1-410-327-7403
Web: http://www.alextom.com

AlfaSystem
Kumamoto city
Japan
Tel: 096-366-5598
Fax: 096-363-5633
Web: http://www.alfasystem.net

Aliasworlds Entertainment
76, Glebky Str.
Minsk, Belarus
Tel: 375 17 250 15 46
Web: http://www.aliasworlds.com

Alpine Studios, Inc.
599 South 500 East
American Fork, Utah 84003
Tel: 1-801-772-0313
Fax: 1-801-756-4564
Web: http://www.alpine-studios.com

Alt.Software Inc.
84 Richmond Street East
Toronto, Ontario
Canada M5C 1P1
Tel: 1-416-203-8508
Fax: 1-416-203-8511
Web: http://www.altsoftware.com

Alt.Software Inc.
104 King St. South
Waterloo, Ontario
Canada N2J 1P5
Tel: 1-519-746-2490
Fax: 1-519-746-1926
Web: http://www.altsoftware.com

Altamira Studios
Level 8, 50 Market Street,
Melbourne, VIC, 3000
Australia
Tel: 61 414 357 221
Web: http://www.tribalempires.com

Altar Interactive
Sedlákova 7
602 00 Brno
Web: http://www.altarinteractive.com

Alternate State Entertainment
Altar interactive
Rezkova 16
602 00 Brno
Czech Republic
Web: http://www.alternatestate.com

Alternative Software
Unit 5 Baileygate Industrial Estate
Pontefract
West Yorkshire
WF8 2LN
ENGLAND
United Kingdom
Tel: 01977 780767
Fax: 01977 790243
Web:
http://www.alternativesoftware.com

Alternatum Studios
22-24 Homecroft Road, Suite 14
Elco House
London N22 5EL

United Kingdom
Tel: +44 (0) 870 321 9537
Web:http://www.alternatum-studios.com

AM2
SEGA Bldg., 2-12-14, Higashi-koujiya
Ohta-ku, Tokyo
144-8532, Japan
Toll Free: (81) 3-5737-7500
Fax: (81) 3-5737-7730
Web: http://www.sega-rd2.com

Amaze Entertainment
12421 Willows Road NE #200
Kirkland, Washington 98034
United States
Tel: 1-425-825-6800
Fax: 1-425-825-6700
Web:
http://www.amazeentertainment.com

Amazing Games
Almveien 20
Fredrikstad N-1659
Torp, Norway
Tel: 47 69 34 84 14
Web: http://www.amazinggames.com

Amazing Studio
9, rue d'Enghien
75010 Paris
France
Web: http://www.amazingstudio.com

Amber Company
Russia
Tel: (007) 095-273-85-87
Fax: (007) 095-273-85-87
Web: http://www.amber.ru

Amber Company Europe
Im Sande 35
D-30926 Seelze
Germany
Tel: +49 511 486 08 20
Tel: +49 171 808 14 85
Mobil: +49 172 54 24 866
Web: http://www.amber.ru

Ambertec Inc.
P.O. Box 61345
Sunnyvale, California 94088-1345
United States
Web: http://www.ambertec.com

Ambrosia Software
P.O. Box 23140
Rochester, New York 14692
United States
Tel: 1-716-325-1910
Fax: 1-716-325-3665
Web: http://www.ambrosiasw.com

AMC Creation
Bucharest, Romania
Tel: +401 2236172
Fax: +401 2236172
Web: http://www.amc.ro

Amusement Vision
144-8532
SEGA sangoukan 3F
2-12-14 Higashikoujiya
Ohta-ku, Tokyo
Japan
Web:http://www.amusementvision.com

Amuze
Vretenvagen 2
s-171 54 Solna, Stockholm
Sweden
Tel: +46 850575700
Fax: +46 850575701
Web: http://www.amuze.com

Anarchy Arts
4994 S. Lincoln Street,
Salt Lake City, Utah, 84107
United States
Tel: 1-801-269-9465
Web: http://www.anarchy-arts.com

Anarchy Enterprises
2 Tree Farm Rd #A-300
Pennington, New Jersey 08534
United States
Web: http://www.anarchyent.com

Anark Corporation
1500 Pearl St., Suite 300
Boulder, Colorado 80302
United States
Web: http://www.anark.com

Anchor Incorporated
3-1-4,Mita Nakajima Bldg.
2F Minato-ku,Tokyo
108-0073,Japan
Tel: (+81)-3-3455-8405
Fax: (+81)-3-5444-6472
Web: http://www.anchorinc.co.jp

Ancient Corp.
3-31-33 Toyoda, Hino-Shi,
Tokyo, Japan
Web: http://www.ancient.co.jp

Anco
Unit 7
Millside Industrial Estate
Lawson Road
Dartford
Kent
DA1 5BH
United Kingdom
Tel: +44 (0) 1322 292513
Fax: +44 (0) 1322 293422
Web: http://www.anco.co.uk

AndNow LLC
213 San Mateo Rd
Half Moon Bay, California 94019
United States
Tel: 1-650-712-6871
Fax: 1-650-726-7621
Web: http://www.andnow.net

Angel Studios
5966 La Place Court
Suite 170
Carlsbad, California 92008
United States
Tel: 1-760-929-0700
Fax: 1-760-929-0719
Web: http://www.angelstudios.com

Animation Technologies
60 Canal Street
Boston, Massachusetts 02114

United States
Tel: 1-617-723-6040
Fax: 1-617-723-6080
Web: http://www.animationtech.com

Animation Technologies
1601 Market Street Suite 380
Philadelphia, Pennsylvania 19103
United States
Tel: 1-215-564-4600
Fax: 1-215-564-4602
Web: http://www.animationtech.com

Animation Technologies
227 West Monroe Street 19th
Floor
Chicago, Illinois 60606
United States
Tel: 1-312-596-8124
Fax: 1-312-596-8638
Web: http://www.animationtech.com

Anim-X
16055 SW Walker Road #144
Beaverton, Oregon 97006-4058
United States
Tel: 1-503-488-0345
Fax: 1-503-617-4763
Web: http://www.anim-x.com

Animedia Entertainment
B1, 551-1 Bescom Tower
Seong-Nae-Dong, Kang-Dong-Gu
Seoul, Korea
134-030
Tel: +82-2-538-3211
Tel: +82-2-483-4363
Fax: +82-476-6902
Web: http://www.animedia.co.kr

Anino Entertainment
Unit 809 Page One Building
Acacia Avenue, Alabang
Muntinlupa, Philippines
Tel: (632)7710144
Web:
http://www.aninoentertainment.com

Aniware AB
Grabergsvagen 27
752 40 Uppsala
Sweden
Tel: +46 (0) 708 83 05 50
Web: http://www.aniware.se

Ansible Software, Inc.
1937 Capistrano Avenue
3rd Floor, Suite B.
Berkeley, California 94707
Tel: 1-510-558-1177
Fax: 1-510-559-8104
Web: http://www.ansiblesoftware.com

Anvil-Soft
Wiesentalstr.5
90419 Nürnberg
Germany
Tel: 0911-93 89 29 2
Fax: 0911-93 89 29 3
Web: http://www.anvil-soft.com

AniVision, Inc.
228 Holmes Avenue, 2nd Floor
Huntsville, Alabama 35801
United States
Web: http://www.anivision.com

Antik Games
Meylan, France
Web: http://www.antikgames.com

Apex Korea., Ltd.
Rm 502, Kookil Bldg 151-1
Inhyun-2ga, Jung Ku
Seoul, Korea
Tel: +82 2 2268 5441
Tel: +82 2 2268 5386~7
Fax: +82 2 2268 5380
Web: http://www.apexgame.co.kr

Apezone
4756 Lalande Blvd
Pierrefonds, Quebec H8Y 1V2
Canada
Tel: 1-514-683-8901
Web: http://www.apezone.com

Apogee Software
P.O. Box 496389
Garland, Texas 75049-6389
United States
Tel: 1-800-APOGEE1
Fax: 1-972-278-4670
Web: http://www.apogee1.com

Apollo Entertainment Software
Rua Pedro Primeiro
4/403 - Centro
Rio de Janeiro
Brazil
Tel: 55-21-2222-4316
Web: http://www.solaris104.com

Appeal
Avenue Bovesse 1
B5100 Namur
Belgium
Fax: +32 81 312 314
Web: http://www.appeal.be

Application Systems Heidelberg
Software GmbH
Pleikartsförsterhof 4/1
69124 Heidelberg
Germany
Tel: 06221-300002
Fax: 06221-300389
Web:http://www.application-systems.de

Apptastic Software Inc.
1010 Polytek Road, Suite 8A
Ottawa, Ontario
Canada
K1J 9H8
Tel: 1-613-748-7066
Fax: 1-613-749-6910
Web: http://www.apptastic.com

Aqua Pacific
23 Dale Street,
Leamington Spa
Warwickshire
CV32 5HH
United Kingdom
Tel: +44 (0) 1926 339100
Fax: +44 (0) 885188
Web: http://www.aqua-pacific.com

Aquaplus
Japan
Web: http://www.aquaplus.co.jp

ArabianOasis, Inc.
1227 N. Allen Ave.,
Pasadnea, California 91104
United States
Tel: 1-626-255-0535.
Web: http://www.arabianoasis.org

Arc Systems Works Co., Ltd
5th Floor
Shin-Yokohama Station Building
2-6-13 Shin-Yokohama
Kohoku-ku, Yokohama
Japan
Web: http://www.arcsy.co.jp

Ardecom inc.
6185, Taschereau.
Brossard, Québec. J4Z 1A6.
Canada
Tel: 1-450-462-5717.
Fax: 1-450-462-0569
Web: http://www.ardecom.com

ArenaNet, Inc.
10020 Main St. #164
Bellevue, Washington 98004
United States
Tel: 1-425-462-9444
Fax: 1-425-671-0589
Web: http://www.arena.net

Argonaut Games PLC
Argonaut House
369 Burnt Oak Broadway
Edgware
Middlesex
HA8 5XZ
United Kingdom
Tel: +44 (020) 8 9516000
Fax: +44 (020) 8 9516050
Web: http://www.argonaut.com

Argos Gameware
600 East Crescent Avenue, Suite 203
Upper Saddle River, New Jersey
07458-1846
United States
Tel: 1-201-934-9411
Fax: 1-201-934-9206
Web: http://www.gameware.com

Arika
141-0031 Tokyo
Japan
Tel: 03-3447-1840
Web: http://www.arika.co.jp

Arithmetic Studios
San Francisco, California
United States
Web:http://www.arithmeticstudios.com

Arkane Studios
20 Bd Eugene Deruelle,
Britannia,bat A, 3ème étage.
69432 Lyon Cedex 03
France
Tel: +33 4 72 19 68 53
Tel: +33 4 78 62 99 01
Fax: +33 4 78 62 91 64
Web:http://www.arkane-studios.com

Art & Bits Corp.
711 S. Carson Street, Ste 4
Carson City, Nevada 89701
United States
Tel: 1-775-881 3426
Web: http://www.artandbits.com

Artdink Corporation
WBG Marive west Bldg
2-6 Nakase, Mihama
Chiba 261-8701
Japan
Web: http://www.artdink.com

Artematica S.r.l.
C.so Dante
50/3 scala B
16043
Chiavari
Italy
Tel: +39 0185/324660

Fax: +39 0185/368490
Web: http://www.artematica.com

Artex Software
Burgstr. 56
60316 Frankfurt
Germany
Web: http://www.artexsoft.com

Artifact Entertainment
4840 East Jasmine, Suite 102
Scottsdale, Arizona 85205
United States
Tel: 1-480-218-1223
Web: http://www.artifact-entertain-ment.com

Artoon Co., Ltd.
YS Bldg. 6F, 2-15-10, Shin-Yokohama, Kouhoku-ku,
Yokohama, Kanagawa 222-0033,
Japan
Tel: +81-45-470-4380
Fax: +81-45-470-4580
Web: http://www.artoon.co.jp

ARUSH Entertainment
13951 N. Scottsdale Road, Suite 233
Scottsdale, Arizona 85254
United States
Tel: 1-480-609-8665
Web: http://www.arushgames.com

Arxel Tribe
20, rue Saint Fiacre
75002 Paris, France
Tel: +33 1 44 76 06 00
Fax: +33 1 44 76 06 19
Web: http://www.arxeltribe.com

ASAP Games LLC.
Costa Mesa, California 92626
United States
Web: http://www.asapgames.com

Ascaron
Dieselstrasse 66, D-33334
Gütersloh, Germany
Tel: (0) 5241-9666-0
Web: http://www.ascaron.com

Ascaron Entertainment UK Ltd
Office #4
Lower Ground Floor
Chantry House
High Street
Coleshill
Birmingham B46 3BP
Tel: +44 (0) 1675 433220
Web: http://www.ascaron.com

Ascension Entertainment
1925 Century Park East Suite 500
Los Angeles, California 90067
United States
Tel: 1-310-789-2111
Web: http://www.maxthrasher.com

Ascension Entertainment
P.O. Box 80822
Portland, Oregon 97280
United States
Tel: 1-503-244-6020
Web: http://www.maxthrasher.com

ASCII Corporation
Toshin Bldg.
4-33-10 Yoyogi
Shibuya-ku
Tokyo 151-8024
Japan
Tel: +81-3-5351-8111
Web: http://www.ascii.co.jp

A Sharp
1517 NW 64th St
Seattle, Washington 98107-2343
United States
Web: http://www.a-sharp.com

A.S.K. Homework
Hungary
Web: http://www.askhomework.hu

Astroll
Shibuya, Tokyo
Japan
Web: http://www.astroll.com

AsUwant Entertainment
21, bis Rue Aristide Briand
92170 Vanves
Tel: + 33 (0)1 41 23 04 80
Fax: + 33 (0)1 46 38 03 65
Web: http://www.asuwant.com

Atari
2230 Broadway Avenue
Santa Monica, California 90404
United States
Web: http://www.atari.com

ATD
Unit 3, Nunhold Business Centre
Dark Lane
Hatton
Warwickshire
CV35 8XB
United Kingdom
Tel: 01926 843444
Fax: 01926 843363
Web: http://www.atd.co.uk

ATGames
1875 Century Park East
Suite #930
Los Angeles, California 90067
United States
Tel: 1-310-286-2222
Fax: 1-310-282-0675
Web: http://www.atgames.net

ATGames
8F, No. 2, Cha Chian Road
Wen-Shan District
Taipei City, Taiwan, 116
Tel: 886-2-2933-5123
Fax: 886-2-2933-2609
Web: http://www.atgames.net

Atlantis Lab LLC.
175 Hawthorne Ave Suite 164
Central Islip, New York 11722
United States
Tel: 1-631-342-8992
Web: http://www.atlantis-lab.com

Atlas Games
P.O. Box 131233
Roseville, Minnesota 55113

United States
Tel: 1-651-638-0077
Fax: 1-651-638-0084
Web: http://www.atlas-games.com

Atlus U.S.A.
15255 Alton Parkway, Suite 100
Irvine, California 92618
United States
Fax: 1-949-788-0433
Web: http://www.atlus.com

Atod AB
Gasverksgatan 9
252 25 Helsingborg
Sweden
Tel: +46 (0)42 271010
Fax: +46 (0)42 271011
Web: http://www.atod.se

Atomic Games, Inc.
PO Box 58186
Houston, Texas 77258-8186
United States
Tel: 1-281-333-1757
Fax: 1-281-335-7141
Web: http://www.atomic.com

Atomic Planet Entertainment ltd.
72-80 Corporation Road
Middlesbrough, Cleveland, TS1
2RF
United Kingdom
Tel: +44 1642 871100
Web: http://www.atomic-planet.com

Atollsoft s.a. /n.v.
Zoning de Saintes
Avenue Ernest Solvay 28
1480 Tubize
Tel :+32 2 391 41 20
Fax: +32 2 391 41 30
Web: http://www.atollsoft.be

Attention to Detail
Unit 3
Nunhold Business Centre
Dark Lane
Hatton
Warwickshire
CV35 8XB

United Kingdom
Tel: +44 (0) 1926 843444
Fax: +44 (0) 1926 843363
Web: http://www.atd.co.uk

Audiogenic Software Limited
PO Box 4004
Stansted
Essex CM24 8JZ
United Kingdom
Web: http://www.audiogenic.com

Auran
P.O. Box 1026
New Farm 4005
QLD
Australia
Web: http://www.auran.com

Avalanche Software
102 West 500 South Suite 502
Salt Lake City, Utah 84101
United States
Web:
http://www.avalanchesoftware.com

Avalon Hill Games
United States
Web: http://www.avalonhill.com

Avaria Corporation
391 Melody Lane
Casselberry, Florida 32707
United States
Tel: 1-407-788-7558
Web:
http://www.endlessagesportal.com

Avery Smartcat Productions
2430 Fulton Road,
Kissimmee, Florida, 34744
United States
Tel: 1-407-932-2604
Tel: 1-407-932-2630
Web: http://www.cybersmart.tv

AWE Games
13798 NW 4th Street
Suite 306-309
Sunrise, Florida 33325
United States
Tel: 1-954-835-9199
Fax: 1-954-835-9196
Web: http://www.awegames.com

Awesome Developments
18a South Bar
Banbury
Oxfordshire
OX16 9AF
United Kingdom
Fax: 01295 276363
Web: http://www.awesome.uk.com

Azursoft
France
Web: http://www.azursoft.fr

Babylon Software
3 Rue Gustave Eiffel
78306 Poissy
France
Tel: 01 39 22 64 14
Web: http://www.babylonsoft.com

Balance Games
PO Box 2103
Malaga 29080
Spain
Tel: +34 952.09.13.51
Web: http://www.balancegames.com

BAM! Entertainment
333 West Santa Clara Street,
Suite 716
San Jose, California 95113
United States
Tel: 1-408-298-7500
Fax: 1-408-298-9600
Web: http://www.bam4fun.com

BAM! Entertainment
Upper Borough Court, 3rd Floor
Upper Borough Walls
Bath, BA1 1RG
England
Tel: +44 (0) 1225 329 298

Fax: +44 (0) 1225 329 241
Web: http://www.bam4fun.com

Bandai Co., Ltd.
5-4, Komagata 2-chome
Taito-ku,
Tokyo 111-8081
Japan
Tel: 03-3847-5005
Fax: 03-3847-5067
Web: http://www.bandai.co.jp

Banpresto
Tokyo, Japan
Tel: 03-3842-1201
Web: http://www.banpresto.co.jp

Barking Dog Studios Ltd.
Rockstar Vancouver
4th Floor - 21 Water Street
Vancouver, BC.
V6B 1A1
Canada
Tel: 1-604-632-9663
Fax: 1-604-632-9664
Web: http://www.barking-dog.com

Barracuda, Inc.
545 2nd Street, Suite 3
Encinitas, California 92024
United States
Tel: 1-760-634-6794
Fax: 1-760-634-6797
Web: http://www.barracudanet.com

BattleAtlantis
1625 SE 39th Ave.,
Portland, Oregon 97214
United States
Tel: 1-503-239-4244
Web: http://www.battleatlantis.com

BattleBorne Entertainment, Inc.
9210 Prototype Dr.
Suite 101
Reno, Nevada 89511
United States
Tel: 1-775-284-0276
Web: http://www.battleborne.com

Battlefront
P.O. Box 307
Dover-Foxcroft, Maine 04426
United States
Web: http://www.battlefront.com

Battlegoat Studios
86 Oneida Blvd
Ancaster, Ontario
Canada L9G 4S5
Tel: 1-905-304-9383
Web: http://www.battlegoat.com

Beam International Limited
55 Claremont St
South Yarra
VIC 3141
Australia
Tel: 61 3 9826 9433
Fax: 61 3 9826 9115
Web: http://www.beam.com.au

Beenox, Inc.
771, St-Joseph Est, Suite 102
Quebec, Canada
G1K 3C7
Tel: 1-418-522-2468
Web: http://www.beenox.com

Beiing xgameworks software
Co.ltd
HuiXin High-rise B-602
Ya Yun Village
Haidian District
Beijing 100101
China
Tel: 086 (010) 84985828-290
Tel: 086 (010) 84985828-291
Fax: 086 (010) 84985828-299
Web: http://www.xgameworks.com

Bellicode
2555 Adams Court,
South San Francisco, California
United States
Tel: 1-650-291-1691
Web: http://www.bellicode.com

Belisa
3, rue Martel
75010 Paris, France
Tel: +33 (1) 47 70 44 74
Fax: +33 (1) 47 70 44 94
Web: http://www.belisa.com

Berigames
4725, Bethany Court
Colorado Springs, Colorado
80918
United States
Tel: 1-719-229-3543
Fax: 1-719-623-0476
Web: http://www.berigames.com

Berkeley Systems
PO Box 85006
Bellevue, Washington 98015-8506
United States
Tel: 1-800-757-7707
Web: http://www.berksys.com

Bethesda Softworks
1370 Piccard Drive, Suite 120
Rockville, Maryland 20850
United States
Phone: 1-301-926-8300
Fax: 1-301-926-8010
Web: http://www.bethsoft.com

Beyond Games
370 E. South Temple, First Floor
Salt Lake City, Utah 84111
United States
Web: http://www.beyondgames.com

Bigben Interactive GmbH
Walter-Gropius-Straße 24
50126 Bergheim
Germany
Tel: 02271 49859-0
Fax: 02271 49859-99
Web:http://www.bigben-interactive.de

Bigben Interactive UK
Parham Drive
Boyatt Wood, Eastleigh
SO50 4 NU
Hampshire

United Kingdom
Tel:+44 2380 653 377
Fax:+44 2380 652 239
Web:http://www.bigben-interactive.de

Bigben Interactive HK Ltd.
13A China Harbour Building
370-374 King's Road, North Point
Hong Kong
Tel:+852 251 23 111
Fax:+852 250 32 865
Web:http://www.bigben-interactive.de

Bigben S.A.
Rue de la Voyette, C.R.T.2
59818 LESQUIN Cedex
France
Web: http://www.www.bigben.fr

Big Blue Box Studios
Southern House
Flambard Way
Godalming
Surrey
GU7 1HH
United Kingdom
Tel: +44 (0) 1483 521700
Fax: +44 (0) 1483 521709
Web: http://www.bigbluebox.com

Big Foot Software
318 North Carson Street Suite 210
Carson City, Nevada
United States
Tel: 1-775-885-2371
Web: http://www.wmsgaming.com

Big Fun Development Company
620 Lake Shore Dr.
Atlanta, Georgia 30096-3038
United States
Tel: 1-770-300-0308
Web: http://bigfun.net

Big Huge Games
1954 Greenspring Drive, Suite 520
Timonium, Maryland 21093
United States
Fax: 1-410-842.0047
Web: http://www.bighugegames.com

Bignet USA Inc.
San Francisco, California
United States
Web: http://www.micronet-japan.com

Big Sky Interactive
600 Round Rock West #205
Round Rock, Texas 78681
United States
Tel: 1-512-733-1711
Web: http://www.bigskyinteractive.com

Big Time Software
P.O. Box 307
Dover-Foxcroft, Maine 04426
United States
Web: http://www.bigtimesoftware.com

bigwheel creative, LLC
161 Harvard Ave., Suite 14A
Allston, Massachusetts, 02134
United States
Tel: 1-617-782-7985
Web: http://www.bigwheelcreative.com

Binary Bards
3 Baldwin Green Common, Suite 108
Woburn, Massachusetts 01801
United States
Tel: 1-781-938-5917
Fax: 1-781-938-5951
Web: http://www.binarybards.com

BioWare Corp.
302 10508 82 Avenue
Edmonton, Alberta
Canada T6E 6H2
Phone: 1-780-430-0164
Fax: 1-780-439-6374
Web: http://www.bioware.com

Bitmap Brothers, The
Wapping
London
United Kingdom
Web:http://www.bitmap-brothers.co.uk

Bitmap Brothers, The
Harrogate
United Kingdom
Web:http://www.bitmap-brothers.co.uk

Bit Managers
Paseo Lorenzo Serra, 4-2-A
08921 Santa Coloma de
Gramanet
Spain
Tel: +34 934662257
Fax: +34 934661269
Web: http://www.bitmanagers.com

Bits Studios
112 Cricklewood Lane
London
NW2 2DP
England
United Kingdom
Telephone: +44 (0) 20 8282 7200
Facsimile: +44 (0) 20 8450 9966
Web: http://www.bitsstudios.com

Bizarre Creations
Energetica Building
18 Faraday Road
Wavertree Technology Park
Liverpool L13 1EH
United Kingdom
Web: http://www.bizarrecreations.com

Black Box Games
Vancouver, British Columbia
V7X 1M6 Canada
Web: http://www.blackboxgames.com

Black Cactus Games Ltd
Athena House
88 London Rd
Morden
Surrey
SM4 5AZ
United Kingdom
Web: http://www.blackcactus.com

Black Element Software
Bezecka 79
169 00 Prague
Czech Republic
Tel: 02/57 21 61 04
Web: http://www.blackelement.com

Black Hammer Productions, Inc.
447 Broadway, 2nd Floor
New York, New York 10013
United States
Tel: 1-212-625-8980
Web: http://www.blackhammer.com

Black Isle Studios
16815 Von Karman
Irvine, California 92606
United States
Tel: 1-949-553-6655
Web: http://www.blackisle.com

Black Label Games
240 West 35th Street, 18th Floor
New York, New York 10001
United States
Tel: 1-212-209-4600
Web: http://www.blacklabelgames.com

Black Label Games
6080 Center Drive, 10th Floor
Los Angeles, California 90045
United States
Tel: 1-310-431-4000
Web: http://www.blacklabelgames.com

Black Label Games
Bâtiment Energy 1 - Porte B
32, avenue de l'Europe
78457 Vélizy - Villacoublay, Cedex
France
Tel: +33 (0) 1.30.67.30.30
Web: http://www.blacklabelgames.com

Black Ops Entertainment
2121 Cloverfield Blvd, #204
Santa Monica, California 90404
United States
Tel: 1-310-828-0682
Fax: 1-310-828-0263
Web: http://www.blackops.com

Black Sea Studios Ltd.
B.I.C. IZOT, 7th. floor, Office 728
7th km, Tzarigradsko shosse, Blvd.
Sofia 1784, Bulgaria
Tel: +359 2 971 84 22
Fax: +359 2 971 81 22
Web: http://www.blackseastudios.com

Blackstar Interactive GmbH
Siegfriedstr. 44
D-67547 Worms
Germany
Tel: ++49 (0)6241 - 93 49 40
Fax: ++49 (0)6241 - 93 49 41
Web: http://www.black-star.de

Blade Interactive Studios
274 Deansgate
Manchester
M3 4JB
England
Tel: +44(0)161 839 6622
Fax: +44(0)161 839 6688
Web: http://www.bladeinteractive.com

Blam!
2511 Van Ness Ave., Suite B
San Francisco, California 94109
United States
Tel: 1-415-351-2526
Fax: 1-415-441-5390
Web: http://www.blam.com

Blissware Entertainment
Römerstraße 13
D-67547 Worms
Germany
Tel: 06241 - 26222
Tel: +49 - 6132 - 58378
Web:
http://www.blissware-entertainment.de

Blitz Games
PO Box 186
Leamington Spa
Warwickshire
CV32 5TX
United Kingdom
Tel: +44 (0) 1926 311284
Fax: +44 (0) 1926 887209
Web: http://www.blitzgames.co.uk
Web: http://www.blitzgames.com

Blizzard Entertainment
P.O. Box 18979
Irvine, California 92623
United States
Tel: 1-949-955-0283
Web: http://www.blizzard.com

Blizzard (Vivendi Universal)
32, avenue de l'Europe
Bâtiment Energy 1 (2e étage)
78 941 Vélizy-Villacoublay cedex
France
Tel: 01 30 67 90 53
Web: http://www.blizzard.fr

Blizzard North
3182 Campus Dr., #502
San Mateo, California 94403
United States
Web: http://www.blizzard.com

Blue Axion Inc.
Waltham, Massachusetts
United States
Web: http://www.blueaxion.com

Blue Byte Software GmbH & Co. KG
Eppinghofer Straße 150
D-45468 Muelheim an der Ruhr
Germany
Tel: +49 (0) 2 08 4 50 88-0
Fax: +49 (0) 2 08 4 50 88-99
Web: http://www.bluebyte.com

Blue Fang Software
One Cranberry Hill, Suite 105
Lexington, Massachusetts 02421
United States
Tel: 1-781-861-7272
Fax: 1-781-862-9335
Web: http://www.bluefang.com

Blue Fang Games, LLC
1601 Trapelo Rd., Suite 12
Waltham, Massachusetts 02451
United States
Fax: 1-781-547-5480
Web: http://www.bluefang.com

BlueInca Studios Ltd.
Cambridge
United Kingdom
Web: http://www.blueinca.co.uk

Blue Planet Software
77 Geary Street, Suite 500
San Francisco, California 94108-

5723
United States
Tel: 1-415-788-5550
Fax: 1-415-477-0616
Web:
http://www.blueplanetsoftware.com

Blue Monkey Studios
Media House
Leeds Road
Huddersfield
West Yorkshire
HD5 0RL
United Kingdom
Tel: +44 1484 353470
Web:
http://www.bluemonkeystudios.com

Bluemoon Design Inc.
8024 Glenwood Avenue, Suite 109
Raleigh, North Carolina 27612
United States
Tel: 1-919-787-3769
Fax: 1-919-420-0497
Web: www.bmdinc.net

Bluemoon Interactive
Ahtri 12
10151 Tallinn
Estonia
Web: http://www.bluemoon.ee

Blue Shift Inc.
200 S. California Ave
Palo Alto, California 94306
United States
Tel: 1-650-614-4855
Fax: 1-650-614-4856
Web: http://www.blueshiftgames.com

Blue Sphere
2 rue auguste Renoir
92290 Châtenay-Malabry
France
Fax: 01 46 32 21 00.
Web: http://www.blue-sphere.fr

Blue Tongue Software Pty Ltd
321 Queensberry Street
North Melbourne
Vic 3051

Australia
Tel: +61 3 9320 8888
Fax: +61 3 9326 5701
Web: http://www.bluetongue.com
Web: http://www.bluetongue.com.au

BMS Modern Games
Handelsagentur GmbH
Pascalstraße 17
52076 Aachen
Tel: +49(0)2408-959-0
Fax: +49(0)2408-959-125
Web: http://www.modern-games.com

Bohemia Interactive
Prague
Czech Republic
Web: http://www.bistudio.com

Bold, by Destineer
400 S Hwy 169, Ste. 101
Minneapolis, Minnesota 55426
United States
Tel: 1-952-697-6055
Web: http://www.boldgames.com

Boolat Games
48 Universitetskaya st., Donetsk,
Ukraine, 83050
Web: http://www.BoolatGames.com

Boss Media AB
P.O. Box 3243
SE-350 53 Växjö
Sweden
Tel: +46 470 70 30 00
Fax: +46 470 70 30 50
Web: http://www.bossmedia.se

Boston Animation, Inc.
14 Red Acre Road
Stow, Massachusetts 01775
Tel: 1-978-897-8180
Fax: 1-978-897-2391
Web:
http://www.bostonanimation.com

Boundless Entertaining Inc.
P.O. Box 2694
Winter Haven, Florida 33883-
2694
United States
Tel: 1-863-298-0209
Fax: 1-863-293-9784
Web:
http://www.boundless-adventures.com

Brainshot Studios
Maure 2258 PB A,
Buenos Aires, 1426
Argentina
Tel: 4855-4220-3434
Fax: 4856-9724
Web: http://www.brainshot.com

Brainsmash Interactive
Rotterdam, The Netherlands
Kvk: 24345015 0000
Web: http://www.brainsmash.net

Brat Designs Ltd.
England
United Kingdom
Tel: 44 (0) 1642 371756
Fax: 44 (0) 1642 3717567
Web: http://www.brat-designs.com

BraveTree Productions
PO Box 1944
Eugene, Oregon 97440
United States
Tel: 1-541-607-7050
Web: http://www.bravetree.com

Bravo Interactive
4 Svyatoshinskaya St, 2
Kiev 03115
Ukraine
Tel: +380 44 516 9364
Web:
http://www.bravointeractive.com

BreakAway Games, Ltd.
10600 York Road Suite 204
Hunt Valley, Maryland 21030
United States
Tel: 1-410-683-1702
Fax: 1-410-683-1706
Web:http://www.breakawaygames.com

Brick House Trading
Los Angeles, California
United States
Web:
http://www.BrickHouseTrading.com

Brightstar Entertainment Limited
2 Oakley Road
Chinnor, Oxon
OX39 4HZ
United Kingdom
Web: http://www.brightstargames.com

Brilliant Digital Entertainment
6355 Topanga Canyon Blvd
Woodland Hills, california 91367
United States
Tel: 1-818-615-1500
Web: http://www.bde3d.com

Broadsword Interactive
8 Science Park
Aberystywth
Ceredigion
Wales
SY23 3AH
United Kingdom
Tal: +44(0)1970 626299
Fax: +44(0)1970 626291
Web: http://www.broadsword.co.uk

Broccoli
Tokyo, Japan
Web: http://www.broccoli.co.jp

Brooklyn Games
132 Crosby St., 4th Floor
New York, New York, 10012
United States
Tel: 1-212-625-8890
Web: http://www.brooklyngames.com

Brownie Brown Co., Ltd.
180-0004 Kichijoji Honmachi 2-1-10
Daiwa Securities Building 6th floor,
Musashino City, Tokyo
Japan
Tel: 0422-23-8135
Fax: 0422-23-8137
Web: http://www.br2.co.jp

Bubble Boy
Tunwells Court
34 Trumpington Street
Cambridge
CB2 1QY
United Kingdom
Telephone: +44 (0) 1223 363000
Facsimile: +44 (0) 1223 312000
Web: http://www.bubbleboyz.com

Bugbear Entertainment Ltd.
Laulukuja 4
00420 Helsinki
Finland
Tel: +358-9-4365 5560
Fax: +358-9-4365 5562
Web: http://www.bugbear.fi

Buka Entertainment
Kashirskoye Shosse 1 Bld.2
Moscow 115230
Russia
Tel: +7 (095) 111 5146
Fax: +7 (095) 111 5440
Web: http://www.buka.com

Bulldog Interactive
166 Lichfield Road
0 Rushall
Walsall
United Kingdom
Tel: 44-0-1922-861314
Fax: 44-0-1922-861314
Web:
http://www.bulldoginteractive.com

Bullfrog
90 Heron Drive
Langley
Berkshire
SL3 8XP
United Kingdom
Web: http://www.bullfrog.com

Bullseye Software
P.O. Box 7900
Incline Village, Nevada 89452
United States
Web: http://www.dogfightcity.com

BumbleBeast
Zeegse
Netherlands
Web: http://www.bumblebeast.com

Bungarra Software
PO Box 253
Mosman Park
Western Australia 6012
Tel: +61 8 9335 8086
Fax: +61 8 9335 9980
Web: http://www.bungarra.com

Bungie Studios
One Microsoft Way
Redmond, Washington 98052
United States
Web: http://www.bungie.com

Bunkasha
Tokyo, Japan
Tel: 03 - 3222 - 5112
Web: http://www.bunkasha-games.com

Burns Entertainment
Marienburger Strasse 26,
Berlin, 10405
Germany
Tel: +49.30.440.502.81
Web: http://www.burns-games.com

Burut Creative Team
32 Kukolkina str. Voronezh
Russia 39-4055
Tel: 7-0732-393-320
Fax: 7-0732-779-339
Web: http://www.burut.ru

Butterfly.net
224 West King St
Martinsburg, West Virginia 25401
United States
Tel: 1-304-260-9520
Fax: 1-304-260-9529
Web: http://www.butterfly.net

Buzz Monkey Software
576 Olive Street, Suite 205
Eugene, Oregon 97401
United States

Tel: 1-541-484-7030
Fax: 1-541-484-7520
Web:
http://www.buzzmonkeysoftware.com

BVM
helmholtzstr. 2-9
d-10587 Berlin
Germany
Tel: +49 (0) 30 390 721-0
Fax: +49 (0) 30 390 721-210
Web: http://www.bvm.de

BVS Development
Voronezh, Russia
Web: http://www.bvssolitaire.com

Bytegeist Software
Sydney, NSW, 2066
Australia
Tel: 79 095 770 988
Tel: 61 4 25 24 3367
Web: http://www.bytegeistsoftware.com

Bytegeist Software
Suite 2603, SOHO
88 Jianguo Rd
Chaoyang, Beijing
100022 China
Tel: +86 10 8580 2197
Fax: +86 10 8580 2808
Web: http://www.bytegeistsoftware.com

Bytegeist Software
London
United Kingdom
Web: http://www.bytegeistsoftware.com

Byte Software
Slovak Republic
Web: http://www.byte.sk

By Thunder
3185 Graveley Street
Vancouver, British Columbia
Canada V5K 3K7
Tel: 1-604-253-8288
Web: http://www.bythunder.com

C4 Pty Ltd
2 / 421 Rathdowne St
Carlton VIC 3053
Australia
Tel: +61 (0)3 9348 2389
Web: http://www.c4-digital.com

Cactus Development Company, Inc.
7301 Burnet Road, Suite 102-114
Austin, Texas 78757-2250
United States
Tel: 1-512-453-1251
Fax: 1-512-453-2022
Web:
http://www.cactusdevelopment.com

Camelot Software Planning
Tokyo, Japan
Tel: 03-3341-7759
Fax: 03-3353-4330
Web: http://www.camelot.co.jp

CAMF Productions
Aignerstrasse 78
AT-5026 Salzburg
Austria
Tel: +43-662-620830
Fax: +43-662-620830-10
Web: http://www.camf.com

Candella Software Ltd
3 Carley Court
103 Friern Park
London
N12 9UG
United Kingdom
Tel: (208) 445 4197
Fax: (208) 445 4197
Web: http://www.candellasoftware.com

Canopy Games
Minneapolis, Minnesota
United States
Web: http://www.canopygames.com

Canopy Games
Orem, Utah
United States
Web: http://www.canopygames.com

Capcom USA.
475 Oakmead Parkway
Sunnyvale, California 94085
United States
Tel: 1-408-774-0500
Fax: 1-408-774-3994
Web: http://www.capcom.com

Capcom Japan
No. 1-3, Uchihiranomachi, 3-Chome
Chuo-ku, Osaka 540-0037
Japan
Tel: 81-6-920-3635
Fax: 81-6-920-5134
Web: http://www.capcom.co.jp

Capcom Tokyo Branch Office
11th floor, Shinjuku Mitsui Building
2-1-1, Nishi-Shinjuku, Shinjuku-ku
Tokyo 163-0411
Japan
Tel: 81-3-3340-0735
Fax: 81-3-3340-0701
Web: http://www.capcom.co.jp

Capcom Asia
Unit 1205-6, 12/F., New East
Ocean Center
9 Science Museum Road,
Tsimshatsui East
Kowloon, Hong Kong
Tel: 852-2366-1001
Fax: 852-2366-1985
Web: http://www.capcomasia.com.hk

Capcom Europe
30-35, Pall Mall
London
SW1Y 5LP
United Kingdom
Tel: 44 (0) 20-7925-2565
Fax: 44 (0) 20-7930-4725
Web: http://www.capcom-europe.com

Captivation Digital Laboratories, Inc.
30 Avenue Portola, 2nd Floor
PO Box 220
El Granada, California 94018
United States
Tel: 1-650-726-1096
Web: http://www.captivation.com

Carapace
14 rue Crespin du Gast
75011 Paris
France
Tel: 33 1 40 210 396
Fax: 33 1 40 215 812
Web: http://www.carapace.fr

Carbon Games
14 decembra 70/6,
Belgrade, , 11000
Yugoslavia
Tel +38 164 111 7775
Web: http://www.carbon-games.com

Carbon6 Entertainment
Sunnyvale, California 94085
United States
Web: http://www.carbon6.com

Cat Daddy Games, LLC
14715 Bel-Red Road Suite 100
Bellevue, Washington 98007
United States
Tel: 1-425-564-8265
Fax: 1-425-746-8206
Web: http://www.catdaddy.com

Catamongus Studios
2430 Fulton Road,
Kissimmee, Florida, 34744
United States
Tel: 1-407-932-2604
Tel: 1-407-932-2630
Web: http://www.cybersmart.tv

Cauldron
Grösslingova 4
814 18 Bratislava
Tel: +421-7-5923 6103
Fax: +421-7-5296 7841
Web: http://www.cauldron.sk

Cave Barn Studios LLC
5109 Steeles Avenue West, Unit
#107A,
Toronto, Ontario
M9L2Y8 Canada
Tel: 1-416-745-1074
Web: http://www.cavebarn.com

Cave Barn Studios LLC
Chicago, Illinois
United States
Tel: 1-773-486-7658
Web: http://www.cavebarn.com

Cavedog Entertainment
3855 Monte Villa Parkway
Bothell, Washington 98021
United States
Web: http://www.cavedog.com

CCP hf.
Klapparstigur 28
101 Reykjavik
Iceland
Tel: +354 511 4999
Fax: +354 511 4998
Web: http://www.ccpgames.com

CDV Software Entertainment AG
Neureuter Straße 37 b
76185 Karlsruhe
Germany
Tel: 0721 / 97 224-0
Fax: 0721 / 97 224-24
Web: http://www.cdv.de

Cecropia, Inc.
57 Bedford St. Suite 120
Lexington, Massachusetts 02420
United States
Tel: 1-781-862-6911
Fax: 1-781-402-2586
Web: http://www.cecropia.com

Celeris
20709 Germain St.
Chatsworth, California 91311
United States
Tel: 1-818-709-2181
Web: http://www.celeris.com

Cenega U.K. Ltd
Weir Bank
Bray-on-Thames
Maidenhead
Berkshire
SL6 2ED
United Kingdom
Tel: 0044 1628 762712
Fax: 0044 1628 762713
Web: http://www.cenega.com

Chaman Productions
52 Avenue Charles de Gaulle
92200 Neuilly sur Seine
Tel: 01 55 62 00 00
Fax: 01 55 62 00 05
Web: http://www.chaman.net

Charybdis
The Cowshed
Strelley Hall
Nottingham
NG8 6PE
United Kingdom
Tel: (0115) 9426962
Fax: (0115) 9299453
Web: http://www.charybdis.co.uk

Check Six Studios
210 Main Street
Venice, California 90291
United States
Tel: 1-310-581-8600
Fax: 1-310-581-8601
Web: http://www.checksixstudios.com

Cheeky Group Ltd.
Cromwell House
Brook Street
Macclesfield
Cheshire, SK11 7AA
United Kingdom
Tel: +44 1625 662152
Fax: +44 1625 662153
Web: http://www.cheekygroup.com

Cheyenne Cloud, LLC
8900 Valdez Dr.
Urbandale, Iowa 50322
United States
Tel: 1-515-278-2087
Web: http://www.destiny3d.com

Chili Con Valley
B.P. 294
82, bd Haussmann
75364 Paris Cedex 08
France
Tel : +33 1 40 08 07 07
Fax : +33 1 43 87 35 99
Web Site: http://www.chiliconvalley.com

ChiselBrain Software
The Netherlands
Web: http://www.chiselbrain.com

Chunsoft
Tokyo, Japan
Tel:03-5272-1711
Fax:03-5272-1710
Web: http://www.chunsoft.co.jp

Cinegram Media Inc.
One Springfield Ave.
Summit, New Jersey 07901
United States
Tel: 1-908-598-4755
Fax: 1-908-598-4756
Web: http://www.cinegram.com

Cinematix Studios, Inc.
4812 South Mill Ave.
Tempe, Arizona 85282-6730
United States
Tel: 1-480-838-0140
Fax: 1-480-838-0215
Web: http://www.cinematix.com

Cinemaware
Redwood City, California
United States
Fax: 1-781-846-6333
Web: http://www.cinemaware.com

City Interactive sp. z o.o.
ul . Zupnicza 17
03-821 Warsaw
Poland
Tel: +48 22 619 63 06
Fax: +48 22 619 99 35
Web: http://www.city-interactive.com

CityRom
18 Sylvester Street,
Toronto, Ontario, M5V 2Z5
Canada
Tel: 1-416-591-5757
Web: http://www.muchmusic.com

Clap Hanz Limited
Japan
Web: http://www.claphanz.co.jp

Claw Design Software
Ludwigstraße 8
D-72474 Winterlingen
Germany
Tel: +49 07434 315126
Fax: +49 07434 315327
Web: http://www.clawdesign.com

CleverMedia
1022 N. Speer Blvd,
Denver, Colorado 80204
United States
Web: http://clevermediastudios.com

Clevers Development
Banhidai ltp 318
Tatabanya
pest
2800
Hungary
Web: http://www.clevers.com

Click Entertainment
777 Florida St. Suite 100
San Francisco, California 94110
United States
Tel: 1-415-643-8650
Tel: 1-415-546-7030
Web: http://www.clickent.com

Climax Group
Fareham Heights
Standard Way
Fareham
Hampshire
PO16 8XT
United Kingdom
Tel: 44 (0) 1329 827777
Fax: 44 (0) 1329 828777
Web: http://www.climax.co.uk

Climax Brighton
Sheridan House
114 Western Road
Hove
East Sussex
BN3 1DD
United Kingdom
Fax: 44 (0) 1273 740819
Web: http://www.climax.co.uk

Climax Nottingham
3-5 High Pavement
Nottingham
Nottinghamshire
NG1 1HF
United Kingdom
Fax: 44 (0) 115 959 6492
Web: http://www.climax.co.uk

Climax London
6&7 Canbury Business Park
Elm Cresent
Kingston
Surrey
KT2 6HJ
Fax: 44 (0) 20 8974 9761
Web: http://www.climax.co.uk

Cobalt Interactive
370 E. South Temple, First Floor
Salt Lake City, Utah 84111
United States
Tel: 1-801-531-8500
Web: http://www.cobaltinteractive.com

CodeFire, Inc.
6 Morgan St. #160
Irvine, California 92618
United States
Tel: 1-949-462-9620
Web: http://www.codefire.com

Codemasters,
P.O. Box 6
Leamington Spa
Warwickshire
CV47 2DL
United Kingdom
Tel: 01926 814132
Fax: 01926 817595
Web: http://www.codemasters.com

Codemasters,
Lower Farm
Stoneythorpe
Southam
Warwickshire
CV47 2DL
United Kingdom
Tel: +44 (0) 1926 814132
Fax: +44 (0) 1926 817595
Web: http://www.codemasters.com

Codemasters
Carnagie Hall Tower
21st Floor
152 West 57th Street
New York, New York 10019
United States
Tel: 1-559-683-4468
Fax: 1-559-683-3633
Web: http://www.codemasters.com

Codemasters
Parc des Aqueducs,
Chemin du Favier
RD42, BP84
69565 Saint Genis Laval
France
Tel: 04.78.56.76.10
Fax: 04.78.56.76.11
Web: http://www.codemasters.com

Codemasters Spain,
C. Orense 85
28020 Madrid
Spain
Tel: +34 915678461
Fax: +34 915714244
Web: http://www.codemasters.com

Code Monkeys Ltd, The
Concourse House
432 Dewsbury Road
Leeds
LS11 7DF
United Kingdom
Tel: +44 (0) 113 271 0996
Fax: +44 (0) 113 271 3572
Web: http://www.codemonkeys.com

Cog Interactive
New Jersey
United States
Web: http://www.coginteractive.com

CogniToy, LLC
236 Central St.
Acton, Massachusetts 01720
United States
Tel: 1-978-264-3945
Fax: 1-978-264-3946
Web: http://www.cognitoy.com

co|interactive
102 East 22nd St #9B
New York, New York 10010
United States
Tel: 1-212-460-5375
Fax: 1-781-735-1070
Web: http://www.cointeractive.com

Collective, The
1900 Quail Street,
Newport Beach, California 92660
United States
Fax: 1-949-724-9667
Web: http://www.collectivestudios.com

Comfy Interactive
14, Baruch Hirsh St.
Bnei Brak 51202, Israel
Tel: 1-972-3-6160046
Fax: 1-972-3-6181876
Web: http://www.comfyland.com

Compile Games
Tokorozawa, Japan
Tel: 042-920-2282
Web: http://www.compile.co.jp

Complex Games Inc.
#410 - 115 Bannatyne Avenue
Winnipeg, Manitoba
R3B OR3
Canada
Web: http://www.complexgames.com

Computer Artworks
144 Buckingham Palace Road
London
SW1W9TR
Telephone: +44 (0) 20 7824 8478
Fax: +44 (0) 20 7824 8578
Web: http://www.artworks.co.uk

Computer House
Kronhusgatan 7
S 411 05 Göteborg
Sweden
Tel: + 46 (0) 31-743 71 00
Fax: + 46 (0) 31-331 44 33
Web: http://www.computerhouse.se

Comverse
100 Quannapowitt Parkway
Wakefield, Massachusetts 01880
United States
Tel: 1-781-246-9000
Fax: 1-781-224-8143
Web:
http://www.comverse.com/Wireles
sGames

Concept Ima
Montreal , Quebec
Canada
Web: http://www.conceptlma.com

Confounding Factor Ltd.
Kingsland House
Gas Lane Bristol
Avon
BS2 0QL
United Kingdom
Web:
http://www.confounding-factor.com

Continuum Entertainment
Curitiba   Paraná
Brazil
Web: http://www.continuum.com.br

Contraband Entertainment Inc.
202 Fashion Lane, Suite 118
Tustin, California 92780
United States
Tel: 1-714-689-2500
Fax: 1-714-689-2501
Web: http://www.contrabandent.com

Core Concepts, Inc.
P.O. Box 297
Temple City, California 91780
United States
Tel: 1-626-446-0159
Tel: 1-877-267-3426
Tel: 1-877-COREGAMES
Fax: 1-626-446-0109
Web: http://www.coregames.com

Core Design
2 Roundhouse Road
Pride Park
Derby

DE24 8JE
United Kingdom
Tel: 01332 227 800
Fax: 01332 227 801
Web: http://www.core-design.com

Coresoft, Inc.
23232 Peralta, Suite 112
Laguna Hills, California 92653
United States
Tel: 1-949-206-0636
Fax: 1-949-206-0676
Web: http://www.coresoftgames.com

Cornered Rat Software
1901 Central Dr.
Suite 400
Bedford, Texas 76021
United States
Tel: 1-817-358-7580
Fax: 1-817-358-7585
Web: http://www.corneredrat.com

Corus Interactive
72 Fraser Avenue, Suite 200
Toronto, Ontario M6K 3J7
M6K 1Y7
Canada
Tel: 1-416-530-5230
Fax: 1-416-530-5177
Web: http://www.www.yabber.net

Cosmic Origins, LLC
335 Talbot Ave., No. 110
Pacifica, California, 94044
United States
Tel: 1-650-342-5522
Tel: 1-650-355-4811
Web: http://cosmicorigins.com

COSMI Corporation
2600 Homestead Place
Rancho Dominguez, California
90220
United States
Tel: 1-310-833-2000
Fax: 1-310-886-3500
Web: http://www.cosmi.com

COSMI Europe, Ltd.
Unit 8A Daimler Close

Royal Oak Industrial Estate
Daventry, North Hamptonshire
NN11 5QJ
United Kingdom
Tel: +44 (0) 1327 879000
Fax: +44 (0) 1327 879888
Web: http://www.cosmi.com

Covert Operations Ltd
241-251 Ferndale Road, Suite
226
Bon Marche Centre
London SW9 8BJ
United Kingdom
Tel: +44 (0)207 924 9995
Web: http://www.covert.co.uk

Coyote Developments Ltd
52 George St, Floors 1&3
Croydon, Surrey, CR0 1PB
United Kingdom
Tel: 0208 681 5000
Web: http://www.coyotedev.com

Crash Masters
PO Box 22012,
Rotterdam, 3003 DA
Netherlands
Tel: +3110 4129999
Fax: +3110 4112101
Web: http://www.crashmasters.com

Crave Entertainment, Inc.
19645 Rancho Way
Los Angeles, California 90220
United States
Tel: 1-310-661-3000
Fax: 1-310.661.3024
Web: http://www.cravegames.com

Crawfish Interactive
8th Floor
Green Dragon House
64-70 High Street
Croydon
Surrey
CR0 9XN
England
Fax: +44 (0) 20 8686 2036
Web: http://www.crawfish.co.uk

Creative Assembly, The
Weald House
Southwater Business Park
Southwater Nr. Horsham
West Sussex
Rh13 - 7he.
United Kingdom
Tel: (+44)(01403) 734473
Fax: (+44)(01403) 734477
Web:
http://www.creative-assembly.co.uk

Creative Assembly, The
Weald House
Southwater Business Park
Southwater Nr. Horsham
West Sussex
RH13 - 9JB.
Tel: (+44)(01403)734473
Fax: (+44)(01403)734477
Web:
http://www.creative-assembly.co.uk

Creative Assembly, The
Level 2, 47 Warner Street
Fortitude Valley QLD 4006
Australia
Tel: +61 (0)7 3252 1359,
Fax: +61 (0)7 3252 3615,
Web:
http://www.creative-assembly.co.uk

Creative Capers
Glendale, California
United States
Web: http://www.creativecapers.com

Creative Edge
P.O. Box 13492
Edinburgh
EH6 6YH
United Kingdom
Tel: +44 (0) 131 555 5366
Web: http://www.edgies.com

Creature Labs Ltd
Quayside
Bridge Street
Cambridge
CB5 8AB
United Kingdom
Web: http://www.creaturelabs.com

Crevace Games
Nigeriastraat 81
Delft
Netherlands
Tel:+31 (0)15 257 44 12
Web: http://www.crevace.com

Criterion Games
Westbury Court
Buryfields
Guildford
Surrey
GU2 4YZ
Tel: +44 (0)1483 406200
Fax: +44 (0)1483 406211
Web: http://www.criterionstudios.com

CrossCut Games
Indianapolis, Indiana
United States
Web: http://www.runesword.com

Croteam
Zagreb
Croatia
Web: http://www.croteam.com

Crowd Control Productions
CCP hf.
Klapparstigur 28
101 Reykjavik
Iceland
Tel: +354 511 4999
Fax: +354 511 4998
Web: http://ccp.cc

Cryo
64 Willow Place,
Paris, , 75018
France
Tel: 01 4465 2565
Web: http://www.cryo-interactive.com

Cryonetworks
Village de la Communication
44-50, Av. du Capitaine Glarner
93585 Saint-Ouen Cedex
France
Tel: +33 1 49 48 69 00
Fax: +33 1 49 48 69 01
Web: http://www.cryo-networks.com

Cryptic Studios
San Jose, California
United States
Web: http://www.CrypticStudios.com

Crystal Dragon
7600 Grand River, suite 299
Brighton, Michigan
United States
Tel: 1-810-844-0434
Web: http://www.crystaldragon.com

Crystal Dynamics
64 Willow Place
Menlo Park, California
United States
Tel: 1-415-473-3400
Fax: 1-415-473-3410
Web: http://www.eidosinteractive.com

Crytek Studios GmbH
Rosenauer Str. 16
96450 Coburg
Germany
Web: http://www.crytek.de

Curly Monsters
Unit 28, Woodside Business Park
Birkenhead
Merseyside
L41 1EL
United Kingdom
Tel: +44 (151) 6490310
Web: http://www.curlymonsters.com

CUTLASS Inc
56 Ludlow Street
New York, New York 10002
United States
Tel: 1-212-388-9121
Web: http://www.ctlss.com

CWR-Spiele
Herrn Rumpf
Zimmerbachstrasse 3
69469 Weinheim
Germany
Web: http://www.cwr-spiele.de

Cyan Worlds
14617 N. Newport Hwy.
Mead, Washington
99021-9378
United States
Tel: 1-509-468-0807
Fax: 1-509-467-2209
Web: http://www.cyan.com

Cyanide Studio
25/27 rue des jeûneurs
75002 Paris
France
Tel: 01 44 88 78 60
Fax: 01 44 88 78 61
Web: http://www.cyanide-studio.com

CyberConcept Inc.
19, Cours le Royer,
Bureau 304
Montreal, Quebec
Canada
H2Y 1W4
Tel: 1-514-281-5706
Fax: 1-514-281-5671
Web: http://www.cyberconcept.com

Cyber Connect Corp.
Fukuoka, Japan
Web: http://www.cyberconnect2.jp

Cyberflix
Knoxville, Tennessee
United States
Web: http://www.cyberflix.com

Cyberfront Corporation
Japan
Tel: 03-5782-7631
Fax: 03-5782-7633
Web: http://www.cyberfront.co.jp

Cyberlore Studios
P.O. Box 181
Northampton, Massachusetts
01061
United States
Tel: 1-413-586-9893
Fax: 1-413-586-0347
Web:http://www.cyberlore-studios.com

Cyber Multimedia (India) Ltd.
Cyber House
B 35, Sector 32 - Institutional
Gurgaon 122002, Haryana
India
Tel: 91 124 6384816
Fax: 91 126 6380694
Web: http://www.cybermm.com

Cyberscape Graphics
P.O. Box 730066
95173 San Jose, California
United States
Tel: 1-408-238-5588
Fax: 1-408-238-7258
Web: http://www.cybgraphics.com

Cyber Warrior Entertainment
Cyber Warrior Inc.
22-08 Route 208 South
Fair Lawn, New Jersey 07410
United States
Tel: 1-201-703-1517
Fax: 1-201-703-6895
Web: http://www.cyberwar.com

Cyclone Arts & Technologies
751, Coté d'Abraham
Québec
G1R 1A2
Canada
Tel: 1-418-522-3906
Fax : 1-418-877-8024
Web: http://www.cyclone.qc.ca

Cyclone Studios
2600 South El Camino Real
Third Floor
San Mateo, California 94403
United States
Tel: 1-415-577-1800
Fax: 1-415-577-1860
Web: http://www.3do.com/upris-
ing/cyclone.htm

CyCo Systems GmbH
P.O.Box 100424
44704 Bochum
Germany
Tel. +49-(0)234-9357951
Fax. +49-(0)234-9357952
Web: http://www.cycosys.com

Cyonex
Hanju Bldg, 6th Floor, 125,
Nonhyun-dong,
Kangnam-gu
Séoul
Korea
135-10
Tel: (822)-511-5353
Fax: (822)-511-6444
Web: http://www.cyonex.com

Dadgum Games
P.O. Box 1154
Issaquah, Washington 98027-
1154
United States
Web: http://www.dadgum.com

Damage Studios
640 second street, 2nd floor
San Francisco, California 94107
United States
Tel: +1 415 495 7384
Fax: +1 415 495 7910
Web: http://www.damagestudios.com

Darkblack Ltd
Unit 7, Follingsby Avenue
Follingsby Park, Gateshead
Tyne & Wear, NE10 8YF
United Kingdom
Tel: +44 (0) 191 418 9900
Fax: +44 (0) 191 418 9901
Web: http://www.darkblack.co.uk

Dark Star Studios
1316 Knob Hill Road
San Marcos, California 92069
United States
Tel: 1-619-807-6712
Fax: 1-619-846-1847
Web: http://www.darkstarstudios.com

Dark Times Multimedia
Str. 1 Decembrie 1918 Nr.3
Bl.313 Ap.15
Brasov 2200
Romania
Tel: +40 92433448
Fax: +40 68476296
Web: http://www.dark-times.com

Darkmonth Studios
25 Satchwell Square
Packington Place
Leamington Spa
Warwickshire
CV31 1EP
Tel : +44 (0) 1926 832931
Web:http://www.darkmonthstudios.com

Darkworks Studio
38 rue du sentier
Paris 75002
France
Tel: 003 31 44 769 500
Web: http://www.darkworks.com
Web: http://www.darkworks-studio.com

Data Becker Corp.
210 Highland Avenue,
Needham Heights,
Massachussets 02494
United States
Tel: 1-781-453-2340
Fax: 1-781-433-2663
Web: http://www.databecker.com

Data Design Interactive
10/11 Birmingham Street
Halesowen
West Midlands
England
B63 3HN
United Kingdom
Tel: +44 (0)121 504 3820
Fax: +44 (0)121 585 1231
Web: http://www.datadesign.uk.com

Data East Corp.
Japan
Tel: 03-5370-0700
Web: http://www.dataeast-corp.co.jp

Datam Polystar Co. Ltd.
Tokyo, Japan
Tel: 00130-6-612643
Web: http://www.datam.co.jp

Davilex
PO box 174
3990 DD Houten
The Netherlands

Tel: +31 (0)30 - 63 54 222
Fax: +31 (0)30 - 63 50 007
Web: http://www.davilex.nl

Dawn Interactive Srl, The
via Pontinia 50
04100 Latina
Italy
Tel: +39-0773-664877
Fax: +39-0773-416786
Web: http://www.thedawn.it

Day 1 Studios, LLC
820 West Jackson Blvd.
Suite 350
Chicago, Illinois 60607
United States
Tel: 1-312-258-0500
Fax: 1-312-258-0600
Web: http://www.day1studios.com

Day 1 Studios, LLC
10955 Golden West Dr.
Suite E
Hunt Valley, Maryland 21031
United States
Tel: 1-410-785-7662
Fax: 1-410-785-7673
Web: http://www.day1studios.com

Daydream Software AB
Box 239
901 05 Umeå
Gösta Skoglunds väg 2
Sweden
Tel: 090 - 70 66 70
Fax: 090 - 70 66 79
Web: http://www.daydream.se

Daylight Productions
1561 Laurel Street, Suite A
San Carlos, California 94070
United States
Tel: 1-650-592-9144
Fax: 1-650-592-9146
Web:
http://www.daylight-productions.com

D'Carlos & Covett Comunicação
Rua Barao Do Triunfo, 520, Suite 11
Sao Paulo 04602-020

Brazil
Tel: (1-940) 387-4189
Web: http://www.yexi.game.new.net

DC Studios
410, Saint Nicolas, bur. 510
Montréal, Québec H2Y 2P5
Canada
Tel: 1-514-849-2555
Fax: 1-514-849-2284
Web: http://www.lienmultimedia.com

Deadline Games Plc.
Sankt Peders Stræde 45, 2nd floor
DK-1453 Copenhagen
Denmark
Tel: +45 3313 1275
Fax: +45 3313 1285
Web: http://www.deadlinegames.com

Deadly Games
PO box 676
Bridgehampton, New York 11932
Tel: 1-631-537-6060
Fax: 1-631-537-3299
Web: http://www.deadlygames.com

DECK13 Interactive GmbH
Sternstr. 23
60318 Frankfurt
Germany
Web: http://www.deck13.com

Deep Red Games Ltd
The Courtyard
Brooklands
Broughton
Milton Keynes
MK16 0HU
United Kingdom
Tel: 44 (0) 1908 393837
Fax: 44 (0) 1908 393951
Web: http://www.deepred.co.uk

Deep Shadows
60 years of Greate October St,
55, room. 131
Kremenchug, ua 02152 UA
Tel: 380-44-539-4885
Fax: 380-44-539-4885
Web: http://www.deep-shadows.com

Deep Space Inc.
Osaka, Japan
Tel: 0727-27-5970
Web: http://deepspace.scei.co.jp

Deibus Studios
Microtime House
Bonny Street
Camden Town
London
NW1 9PG
United Kingdom
Tel: +44 020 7267 4667
Fax: +44 020 7267 4399
Web: http://www.deibus.com

Delphine Software
150 Boulevard Haussmann
75008 Paris
France
Web: http://www.delphinesoft.com

Delta Tao
8032 Twin Oaks Ave.
Citrus Heights, California 95610
United States
Fax: 1-408-884-2345
Web: http://www.deltatao.com

Demiurge Studios
429 First Ave. Floor 1
Pittsburgh, Pennsylvania 15219
United States
Tel: 1-412-433-9834
Web: http://www.demiurgestudios.com

Denki Ltd.
Level 5
The EPICentre
9 West Bell Street
Dundee DD1 1HG
United Kingdom
Tel: (+44) (0) 1382 308686
Fax: (+44) (0) 1382 308688
Web: http://www.denki.co.uk

DEreditaSoft Gaming
Staten Island, New York
United States
Tel: 1-718-227-5226
Web: http://dereditasoft.com

Destination Games
7000 N. Mopac Expwy, Suite 2004
Austin, Texas 78731
United States
Tel: 1-512-514-6645
Web:http://www.destination-games.com

Destination Software, Inc.
400 North Church Street, Suite 260
Moorestown, New Jersey 08057
United States
Tel: 1-888-654-4447
Web: http://www.destinationsoftwareinc.com

Destrax Entertainment Software
Herforderstrasse 260
33609 Bielefeld
Germany
Tel: 0179-63 73 98 4
Web: http://www.destrax.de

Detalion games developers
Rzeszow, Poland
Web: http://www.detalion.com

Dexterity Software
P.O. Box 571961
Tarzana, California 91357-1961
United States
Web: http://www.dexterity.com

Dexterity Software
20944 Elkwood St.
Canoga Park, California 91304
United States
Tel: 1-818-341-5133
Fax: 1-530-579-7241
Web: http://www.dexterity.com

DeVisions
Turkenstrasse 55 - 57
80799 München
Germany
Tel: 089-27 77 76 -18 (-0)
Fax: 089-27 77 76 -76
Web: http://www.devisions.de

Dhruva Interactive
#67, 4th Main,
1st Cross
Domlur 2nd Stage
Bangalore
560 071, India
Tel: +91 80 535 6644
Fax: +91 80 535 3151
Web: http://www.dhruva.com

Diavlo, Inc.
11734 Wilshire Blvd.,
Los Angeles, California 90025
United States
Tel: 1-310.445.0032
Web: http://www.diavlo.com

DICE
Box 531 60
400 15 Gothenburg
Tel: 031- 60 98 00
Fax: 031- 60 98 10
Web: http://www.dice.se

DICE
Maria Skolgata 83 TR 5
118 53 Stockholm
Tel: 08- 54 51 84 80
Fax: 08- 54 51 84 97
Web: http://www.dice.se

DICE
148 Fullarton St.
Unit 406, London, Ontario
Canada N6A 5P3
Tel: +1 (519) 675 9993.
Web: http://www.dice.se

die multimedia schmiede
Gesellschaft für Medienlösungen mbH
Baaderstraße 79
D-80469 München
Germany
Tel: ++ 49 / 89 / 65 12 45 - 0
Fax: ++ 49 / 89 / 65 12 45 - 29
Web: http://www.dmms.de

DiezelPower Studios
Nice, France
Web: http://www.diezelpower.com

DiezelPower Studios
Yokohama, Japan
Web: http://www.diezelpower.com

DiezelPower Studios
San Francisco, California
United States
Web: http://www.diezelpower.com

Digital ADventure
Shaw Court
630 3rd Av SW, Suite 501,
Calgary, AB T2P 4L4
Canada
Tel: 1-403-444-4243
Web:
http://www.www.digital-adventure.com

Digital Amuse Network
rice field town 2-19 D2 building
Chiyoda Ku Kanda
Tokyo, Japan
Tel: 03-5207-6651
Fax: 03-5207-6652
Web: http://www.dams.co.jp

Digital Amuse Network
2-21 Awazi Cho MH building 1f B1
Chiyoda Ku Kanda
Tokyo, Japan
Tel: 03-5256-5391
Fax: 03-5256-5392
Web: http://www.dams.co.jp

Digital Animations plc
The Lighthouse
70 Mitchell Street
Glasgow
G1 3LX
Tel: +44 (0) 141 582 0600
Fax: +44 (0) 141 582 0699
Web:http://www.digital-animations.com

Digital Anvil
316 Congress Avenue
Austin, Texas 78701
United States
Tel: 1-512-457-0129
Fax: 1-512-457-0404
Web: http://www.digitalalvil.com

Digital Complete
1720 Yucca Rd,
Oceanside, California 92054
United States
Tel: 1-760-722-0266
Web: http://www.digitalcomplete.com

Digital Design Multimedia
Via Malaspina, 30
90145 Palermo
Italy
Tel: 39 091 6812443
Web: http://www.netdigitaldesign.com

Digital Dialect
Calabasas, California
United States
Web: http://www.digitald.com

Digital Dream Studios
553-3 Dogok-Dong, Kangnam-gu
135-270 Seoul, Korea
Tel: (822)2140-4000
Fax: (822)578-0933
Web: http://www.ddsdream.com

Digital Eclipse Software, Inc U.S.
5515 Doyle Street
Suite No. 1
Emeryville, California 94608
United States
Tel: 1-510-547-6101
Fax: 1-510-547-6104
Web: http://www.digitaleclipse.com

Digital Eclipse Software, Inc
Canada
1965 West 4th Ave #201
Vancouver, British Columbia
V6J1M8
Canada
Tel: 1-604-738-9292
Fax: 1-604-738-9294
Web: http://www.digitaleclipse.com

Digital Extremes
1807 Wonderland Rd. N.
London, Ontario
Canada
N6G 5C2
Tel: 1-519-656-4260

Fax: 1-519-471-9972
Web: http://www.digitalextremes.com

Digital Fiction
215, St-Jaques Ouest, bur. 220
Montréal, Québec H2Y 1M6
Canada
Tel: 1-514-281-5701
Fax: 1-514-281-5671
Web: http://www.digital-fiction.com

DigitalFlux Entertainment, LLC
New York, New York
United States
Web: http://www.digitalflux.com

Digital Fusion Inc.
1590 Benedict Canyon Dr.
Beverly Hills, California 90210
United States
Fax: 1-310-274-3289
Web: http://www.fusiongames.com

Digital Gamecraft
Post Office Box 4936
East Lansing, Michigan 48826-
4936
United States
Tel: 1-517-337-3905
Fax: 1-517-337-4420
Web: http://www.digitalgamecraft.com

Digital Illusions CE AB
P.O. Box 531 60
400 15 Gothenburg
Sweden.
Tel: +46 (0)31 60 98 00
Fax: +46 (0)31 60 98 10
Web: http://www.dice.se

Digital Illusions CE Stockholm AB
Maria Skolgata 83, 5th floor
118 53 Stockholm
Sweden
Tel: +46 (0)8 545 184 80
Fax: +46 (0)8 545 184 97.
Web: http://www.dice.se

Digital Illusions Canada Inc (CE)
148 Fullarton St.
Unit 406
London, Ontario
Canada N6A 5P3
Tel: +1 (519) 675 9993
Fax: +1 (509) 694 81 28
Web: http://www.dice.se

Digital Impact
Nevada
United States
Fax: 1-775-402-4814
Web: http://www.game-club.com

Digital Integration
Watchmoor Trade Centre
Watchmoor Road
Camberley, Surrey
GU15 3AJ
United Kingdom
Web: http://www.digint.co.uk

Digital Knights
938 54th St. Suite B-1
Brooklyn, New York 11219
United States
Web: http://www.digitalknights.com

Digital Legends Entertainment
C/ Casp,nº 116
Barcelona
08013
Spain
Tel: +34-932444151
Fax: +34-932444151
Web: http://www.digital-legends.net

Digital Leisure Inc.
33 Cedar Ridge Road
Gormley, Ontario
Canada L0H 1G0
Web: http://www.digitalleisure.com

Digital Plans Entertainment Co.
609 Unit, Hangang Bldg, 16-91
Hangang Ro 3Ga, Yong San Ku
Seoul Korea, Seoul
Tel: +82-2-6354-5824
Fax: +82-2-6354-5825
Web: http://www.digitalplans.co.kr

Digital Reality
Roppentyu utca 53.
LogoTrade Centre, 2nd floor
1139 Budapest
Hungary
Tel: +36 1-2884080
Fax: +36-1-2884085
Web: http://www.digitalreality.hu

Digital Soapbox
1509 Moravian St.
Philadelphia, Pennsylvania 19102
United States
Web: http://www.digital-soapbox.com

Digital Soapbox
31 Harrow Road
Levittown, Pennsylvania 19056
United States
Tel: 1-215-563-9595
Web: http://www.digital-soapbox.com

Digital Tainment Pool GmbH
Usedomstraße 19
22047 Hamburg
Tel.: +49-(0)40 / 66 99 10 - 0
Fax: +49-(0)40 / 66 99 10 - 10
Web: http://www.dtp-ag.de

Digital Tome L.P.
P.O. Box 8759
Spring, Texas 77387-8759
United States
Web: http://www.digital-tome.com

Digital Velocity, LLC
7414 Inwood Road,
Catonsville, Maryland, 21228
United States
Tel: 1-410-747-8611
Web: http://www.digitalvelocity.com

Digitalo studios, inc.
9144 nw 53rd manor
Coral Springs, Florida 33067
United States
Tel: 1-954-646-5613
Web: http://www.digitalo.com

Digitalo studios, inc.
6365 nw 6 way suite 140
Fort lauderdale, Florida 33309
United States
Tel: 1-954-646-5613
Web: http://www.digitalo.com

Digitalo Japan:
digitalo studios, inc.
arc villa K B105
307-1 kurono 501-1131
Gifu
Japan
Web: http://www.digitalo.com

Dimps Corp.
7F, Daiichi Kasai Bldg.,
1-1-8, Shinsenrinishi-machi,
Toyonaka, Osaka
Web: http://www.dimps.co.jp

Dimsdale & Kreozot United
Games Manufacture
11 Sunnyvale Place
Belmont,
4153 QLD
Australia
Web:http://www.dimsdale-kreozot.com

Dimsdale & Kreozot United
Games Manufacture
29 chadford street
Macgregor,
4109 QLD
Australia
Web:http://www.dimsdale-kreozot.com

Dinamic Multimedia S.A.
Saturno 1
Pozuelo de Alarcón (28224)
Spain
Tel: 902480 482
Fax: 902 380 382
Web: http://www.dinamic.com

Discovery Channel Multimedia
Bethesda, Maryland 20814
United States
Tel: 1-301-986-0444
Web: http://multimedia.discovery.com

Discreet Monsters
Turkenstrasse 55 - 57
80799
Munich
Germany
Tel: +49 - (0) 89 - 27 77 76 - 0
Fax: +49 - (0) 89 - 27 77 76 - 76
Web:http://www.discreetmonsters.com

Disney Interactive
Burbank, California
United States
Tel: 1-818-553-5000
Web:http://www.disneyinteractive.com

DistantStar Productions
709 Henry Street,
Roanoke Rapids, North Carolina,
27870
United States
Web:
http://www.distantstarproductions.com

Distinctive Developments Ltd
Sheffield Science Park
Arundel Street
Sheffield
South Yorkshire
S1 2NS
United Kingdom
Tel: +44 (0)114 281 2208
Fax: +44 (0)114 281 2207
Web: http://www.distdevs.co.uk

Diversions Entertainment, Inc.
12118 Panama City Beach
Parkway
Panama City Beach, Florida
United States
Web: http://www.omf.com

Divide by Zero
P.O. Box 654
Bel Air, Maryland 21014-0654
United States
Tel: 1-410-879-3924
Fax: 1-410-879-0561
Web: http://www.dividebyzero.com

DivoGames
Novgorod
Russia
Web: http://www.divogames.com

Dmagic
Parkvej 7 B
8660 Skanderborg
Denmark
Tel: (+45) 86 51 14 79
Web: http://www.dmagic.dk

Dodekeadron Software Creations,
Inc.
PL 143
01511 Vantaa
Finland
Web:
http://www.megabaud.fi/~teemut

Doki Denki Studio
21, Boulevard Yves Farge
69007 Lyon
France
Tel : +33 (0)4 72 71 46 46
Fax : +33 (0)4 72 71 16 50
Web: http://www.dokidenki.com

Domark
Ferry House, 51-57 Lacy Road
Putney
London
SW15 1PR
Tel: 44(0) 181-780 2222
Fax: 44(0) 181-780 1540

Double Click Pte., Ltd.
65 Rimrock Road
168121 Singapore
Web: http://www.town4kids.com

Double Fine Productions, Inc.
San Francisco, California
United States
Web: http://www.doublefine.com

DPVG Ltd.
United Kingdom
Web: http://www.dpvg.co.uk

Dragonfly GF Co., Ltd.
FI.30 Prime Center
546-4 Ku-ui-dong
Kwangjin-gu
Seoul
Korea
Tel: 02-3424-7722
Fax: 02-3424-7723
Web: http://www.dragonflygame.com

Dragonlight
19100 Ventura Blvd., Suite 10
Tarzana, California 91356
United States
Tel: 1-818-343-1701
Fax: 1-818-343-1826
Web: http://www.dragonlight.com

Dragonstone Software
660 N. Diamond Bar Blvd., Suite
200
Diamond Bar, California 91765
United States
Tel: 1-909-396-1978
Fax: 1-909-396-0468
Web: http://www.dragonstone.com

Drakan
Russia
Web: http://www.drakan.ru

Drakssen
Rodriguez Peña 1442,
Castelar, Buenos Aires, 1712
Argentina
Tel: +54-1146281682
Web: http://www.drakssen.com.ar

DreamCatcher Interactive
5000 Dufferin Street
Toronto, Ontario M3H 5T5
Canada
Tel: 1-416-638-5000
Web:
http://www.dreamcatchergames.com

Dream Design
Gernot Frisch
Niederfelder Str. 62
85077 Manching
Germany
Web: http://www.dream-d-sign.de

Dream Enterprise
Korea
Tel: 02-545-9532
Fax: 02-3442-2675
Web: http://www.dream21c.co.kr

Dream Factory Co., Ltd
Tokyo, Japan
Tel: 03-5449-2151
Fax: 03-5449-2152
Web: http://www.drf.co.jp

DreamForge Intertainment Inc.
RD#12 Box #204
Donahue Rd.
Greensburg, Pennsylvania
15601-9217
United States
Web: http://www.dreamforge.com

Dreams Interactive B.V.
London, England
United Kingdom
Web:
http://www.dreams-interactive.com

Dreamworks Interactive
P.O. Box 492147
Los Angeles, California 90049
United States
Fax: 1-310-234-7201
Web:
http://www.dreamworksgames.com

DTI
388, St-Jacques, 1er étage
Montréal, Québec H2Y 1S1
Canada
Tel: 1-514-499-0910
Fax: 1-514-499-0715
Web: http://www.dtisoft.com

Dungeon Crawl Software
710 Old Sambro Road
Halifax, Nova Scotia
B3V 1A2
Canada
Web:http://www.dungeon-crawl.com

Dynamic Animation Systems, Inc.
12015 Lee Jackson Highway,
Suite 200
Fairfax, Virginia 22033
United States
Tel: 1-703-503-0500
Fax: 1-703 425-2204
Web: http://www.d-a-s.com

Dynamic Animation Systems, Inc.
6035 Burke Center Parkway,
Suite 200
Burke, Virginia 22015
United States
Tel: 1-703-503-0500
Fax: 1-703-425-2204
Web: http://www.d-a-s.com

Dynamix - Sierra
3380 146th Place SE, Suite 300
Bellevue, Washington 98007
United States
Web: http://www.dynamix.com

DynoTech Software
35899 Leon Street
Livonia, Michigan 48150-2550
United States
Tel: 1-573-336-3390
Fax: 1-734-838-0074
Web: http://www.dynotech.com

DynoTech Software
PO BOX 4188
Waynesville, Missouri 65583
United States
Tel: 1-800-396-6832
Fax: 1-734-838-0074
Web: http://www.dynotech.com

Eagle Claw, Inc.
Bishop Ranch #6, 2440
Camino Ramon, Suite #225
San Ramon, California 94583
United States
Tel: 1-510-651-2413
Tel: 1-925-866-4182
Web:
http://www.eagleclawstudios.com

eBrainyGames, LLC
Germantown, Maryland 20874
United States
Web: http://www.ebrainygames.com

Eclipse Software Design
Austria
Web: http://www.eclipse.at

Eclypse Entertainment
c/o Creactive Media GmbH
Gaswerkstr. 11
D-26789 Leer
Germany
Tel.: 0491-92806-0
Fax : 0491-92806-18
Web: http://www.eclypse.de

Ecolotech Ltd.
2-9-22, Tamagawa, Ota-ku
Tokyo 146-0095
Japan
Tel: 81-3-5482-7211
Web: http://www.namco.co.jp

Edash
Oakland, California
United States
Web: http://www.edash.com

Eden Studios
83 - 85 Boulevard Vivier Merle
69487 Lyon Cedex 03
France
Tel: + 33(0) 4 72 91 75 75
Fax: +33(0) 4 72 91 75 70
Web: http://www.eden-studios.fr

Edge of Reality
6101 W. Courtyard Drive
Building 1, Suite 200
Austin, Texas 78730
United States
Web: http://www.edgeofreality.com

Edgies,
24 Broughton Street,
Edinburgh,
Scotland.
EH13RH
United Kingdom
Tel: +44 (0)131 477 3801
Fax: +44 (0)131 477 3802
Web: http://www.edgies.com

Edgies
San Francisco, California
United States
Web: http://www.edgies.com

Edmark
Enterprise Centre
P.O. Box 97021
Redmond, Washington 98073-9721
United States
Tel: 1-800-691-2986
Fax: 1-425-556-8430
Web: http://www.edmark.com

eGames
2000 Cabot Boulevard, Suite 110
Langhorne, Pennsylvania 19047-
1811
United States
Tel: 1-215-750-6606
Web: http://www.egames.com

eGenesis
Pittsburgh , Pennsylvania
United States
Tel: 1-412-247-3562
Web: http://www.egenesis.com

Egosoft
Heidestrasse 4
Würselen
52146
Germany
Tel: (49) 02405 / 4239970
Fax: (49) 02407 / 4239976
Web: http://www.egosoft.com

Eidos Interactive
London
United Kingdom
Tel: +44 (0) 181 636 3000

Fax: +44 (0) 181 636 3001
Web: http://www.eidosinteractive.com

Eigenocity, Inc.
2064 Woodbury Avenue, Suite 204
Portsmouth, New Hampshire 03801
United States
Tel: 1-603-373-6288
Fax: 1-603-559-9351
Web: http://www.eigenocity.com

EKKLA Research
22, rue du Docteur Lucas
Championnière
Paris 75013
France
Tel: 06-15312583
Web: http://www.ekkla-research.com

Eko Software
16, avenue Jean-Jaurès
94600 Choisy le Roi
Tel: 01 48 84 44 42
Fax: 01 48 84 44 41
Web: http://www.ekosystem.com

eku interactive e.K.
fuggerstrasse 37
10777 berlin
Germany
Tel: 030 - 217 76 85
Fax: 030 - 217 64 93
Web: http://www.eku.de

Electric Funstuff
27 W. 20th Street #501
New York, New York 10011
United States
Tel: 1-212-463-7559
Fax: 1-212-352-9071
Web: http://www.electricfunstuff.com

Electronic Arts, Inc.
209 Redwood Shores Parkway
Redwood City, California 94065
United States
Tel: 1-650-628-1500
Fax: 1-650-628-1380
Web: http://www.ea.com

Electric Storm Studios
Buchenstr.4
85276 Pfaffenhofen
Germany
Tel: 08441 490455
Fax: 08441 490457
Web: http://www.es-studios.com
Web: http://www.electric-storm.de

Electro Mechanic Games
Lyon, France
Web: http://www.emg.fr

Elite Systems Ltd UK
Prospect House
Prospect Road
Burntwood
Staffs WS7 0AL
England
United Kingdom
Fax: +44 (0) 703 115 1536
Web: http://www.elite-systems.co.uk

Elite Systems Ltd USA
34813 Candice Court
Fremont
California 94555
United States
Web: http://www.elite-systems.co.uk

Elixir Studios Ltd
4th Floor, The Forum
74 - 80 Camden Street
London NW1 0EG
United Kingdom
Tel (020) 7681 0000
Fax (020) 7681 0010
Web: http://www.elixir-studios.co.uk

elkware GmbH
Grenzweg 1
22880 Wedel
Germany
Tel: 0 41 03 - 90 20 90
Fax: 0 41 03 - 90 20 910
Web: http://www.elkware.com

Elo Interactive Media GmbH
Münsterstrasse 50
49176 Hilter
Germany
Tel: +49-5424-21373-0
Fax: +49-5424-21373-11
Web: http://www.elo-interactive.de

Elpin Systems, Inc.
1363 Jacklin Rd.
Milpitas, California 95035
United States
Tel: 1-800-723-9038
Tel: 1-408-956-0720
Fax: 1-408-956-0729
Web: http://www.elpin.com

Elsinore Studio
A division of Activision
9425 Sunset Drive Suite 150
Miami, Florida 33173-3248
United States
Tel: 1-305-503-3500
Fax: 1-305-503-3550
Web: http://www.activision.com

EMA Multimedia, Inc.
1800 Ave. of the Stars, Suite 430
Century City, California 90067
United States
Tel: 1-310-277-7379
Fax: 1-310-277-7378
Web:http://www.emamultimedia.com

Emperor Studios
Germany
Web: http://www.emperor-studios.de

Empire Interactive U.K.
The Spires, 677 High Road,
North Finchley,
London N12 0DA
United Kingdom
Tel: +44 (0) 20 8343 7337
Fax: +44 (0)20 8343 7447
Web:
http://www.empireinteractive.com

Empire Interactive U.S.A
16th Floor
580 California Street

San Francisco, California 94104
United States
Tel: 1-415-439-4854
Fax: 1-415-439-4928
Web: http://www.empireinteractive.com

Empire Interactive Germany
Lochhamer Str.9,
D-82152 Planegg b.
Munich
Germany
Tel: +49 (0) 89 857 95 131
Fax: +49 (0) 89 857 95 169
Web: http://www.empireinteractive.com

Empire Interactive Italy
Palazzo "Transatlantico"
Via Sinigaglia, 1
22100 Como CO
Italy
Tel.+39 031 576226
Fax: +39 031 576226
Web: http://www.empireinteractive.com

Encore Software, Inc.
16920 South Main Street
Gardena, California 90248
United States
Tel: 1-310-768-1800
Fax: 1-310-768-1822
Web: http://www.encoresoftware.com

Enigma Interactive
7-15 Pink Lane
Newcastle upon Tyne
United Kingdom
NE1 5DW
Tel: +44 191.26.12.99.1
Fax: +44 191.26.12.37.8
Web:
http://www.enigma-interactive.co.uk

Enix
4-31-8Yoyogi
Shibuya-ku
Tokyo
151-8544 Japan
Tel: 03-5352-6411
Web: http://www.enix.co.jp

Enix
Kourakuen Shinjuku Bldg 3F
4-15-7, Nishi-Shinjuku
Shinjuku-ku, Tokyo
160-8307 Japan
Tel: 03-5352-6404
Web: http://www.enix.co.jp

Enix
Yotsubashi Central Bldg,1-3-12
Shinmachi, Nishi-ku, Osaka
550-0013 Japan
Tel: 06-6535-0671
Web: http://www.enix.co.jp

Enix - BMF Corp.
11-2,Minamikurokawa
Asao-ku
Kawasak-shi
Kanagawa
215-0034 Japan
Tel: 044-989-5511
Web: http://www.enix.co.jp

Enix
Digital Entertainment Academy
Corporation
Satou Bldg,1-5-2,Kitashinjuku
Shinjuku-ku, Tokyo
169-0074 Japan
Tel: 03-5330-2870
Web: http://www.enix.co.jp

Enix America Inc.
1520 Eastlake Ave. E #205
Seattle, Washington 98102-3717
United States
Tel: 1-206-861-1274
Web: http://www.enix.com

enjoy Entertainment
Hollerather Str. 17
50937 Köln
Germany
Tel: 0221 / 9435059
Fax: 0221 / 9435059
Web: http://www.enjoy-e.de

Enlight Software
22/F, One Capital Place
18 Luard Road,
Wanchai
Hong Kong
Tel: (852) 2116-7575
Fax: (852) 2116-7576.
Web: http://www.enlight.com

Enlight Software
14/F, Great Smart Tower,
230 Wanchai Road,
Hong Kong.
Tel: (852)2575-2929
Fax: (852)2575-3500
Web: http://www.enlight.com

Enlightment Entertainment Ltd.
Lautatarhankatu 6, 4th floor
Helsinki 580
Finland
Tel: +358 9 774 1255
Web: http://www.enlightment.fi

Ensemble Studios
Suite 1600 - 10440 N Central
Expressway
Dallas, Texas 75231
United States
Web:http://www.ensemblestudios.com

Entale Aps
Søndergade 44, 3
8000 Aarhus C
Denmark
Tel: +45 26 796 794
Web: http://www.entale.com

Enterbrain, Inc.
Mikami Building
1-18-10 Wakabayashi
Setagaya-ku
Tokyo, 154-8528
Japan
Web: http://www.enterbrain.co.jp

Entertaining Games, Inc.
14N849 Lac Du Beatrice
West Dundee, Illinois 60118
United States
Tel: 1-847-836-8158

Fax: 1-847-836-8159
Web:http://www.entertaininggames.com

Epic Games, Inc.
5511 Capital Center Drive, Suite 675
United States
Raleigh, North Carolina 27606
Tel: 919-854-0070
Web: http://www.epicgames.com

Epic Megagames
110 Horizon Dr.
Raleigh, North Carolina 27615
United States
Tel: 1-919-676-6908
Web: http://www.epicgames.com

E-Pie Entertainment &
Technology Co., Ltd
Beijing
China
Tel: 86-10-62658399
Tel: 86-10-62658400
Fax: 86-10-62658380
Web: http://www.epiegame.com

EPSITEC
Switzerland
Web: http://www.epsitec.ch

Epix Interactive Studios
904 S. Roselle Rd. Box 111
Schaumburg, Illinois 60193
United States
Tel: 1-847-397-0837
Web: http://www.epixinteractive.com

Epoch Inc.
Tokyo, Japan
Tel: 03 3843 8812
Web: http://www.epoch.gr.jp

Escape Factory, Ltd.
1016 East Pike St, Suite #100
Seattle, Washington 98122
United States
Tel: 1-206-709-0107
Fax: 1-206-709-0107
Web: http://www.escapefactory.com

eSim Games
PO Box 4443
Mountain View, California 94040
United Stated
Web: http://www.esimgames.com

Espaço Informática Ltda.
Rua Voluntários da Pátria
1152 sala 25
Venâncio Aires - RS
CEP: 95.800-000
Brasil
Tel: +55 +51 37414833
Web: http://www.hades2.com

ESP Software
PC House
St. John's Road
Westcliff-on-Sea
Essex
SS0 7JY
England
Tel: 01702 434600
Fax: 01702 434888
Web: http://www.espsoftware.co.uk

Ethermoon Entertainment
P.O. Box 519
Edgemont, Pennsylvania 19028
United States
Web: http://www.ethermoon.com

Etranges Libellules
17 rue des Archers
69002 Lyon
France
Tel: 33 (0)4 72 40 24 72
Fax: 33 (0)4 72 40 27 19
Web: http://www.etranges-libellules.fr

Eugen Systems
20, rue Saint Fiacre
75002 Paris
France
Tel: + 33 (0)1 40 13 84 80
Web: http://www.eugensystems.com

Eurocom Entertainment Software
Eurocom House
Ashbourne Road
Mackworth
Derby
DE22 4NB
United Kingdom
Tel: + 44 (0) 1332 825100
Fax: + 44 (0) 1332 824823
Web: http://www.eurodltd.co.uk

Europress Software
Thomas House
Hampshire International
Business Park
Basingstoke
Hampshire
RG24 8WH
United Kingdom
Tel: +44 (0)1256-707727
Web: http://www.europress.co.uk

Eutechnyx Ltd.
Metro Centre East Business Park
Waterside Drive
Gateshead
Tyne & Wear
NE11 9HU
United Kingdom
Web: http://www.eutechnyx.com

Evermore88
583 D'Onofrio Dr. Suite #4
Madison, Wisconsin 53719
United States
Fax: 1-608-827-0065
Web: http://www.evermore88.com

Evillusion
1910, Marchand
Laval Québec H7G 4V6
Canada
Tel: 1-514-231-9339
Web: http://www.evillusion.com

Evolution Games
PO BOX 1682
Fortitude Valley 4006
Australia
Tel: + 61-7-3252-2321
Web: http://www.evolutiongames.com

Evolution Studios,
Unit 2 King's Court,
Manor Park,
Manor Farm Road,
Runcorn,
Cheshire,
WA7 1HR
England
United Kingdom
Web http://www.evos.net

Evolvestudios
21 Canmore Park
Stonehaven
Aberdeenshire AB39 2WH
United Kingdom
Tel: 01569 766620
Web: http://www.evolvestudios.co.uk

Evryware
8142 Kerbaugh Rd.
Olympia, Washington 98516
United States
Web: http://www.evryware.com

EXAKT Entertainment, Inc.
5757 West Century Boulevard, Suite 514
Los Angeles, California 90045-6406
Tel: 1-310-337-8480
Fax: 1-310-641-8711
Web: http://www.exaktent.com

Exood4 Studios
17, Rue de la Caravelle, appt 554
Toulouse, 31500
France
Tel: (33) 5 61 26 21 53
Web: http://www.exood4.com

Exortus Software GmbH
Im Sande 35
30926 Seelze, Germany
Tel: +49 511 486 08 20
Fax: +49 511 48 23 08
Web: http://www.exortus.com

Exortus Software GmbH
Im Sande 35
30926 Seelze, Germany
Tel: +49 (0) 511 486 08 20
Fax: +49 (0) 511 486 08 18
Web: http://www.exortus.com

Expedition Games
P.O. Box 8759
Woodlands, Texas 77387-8759
United States
Tel: 1-281-216-6503
Web:http://www.expedition-games.com

Expert Software
7646 Golden Triangle Dr
Eden Prairie, Minnesota 55344
United States
Tel: 1-952-918-9400
Fax: 1-952-918-9560
Web: http://www.expertsoftware.com

Expotato Corporation
135-080 Dae-Myung Bldg. 3F
725-4 Yuksam-dong
Kangnam-gu
Seoul, Korea
Tel: +82-2-553-9111
Fax: +82-2-521-6277
Web: http://www.expotato.com

Extreme FX
Plaza One
Telford Plaza
Irnomasters Way
Telford
Shropshire
TF3 4NT
United Kingdom
Web: http://www.extremefx.co.uk

Eyecon Pty., Ltd.
First Floor
197b Boundary Street
West End
Queensland 4101
Australia
Tel: +61 7 3846 0399
Fax: +61 7 3846 0399
Web: http://www.eyecon.com.au

EyeOne
Sørkedalsveien 10A
Oslo 304
Norway
Tel: +47 23331970
Web: http://www.eyeone.com

Eye One AS
Parc de l'Esplanade
12, rue Enrico Fermi
77462 Lagny sur Marne Cedex.
France
Tel: (+33) 1 60 31 04 03
Fax: (+33) 1 60 31 07 08
Web: http://www.eyeone.com

Factor 5, LLC
Entertainment Software
101 Lucas Valley Rd., Suite 300
San Rafael, California 94903
United States
Tel.: 1-415-492-5900
Fax: 1-415-492-5901
Web: http://www.factor5.com
GPS:
38°01'23" N
122°32'30" W

Fakeworlds
4343 Ocean View Blvd - Suite 150
Montrose, California 91020
United States
Tel: 1-818-957-0804
Web: http://www.fakeworlds.com

Fakt Software GmbH
Rosa-Luxemburg-Str. 76
08058 Zwickau
Germany
Tel: +49 (375) 2000 557
Fax: +49 (375) 2040 763
Web: http://www.fakt-software.com

FarSight Studios
611 Spruce Rd.,
Big Bear Lake, California 92315
United States
Tel: 1-909-866-0501
Fax: 1-909-866-0539
Web: http://www.farsightstudios.com

Fantasy Interfaces
Nygrand 10
PO Box 2258
Gamala Stan
103 16 Stockholm
Sweden
Tel: +46 8 402 43 21
Fax: +28 8 402 43 01
Web: http://www.fantasyinterfaces.com

Fantasy Studio
Poprad, Slovakia
Web: http://www.fantasystudio.sk

FASA Studio
One Microsoft Way
Redmond, Washington 98052
United States
Web: http://www.fasastudio.com

Fate Studios
Toronto, Canada
Web: http://www.FateStudios.com

Faust Logic, Inc.
4724 Wentworth Avenue South
Minneapolis, Minnesota, 55409
United States
Tel: 1-612-823-8137
Web: http://www.faustlogic.com

Fever Pitch Studios Inc
7000 West William Cannon, Suite 2150
Austin, Texas 78735
United States
Tel: 1-512-899-1889
Fax: 1-512-899-2672
Web: http://www.feverpitchstudios.com

Flight World
CH1217 Mayrin
Geneva
Switzerland
Web: http://www.flightworld.org

Flipside Network
240 West 35th Street, 18th floor
New York, New York 10001
United States
Tel: 1-212-209-4600
Fax: 1-212-209-4620
Web: http://www.flipside.com

Flipside Network
10940 Wilshire Blvd., 11th Floor
Los Angeles, California 90024
United States
Tel: 1-310-264-4300
Fax: 1-310-264-4399
Web: http://www.flipside.com

Fluent Entertainment
1701 Novato Boulevard, Suite 300
Novato, California 94947
United States
Tel: 1-415-493-2300
Fax: 1-415-493-2326
Web: http://fluentsolutions.com

Fluid Games
Monticello C. Otto
Italy
Web: http://www.fluidgames.net

FifthAxis Interactive Systems Inc.
1227 Valentine Drive
Cambridge, Ontario N3H-2P1
Canada
Tel: 1-519-241-5952
Fax: 1-509-463-9921
Web: http://www.fifthaxis.com

FifthAxis Interactive Systems Inc.
1114 W. Addison
Chicago, Illinois 60613
United States
Tel: 1-773-865-7534
Fax: 1-509-463-2032
Web: http://www.fifthaxis.com

Firaxis Games
11350 McCormick Road
Executive Plaza III, 12th Floor
Hunt Valley, Maryland 21031
United States
Web: http://www.firaxis.com

Fire Phoenix Co.ltd.
Unit 6A, Lianyi Building
NO.266 Heshan Road
Huli District, Xiamen
361009 China
Tel: +86-592-5529367
Fax: +86-592-5564527
Web: http://www.firephoenix.com.cn

FireFly Studios
Shakespeare House
168 Lavender Hill
London
SW11 5TG
United Kingdom
Web: http://www.fireflyworlds.com

Fireline Interactive, LLC
1650 W. 11th Ave. Suite 8
Eugene, Oregon 97402
United States
Tel: 1-541-684-7772
Web: http://www.firelineinteractive.com

Firetoad Software, Inc.
#222, 7260 12th Street SE
Calgary, Alberta, Canada
T2H 2S5
Tel: 1-403-686-6732
Fax: 1-403-640-4255
Web: http://www.firetoads.com

First Star Software, Inc.
24 Tanglewild Road
Chappaqua, New York 10514
United States
Tel: 1-914-238-3073
Fax: 1-914-238-3076
Web: http://www.firststarsoftware.com

Fishtank Interactive
möhlstrasse 23
81675 münchen
Germany
Fax: +49 (0)89-99 72 71 98
Web:http://www.fishtank-interactive.com

Flight Sim Central
820 Cartwright Road - Suite 101
Reno, Nevada 89511
United States
Tel: 1-800-477-7467
Web: http://www.fscentral.com

Flipside Network World
Headquarters
240 West 35th Street, 18th floor
New York, New York 10001
United States
Tel: 1-212-209-4600
Fax: 1-212-209-4620
Web: http://www.flipside.com

The Flipside Network
10940 Wilshire Blvd., 11th Floor
Los Angeles, California 90024
United States
Tel: 1-310-893-7000

Fax: 1-310-893-7094
Web: http://www.flipside.com

Fluid Games
Italy
Web: http://www.fluidgames.net

Flying Lab Software
1905 Queen Anne Ave North Suite 300
Seattle, Washington 98109-2549
United States
Tel: 1-206-272-9815
Fax: 1-206-272-9818
Web: http://www.flyinglab.com

Flying Rock Enterprises, LLC
488 Kennesaw Avenue
Marietta, Georgia
United States
Tel: 1-770-426-1581
Fax: 1-770-425-3226
Web: http://www.flyingrockllc.com

Flying Tiger Development
1901 E. Lambert Rd. Suite 111
La Habra, California 90631
United States
Fax: 1-562-697-7736
Web: http://www.ftdgames.com

Force 12 Studios
Denver, Colorado
United States
Web: http://www.g2interactive.com

Force 85
1418 North Carolina Ave NE
Washington, DC 20002
United States
Web: http://www.force85.com

Fortyfive Co. Ltd.
Shinjuku, Japan
Tel: 03-3350-1541
Web: http://www.xlv.co.jp

Fox Interactive
P.O. Box 900

Beverly Hills, California 90213-0900
United States
Web: http://www.foxinteractive.com

Fox Interactive
2121 Avenue of the Stars, 25th Flr
Los Angeles, California 90067
United States
Web: http://www.foxinteractive.com

Freedom Games
P. O. Box 43273
Baltimore, Maryland 21236-0273
United States
Web:http://www.freedomgamesinc.com

Free Mind software
ul. Bularnia 5
31-222 Kraków
Poland
Tel: +48 12 4200428
Fax: +48 12 4200427
Web:http://www.freemindsoftware.com

Free Radical Design
Unit 1 Interchange 25
Bostocks Lane
Sandiacre
Nottingham
NG10 5QG
United Kingdom
Web: http://www.frd.co.uk

Freeverse Software
447 West 24th Street
New York, New York 10011
United States
Web: http://www.freeverse.com

Friendly Software Corporation
Maumee, Ohio
United States
Tel: 1-419-868-6090
Fax: 1-419-868-6099
Web:http://www.friendlysoftware.com

Frog City Software
2002 Irving Street
San Francisco, California 94122
United States
Tel: 1-415-661-8221
Fax: 1-415-731-5398
Web: http://www.frogcity.com

Frogwares Ireland
22 Northumberland Road
Ballsbridge, Dublin 4, Ireland
Tel: 353 1 679 44 79
Fax: 353 1 679 44 79
Web: http://www.frogwares.net

Frogwares France
109 Avenue Foch,
94120, Fontenay sous Bois
Paris, France
Tel: 33 (0) 1 48 76 66 30
Fax: 33 (0) 1 48 76 66 30
Web: http://www.frogwares.net

Frogwares Ukraine
of. 607, 83-a Melnikova
Kiev, Ukraine
Tel: 380 44 495 25 46
Fax: 380 44 495 25 46
Web: http://www.frogwares.net

From Software Inc.
Japan
Tel: 03-3320-6071
Web: http://www.fromsoftware.co.jp

Front Fareast Industrial Corp.
4F-2, No. 190, Chung-Hsing Road Sec. 2
Hsin-Tien City, Taipei, Taiwan
R.O.C.
Tel: 886-2-2138409
Web: http://www.front.com.tw

Frontier Developments Ltd.
Saxon Farm, Longmeadow, Lode
Cambridge, England
CB5 9HA
United Kingdom
Tel: +44 1223 811753
Fax: +44 1223 812780
Web: http://www.frontier.co.uk

Full-Fat
14th Floor
Coventry Point
Market Way
Coventry
West Midlands,CV1 1EA
United Kingdom
Web: http://www.full-fat.com

Full-On Amusement
pmb 5, 205 De Anza Boulevard
San Mateo, California 94402
United States
Web: http://www.full-on.com

Funatics Developments
Aktienstrasse 212
45473 Mülheim an der Ruhr
Germany
Tel: +49(0)208 439 270 60
Tel. +49 (0) 208 388 1015
Fax: +49(0)208 439 270 61
Fax. +49 (0) 208 388 1017
Web: http://www.funatics.de

Funcom Inc.
PO Box 14390
Durham, North Carolina 27709-14390
United States
Web: http://www.funcom.com

Funcom Oslo A/S
Karenslyst Alle 5
N-0277 Oslo, Norway
Phone: +47 2242 0102
Fax: +47 2242 0302
Web: http://www.funcom.com

Funcom Switzerland GmbH
Dufourstrasse 131
8008 Zurich
Switzerland
Phone: +41 1 422 8977
Fax: +41 1 422 8984
Web: http://www.funcom.com

Fun Labs
8 Unirii Blvd.
Bl. 7A, District 5
Bucuresti 76104
Romania
Web: http://www.funlabs.com

Fungus Amungus, Inc.
261 Jersey Street
San Francisco, California 94114
United States
Web:http://www.fungusamungus.com

Funny Garbage
73 Spring Street, Suite 406
New York, New York 10012
United States
Tel: 1-212-343-2534
Fax: 1-212-343-3645
Web: http://www.funnygarbage.com

Furious Entertainment
Suite 200, 1111 Homer Street
Vancouver, BC, Canada
V6B 2Y1
Tel: 1-604-647-0422
Fax: 1-604-893-8801
Web:http://www.furiousentertainment.com

Furious Games
355 East 50 South
American Fork, Utah 84003
United States
Tel: 1-801-756-1955
Web: http://www.furiousgames.com

Future Interactive
Von-der-Recke Str. 131b
58300 Wetter (Ruhr)
Germany
Tel: 02335-963894
Web: http://www.futureint.de

Fusion Games
Digital Fusion Inc.
1590 Benedict Canyon Dr.
Beverly Hills, California 90210
United States
Fax: 1-310-274-3289
Web: http://www.fusiongames.com

G2 Interactive
Seattle, Washington
United States
Web: http://www.g2interactive.com

G5 Software
Moscow, Russia
Tel: +7 (095) 258-35-86
Fax: +7 (095) 258-35-86
Web: http://www.G5Software.com

Gabriel Interactive
401 N. College, Suite A
Indianapolis, Indiana 46202
United States
Tel: 1-317-396-0777
Fax: 1-317-396-0778
Web:http://www.gabrielinteractive.com

Gainax
Tokyo, Japan
Tel: 0422-53-5568
Fax: 0422-53-5565
Web: http://www.gainax.co.jp

Galactic Village Games
405 Waltham Street, Suite 342
Lexington, Massachusetts 02421
United States
Web: http://www.galactic-village.com

Galcom
13788 NW 22nd Plc
Fort Lauderdale, Florida 33323
United States
Web: http://www.3000ad.com

Galilea
12, rue Ampere
Grenoble
France
38000
Tel: +33 4.38.12.99.0
Fax: +33 4.38.12.99.2
Web: http://www.galilea.com

GameAgents Corp
1633 Mountain Rd. Suite 12
Moncton, NB
Canada E1G1A5
Tel: 1-877-GameAgent
Tel: 1-506-855-4945
Fax: 1-506-852-9510
Web: http://www.gameagents.com

Game Arts Co. Ltd.
2 Chome 9th 9 First Ikebukuro
White Building 7f
Toshima Ku south Ikebukuro
Tokyo 171-0022
Japan
Tel: (03) 3984-1136
Tel: (03) 3984 8031
Fax: (03) 3984 7939
Web: http://www.gamearts.co.jp

GameBrains
Level 62 Tower 2
Petronas Twin Towers
Kuala Lumpur City Centre
Kuala Lumpur 50088
Malaysia
Tel: +60-3-7490-4566
Fax: +60-3-7490-4568
Web: http://www.gamebrains.com

Gamecity GmbH
Kanzleistr. 120
CH-8004 Zürich
Switzerland
Tel: +41-1-298 20 80
Web: http://www.infogrames.com

Gameday Software LLC
P. O. Box 1242
Fremont, California 94538
United States
Tel: 1-510-894-1618
Web: http://www.gamedayonline.com

GameEDU
Vasundhra Enclave
Mayur Vihar, 29
Delhi, 110096
India
Tel: 9811199402
Web: http://www.gameedu.net

GameEDU
252-A, East of Kailash
Sant Nagar, Lakshyadeep Plaza
New Delhi, 110096
India
Tel: 6405387
Web: http://www.gameedu.net

Game Freak Inc.
Tokyo, Japan
Tel: 03 3515 6846
Web: http://www.gamefreak.co.jp

GameFX Technology
35 Hartwell Avenue
Lexington, Massachusetts 02421-3102
United States
Web: http://www.gamefx.com

gameLab
368 broadway #210
New York, New York 10013
United States
Tel: 1-646-827-6644
Fax: 1-646-827-6645
Web: http://www.gmlb.com

Gameloft
45 West 25th Street, 9th Floor
New York, New York 10010
United States
Tel: 1-212-993-3000
Fax: 1-212-414-1460
Web: http://www.gameloft.com

Gameloft
625 Third Street, 3rd floor
San Francisco, California 94107
United States
Tel: 1-415-547-4000
Fax: 1-415-547-4001
Web: http://www.gameloft.com

Gameloft
5505 blvd St-Laurent, Suite 5000
Montreal, Quebec
H2T 1S6 Canada
Tel: 1-514-490-2040
Fax: 1-514-490-0882
Web: http://www.gameloft.com

Gameloft
35 rue Greneta
75002 Paris
France
Tel : + 33 (0)1 58 16 20 40
Fax : + 33 (0)1 58 16 20 41
Web: http://www.gameloft.com

Gameloft
Zimmerstr. 19
40215 Düsseldorf
Gemany
Tel : + 49(0)211-33800-600
Fax : + 49(0)211-33800-650
Web: http://www.gameloft.com

Gameloft
Vialle Cassala 22
20143 Milan
Italy
Tel: + 39 02 83 312 1
Fax: + 39 02 83 312 341
Web: http://www.gameloft.com

Gameloft
Avda Ragull, 60 2nd Floor
08190 Sant Cugat del Vallès
Barcelona
Spain
Tel: 34 93 544 15 00
Fax: 34 93 589 56 60
Web: http://www.gameloft.com

Gameloft
3F Kaiyuan Business Building
28 Zhichunli Haidan District
Beijing, 100086 PR
China
Tel : + 86 10 6254 2446
Fax : 86 10 8261 7417 0
Web: http://www.gameloft.com

Gameloft (UK) Limited
Suite 117
2 Lansdowne Row
London
W1J 6HL
United Kingdom
Tel: +44 7789 176 319
Web: http://www.gameloft.com

GamLogik
G419, Boul. Lafayette, bur.26
Longueuil, Québec J4K 3A4
Canada
Tel: 1-450-651-5723
Web: http://www.gamlogik.com

Game Makers
38 Arrowhead Drive
Burlington, New Jersey 08016
United States
Tel: 1-609-239-9344
Web: http://www.game-makers.com

Gameness Art Software, Inc.
Taipei, Tiawan
Tel: 8369-5660
Fax: 8369-5661
Web: http://www.gamenessart.com

GameOne Systems Limited
5/F Island Place Tower, 510 King's Road
North Point, Hong Kong
Tel: (852) 2314 7627
Fax: (852) 2907 8838
Web: http://www.gameone.com

Games Kitchen Ltd., The
1 Michaelson Square
Livingston
Scotland
EH54 7DP
United Kingdom
Tel: +44 (0) 1506 20 30 20
Fax: +44 (0) 1506 47 22 09
Web: http://www.gameskitchen.com

Gamesquad
Le Sextant 150, Grande Rue de
Saint-Clair
69300 Caluire - France
Tel: +33 (0)4 37 40 2000
Fax: +33 (0)4 37 40 2019.
Web: http://www.gamesquad.fr

Game Web design
Office 25
33 Zolotodolinskaya St.
Novosibirsk, 630090
Russia
Tel: +7(3832) 330547
Web: http://www.gamewebdesign.com

Gamesworks Limited
The American Barns
Banbury Road
Lighthorne
Warwick

Warwickshire
CV35 0AE
United Kingdom
Tel: +44 (0) 1926 652800
Fax: +44 (0) 1926 650111
Web: http://www.gamesworks.co.uk

Gameworld Seven Ltd.
The Studio
12 Goat Street
Haverfordwest
SA61 1PX
United Kingdom
Tel: 01437 760837
Web: http://www.gw7.co.uk

GammanSoft Corporation
unit 617, Blanco Center
119 LP Leviste St., Salcedo Village
Makati City, Philippines 1200
Tel: (63)(02) 812-3701
Fax: (63)(02) 812-3499
Web: http://www.gammansoft.com

Gangster Games
Niagara, Falls Ontario
Canada
Tel: 1-905-325-FEAR
Web: http://www.gangstergames.com

Game Titan
820 West 3rd ST #1105,
Austin, Texas 78701
United States
Tel: 1-512-494-9287
Web: http://www.gametitan.com

GameTronics
59 Romina Drive
Concord, Ontario L4K 4Z9
Canada
Tel: 1-905-738-5400
Fax: 1-416-738-5414
Web: http://www.gametronics.com

Ganymede Technologies s.c.
Al. 29 Listopada 45A/11
31-425 Kraków, Poland
Tel: +48 12 412 69 29
Fax: +48 12 412 69 29
Web: http://www.ganymede.com.pl

GarageGames
Eugene, Oregon
United States
Web: http://www.garagegames.com

Garfield Games
5440 East 450
North Albany, Indiana 47320
United States
Tel: 1-765-287-2292
Fax: 1-765-287-2329
Web: http://www.garfieldgames.com

Gas Powered Games
PMB 473
218 Main Street
Kirkland, Washington 98033
United States
Web: http://www.gaspowered.com

Gatehouse Games Ltd.
St. Michaels Studio
Derby
DE1 3SU
United Kingdom
Tel: 01332 616160
Web:http://www.gatehousegames.com

Gathering of Developers
Dallas, Texas
United States
Tel: 1-212-696-2000
Web: http://www.godgames.com

Gatorhole AB
Kocksgatan 52
116 29 Stockholm
Sweden.
Tel: +46-8-6410560
Web: http://gatorhole.com

Gearbox Software
101 East Park Blvd., Suite 1069
Plano, Texas 75074
United States
Tel: 1-972-312-8202
Fax: 1-972-312-8318
Web: http://www.gearboxsoftware.com

Genepool
Bruntwood Hall
Bruntwood Park
Cheadle, Cheshire, SK8 1HX
United Kingdom
Tel: +44(0) 161 495 7110
Web: http://www.genepool-uk.com

Gekko Software GmbH
P.O. Box 24 24
D-55014 Mainz
Germany
Fax: +49/6136-994910
Web: http://www.gekko-software.de

General Entertainment Co.
Tokyo, Japan
Tel: 03-5414-2369
Tel: 03-3248-2019
Web: http://www.genet.co.jp

Genetic Anomalies
35 Hartwell Avenue
Lexington, Massachusetts 02421
United States
Tel: 1-888-ANOMALIES
Tel: 1-781-863-8868
Fax: 1-617-531-2042
Web: http://www.geneticanomalies.com

GeneX Corp.
Sakura Building 4F 4-6-1 Ohi
Shinagawa-ku
Tokyo
Japan 140-0014
Web: http://www.generation-x.co.jp

Genki Co.,Ltd.
Shinjuku Lambdax Bldg.
2-4-12, Okubo
Shinjuku-ku, Tokyo
169-0072, Japan
Web: http://www.genki.co.jp

Ghost 3D, LLC
17155 Robey Drive
Castro Valley, California 94546
United States
Tel: 1-510-481-1146
Fax: 1-510-481-1176
Web: http://www.ghost3d.com

Gigantic Games
815-a Brazos Street #313
Austin, Texas 78701-9996
United States
Web: http://www.giganticgames.com

Gigantic Designs
211 E 7th Street Suit 640
Austin, Texas 78701
United States
Web: http://www.giganticdesigns.com

Gigawatt Studios
6255 Sunset Blvd. Suite 1111
Hollywood, California 90028
United States
Tel: 1-323-856-5245
Fax: 1-323-856-5240
Web: http://www.gwatt.com

GIME International Pte Ltd
38c North Canal Road
Singapore
Tel: +65 6874 3508
Web: http://www.gime.org

Gizmo Games
Los Angeles, California
United States
Web: http://www.gizmogames.com

Glass Egg Digital Media
E-Town.
7th Floor, 364 Cong Hoa St.
Tan Binh District
Ho Chi Minh City
Vietnam
Tel: 84 8 810 9018
Fax: 84 8 810 9013
Web: http://www.glassegg.com

Glass Eye Entertainment
701 Brazos Ave. Suite 710
Austin, Texas 78701
United States
Tel: 1-512-457-8647
Fax: 1-512-472-1561
Web: http://www.glasseye.net

GLIPS Entertainment, Inc.
102 West Vance St.
FuQuay-Varina, North Carolina
27526
United States
Tel: 1-919-557-3030
Web:
http://www.glipsentertainmentinc.com

GM-Squared
Schwackendorf 33
24376 Hasselberg
Germany
Tel: 04642-96 51 52
Fax: 04642-96 51 53
Web: http://www.gm-squared.de

GMMEntertainment s.r.l.
Strada Statale Savonesa 9,
15050
Rivalta Scrivia (AL)
Italy
Tel: 0131-860258
Fax: 0131-860607
Web:
http://www.gmmentertainment.com

Global A Entertainment, Inc.
Tokyo, Japan
Tel: 0422-23-8720
Tel: 0422-41-5119
Fax: 0422-23-8730
Fax: 0422-41-5129
Web: http://www.gae.co.jp

Global Star Software Ltd.
6225 Kenway Drive
Mississauga, Ontario - L5T 2L3
Canada
Phone: 1-905-795-9880
Fax: 1-905-795-3237
Web:http://www.globalstarsoftware.com

GMM Entertainment s.r.l.
Ripa di Porta Ticinese, 91
20143 Milano
Italy
Tel: +39-02-8393374
Fax: +39-02-58103485
Web:
http://www.gmmentertainment.com

GMM Entertainment s.r.l.
Strada Statale Savonesa 9
15050 Rivalta Scrivia (AL)
Italy
Tel: +39-0131-860258
Fax: +39-0131-860607
Web:
http://www.gmmentertainment.com

GMX Media
78 York Street
London
W1H 1DP
United Kingdom
Web: http://www.gmxmedia.net

Gnostic Labs
256 Mathilda Dr. #8
Goleta, California 93117
United States
Tel: 1-805-685-5571
Fax: 1-630-477-0313
Web: http://www.gnosticlabs.com

GodGames
Dallas, Texas
United States
Tel: 1-212-696-2000
Web: http://www.godgames.com

GodGames
Austin, Texas
United States
Tel: 1-212-696-2000
Web: http://www.godgames.com

Goldtree Enterprises
4071 Crest Road
Pebble Beach, California 93953
United States
Web: http://www.goldtree.com

GolemLabs Laboratories
2100, rue King Ouest, bur. 240
Sherbrooke, Québec
J1L 2E8
Canada
Web: http://www.golemlabs.com

Gorilla Systems Corporation
4023 Tampa Road, Suite 2000
Oldsmar, Florida 34677
United States
Fax: 1-813-854-1320
Web: http://www.gorilla.com

Got Game Entertainment
33 Birch Hill Road
Weston, Connecticut 06883
United States
Web:http://gotgameentertainment.com

Gotham Games
New York, New York 10012
United States
Fax: 1-212-334-6644
Web: http://www.gothamgames.com

Graphic Simulations Corporation.
15400 Knoll Trail Dr. Suite #104
Dallas, Texas 75248
United States
Tel: 1-972-386-7575
Fax: 1-972-386-7875
Web: http://www.graphsim.com

Graphic State
5 Russell Street
Leamington Spa
Warwickshire
CV32 5QA
England
United Kingdom
Tel: +44 (0)1926 335935
Fax: +44 (0)1926-336812
Web: http://www.graphic-state.com

Gratuitous Games Inc
8989 Rio San Diego Dr.
Suite 170
San Diego, California 92108
United States
Tel: 1-619-297-6160
Web:
http://www.gratuitousgames.com

Gravity Corp.
5-6F Shingu Bldg.
620-2 Shinsa-Dong
Gangnam-Gu
Seoul
Korea 135-894
Web: http://www.gravity.co.kr

Gray Design Associates
P.O. Box 333
Northboro, Massachussets 01532
United States
Web: http://www.dgray.com

Gray Matter Studios
2038 Armacost Avenue
Los Angeles, California 90025
United States
Tel: 1-310-207-2899
Fax: 1-310-207-1229
Web: http://www.gmistudios.com

Green Dragon Creations, Inc.
301 Main Street
Water Valley, Mississippi 38965
United States
Tel: 1-662-473-HACK
Fax: 1-662-473-2122
Web: http://www.greendragon.com

Greenwood Enternainment
Phenomedia AG
Josef-Haumannstr. 10
44866 Bochum,
Germany
Tel: 02327 - 99 73 80
Fax: 02327 - 99 73 11
Web: http://www.greenwood.de

Grin
Stockholm, Sweden
Web: http://www.grin.se

Grip Studios Interactive
Kristianinkatu 15
00170 Helsinki
Finland
Tel: +358 9 5657 640
Fax: +358 9 5657 6410
Web: http://www.gripstudios.com

Groove
66 Dupont Street
Toronto, Ontario
Canada
M5R 1V2
Tel: 1-416-324-9894
Fax: 1-416-324-9790
Web: http://www.groovegames.com

Groove Alliance, The
6464 Sunset Blvd., Ste. 910
Hollywood, California 90028
United States
Tel: 1-323-962-3456
Fax: 1-323-962-5820
Web: http://www.3dgroove.com

GSC Game World
Lepse st, 4 ap. 516-518
Kiev
03067
Ukraine
Tel: +38 044 4410665
Web: http://www.gsc-game.com

GT Interactive Software
Corporation
417 5th Avenue
New York, New York 10016
United States
Web: http://www.gtinteractive.com

GU Inc.
Tokorozawa, Japan
Web: http://www.gu-inc.com

Gunnar Games
7210 SW 57 Avenue
Suite 210
Miami, Florida 33143
United States
Tel: 1-305-661-1639
Fax: 1-305-661-1739
Web: http://www.gunnargames.com

Gust
Nagano, Japan
Web: http://www.gust.jp

H2O Entertainment
12th Floor, 570 Granville St.
Vancouver, B.C.
Canada
V6C 3P1
Tel: 1-604-609-0925
Fax: 1-604-609-0938
Web: http://www.h2oent.com

Habitat North AB
Magasinsgatan 3,
SE-411 18, Gothenburg
Sweden
Tel: +46(0)31 136657
Web: http://www.habitatnorth.com

Haemimont Games
BIC IZOT, Fl. 4
Tzarigradsko Chaussee 7th km, Blvd.
Sofia 1784, Bulgaria
Tel: (+359 2) 965 0650,
Fax: (+359 2) 974 3469
Web: http://www.haemimont.bg

Hailstorm Entertainment Limited
12b South Bar
Banbury
Oxfordshire
OX16 9AA
United Kingdom
Tel: +44(0) 1295 70 9899
Fax: +44(0) 1295 70 9663
Web: http://www.hailstorm.co.uk

HAL Laboratory, Inc.
Tokyo, Japan
Web: http://www.hallab.co.jp

Hammerhead Ltd
Unit 12,
The Shakespeare Centre
Shakespeare Street
Southport
Merseyside
PR8 5AB
United Kingdom
Web: http://www.hammerhead.ltd.uk

Hamumu Software
PO Box 893172
Temecula, California 92589
United States
Web: http://hamumu.com

Handheld Games
16000 Bothell-Everett Highway,
Suite 2000
Mill Creek, Washington 98012
United States
Tel: 1-425-337-5958
Fax: 1-425-316-3897
Web:http://www.handheldgames.com

Handy Games
Kilianstr. 3
97437 Hassfurt
Germany
Tel: (+49) 9521 / 951 473
Fax: (+49) 9521 / 951 573
Web: http://www.handy-games.com

Happy-Grafix GbR
c/o Second Evolution Team
Rohrweg 7
08547 Plauen OT Jößnitz
Germany
Tel: 03741-529598
Fax: 03741-528674
Web: http://www.second-evolution.de

Happy Hour Entertainment LLC
1330 NW 14th Ave.
Portland, Oregon 97209
United States
Tel: 1-503-295-6800
Fax: 1-503-295-6636
Web:
http://www.happyhour-entertainment.com

Harmonic Vision
68 E. Wacker Place, 8th floor
Chicago, Illinois 60601
United States
Tel: 1-312-332-9200
Tel: 1-800-474-0903
Fax: 1-312-726-1946
Web: http://www.harmonicvision.com

Harmonix
675 Massachusetts Avenue, 6th Floor
Cambridge, Massachussets 02139
United States
Tel: 1-617-491-6144
Fax: 1-617-491-7411
Web: http://www.harmonixmusic.com

HB Studios
The Hive
Box 725, Lunenburg
Nova Scotia
Canada, B0J 2CO
Tel: 1-902-634-8316
Web: http://www.hb-studios.com

Head Games
7646 Golden Triangle Dr
Eden Prairie, Minnesota 55344
United States
Web: http://www.headgames.net

Headfirst Productions
Unit 3, Priory, Old London Road
Canwell, Sutton Coldfield
West Midlands
B75 5SH
United Kingdom
Tel: +44 (0) 121 308 8900
Fax: +44 (0) 121 308 8815
Web: http://www.headfirst.co.uk

Headgate Studios
1596 S. 500 W.
Bountiful, Utah 84010
United States
Tel: 1-801-298-3800 ext. 22
Fax: 1-801-298-9169
Web: http://www.headgatestudios.com

Heart-Line
Germany
Web: http://www.heart-line.de

Heavy3d Ltd.
Floor 3
134 Shoreditch Hight Street
London E1 6JE
United Kingdom
Tel: +44 (0)7950 4000 65
Web: http://www.heavy3d.com

Heavy Iron Studios
Culver City, California
United States
Web: http://www.heavy-iron.com

Heliogame Production
21, Boulevard Yves Farge
69007 Lyon
France
Tel: +33 (0)4 72 71 46 46
Fax: +33 (0)4 72 71 16 50
Web: http://www.heliogame.com

Helixe Games/THQ Inc.
35 Hartwell Ave.
Lexington, Massachusetts 02421
United States
Tel: 1-781-863-8868
Fax: 1-781-863-8878
Web: http://www.helixe.com

Her Interactive, Inc.
11808 Northup Way, Suite W-160
Bellevue, Washington 98005
United States
Tel: 1-425-889-2900
Fax: 1-425-822-6121
Web: http://www.herinteractive.com

Heuristic Park
1900 Century Blvd., Suite 17
Atlanta, Georgia 30345
United States
Web: http://www.heuristicpark.com

Hexacto Games Inc.
33 rue Prince, # 280
Montreal, Québec
H3C 2M7
Canada
Tel: 1-514-395-2882
Fax: 1-514-395-1120
Web: http://www.hexacto.com

Hi2 Limited
Harwell Innovation Centre
173 Curie Avenue
Harwell International Business Centre
Oxfordshire OX11 0QG
United Kingdom
Tel: +44 (0)1235 838516
Fax: +44 (0)1235 838517
Web: http://www.hi2.com

Hi Corporation
1-6-5 Higashiyama, Meguro-ku,
Tokyo 153-0043
Japan
Tel: +81-3-3710-2843
Fax: +81-3-3710-2844
Web: http://www.hicorp.co.jp

Hidden Dinosaur AB
Dalagatan 30
11329 Stockholm
Sweden
Web: http://www.hiddendinosaur.com

High Voltage Software, Inc.
2345 Pembroke Ave.
Hoffman Estates, Illinois 60195
United States
Fax: 1-847-490-9951
Web: http://www.high-voltage.com

HIPnTASTY, Inc.
80 Wall Street, 11th floor
New York, New York 10005
United States
Tel: 1-646-498-7055
Fax: 1-208-275-1642
Web: http://www.hipntasty.com

HiTech Creations, Inc.
210 Park Blvd., Suite 100
Grapevine, Texas 76051
United States
Tel: 1-817-251-1540
Fax: 1-817-251- 6731
Web: http://www.hitechcreations.com

Hitmaker Co., Ltd.
2-12-14 Higashikoujiya
Ohta-ku, Tokyo 144-0033
Japan
Web: http://www.hitmaker.co.jp

Holistic Design
5295 Hwy 78
D-337
Stone Mountain, Georgia 30087
United States
Web: http://www.holistic-design.com

Hoopla Entertainment
6545 E 4th Street
Scottsdale, Arizona 85251
United States
Tel: 1-480-874-0116
Fax: 1-480-874-0118
Web:http://www.whatsthehoopla.com

Horizont Entertainment OHG
Lohberg 44
47589 Uedem
Germany
Tel: 0221-589 08 79
Mobil: 0173- 543 47 30
Web:
http://www.horizont-entertainment.com

HOT-B USA, Inc.
1255 Post Street, Suite 1040
San Francisco, California 94109
United States
Tel: 1-415-567-9501
Web: http://www.hotb.com

Hot House
5th Floor
The Colston Tower
Colston Street
Bristol
BS1 4XE
United Kingdom
Web: http://www.hothouse.org

HotGen Studios
NLA Tower
12-16 Addiscombe Road
Croydon
Surrey
CRO OXT
Tel: +44 (0)20 8603 0555
Fax: +44 (0)20 8667 9592
Web: http://www.hotgen.com

Hothouse Creations Ltd
5th Floor, The Colston Tower
Colston Street
Bristol
BS1 4XE
United Kingdom
Tel: +44 (0)117 901 5100
Fax: +44 (0)117 901 5115
Web: http://www.hothouse.org

House of Tales
Germany
Web: http://www.house-of-tales.com

Housemarque
Kaisaniemenkatu 1D
00100 Helsinki
Finland
Tel: +358 9 637 586
Fax: +358 9 637 890
Web: http://www.housemarque.com

How in the World?
PO Box 5772
Deltona, Florida 32728-5772
United States
Web: http://www.howintheworld.com

HPS Simulations
PO Box 3245
Santa Clara, California 95055-3245
United States
Tel: 1-408-554-8381
Fax: 1-408-241-6886
Web: http://www.hpssims.com

Hudson Soft: Head office
Hudson Bldg.,5-4-22, Hiragishi 3-jo
Toyohira-ku
Sapporo City
Hokkaido 062-8622
Japan
Tel: 011-841-4622
Web: http://www.hudson.co.jp

Hudson Soft: Hudson Central
Laboratory / Hu-LAB
3-C62, Geijutsu-no-mori
Minami-ku
Sapporo City 005-0864
Japan
Tel: 011-591-4622
Web: http://www.hudson.co.jp

Hudson Soft: Hudson Studio
Shin Hokkaido Bldg.
Nishi, 4-3-1, Kita 7-jo, Kita-ku
Sapporo City, Hokkaido 060-0807
Japan
Tel: 011-746-4622
Web: http://www.hudson.co.jp

Hudson Soft: Hudson Tokyo
Ginza Ohno Bldg., 4-1-17, Tsukiji
Chuo-ku, Tokyo 104-8446
Tel: 03-3542-4622
Web: http://www.hudson.co.jp

Human Head Studios, Inc.
6325 Odana Road
Madison, Wisconsin 53719
United States
Tel: 1-608-298-0644
Web: http://www.humanhead.com

Humansoft Corporation
411 Borel Avenue
Suite 507
San Mateo, California 94402
United States
Tel.: 1-650-577-1000
Fax: 1-650-577-1035
Web: http://www.humansoft.com

Humongous Entertainment
3855 Monte Villa Parkway
Bothell, Washington 98021
United States
Tel: 1-425-486-9258
Fax: 1-425-951-1903
Web: http://www.infogrames.com

Hunex
Tokyo, Japan
Tel: 0422-23-1310
Web: http://www.hunex.co.jp

Hydravision Entertainment
31 rue de la Fonderie
59200 Tourcoing
France
Tel: +33 (0) 3 20 68 42 20
Fax: +33 (0) 3 20 68 42 21
Web: http://www.hydravision.com

HydraVision Entertainment
BP 2000
Tourcoing, France
59 203
Tel: +33 3 20 68 42
Fax: +33 3 20 68 42
Web: http://www.hydravision.com

Hyperion Entertainment
Belgium and Germany
Web:
http://www.hyperion-entertainment.com

Hypermedia
Office 101
Trinity House
40 - 42 Byzantiou Street
2064 Strovolos, Nicosia
Cyprus
Tel: +357-22667112
Fax: +357-22667187
Web: http://www.hyper.com.cy

Hyperspace Cowgirls
857 Broadway
New York, New York 10003
United States
Tel: 1-212-741-1350
Fax: 1-212-627-0615
Web: http://www.hygirls.com
http://www.hyperspacecowgirls.com

Hypnos Entertainment, Inc.
P.O. Box 1091
Soquel, California 95073
United States
Tel: 1-831-476-4102
Fax: 1-831-476-4126
Web:
http://www.hypnos-entertainment.com

Hypnotix
Little Falls, New Jersey
United States
Web: http://www.hypnotix.com

i4 Corporation
IK Building 2-24-9
Kamiosaki Shinagawa-ku Tokyo
141-8670 JAPAN
Tel: 03-5436-7850
Fax: 03-5436-7866
Web: http://www.ifour.co.jp

iBeta Software
2101 S. Blackhawk Street, Suite 100
Aurora, Colorado 80014
United States
Tel: 1-303-627-1110
Web: http://www.ibeta.com

Icarus Studios
Raleigh, North Carolina
United States
Web: http://icarusstudios.com

I.C.E. Division Multimédia
2775, Rolland Street, Suite 100
Ste-Adèle, Québec
Canada J8B 1C9
Tel: 1-450-229-9220
Fax: 1-450-922-9322
Web: http://www.icemultimedia.com

ICE Technology Corp.
12F-1, No. 9, Sec. 2 Luosfu Rd.
Taipei, 100 Taiwan
Tel: +886 2 23961880
Fax: +886 2 23961881
Web: http://terazona.icetech.com.tw

id Software, Inc.
3819 Towne Crossing Blvd, Suite 222
Mesquite, Texas 75150
United States
Tel: 1-972-613-3589
Fax: 1-972-686-9288
Web: http://www.idsoftware.com

Idea Factory Co. Ld.
Wacore Kanamecho 5,6F
11-2 Nakamaru-cho
Itabashi-ku
Tokyo
Japan 173-0026
Tel: +81-3-5995-4301
Fax: +81-3-5995-4302
Web: http://www.ideaf.co.jp

Ideas From the Deep
P.O.Box 7855
Pueblo West, Colorado 81007
United States
Web: http://www.ifd.com

Ideas Included
6 Wallbridge,
Frome,
BA11 1QY
United Kingdom
Tel:+44 (1373) 453338
Web: http://www.ideasincluded.com

Ideas That Play
ITP Entertainment Inc.
P.O. Box 4277
349 West Georgia Street
Vancouver, British Columbia
Canada V6B 3Z7
Tel: 1-604-682-2626
Fax: 1-604-682-2672
Web: http://www.ideasthatplay.com

IdolEyes Entertainment
82 Summer St.
Everett, Massachusetts 02149
United States
Web: http://www.idoleyes.net

Idol FX AB
Söder Mälarstrand 21
S-118 20 Stockholm
Sweden
Tel: +46-8-644 30 51
Fax: +46-8-442 04 66
Web: http://www.idolfx.se

Idol Minds
363 Centennial Pkwy Suite 200
Louisville, Colorado 80027
United States
Web: http://www.idolminds.com

Idryonis Studios
49 James Road
Hatboro, Pennsylvania 19040
United States
Tel: 1-215-479-7728
Fax: 1-215-479-7728
Web: http://www.idryonis.com

iEntertainment Network
124-126 Quade Drive
Raleigh, North Carolina 27513
United States
Tel: 1-919-678-8301
Fax: 1-919-678-8302
Web: http://www.iencentral.com

IG Ltd
IG House
Palliser Road
London W14 9EB
Tel: 020 73863000

Fax: 020 73860404
Web: http://www.igl.co.uk

Iguana Entertainment Inc.
3410 Far West Blvd
Austin Texas 78731-3194
United States
Tel: 1-512-338-8161
Web: http://www.acclaim.net

I-Imagine Interactive
Unit 3 Sunninghill Office Park
167 Peltier Road
Sunninghill
Johannesburg
South Africa
2157
Tel: +27 (0)11 785 9800
Fax: +27 (0)11 785 9828
Web: http://www.i-imagine.com

Ikarion Software GmbH
Bahnhofstr. 18-20
D-52064 Aachen
Germany
Tel: +49 241 47 01 50
Fax: +49 241 47 01 525
Web: http://www.ikarion.com

ILL Clan Productions
236 Leonard St., #2
Brooklyn, New York 11211
United States
Tel: 1-718-599-2591
Web: http://www.illclan.com

Illusion Softworks, a.s.
Kastanova 143
617 00 Brno
Czech Republic
Tel: +420 5 4325 0161
Tel/Fax: +420 5 4325 0160
Web: http://www.illusionsoftworks.com

Image Space Incorporated
206 South Main Street Suite 206
Ann Arbor, Michigan 48104
United States
Tel: 1-313-662-3660
Fax: 1-313-662-3028
Web: http://www.imagespaceinc.com

Image Space Incorporated
209 East Washington Street
Ann Arbor, Michigan 48104
United States
Tel: 1-313-662-3660
Fax: 1-313-662-3028
Web: http://www.imagespaceinc.com

Imagineer CO and Ltd.
Tokyo
Japan
Tel: 03-3343-8911
Fax: 03-3343-8915
Web: http://www.imagineer.co.jp

Imagine Games
2/24 Beach Road
Bondi
NSW 2026
Sydney
Australia
Tel: 04 1616 4570
Fax: 02 9365 7252
Web: http://www.imaginegames.com.au

Imaginengine Corp.
3025 Fillmore St.
San Francisco, California 94116
United States
Tel: 1-415-567-6158
Fax: 1-415-567-8081
Web: http://www.imaginengine.com

Impressions Games
222 Third Street - Suite 4100
Cambridge, Massachusetts
02142
United States
Fax: 1-617-225-0993
Web:http://www.impressionsgames.com

Incredible Simulations
P.O. Box 411237
Chicago, Illinois 60641
United States
Tel: 1-773-804-7403
Web:http://www.incrediblesimulations.com

Incredible Technologies, Inc.
3333 North Kennicott Avenue
Arlington Heights, Illinois 60004-1429
United States
Tel: 1-847-870-7027
Fax: 1-847-870-0120
Web: http://www.itsgames.com

Independent Arts
Gebaude 4, Munsterstr. 5,
59065 Hamm
Germany
Tel: +49 2381 688292
Fax: +49 2381 688293
Web:
http://www.independent-arts-software.de

Indiagames.com Ltd.
B/423, Shrikant Chambers
Next to RK Studios
V N Purav Marg
Chembur
Mumbai 400071
India
Tel: +91-22-25201127-29-30
Web: http://www.indiagames.com

Inertia, LLC
2019 N Lamar St
Suite 240
Dallas, Texas 75202-1704
United States
Tel: 1-214-855-5955
Web: http://www.inertiagames.com

Inevitable Entertainment
Echelon IV 9430 Research Blvd.,
#200
Austin, Texas 78759
United States
Tel: 1-512-682-0600
Fax: 1-512-682-0666
Web: http://www.inevitable.com

InfiKnowledge
720-724 Main Street
Second Floor
Moncton, NB, E1C 1E4
Canada
Tel: 1-506-855-2991
Web: http://www.infiknowledge.com

Infinential Interactive
Toronto, Ontario
Canada
Web: http://www.infinential.com

Infinite Dreams
Kaczyniec 7,
Gliwice, 44-100
Poland
Web: http://www.idreams.com.pl

Infinite Interactive Pty. Ltd.
PO Box 478
Altona, Victoria
Australia 3018
Web: http://www.infinite-interactive.com

Infinite Machine, Inc.
2560 9th Street Suite 220A
Berkeley, California 94710
United States
Web: http://www.infinite-machine.com

Infinite Monkey Systems, Inc.
58 Burr Avenue
Middletown, Connecticut 06457
United States
Fax: 1-860-704-8306
Web: http://www.imonkey.com

Infinite Ventures, Inc.
P.O. Box 394
Philomont, Virginia 20131
United States
Tel: 1-703-995-0498
Fax: 1-703-995-0498
Web:
http://www.infiniteventures.com

InfoBank Tecnology Corp.
5th Fl., No.192 Rueiguang Rd.
Neihu Chiu
Taipei
Taiwan R.O.C.
Tel: (886)2-2799-5855
Fax: (886)2-2799-5250
Web: http://www.ifb.com.tw

Infogrames, Inc. Head Office
417 Fifth Ave.

New York, New York 10016
United States
Tel: 1-212-726-6500
Web: http://www.infogrames.com

Infogrames, Inc.
50 Dunham Road
Beverly, Massachusetts 01915
United States
Tel: 1-978-921-3700
Web: http://www.infogrames.com

Infogrames, Inc. (Humongous
Entertainment)
3835 Monte Villa Parkway
Bothell, Washington 98021
United States
Tel: 1-425-486-9258
Web: http://www.infogrames.com

Infogrames Hunt Valley
180 Lakefront Drive
Hunt Valley, Maryland 21030
United States
Tel: 1-410-771-0440
Fax: 1-410-527-0541
Web: http://www.infogrames.com

Infogrames, Inc.
(Wizardworks & Macsoft)
2155 Niagara Lane North Suite 150
Plymouth, Minnesota 55447
United States
Tel: 1-763-249-7600
Web: http://www.infogrames.com

Infogrames, Inc.
2230 Broadway
Santa Monica, California 90404
United States
Tel: 1-310-595-2100
Web: http://www.infogrames.com

Infogrames, Inc.
613 Tasman Drive, Suite B
Sunnyvale, California 94089
United States
Tel: 1-408-212-7800
Web: http://www.infogrames.com

Infogrames do Brasil Ltda.
Rua Voluntários da Pátria, 4649
02401-400 - São Paulo   Sp
Brasil
Web: http://www.infogrames.com.br

Infogrames Entertainment
1 Place Verazzano
69252 Lyon Cedex 09
France
Tel: +33 (0)4 37 64 30 00
Fax: +33 (0)4 37 64 30 01
Web: http://www.infogrames.fr

Infogrames France
Infogrames Entertainment (&
Europe)
1 Place Verazzano
69252 Lyon Cedex 09
France
Tel: +33 (0)4 37 64 37 64
Web: http://www.infogrames.fr

Infogrames UK
Landmark House
Hammersmith Bridge Road
London
United Kingdom
W6 9DP
Tel: +44 (0) 20 8222 9700
Web: http://www.infogrames.co.uk

Infogrames Deutschland GmbH
Robert-Bosch-Straße 18
63303 Dreieich-Sprendlingen
Deutschland
Tel: +49 6103 334 100
Web: http://www.infogrames.de

Infogrames Nordic
Gunnebogatan 32
SE-163 53 Spanga
Sweden
Tel: +46 8 761 10 01
Web: http://www.infogrames.com

Infogrames Benelux BV
Parklaan 81a, 5613 BB
Eindhoven
PO Box 2367, 5600 CJ
Eindhoven
The Netherlands

Tel: +31 40 2393 555
Web: http://www.infogrames.com
Infogrames Italia
Viale Italia, 82
20020 Lainate (MI)
Italia
Tel: +39 02 93 76 71
Web: http://www.infogrames.it

Infogrames Spain
Cañada Real de las Merinas, 3,
planta 5ª
Nudo Eisenhower, Edificio 4
28042 Madrid
ESPAÑA
Tel: +34 91 329 42 35
Fax: +34 91 329 21 00
Web: http://www.es.infogrames.com

Infogrames Portugal
Suporte Técnico
Estrada Principal c/ Rua Almada
Negreiros
Bicesse 2765 Estoril
Portugal
Tel: +35 1 21 460 8585
Web: http://www.pt.infogrames.com

Infogrames Hellas
Panagouli 73 Agia Paraskevi
15343 Athens
Greece
Tel: +301 601 8801
Web: http://www.infogrames.com

Infogrames Gamecity GmbH
Kanzleistr. 120
CH-8004 Zürich
Switzerland
Tel: +41-1-298 20 80
Web: http://www.infogrames.com

Infogrames Israel
21 Atir Yeda St.
P.O.B. 2358 Kefar Saba
44641 Israel
Tel: 972-9-7679-777
Fax: 972-9-7679-947
Web: http://www.il.infogrames.com

Infogrames Australia
Melbourne House

Level 11, 14 Queens Road
Melbourne, Victoria
Australia
3004
Tel: +61 (0) 3 9867 0700
Fax: +61 (0) 3 9867 0800
Web: http://www.infogrames.com

Infogrames Asia Pacific Pty Ltd
32 Bowden St
Alexandria
Australia
2019
Tel: +61 (0) 2 8303 6800
Fax: +61 (0) 2 8303 6830
Web: http://www.infogrames.com

Infogrames Korea Limited
Namgok B/D 6F, 650-1
Yeoksam-dong, Kangnamgu
Seoul
Korea
135-080
Tel: +82 2 545 4555
Fax: +82 2 555 0912
Web: http://www.infogrames.co.kr

Infogrames Korean Office
Seoul, South Korea
Phone: + 82 2 545 4555
Fax: +82 2 555 0912
Web: http://www.infogrames.co.kr

Infogrames Taiwan Limited
Room 1521, 13 Floor,
144 Ming Chuan East Road
Sec.3, Taipei
Taiwan
Tel: +886 2 2717 0777
Fax: +886 2 2545 6060
Web: http://www.tw.infogrames.com

Infogrames Taiwan Limited
RM 1521,13F, No 144
Ming-Chuan E. RD.
Sec.3, Taipei 105
Taiwan
Tel: +886-2-2717-0777
Fax: +886-2-2545-6060
Web: http://www.tw.infogrames.com

Infogrames Japan
Kamiyacho Tower 701
5-2-5 Toranomon, Minato-ku
Tokyo, Japan 105-0001
Tel: 03-5777-0561
Web: http://www.jp.infogrames.com

Infomedia
00-515 W-wa
ul.Zurawia 22
Poland
Tel: (022)6270459
Web: http://www.strefacd.pl

INGENIO filiale de Loto-Québec
500, rue Sherbrooke Ouest,
bur.2100
Montréal, Québec
H3A 3G6
Canada
Tel: 1-514-282-0210
Fax: 1-514-282-2028
Web: http://www.ingenio-quebec.com

Ingenuity Works Inc.
560 Beatty Street, Unit L-200
New!
Vancouver, B.C. V6B 2L3
Tel: 1-604-484-8053
Tel: 1-800-665-0667
Fax: 1-604-484-8096
Web: http://www.ingenuityworks.com

Ingenuity Works Inc.
1123 Fir Avenue
Blaine, Washington 98230-9702
United States
Web: http://www.ingenuityworks.com

In Images
Poland
http://www.inimages.pl

Inmar Software Ltd.
Piippukatu 11
40100 Jyväskylä
Finland
Tel: +358 40 586 7512
Fax: +358 14 283 795
Web: http://www.inmarsoftware.com

Innerloop Studios
Øvre Slottsgate #27
N-0157 Oslo
Norway
Tel: +47 - 22 47 90 00
Fax: +47 - 22 47 90 09
Web: http://www.innerloop.no

Innonics
Moocksgang 5
Hanover
30169
Germany
Tel: 05 11 / 33 61 37 - 0
Fax: 05 11 / 33 61 37 - 77
Web: http://www.innonics.de

Insomniac Games
Los Angeles, California
United States
Web:http://www.insomniacgames.com

Interactif Factory
50 Bd menilmontant
Paris, 75020
France
Tel: 33 1 43 15 98 80
Web: http://www.interactifactory.com

Interlex
Tokyo, Japan
Tel: 03-5232-5850
Fax: 03-3798-2286
Web: http://www.interlexinc.com

Intermedia Design Inc.
129 Franklin Street #210
Cambridge, Massachusetts
02139
United States
Tel: 1-617-494-9278
Web: http://www.imd.com

Intrepid Games
Unit 3
Woodman Works
204 Durnsford Road
London
SW19 8DR
United Kingdom
Web: http://www.intrepidgames.com

IG Ltd
IG House
Palliser Road
London
W14 9EB
United Kingdom
Tel: 020 73863000
Fax: 020 73860404
Web: http://www.igl.co.uk

I-Imagine Interactive
Unit 3 Sunninghill Office Park
167 Peltier Road
Sunninghill
Johannesburg
South Africa
2157
Tel: +27 (0)11 785 9800
Fax: +27 (0)11 785 9828
Web: http://www.i-imagine.com

Insane Logics
1303 Grene Avenue, Suite 200
Montreal Quebec
Canada, H3Z 2A7
Tel: 1-514-939-0799
Fax: 1-514-939-2321
Web: http://www.insanelogics.com

Inter Adventure
P.O. Box 4133
Burlington, Vermont 05406
United States
Web: http://www.interadventure.com

Interactive Entertainment
United Kingdom
Web:
http://www.interactive-entertainment.co.uk

Interactive Imagination Corp.
81 South Main Street,
Seattle, Washington 98104
United States
Tel: 1-206-264-7598
Fax: 1-206-264-9974
Web:
http://www.interactiveimaginationcorp.com

Interactive Magic
124-126 Quade Drive
Raleigh, North Carolina 27513
United States
Tel: 1-919-678-8834.
Tel: 1-919-678-8301
Fax: 1-919-678-8302
Web: http://www.warbirdsiii.com

Interactive Media Worx
Lindenstraße 65
59505 Bad Sassendorf
Germany
Web: http://www.imx-online.de

InterActive Vision A/S
Nørreskov Bakke 14
DK-8600 Silkeborg
Denmark
Tel: +45 8680 2700
Fax: +45 8680 0692
Web: http://www.iavgames.com

Interbet
Bethany, Connecticut, 6524
United States
Tel: 1-203-393-2291
Tel: 1-203-393-2000
Web: http://www.interbetcasino.com

Interplay Entertainment Corp.
16815 Von Karman
Irvine, California 92606
United States
Tel: 1-949-553-6655
Tel: 1-800-INTERPLAY
Fax: 1-949-252-2820.
Web: http://www.interplaysports.com

Interplay Entertainment Corp.
PTY Ltd.
Level 3, Unit 1
39 Herbert Street
St Leonards, NSW 2065
Australia
Tel: +61 (0)2 9431-1311
Web: http://www.interplay.com

Interplay Productions Ltd
Virgin Interactive Entertainment Ltd.
74a Charlotte Street

London
W1T 4QN
United Kingdom
Web: http://www.interplay.com

Interplay/Virgin Interactive
233 rue de la Croix Nivert
75015 Paris
France
Fax: 01 41 11 64 24
Web: http://www.interplay.com

InterScape Creations Inc.
239 East Georgia Street
Vancouver, British Columbia
Canada
Web: http://www.icgamesoft.com

InterScape Creations Inc.
Shanghai ZhongYi Technology
Consulting Co., Ltd.
704-1080 Qiu Jiang Road
Shanghai, China
Tel: (8621)56630996
Web: http://www.icgamesoft.com

Intrepid Computer Entertainment
Ltd.
Unit 3
Woodman Works
204 Durnsford Road,
London SW19 8DR
United Kingdom
Web: http://www.intrepidgames.com

Introversion Software
PO Box 3210
Glastonbury
BA6 8WF
United Kingdom
Web: http://www.introversion.co.uk

Intulo
Am Schuetzenholz 25
D-29643 Neuenkirchen
Germany
Tel: +49 5195 972 690
Fax: +49 5195 972 691
Web: http://www.intulo.de

In Utero
67, avenue de la République
75011 Paris
France
Tel: 33 (0) 1 49 29 59 29
Fax: 33 (0) 1 49 29 59 15
Web: http://www.in-utero.com

Inverse Entertainment GmbH
Henriettenstr. 10-14
20259 Hamburg
Germany
Tel: +49-(0)700 / CODEFABRIK
Tel: +49-(0)40 / 43 09 26 16
Fax: +49-(0)40 / 43 09 26 17
Web:
http://www.inverse-entertainment.de

Invictus Games Kft.
Nyulas u. 8/c
Debrechen, 4032
Hungary
Tel: +36-52-485-034
Fax: +36-52-485-034
Web: http://www.invictus.hu

IO Interactive
Farvergade 2
1463 Copenhagen K Denmark
Tel: +45 33 73 29 00
Fax: +45 33 33 02 15
Web: http://www.ioi.dk

Ionside Interactive, Inc.
The Bell Building
15 West Montgomery Avenue,
Suite 300
Rockville, Maryland 20850
United States
Web:http://www.ionside.com

Ion Storm
8303 MoPac Expressway North,
Ste A210
Austin, Texas 78759
United States
Fax: 512-531-3560
Web: http://www.ionstorm.com

IPC Software
1518 Seattle Hill Road
Bothell, Washington 98012-6001
United States
Tel: 1-425-402-7000
Fax: 1-425-402-1900
Web: http://www.ipc-software.com

Irem Software Engineering, Inc.
Fukudome 655 Matto
Ishikawa 924-0051 Japan
Tel: (076)277-3800
Fax: (076)277-3622
Web: http://www.irem.co.jp

Iridon Interactive AB
Bultgatan 40A
442 40 Kungälv
Sweden
Tel: +46(0)303 579 53
Fax: +46(0)303 148 92
Web: http://www.iridon.com

iRock Interactive
114 MacKenan Drive, Suite 100
Raleigh, North Carolina, 27511
United States
Phone: 1-919-467-9700
Fax: 1-919-468-2035
Web: http://www.irock.com

Iron Fusion
20 Marlatts Rd.
Thorold, Ontario
L2V 1N1
Canada
Tel: 1-905-680-0436
Fax: 1-905-227-4426
Web: http://www.ironfusion.com

Iron Lore Entertainment
29 Hudson Road
Sudbury, Massachusetts 01776
United States
Tel: 1-978-443-1309
Fax: 1-978-443-3194
Web: http://www.ironlore.com

Irrational Games Boston
125 B Street
Second Floor

Boston, Massachusetts 02127
United States
Tel: 1-617-269-0424
Fax: 1-617-269-0724
Web: http://www.irrationalgames.com

Irrational Games Australia
PO Box 66
Braddon, ACT 2612
Australia
Tel: +61 02 6230 4240
Fax: +61 02 6230 4231
Web: http://www.irrational.com.au

Irrational Games Australia
Unit 10, 18 Lonsdale St
Braddon, ACT
Australia
Tel: +61 02 6230 4240
Fax: +61 02 6230 4231
Web: http://www.irrational.com.au

iSeeSoft
1776 Mentor Ave, Suite 179
Cincinnati, Ohio 45212
United States
Tel: 1-513-351-0000
Web: http://www.iseesoft.com

Isonic Online Corp
Seocho E-Biz Tower 5F
23 Yangjae-dong Seocho-ku
Seoul ,Korea
Tel: 82-2-3460-1692
Web: http://www.isoniconline.com

Italian Tomato Ltd.
9-6-24, Akasaka, Minato-ku
Tokyo 107-0052
Japan
Tel: 81-3-3404-2681
Web: http://www.namco.co.jp

Jack in the Box Computing Game
Development
Porto Alegre
Brazil
Web: http://www.jackbox.com

Jack Of All Games
8800 Global Way
West Chester, Ohio 45069
United States
Tel: 1-888-522-5467
Tel: 1-513-326-3020
Web: http://www.jackofallgames.com

Jadeware
France
Web: http://www.jadeware.org

Jagex Software
Cambridge and London, England
United Kingdom
Web: http://www.jagex.com

Jaleco Entertainment
119 W. Tupper Street
Buffalo, New York 14202
United States
Tel: 1-716-853-7529
Fax: 1-716-853-3290
Web: http://www.jaleco.com

Jamie System Development Co. Ltd.
2nd F, Rosedale Bldg.
#724 Suseo-Dong
Kangnam-Ku
Seoul 135-885, Korea
Web: http://www.jamie.co.kr

Jane's Combat Simulations
United States
Web: http://www.janes.ea.com

Jarhead Games
502-580 Granville Street
Vancouver, Canada
V6C 1W6
Web: http://www.jarheadgames.com

JCEntertainment Corp
Rosedale Building 4th Floor
724 Suseo-Dong
Kangnam-Ku
Seoul, Korea
Tel : 82-2-2040-1116
Fax: 82-2-2040-1109
Web: http://www.jceworld.com

JC Entertainment Corp
World Netgames, Inc.
18 Technology Drive, Suite165
Irvine, California 92618
United States
Tel: 1-949-727-4240
Fax: 1-949-727-4260
Web: http://www.jceworld.com

JDS Games
716 NE 8th Street #5
Hallandale, Florida 33009
United States
Tel: 1-954-454-7782
Web: http://www.jdsgames.com

Jellyvision, Inc.
848 W. Eastman St.
Suite 104
Chicago, Illinois 60622
United States
Tel: 1-312-266-0606
Fax: 1-312-266-0088
Web: http://www.jellyvision.com

Jester Interactive @ Hawarden
Francis Smith House
Manor Lane
Hawarden
Flintshire
CH5 3PP
Tel: +44 (0) 1244 537770
Fax: +44 (0) 1244 537771
Web: http://www.jesterinteractive.com

Jester Interactive @ Liverpool
3rd Floor
Port of Liverpool Building
Pier Head
Liverpool
Merseyside
L31BY
Tel: +44 (0) 151 236 8840
Fax: +44 (0) 151 236 8850
Web: http://www.jesterinteractive.com

JFP Inc.
Kinsan Bldg. 2F
Zaimokucho 2-26
Morioka-City
Iwate, Japan
020-0063

Tel: +81-19-623-3613
Fax: +81-19-623-4028
Web: http://www.jfpinc.com

JFP Inc.
Marios Building 7F
Morioka Station Nishi-Dori 9-1
Morioka City
Iwate Prefecture, Japan
020-0045
Tel: +81-19-621-8370
Fax: +81-19-621-5286
Web: http://www.jfpinc.com

JFP Inc.
Nankai Tokyo Bldg.
Iwate Ginga Plaza
Chuo-ku Ginza 5-15-1
Tokyo, Japan
104-0061
Tel: +81-3-3524-8265
Fax: +81-3-3524-8291
Web: http://www.jfpinc.com

JoyCity (JCEntertainment U.S.A)
18 Technology Dr. #165
Irvine, California 92618
United States
Tel: 1-949-727-4240
Fax: 1-949-727-4260
Web: http://www.joycity.com

JoWooD Productions Software AG
Technologiepark 4a
A-8786 Rottenmann
Phone: +43 3614 2966-0
Fax: +43 3614 2966-1064
Web: http://www.jowood.com

JoWooD Productions Germany
D-63263 Neu-Isenburg
Martin-Behaim-Str. 19-21
Germany
Tel: +49 6102 8168-0
Fax: +49 6102 8168-010
Web: http://www.jowood.com

JoWooD Productions UK Ltd.
2 Gayton Road
Harrow, Middlesex, HA1 2 XU
United Kingdom

Tel: +44 20 8901 7300
Fax: +44 20 8901 7305
Web: http://www.jowood.com

JoWooD Productions Vienna
A-1070 Wien
Schottenfeldgasse 29/1
Vienna
Tel: +43 1 522 1866 0
Fax: +43 1 522 1866 20
Web: http://www.jowood.com

JoWooD Productions Ebensee
A-4802 Ebensee
Bahnhofstrasse 22
Austria
Tel: +43 6133 8430 0
Fax: +43 6133 8430 14
Web: http://www.jowood.com

Joylabs
Loorweg 105c
D-51143 Koeln
Germany
Tel: +49 (0) 2203 9803019
Fax: +49 (0) 2203 503462
Web: http://www.joylabs.de

Joymania Entertainment
Ohlmann&Sprys GbR
Lindenstrasse 64
45478 Muelheim
Germany
Web: http://www.joymania.de

JRC s.r.o.
Naskové 3, 150 00 Praha 5
IO: 257 64 683
Czech Republic
Tel: +420 2 57189501
Tel: 02 57 18 95 00
Fax: + 420 2 57216544
Web: http://www.jrc.cz

JSC Gamos
Bldg 27, Bolshaya Kommunisticheskaya str.
Moscow
109004, RUSSIA.
Tel: 7(095) 912-66-24
Fax: 7(095) 912-66-24
Web: http://www.gamos.ru

Junction-18 Limited
Lord Hope Building
141 St. James Road
Glasgow, G4 0LT
United Kingdom
Tel: 0141 303 8300
Fax: 0141 552 3886
Web: http://www.junction-18.com

Junglevision Software
1412 Addison St.
Berkeley California 94702
United States
Tel: 1-510-848-5211
Fax: 1-510-649-0452.
Web: http://www.junglevision.com

Just Add Monsters Limited
St John's Innovation Centre
Cowley Road
Cambridge
CB4 0WS
Tel: +44 (0) 1223 422130
Fax: +44 (0) 8701 324500
Web: http://www.justaddmonsters.com

Just Flight Ltd.
Units A2/A3
Edison Road
St. Ives
Cambridgeshire
PE27 3LD
United Kingdom
Tel: +44 (0)1480 468075
Fax: +44 (0)1480 463070
Web: http://www.justflight.com

JV Games
PO Box 97455
Las Vegas, Nevada 89193
United States
Tel: 1-702-433-9689
Web: http://www.jvgames.com

Kaboom Studios LTD
The American Barns
Banbury Road
Lighthorne
Warwickshire
CV35 0AE
Web: http://www.kaboomstudios.com

Kainai.Net GmbH
Märkische Str. 59
44141 Dortmund
Germany
Tel: +49 - (0) 231 - 206 3747
Fax: +49 - (0) 231 - 206 3767
Web: http://www.kainai.de

Kalisto Bordeaux
Cité Mondiale
Parvis des Chartrons
33074 Bordeaux Cedex
France
Tel : +33 5 5648 6030
Fax : +33 5 5648 6033
Web: http://www.kalisto.com

Kalisto Paris studio
74 Rue Stendhal
75020 Paris
France
Tel: 01 40 33 75 00
Fax: 01 40 33 75 01
Web: http://www.kalisto.com

Kalisto USA Studios
600 Round Rock West Drive
Suite 205
Round Rock, Texas 78681
United States
Tel: 1-310-454-7647
Fax: 1-310-454-6807
Web: http://www.kalisto.com

Kalisto Japan
Park Avenue Jinnan 703,
Jinnan 1-13-8,
Shibuya-Ku,
Tokyo 150-0041
Web: http://www.kalisto.com

Kama Digital Entertainment
Sam-Chang Bldg. 109
Samsung-Dong
Kangnam-Ku
Seoul, 135-091
Korea
Tel: +822-544-6800
Fax: +822-544-6007
Web: http://www.kama.co.kr

Kamehan Studios
26 Rue Martial Boudet Chaville
Haut de Seine 92370
France
Tel: 01 41 15 24 00
Web: http://www.kamehan.com

Karma Labs Inc.
163 Amsterdam Avenue, #358
New York, New York 10023
Tel: 1-212-937-2228
Fax: 1-212-937-2228
Web: http://www.karmalabs.com

Karma Studios
Nieuwstad 62
6811 BM Arnhem
The Netherlands
Tel: +31 26 4461563
Fax: +31 26 4461567
Web: http://www.karma-studios.com

Kaolink
51 rue de Verdun
92158 Suresnes Cedex
France
Tel: 01 46 97 21 99
Fax: 01 46 97 20 10
Web: http://www.kaolink.com

Kaon Interactive
2 Clock Tower Place
Suite 100
Maynard, Massachusetts 01754
United States
Tel: 1-978-823-0111
Web: http://www.kaon.com

KaosKontrol, Inc.
Nice, France
Web: http://www.kaoskontrol.com

Kapooki Games Ltd.
No.5 Talbot Street
Dublin 1
Ireland
Tel: +353 (0)1 8745848
Fax: +353 (0)1 8787919
Web: http://www.kapookigames.com

KCE Tokyo
3-25, Kanda Jimbocho
Chiyoda-ku
Tokyo 101-0051, Japan
Fax: 81 (03) 3264-5256
Web: http://www.kcetokyo.com

KD-Lab
Telmana St., 73
236008 Kaliningrad
Russia
Tel: +7 (0112) 275378, 364749
Fax: +7 (0112) 275378, 364749
Web: http://www.kdlab.com

Kellogg Creek Software, Inc.
3808 SE Licyntra Ct.
Portland, Oregon 97222
United States
Tel: 1-503-653-2544
Web: http://www.spiritwars.com

KEMCO Japan
East capital
1 Chome 8th 1 Ohashi
station building 3f
Shinjuku Ku Shinjuku, Tokyo
160-0022 Japan
Tel: 03 3225 3456
Fax: 03 3225 5445
Web: http://www.kemco-games.com

KEMCO Japan
The Hiroshima prefecture
Kure city book 2
Chome 6th 3
Kure Chamber of Commerce
and Industry building 5f
Kure 737-0045
Japan
Tel: 0823 21 3456
Fax: 0823 21 8800
Web: http://www.kemco-games.com

KEMCO Japan
The Hiroshima prefecture
Hiroshima city
Ku silver mountain town
3rd 17 2nd Suehiro building 301
wide island
730-0022 Japan
Tel: 082 541 0661

Fax: 082 249 2352
Web: http://www.kemco-games.com

KEMCO U.S.A., INC.
14711 NE 29th Place Suite 215
Bellevue, Washington 98007
United States
Tel: 1-425-869-8000
Web: http://www.kemco-games.com

Kinesoft
2201 Donley Drive, Suite 305
Austin, Texas 78758
United States
Tel: 1-512-833-8086
Fax: 1-512-833-8102
Web: http://www.kinesoft.com

King of the Jungle Ltd
Unit 20 Berghem Mews
Blythe Road
London W14 OHN
United Kingdom
Tel: +44(0)20 7 371 3710
Fax: +44(0)20 7 371 3711
Web: http://www.kingofthejungle.co.uk

Klik Animation
5524, Saint-Patrick, bur. 302
Montréal, Québec H4E 1A8
Canada
Tel: 1-514-842-6602
Fax: 1-514-842-6603
Web: http://www.klikanimation.com

Knight Bridging Korea
2F, Channel Bldg.
206-4 poi-Dong
kangnam-Gu
Seoul, Korea
Tel: 82-2-574-9097
Fax: 82-2-574-9098
Web: http://www.kbk21.com

KnightSoft Technologies
Montreal, Canada
Web: http://knightsoft.ca

Knowble Design
Portland, Oregon

United States
Tel: 1-503-684-8232
Web: http://www.knowbledesign.com

KnowWonder Digital Mediaworks
12421 Willows Road NE #200
Kirkland, Washington 98034
United States
Tel: 1-425-825-6800
Fax: 1-425-825-6700
Web: http://www.knowwonder.com

KOCH Media
Thomas House
Hampshire International Business Park
Basingstoke
Hampshire, RG24 8WH
United Kingdom
Tel: 01256 707767
Fax: 01256 707377
Web: http://www.kochmedia.co.uk

Kodiak Studios
4001 South, 700 East, Suite 301
Salt Lake City, Utah 84107
United States
Tel: 1-801-266-5400
Fax: 1-801-266-5570
Web: http://www.kodiakgames.com

KOEI Co., Ltd.
1-18-12, Minowa-cho
Kohoku-ku, Yokohama City
223-8503 Japan
Web: http://www.koei.co.jp

KokoHead Studios Inc.
1107 - 1060 Alberni Street
Vancouver, British Columbia
Canada V6E 4K2
Tel: 1-778-883-7928
Fax: 1-604-692-5588
Web: http://www.kokoheadstudios.com

Konami Headquarters
3-1, Toranomon 4-chome, Minato-ku,
Tokyo 105-6021, Japan
Tel: (03) 3578-0573
Fax: (03) 3432-5679
Web: http://www.konami.co.jp

Konami Kobe Building
3-2, Minatojimanakamachi 7-chome, Chuo-ku,
Kobe-shi, Hyogo 650-0046,
Japan
Tel: (078) 303-0573
Fax: (078) 303-1230
Web: http://www.konami.co.jp

Konami Amusement Machines
Division s Head Office
5-1, Nishi-Shinjuku 6-chome,
Shinjuku-ku,
Tokyo 163-1334, Japan
Tel: (03) 5339-0573
Fax: (03) 5339-0574
Web: http://www.konami.co.jp

Konami Amusement Machines
Division s Kobe Office
6-3, Takatsukadai, Nishi-ku, Kobe-shi,
Hyogo 651-2271, Japan
Tel: (078) 993-0573
Fax: (078) 993-2520
Web: http://www.konami.co.jp

Konami Consumer-Use Software
Division s Head Office
4-30, Roppongi 1-chome, Minato-ku,
Tokyo 106-0032, Japan
Tel: (03) 3588-0573
Fax: (03) 5575-3457
Web: http://www.konami.co.jp

Konami Gaming Machines
Division s Head Office
1-1, Higashihara 5-chome, Zama-shi,
Kanagawa 228-0004, Japan
Tel: (046) 298-0573
Fax: (046) 298-0574
Web: http://www.konami.co.jp

Konami Creative Products
Divison s Head Office
12-1, Dogenzaka 1-chome,
Shibuya-ku,
Tokyo 150-0043, Japan
Tel: (03) 5458-0573
Fax: (03) 5458-1040
Web: http://www.konami.co.jp

Konami Health Entertainment
Divison s Head Office
6-1, Nishi-shinjuku 1-chome,
Shinjuku-ku,
Tokyo 163-1525, Japan
Tel: (03) 3349-0573
Fax: (03) 3348-5730
Web: http://www.konami.co.jp

Konami of America, Inc.
1400 Bridge Parkway, Suite 101
Redwood City, California, 94065-1567
United States
Tel: 1-888-212-0573
Fax: 1-650-654-5690
Web: http://www.konami.com/usa

Konami Gaming, Inc.
7140 South industrial Rd., Suite A1-A6
Las Vegas, Nevada 89118
United States
Tel: 1-702-367-0573
Fax: 1-702-367-0007
Web: http://www.konami.com/usa

Konami Reno
4750 Longly Lane
Reno, Nevada 89502
United States
Tel: 1-775-823-7900
Web: http://www.konamigaming.com

Konami Mississippi
254 E. Second St.
Pass Christian, Mississippi 39571
Tel: 1-228-216-0288
Fax: 1-228-452-7202
Web: http://www.konamigaming.com

Konami St. Louis
3209 Fairview
St. Louis, Missouri 63129
United States
Tel: 1-314-892-8411
Web: http://www.konamigaming.com

Konami Computer Entertainment
America, Inc.
Honolulu Studio
2222 Kalakaua Ave., Suite 1500

Honolulu, Hawaii 96815
United States
Tel: 1-808-923-0573
Fax: 1-808-921-2244
Web: http://www.konami.com/usa

Konami of Europe GmbH
Frankfurt Head Office
Berner Str. 103-105
60437 Frankfurt am Main
Germany
Tel: 069 985 573 0
Fax: 069 985 573 77
Web: http://www.metalgear.de

Konami Amusement of Europe, Ltd.
Konami House
54A Cowley Mill Road
Uxbridge, Middlesex, UB8 2QE
United Kingdom
Tel: 01895 200 573
Fax: 01895 200 500
Web: http://www.konami.co.uk

Konami Marketing (Asia) Ltd.
Suite 2007, Tower 1, The Gateway
25 Canton Road, Tsim Sha Tsui,
Kowloon, Hong Kong, People's
Republic of China
Tel: 2956 0573
Fax: 2956 2300
Web: http://www.konami.com.hk

Konami Singapore
Singapore
Tel: 65 587 0968
Fax: 65 587 0967
Web: http://www.konami.com.hk

Konami Korea
P.O. Box 573, Yeoido Post Office
Yeoido-dong, Yungdeungpo-ku,
Seoul, Korea
Web: http://www.konami.com.hk

KraiSoft Entertainment
1703 Saratoga Court
Allentown, Pennsylvania 18104
United States
Web: http://www.kraisoft.com

Kritzelkratz 3000 GmbH
Martinstrasse 21
D-97070 Würzburg
Germany
Tel: +49 (0) 931/ 3 53 60 91
Fax: +49 (0) 931/ 3 53 60 89
Web: http://www.kritzelkratz.de

Krome Studios
PO Box 1639
Fortitude Valley
Brisbane
Queensland 4006
Australia
Tel: +61 (0) 7 3257 2377
Fax: +61 (0) 7 3257 1168
Web: http://www.kromestudios.com

Kronos Digital Entertainment
150 South Arroyo Parkway
Pasadena, California 91105
United States
Tel: 1-626-666-1138
Fax: 1-626-666-1136
Web: http://www.kronosdigital.com

Kuju Entertainment Ltd.,
Unit 10 Woodside Park,
Catteshall Lane,
Godalming,
Surrey.
GU7 1LG.
United Kingdom.
Tel: +44 (0)1483 414 344
Fax: +44 (0)1483 414 287
Web: http://www.kuju.com

Kuju Entertainment Ltd.
157-168 Blackfriars Rd
London
SE1 8EZ
Tel: 020 7401 9969
Fax: 020 7261 9179
Web: http://www.kuju.com

Kuju Entertainment Ltd.
Blades Enterprise Centre,
Sandygate Suite,
Sheffield United Football Ground,
Bramall Lane,
Sheffield
S2 4SU

United Kingdom
Tel: 0114 292 2111
Web: http://www.kuju.com

Kutoka Interactive
1001 Sherbrooke Street East
Suite 400
Montreal , Quebec
H2L 1L3
Canada
Tel: 1-514-849-4800
Tel: 1-877-8KUTOKA
Fax: 1-514-849-9182
Web: http://www.kutoka.com

Laboratorium Komputerowe
Avalon
ul. Targowa 1/1010
Rzeszow, Poland
35-064
Web: http://www.lkavalon.com

LaFond Studios
9965 Miramar Parkway, PMB 284
Miramar, Florida 33025
United States
Web: http://www.lafondent.com

Lago Looking Ahead
Viale Masia 79 Como
Italy 22100
Tel: +39 0332 874111
Fax: +39 0332 870890
Web: http://www.lagoonline.com

Laminar Research
1005 Brentwood Court
Columbia, South Carolina, 29206
United States
Tel: 1-803-738-0910
Web: http://www.x-plane.com

Lankhor
130-136 Avenue Joseph Kessel
Voisins-le-Bretonneux
78960
France
Web: http://www.lankhor.com

Large Animal Games
27 w. 24th st. #10-d
New York, New York 10010
United States
Tel: 1-212-989-4312
Web: http://www.largeanimal.com

Larian Studios
Doorn 17 bis
B-9700 Oudenaarde
Belgium
Fax: +32(0)55-23.99.17
Web: http://www.larian.com

LatticeWork Software
Lafayette Hill, Pennsylvania
United States
Web: http://www.latticeworksw.com

LavaMind
2630 34th St.
Santa Monica, California 90405
United States
Web: http://www.lavamind.com

Left Field Productions
2900 Townsgate Road
Suite # 210
Weslake Village, California 91361
United States
Web: http://www.left.com

Leaping Lizard Software
18219-D Flower Hill Way
Gaithersburg, Maryland 20879
United States
Tel: 1-301-963-8230
Fax: 1-301-963-9016
Web: http://www.lplizard.com

Learn Technologies Interactive
361 Broadway, Suite 610
New York, New York 10013
United States
Tel: 1-212-334-2225
Fax: 1-212-334-1211
Web: http://www.learntech.com

Legacy Interactive, Inc.
6834 Hollywood Blvd, Suite 400
Los Angeles, California 90028
United States
Tel: 1-323-463-0300
Tel: 1-410-568-3636
Fax: 1-323-463-1300
Web:http://www.legacyinteractive.com

Legend Entertainment
4449-C Brookfield Corporate Dr.
Chantilly, Virginia 20151
United States
Tel: 1-703-227-1927
Fax: 1-703-227-1921
Web: http://www.legendent.com

Legend Studios S.L.
Corregidor Francisco Molina Nº
11 Piso 2
Puerta 4
29006 Málaga
Spain
Tel: +34 952 08 76 06
Fax: +34 952 08 76 06
Web: http://www.lsgames.com

Lemon Interactive Sp. z o.o.
Ul. Powstancow Slaskich 85 u6
01-355 Warsaw, Poland
Tel: +48 22 666 19 66
Fax: +48 22 666 19 77
Web: http://www.lemon-interactive.com
Web: http://www.lemon-interactive.pl

Leisuresoft GmbH
Robert Bosch Str. 1
59199 Bönen
Germany
Tel: +49 2383/69-0
Fax: +49 2383/69-500
Web: http://www.leisuresoft.de

LestaStudio
18 Moskovski Prospekt, Office 1
St.Petersburg
198013 Russia
Tel: +7(812) 3165056
Fax: +7(812) 3208445
Tel: http://www.lesta.ru

Level-5 Inc
Kyukan Daimyo Bldg. 6F
2-6-28 Daimyo Chuo-ku Fukuoka-shi
810-0041 Japan
Tel: +81-92-736-3150
Fax: +81-92-736-3151
Web: http://www.level5.co.jp

Life Line Entertaiment SL
C/ Claudio Coello, 76, sc.
Madrid, 28001
Spain
Tel: +34 915.772774
Fax: +34 915.772774
Web: http://www.revistronic.com

LightBrain GmbH
Moorweg 9a
24640 Schmalfeld
Germany
Tel: +49 (0)4191 959850
Fax: +49 (0)4191 958108
Web: http://www.lightbrain.de

LIGHTCUBE GmbH
Stresemannstr. 342
22761 Hamburg
Germany
Tel: 040-401 87 94 - 9
Fax: 180-50 52 55 21 33 47
Web: http://www.lightcube.com

Lightplay Studios
6709 W. 119th Street, Suite 204
Overland Park, Kansas 66209
United States
Tel: 1-913-685-9442
Fax: 1-913-814-9442
Web: http://www.lightplay.com

Lightspeed Games, Inc.
830 Hillview Court, Suite 210
Milpitas, California 95035
United States
Tel: 1-408-262-8505
Fax: 1-408-904-5388
Web:http://www.lightspeedgames.com

Lightweight
Shinjuku, Japan
Tel: 03-5292-3181

Fax: 03-5292-3182
Web: http://www.lightweight.co.jp

Linden Lab
577 Second Street, Suite 200
San Francisco, California 94107
United States
Tel: 1-415-243-9000
Fax: 1-415-243-9045
Web: http://lindenlab.com

Liquid Fire
17 DaCosta Ave Prospect
Adelaide, South Australia 5082
Australia
Web: http://www.liquidfiregames.com

Lionhead Studios
2nd Floor
1 Occam Court
Occam Road
Surrey Research Park
Guildford
Surrey
GU2 7YQ
United Kingdom
Web: http://www.lionhead.co.uk

Liquid Edge Games Ltd
141B Jervois Road
Herne Bay
Auckland
New Zealand
Tel: +64 25 271 1386
Fax: +64 9 360 7184
Web: http://www.roboforge.com

Liquid Entertainment
29800 Agoura Road, Suite 205
Agoura Hills, California 91310
United States
Tel: 1-818-991-3260
Fax: 1-818-991-5280
Web:
http://www.liquid-entertainment.com

Little Rocket Studios
25kV gebouw
lloydstraat 13b
3024EA Rotterdam
Netherlands
Tel: 010 476 60 30
Fax: 010 477 30 15
Web:http://www.littlerocketstudios.com

LittleWing Co. LTD.
P.O. BOX 30
Toyama Minami
939-8691 Japan
Fax: +81-764-22-6107
(Dial 001-81-764-22-6107 from USA)
Web: http://www.littlewing.co.jp

Live Media
Standingford House, Cave Street
Oxford
OX4 1BA
United Kingdom
Tel: +44(0)1865 247714
Fax: +44(0)1865 247715
Web: http://www.livemedia.co.uk

L.K. Avalon
skr. poczt. 66
35-959 Rzeszów
Ploand
Tel: (017) 856 77 67
Fax: (017) 856 99 12
Web: http://www.lkavalon.com

Locatha Industries
Jacksonville, Flordia
United States
Tel: 1-904-772-0540
Web: http://www.locatha.com

Logic Factory
2300 NW Thurman
Portland, Oregon 97210
United States
Tel: 1-503-517-2198
Web: http://www.logicfactory.com

Logic Factory, The
100 Dolores Street #251
Carmel, California 93923
United States

Tel: 1-408-625-5777
Fax: 1-408-625-5818
Web: http://www.logicfactory.com

Lonely Cat Games
Preslova 80
Brno, 602 00
Czech republic
Tel: +420 - 5 - 4323 6151
Fax: +420 - 5 - 4323 6151
Web: http://www.lonelycatgames.com

Longbow Digital Arts
4 MaryJane Street
Providence Bay, Ontario
P0P 1T0
Canada
Tel: 1-705-377-4500
Tel: 1-800-414-4268
Fax: 1-705-377-5372
Web:http://www.longbowdigitalarts.com

Lore Crafters
8347 Bent Waters,
San Antonio, Texas 77849
United States
Tel: 1-210-599-8290
Web: http://www.lorecrafters.com

Lost Boys games B.V.
Prins Hendrikkade 139
1011 AS Amsterdam
The Netherlands
Tel: +31 20 427 22 77
Fax: +31 20 427 40 40
Web: http://www.games.lostboys.com

Lost Minds
Djäknegatan 15,
Uppsala
Sweden
Tel: : 0736753843
Web: http://www.lostminds.com

Lost Toys LTD
Alexandra House
Alexandra Terrace
Guildford
Surrey
United Kingdom
GU1 3DA

Tel: +44 (0) 1483 449110
Fax: +44 (0) 1483 449190
Web: http://www.losttoys.com

Lovedelic
Japan
Tel: 03-5771-2721
Fax: 03-5771-2722
Web: http://www.lovedelic.co.jp

LSP
8 rue Wulfram Puget
13008 MARSEILLE
France
Tel: 04 91 29 32 60
Fax: 04 91 29 32 74
Web: http://www.lspgames.com

LTI Gray Matter
3325 Cochran Street Suite #200
Simi Valley, California 93063
United States
Voice: 1-805-584-1172
Fax: 1-805-584-1214
Web: http://www.livetech.com

LTStudios Ltd
Cherwell Innovation Centre
77 Heyford Park
Upper Heyford
Bicester
Oxfordshire
OX25 5HD
United Kingdom
Tel: +44 (0) 1869 238370
Tel: +44 (0) 1869 238371
Fax: +44 (0) 1869 238372
Web: http://www.ltstudios.com

LucasArts Entertainment
Company LLC
PO Box 10307
San Rafael, California 94912
United States
Fax: 1-415-444-8438
Web: http://www.lucasarts.com

Lucas Learning Ltd.
PO Box 10667
San Rafael, California 94912
United States
Tel: 1-415-444-8800
Web: http://www.lucaslearning.com

Lucky Chicken Games
2409 Main Street
Santa Monica, California 90405
United States
Tel: 1-310-396-6399
Fax: 1-310-396-6070
Web: http://www.luckychicken.com

Lud IQ
1457, Darling
Montréal, Québec H1W 2W2
Canada
Tel: 1-514-596-1640
Web: http://www.ludiq.com

Lunar Cheese Technologies
66 rue Villon,
69008 LYON
France
Tel: (33) 04 37 90 53 53
Fax: (33) 04 37 90 53 54
Web: http://www.lunarcheese.com

The Lunny Group
20th Floor
1500 West Georgia Street
Vancouver, British Columbia
V6G 2Z6 Canada
Tel: 1-604-669-0333
Fax: 1-604-662-7500
Web: http://www.lunny.com

Lupine Games
335 Timberhead Lane
Foster City, California 94404
United States
Tel: 1-650-345-2525
Web: http://www.lupinegames.com

Luxoflux Corp.
2850 Ocean Park Blvd. #240
Santa Monica, California 90405
United States
Tel: 1-310-314-3876

Fax: 1-310-314-3879
Web: http://www.luxoflux.com

Lyra Studios LLC
1800 Butler Ave #105
Los Angeles, California 90034
United States
Web: http://www.lyrastudios.com

Lyra Studios, LLC
Post Office Box 1494
El Segundo, California 90245
United States
Web: http://www.lyrastudios.com

M4 Limited
Unit 12
The Dove Centre
109 Bartholomew Road
London
NW5 2BJ
United Kingdom
Web: http://www.m4.co.uk

Macnetic GmbH
Wellingsbütteler Landstr. 234b
22337 Hamburg
Germany
Tel: 040 / 500 533 25
Fax: 040 / 500 533 26
Web: http://www.macnetic.de

MacPlay
2019 North Lamar St, Ste 240
Dallas, Texas 75202-1704
United States
Tel: 1-214-855-5955
Fax: 1-214-855-5980
Web: http://www.macplay.com

Madcat Interactive Software GmbH
Multimedia Internetpark
Gebäude 71
66482 Zweibrücken
Germany
Tel: 0 63 32 / 79 13 20
Fax: 0 63 32 / 79 13 21
Web: http://www.madcat.de

Mad Data
Lenaustr. 24
40699 Erkrath
Germany
Tel: +49 211 3840564
Fax: +49 211 3840568
Web: http://www.mad-data.com

Mad Doc Software, LLC
15 Union St.
Lawrence, Massachusetts 01840
United States
Tel: 1-978-687-8405
Fax: 1-978-687-8295
Web: http://www.maddocsoftware.com

Made By KIDDIES, Inc.
3701 Wilshire Blvd., Penthouse 1130
Los Angeles, California 90010
United States
Tel: 1-213-383-4448
Fax: 1-213-383-1776
Web: http://www.madebykiddies.com

Magenta Software Ltd
Suite 34
The Colonnades
Albert Dock
Liverpool
L3 4AA
United Kingdom
Web:http://www.magentasoftware.com

Magic Lantern Playware
Monmouth
The Patton Block Center
Monmouth, Illinois 61462
United States
Web: http://www.mlantern.com

Magic Lantern Playware
Richardson
2031 Cap Rock Drive
Richardson, Texas 75080
United States
Web: http://www.mlantern.com

Magic Systems Oetiker & Co.
Germanenstrasse
4313 Möhlin
Switzerland
Tel: +41 (0)61 851 40 70
Web: http://www.magicsystems.ch

Magique Productions
5481 Poker Face Court
Las Vegas, Nevada 89118
United States
Tel: 1-702-365-0221
Web:http://www.magiqueproductions.com

Magitech Corp.
Toronto, Canada
Web: http://www.ezgame.com

Magnetic Fields
Unit 4B Bridgegate North
The Pavilions
Chester Business Park
Chester
CH4 9QH
United Kingdom
Tel: +44 (0) 1244 679555
Fax: +44 (0) 1244 678998
Web: http://www.magneticfields.co.uk

Magnum 33
Rua Humberto Maderia
No2 2o andar
2745-663 Queluz de Baixo
Portugal
Tel: +351 21 434 69 60
Fax: +351 21 434 69 69
Web: http://www.magnum33.pt

Magus Soft
Room 1021 Hua Tai Building
No 1 Xin Wai Street
Hai Dian District
Beijing
China
Tel: +86 10 62017552
Fax: +86 10 62011571
Web: http://www.magus-soft.com

Magus Soft
Room 13A1, Jian Jing Building
1399 Bejing(West) Road
Shanghai 200040

Tel: +86 21 62794737
Fax: +86 21 62794738
Web: http://www.magus-soft.com

Majesco Games
160 Raritan Center Parkway Suite #1
Edison, New Jersey 08837
United States
Tel: 1-732-225-8910
Fax: 1-732-225-8408
Web: http://www.majescogames.com

Majorem
Maklef 6
Holon, 58672
Israel
Tel: 972-54-882198
Web: http://www.majorem.com

Majorem Ltd.
AM-SHAV Technological Applied
Development Center -
Technological Incubator
Midreshet Sde Boker
Israel, 84990
Tel: 03-6191412
Fax: 03-5700221
Web: http://www.majorem.com

Majority Productions
2700 Baycliff Court, Suite 201
Las Vegas, Nevada 89117
United States
Tel: 1-702-838-6928
Fax: 1-702-838-1029
Web:http://www.majorityproductions.com

Makonin Consulting Corp.
3185 Graveley Street
Vancouver, British Columbia
Canada V5K 3K7
Tel: 1-604-253-8288
Web: http://www.makonin.com

Malfador Machinations
PO Box 471885
San Francisco, California 94147-1885
United States
Tel: 1-415-281-9971
Web: http://www.malfador.com

Mango Grits
San Jose, California
United States
Web: http://www.mangogrits.com

Maratron
Limmatauweg 2
CH-4508 Ennetbaden
Switzerland
Tel: +41.(0)56.222.86.09
Fax: +41.(0)56.222.86.09
Web: http://www.maratron.com

Marcnamara Network Ltda.
Rua 6, 370 sala 310
Ed. Empire Center
Goiania 74115-070
Brazil
Tel: 55 (62) 215-4528
Web: http://www.realflight.com.br

Mare Crisium Studios
700 NE 22 Ave.
Portland, Oregon 97232
United States
Tel: 1-503-239-1174
Fax: 1-503-239-7599
Web: http://www.crisium.com

MARI Korea
638-1 Yeoksam-dong
Kangnam-ku
Seoul
Korea
Tel: 82-2-559-9600
Fax: 572-4290
Web: http://www.maritel.com

MARI USA
3003 N. First Street Suite 206
San Jose, California 95132
United States
Tel: 1-408-519-5735
Fax: 1-408-519-5804
Web: http://www.maritel.com

MARI Japan
11th Mori Bldg 9F Toranomon 2-6-4
Minato-Ku Tokyo
105-0001 Japan
Tel: 03-3519-8804
Fax: 03-5501-3234
Web: http://www.maritel.com

marune GmbH
Inselkammerstraße 8a
82008 Unterhaching
Tel: 089-62299880
Fax: 089-62299889
Web: http://www.marune.de

Marvelous Entertainment, Inc.
Oak Minami-Azabu Bldg. 13F 19-23
Minami-Azabu 3-Chome Minato-ku
Tokyo ,Japan
Tel: +81-3-5793-3377
Fax: +81-3-5793-3379
Web: http://www.mmv.co.jp

MASA France
24 Bd de l'Hôpital
75005 Paris
France
Tel: +33 (0)1 55 43 13 20
Fax: +33 (0)1 55 43 13 49
Web: http://www.animaths.com

MASA UK
Sussex Innovation Centre
Science Park Square
Falmer, Brighton BN1 9SB
United Kingdom
Tel: +44 (0)1273 234653
Fax: +44 (0)1273 704499
Web: http://www.animaths.com

MASA USA
15 Mercer St, #6
New York, New York 10013
United States
Tel: 1-212-343 8838
Fax: 1-212-343 9302
Web: http://www.animaths.com

Mass Media Inc.
357 Science Drive
Moorpark, California 93021

Tel: 1-805-531-9399
Fax: 1-805-531-9393
Web: http://massmedia.com

Massive Development GmbH
Joseph-Meyer-Str. 13-15
68167 Mannheim
Germany
Tel: 0621 - 33 86 4 0
Fax: 0621 - 33 86 4 29
Web: http://www.massive.de

Massive Entertainment AB
Box 4297
SE-203 14 Malmo
Sweden
Tel: +46(0)40 600 1000
Fax: +46(0)40 600 1099
Web: http://www.massive.se

Massive Entertainment AB
Södra Tullgatan 4a
SE-211 40 Malmo
Sweden
Tel: +46(0)40 600 1000
Fax: +46(0)40 600 1099
Web: http://www.massive.se

Matahari Studios Pty Ltd
49 Kew Street
Welshpool
Western Australia 6106
Australia
Tel: +61-8-9362-0800
Fax: +61-8-9362-0888
Web:http://www.mataharistudios.com

Matahari Studios
(PT Studiosoft)
Karawaci Office Park # I-39
Lippo Karawaci
Tangerang 15810
Banten, Indonesia
Tel: +62-21-5579-9722
Fax: +62-21-5579-9723
Web:http://www.mataharistudios.com

Matrix Games
3835 Richmond Avenue
Suite 192
Staten Island, New York 10312

United States
Tel: 1-888-280-7782
Web: http://www.matrixgames.com

Maverick Developments
31 High Street
Cawston
Norwich
Norfolk
NR10 4AE
England
United Kingdom
Tel: +44 (0) 1603-879-378
Fax: +44 (0) 1603-879-380
Web: http://www.maverickdev.com

Max Design
Austria
Web: http://www.max-design.at

Maxim Software
Bucharest,Romania
Tel: 40744331327
Web: http://www.realmsoftorment.net

Maximum Charisma Studios Inc.
5400 Ward Road
Bld#5 Suite#100
Arvada, Colorado 80002
United States
Tel: 1-303-432-0286
Fax: 1-303-432-9839
Web: http://www.mcszone.com

Maxis
2121 N. California Blvd.
Suite 600
Walnut Creek, California 94596
United States
Tel: 1-925-933-5630
Fax: 1-925-927-3736
Web: http://www.maxis.com

Mayhem Studios s.r.o.
Sastínska 37
Bratislava, Slovak Republic
Web: http://www.mayhem.sk

Mayhem Studios s.r.o.
Robotnícka 5
Bratislava, Slovak Republic
Web: http://www.mayhem.sk

Mayhem Studios s.r.o.
PO Box 72
817 72, Bratislava
Slovak Republic
Web: http://www.mayhem.sk

MBA Studios
63500 Seligenstadt
Germany
Tel: +49 6182 200940
Fax: +49 6182 200948
Web: http://www.mba-studios.de

MECHA Software, LLC
4L Hopkins RD
Taunton, Massachusetts 02780
United States
Web: http://www.mechasoftware.com

Mediamond Tmi
PL 14
02151 Espoo
Finland
Web: http://www.mediamond.fi

MEG Studio, Inc.
Kangnam-Ku, Seoul
South Korea
Tel: 82-11-415-1818
Fax: 82-2-518-1308
Web: http://www.megstudio.com

Mekada
717 Twinridge Ln.
Richmond, Virginia 23235
United States
Web: http://www.mekada.com

Melbourne House Pty Ltd
(Infogrames)
Level 11
14 Queens Road
Melbourne
Victoria
3004

Australia
Tel: +61 3 9867 0700
Fax: +61 3 9867 0800
Web:http://www.melbournehouse.com

MercurySteam Entertainment
C/. Ricardo de la Vega nº 12A
28028 MADRID
Spain
Tel: +34 91 725 16 11
Web: http://www.mercurysteam.com

Meridian'93
#33, Vatutina block
Lugansk 91040
Ukraine
Tel: (380)-642-46-13-09
Tel: (380)-642-34-48-47
Web: http://www.meridian.com.ua

Metro3D, Inc.
12 South First Street, 10th floor
San Jose, California, 95113
United States
Tel: 1-408-286-2900
Fax: 1-408-286-2970
Web: http://www.metro3d.com

Metro3D, Inc.
5-3-601 Maruyama-Cho
Shibuya-Ku, Tokyo, Japan
Tel: 03-3770-3376
Web: http://www.metro3d.com

Metro3D Europe Ltd.
Suites 508-510
Elder House, Elder Gate
Central Milton Keynes
MK9 1LR
United Kingdom
Tel: +44 1908 550 298
Web: http://www.metro3d.com

Metropolis Software House
ul. Podstaroscich 4 lok.2
1573 Warsaw
Poland
Tel: 48-22-39-33-54
Fax: 48-22-39-33-54
Web: http://www.metropolis.com.pl

Metropolis Software Sp. z o. o.
Rydygiera 8
01-793 Warsaw
Poland
Tel: +48 22 832-24-95
Fax: +48 22 832-24-95
Web: http://www.metropolis-software.com

MDO Games
Oberbüngstraße 5
56566 Neuwied
Germany
Tel: +49-2622-972877
Fax: +49-2622-972878
Web: http://www.mdo-games.de

Microcabin Corp
Japan
Tel: 0593-53-3811
Fax: 0593-54-5838
Web: http://www.microcabin.co.jp

Micro Forté Canberra
National Institute of Design
Phillip Avenue
Watson
Canberra A.C.T. 2602
Australia
Phone: +61-2-6242 5040
Facsimile: +61-2-6242 5090
Web: http://www.microforte.com.au

Micro Forté Sydney
95 Rose Street Chippendale
Sydney NSW 2008, Australia
Phone: +61-2-9319 3047
Facsimile: +61-2-9319 7590
Web: http://www.microforte.com.au

Microforum s.p.a.
Via del Casale Ghella 4
00189 Roma
Italy
Tel: (+39)0633251274
Fax: (+39)0633251475
Web: http://www.microforum.it

MICROïDS France
Vélizy Plus -
1 bis, rue du Petit Clamart
78140 Vélizy
France
Tel: (33) 1 46 01 54 01
Fax: (33) 1 46 32 25 64
Web: http://www.microids.com

MICROïDS Canada INC 87 rue
Prince,
Suite 140
Montréal, Québec
H3C 2M7
Canada
Tel: 1-514-390-0333
Fax: 1-514-526-6717
Web: http://www.microids.com

MICROïDS LTD UK
Windrush Barn,
Stantonbury Park Offices,
Great Linford,
Milton Keynes
MK14 5AT
England
United Kingdom
Tel: (44) (0) 1908 223377
Fax: (44) (0) 1908 227567
Web: http://www.microids.com

MICROïDS Italia
Corso Sempione 9
20145 Milano
Italia
Tel: (39) 02 345 92 392
Fax: (39 02 345 92 469
Web: http://www.microids.com

Microprose Software
100 Europa Drive
Chapel Hill North Carolina, 27514
United States
Fax: 1-919-933-5709
Web: http://www.microsoft.com

Microsoft Corp
One Microsoft Way
Redmond, Washington 98052
United States
Tel: 1-425-882-8080
Web: http://www.microsoft.com

Micronet Co., Ltd.
Sapporo, Japan
Web: http://www.micronet-japan.com
Micronet Software Manila, Inc.
Metro Manila, Philippines
Web: http://www.micronet-japan.com

Micronet (Bignet USA Inc.)
San Francisco, California
United States
Web: http://www.micronet-japan.com

Midas Interactive Entertainment Ltd
Unit 14, Stansted Business
Centre
Bishops Stortford
Hertfordshire
CM22 7DG
United Kingdom
Tel: 01279-858000
Fax: 01279-508841
Web: http://www.midasinteractive.com

Midnight Synergy
Regina , Canada
Web: http://www.midnightsynergy.com

Midway Games Inc.
2704 West Roscoe Street
Chicago, Illinois 60618
United States
Tel: 1-773-961-2222
Fax: 1-903-874-0434
Web: http://www.midway.com

Midway Amusement Games, LLC
2727 West Roscoe Street.
Chicago, Illinois 60618
United States
Tel: 1-773-961-2222
Web: http://www.midway.com

Midway Games West Inc.
PO BOX 360839
Milpitas, California 95036-0839
United States
Tel: 1-408-434-3700
Web: http://www.midway.com

Midway Home Entertainment Inc.
10110 Mesa Rim Road
San Diego, California 92121
United States
Tel: 1-858-658-9500
Web: http://www.midway.com

Mil Ltd.
2-1-21, Yaguchi, Ota-ku
Tokyo 146-8655
Japan
Tel: 81-3-3756-1851
Web: http://www.namco.co.jp

MILESTONE S.r.l.
Via Fara 35
20124 Milano
Italy
Web: http://www.milestone.it

MindArk AB
Järntorget 8, pl:22
SE - 413 04 Gothenburg
Sweden
Tel: +46 31 60 72 60
Fax: +46 31 136 016
Web: http://www.mindark.se

Mind Control Software
230 Emerystone Terrace
San Rafael, California 94903
United States
Tel: 1-415-491-1544
Web: http://www.mind-control.com

Mind Engine
300 East 4th St.
New York, New York 10009
United States
Tel: 1-212-673-7297
Web: http://www.mindengine.com

Mindflex
566 Dutch Valley Road
Atlanta, Georgia 30324
United States
Tel: 1-404-892-6232
Tel: 1-877-646-3353
Fax: 1-404-892-6076
Web: http://www.mindflex.com

Minds-Eye Productions
Ground Floor
Westfalia house
Old Wolverton Rd
Milton Keynes
MK12 5PY
United Kingdom
Tel: 01908 318315
Web: http://www.minds-eye.net

Mindscape, Inc.
88 Rowland Way
Novato, California 94945
United States
Tel: 1-415-895-2000
FaxL 1-415-895-2102
Web: http://www.learningco.com

Mind Shear Software, Inc.
606 Common Street
Shreveport, Louisiana 71101
United States
Tel: 1-318-221-8718.
Web:
http://www.softdisk.com/comp/mss

MindSpan Technologies Corp.
PO Box 18034 Kerrisdale
Vancouver
British Columbia
V6M 4L3 Canada
Web: http://www.mindspan.com

Mindware Studios s.r.o.
Belohorska 43
Prague 6
169 00
Tel: (420) 2 333 500 58
Web:http://www.mindwarestudios.com

Miracle Designs N.V.
Ottergemsesteenweg 379
9000 Gent
Belgium
Tel: +3293244017
Fax: +3293244018
Web: http://www.miracle-designs.com

Mirage Interactive Sp. z o.o.
ul. ObroDców 2c
03-933 Warszawa

Poland
Tel: (22) 616 1551
Fax: (22) 617 9321
Web: http://www.mirage.com.pl

MiST Land
Russia
Web: http://www.mistgames.ru

MitCom Neue Medien GmbH
Anglerstraße 6 D
80339 München
Germany
Tel: +49 89 500 332 0
Fax: +49 89 500 332 22
Web: http://www.mitcom.de

Mithis Games Ltd.
Kecskeméti u. 2.
H-1053 Budapest, Hungary
Tel: +36 1 266 1533
Tel: +36 1 266 1544
Fax: +36 1 266 1545
web: http://www.mithis.hu

MM3D
9815 Copper Creek Drive
Austin, Texas 78729
United States
Tel: 1-512-249-4448
Web: http://www.mm3d.com

Mobile Active Digital
102 Hamilton Avenue
Craighall Park
Johannesburg, 2196
South Africa
Tel: +27 11 327 0188
Fax: +27 11 327 0188
Web: http://www.mobileactive.co.za

Mobius Entertainment
St Pauls House
Richardshaw Lane
Pudsey
LS28 6BN
United Kingdom
Web: http://www.mobiusent.com

Modern Games
Handelsagentur GmbH
Pascalstraße 17 - 52076 Aachen
Tel: +49(0)2408 - 959 - 0
Fax: +49(0)2408 - 959 - 125
Web: http://www.modern-games.com

Modstar
628 E 11th Street, Suite 1B
New York, New York 10009
United States
Tel: 1-212-598-1868
Fax: 1-212-598-9920
Web: http://www.modstar.com

Mogility, Inc.
21715 Redwood Road
Castro Valley, California 94546
United States
Tel: 1-510-538-1382
Web: http://www.mogility.com

Mondo Media
135 Mississippi St.
San Francisco, California 94107
United States
Tel: 1-415-865-2700
Fax: 1-415-865-2645
Web: http://www.mondomedia.com

Monkey Byte
P.O. Box 15959
San Luis Obispo, California 93406
United States
Tel: 1-805-545-7860
Fax: 1-805-545-7860
Web: http://www.mbyte.com

Monkeystone Games Inc.
8307 Private Road 2409
Quinlan, Texas 75474
United States
Tel: 1-903-356-0078
Web: http://www.monkeystone.com

Monolith Productions
10516 NE 37th Circle
Kirkland, Washington 98033
United States
Tel: 1-425-739-1500
Fax: 1-425-827-3901
Web: http://www.lith.com

Monolith Software Inc.
1-1-32, Shinurashima-cho,
Kanagawa-ku
Yokohama 221-0031
Japan
Tel: 81-45-450-2227
Web: http://www.namco.co.jp

Monster Studios
Eugene, Oregon.
United States
Web: http://www.monsterstudios.com

Monsterland Produktion
Katarina Bangata 69
116 42 Stockholm
Sweden
Tel: 08-640 70 57
Tel: 0705-46 71 41
Web: http://www.monsterland.se

Monte Cristo
42, rue des Jeûneurs
75002 Paris
France
Tel: +33 (0)1 40 39 11 11
Fax: +33 (0)1 40 39 00 10
Web:http://www.montecristogames.com

Moosehill Productions AB
Sweden
Tel: 0707-427902
Web: http://www.moosehill.se

MoraffWare
P.O. Box 46669
Tampa, Florida 33647
United States
Tel: 1-877-842-6858
Tel: 1-813-994-7700
Fax: 1-813-994-7800
Web: http://www.moraff.com

Morpheme Ltd.
4th Floor
Linton House
39-51 Highgate Road
London
NW5 1RS
United Kingdom
Tel: +44 (0) 207 428 7703

Fax: +44 (0) 705 069 5392
Web: http://www.morpheme.co.uk

Morphonix
104 Wimbledon Way
San Rafael, California 94901
United States
Fax: 1-415-456-1433
Tel: 1-415-456-2561
Web: http://www.morphonix.com

Moto1, Inc.
100 E. Royal Ln,
Ste. 130
Irving, Texas 75039
United States
Tel: 1-972-910-8866
Fax: 1-972-910-8216
Web: http://www.moto1.net

Motorsims
100 East Royal Lane, Ste. 13
Irving, Texas, 75039
United States
Fax: 1-972-910-8216
Web: http://www.motorsims.com

Mountain King Studios Inc.
2466 Forest Drive #212
Woodridge , Illinois 60517
Tel: 1-630-985-8603
Fax: 1-630-985-8603
Web: http://www.mking.com

Moxze Games
507 East, 10 Langjiayuan
Jianguomenwai Avenue
Beijing, China 100022
Tel: +86.10.6538.2800
Fax: +86.10.8580.0242
Web: http://www.moxze.com

Mucky Foot Productions Ltd.,
1st Floor, Albany House,
Woodbridge Meadows,
Guildford,
Surrey,
United Kingdom
GU1 1BA
Web: http://www.muckyfoot.com

Mumbo Jumbo
(United Developers)
2019 N Lamar St Ste 240
Dallas, Texas 75202-1704
United States
Tel: 1-214-871-0400
Fax: 1-214-871-7390
Web: http://www.mumbojumbo.com

Mumbo Jumbo
(United Developers)
Irvine, California
United States
Web: http://www.mumbojumbo.com

MVP Software, Inc.
1035 Dallas, SE
Grand Rapids, Michigan 49507
United States
Tel: 1-616-831-7981.
Web: http://www.mvpsoft.com

Mythic Entertainment
4035 Ridge Top Road, 8th Floor
Fairfax, Virginia 22030
United States
Web:
http://www.mythicentertainment.com

Mythic Entertainment
3919 Old Lee Highway
Suite 82A
Fairfax, Virginia 22030
United States
Tel: 1-703-934-0453
Fax: 1-703-934-0447
Web: http://www.mythicgames.com

My Virtual Model Inc.
1001 Sherbrooke Street East,
Suite 700
Montreal, Québec
H2L 1L3
Canada
Tel: 1-514-523-9966
Fax: 1-514-523-0100
Web:
http://www.monmannequinvirtuel.com

Mzone Studio
7, boulevard de Linz
44210 Pornic
France
Tel : +33 2 28 53 04 60
Web: http://www.mzonestudio.com

N'Lightning Software
Development, Inc.
1050 Crater Lake Ave. Suite E
Medford, Oregon 97504
Toll Free: 1-877-672-0031
Tel: 1-541-245-9309
Fax: 1-541-245-4896
Web: http://www.awesomegame.com
Web: http://www.n-lightning.com

n-Space, Inc.
7035 Grand National Drive
Orlando, Florida 32819
United States
Tel: 1-407-352-5333
Fax: 1-407-352-5571
Web: http://www.n-space.com

Naked Sky Entertainment
Los Angeles, California
United States
Web: http://www.nakedsky.com

Namco Corporate Headquarters
Tokyo
2-1-21, Yaguchi, Ota-ku
Tokyo 146-8655
Japan
Tel: 81-3-3756-2311
Web: http://www.namco.co.jp

Namco Toranomon
7F, Toranomon 5 Mori Building, 1-17-1, Toranomon
Minato-ku, Tokyo 105-0001
Japan
Tel: 81-3-3504-1321
Web: http://www.namco.co.jp

Namco Tamagawa
2-9-22, Tamagawa, Ota-ku
Tokyo 146-0095, Japan
Tel: 81-3-3756-2311
Web: http://www.namco.co.jp

Namco Yokohama Creative
Center
1-1-32, Shinurashima-cho,
Kanagawa-ku, Yokohama 221-0031
Japan
Tel: 81-45-461-8049
Web: http://www.namco.co.jp

Namco
Yokohama Mirai-Kenkyusho
15-1, Shinei-cho, Tsuzuki-ku,
Yokohama 224-0035
Japan
Tel: 81-45-593-0711
Web: http://www.namco.co.jp

Namco Technical Center
2-1-60, Taru-machi, Kohoku-ku,
Yokohama 222-0001
Japan
Tel: 81-45-547-4000
Web: http://www.namco.co.jp

Namco Yaguchi
2-4-6, Yaguchi, Ota-ku
Tokyo 146-0093
Japan
Tel: 81-3-3756-2311
Web: http://www.namco.co.jp

Namco Kansai
1-21-26, Esaka-cho, Suita
Osaka 564-0063
Japan
Tel: 81-6-6338-6636
Web: http://www.namco.co.jp

Namco America Inc.
2055 Junction Avenue
San Jose, California 95131
United States
Tel: 1-408-383-3900
Web: http://www.namcoarcade.com

Namco Hometek Inc.
2055 Junction Avenue
San Jose, California 95131
United States
Tel: 1-408-922-0712
Web: http://www.namco.com

Namco Cybertainment Inc.
877 Supreme Drive
Bensenville, Illinois 60106-1106
United States
Tel: 1-630-238-2200
Web: http://www.namcoarcade.com

Namco XS Entertainment Inc.
c/o: Namco Cybertainment Inc.
Musicplayground Inc.
3 Riverside Drive
Andover, Massachusetts 01810
United States
Tel: 1-978-688-8800
Web: http://www.namcoarcade.com

Namco Europe Ltd.
Namco House
Acton Park Estate
The Vale
London
W3 7QE
United Kingdom
Tel: 44-20-8324-6000
Web: http://www.namco.co.uk

Namco Operations Spain S.L.
c/Buenavista, 3, 28220,
Majadahonda
Madrid
Spain
Tel: 34-91-634-29-61
Web: http://www.namco.com

Namco Operations France S.A.
29, Rue Cartier Bresson
93500 Pantin
France
Tel: 33-1-49910792
Web: http://www.namcoarcade.com

Namco Operations Germany
GmbH
Centro-Allee 267 46047
Oberhausen
Germany
Tel: 49-208-805-656
Web: http://www.namcoarcade.com

Namco Enterprises Asia Ltd.
Shop p501, Podium 5, World
Trade Center, 280 Gloucester
Road,
Causeway Bay
Hong Kong
Tel: 852-2516-6610
Web: http://www.namcoarcade.com

Namco: JPN-Namco Taiwan Co., Ltd.
Shin Kong Mitsukoshi Kaoshiung
Store 14F, No.213
Santou 3 Road, Kaoshiung
Taiwan, R.O.C.
Tel: 886-7-330-8915
Web: http://www.namcoarcade.com

Namco Shanghai Ltd.
No. 258-23, Caoshi Road
Shanghai, 200233
China
Tel: 86-21-6495-3248
Web: http://www.namcoarcade.com

Namco/Monolith Software Inc.
1-1-32, Shinurashima-cho,
Kanagawa-ku
Yokohama 221-0031
Japan
Tel: 81-45-450-2227
Web: http://www.namco.co.jp

Namco Italian Tomato Ltd.
9-6-24, Akasaka, Minato-ku
Tokyo 107-0052
Japan
Tel: 81-3-3404-2681
Web: http://www.namco.co.jp

Namco T&E Co., Ltd.
1273-1, Aoyagi, Ichihara
Chiba 299-0102
Japan
Tel: 81-436-23-2701
Web: http://www.namco.co.jp

Namco Mil Ltd.
2-1-21, YaguchiOta-ku
Tokyo 146-8655
Japan
Tel: 81-3-3756-1851
Web: http://www.namco.co.jp

Namco Wonder Seven Ltd.
3-10-10, Akasaka, Minato-ku
Tokyo 107-0052
Japan
Tel: 81-3-5562-5200
Web: http://www.namco.co.jp

Namco St. Tropez Ltd.
3-10-10, Akasaka, Minato-ku
Tokyo 107-0052
Japan
Tel: 81-3-5562-5400
Web: http://www.namco.co.jp

Namco Nikkatsu Corp.
3-28-12, Hongo, Bunkyo-ku
Tokyo 113-0033
Japan
Tel: 81-3-5689-1002
Web: http://www.namco.co.jp

Namco Yunokawa Kanko Co., Ltd.
2-4-20, Yunokawa-cho, Hakodate
Hokkaido 042-0932
Japan
Tel: 81-138-57-1188
Web: http://www.namco.co.jp

Namco Ecolotech Ltd.
2-9-22, Tamagawa, Ota-ku
Tokyo 146-0095
Japan
Tel: 81-3-5482-7211
Web: http://www.namco.co.jp

Namco Nihon I-Tec K.K.
Bancho Gloria Building, 7
Rokubancho, Chiyoda-ku
Tokyo, 102-0085
Japan
Tel: 81-3-3288-5521
Web: http://www.namco.co.jp

NapsTeam snc
P.O. BOX 118
98100 Messina
Italy
Tel: 0039-090-6401000
Web: http://www.napsteam.com

Natsume Inc.
1818 Gilbreth Road, Suite 229
Burlingame, California 94010
United States
Tel: 1-650-692-1941
Web: http://www.natsume.com

Naughty Dog, Inc.
Santa Monica, California
United States
Web: http://www.naughtydog.com

NAWAR Ltd.
Kosciuszki 27
85079
Bydgoszcz
Poland
Tel: +48 52 321 55 45 ext. 14
Fax: +48 52 584 13 09
Web: http://www.nawar.com.pl

NCsoft Corp.
Seung Kwang Bldg
143-8, Samsung-dong
Kangnam-gu, Seoul
135-090, Seoul, Korea
Tel: +82-2-2186-3300
Fax: +82-2-2186-6206
Web: http://www.ncsoft.co.kr

Near Death Studios Inc.
1745 Pilgrim Ave
Mountain View, California 94040
United States
Tel: 1-650-948-2839
Fax: 1-650-745-9842
Web: http://www.neardeathstudios.com

Nebula Entertainment
Seville, Spain
Web: http://web.jet.es/wisefox

NEC Interchannel, Ltd.
Mita Kokusai Building. 21st Floor.
4-28 Mita 1-Chome
Minato-ku Tokyo 108, Japan
Tel: +81 3 5440 0755
Fax: +81 3 5440 0758
Web: http://www.neic.co.jp

Nemosoft
115, rue Aimé Grumbach
30900 NIMES
France
Tel: 04 66 84 03 03
Fax: 04 66 29 65 38
Web: http://www.nemosoft.fr

Nemosoft Paris
52, rue d'Aguesseau
92774 BOULOGNE
BILLANCOURT Cedex
Tel : 01 46 99 14 14
Fax : 01 46 99 14 00
Web: http://www.nemosoft.fr

neo media
neo Consulting Neue Medien
Software Produktions GmbH
Business Park Vienna
Wienerbergstraße 9, 1. OG
A-1100 Vienna
Austria
Tel: +43-1-607 6060 0
Fax: +43-1-607 4080 6
Web: http://www.neo.at

Neon Software
Deutschherrnufer 32
60594 Frankfurt / Main
Tel: 069-61 99 43 60
Fax: 069-61 99 43 81
Web: http://www.neon-online.de

Nerve Lab Software AB
Observatoriegatan 6, first floor
S-113 29 Stockholm
Sweden
Telephone: +46 -8- 6118822
Web: http://www.nervelab.com

Nerve Software
18601 Lbj Freeway #200
Mesquite, Texas 75150
United States
Tel: 1-972-270-2304
Web: http://www.nervesoftware.com

Netamin Communication Corp.
20955 Pathfinder Road #210
Diamond Bar, California 91765

United States
Tel: 1-909-598-7177
Fax 1-909-598-7404.
Web: http://www.netamin.com

NetDevil
890 W. Cherry Street, Suite 240
Louisville, Colorado 80027
United States
Tel: 1-720-890-0411
Fax: 1-720-890-0415
Web: http://www.netdevil.com

NetDevil
2051 Dogwood Street, Suite 240
Louisville, Colrado 80027
United States
Tel: 1-720-890-0411
Fax: 1-720-890-0415
Web: http://www.netdevil.com

NetDragon WebSoft, Inc.
58 Hotspring Branch Road
Fuzhou, China
350001
Tel: +86 591.75.19.19.8
Fax: +86 591.76.06.70.4
Web: http://www.ndchina.com

Net Games
Englschalkinger Strasse 14
Munich
Germany
81925
Web: http://www.net-games.com

Net-Lines
61 rue Sully
69006 Lyon
France
Tel: 33+472 829 777
Fax: 33+472 829 897
Web: http://www.net-lines.com

NET-VR
Mythenquai 353
CH-8038 Zurich
Switzerland
Tel: +41 433 99 99 01
Web: http://www.net-vr.com

Neuron Entertainment, Inc.
P.O. Box 31601
Colorado Springs, Colorado
80931-1601
United States
Tel: 1-719-391-8230
Web:
http://www.neuronentertainment.com

Never-Land Company, Inc.
Tokyo, Japan
Web: http://www.n-land.co.jp

Neversoft Entertainment
20335 Ventura Blvd, Suite 320
Woodland Hills, California 91364
United States
Tel: 1-818-610-4100
Fax: 1-818-610-4101
Web: http://www.neversoft.com

Nevolution
167 Eagle Glen Dr.
Woodstock, Georgia 30189
United States
Web: http://www.nevolution.net

Nevrax Limited UK
60 Lombard Street
London
EC3V9EA
United Kingdom
Tel: +44 20 7464 8408
Fax: +44 20 7464 8656
Web: http://www.nevrax.com

Nevrax Limited France
Paris, France
Web: http://www.nevrax.com

New Corp.
Japan
Tel: 0471-60-1131
Fax: 0471-60-1132
Web: http://www.new.co.jp

New Generation Software
Neuenkirchen
Germany
Web: http://www.newgsoft.com

New Horizon Studios S.L.
Sevilla
41927 Spain
Web: http://www.new-hs.com

NewKidCo International Inc,
250 West 57th Street
Suites 1020 and 1502
New York, New York 10107
United States
Tel: 1-212-581-1555
Fax: 1-212-265-1620
Fax: 1-212-581-9298
Web: http://www.newkidco.com

New Media Generation
3 Rimskogo-Korsakova str.
Moscow, 127566
Russia
Tel: +007(095)-903-30-50
Fax: +007(095)-903-80-98
Web: http://www.nmg.ru

New Pencil
80 Liberty Ship Way, Suite 6
sausalito, California 94965
United States
Tel: 1-415-339-1800
Fax: 1-415-339-1803
Web: http://www.newpencil.com

New World Computing
Agoura, California
United States
Tel: 1-408-988-7571
Fax: 1-408-988-7677
Web: http://www.nwcomputing.com

New World Computing
600 Galveston Drive
Redwood City, California 94063
United States
Web: http://www.nwcomputing.com

Nexon U.S.A.
1095 East Duane Avenue Suite 209
Sunnyvale California 94086
United States
Tel: 1-408-736-1755
Fax: 1-408-737-9351
Web: http://www.nexon.net

Ne-XS Interactive
14 Twin Pond Lane
Sudbury, Massachusetts 01776
United States
Tel: 1-978-440-7283
Web: http://www.nexsinteractive.com

Nexus
560 Henri-Bourassa West Suite
312
Montreal, Quebec,
H3L 1P4
Canada
Tel.: 1-514-334-8715
Fax: 1-514-334-5288
Web: http://www.nexus-is.qc.ca

nFusion Interactive LLC
66 Brunswick Woods Drive
East Brunswick, New Jersey
08816
United States
Web: http://www.n-fusion.com

nGame Limited
Logic House
Newmarket Road
Cambridge, CB5 8HA
England
United Kingdom
Tel: +44 (0) 1223 707707
Fax: +44 (0) 1223 707709
Web: http://www.ngame.com

nGame Inc.
41 Sussex Unit A
San Francisco, California 94131
United States
Tel: +1 415 584 1400
Fax: +1 415 276 3060
Web: http://www.ngame.com

Nicely Crafted Entertainment
PO BOX 142, Cambridge,
England
CB5 8ZG
United Kingdom
Web: http://www.nicelycrafted.com

Niels Bauer Software Design
Software Entwicklung

Sickingenstraße 37
79117 Freiburg
Tel: 0172-62 40 09 3
Fax: 0761-66 69 3
Web: http://www.nbsd.de

Niemo Entertainment ApS
Møllebovej 6
2640 Hedehusene
Denmark
Tel: +4546563861
Web: http://www.niemo.com

Nihilistic Software
371 Bel Marin Keys Blvd. Suite 110
Novato, California 94949
United States
Web: http://www.nihilistic.com

Nihon Falcom Corp.
1-14-13, Akebono-cho
Tachikawa-shi, Tokyo
190-0012, Japan
Tel: 042-527-0555
Fax: 042-528-2714
Web: http://www.falcom.com

Nihon I-Tec K.K.
Bancho Gloria Building, 7
Rokubancho, Chiyoda-ku,
Tokyo, 102-0085
Japan
Tel: 81-3-3288-5521
Web: http://www.namco.co.jp

Nikita Interactive
1a Kolomensky proyezd
115446 Moscow
Russia
Tel: +7 (095) 115 97 43
Tel: +7 (095) 115 97 77
Fax: +7 (095) 112 70 94
Web: http://www.nikita.ru
http://www.nikitainteractive.com

Nikitova Games
1205 Prospect 101
St. Petersburg
Russia
Tel: +1 (847) 541 2863
Web: http://www.nikitova.com

Nikitova Games
581 North Wolf Road
Chicago, Illinois 60090
United States
Tel: 1-773-336-7739
Tel: 1-866-NIKITOVA
Fax: 1-773-442-0693
Web: http://www.nikitova.com

Nikitova Games
1307 Block 203
Kiev
Ukraine
Tel: +1 (847) 541 2863
Web: http://www.nikitova.com

Nikkatsu Corp.
3-28-12, Hongo, Bunkyo-ku
Tokyo 113-0033
Japan
Tel: 81-3-5689-1002
Web: http://www.namco.co.jp

Ninjaneering
1506 Travis Heights
Austin, Texas 78704
United States
Tel: 1-512-796-4363
Web: http://www.ninjaneering.com

Nine Dragons Software
351 Ulloa Street
San Francisco, California 94127
United States
Tel: 1-415-664-3474
Fax: 1-415-564-3161
Web: http://www.ninedragons.com

Nintendo of America
PO Box 957
Redmond, Washington 98073
United States
Job line: 1-425-861-2170
Web: http://www.nintendo.com

Nintendo Company, Ltd. Japan
11-1 kamitoba-hokotate-cho,
minami-ku
Kyoto 601-8501
Japan
Tel: 011 81 75 662-9600

Fax: 011 81 75 662-9620
Web: http://www.nintendo.co.jp

Nintendo Australia Pty. Limited
Scoresby Industrial Park
804 Stud Road
Scoresby 3179
Victoria
Australia
Web: http://www.nintendo.com.au

Nintendo Australia Pty. Limited
Mailing Address
P.O. Box 804
Scoresby 3179
Victoria
Australia
Tel: 011 61 3 9730 9900
Fax: 011 61 3 9730 9922
Web: http://www.nintendo.com.au

Nintendo of Canada LTD. (NOCL)
110-13480 Crestwood Place
Richmond, British Columbia V6V 2J9
Canada
Web: 1-604-279-1600
Fax 1-604-279-1649
Web: http://www.nintendo.ca

Nintendo España, S.A
Azalea, 1-Edificio D
Miniparc 1-El Soto de La Moraleja
28109 Alcobendas (Madrid)
Spain
Tel: 011 34 91 659 74 00
Fax: 011 34 91 659 7401
Web: http://www.nintendo.es

Nintendo of Europe GmbH
Nintendo Center
63760 Großostheim
Federal Republic of Germany
Tel: 011 49 6026 950 0
Fax: 011 49 6026 950 301
Web site: http://www.nintendo.de

Nintendo France S.A.R.L.
le Mercury
1 rue de la Croix des Maheux
Cergy Pontoise 95031
France

Tel: 011 33 1 34 35 46 00
Fax: 011 33 1 34 35 46 35
Web: http://www.nintendo.fr

Nintendo Netherlands B.V.
(Nintendo Benelux B.V.)
Krijtwal 33
3432 ZT Nieuwegein
The Netherlands
Tel: 011 31 3060 971-00
Fax: 011 31 3060 51110
Web: http://www.nintendo.nl

Nintendo Netherlands B.V.
(Nintendo Benelux B.V.)
P.O. Box 564
3430 AN Nieuwegein
The Netherlands
Tel: 011 31 3060 971-00
Fax: 011 31 3060 51110
Web: http://www.nintendo.nl

Nippon Ichi Software
Kamigahara, Japan
Tel: 0583-71-7275
Fax: 0583-71-7212
Web: http://www.nippon1.co.jp

Nitro Software
Pfefferackerstr. 2a
45894 Gelsenkirchen
Tel: 02 09 / 60 47 8-0
Fax: 02 09 / 60 47 8-29
Web: http://www.nitro-software.de

Nival Interactive
10a bld. 5, 1st Volokolamsky
proezd
Moscow 123060
Russia
Tel: +7 (095) 363 9630
Fax: +7 (095) 363 9631
Web: http://www.nival.com

Nixxes Software BV
Nieuwegracht 17
3512 LC UTRECHT
The Netherlands
Web: http://www.nixxes.com

N'Lightning Software
Development, Inc.
1050 Crater Lake Ave. Suite E
Medford, Oregon 97504
United States
Tel: 1-541-245-9309
Tel: 1-877-672-0031
Fax: 1-541-245-4896
Web: http://www.n-lightning.com

NO.2 Games
359 Howell Ave.
Cincinnati, Ohio 45220
Tel: 1-513-238-1049
Fax: 1-513-751-3770
Web: http://www.no2games.com

NO.2 Games
1148 Main Street
Cincinnati, Ohio 45202
Tel: 1-513-238-1049
Fax: 1-513-751-3770
Web: http://www.no2games.com

Nordisk Film Production A/S
Mosedalvej 14
Valby, Denmark
2500
Tel: +45.36.18.82.00
Web: http://www.nordiskfilm.dk

NovaLogic, Inc.
26010 Mureau Rd., Suite 200
Calabasas, California 91302
United States
Fax: 1-818-880-1998
Web: http://www.novalogic.com

Novarama Studios
Barcelona, Spain
Web: http://www.novarama.com

NovaTrix GmbH
Konzeption und Entwicklung
interaktiver digitaler Medien
Ettishofer Straße 10c
88250 Weingarten
Germany
Tel: ++49 (0)751/50921-30
Fax ++49 (0)751/50921-31
Web: http://www.novatrix.de

Novus Delta
Clearwater, Florida
United States
Web: http://www.novusdelta.com

Now Production Co., Ltd.
Osaka, Japan
Tel: 06 6232 1660
Fax: 06 6232 1661
Web: http://www.nowpro.co.jp

Now Production Co., Ltd.
Tokyo, Japan
Tel: 03 5312 7688
Fax: 03 5312 7699
Web: http://www.nowpro.co.jp

NPCube SARL
1 bis, voie de liaison portuaire
97420 Le Port
Reunion Island - France
Tel: +262 262 22 52 64
Fax: +262 262 43 90 68
Web: http://www.npcube.com

n-Space, Inc.
7035 Grand National Drive
Orlando, Florida 32819
United States
Tel: 1-407-352-5333
Fax: 1-407-352-5571
Web: http://www.n-space.com

NTN Communications, Inc.
5966 La Place Court, Suite 100
Carlsbad, California 92008
United States
Tel: 1-760-438-7400
Fax: 1-760-438-7470
Web: http://www.ntn.com

N U C L E A R V I S I O N
Entertainment GmbH
Körnerstraße 9
38102 Braunschweig
Germany
Tel: (0049) 0531 701 89 840
Fax: (0049) 0531 701 89 846
Web: http://www.nuclearvision.de

NuFX, Inc.
2353 Hassell Road, Suite 115
Hoffman Estates, Illinois 60195
United States
Tel: 1-847-884-2000
Fax: 1-847-884-2002
Web: http://www.nufx.com

O3 Games AB
Kristallen
754 51 Uppsala
Sweden
Tel: 018-12 28 00
Fax: 018-12 28 05
Web: http://www.o3games.com

Object Software Beijing
South 401, Yinhai Mansion, Jia 10
South Avenue, Zhongguancun
Haidian District, Beijing
China 100081
Fax: 8610-68910085
Tel: 8610-68910190
Web: http://www.object.com.cn

Object Software Hong Kong
Suite 4A, No.6 Knutsford Terrace
Tsimshatsui
Kowloon
Hong Kong
Fax: 852-2956-0576
Tel: 852-2336-3017
Web: http://www.objectsw.com

OC3 Entertainment
1133 Winter Walk Circle
Raleigh, North Carolina 27560
United States
Tel: 1-919-460-4564
Web: http://www.oc3ent.com

Ocean Software
Landmark House
Hammersmith Bridge Road
London
United Kingdom
W6 9DP
Tel: +44 (0) 20 8222 9700
Web: http://www.ocean.co.uk

Oceanus Communications Inc.

50 Kaymar Drive
Ottawa, Ontario
Canada
K1J 7C7
Tel: 1-613-261-6735
Web: http://www.nekonline.com

Octoplus Entertainment
Mumbai, India
Tel: +91 22 82099
Web: http://www.octopluse.com

Octopus Motor Games
Pacifica, California
United States
Web:
http://www.theycamefromhollywood.com

Oddworld Inhabitants
869 Monterey Street
San Luis Obispo, California
93401
United States
Web: http://www.oddworld.com

Oeil pour Oeil
66 Rue d'Angleterre
59800 Lille
France
Web: http://www.oeilpouroeil.fr

OMG Games
177 Manorville Road
Saugerties, New York 12477
United States
Web: http://www.omg-games.com

On Deck Interactive
2700 Fairmount St.
Dallas, Texas 75201
United States
Tel: 1-214-880-0001
Fax: 1-214-871-7934
Web: http://www.odigames.com

OneWorld BDC
5151 Collins Avenue Suite 326
Miami Beach, Florida 33140
United States
Web: http://www.oneworldbdc.com

Oniros Illusions Studio SPRL
37, rue du Prince Royal
1050 Brussels
Belgium
Tel: +322 534 84 08
Fax : 322 534 87 73
Web: http://www.oniros.com

OpenPath
Baltimore, Maryland
United States
Tel: 1-410-263-1962
Fax: 1-410-263-7412
Web:http://www.openpathproducts.com

Optical Realities
105 Gainford
Chester-Le-Street
Durham, DH2 2EP
United Kingdom
Web: http://www.opticalrealities.com

Opus Corporation
5-7-14 Okusawa
Setagaya-ku
Tokyo
158-0083 Japan
Web: http://www.opus.co.jp

Opus Corporation
Inoue Bld. 5F
3-14-12 Kamiosaki
Shinagawa-ku
141-0021 Japan
Tel: 03-5447-1700
Fax: 03-5447-1770
Web: http://www.opus.co.jp

Oquirrh Productions
1800 S. West Temple Street, Suite 115
Salt Lake City, Utah 84115
United States
Web: http://www.oquirrh.com

Orange Games
Herengracht 410
1017 BX Amsterdam
The Netherlands
Tel: +31 20 427 22 77
Fax: +31 20 427 40 40
Web: http://www.orangegames.com

Orbital Frog Productions
5351 Ladera Crest Dr
Los Angeles, California 90056
United States
Tel: 1-310-649-1112
Fax: 1-520-223-0794
Web: http://www.orbitalfrog.com

Origin Systems
5918 W. Courtyard Drive
Austin, Texas 78730
United States
Fax: 1-512-346-7905
Web: http://www.origin.ea.com

OtherWorlds Interactive
Springfield Missouri
United States
Web:
http://www.otherworldsonline.com

OtherWorlds Interactive
Grand Prairie, Texas
United States
Web:
http://www.otherworldsonline.com

Outlaw Studios
103 e. 5th ST
Austin Texas, 78701
United States
Tel: 1-512-494-9966
Web: http://www.outlawstudios.com

Outline Development
Ringstraße 58
57234 Wilnsdorf
Tel: +49 (0) 2739 - 470240
Fax: +49 (0) 2739 - 479830
Web:
http://www.outline-development.de

OuterBound Games
2000 Cabot Blvd. Suite 110
Langhorne, Pennsylvania 19047
United States
Tel: 1-215-750-6606
Web: http://www.outerbound.com

Out of the Park Developments
P. O. Box 837
Graysville, Tennessee 37338
United States
Web: http://www.ootp.net
Web: http://www.ootp4.com

Out of the Park Developments
Raht, Trusheim, Heinsohn GbR
Out of the Park Developments
Kirchenstr. 35
21723 Hollern-Twielenfleth
Germany
Web: http://www.ootp4.com

Outrage Entertainment
330 E. Liberty St. Suite 4
Ann Arbor, Michigan 48104-2238
United States
Tel: 1-734-663-9120
Fax: 1-734-663-6702
Web: http://www.outrage.com

Outsider Development
Slovakia
Web:
http://www.outsiderdevelopment.sk

Overworks, Ltd.
Tokyo, Japan
Web: http://www.o-works.co.jp

Ozo Interactive
PO Box 10531
Eugene, Oregon 97440
United States
Tel: 1-541-683-3121
Web: http://www.ozointeractive.com

Pacific Coast Power and Light
5225 Betsy Ross Drive
Santa Clara, California 95054
United States
Tel: 1-408-330-0100
Fax: 1-408-855-8940
Web: http://www.pcpandl.com

Page 44 Studios
410 Jesse St. 3rd Floor
San Francisco, California 94103
United States
Tel: 1-650-787-6824
Web: http://www.page44.com

Palestar
1500 Scenic Drive, Suite 105
Austin, Texas 78703
United States
Tel: 1-512-476-9336
Web: http://www.palestar.com

Pandemic Studios
1920 Main Street
Santa Monica, California 90405
United States
Tel: 1-310-450-5199
Fax: 1-310-450-5190
Web: http://www.pandemicstudios.com

Pangea Software, Inc.
12405 John Simpson Court
Austin, Texas 78732
United States
Tel: 1-512-266-9991
Web: http://www.pangeasoft.net

Panther Software
Tokyo
Japan
Tel: 03-5232-5850
Tel: 03-5443-7811
Fax: 03-3798-2286
Web: http://www.panther.co.jp

PAN Vision AB
TegnÈrgatan 34
P. O. Box 6809
Stockholm
Sweden
113 86
Tel: +46 8 59 79 62 81
Tel: +46 8 57 99 62 50
Web: http://www.panvision.com

PAN Vision AB
Varbergsvägen 44
BOX 1150
501 11 Borås
Sweden
+46 (0)33-44 25 00
Web: http://www.paninteractive.se

PAN Vision AB
Järntorget 3
413 04 Göteborg
Sweden
+46 (0)13-12 89 55
Web: http://www.paninteractive.se

Pan Vision
Strandboulevarden 122, 5 sal
2100 Copenhagen
Denmark
+45 4814 6969
Web: http://www.paninteractive.se

PAN Vision AB
St. Olavs gatan 21 A
0165 Oslo
Norway
+47 2236 5800
Web: http://www.paninteractive.se

PAN Vision AB
Vattuniemenkatu 27
00210 Helsinki
Finland
+358 9 25340500
Web: http://www.paninteractive.se

Papaya Studio
17050 Bushard Street #350
Fountain Valley, California 92708
United States
Web: http://www.papayastudio.com

Papyrus Racing Games
200 Baker Ave, Suite 210
Concord, Massachusetts 01742
United States
Phone: 1-978-402-1100
Fax: 1-978-402-1101
Web: http://www.papy.com

Paradigm Entertainment, Inc.
1628 Valwood Parkway, Suite 110
Carrollton, Texas 75006
United States
Tel: 1-972-857-1383
Fax: 1-972-488-6300
Fax: 1-972-488-6317
Web: http://www.pe-i.com
Web: http://www.infogrames.com

Paradox Entertainment AB
Hitechbuilding
SE101 52 Stockholm
Sweden
Tel: +46 8 56 61 48 00
Fax: +46 8 56 61 48 19
Web:
http://www.paradox-entertainment.com

Paragon 5, Inc.
3 Polo Drive
S. Barrington, Illinois, 60010
United States
Tel: 1-847-858-8584
Web: http://www.paragon5.com

Paradox Development
5400 Tech Circle Drive
Moorpark, California 93021
United States
Web: http://www.px.com

Paraworld AG Dieburg
Am Bauhof 18
D-64807 Dieburg
Germany
Phone: +49 (0) 60 71 / 210-0
Fax: +49 (0) 60 71 / 210-222
Web: http://www.paraworld.com

Paraworld AG Hamburg
Niederlassung Hamburg
Mühlenkamp 31
D-22303 Hamburg
Germany
Phone: +49 (0) 40 / 27 88 19 54
Fax: +49 (0) 40 / 27 88 19 61
Web: http://www.paraworld.com

Paraworld (APAC) Pte Ltd
Singapore

9A & B, Ann Siang Road
Singapore 069690
Singapore
Phone: +65 339 / 38 10
Fax: +65 339 / 43 69
Web: http://www.paraworld.com

ParityBit
Japan
Web: http://www.paritybit.co.jp

Parsec
Vienna, Austria
Web: http://www.parsec.org

ParSoft Interactive
2019 North Lamar Street, Suite 220
Dallas, Texas 75202-1744
United States
Tel: 214-871-0400
Fax: 214-871-7390
Web: http://www.parsoft.com

Particle Systems Ltd.
12 Turners Lane
Broomhill
Sheffield
S10 1BP
United Kingdom
Web: http://www.particle-systems.com

Patch Products, Inc.
PO Box 268
Beloit, Wisconsin 53512-0268
United States
Tel: 1-800-524-4263
Tel: 1-608-362-6896
Web: http://www.patchproducts.com

Pendulo Studios
c/ Comercio 6
28007 Madrid
Spain
Web: http://www.pendulostudios.com

People Can Fly
Warszawa, Poland
Web: http://www.peoplecanfly.com

Perception PTY Ltd.
Suite 4001,
376 Bay Street,
Brighton Le Sands, 2216
Australia
Tel: (+612) 9556 3100
Fax: (+612) 9556 3200
Web: http://www.perception.com.au

Perceptum
Santo Andre
Brazil
Web: http://www.perceptum.com

Periscope3 North Carolina
1400 Crescent Green
Suite 230
PO Box 5488
Raleigh, North Carolina 27511
United States
Tel: 1-919-816-1700
Fax: 1-919-816-1710
Web: http://www.periscope3.com

Periscope3 Virginia
520 Herndon Parkway
Suite 200
Herndon, Virginia 20170
United States
Tel: 1-703-471-8367
Fax: 1-703-471-8364
Web: http://www.periscope3.com

Persei Entertainment
Frankrigsgade 31, 4. Th
2300 Copenhagen S
Denmark
Web: http://www.persei.dk

Petroleum Entertainment Group
Box 47571
1227 Barton Street East
Hamilton, Ontario
Canada L8H 2V4
Tel: 1-905-547-0017
Web: http://www.pyrostar.com

Phantagram
11F HaeSung Building
Dae-Chi 3, 942 Kang-Nam
Seoul
Korea
Tel: 82-2-528-2282
Fax: 82-2-528-2289
Web: http://www.phantagram.com

Phantagram Limited Korea
13F Star Tower, Yeoksam 737,
Kangnam
Seoul, 135-984
Korea
Tel: 82 - 2 - 2112 - 2490
Fax: 82 - 2 - 2112 - 2480
Web: http://www.phantagram.com

Phantagram Entertainment Inc.
USA
130 N. Brand Blvd.
Glendale, California 91203
United States
Fax: 1-818-553-1681
Web: http://www.phantagram.com

Phantom EFX
Cedar Repids, Iowa
United States
Tel: 1-319-266-1999
Web: http://www.phantomefx.com

Pharaoh Productions
1355 S. Boulder Road #F109
Louisville, Colorado 80027
United States
Tel: 1-303-604-1335
Web:
http://www.pharaoh-productions.com

Phase 3 Studios
Floor 1,
Gainsborough Business Centre
100 Pall Mall
St James's
London
SW1Y 5HP
United Kingdom
Tel: +44 207 664 8798
Fax: +44 207 664 8799
Web: http://www.phase3studios.com

Phenomedia AG
Josef-Haumann-Str. 10
4866 Bochum
Germany
Phone: + 49 (02327) 997-0
Fax: + 49 (02327) 997-411
Web: http://www.phenomedia.com

Phenomic Game Development
Gehauweg 1
55218 Ingelheim am Rhein
Germany
Web: http://www.phenomic.de

Philos Entertainment
126-128 Bécsi str.
Budapest H-1034
Hungary
Tel: +36 (1) 388 3795 / 500
Fax: +36 (1) 388 3795 / 501
Web: http://www.philoslabs.com

Phoenix Entertainment
Charleston, South Carolina
United States
Web:
http://www.underworldgame.com

Phoenix Simulation
United Kingdom
Web:
http://www.phoenix-simulation.co.uk

Pimpernel Online Games
Zutphen, The Netherlands
Tel: 00-31-(0)78-613 38 21
Web: http://www.pimpernel.com

Pipeworks Software, Inc.
260 E. 11th Ave. Suite 3D
Eugene, Oregon 97401
United States
Tel: 1-541-685-0644
Fax: 1-541-685-0671
Web:
http://www.pipeworkssoftware.com

Piranha Bytes Software GmbH
Josef-Haumann-Str. 10
44866 Bochum

Germany
Web: http://www.piranha-bytes.com

Piranha Bytes Software
Lohrheidestrasse 1
44866 Bochum
Germany
Web: http://www.piranha-bytes.com

Piranha Games
501-580 Granville Street
Vancouver, British Columbia
V6C 1W6
Canada
Web: http://www.piranha-games.com

The Pitbull Syndicate
North East England
United Kingdom
Web: http://www.pitbull.co.uk

Pivotal Games
Unit 24, Church Farm Business
Park
Corston
Bath
BA2 9AP
United Kingdom
Tel: 01225 874448
Fax: 01225 874401
Web: http://www.pivotalgames.com

Pixelbrothers
35 Kingsland Road
London E2 8AA
United Kingdom
Tel: 020 76134707
Web: http://www.pixelbrothers.co.uk

Pixel-Grip, Inc.
7500 East Deer Valley Road,
Suite #162
Scottsdale, Arizona 85255
United States
Web: http://www.pixel-grip.com

Pixel Logic
2nd Floor 111 Charles Street
Sheffield
S1 2ND
United Kingdom
Tel: (0114) 275 4428
Fax: (0114) 275 8741
Web: http://www.pixelogic.co.uk

Pixelstorm, Trecision S.p.A.
C.so Assereto 15
16035 Rapallo (GE)
Italy
Tel: (+39) 0185 23 20 22
Fax: (+39) 0185 237 592
Web: http://www.trecision.com

Plaid World Studios, LLC
1626 14th Ave South
St. Cloud, Minnesota 56301
United States
Web: http://www.plaidworld.com

Planet Moon Studios
1750 Bridgeway STE A200
Sausalito, California 94965
United States
Web: http://www.planetmoon.com

Planet, The
Klerkegade 19,
Copenhagen, 1308
Denmark
Tel: +45 33930020
Web: http://www.planet.dk

Plastic Reality Technologies, s. r.
o.
Radova 9
623 00 Brno
Czech Republic
Tel: +42 0 604201082
Web: http://www.preality.com

Playmore Corp.
Esaka Sekishu Bldg. 15-11
Toyotsu-cho,
Suita-shi, Osaka 564-0051 Japan
Tel: (06) 6339-6362
Fax: (06) 6378-6360
Web: http://www.playmore.co.jp

Playmates Interactive
611 Anton Blvd., Suite 555
Costa Mesa, California 92626
United States
Web: http://www.playmatestoys.com

Playnet Inc.
1901 Central Dr., Suite 400
Bedford, Texas 76021
United States
Tel: 1-817-358-7580
Fax: 1-817-358-7585
Web: http://www.playnet.com

Playscape Research
Valnoeddegaarden 33
2620 Albertslund
Denmark
Tel: 0045 43 66 19 90
Web: http://www.playscape.dk

Playstos
Corso Sempione, 63
20149 Milano
Italy
Tel: +39 02 3314153
Fax: +39 02 315678
Web: http://www.playstos.com

Plutonium Games
9135 Katy Freeway, Suite 229
Houston, Texas 77024
United States
Tel: 1-713-722-8867
Tel: 1-713-984-8164
Web:http://www.plutoniumgames.com

Pocket Studios
Burnhill Business Centre
50 Burnhill Road
Beckenham
Kent
BR3 3LA
Tel: +44 (0) 20 8249 6074
Fax: +44 (0) 20 8249 6006
Web: http://www.pocket-studios.com

Point Blank Development
Midskogsgränd 11, 1tr
S115 43 Stockholm
Sweden

Telephone: +46 (0)8 442 70 20
Fax: +46 (0)8 664 12 90
Web: http://www.pointblankgames.com

Point of View, Inc. Tustin Office
15641 Redhill Ave. Suite 205
Tustin, California 92780
United States
Tel: 1-714-258-7350
Web: http://www.pov-inc.com

Point of View, Inc. Austin Office
5000 Plaza On The Lake
Austin, Texas 78746
United States
Tel: 1-512-330-9991
Web: http://www.pov-inc.com

Polygon Magic, Inc
Tokyo, Japan
Tel: 03-5207-6631
Fax: 03-5207-6639
Web: http://www.polygonmagic.com

Polygon Studio
9 rue de l'Association
75016 Paris
France
Tel: +33 (0) 1 55 74 70 00
Fax: +33 (0) 1 55 74 70 09
Web: http://www.polygonstudio.com

Ponos Corp.
Osaka, Japan
Tel: (06) 6242 2677
Fax: (06) 6242 2675
Web: http://www.ponos.co.jp

Pop
425 West 13th Street, Suite #8
New York, New York 10014
United States
Tel: 1-646-230-1430
Web: http://www.popnyc.com

PopTop Software
1714 Gilsinn Dr.
Fenton, Missouri 63026
United States
Web: http://www.poptop.com

Positech
United Kingdom
Web: http://www.positech.co.uk

Power Media, Inc.
11101 SW Greenburg Road
Tigard, Oregon 97223
United States
Tel: 1-503-684-8232
Fax: 1-503-684-6298
Web: http://www.powermedia.com

Powerhead Games
New York, New York
United States
Web: http://www.powerheadgames.com

PowerUp Studios
4 - 597 St. Clair Avenue West
Toronto, Ontario
M6C 1A3 Canada
Tel: 1-416-656-4331
Web: http://www.powerupstudios.com

Precision Manuals
708 North Howard Street #204
Alexandria, Virginia 22304
United States
Web: http://www.precisionmanuals.com

Prelusion Games
Prästgatan 41-43
SE 831 31 Östersund
Sweden
Tel: +46(0)63-106564
Fax: +46(0)63-575850
Web: http://www.prelusion.com

Presto Studios, Inc.
5414 Oberlin Drive, Suite 200
San Diego, California 92121
United States
Tel: 1-858-622-0500
Fax: 1-858-622-0310
Web: http://www.presto.com

Primal Interactive
Manchester, New Hampshire
United States
Web: http://www.primalinteractive.com

Primal Software
Moscow, Russia
Web: http://www.primal-soft.com

ProbeGames
Suite 1607
16-19 Southampton Place
London
England
WC1A 2AJ
Tel: 0044 (0) 20 7745 7284
Fax 0044 (0) 20 7745 7220
Web: http://www.probe-it.com

Production I.G Inc.
ING Studio, 3-4-5, Minami Cho,
Kokubunji-shi, Tokyo 185-0021
Web: http://www.production-ig.co.jp

Prograph Research S.r.l.
Zona Industriale, 24
32013 Longarone (BL)
Italy
Tel: (+39) 0437 573558
Fax: (+39) 0437 576267
Web: http://www.prograph.it

Progress Software
14 Oak Park
Bedford, Massachusetts 01730
United Stateds
Tel: 1-800-477-6473
Web: http://www.progress.com

Prolific Publishing, Inc.
1400 W. Burbank Blvd.
Burbank, California 91506-1308
United States
Tel: 1-818-562-8400
Fax: 1-818-562-8410
Web: http://www.prolific.com

Pronto Games, Inc.
1500 Park Ave, Suite 225
Emeryville, California 94608
United States
Tel: 1-510-654-4350
Web: http://www.prontogames.com

Prophecy Gaming Studios
Waterleikens 32
B-8501 Heule
Belgium
Fax: +32 261 279 50
Web: http://prophecy.now.nu

ProSIM
94-636 Kauakapuu Loop
Mililani, Hawaii 96789
United States
Tel: 1-808-623-2361
Fax: 1-808-623-2361
Web: http://www.prosimco.com

Pseudo Interactive Inc.
80 Bloor Street West, Suite 400
Toronto, Ontario, Canada
M5S 2V1
Tel: 1-416-966-1142
Fax: 1-416-966-2075
Web: http://www.pseudointeractive.com

Psikyo Co. Ltd.
Tokyo, Japan
Tel: 03-5340-8768
Fax: 03-5340-8968
Web: http://www.psikyo.co.jp

Psyonix
476 Highway A1A, Suite #6
Satellite Beach, Florida 32937
United States
Tel: 1-321-917-4852
Web: http://www.psyonix.com

Pterodon s.r.o.
Kastanova 143
617 00 Brno
Czech republic
Tel.: +420-5-43321326
Web: http://www.pterodon.cz

Pulsar Interactive Corporation
49234 Golden Oak Drive Suite 106
Oakhurst, California 93644
United States
Tel: 1-559-642-3080
Fax: 1-559-683-7657
Web: http://www.pulsarinteractive.com

Pulsar Interactive Corporation
P.O. Box 2838
Oakhurst, California 93644
United States
Tel: 1-559-642-3080
Fax: 1-559-683-7657
Web: http://www.pulsarinteractive.com

Pulse Headquarters
654 Mission Street
San Francisco, California 94105
United States
Tel: 1-415-348-4000
Fax: 1-415-348-4001
Web:http://www.pulseentertainment.com

Purple Software Limited (UK)
Purple House
12 Corporation Street
High Wycombe
Buckinghamshire
HP13 6TQ
England
United Kingdom
Tel: +44 (0) 1494 750300
Fax: +44 (0) 1494 750301
Web: http://www.purplesoftware.com

Purple Software Limited (Japan)
437-29 Komyo-cho
Ikoma-shi
Nara-ken
630-0201
Japan
Tel: +81 (0) 743 70 8126
Fax: +81 (0) 743 70 8127
Web: http://www.purplesoftware.com

Pyro Studios
Avda. de Burgos 16-D, 1° planta
28036 Madrid
Spain
Tel: 34 91 3846880
Fax: 34 91 7666474
Web: http://www.pyrostudios.com

QASoft
33401 Central Avenue
Union City, California 94587
United States
Web: http://www.qasoft.com

Qove Studios
1616 Anderson Rd, Suite 324
McLean, Virginia 22102
United States
Tel: 1-703-286-0759
Web: http://www.qove.com

Quantic Dream
56, Boulevard Davout
75020 Paris
France
Tel: (33) 01 44 64 00 90
Fax: (33) 01 44 64 00 89
Web: http://www.quanticdream.com

QuantumWorks Corporation
San Diego, California
United States
Tel: 1-858-483-9700
Fax: 1-858-483-9717
Web: http://quantumworks.com

Qwato Interactive Studios
Falls Church, Virginia
United State
Fax: 1-703-852-4306
Web: http://www.qwato.com

Qube Corporation
105-109 Sumatra Road
West Hampstead
London
NW6 1PL
United Kingdom
Tel: +44 (0) 20 7431 9995
Fax: +44 (0) 20 7431 9992
Web: http://www.qubesoft.com

Quicksilver Software, Inc.
17881 Sky Park Circle Suite H
Irvine, California
92614
Tel: 1-949-474-2150
Web: http://www.quicksilver.com

R3 Interactive
264 Richmond Road
Marleston
South Australia
Australia 5033
Tel: 61 (0)8 8351 8399

Fax: 61 (0)8 8351 8499
Web: http://www.r3interactive.com

R/GA Interactive New York
350 West 39th Street
New York, New York 10001
United States
Tel: 1-212-946-4000
Fax: 1-212-946-4010
Web: http://www.rga.com

R/GA Interactive Los Angeles
1888 Century Park East, 5th Floor
Los Angeles, California 90067
United States
Tel: 1-800-683-9487
Fax: 1-310-788-6600
Web: http://www.rga.com

Radical Entertainment
8th Floor, 369 Terminal Ave.
Vancouver, British Columbia
V6A 4C4
Canada
Tel: 1-604-688-0606
Fax: 1-604-685-0298
Web: http://www.radical.ca

Radon Labs GmbH
Kastanienalle 26
10435 Berlin
Germany
Web: http://www.radonlabs.de

Rage Software PLC
Martins Building
Water Street
Liverpool
L2 3SP
United Kingdom
Tel: +44 (0)151 237 2200
Fax: +44 (0)151 237 2201
Web: http://www.rage.co.uk

Rainbow Studios
3830 N. 7th St.
Phoenix, Arizona 85014
United States
Tel: 1-602-230-1300
Fax: 1-602-230-2553
Web: http://www.rainbo.com

Rapid Eye Entertainment
6215 Ferris Square, Suite 201
San Diego, California 92121
United States
Tel: 1-858-453-5100
Fax: 1-858-453-5121
Web: http://www.rapideyegames.com

Raptor Entertainment Pvt. Ltd.
#845, 6th Main, 3rd Cross
J.P.Nagar II Phase
Bangalore 560078, India
Tel: 091-080-6584624
Web:
http://www.raptorentertainment.com

Rare Ltd.
Manor Park
Nr. Twycross
Warks. CV9 3QN
United Kingdom
Web: http://www.rareware.com

Ra Studios
2158 Plainfield Pike, Unit 1
Cranston, Rhode Island 02920
United States
Tel: 1-888-SUNGOD-1
Web: http://www.rastudios.com

Ratbag
Level 8
63 Pirie Street
Adelaide, South Australia
5000
Tel: +61 8 8223 5830
Fax: +61 8 8223 5746
Web: http://www.ratbaggames.com

Ratloop, Inc.
717 Twinridge Ln.
Richmond, Virginia 23235
United States
Tel: 1-804-327-8444
Fax: 1-804-327-8445
Web: http://www.ratloop.com

Ravensburger AG
Grundstraße 9
5436 Würenlos
Switzerland

Tel: 0041-564368484
Fax: 0041-564368485
Web: http://www.ravensburger.com

Ravensburger spol. s.r.o.
Smetanova 66
46601 Jablonec Nad Nisou
Czech Republic
Tel: 0042-0428443311
Fax: 00420428443323
Web: http://www.ravensburger.com

Ravensburger S.A. / N.V.
International Trade Mart
Atomiumsquare/Bologna 274-275
1020 Brüssel
Belgium
Tel: 0032-(0)2-4 78 49 75
Fax: 0032-(0)2-4 78 54 40
Web: http://www.ravensburger.com

Ravensburger S.A.
24, rue de Paris
68220 Attenschwiller
France
Tel: 0033-389687800
Fax: 0033-389687807
Web: http://www.ravensburger.com

Ravensburger B.V.
Neonweg 2A
Postbus 289
3800 AG Amersfoort
Netherlands
Tel: 0031-334611445
Fax: 0031-334618145
Web: http://www.ravensburger.nl

Ravensburger Ges.m.b.H.
Ricoweg 24
A-2351 Wiener Neudorf
Austria
Tel: +43-2236-72 05 05
Fax: +43-2236-72 059
Web: http://www.ravensburger.com

Ravensburger Karton s.r.o.
Stritezska 968
57201 Policka
Czech Republic
Tel.: 0042-0463722125

Fax.: 0042-046322867
Web: http://www.ravensburger.com

Ravensburger Ltd.
Unit 1
Avonbury Business Park
Howes Lane
Bicester OX26 2UB
United Kingdom
Tel: 0044-1869363830
Fax: 0044-1869363835
Web: http://www.ravensburger.com

Ravensburger S.p.A.
Via Enrico Fermi
20- I-20090 Assago-MI
Italy
Tel: +39-(0)2/4577131
Fax: +39-(0)2/45713400
Web: http://www.ravensburger.com

Raven Software
Three Point Place, Suite 1
Madison, Wisconsin 53719
United States
Web: http://www.ravensoft.com

Raylight Studios s.r.l.
via Panoramica 16
82010 S. Angelo a Cupolo (BN)
Italy
Tel: +39-081-5635201
Fax: +39-081-5635201
Web: http://www.raylight.it

RayLogic
130 Maple Drive North
Hendersonville, Tennessee 37075
United States
Tel: 1-615-264-8038
Web: http://www.raylogic.com

Razorwax AS
PO Box 2194
Grunerlokka
0505 Oslo
Norway
Phone: +47 22 71 74 10
Fax: +47 22 80 77 99
Web: http://www.razorwax.com

Razorworks
The Kidlington Centre
High St, Kidlington
OX5 2DL
United Kingdom
Web: http://www.razorworks.com

Reactor Software
P.O. Box 248
Boxford, Massachusetts 01921
United States
Web: http://www.reactorsoftware.com

Reakktor Media Ltd.
Walderseestr. 30
30177 Hannover
Germany
Tel.: +49 - (0) 511 - 540 98 - 0
Fax.: +49 - (0) 511 - 540 98 - 70
Web: http://www.reakktor.com

Real Games
2601 Elliott Avenue, Suite 1000
Seattle, Washington 98121
United States
Tel: 1-206-674-2700
Web: http://games.real.com

Reality Pump
Zuxxez Enterainment AG
Shonauer Strasse 4a
67547 Worms
Germany
Tel: (+49) 06241-2688-0
Fax: (+49) 06241-2688-88
Web: http://www.realitypump.com
Web: http://www.zuxxez.com

ReAllis Inc.
P.O. Box 632
Piscataway, New Jersey 08855
United States
Web: http://www.reallis.com

Realm Interactive
931 East Southern Ave, Suite 206
Mesa, Arizona 85204
United States
Web: http://www.realminteractive.com

Realtime Gaming
Atlanta, Georgia
United States
Web: http://www.realtimegaming.com

Regulator Studios, LLC
Atlanta, Georgia
United States
Web: http://www.regulatorstudios.com

Related Designs Software GmbH
Fuststr.15
55116 Mainz
Tel.: 06131 - 554470
Web: http://www.related-designs.de

Realtime Associates Inc.
5757 W. Century Blvd, Suite 800
Los Angeles, California 90045
United States
Tel: 1-310-414-8555
Fax 1-310-414-8544
Web: http://www.rtassoc.com

Real Time Studios Pty Ltd
4/8 John Street,
Elwood, Victoria, 3184
Australia
Tel: +61 3 9525 6695
Tel: +61 3 9826 9811
Web: http://www.rtstudios.com.au

Real Virtuality Labs
Skolni 3054
76001 Zlin
Czech Republic
Web: http://www.rvlsoftware.com

Rebellion
The Studio
Brewer Street
Oxford
OX1 1QN
United Kingdom
Web: http://www.rebellion.co.uk

Rebelmind
Spacerowa 2
Warsaw
39-200

Poland
Tel: +48 22 8394935
Fax: +48 22 8394935
Web: http://www.rebelmind.com

Rebel Software
21 James St.
Prospect
South Australia
Australia 5082
Web: http://www.rebel.com.au

RedBedlam
15 Surrey Street
Brighton
East Sussex
BN1 3PA UK
United Kingdom
Tel: +44 7711 562 486
Web: http://www.redbedlam.com

Red Company
Japan
Web: http://red-universe.com

Red Eye Studio
2155 Stonington Ave #122
Hoffman Estates, Illinois 60195
United States
Tel: 1-847-843-2438
Web: http://www.redeye-studio.com

Red Eye Studios
One Grove Street, Suite 122A
Pittsford, New York 14534
United States
Web: http://www.redeyestudios.com

Red Lemon Studios
175 West George Street
Glasgow
Scotland
G2 2LB
United Kingdom
Web: http://www.redlemon.com

Red Storm Entertainment
2000 Aerial Center, S110
Research Triangle Park
Raleigh, North Carolina, 27560
United States
Tel: 1-919-460-1776
Fax: 1-919-468-3305
Web: http://www.redstorm.com

RedZone Interactive, Inc.
919 E. Hillsdale Blvd.
Foster City, California 94404
United States
Tel: 1-650-655-8000
Fax: 1-650-655-8042
Web: http://www.redzonegames.com

Reflections Interactive
Kingfisher House Ste. #5
Team Valley
GatesHead
Tyne & Wear
New Castle
NE11 0JQ
United Kingdom
Tel: 011 44 191 482 4494
Web: http://driver.gtgames.com

Reflections Interactive
Central Square South
Orchard Street
Newcastle upon Tyne
NE1 3AZ
United Kingdom
Phone: +44 (0) 191 277 2222
Fax: +44 (0) 191 277 2223
Web: http://www.infogames.com

Reflexive Entertainment
21068 Bake Parkway Ste# 100
Lake Forest, California 92630
United States
Web: http://www.reflexive.net

Related Designs Software GmbH
Fuststr.15
55116 Mainz
Germany
Tel.: +49 (0)6131 - 55447-0
Web: http://www.related-designs.de

Relic Entertainment
#400 - 948 Homer Street
Vancouver, British Columbia
Tel: 1-604-801-6577
Fax: 1-604-801-6578
Web: http://www.relic.com

reLINE Software
Friedrich-Ebert-Str. 61
D-30459 Hannover
Germany
Tel: +49 511 3885099
Fax: +49 511 3885089
Web: http://www.reline.de

Remedy Entertainment, Ltd.
Kappelitie 6
Espoo, Finland
02200
Tel: +358-9-435 5040
Fax: +358-9-435 50444
Web: http://www.remedy.fi

Retro Studios
1835A Kramer Lane, Suite 100
Austin, Texas 78758
United States
Tel: 1-512-493-4600
Fax: 1-512-493-4602
Web: http://www.retrostudios.com

Retro64, L.L.C.
311 Jackson #3
East Dundee, Illinois 60118
United States
Web: http://www.retro64.com

Revelation Interactive
Houston, Texas 77071
United States
Web:http://www.revelation-interactive.com

Revistronic
Claudio Coello, 76, Sc.
28006 Madrid
Spain
Tel: +34 915 772774
Fax: +34 915 772774
Web: http://www.revistronic.com

REVOgames
Germany
Web: http://www.revogames.de

Revolt Games
Moscow, Russia
Web: http://www.revoltgames.com

Revolution Software
Kings House
King Street
York
YO1 9SP
England
United Kingdom
Web: http://www.revolution.co.uk

Ripcord Games
4701 Patrick Henry Dr. Bungalow
Number 13
Santa Clara, California 95054-1863
United States
Web: http://www.ripcordgames.com

Ritual Entertainment
2019 N. Lamar St.
Suite 220
Dallas, Texas 75202
United States
Web: http://www.ritual.com

Rival Interactive
4501 Ford Avenue, Suite 240
Alexandra, Virginia 22302-1435
United States
Tel: 1-703-575-4264
Web: http://www.rivalinteractive.com

Riverdeep, Inc
399 Boylston Street
Boston, Massachusetts 02116
United States
Tel: 1-617-778-7600
Fax: 1-617-778-7601
Web: http://www.riverdeep.net

Riverdeep Interactive Learning Ltd
Styne House
3rd Floor
Upper Hatch Street
Dublin 2
Ireland
Tel: 353-1-6707570
Fax: 353-1-6707626
Web: http://www.riverdeep.net

RoboForge Limited
North Shore, Auckland
New Zealand
Web: http://www.roboforge.net

Rocketsnail Games
9-1481 Inkar Rd
Kelowna British Columbia
V1Y 8J1 CANADA
Tel: 1-250-717-9091
Web: http://www.rocketsnail.com

Rogue Entertainment
2019 N. Lamar St., Suite 240
Dallas, Texas 75202-1704
United States
Tel: 1-214-855-5955
Fax: 1-214-855-5980
Web: http://www.rogue-ent.com

Rock Solid Studios AB
Midskogsgränd 11, 1tr
S115 43 Stockholm
Sweden
Tel: +46 (0)8 442 70 20
Fax: +46 (0)8 664 12 90
Web: http://www.rocksolidstudios.com

Rockstar Studios
Second Floor
Links House
15 Links Place,
Leith, Edinburgh
EH6 7EZ
Tel: +44 (0) 131 454 2000
Fax: +44 (0) 131 454 2023
Web:http://www.rockstarstudios.com

Rockstar Vancouver
Barking Dog Studios Ltd.
4th Floor - 21 Water Street

Vancouver, BC.
V6B 1A1
Canada
Tel: 1-604-632-9663
Fax: 1-604-632-9664
Web: http://www.barking-dog.com

Rockstar Vienna
neo Software Produktions GmbH
Business Park Vienna
Wienerbergstraße 7/7.OG
A-1810 Vienna
Austria
Tel: +43/1/607 40 80
Fax: +43/1/607 40 80-6
Web: http://www.rockstarvienna.com

Ronin Entertainment
7595 Redwood Blvd., Suite 207
Novato, California 94945
United States
Fax: 1-415-893-1735
Web: http://www.roningames.com

RPM Studios inc.
4710 St. Ambroise
Suite 213
Montréal, Québec
H4C 2C7
Canada
Tel: 1-514-937-0606
Web: http://www.rpmstudiosinc.com

RT Soft: Robinson
Technologies.Inc
Makuyama, Fukuyama
Japan
Web: http://www.rtsoft.com

Runecraft Ltd Dewsbury
The Old Eightlands Well
Eightlands Road
Dewsbury
West Yorkshire
WF13 2PF
United Kingdom
Tel: +44 (0) 1924 500817
Fax: +44 (0) 1924 500898
Web: http://www.runecraft.co.uk

Runecraft Ltd Leeds
Coverdale House
15 East Parade
Leeds
West Yorkshire
LS1 2BH
United Kingdom
Tel: +44 (0) 113 220 6300
Fax: +44 (0) 113 220 6301
Web: http://www.runecraft.co.uk

Runecraft Ltd Boston
380 Lowell Street
Suite 202B
Wakefield, Massachusetts 01880
United States
Tel: 1-781-245-1714
Fax: 1-781-245-1353
Web: http://www.runecraft.com

Running With Scissors
P.O. Box 64309
Tucson, Arizona 85728-4309
United States
Web:
http://www.runningwithscissors.com

Ruske & Pühretmaier
Edutainment GmbH
Leberberg 10
D 65193 Wiesbaden
Tel: (+49) 06 11/95 04 0-0
Fax: (+49) 06 11/95 04 0-16
Web: http://www.edutainment.de

Russobit-M Co.
Petrovsko-Razumovsky pr. 7
Moscow 125083
Russia
Tel: +7 095 212 4232
Web: +7 095 212 0181
http://www.russobit-m.ru

RVL, s.r.o.
Skolni 3054
76001 Zlin
Czech Republic, Europe
Web: http://www.rvlsoftware.com

S2 Games
120 Avram Avenue, Suite 204
Rohnert Park, California 94928
United States
Web: http://www.s2games.com

Saber Interactive
350 5th Avenue Suite 4222
New York, New York 10118
United States
Tel: 1-212-736-2000
Fax: 1-212-736-6826
Web: http://www.saber3d.com

Sacnoth Digital Entertainment
Tokyo, Japan
Tel: 03-3280-4561
Fax: 03-3280-4540
Web: http://www.sacnoth.co.jp

Saffire Corporation
734 East Utah Valley Drive
American Fork, Utah 84003
United States
Tel: 1-801-847-1400
fax: 1-801-847-1401
Web: http://www.saffire.com

Sales Curve Interactive
11 Ivory House
Plantation Wharf
Clove Hitch Quay
Battersea
London
SW11 3TN
United Kingdom
Tel: +44 (0)20 7585 3308
Fax: +44 (0)20 7924 3419
Web: http://www.sci.co.uk

Salsa Shark Productions
Jobs, P.O. Box 66796
Houston, Texas 77266
United States
Web: http://www.salsagames.com

Sammy Corporation
2-23-2 Higashi Ikebukuro
Toshima-ku, Tokyo
Japan
Web: http://www.sammy.co.jp

Sammy Studios, Inc.
5650 El Camino Real, Suite 225
Carlsbad, California 92008
United States
Tel: 1-760-448-3000
Fax: 1-760-448-3500
Web: http://www.sammystudios.com

Santa Cruz Games
Santa Cruz, California
United States
Web: http://www.santacruzgames.com

Sarbakan
420, boul. Charest Est, bur. 300
Québec G1K 8M4
Canada
Tel: 1-418-682-0601
Fax: 1-418-682-2832
Web: http://www.sarbakan.com

Savage Entertainment
4079B Redwood Ave
Los Angeles, California 90066
United States
Tel: 1-310-306-1828
Fax: 1-310-306-1883
Web: http://www.savagesite.com

Savannah A/S
Ravnsborggade 8 B
Copenhagen, Denmark
2200
Tel: +45.35.24.78.00
Fax: +45.35.39.78.33
Web: http://www.savannah.dk

Savoir Fair
Paris, France
Web: http://www.savoirfair.com

Schwerpunkt
2483 Woodbury, Ste. 150
Pearland, Texas 77584
United States
Tel: 1-281-997-1209.
Web: http://www.ghg.net/schwerpt

Scholastic Interactive
555 Broadway

New York, New York 10012
United States
Tel: 1-212-343-6100
Web: http://www.scholastic.com

School Zone Interactive
Grand Haven, Michigan
United States
Web: http://www.schoolzone.com

Schwerer-als-Luft
Hugstraße 27 b
D-14469 Potsdam
Germany
Tel: +49 (0) 331 5050291
Web: http://www.schwerer-als-luft.de

SCI Entertainment
11 Ivory House
Plantation Wharf
Clove Hitch Quay
Battersea
London
SW11 3TN
United Kingdom
Tel: +44 (0) 20 7585 3308
Fax +44 (0) 20 7924 3419
Web: http://www.sci.co.uk

Scion Studios
5511 Capital Center Dr, Suite 625
Raleigh, North Carolina 27606
United States
Tel: 1-919-233-2004
Web: http://www.scionstudios.com

Screaming Games LLC
Anthem, Arizona 85086
United States
Tel: 1-623-551-4263
Fax: 1-623-551-4264
Web: http://www.screaminggames.com

SCS Software
1 Jagellonska
130 00 Prague 3
Czech Republic
Tel: (++420) 222 710 670
Fax: (++420) 222 720 431
Web: http://www.scssoft.com

Secret Level Inc.
870 Market Street, Suite 1015
San Francisco, California 94102
United States
Tel: 1-415-421-1249
Fax: 1-415-421-1284
Web: http://www.secretlevel.com

Sega of America
650 Townsend Street, Suite 650
San Francisco, California 94103-4908
United States
Web: http://www.sega.com

Sega.com & SEU
650 Townsend Street, Suite 550
San Francisco, California 94103-4908
United States
Web: http:// www.segaarcade.com

Sega Corporation Head Office
2-12, Haneda 1-chome
Ohta-ku
Tokyo 144-8531
Japan
Tel: (03) 5736-7111
Web: http://www.sega.jp

Sega Europe Ltd.
Canberra House
Gunnersbury Avenue
London
W4 5QB
United Kingdom
Tel: 44-208-995-3399
Web: http://www.sega-europe.com

Sega Amusements Europe Ltd.
Unit 2, Industrial Estate
Leigh Close
New Malden
Surrey
KT3 3NL
United Kingdom
Tel: 44-208-336-1222
Web: http://www.sega-europe.com

Sega Rosso Co. Ltd.
4th Floor
2-12-14 Higashi-koujiya

Ohta-ku, Tokyo
Japan 144-0033
Web: http://www.segarosso.com

Seimentech
Korea
Web: http://www.siemen.co.kr

Seismic Studios, Inc.
1534 Santa Rosa Street
Davis, California 95616
United States
Tel: 1-650-346-6329
Web: http://www.seismicstudios.net

SEK.ost
Köpenicker Straße 154a
10997 Berlin-Kreuzberg
Germany
Tel: 030 - 61 62 66 46
Fax: 030 - 61 62 66 45
Web: http://www.sek-ost.de

Sennari Interactive, LLC
5301 Beethoven Street, Suite 155
Los Angeles, California 90066
United States
Tel: 1-310-821-7880
Fax: 1-310-306-1739
Web: http://www.sennarigames.com

Sensible Software Company, The
Firlands Cottage
Cuckfield Road
Burgess Hill
RH15 8RE
United Kingdom
Telephone: 07941 149 305
Web: http://www.sensiblesoftware.co.uk

Sentient Machine Games LLC
2069 Argyle Ave Suite 515
Hollywood, California 90068
United States
Web: http://www.sentientmachine.com

Seta Corporation
Tokyo, Japan
Web: http://www.seta.co.jp

Shaba Games, LLC.
24 Shotwell
San Francisco, California 94103
United States
Tel: 1-415-332-1960
Fax: 1-415-332-1959
Web: http://www.shaba.com

Shade Inc.
Tokyo, Japan
Web: http://www.shade.co.jp

ShaRevolution
Tannenweg 19
21683 Stade
Germany
Tel: 04141 - 786504
Web: http://www.sharevolution.de

SharkByte Software Inc.
1245 W. 18th St.
Houston, Texas 77008
United States
Tel.: 1-713-426-4040
Fax: 1-713-426-4045
Web: http://www.sharkbyte.com

Sherer Digital Animation
71-956 Magnesia Falls Drive,
Rancho Mirage, California, 92270
United States
Tel: 1-760-346-7234
Fax: 1-760-340-3170
Web: http://www.shererdigital.com

Shine Studio
2203 wellborne Comm, Centre
North Point
Hong Kong
Web: http://www.shinestudio.com

Shiny Entertainment, Inc.
1088 North Coast Highway
Laguna Beach, California 92651-1338
United States
Fax: 1-949-376-8343
Web: http://www.shiny.com

Shrapnel Games
PMB #164
952 US Hwy 64 West
Raleigh, North Carolina 27502
7184
United States
Web: http://www.shrapnelgames.com

Shoeisha Co., Ltd.
Japan
Web: http://www.shoeisha.co.jp

Shadowpool Studios LLC
13830 54th Dr NE
Marysville, Washington 98271
United States
Web: http://www.shadowpool.com

Sidhe Interactive
Level 7, Willbank House
57 Willis Street
Wellington
New Zealand
Tel: +64 4 4712638
Fax: +64 4 4712639
Web: http://www.sidhe.co.nz

Sierra On-Line, Inc.
4247 S Minnewawa Ave
Fresno, California 93725
United States
Tel: 1-310-649-8008
Web: http://www.sierra.com

Sierra On-Line, Inc. Europe
32 avenue de l'Europe (Imm Energy
1)
78740 Velizy
Tel: 01 30 67 90 14
Fax: 01 30 67 90 01
Web: http://www.sierra.com

Sightline Vision AB
Liljeholmstorget 7
117 63 Stockholm
Sweden
Tel: +46(0)8 556 752 60
Fax: +46 (0) 8 556 752 65
Web: http://www.sightline.se

Sigil Games Online, Inc.
11315 Rancho Bernardo Drive
Suite 126
San Deigo, California 92128
United States
Web: http://www.sigilgames.com

Silent Software, Inc.
1400 W. Burbank Blvd.
Burbank, California 91506
United States
Web: http://www.silentsoftware.com

Silicon Dreams Studio
Unit 1
Somerville Court
Banbury Business Park
Adderbury
Nr. Banbury
Oxon
OX17 3SN
United Kingdom
Fax: +44 (0) 1295 812295
Tel: +44 (0) 1295 812916
Web: http://www.sdreams.co.uk

Silicon Knights, Inc.
1 St. Paul Street, Suite 800
St. Catharines, Ontario
L2R 7L2 Canada
Tel: 1-905-687-3334
Fax: 1-905-687-4055
Web: http://www.siliconknights.com

Silmarils
22, rue de la Maison Rouge
77185 Lognes - Marne La Vallee
France
Tel: (+33) 01 60 17 15 24
Fax: (+33) 01 60 17 36 76
Web: http://www.silmarils.com

Silver Creek Entertainment
PO Box 518
Grants Pass, Oregon 97528
United States
Web: http://www.silvercrk.com

Silverfish Studios
Birmingham, Alabama

United States
Web: http://www.silverfishstudios.com

Silver Lightning Software
5 Mitra Loop
Beechboro
6063
Australia
Tel: (08) 9378 7060
Web: http://www.silverlightning.com

Silver Style Entertainment e.K.
Wachsmuthstraße 9
13467 Berlin
Germany
Web: http://www.silverstyle.de

Silverback Entertainment
1430 north 6th avenue
Tucson, Arizona 85719
United States
Tel: 1-520-324-0472
Web: http://www.silverbackgames.com

Similis Software GmbH
Lessingstraße 6
D-46149 Oberhausen
Tel: 0208-767 12 89
Fax: 0208-767 12 91
Web: http://www.similis.com

Simis
Kuju Entertainment Ltd.,
Unit 10 Woodside Park,
Catteshall Lane,
Godalming,
Surrey.
GU7 1LG.
United Kingdom
Tel: +44 (0)1483 414 344
Fax: +44 (0)1483 414 287
Web: http://www.simis.co.uk

Simon & Schuster Interactive
1230 Avenue of the Americas
New York, New York 10020
United States
Web:
http://www.simonsays.com/cddomain

Similis Software GmbH
Vienna
Austria
Web: http://www.similis.com

Simis
Unit 10 Woodside Park
Catteshall Lane
Godalming
Surrey.
GU7 1LG.
United Kingdom.
Tel: +44 (0)1483 414 344
Fax: +44 (0)1483 414 287
Web: http://www.simis.co.uk

SIMS Co., Ltd.
Tokyo, Japan
Tel: 03-5459-3693
Fax: 03-5459-3696
Web: http://www.sims.co.jp

Simutronics Corporation
1500 Wall Street
St. Charles, Missouri 63303
United States
Tel: 1-314-925-3172
Web: http://www.play.net

Singularity Software
Geibel Str. 18
81679 Munchen
Germany
Tel: +49 (0) 89 4190 2242
Fax: +49 (0) 89 4190 2243
Web:
http://www.singularitysoftware.co.uk

Sinister Games
510 Glenwood Ave
Raleigh North Carolina 27603
United States
Tel: 1-919-402-8937
Web: http://www.sinistergames.com

Sinister Systems
Stefanova 15
1000 Ljubljana
Slovenija
Web: http://www.sinistersystems.com

Siren Games
West Roxbury, Massachusetts
United States
Web: http://www.sirengames.com

Sirtech Canada Ltd.
1645 Russell Rd. Unit 2, Suite 205
Ottawa
K1G 4G5
Canada
Tel: 1-613-736-5362
Fax: 1-613-736-5301
Web: http://www.sir-tech.com

Sismoplay
83 rue Masséna
69006 Lyon
France
Tel: 00 33 4 72 83 75 10
Fax: 00 33 4 72 83 75 12
Web: http://www.sismoplay.com

Skizoid
GPO Box 984
Brisbane
Queensland 4001
Australia
Tel: +61 7 3229 0594
Web: http://www.schizomedia.com.au

Skunkworks Studios
Hull Avenue
Redwood City, California
United States
Tel: 1-415-235-3235
Web: http://www.skunkstudios.com

Sleepless Software
Port Orchard, Washington
United States
Web: http://www.sleepless.com

Slitherine Software UK Ltd.
Wimbledon Village Business
Centre
Thornton House
Thornton Road
Wimbledon
London
SW19 4NG
United Kingdom

Tel: 020 8405 6434
Web: http://www.slitherine.co.uk

Small Fry Studios
Cambridge, Massachusetts
United States
Web: http://www.smallfrystudios.com

Slingshot Game Technology, Inc.
15 Mercer Rd
Natick Massachusetts 01760
United States
Tel: +1 508 655-3232
Fax: +1 508 655-3737
Web: http://www.soulride.com

Small Planet Ltd
Kaisaniemenkatu 3 B (3rd Floor)
FIN-00100 Helsinki
Finland
Tel: +358 9 5420 1100
Fax: +358 9 5420 1120
Web: http://www.smallplanet.fi

Small Rockets
The Old Magistrates Court
71 North Street
Guildford
Surrey
GU1 4AW
England
United Kingdom
Tel: +44 (0) 1483 445440
Fax: +44 (0) 1483 445444
Web: http://www.smallrockets.com

Smartdog
Leamington Spa
United Kingdom
Tel: 01926 335400
Fax: 01926 335460
Web: http://www.smartdog.co.uk

Smarterville (Esmart, LLC.)
810 Crescent Center Drive, Suite
120
Franklin, Tennessee 37067
United States
Web: http://www.smarterville.com

Smart Games, Inc.
49 Atlantic Avenue
Marblehead, Massachusetts
01945
United States
Web: http://www.smartgames.com

Smilebit Corporation
SEGA #2BLDG 5F, 1-2-12, Ohta-ku
Haneda, Tokyo
144-0043
Japan
Web: http://www.smilebit.com

Smilie Ventures Ltd.
Talisman House
13 North Park Road
Harrogate, North Yorkshire
HG1 5PD, England
United Kingdom
Tel: +44 (0)1423 565808/858230
Fax: +44 (0)845 4580360
Web: http://www.smilie.com

Smoking Gun Productions
Mede House
Salisbury Street
Southampton
SO15 2TZ
England
United Kingdom
Web: http://www.smoking-gun.co.uk

Snarl-up Software
Nöbbelövs Torg 29, 2606
226 52 Lund
Sweden
Tel: (+46) 070-6407040
Web: http://www.snarl-up.com

Snowball Interactive
Russsia
Web: http://www.snowball.ru

Snowball Group USA
Box #396 c/o IPS
PMB 572, 666 Fifth Avenue
New York New York 10103-0001
United States
Web: http://www.snowball.ru

Snowball Group UK
Box #396
c/o Post International
2 Gales Gardens
Birkbeck Street
London
E20 EJ
United Kingdom
Web: http://www.snowball.ru

Snowball Interactive De France
Box #396, c/o Post International
Sodexi Zone De Eret 4 Bat. Air
France Express
Rue Des Voyelles
Bp. 10041 Tremblay En France
95723 Roissy CDG Cedex,
France.
Web: http://www.snowball.ru

Snowblind Studios
777 108th Ave. NE, Suite 1550
Bellevue, Washington 98004
United States
Tel: 1-425-635-7781
Fax: 1-425-635-7774
Web: http://www.snowblindstudios.com

SN Systems Ltd
4th Floor - Redcliff Quay
120 Redcliff Street
Bristol
BS1 6HU
United Kingdom
Tel: +44 (0)117 929 9733
Fax: +44 (0)117 929 9251
Web: http://www.snsys.com

Soap Bubble Productions
530 rt 517
Sussex, New Jersey 07461
United States
Web: http://www.soapbubble.com

Softdisk, L.L.C.
PO Box 1240
Shreveport, Louisiana 71163
United States
Tel: 1-318-221-8718
Tel: 1-800-831-2694
Web: http://www.softdisk.com

Soft Enterprises GmbH
Hinter der Komödie 13-17
34117 Kassel
Germany
Web: http://www.se-games.com
Soft Enterprises
Wiegelsweg 2
34613 Treysa
Tel: 06691-91 98 06
Fax: 06691-91 98 07
Web: http://www.soft-enterprises.com

Softgame Company
107 Irving Drive
Weare, New Hampshire 03281
United States
Web: http://www.softgame.net

Soft-iK Co., Ltd
151-069 GiGwang B/D 5F
Bongcheon-Dong 949-20
Gwan-Ak Gu, Seoul, Korea
Tel: +82-2-889-9177
Fax: +82-02-885-9887
Web: http://www.soft-ik.com

SoftLab-NSK Ltd.
Universitetskii pr. 1
Novosibirsk
630090
Russia
Tel: 7(3832) 399220
Tel: 7(3832) 331067
Fax: 7(3832) 332173
Web: http://www.softlab-nsk.com

Softmax.Co.,Ltd
C&S Venture Bldg.
Nonhyun-Dong, 221-2
Kangnam-Ku, Seoul
135-829 Korea
Tel: 82-2-598-2554
Fax: 82-2-598-2555
Web: http://www.softmax.co.kr

Soft Spot Software
214, Chorley New Road
Bolton
Lancashire Bl1 5AA
United Kingdom
Web: http://www.softspotsoftware.com

Software 2000
Max-Planck-Straße 9
23701 Eutin
Tel: +49-4521-80040
Fax: +49-4521-800488
Web: http://www.software2000.de

Software Dynamics, inc.
PO Box 53506
310 - 777 Royal Oak Drive
Victoria, Brittish Columbia
V8X 5K2 CANADA
Tel: 1-250-721-2206
Web: http://www.sdispace.com

Soleau software, Inc.
163 Amsterdam Ave. #213
New York, New York 10023
United States
Tel: 1-212-721-2361
Fax: 1-212-873-4994
Web: http://www.soleau.com

Solecismic Software
Amherst, New Hampshire
United States
Web: http://www.solecismic.com

Sonalysts, Inc.
215 Parkway North
P.O. Box 280
Waterford, Connecticut 06385
United States
Web: http://www.sonalysts.com

Sony Computer Entertainment America
919 East Hillsdale Blvd., 2nd Floor
Foster City, California 94404
United States
Toll Free: 1-800-345-SONY
Tel: 1-800-345-SONY
Web: http://www.playstation.com

Sony Computer Entertainment UK Ltd
Stephenson Way
Wavertree Technology Park
Liverpool
L13 1HD
Tel: 44-1932-816-107
Web: http://www.scee.com

Sony Computer Entertainment
Europe
30 Golden Square
London
W1F 9LD
Tel: 020 7859 5000
Web: http://www.scee.net

Sony Computer Entertainment
Italia SPA
Via Flaminia 872
Roma, Italy
Tel: 06 330741
Web: http://www.playstationplanet.it

Sony Computer Entertainment
España SA
C/ Hernández de Tejada, 3
28027 Madrid
Spain
Tel: 91-377-11-00
Tel: 39-02-618381
Web: http://es.scee.com

Sony Computer Entertainment
Austria Ges. M.b.H.
Laxenburger Straße 254
1239 Wien
Austria
Tel: 43-1-61050-0
Web: http://www.playstation.at

Sony Computer Entertainment
(Benelux) BV
The Netherlands
Tel: 31-20-658-1911
Web: http://nl.scee.com

Sony Computer Entertainment
Australia Pty Ltd
Australia
Tel: 61-2-9887-6666
Web: http://au.playstation.com

Sony Computer Entertainment
France SA
92 avenue de Wagram, 75017
Paris
France
Tel: 33-1-55-90-30-00
Web: http://fr.scee.com

Sony Computer Entertainment
Deutschland GmbH
Frankfurter Str. 233
63263 Neu-Isenburg
Germany
Tel: 49-221-537-0
Tel: 06-102-433-0
Web: http://www.playstation.de

Sony Computer Entertainment
Switzerland AG
Flugplatzstr. 5
8404 Winterthurtr
Switzerland
Tele: 052 / 245 18 18
Fax: 052 / 245 18 19
Web: http://ch.scee.com

Sony Computer Entertainment
New Zealand
Tel: 64-9-488-6188
Web: http://nz.scee.com

Sony Computer Entertainment Inc.
7-1-1, Akasaka
Minato-ku
Tokyo, 107
Japan
Web: http://www.scei.co.jp

Sony Online Entertainment Inc.
San Diego California
United States
Tel: 1-858-537-0898
Web: http://www.station.sony.com

Southend Interactive
Verkstadsgatan 2
211 42 Malmö
Sweden
Web:http://www.southend-interactive.com

Southpeak Interactive
2900 Polo Pkwy, Suite 104
Midlothian, Virginia 23113
United States
Web: http://www.southpeak.com

Space Ewe Software
Dapci 218a
Cazma
Hrvatska
43240
Croatia
Web: http://www.space-ewe.com

Space Time Foam
Skyttegade 7, 3tv
2200 Copenhagen N
Denmark
Tel: (+45) 35301058
Fax: (+45) 35359340
Web: http://www.spacetimefoam.com

Spark Unlimited
15000 Ventura Boulevard Suite 202
Sherman Oaks, California 91403
United States
Tel: 1-818-455-0302
Fax: 1-818-455-0457
Web: http://www.sparkunlimited.com

Speedy Bullet Game Design
28788 Commerce St.
Manasass, Virginia 22110
United States
Tel: 1-877-555-3344
Web: http://www.sbdesign.org

Spelchan Software
2601 Pheasant Ridge Drive,
Armstrong, British Columbia
V0E 1B2 Canada
Tel: 1-250-546-9625
Web: http://www.blazinggames.com

Spellbound Entertainment
Weststrasse 15
77694 Kehl am Rhein
Tel: 07851-99 16 60
Fax: 07851-99 16 61
http://www.spellbound.de

Spellcraft Studio GmbH
Danziger Str. 139
10407 Berlin
Germany
Tel.: 030 / 46 79 46 83
Fax: 0721 - 151 47 95 74
Web: http://www.spellcraft.de

Spider Web Software Inc.
P.O. Box 85659
Seattle, Washington 98145
United States
Tel: 1-206-789-4438
Fax: 1-206-789-4016
Web:
http://www.spiderwebsoftware.com

Sports Interactive
Suite 6, Islington House
313-314 Upper St
London
N1 2XQ
United Kingdom
Tel: 020 7704 0091
Fax: 020 7704 0094
Web: http://www.sigames.com

Sports Mogul Inc.
196 Boston Avenue, Suite 2500
Medford, Massachusetts 02155
United States
Tel: 1-781-395-9860
Fax: 1-781-395-9865
Web: http://www.sportsmogul.com

Sproing Interactive Media GmbH
Fernkorngasse 10
1100 Vienna
Austria
Tel: +43 1 6043028
Fax: +43 1 6043028-50
Web: http://www.sproing.at

Squaresoft USA
Square Soft Inc
6060 Center Drive
Los Angeles, California 90045
United States
Web: http://www.squaresoft.com

Squaresoft Inc.
949 South Coast Drive, Suite 200
Costa Mesa, California 92626
United States
Tel: 1-714-438-1700
Fax: 1-714-438-1705
Web: http://www.squaresoft.com

Squaresoft Japan
Arco Tower, 1-8-1 Shimomeguro

Meguro-ku
Tokyo, 153
Japan
Tel: 81-3-5496-7525
Fax: 81-3-5496-7049
Web: http://www.squaresoft.com

Square Europe
London, England
United Kingdom
Web: http://www.square-europe.com

SRP Inter@ctive Inc.
440, Armand-Frappier, suite 190
Laval, Quebec
H7V 4B4
Canada
Web: http://www.strategicracing.com

SSG
Sydney, Australia
Web: http://www.ssg.com.au

Stagecast Software, Inc.
1325 Howard Avenue #705
Burlingame, California 94010-4212
United States
Tel: 1-877-STAGECAST
Tel: 1-877-782-4322
Tel: 1-650-599-0399
Fax: 1-650-599-0355
Web: http://www.stagecast.com

Stainless Games
Unit L
Innovation Centre
St Cross Business Park
Monks Brook Way
Newport
Isle of Wight
PO30 5WB
United Kingdom
Tel: +44 (0)1983 550440
Fax: +44 (0)1983 550444
Web: http://www.stainless.co.uk

Stainless Steel Studios
139 Main St., Kendall Square
Cambridge, Massachusetts 02142-1528
United States
Web:
http://www.stainlesssteelstudios.com

Stalker Entertainment
3439 Winecork Way - 685 clyde ave.
San Jose, California 95124
United States
Web:
http://www.stalkerentertainment.com

Starbreeze Studios
O3 Games AB
Sysslomansgatan 7
S-75311 Uppsala
Sweden
Tel: +46(0)18-122800
Tel: +46(0)18-122845
Fax: +46(0)18-122805
Web: http://www.starbreeze.com

Stardock
17292 Farmington Rd.
Livonia Michigan 48152
Tel: 1-734-762-0687
Fax: 1-734-762-0690
Web: http://www.stardock.net

Starfire
5235 West 139th Street
Savage, Minnesota 55378
United States
Tel: 1-952-890-5367
Web: http://www.starfireresearch.com

Stargames
13 Sheridan Close
Milperra NSW 2214.
Australia
Tel: +612 9773 0299
Fax: +612 9773 0828
Web: http://www.stargames.com.au

Stargames
PO Box 4516
Milperra NSW 1891.
Australia
Tel: +612 9773 0299

Fax: +612 9773 0828
Web: http://www.stargames.com.au

Starsphere Interactive, Inc.
P.O. Box 7551
Porter Ranch, California 91326
United States
Fax: 1-818-831-2043
Web: http://www.starsphere.com

Steel Monkeys
Tara House
46 Bath Street
Glasgow
G2 1HG
United Kingdom
Tel: +44 (0) 141 572 7272
Fax: +44 (0) 141 572 7373
Web: http://www.steelmonkeys.com

Stentec B.V.
Hollingerstr. 14
8621 CA Heeg
The Netherlands
Tel: +31 515 443515
Fax: +31 515 442824
Web: http://www.stentec.com

Sting
Tokyo, Japan
Tel: 03-5616-5791
Fax: 03-5616-5792
Web: http://www.sting.co.jp

Stock's Eye
148 West Street
Granby, Massachusetts 01033
United States
Tel: 1-413-467-2761
Web: http://www.stocks-eye.com

Stormfront Studios
4040 Civic Center Dr., Third floor
San Rafael, California 94903
United States
Tel: 1-415-479-2800
Fax: 1-415-479-2880
Web: http://www.stormfront.com

Stormregion Game Developers
Wesselenyi u. 21
Budapest, BP 1077
Hungary
Web: http://www.stormregion.com

Strategic Studies Group
Australia
Web: http://www.ssg.com.au

Strategic Studies Group
1612 9th Ave. NE
Rochester, Minnesota 55906
United States
Tel: 1-507-529-7937
Web: http://www.ssgus.com

Strategic Studies Group
6054 S. Lostan Ave
Tucson, Arizona 85706-4304
United States
Tel: 1-520-531-9799
Web: http://www.ssgus.com

Strategy First
147 St. Paul West
Suite 300
Montreal, Quebec
Canada
H2Y 1Z5
Tel: 1-514-844-3040
Fax: 1-514-844-4337
Web: http://www.strategyfirst.com

Streamline Studios
Digital Imaging and Animation
Egelstraat 6
1216AB Hilversum
The Netherlands
Tel: +31 (0) 35 772 5608
Fax: +31 (0) 35 772 5608
Web: http://www.streamline-studios.com

St. Tropez Ltd.
3-10-10, Akasaka, Minato-ku
Tokyo 107-0052
Japan
Tel: 81-3-5562-5400
Web: http://www.namco.co.jp

Studio 3
90 Long Acre
Covent Garden
WC2E
London
United Kingdom
Tel: 0207 849 3080
Fax: 0207 849 3081
Web: http://www.studio3.co.uk

Studio 3 Interactive Limited
66 College Road
Harrow,
Middlesex
HA1 1BX
England
Tel: +44 (0)181 863 5056
Fax: +44 (0) 181 863 5057
Web: http://www.studio3.co.uk

Studio 33 (UK) Ltd.
Nautilus House
Columbus Quay
Riverside Drive
Liverpool
L3 4DB
United Kingdom
Tel: 44 (151) 727 2787
Fax: 44 (151) 727 7337
Web: http://www.studio33.co.uk

Studio Gigante, Inc.
Chicago, Illinois
United States
Web: http://www.studiogigante.com

Studio Mythos
20817 S. Western Avenue
Torrance, California 90501
United States
Tel: 1-310-533-0668
Fax: 1-310-533-0638
Web: http://www.studiomythos.com

Studio SAN (SleepTeam Labs)
Chomutov, Czech republic
Web: http://www.sleepteam.com

Stunt Puppy Entertainment Inc.
1690 Woodside Road, Suite 104
Redwood City California 94061

United States
Tel: 1-650-363-5777
Fax: 1-650-363-0552
Web: http://www.stuntpuppy.com

Sucker Punch
14575 Bel-Red Road, Suite #200
Bellevue, Washington 98007
United States
Fax: 1-425-614-2795
Web: http://www.suckerpunch.com

Sudden Presence, LLC
1012 N. Alexandria Ave.
Los Angeles, California 90029
United States
Tel: 1-818-510-1782
Fax: 1-435-603-5517
Web: http://www.suddenpresence.com

Sunburst Technology
101 Castleton Street, Suite 201
Pleasantville, New York 10570
United States
Tel: 1-914-747-3310
Fax: 1-914-747-4109
Web: http://www.hminet.com

Sunflowers Interactive
Entertainment Software GmBH
Ohmstrasse 2
63225 Langen
Germany
Telephone: +49 (0) 6103 - 2063 0
Fax: +49 (0) 6103 - 2063 217
Web: http://www.sunflowers.de

Super X Studios
31708 7th Ave S
Federal Way, Washington 98003
United States
Tel: 1-619-733-8332
Fax: 1-425-696-9820
Web: http://www.superxstudios.com

Sunspire Studios
Waterloo, Ontario
Canada
Web: http://www.sunspirestudios.com

Sunstorm Interactive
120 East Market St
Suite 1100
Indianapolis, Indiana 46204
United States
Web: http://www.sunstorm.net

Supedo
2 andrews road
London
E8 4QL
United Kingdom
Tel: +44(0)20 7241 7012
Web: http://www.supedo.co.uk

Superempire Interactive Inc.
6319 - 151st Avenue South East
Bellevue, Washington 98006
United States
Tel: 1-425-443-6129
Fax: 1-425-643-7413
Web: http://www.superempire.com

Superempire Interactive Inc.
Chasovaya street 16 , Office 216
Moscow, Russia
Tel: +7 (095) 136-8734
Fax: +7 (095) 152-4820
Web: http://www.superempire.com

Superscape Inc.
131 Calle Iglesia
Suite 200
San Clemente, California 92672
United States
Tel: 1-800-965-7411
Fax: 1-949-940-2841
Web: http://www.superscape.com

Superscape Inc.
316 Eisenhower Parkway
Livingston, New Jersey 07039
United States
Tel: 1-973-992-7030
Fax: 1-973-992-8130
Web: http://www.superscape.com

Superscape Ltd
Cromwell House
Bartley Wood Business Park
Hook
Hampshire
RG27 9XA
United Kingdom
Tel: +44 (0)1256 745 745
Fax: +44 (0)1256 745 777
Web: http://www.superscape.com

Superscape KK
Level 18
Yebisu Garden Place Tower
4-20-3 Yebisu
Shibuya-ku
Tokyo 150-6018
Japan
Tel: +81 3 5789 5775
Fax: +81 3 5789 5757
Web: http://www.superscape.com

Superscape Sarl
4 Rue Miromesnil
75008 Paris
France
Tel: +33 1 42 68 04 04
Fax: +33 1 42 68 04 10
Web: http://www.superscape.com

Superscape RTZ S.L.
Moll De Barcelona
The World Trade Center
6th Floor
08039 Barcelona
Tel: +34 90 250 0777
Fax: +34 93 508 8780
Web: http://www.superscape.com

Supersonic Software Ltd
Supersonic House
23 Adelaide Road
Leamington Spa
Warwickshire
CV31 1PD
United Kingdom
Web:
http://www.supersonic-software.com

Super X Studios
31708 7th Ave S
Federal Way, Washington 98003

United States
Voice: 1-206-799-0604
Fax: 1-425-696-9820
Web: http://www.superxstudios.com

Sunflowers Interactive
Entertainment Software GmBH
Seligenstädter Grund 1
63150 Heusenstamm
Germany
Tel: +49 (0) 6104 - 948 20
Fax: +49 (0) 6104 - 948 217
Web: http://www.sunflowers.de

Sunny Games LLC
10651 N.E. 11th Court
Miami Shores, Florida 33138
United States
Web: http://www.sunnygames.com

Sunstorm Interactive
120 East Market Street, Suite
1100
Indianapolis, Indiana 46204
United States
Tel: 1-317-843-2690
Fax: 1-317-843-0474
Web: http://www.sunstorm.net

Surreal Software, Inc.
701 N. 34th Street, Suite 301
Seattle, Washington 98103
United States
Tel: 1-206-587-0505
Fax: 1-206-587-5608
Web: http://www.surreal.com

SWING! Entertainment Media AG
Industriestr. 8
41564 Kaarst
Germany
Tel.: +49 (0) 2131 / 4066   0
Fax: +49 (0) 2131 / 4066   440
Web: http://www.swing-ag.de

SW Games
6445 Westgate
Ft. Worth, Texas 76180-4705
United States
Web: http://www.swgames.com

Swamiware LLC.
1657 Abigail Way
Ann Arbor, Michigan 48103
United States
Tel: 1-734-996-9161.
Web: http://www.swamiware.com

Swingin' Ape Studios, Inc.
26895 Aliso Creek Road, Suite B #471
Aliso Viejo, California 92656
United States
Fax: 1-949-716-8218
Web: http://www.swingingape.com

Sylum Entertainment Ltd.
92 Seward Avenue
Middletown, New York 10940
United States
Tel: 1-845-341-0195
Fax: 1-845-342-0477
Web: http://www.sylum.com

Synaptic Soup
London, England
United Kingdom
Web: http://www.synapticsoup.com

Synergenix Interactive AB
Solna strandväg 96, Plan 6
17154 Solna
Sweden
Tel: +468 764 9196
Web: http://www.synergenix.se

Synetic - The Funfactory
Auf der Haar 47
33332 Gütersloh
Germany
Telephone: +49 (0)5241 400990-0
Fax: +49 (0)5241-400990-9
Web: http://www.synetic.de

SYNOTEC
New media solutions
Marktallee 20
48165 Munster
Germany
Tel: 02501 964774
Fax: 02501 964769
Web: http://www.synotec-newmedia.de

Synovial, Inc.
1669-2 Hollenbeck Avenue, #227
Sunnyvale, California 94087
United States
Web: http://www.synovial.com

Synthetic Dimensions
Silver Birches House
72 Wergs road
Tettenhall
Wolverhampton
WV6 8TH
United Kingdom
Tel: 01902 742442
Web: http://www.syndime.com

Syscom Entertainment Inc.
SEF BLDG 1-3-5 MATsugaya
taito-ku Tokyo
Japan 111-0036
Tel: +81-3-5626-7770
Fax: +81-3-5826-7778
Web: http://www.syscom.co.jp

T&E Co., Ltd.
1273-1, Aoyagi, Ichihara
Chiba 299-0102
Japan
Tel: 81-436-23-2701
Web: http://www.namco.co.jp

T-Bot
39A Rue de la Grange aux Belles
75010 Paris
France
Web: http://www.t-bot.fr

Tactical Soft Inc
CP 69 Delorimier
Montreal, Quebec
H2H 2N6
Canada
Web: http://www.tacticalsoft.com

Taito Corporation
Tokyo, Japan
Tel: 03 - 3222 - 4825
Web: http://www.taito.co.jp

Takara
230 Fifth Avenue
Suite 1201-6
New York, New York 10001
United States
Web: http://www.takaratoys.co.jp

Takara
Tokyo, Japan
Tel: 03-3-603-2131
Tel: 81-3-5680-2041
Fax: 81-3-5680-8627
Web: http://www.takaratoys.co.jp

Take-Two Interactive Software,
Inc.
622 Broadway
New York, New York 10012
United States
Tel: 1-646-536-2842
Web: http://www.take2games.com

Take Two UK
Saxon House
4 Victoria Street
Windsor
Bershire
SL4 1EN
United Kingdom
Tel: 01753 496 600
Web: http://www.take2games.com

Takumi Corp.
Tokyo, Japan
Tel: 03-5269-3571
Fax: 03-5269-3572
Web: http://www.takumi-net.co.jp

Takuyo
Kanagawa prefecture
Yokosuka
Japan
Tel: 046-841-6028
Tel: 046-846-1127
Web: http://www.takuyo.co.jp

Takuyo
Tokyo, Japan
Tel: 03-5439-9253
Web: http://www.takuyo.co.jp

Taldren
1520 Nutmeg Place Suite #250
Costa Mesa, California 92626-
2501
United States
Tel: 1-714-43-1042
Fax: 1-714-438-2469
Web: http://www.taldren.com

TalonSoft
9900 Franklin Square Drive, Suite
A
White Marsh, Maryland 21236
United States
Tel: 1-410-933-9191
Fax: 1-410-933-1740
Web: http://www.talonsoft.com

Talking Birds Ltd
5 Minster Close
Rayleigh
Essex. SS6 8SF
England
United Kingdom
Web: http://www.talking-birds.co.uk

Tamsoft Corp.
Tokyo, Japan
Tel: 03-5828-5592
Fax: 03-5828-5595
Web: http://www.tamsoft.co.jp

Tannhauser Gate
ul. Mielczarskiego 60a
51-663 Wroclaw
Poland
Tel: +48 71 345-16-19
Fax: +48 71 345-21-39
Web: http://www.thgate.com

Tantalus Interactive
Level 5 'The Tea House'
28 Clarendon St
South Melbourne 3205
Victoria Australia
Tel: +61 3 9674 5955
Fax: +61 3 9674 5966
Web: http://www.tantalus.com.au

Tantrum
16815 Von Karman Ave.
Irvine, California 92606
United States
Tel: 1-949-553-6655
Fax: 1-949-252-2820
Web: http://www.tantrum.com

Targem
Ekaterinburg
Highland 12
of.213
Russia
Tel: (3432) 428172
Web: http://www.targem.ru

Targetware
San Francisco, California
United States
Web: http://www.targetware.net

Tasman Studios
Sydney, Australia
Web: http://www.tasman-studios.com

Tatanka
ul . Zupnicza 17
03-821 Warsaw
Poland
Tel: +48 22 619 63 06
Fax: +48 22 619 99 35
Web: http://www.tatanka.pl

TDC Games, Inc.
1456 Norwood Avenue
Itasca, Illinois 60143
Tel: 1-800-292-7676
Fax: 1-630-860-9977
United States
Web: http://www.tdcgames.com

TDK Mediactive Inc.
26115 Mureau Road, Suite B
Calabasas, California 91302-3126
United States
Tel: 1-818-878-0505
Web: http://www.tdk-mediactive.com

TDK Mediactive, Inc.
4373 Park Terrace Drive

Westlake Village, California
91361
United States
Tel: 1-818-707-7063
Fax: 1-818-707-1450
Web: http://www.tdk-mediactive.com

Team17 Software Limited
Longlands House
Wakefield Road
Ossett
West Yorkshire
WF5 9JS
United Kingdom
Web: http://www.team17.com

Team Evolve
4145 E. Vera Drive
Suite #102
Indianapolis, Indiana 46220-5248
United States
Tel: 1-317-253-2541
Web: http://www.teamevolve.com

Techland Software
Zolkiewskiego 3
63400 Ostrow Wlkp
Poland
Tel: +48 (62) 7372748
Fax: +48 (62) 7372749
Web: http://www.techlandsoft.com

Technyat3D
P.O. Box 2051
Damascus, Syria
Tel: +963 11 232 36 88
Web: http://www.zoyagame.com

Technyat3D
Dubai, United Arab Emirates
Tel: +971 4 269 53 05
Web: http://www.zoyagame.com

Tecmo Inc.
PO Box 5553
21213-B Hawthorne Blvd.
Torrance, California 90503
United States
Tel: 1-310-944-5005
Fax: 1-310-944-3344
Web: http://www.tecmogames.com

Tecmo Inc.
North 4 Chome 1st
102-8230 Tokyo Chiyoda Ku
Japan
Tel: 34 03-3222-7645
Web: http://www.tecmo.co.jp

Telegames, Inc.
P.O. Box 1855
DeSoto, Texas 75123
United States
Tel: 1-972-228-0690
Fax: 1-972-228-0693
Web: http://www.telegames.com

Templar Studios
157 Ludlow Street
New York, New York 10002
United States
Tel: 1-212-982-9360
Fax: 1-212-982-9370
Web: http://www.templar.com

Terabyte Inc.
3F Daimex Sapporo Minami 2Jo
Bldg.
Minami 2Jo Nishi 10 Chome, Chuo-ku
Sapporo, 060-0062
Japan
Tel: +81(11)280-2180
Fax: +81(11)280-2181
Web: http://www.tera-byte.co.jp

Terminal Reality, Inc.
2274 Rockbrook Drive
Lewisville, Texas 75067
United States
Tel: 1-972-315-8089
Fax: 1-972-315-8091
Web: http://www.terminalreality.com

Terminal Studio
Seattle, Washington
United States
Tel: 1-206-98-GAMES
Tel: 1-206-984-2637
Web: http://www.terminalstudio.com

Termite Games
Adelgatan 11
Malmo
Sweden
Web: http://www.termite-games.com

Terratools Software und
Filmproduktions GmbH
Rudolf-Breitscheid-Straße 162
D-14482 Potsdam-Babelsberg
Tel: +49 (331) 62 01 -20
Fax: +49 (331) 62 01 -299
Web: http://www.terratools.de

Tesseraction Games Inc.
39747 Little Fall Creek Rd.
Fall Creek, Oregon 97438
United States
Tel: 1-541-686-4200
Tel: 1-541-726-3077
Tel: 1-541-485-5151
Fax: 1-888-663-3350
Web: http://www.tesseractiongames.com

Thalamus Interactive Ltd.
314 Linthorpe Road
Middlesbrough
TS1 3QX
United Kingdom
Web:
http://www.thalamusinteractive.com

ThatGame
Melbourne, Victoria
Australia
Web: http://www.thatgame.com

The 3DO Company
200 Cardinal Way
Redwood City, California 94063
United States
Tel: 1-650-385-3000
Fax: 1-650-385-3183
Web: http://www.3do.com

The Bitmap Brothers
Wapping, London
United Kingdom
Web: http://www.bitmap-brothers.co.uk

The Bitmap Brothers
Harrogate
United Kingdom
Web: http://www.bitmap-brothers.co.uk

The Code Monkeys Ltd
Concourse House
432 Dewsbury Road
Leeds
LS11 7DF
United Kingdom
Tel: +44 (0) 113 271 0996
Fax: +44 (0) 113 271 3572
Web: http://www.codemonkeys.com

The Collective,
1900 Quail Street,
Newport Beach, California 92660
United States
Fax: 1-949-724-9667
Web: http://www.collectivestudios.com

The Creative Assembly
Weald House
Southwater Business Park
Southwater Nr. Horsham
West Sussex
Rh13 - 7he.
United Kingdom
Tel: (+44)(01403) 734473
Fax: (+44)(01403) 734477
Web: http://www.creative-assembly.co.uk

The Creative Assembly
Sydney, Australia
Web: http://www.creative-assembly.co.uk

The Dawn Interactive Srl
via Pontinia 50
04100 Latina
Italy
Tel: +39-0773-664877
Fax: +39-0773-416786
Web: http://www.thedawn.it

The Games Kitchen Ltd.
1 Michaelson Square
Livingston
Scotland
EH54 7DP
United Kingdom

Tel: +44 (0) 1506 20 30 20
Fax: +44 (0) 1506 47 22 09
Web: http://www.gameskitchen.com

The Game Design Studio
7 avenue des Pavillons
92700 Colombes
France
Tel: +33 (0)1 47 85 74 36
Web: http://www.gamedesignstudio.com

The Groove Alliance
6464 Sunset Blvd., Ste. 910
Hollywood, California 90028
United States
Tel: 1-323-962-3456
Fax: 1-323-962-5820
Web: http://www.3dgroove.com

The Logic Factory
100 Dolores Street #251
Carmel, California 93923
United States
Tel: 1-408-625-5777
Fax: 1-408-625-5818
Web: http://www.logicfactory.com

Themis
2530 Meridian Parkway 2nd Floor
Durham, North Carolina 27713
United States
Tel: 1-919-806-4477
Web: http://www.themis-group.com

Themis
27 Signal Road
Stamford, Connecticut 06902
United States
Web: http://www.themis-group.com

The Other Guys
Franzengatan 14
871 31 Härnösand
Sweden
Tel: 46-611-22334
Fax: 46-611-22334
Web: http://www.otherguys.com

The Planet
Klerkegade 19,
Copenhagen, 1308
Denmark
Tel: +45 33930020
Web: http://www.planet.dk

There.com
165 Jefferson Drive
Menlo Park, California 94025
United States
Tel: 1-650-433-4000
Web: http://www.prod.there.com

The Software Refinery
21 Wharf Street
Leeds
LS2 7EQ
United Kingdom
Tel: +44 (0) 113-2444702
Web: http://www.refinery.co.uk

The VIP Group
111 Dunlop St East, Suite 1204
Barrie, Ontario L4M6J5
Canada
Web: http://www.shop-vip.com

The Whole Experience, Inc
307 3rd Avenue South, Suite 520
Seattle, Washington 98104
United States
Tel: 1-206-287-9146
Web: http://www.wxp3d.com

TheyerGFX Pty Ltd
33 Pinnaroo Street
Santa Barbara, QLD 4212
Australia
Tel: +61 7 5530 8752
Fax: +61 7 5530 1024
Web: http://www.theyergfx.com

Think Tank Studios
3 Eden Court, 55 Standen Rd
Southfields
London
SW18 5TH
United Kingdom
Tel: +44 (0)7712 885 934
Web: http://www.thinktankstudios.co.uk

Third Law Interactive
14860 Montfort Drive Suite 250
Dallas, Texas 75254
United States
Tel: 1-972-960-1102
Web: http://www.thirdlaw.com

Third Wire Productions, Inc.
3355 Bee Cave Road, Suite 302
Austin, Texas 78746
United States
Tel: 1-512-327-8052
Fax: 1-512-328-0166
Web: http://www.thirdwire.com

Thot'em Interactif
88 Boulevard de la Villette
75019 Paris
France
Tel: 01-42-08-33-45
Fax: 01-42-08-33-84
Web: http://www.thot-em-interactif.com

Thought Guild
530 Showers Dr., Suite 7-294
Mountain View, California 94040
United States
Tel: 1-650-568-2710
Fax: 1-650-960-0921
Web: http://www.t-guild.com

THQ Inc.
27001 Agoura Road, Ste 325
Calabasas Hills, California 91301
United States
Tel: 1-818-871-5000
Web: http://www.thq.com

THQ Inc.
35 Hartwell Avenue
Lexington, Massachusetts 02421
United States
Tel: 1-781-863-8868
Web: http://www.thq.com

THQ International Ltd.
Dukes Court
Duke Street
Woking
Surrey
GU21 5BH

England
United Kingdom
Tel: +44 (0)1483 767656
Fax: +44 (0)1483 770727
Web: http://www.thq.co.uk

THQ Entertainment GmbH
z. Hd. Frau Wörner
Daimlerstr. 8
41564 Kaarst
Tel: 0 21 31 / 607 122
Web: http://www.thq.de

THQ France
32, rue de Paradis
75010 Paris
France
Tel: 01 45 23 99 72
Fax: 01 45 23 99 90
Web: http://www.thq.fr

THQ Asia Pacific Pty Ltd.
Level 2, 578 St. Kilda Road
3004, Melbourne, Victoria
Australia
Tel: 61 3 9573 9200
Web: http://www.thq.com.au

Thrive Media, Inc.
5th Floor, 856 Homer Street
Vancouver, British Columbia
V6B 2W5 Canada
Tel: 1-604-681-2858
Web: http://www.thrivemedia.com

Thrushwave
31708 7th Ave S
Federal Way, Washington 98003
United States
Tel: 1-619-733-8332
Fax: 1-425-696-9820
Web: http://www.thrushwave.com

Tibo Software
Varsavska 238
Pardubice 53009
Czech Republic
Web: http://www.tibosoftware.com

Tiburon - Electronic Arts
2301 Lucien Way, Suite 395
Maitland, Florida 32751
United States
Fax: 1-407-838-8899
Web: http://www.tiburon.com

Tiertex Design Studios
The Yews
67 Palatine Road
Didsbury
Manchester
M20 3LJ
United Kingdom
Tel: +44 (0) 161 446 2251
Fax: +44 (0) 161 446 2259
Web: http://www.tiertex.co.uk

Tigon Software Ltd.
Taunfield
South Road
Taunton
Somerset
TA1 3ND
United Kingdom
Tel: (+44) 01823 326314
Fax: (+44) 01823 350726
Web: http://www.tigon.co.uk

Tilted Mill
9 Carter Drive
Natick, Massachusetts 01760
United States
Web: http://www.tiltedmill.com

Tilted Mill U.S.
141 Linden Street
Wellesley, Massachusetts 02482-7925
United States
Web: http://www.tiltedmill.com

TimeGate Studios, Inc.
14140 Southwest Freeway Suite 400
Sugar Land, Texas 77478
United States
Tel: 1-281-295-GAME
Fax: 1-281-295-4050
Web: http://www.timegate.com

Time Travel Games
1558 Forrest Trail Circle

Toms River, New Jersey 08753
United States
Web: http://www.timetravelgames.com

Tinkering.net LLC
P.O. Box 59
New York, New York 10021-0030
United States
Tel: 1-917-509-7554
Web: http://www.tinkering.net

Titan Software
Mahndorfer Heerstrasse 80A
D-28307 Bremen
Germany
Tel: +49 (0)421 48 16 20
Fax: +49 (0)421 43 88 29
Web: http://www.titan-
computer.com

Titus Interactive,
Parc de I Esplanade
12 rue Enrico Fermi
Saint-Thibault des Vignes
77462 Lagny-sur-Marne
France
Tel: 01 60 31 04 03
Fax: 01 60 31 07 08
Web: http://www.titus-
interactive.com

Titus Software Corporation
20432 Corisco Street
Chatsworth, California, 91311
United States
Tel: 1-818-709-3692
Fax: 1-818-709-6537
Web: http://www.titus-
interactive.com

Titus Software UK Limited
162a The Parade
Leamington Spa
Warwickshire
England CV32 4AE
United Kingdom
Tel: 01926 335400
Fax: 01926 335460
Web: http://www.titus-interactive.com

Titus Japan K.K.
Kotubuki Dogenzaka Bldg 8F
1-19-11 Dogenzaka
Shibuyaku 1500043
Japan
Web: http://www.titus-interactive.com

Tiwak
PIT de la Pompignane
rue de la Vieille Poste - Bât. T2
34055 Montpellier cedex 1
France
Tel: +33 (0)4 99 52 85 90
Fax: +33 (0)4 99 52 29 95
Web: http://www.tiwak.com

TKO Software, Inc.
207 McPherson St. Suite D
Santa Cruz, California 95060
United States
Tel: 1-831-457-8560
Fax: 1-831-457-8563
Web: http://www.tko-software.com

ToeJam & Earl Productions, Inc.
One Thorndale Drive, Suite 225
San Rafael, California 94903
United States
Web: http://www.tjande.com

Toka
33, rue Faidherbe
75011 Paris
France
Tel: 33 (0) 1 42 79 38 62
Fax: 33 (0) 1 42 79 39 71
Web: http://www.toka.fr

Toka
Muse Nishi Ikeburo 6 Gousitsu
Nagasaki 1-28-3 Toshima-ku
Tokyo, Japan
Tel: (03)-5964-5901
Fax: (03)-5964-5901
Web: http://www.toka.fr

TOMY Company, Ltd.
7-9-10 Tateishi, Katsushika-ku,
Tokyo 1 24-8511 Japan
Tel: +81 3 3693 8660
Web: http://www.tomy.com

TOMY Corporation
4695 MacArthur Court Suite
130, Newport Beach, California
92660
United States
Web: http://www.tomy.com/usa

Tommy's Toys
P.O. Box 11261
Denver, Colorado 80211-0261
United States
Web: http://www.tommystoys.com

tomgamesDE
Europe
Tel: 0173 3939577
Web: http://www.tomgames.de

Topware Interactive
Markircher Strasse 25
68229 Mannheim
Germany
Tel: +49 621 - 48 05 0
Fax: +49 621 - 48 05 200
Web: http://www.topware.com

Topics Entertainment Inc.
1600 S.W. 43rd St.
Renton, Washington 98055
United States
Tel: 1-425-656-3621
Web: http://www.topics-ent.com

Topware Poland Sp. z
ul. KamiDskiego 19
43-300 Bielsko-BiaBa
Poland
Web: http://www.topware.pl

Torn Space
10 E 29th Street, Suite 10G
New York, New York 10016
United States
Tel: 1-212-779-0597
Web: http://www.tornspace.com

Torus Games
6-8 Floriston Road
3155 Boronia, Victoria
Australia

Tel: +61 3 9762 0522
Fax: +61 3 9762 0533
Web: http://www.torus.com.au

Total ArKade Software (T.A.K.S)
30 Berrylands
Raynes Park
London SW20 9HD
United Kingdom
Web: http://www.taks.co.uk

Totally Games
PO Box 6248
Terra Linda, California 94903-0248
United States
Fax: 1-248-671-0867
Web: http://www.totallygames.com

Tournament Games
Lebanon, Tennessee
United States
Web: http://www.tournamentgames.com

Toy's for Bob
San Fransisco, California
United States
Tel: 1-415-898-1060
Fax: 1-415-898-2490
Web: http://www.toysforbob.com

Train Wreck Studios
8282 S. Memorial Drive, Suite 104
Tulsa, Okholoma 74133
United States
Tel: 1-918-252-2015
Web: http://www.trainwreckstudios.com

Travellers Tales
Cheshire
United Kingdom
WA16 0SR
Tel: 00 44 01565 757 300
Web: http://www.t-tales.com

Treasure
Tokyo, Japan
Tel: 03-3361-8132
Fax: 03-3361-8152
Web: http://www.treasure-inc.co.jp

Trecision S.p.A.
C.so Assereto 15
16035 Rapallo (GE)
Italy
Tel: (+39) 0185 23 20 22
Fax: (+39) 0185 237 592
Web: http://www.trecision.com

Treyarch
3420 Ocean Park Blvd., Suite 2000
Santa Monica, California 90405
Tel: 1-310-581-4700
Fax: 1-310-581-4702
Web: http://www.treyarch.com

tri-Ace Inc.
4-31-8 Yoyogi
Shibuya-ku, Tokyo 151-0053
Japan
Tel: 03-3320-9671
Web: http://www.tri-ace.com

Tricium Factory
Müllerstraße 38
15370 Petershagen
Tel: 033439-80 58 8
Fax: 033439-80 58 8
Web: http://www.tfactory.de

Triggerlab
Sternstr. 23
60318 Frankfurt
Germany
Web: http://www.triggerlab.de

Triglow Pictures Ltd.
3F Gunbok B/D., 924-13
BangBae-dong
Seocho-gu
Seoul, Korea
Web: http://www.triglow.co.kr

Trillium Group
903 Colorado Ave. Suite 220
Santa Monica, California 90401
United States
Tel: 1-310-260-1102
Fax: 1-310-260-6496
Web: http://www.thetrilgroup.com

Trilobite Graphics Doctor Gómez
Ulla, 14
28028 - Madrid
Spain
Tel: +34 91 726 72 87
Tel: +34 91 725 18 98
Fax: +34 91 726 87 73
Web: http://www.trilobitegraphics.com

Trilobyte
Rockwall, Texas
United States
Web: http://www.tbyte.com

TriNodE Entertainment GmbH
Universitätsstraße 90
44789 Bochum
Tel: (+49) +234 91 29 25 6
Fax: (+49) +234 91 29 25 7
Web: http://www.trinode.de
Web: http://www.trinode.com
Web: http://www.trinode.net

TriStrip
19425 Soledad Canyon Road,
Suite B #209
Santa Clarita, California 91351
United States
Tel: 1-818-601-4562
Fax: 1-818-688-3986
Web: http://www.tristrip.com

Triumph Studios
Slot de Houvelaan 39
Maasland
ZH 3155 VR
Netherlands
Tel: 078-6815053
Web: http://www.triumphstudios.com

Tri Synergy Inc.
22 Forest Street
Upton, Massachusetts 01568
United States
Web: http://www.trisynergy.com

Tri Synergy Inc
Dallas, Texas
United States
Web: http://www.trisynergy.com

Troika Games
2680 Walnut Avenue, Suite A
Tustin, California 92780
United States
Web: http://www.troikagames.com

Trymedia Systems
1516 Folsom St.
San Francisco, California 94103
Tel: 1-415-255-3060
Fax: 1-415-255-0910
Web: http://www.trymedia.com

TS Group Entertainment LLC.
#601, Vilnysskaya st. 8/2
Moscow, Russia
117574
Web: http://www.tsgroup-inc.com

Tuna Technologies
Redlands Business Centre
3-5 Tapton House Road
Sheffield
South Yorkshire
England S10 5BY
United Kingdom
Tel: +44 (0)114 2662211
Web: http://www.tunatech.com

Turbine Entertainment Software
60 Glacier Drive, Suite 4000
Westwood, Massachusetts 02090
United States
Tel: 1-781-407-4000
Fax: 1-781-FAX-LINE
Fax: 1-781-329-5463
Web: http://www.turbinegames.com

Twilight Games
1916 Notre-Dame Ouest
Montreal, Quebec
Canada, H3J 1M6
Web: http://www.twilightgames.com

Twilight Software
PO Box 304
Milsons Point NSW
2061 Australia
Web: http://www.twilightsoftware.com

Ubi Soft Entertainment inc. Canada
5505, St-Laurent Blvd., Office 5000
Montreal, Quebec, H2T 1S6
Canada
Tel: 1-514-490-2000
Fax: 1-514-490-0882
Web: http://www.ubisoft.qc.ca

Ubi Soft San Francisco, USA
625 Third Street, 3rd Floor
San Francisco, California 94107
United States
Tel: 1-415-547-4000
Fax: 1-415-547-4001
Web: http://www.ubi.com

Ubi Soft Entertainment Inc. New York
45 West 25th Street, 9th Floor
New York, New York 10001
United States
Tel: 1-212-993-3000
Fax: 1-212-414-1460
Web: http://www.ubi.com

Ubi Soft Entertainment Ltda Brazil
Alameda Lorena, 638
Cep 01424-000 Sao Paulo
Brazil
Tel: 00 55 11 3051 3317
Fax: 00 55 11 889 9827

Ubi Soft entertainment SA France
28 rue Armand Carrel
93108 Montreuil sous Bois Cedex
France
Tel: 33 1 48 18 50 00
Fax: 33 1 48 57 07 41
Web: http://www.ubisoft.fr

Ubi Soft Entertainment Ltd
London, UK
Vantage House
1 Weir Road
Wimbledon
London
SW19 8UX
United Kingdom
Tel: 44 208 944 9000
Fax: 44 208 944 9300
Web: http://www.ubisoft.co.uk

Ubi Studios Ltd. Oxford, UK
60 St Aldates
Oxford
OX1 1ST
United Kingdom
Tel: 44 186 5 26 48 00
Fax: 44 186 5 24 57 30
Web: http://www.ubisoft.co.uk

Ubisoft - Gamebusters
Warenhandels GmbH
Hannakstr. 23
A - 5023 Salzburg
Austria
Tel: 43 662 440144
Fax: 43 662 44014414
Web: http://www.ubisoft.de

Ubi Soft Entertainment GmbH
Zimmerstraße 19
40215 Düsseldorf
Germany
Tel: 49 211 33 800 150
Fax: 49 211 33 800 151
Web: http://www.ubisoft.de

Ubisoft - Blue Byte Software
GmbH & Co. KG
Eppinghofer Strasse 150
D-45468 Muelheim an der Ruhr
Germany
Tel: 49 2 08 4 50 880
Fax: 49 2 08 4 50 8899
Web: http://www.bluebyte.net

Ubi Studios SL
Edificio Horizon,
Ctra de Rubi n°72-74
08190 Sant Cugat del Vallès,
Barcelona
Spain
Tel: 34 93 544 15 00
Fax: 34 93 589 56 60
Web: http://www.ubisoft.es

Ubi Soft Entertainment S.A.
Via de las dos Castillas, 15
Edificio Cantro Plaza Urbis
Oficinas I-J Sur
28224 Pozuelo de Alarcon
Madrid
Spain

Tel: 34 91 141 60 09
Fax: 34 91 351 48 36
Web: http://www.ubisoft.es

Ubi Soft SpA
Ubi Studios Srl
Viale Cassala 22
20143 Milan
Italy
Tel: 39 02 83 312 1
Fax: 39 02 83 312 300
Web: http://www.ubisoft.it

Ubi Soft Entertainment
Chaussée de Louvain 775
1140 Brussels
Belgium
Tel: 32 27 35 23 63
Fax: 32 37 35 31 89
Web: http://www.ubisoft.be

Ubi Soft Entertainment B.V.
Huizemaatweg 3A
1273 NA Huizen
The Netherlands
Tel: 31 35 528 88 00
Fax: 31 35 525 28 72
Web: http://www.ubisoft.nl

Ubisoft Denmark
Nordre Fasanvej 108, 4th Floor
DK-2000 Frederiksberg
Denmark
Tel: 45 38 3 03 00
Fax: 45 38 33 34 49
Web: http://www.ubisoft.dk

Ubi Soft Sweden
Ekbackvägen 22
S-168 69 Bromma
Sweden
Tel: 46 8 564 351 30
Fax: 46 8 704 03 43
Web: http://www.ubisoft.se

Ubi Soft SRL
51 Bd Primaveri
Sector 1
Bucharest
Romania
Tel: 00 401 231 67 62 (to 65)

Fax: 00 401 231 67 66
Web: http://www.ubisoft.com

Ubi Soft Entertainment SARL
62 Bd. d'Anfa,
angle Moulay Youssef
Casablanca
Morocco
Tel: 212 22 20 85 87
Fax: 212 22 20 85 86
Web: http://www.ubi.com

Ubi Soft KK
Ubi Studios KK
Three F Minami Aoyama Bldg, 5F
6-11-1, Minami Aoyama
Minato-ku
Tokyo 107-0062
Japan
Tel: 81 3 5468 2751
Fax: 81 3 5468 1360
Web: http://www.ubisoft.co.jp

Ubi Soft Entertainment
17 F Times Square
500 Zhangyang Road
Pudong 200122 - Shanghai
China
Tel: 86 21 58 78 89 69
Fax: 86 21 58 36 70 21
Web: http://www.ubisoft.com.cn

Ubi Soft Entertainment Ltd.
2nd Floor, Silver Tech Tower
26 Cheung Lee Street
Chai Wan
Hong Kong
China
Tel: 852 2886 8037
Fax: 852 2886 8152
Web: http://www.ubisoft.com.cn

Ubi Computer Software Co., Ltd.
3rd Floor, Kaiyuan Building
28, Zhi Chun Li
Haidian District
100086 Beijing
China
Tel: 86 10 82617418
Fax: 86 10 62641444
Web: http://www.ubisoft.com.cn

Ubi Soft Entertainment Pty Ltd
Level 3
111-117 Devonshire Street
Surrey Hills
Sydney
NSW 2010
Australia
Tel: 61 2 8303 1800
Fax: 61 2 9319 0322
Web: http://www.ubi.com

UDS
Västgötegatan 13
60221 Norrköping
Sweden
Tel +46(0) 11 470 51 00
Fax +46(0) 11 123160
Web: http://www.uds.se

UDS Globalfun
Drakegatan 5
41250 Göteborg
Sweden
Tel +46(0)11 470 51 00
Fax +46(0)31 406 952
Web: http://www.uds.se

UGA (United Game Artists)
Shibuya 1-12-1
Nextcom Building
Sibuya-Ku, Tokyo
Japan
Web: http://www.u-ga.com

Ugly Studios
Beavis Lodge
Whitwell Road
Sparham
Norwich
Norfolk NR9 5PN
United Kingdom
Tel: +44 (0) 1603 492219
Fax: +44 (0) 1603 492219
Web: http://www.uglystudios.com

Ultimation Inc.
204 G. Street
Suite 202
Petaluma, California 94952
United States
Tel: 1-707-789-0622
Web: http://www.ultimation.com

UltraFish
204 S Topanga Cyn Blvd
Topanga, California 90290
United States
Tel: 1-310-455-3220
Web: http://www.ultrafish.com

Ultra United
Austin, Texas
United States
Web: http://www.ultra-united.com

United Bytes
Kristallweg 13
70619 Stuttgart
Germany
Web: http://www.unitedbytes.de

United Developers USA
2019 N. Lamar St., Suite 240
Dallas, Texas 75202-1704
United States
Tel: 1-214-855-5955
Fax: 1-214-855-5980
Web: http://www.udgames.com

United Developers Limited
Europe
12 York Gate
Regent's Park
London
NW1 4QS
United Kingdom
Web: http://www.udgames.com

United Game Artists Inc.
Shibuya Tokyo, Japan
Web: http://www.u-ga.com

Universal Interactive Studios
Los Angeles, California 90045
United States
Web:
http://www.universalinteractive.com

UnoTechnology Inc.
Kwangjin-gu
Gui-dong
Techno Mart Bldg. 34th FL. #8
Seoul, Korea

Tel: (02)3424-2739
Fax: (02)3424-2736
Web: http://www.unotac.com

Unplugged
2625 Alcatraz Ave #608
Berkeley, California 94705
United States
Web: http://www.ungames.com

Unreal Studios
San Antonio, Texas
United States
Web: http://www.unrealstudios.net

Vae Victis Incorporated
Illinois
United States
Web: http://www.vaevictisgames.com

Valkyrie Studios
Chicago, Illinois
United States
Web: http://www.valkyriestudios.com

ValuSoft
711 S. Pine Street
Waconia, Minnesota 55387
United States
Web: http://www.valusoft.com

Valve Software
520 Kirkland Way #201
Kirkland, Washington 98033
United States
Tel: 1-425-827-4843
Fax: 1-425-827-484
Web: http://www.valvesoftware.com

Variant Interactive
PO Box 1272
East Lansing, Michigan 48826
United States
Tel: 1-517-862-1761
Web: http://www.variantinteractive.com

VCC Entertainment / Milk Studios
Waterloohain 6-8
22769 Hamburg
Germany
Web: http://www.vcc-entertainment.de

VCC Berlin
Berlin, Germany
Tel: +49 30.20.20.96.0
Web: http://www.vcc.de

VCC Perfect Pictures Babelsberg
Babelsberg, Germany
Tel: +49 33.17.21.36.0
Web: http://www.vcc.de

Vector Com Development
Woehlerstrasse 40
30163 Hanover
Germany
Web: http://www.vectorcom.de

Verant Interactive, Inc.
8958 Terman Court
San Diego, California 92121
United States
Tel: 1-310-840-8753
Tel: 1-858-577-3100
Fax: 1-858-577-3200
Web: http://www.verantinteractive.com

Verge Entertainment
New York, New York
United States
Tel: 1-917-532-6675
Web: http://www.vergeentertainment.com

Vertige Next E-volution Arts
37 rue Chrétien, Bureau Z-1
Gaspé, Québec
G4X 1E1
Canada
Web: http://www.vertige.ca

Vibes S.A.
8 rue du Fbg Poissonnière
75010 Paris
France
Web: http://www.vibes.net

Vicarious Visions Inc.
350 Jordan Road
Troy, New York 12180
United States
Fax: 1-518-283-4095
Web: http://www.vvisions.com

Vicious Cycle
6330 Quadrangle Drive, Suite 100
Chapel Hill, North Carolina 27517
United States
Tel: 1-919-370-3000
Fax: 1-919-370-3010
Web: http://www.viciouscycleinc.com

Vicious Software
498 London Road
Newmarket, Ontario
L3Y6h2
Canada
Tel: 1-905-898-6418
Fax: 1-905-836-5705
Web: http://www.vicioussoftware.com

Victor Interactive Software Inc.
Tokyo, Japan
Tel: 03 5466 1757
Web: http://www.vis.co.jp

Victory Simulations, Inc.
Laguna Niguel, California 92677
United States
Web: http://www.victorysims.com

Vinayak Computer Entertainment
50 North 3rd Street.
Fairfield, Iowa 52556
United States
Tel: 1-641-472-5625
Web: http://www.4dgames.com

Vin Unjal Interactive P Ltd.
K. Aravindan
Vin Unjal Interactive
31 Muniappa Mudali Street,
Chennai 600 079
Tel: 044-2520 2241
Web: http://www.vinunjal.com

VIP Group, The
111 Dunlop St East, Suite 1204
Barrie, Ontario L4M6J5
Canada
Web: http://www.shop-vip.com

Vir2L Studios
1370 Piccard Drive, Suite 120
Rockville, Maryland 20850
United States
Tel: 1-301-963-2000
Fax: 1-301-948-2253
Web: http://www.vir2l.com

Vir2L Studios
10950 Washington Blvd. Suite 240
Culver City, California 90232
Tel: 1-310-237-3180
Fax: 1-310-237-3181
Web: http://www.vir2l.com

Vir2L Studios Europe
54/56 Wharf Road
Islington
London
N1 7SF
United Kingdom
Tel: +44 207 336 1333
Fax: +44 207 608 1873
Web: http://www.vir2l.com

Vircom
2055 Peel, Suite 200
Montréal (Québec)
H3A 1V4
Canada
Tel: 1-514-845-1666
Fax: 1-514-845-6922
Web:
http://www.vircom.com/interactive

Virgin Interactive
74A Charlotte Street
London
W1T 4QN
Tel: 0207 551 0000
Fax: 0207 551 0001
Web: http://www.virgininteractive.com

Virgin Interactive
233 rue de la Croix Nivert
75015 Paris
France
Fax : 01 41 11 64 24
Web: http://www.virgininteractive.com

Virgin Interactive Entertainment
GmbH
Borselstr. 16 C
22765 Hamburg
Germany
Tel: 040/ 89703300
Web: http://www.virgininteractive.com

Virgin Interactive Entertainment
ESPAÑA, S.A.
Paseo de la Castellana, 9 -11
Bajo
28046 Madrid
Spain
Tel: (91) 789.35.50
Fax: (91) 789.35.60
Web: http://www.virgininteractive.com

Virtual Heaven
Erkelenzdamm 59-61
10999 Berlin
Germany
Tel: 030-61 67 84 10
Fax: 030-61 67 84 99
Web: http://www.virtualheaven.de

Virtucraft Ltd
21/23 Silverwell Street
Bolton
Lancashire
England
BL1 1PP
Tel: +44 (0)1204 528060
Fax: +44 (0)1204 524297
Web: http://www.virtucraft.com

Visco Corporation
Kyoto, Japan
Tel: 075-464-2676
Fax: 075-463-6163
Web: http://www.visco.co.jp

Visco Corporation
Tokyo, Japan
Tel: 03-3554-0121
Fax: 03-3554-0150
Web: http://www.visco.co.jp

VIS Entertainment
Seabraes Mill
Perth Road
Dundee
DD1 4LN
Tel: 44 (0)1382 341 000
Fax: 44 (0)1382 341 045
Web: http://www.visentertainment.com

VIS Games
Seabraes Mill
Perth Road
Dundee
DD1 4LN
United Kingdom
Tel: +44 (0) 1382 341 000
Fax: +44 (0) 1382 341 045
Web: http://www.vis-plc.com
Web: http://www.visentertainment.com

VIS Games
Izatt Avenue
Dunfermline
KY11 3BZ
United Kingdom
Tel: +44 (0) 1383 845 300
Fax: +44 (0) 1383 845 345
Web: http://www.vis-plc.com
Web: http://www.visentertainment.com

VIS Games
Park Place Farm
Calbourne Road Newport
Isle of Wight
PO30 4HP
United Kingdom
Tel: +44 (0)1983 827 777
Fax: +44 (0)1983 827 799
Web: http://www.vis-plc.com
Web: http://www.visentertainment.com

Vision Games
1310 SW Kings Byway
Troutdale, Oregon 97206
United States
Web: http://www.vision-games.com

Vision Media Engineering GmbH
Berner Straße 117
D-60437 Frankfurt
Germany
Tel: +49 - 69 952 - 181 - 58
Fax: +49 - 69 952 - 181 - 42
Web: http://www.vme.de

Vision Park Entertainment AB
Riddargatan 19, 2tr
114 57 Stockholm
Sweden
Tel: +46 8 545 892 00
Fax: +46 8 545 892 27
Web: http://www.visionpark.com

Vision Park i Göteborg AB
Järntorget 3
413 04 Gothenburg
Sweden
Tel: +46 31 12 89 55
Fax: +46 31 12 89 87
Web: http://www.visionpark.com

Vision Park - Innerloop Studios A/S
Øvre Slottsgate 27
0157 Oslo
Norway
Tel: +47 22 47 90 00
Fax: +47 22 47 90 09
Web: http://www.visionpark.com

Vision Park Entertainment AB
Riddargatan 19, 2tr
114 57 Stockholm
Sweden
Tel: +46 8 545 892 00
Fax: +46 8 545 892 27
Web: http://www.visionpark.com

Vision Park Online
Riddargatan 19, 2 tr
114 57 Stockholm
Sweden
Tel: +46 8 545 892 00
Fax: +46 8 545 892 27
Web: http://www.visionpark.com

Vision Scape Int.
12840 Danielson Ct.
Poway, California 92064
United States
Tel: 1-858-391-1300
Fax: 1-858-391-1301
Web: http://www.vision-scape.com

Visionary Media, Inc.
233 Tamalpais Drive, Suite B,
Corte Madera, California 94925
United States
Tel: 1-415-927-6636
Web: http://www.vmisoft.com

Visiware
2 rue Troyon
92316 Sevres Cedex
France
Tel: +33.(0)1 46 29 39 00
Fax: +33.(0)1 46 29 39 01
Web: http://www.visiware.com

Visual Concepts Entertainment, Inc.
One Thorndale Drive
San Rafael, California 94903
United States
Tel: 1-415-479-3634
Web: http://www.Sega.com

Visual Impact Productions
119 Rue Damremont
75018 Paris
France
Tel: +33 (0)1 53 09 24 44
Fax: +33 (0)1 53 09 24 00
Web: http://www.viprod.com

Visual Sciences
7 Luna Place
Gateway West
Dundee Technology Park
Dundee DD 1XF
United Kingdom
Tel: +44 (0) 1382 422100
Fax: +44 (0) 1382 422101
Web: http://www.vissci.com

Vivarium Inc.
Tokyo, Japan
Web: http://www.vivarium.co.jp

Vivid Design
ul. Ogrody 22/4
85-870 Bydgoszcz
Poland
Tel: 052 362 06 96
Fax: 052 362 06 96
Web: http://www.vdb.pl

Vivid Image
Istanbul, Turkey
Web: http://www.vividimage.co.uk

Volition, Inc.
2004 Fox Drive Suite B
Champaign Illinois, 61820
United States
Tel: 1-217-355-0320
Fax: 1-217-355-0767
Web: http://www.volition-inc.com

Vortigern Strategic Software
P.O Box 1081
Lismore NSW 2480
Australia
Tel: 02 6689 1919
Fax: 02 6689 1919
Web: http://vortigern.com.au

Voxar Inc.
945 Concord Street
Framingham, Massachusetts 01701
United States
Tel: 1-877-Voxar-3D
Tel: 1-508-620-9446
Fax: 1-508-620-9447
Web: http://www.voxar.com

VR1 Entertainment USA
5775 Flatiron Parkway, Suite 100
Boulder, Colorado 80301
United States
Tel: 1-720-564-1000
Fax: 1-720-564-1090
Web: http://www.vr1.com

VR1 Japan, Inc.
DS Bldg. 6th Floor
5-15-5 Sendagaya
Shibuya-ku
Tokyo, 151-0051 Japan
Tel: 03-5363-5271

Fax: 03-5363-5274
Web: http://www.vr1.com

VRmagic GmbH
B6, 23 29 C
68032 Mannheim
Germany
Tel: +49 (0) 621 - 181 2765
Fax: +49 (0) 621 - 181 2591
Web: http://www.vrmagic.com

VSLKorea
Kwangjingu Jayangdong Donho
b/d 5th floor
Seoul, Korea 219-25
Tel: (02)3436-7811
Fax: (02)3436-7511
Web: http://www.vslk.co.kr

Vulcan Software Ltd.
Portsmouth
Hampshire
United Kingdom
Tel: +44 (0)23 9267 0269
Web: http://www.vulcan.co.uk

Vulpine GmbH
3D Technologies
Birnenweg 15
72766 Reutlingen
Tel: 07121-144935-0
Fax: 07121-144935-9
Web: http://www.usf.de

Waggaworld Entertainment
11 Charlotte St. - 2nd Floor
Toronto, Ontario M5V 2H5
Canada
Tel: 1-416-591-2200
Fax: 1-416-591-3818
Web: http://www.waggaworldent.com

Wahoo Studios, Inc.
405 S. 100 E., Suite 13
Pleasant Grove, Utah 84062
United States
Tel: 1-801-796-5904
Web: http://www.wahoo.com

Walker Boys Studio
116 Ace Dr.
Desoto, Texas 75115
United States
Phone: 1-972-223-3726
Web: http://www.walkerboystudio.com

Walrus Ltd.
410 Victory Business Centre
Somers Road North
Portsmouth
Hampshire
England
PO1 1PJ
Tel: +44 (0)23 9283 1777
Fax: +44 (0)23 9281 6279
Web: http://www.walrus.uk.com

Wanadoo Edition
France
Web: http://www.wanadoo-edition.com

Wargaming
909 Poydras Street, Suite 2600
New Orleans, Louisiana 70112
United States
Web: http://www.wargaming.net

Warlock Studio
Penza, Russia
Web: http://www.warlockstudio.com

Warthog
10 Eden Place
Cheadle, Cheshire
SK8 1AT
United Kingdom
Tel: +44 (0) 161 491 5131
Fax: +44 (0) 161 610 3033
Web: http://www.warthog.co.uk

Watermarks Ltd.
Hiroo Person 302 5-9-25 Hiroo
Shibuyaku
Tokyo 150-0012 Japan
Tel: 813-5447-5058
Fax: 813-544-5059
Web: http://www.watermarks.com

Waterproofs Entertainment
7328 Papineau Ave.
Montreal, Québec
H2E 2G6 Canada
Tel: 1-514-721-9256
Web: http://www.water-proofs.com

WayForward
24300 Town Center Dr. Suite 370
Valencia, California 91355-1332
United States
Tel: 1-661-286-2769
Fax: 1-661-286-1234
Web: http://www.wayforward.com

WaywardXS Entertainment S.r.l.
Via Pirandello 1A/1
17100 Savona
Italy
Tel: +39 019 80 59 54
Fax: +39 019 88 25 60
Web: http://www.waywardxs.com

Way-X
Neubrückstr. 3
40213 Düsseldorf
Germany
Tel: 0221/8306-160
Fax: 0221/8306-160
Web: http://way-x.got-game.org

Webfoot Technologies, Inc.
P.O. Box 15
Lemont, Illinois 60439
United States
Tel: 1-815-836-1224
Web: http://www.webfootgames.com

Webzen, Inc.
6F, Daelim Acrotel
467-6, Dogok-Dong
Kangnam-Gu
Seoul, South Korea
135-971
Tel: +82 2.34.98.16.18
Fax: +82 2.20.57.25.68
Web: http://www.webzen.co.kr

Westbyte
Boyarka, Kiev
Motovilovka

Ukraine
Web: http://www.westbyte.com

Werd Interactive
1717 Wakefield Drive,
Huntsville, Alabama 35811
United States
Tel: 1-256-534-3798
Web: http://www.werdinteractive.com

West Racing
21 Fountain Court, Oldfield Wood
Woking Surrey, Maybury Hill
GU228AN
United Kingdom
Tel: +44 (0) 148 383 4298
Web: http://www.west-racing.com

Westka Interactive GmbH
Neusser Str, 159
50733 Cologne, Germany
Europe
Web: http://www.westka.de

Westlake Interactive
5114 Balcones Woods Dr.
Suite 307-339
Austin, Texas 78759
United States
Web: http://www.westlakeinteractive.com

Westwood
2400 N Tenaya Way
Las Vegas, Nevada 89128
United States
Web: http://www.westwood.com

Whatif Productions LLC
Belmont, Massachusetts
United States
Web: http://whatif-productions.com

Whiptail Interactive
West Chester, Pennsylvania
United States
web: http://www.whiptailinteractive.com

White Knuckle Games
13300-74 Morris Rd
Alpharetta, Georgia 30004
United States
Tel: 1-678-230-9124
Web:
http://www.whiteknucklegames.com

Whoopee Camp Corp., Ltd.
Osaka, Japan
Tel: 0727-27-5673
Fax: 0727-27-5674
Web: http://www.whoopeecamp.co.jp

Wicked Witch Software
Central avenue Boronia
Melbourne, Victoria
Australia
Tel: (03) 87040497
Web: http://www.wicked-witch.com.au

Wide Games Ltd
24 Old Steine
Brighton
Sussex
BN1 1EL
United Kingdom
Tel: +44 (0) 1273 818 600
Fax: +44 (0) 1273 818 652
Web: http://www.widegames.com

Wide Games Ltd
Surrey House
Surrey Street
Croydon
Surrey
CR0 1SZ
United Kingdom
Web: http://www.widegames.com

Widescreen Games
16 rue Crillon
69006 Lyon
France
Tel: +33 (0) 4 37 47 27 47
Fax: +33 (0) 4 37 47 27 49
Web: http://www.wsg.fr

Wilco
P.O. Box 30
1620 Drogenbos

Belgium
Fax: +32.2.331.07.51
Web: http://www.wilcopub.com

Wild Child Studios, Inc.
3101 Landing Lane
Moon Township, Pennsylvania 15108
United States
Tel: 1-412-908-8898
Web:
http://www.wildchildstudios.com

Wildfire Studios
19 Southerden Ave
Grange 4051
Brisbane, Queensland
Australia
Tel: +61 (0)7 3844 1000
Fax: +61 (0)7 3856 2147
Web: http://www.wildfire.com.au

Wild Tangent
18578 NE 67th Court
Building 5, Redmond East Office
Complex
Redmond, Washington 98052
United States
Tel: 1-425-497-4500
Fax: 1-425-497-4501
Web: http://www.wildtangent.com

Windward Studios, Inc.
PMB 115
637 B South Broadway
Boulder, Colorado 80305
United States
Tel: 1-303-499-2544
Web: http://www.windward.net

Wings Simulations
Werkstrasse 15
45527 Hattingen
Tel: 02324-56 62 0
Fax: 02324-56 62 8
Web: http://www.wingssimulations.com

WinkySoft
Japan
Web: http://www.winky.co.jp

Wintervalley Software
Unit A 2822 Tudor Ave.
Victoria, British Columbia V8N 1L8
Canada
Tel: 1-250-382-8073
Web: http://www.wintervalley.com

Wired Realms
3 Copse Hill, First Floor
London, SW20 0NA
United Kingdom
Tel: +44 (0) 89447610
Web: http://www.wiredrealms.com

Wit Entertainment
Gotlandsresan 174
Uppsala, n/a 75754
Sweden
Tel: +46 (0) 708 245823
Web: http://www.witentertainment.com

Witan Entertainment, BV
Wagenweg 16
Haarlem, Noord Holland, 2012 ND
Netherlands
Tel: 31-23-534-5566
Web: http://www.witan.nl

Wizard Soft Ltd.
Wizard Soft Building
192-9 Bang-yi, Songpa
Seoul 138-051, Korea
Tel: 82-2-418-7711
Fax: 82-2-418-7712
Web: http://www.wzsoft.com

Wizard Soft, Inc. US Office
3003 North First Street, Suite 224
San Jose, California 95134
United States
Tel: 1-408-232-5473
Tel: 1-408-202-5263
Fax: 1-408-232-5474
Web: http://www.wzsoft.com

Wizardworks & Macsoft
2155 Niagara Lane North Suite 150
Plymouth, Minnesota 55447
United States
Tel: 1-763-249-7600
Web: http://www.infogrames.com

Wizbang !
2955 80th Avenue SE, Suite 102
Mercer Island, Washington 98040
United States
Web: http://www.wizbang.com

WizCom
Bahnhofstr. 110
8001 Zurich
Switzerland
Tel: 411 215 17 80
Fax: 411 215 17 81
Web: http://www.wizcom.net

WizCom
Untere Roostmatt 8
6300 Zug
Switzerland
Tel: +41 61 283 50 10
Fax: +41 61 283 50 01
Web: http://www.wizcom.net

WizCom
7 Hristo Belchev Street
Sofia 1000
Bulgaria
Tel: +359 2 981 2282
Fax: +359 2 986 5664
Web: http://www.wizcom.net

WKG
13300-74 Morris Rd
Alpharetta, Georgia 30004
United States
Tel: 1-678-230-9124
Web:
http://www.whiteknucklegames.com

WMS Gaming, Inc
3401 N. California Ave.
Chicago, Illinois 60618
United States
Tel: 1-773-961-1879
Tel: 1-773-961-1620
Fax: 1-773-961-1025
Web: http://www.wmsgaming.com

WolfPack Studios, Inc.
1 Chisholm Trail, Ste 400
Round Rock, Texas 78681
United States
Web: http://www.wolfpackstudios.com

Wonder Seven Ltd.
3-10-10, Akasaka
Minato-ku
Tokyo 107-0052
Japan
Tel: 81-3-5562-5200
Web: http://www.namco.co.jp

Wonder Show Studios Inc.
10620 SW Davies Rd., Suite #13
Beaverton, Oregon 97008
United States
Tel: 1-503-579-2629
Web:
http://www.wondershowstudios.com

Working Designs
PO Box 494340
Redding, California 96049-4340
United States
Tel: 1-530-243-3417
Fax: 1-530-244-3416
Web: http://www.workingdesigns.com

World Fusion
2900 Bristol Street, Suite H-103
Costa Mesa, California 92626
United States
Tel: 1-714-708-7400
Fax: 1-714-708-7401
Web: http://www.worldfusion.com

Worldwide MicroTronics, Inc.
P.O. Box 8759
Spring, Texas 77387-8759
United States
Tel: 1-281-296-2880
Web: http://www.microtronics.com

WorldWinner
Los Angeles, California
United States
Web: http://www.worldwinner.com

Wow Entertainment Inc.
Tokyo, Japan
Web: http://www.wow-ent.co.jp

WXP Entertainment
95 South Jackson Street, Suite 200
Seattle, Washington 98104
United States
Tel: 1-206-287-9146
Web: http://www.wxp3d.com

WXP (The Whole Experience, Inc)
307 3rd Avenue South, Suite 520
Seattle, Washington 98104
United States
Tel: 1-206-287-9146
Web: http://www.wxp3d.com

XadrA LLC
3217 Upper Lock Ave
Belmont, California 94002
United States
Tel: 1-650-591-5515
Fax: 1-650-591-5514
Web: http://www.xadra.com

X-ample Architectures
Im Bauernholz 9a
21244 Buchholz i.d.N.
Germany
Web: http://www.xap.de

Xantera, Inc.
407 Veronica Dr.
Paso Robles, California 93446
United States
Tel: 1-805-610-5483
Fax: 1-805-238-1215
Web: http://www.xantera.com

Xcreate Company Limited
Ft4 7/F Ping Fai Bldg 312 Un
Chau Street
Sham Shui Po
Kowloon
Hong Kong
Tel: (852) 2720 8812
Tel: (852) 2720 8109
Fax: (852) 2720 816
Web: http://www.xcreate.com

Xdyne Inc.
1785 South Paw Paw Rd.
Earlville, Illinois 60518
United States
Tel: 1-815-246-6981
Fax: 1-815-246-4981
Web: http://www.xdyne.com

Xenopi Studios, Inc.
1509 SW Sunset Blvd.
Suite 1-H
Portland, Oregon 97201
United States
Web: http://www.xenopi.com

XGame Works
zhongyu business garden
NO.42 fucheng road
Haidian District
Beijing, 100036
China
Tel: +86-10-88142188
Web: http://www.xgameworks.com

Xgameworks software Co.ltd
HuiXin High-rise B-602
Ya Yun Village
Haidian District
Beijing 100101
China
Tel: 086 (010) 84985828-290
Tel: 086 (010) 84985828-291
Fax: 086 (010) 84985828-299
Web: http://www.xgameworks.com

Xicat Interactive
1st Floor
17/18 Great Sutton Street
London EC1V ODP
Tel: +44 (0)207 251 8000
Fax: +44 (0)207 253 7445
Web: http://www.xicat.com

Xicat Interactive
800 East Broward Boulevard - Suite 700
Fort Lauderdale, Florida 33301
United States
Web: http://www.xicat.com

Xicat Interactive
Via San Bastiaun 5
Samedan
Switzerland
Web: http://www.xicat.com

Xilam Animation
25 rue Yves Toudic
75010 Paris
France
Tel: (33) 01 40 18 72 00
Fax: (33) 01 40 03 02 26
Web: http://www.xilam.com

Xpiral
C/ Alfonso I, 36
50003 Zaragoza
Spain
Tel: +34 976393250
Fax: +34 976393250
Web: http://www.xpiral.com

X-Ray Interactive Sp. z o.o.
37-310 Nowa Sarzyna
ul. Chopina 1
Poland
Tel: +48 (0) 17 24-11-458
Web: http://www.x-ray.com.pl

XSRD
927 Sunnybrae Lane
Novato, California 94947
United States
Tel: 1-415-897-7922
Web: http://www.xsrd.com

XSRD
117 38th Street, Suite 1
Manhattan Beach, California
90266
United States
Tel: 1-310-545-3197
Web: http://www.xsrd.com

Xtreme Games LLC
PO Box 641744
San Jose, California 95164-1744
United States
Tel: 1-925-736-2098
Web: http://www.xgames3d.com

YAGER Development GmbH
Gubener Straße 46
10243 Berlin
Germany
Tel: +49 (30) 29367594
Fax: +49 (30) 29367596
Web: http://www.yager-develop-ment.com

Yamisoft Entertainment Inc.
Vancouver
British Columbia
Canada
Web: http://www.yamisoft.com

Yes Ten Style Ltd.
Al. Solidarnosci 72/84
Warsaw, 00-090
Poland
Tel: +48 22 831 34 25
Fax: +48 22 636 75 35
Web: http://www.yes10.pl

YetiSoft Limited
Room 1001
Morecrown Commercial Building
108 Electric Road
North Point
Hong Kong
Tel: 852-2503-4343
Fax: 852-2503-5040
Web: http://www.yetisoft.com.hk

Yuke's Future Media Creators
4-45-1 Ebisujima
Sakai Osaka
590-0985 Japan
Tel: 81-72-224-5155
Fax: 81-72-224-1397
Web: http://www.yukes.co.jp

Yuke's Future Media Creators
6-6 Kinkoucho
Kanagawa-ku
Yokohama
221-0056 Japan
Tel: 81-45-451-5558
Fax: 81-45-440-1533
Web: http://www.yukes.co.jp

Yuki Enterprise Inc.
Tokyo, Japan
Tel: 03-5961-8301
Fax: 03-5961-8302
Web: http://www.yuki-web.co.jp

Yunokawa Kanko Co., Ltd.
2-4-20, Yunokawa-cho, Hakodate
Hokkaido 042-0932
Japan
Tel: 81-138-57-1188
Web: http://www.namco.co.jp

ZAQ Interactive Solutions
297 St. Paul Street West, Suite 007
Montreal, Quebec
Canada
H2Y 2A5
Tel: 1-514-282-7073
Fax: 1-514-282-8011
Web: http://www.zaq.com

Z-AXIS, Ltd.
21021 Corsair Blvd
Suite 200
Hayward, California 94545
United States
Tel: 1-510-887-7900
Fax: 1-510-887-7912
Web: http://www.z-axis.com

Zed Two Game Design Studio
Portland Chambers
131-133 Portland Street
Manchester
M1 4PZ
United Kingdom
Tel: +44 (0)161 236 2166
Fax: +44 (0)161 236 0601
Web: http://www.zedtwo.com

Zetha gameZ
18/22 Avenue de la Gare
95150 Taverny
Paris
France
Web: http://www.zetha.com

ZeniMax Productions
10950 Washington Blvd. Suite 240
Culver City, California 90232

Tel: 1-310-237-3180
Fax: 1-310-237-3181
Web: http://www.vir2l.com

Zenith Studios
Illweg 10
A-6714 Nueziders
Austria
Web: http://www.zenithstudios.com

Zero Gravity
5051 Westheimer, Ste. 600
Post Oak Tower @ The Galleria
Houston, Texas 77056
United States
Tel: 1-281-364-0602
Fax: 1-281-364-0102
Web: http://www.zero-gravity.com

Zeroscale GmbH & Co. KG
Frankfurter Allee 73d
10247 Berlin
Germany
Tel: +49-(0) 30-4281-8001
Fax: +49-(0) 30-4281-8008
Web: http://www.zeroscale.com

Zero Sum Software
Eldorado, Texas
United States
Web: http://www.zero-sum.com

Zetha gameZ
18/22 Avenue de la Gare
95150 Taverny
France
Tel: 01.30.40.14.45
Fax: 01.30.40.14.46
Web: http://www.zetha.com

ZForm LLC
30 Industrial Drive East
Northampton, Massachusetts
01060
United States
Web: http://www.zform.com

Zima Software
Pod Turnovskou tratí 18
198 00 Praha 9

Czech Republic
Tel: 00420 2 81863804
Fax: 00420 2 81861251
Web: http://www.zima-software.cz

ZIOSoft, Inc.
18625 Sutter Boulevard, Suite 200
Morgan Hill, California 95037
United States
Tel: 1-408-778-6500
Fax: 1-408-778-2737
Web: http://www.ziosoft.com

Zipper Interactive
8314 154th Ave. N.E.
Redmond, Washington 98052
United States
Fax: 1-425-556-4382
Web: http://www.zipperint.com

Zoesis Studios
246 Walnut Street, Suite 301
Newton, Massachusetts 02460
United States
Tel: 1-617-969-5700
Fax: 1-617-969-4472
Web: http://www.zoesis.com

ZOIment
TechnoMart 30Fl.
546-4 Kuui-dong
Kwangin-gu
Seoul
Korea 143-200
Tel: 82-2-3424-1766
Fax: 82-2-3424-1765
Web: http://www.zoiment.com

Zombie
114 1/2 First Ave South
Seattle Washington 98104
United States
Tel: 1-206-623-9655
Fax: 1-206-623-9714
Web: http://www.zombie.com

Zona Headquarters
2606 Bayshore Parkway
Mountain View, California 94043
United States
Tel: 1-650-964-1133
Fax: 1-650-961-8833
Web: http://www.zona.net

Zona Korea
Aname Tower 1219
702-10 Yeoksam, Kangnam
Seoul, Korea
Tel: 02-557-9360-1
Fax: 02-557-9362
Web: http://www.zona.net

Zona Japan
AIOS Bldg. 707
1-11-2 Hiroo, Shibuya
Tokyo 150-0012 Japan
Tel: 03-5798-2859
Fax: 03-5798-2869
Web: http://www.zona.net

Zong Chin Technology
16F No. 175, Jungjeng 2nd Road
Lingya District, Kaohsiung
Taiwan
Tel: +886-7-2232091
Fax: +886-7-2247415
Web: http://www.zct.com.tw

Zono, Inc.
3140 Red Hill Avenue
Suite 200 Costa Mesa, California
92626
United States
Web: http://www.zono.com

Zoomorphix Systems
PO BOX 208
Carnegie Vic. 3163
Melbourne, Australia
Tel: +61 +3 9543 6610
Fax: +61 +3 9543 9938
Web: http://www.zoomorphix.com.au

Zuxxez Enteratinmant AG
Schonauer Strasse 4a
67547 Worms
Germany

Tel: (+49) 06241-2688-0
Fax: (+49) 06241-2688-88
Web: http://www.zuxxez.com

ZReality, Inc.
Raleigh, North Carolina
United States
Fax: 1-919-874-0056
Web: http://www.zreality.com

ZZICT
Laan van Mertersem 64
4813 GH Breda
The Netherlands
Tel: +31 76 5155409
Fax: +31 76 5155412
Web: http://www.zzict.com

ZZICT
Fonteinstraat 57
3000 Leuven
Belgium
Tel: +32 468 830968
Fax: +31 76 5155412
Web: http://www.zzict.com

© CHARLES BARSOTTI

Wow! What a huge list of companies!
Looks like we've got to get to work.

*Send in your changes
and Phil will put them into the book.*

We want to hear from you!
Please tell if this list is missing anything.

Companies come and go. This list may be missing your favorite game company or may include companies that have gone out of business or changed their name. If you noticed errors in this list please report them. We take your comments, as well as all the others like yours, and do our best to implement them into the next version of the book. If you are the first one to report an error or to make a suggestion, we will acknowledge you in the next printing. (Unless you specify otherwise.)

Due to the extremely high volume of mail we may not get back to you immediately. You can be sure that your e-mail will be answered.

Web site: www.EdHarriss.com

Email: EdHarriss@EdHarriss.com

Fax: 1-603-691-6470

Mailing Address:

EdHarriss.com
90154
Raleigh, NC 27675-90154
United States

Sure is easier than grading tests.

RESOURCES - Computer Animation Schools

3D Exchange
140 Lakewood Drive
Frazier Park, California 93225
United States
Tel: 1-661-245-2240
Fax: 1-661-245-2218
Web: http://www.3dexchange.com

3DMIRAGE
208 W. 29th St. Suite 601
New York, New York 10001
United States
Tel: 1-212-967-7777
Fax: 1-212-208-6886
Web: http://www.3dmirage.com

3D-Online
820 Manhattan Ave., Suite 104
Manhattan Beach, California 90266
United States
Tel: 1-310-406-1169
Fax: 1-509-278-3400
Web: http://www.3d-online.com

Abram Friedman Occupational
Center
1646 South Olive Street
Los Angeles, California 90015
United States
Tel: 1-213-745-2013
Fax: 1-213-748-7406
Web: No Site

Academy Education Center, Inc.
3050 Metro Drive
Minneapolis, Minnesota 55425
United States
Tel: 1-612-851-0066
Fax: 1-612-851-0094
Web:http://www.academyeducation.com

Academy of Art College
79 New Montgomery St.
San Francisco, California 94105
United States
Tel: 1-800-544-ARTS
Fax: 1-415-263-4130
Web: http://www.academyart.edu

Academy of Digital Animation,
Cerro Coso College
3000 College Heights Boulevard
Ridgecrest, California 93555
United States
Tel: 1-661-301-0652
Fax: 1-760-375-4776
Web: http://www.coyote3d.com

Academy of Entertainment & Technology
1660 Stewart Street
Santa Monica, California 90404
United States
Tel: 1-310-434-3700
Fax: 1-310-434-3709
Web:http://www.smc.edu

Academy of Fine Arts
Ilica 85 (Administrative Building)
Zagreb
10000
Croatia
Tel: 38 5137 77 300
Fax: 38 5137 73 401
Web: http://www.alu.hr

Academy of Fine Arts and Design
Hviezdoslavovo nám. 18
Drotárska Cesta 44
Bratislava
Slovakia
Tel: +421 2 5444519
Fax: +421 2 54432340
Web: http://www.afad.sk

Academy of G.E.T.
6311 Romaine St., Suite 7111
Hollywood, California 90038
United States
Tel: 1-323-466-4300
Fax: 1-323-466-4368
Web: http://www.academyofget.com

Academy of Media Arts
Peter-Welter-Platz 2
Koln
D-50676
Germany
Tel: 49 22 12 01 89 0
Fax: 49 22 12 01 89 17
Web: http://www.khm.de

ADAC - Ville de Paris
Centre des Beaux-Arts
5, rue des Beaux-Arts
Paris, France
75006
Tel: 33 1 42 22 37 41
Web: http://adacparis.com

AFIDE
9, rue Rataud
Paris, France
75005
Tel: 33 1 45 35 60 92
Fax: 33 1 45 35 42 81
Web: http://www.afide.fr

AFIDE
83 Bd du Port Royal
Paris, France
75013
Tel: 33 1 42 17 47 67
Web: http://www.afide.fr

AGA Digital Studios, Inc.
542 West Campus Drive
Arlington Heights, Illinois 60004-1408
United States
Tel: 1-847-222-9454
Fax: 1-847-222-9455
Web: http://www.agadigital.com

Akademia Sztuk Pieknych W
Poznaniu
Department of Multimedia
Communication
ul Aleje Marcinkowskiego 29
Poznan
60-967
Poland
Tel: 48 61 855 25 21
Fax: 48 61 852 23 09
Web: http://www.asp.poznan.pl

Akademie der Bildenden Kunste
Akademiestrasse 2
Munchen 40
D-80799
Germany
Tel: 49 89 38 52 0
Fax: 49 89 38 52 206
Web: http://www.adbk.mhn.de

Akademie der Bildenden Kunste
Schiller Platz, 3
Wien
A-1010
Austria
Tel: 43 1 58 81 60
Fax: 43 1 58 81 61 37
Web: http://www.akbild.ac.at

Alberta College of Art & Design
Fine Arts, Visual Communications
Design,
and Media Arts & Digital
Technologies (MADT)
1407 14 Avenue N.W.
Calgary
Alberta
T2N 4R3
Canada
Tel: 403 284 7617
Fax: 403 284 7644
Web: http://www.acad.ab.ca

Albuquerque TVI Community College
525 Buena Vista SE
Albuquerque, New Mexico 87106
United States
Tel: 1-505-224-3000
Fax: 1-505-272-7969
Web: http://www.tvi.cc.nm.us

Algonquin College
School of Media & Design
1385 Woodroffe Avenue
Ottawa
Ontario
K1K 1C2
Canada
Tel: 1-613-727-4723
Fax: 1-613-727-7707
Web: http://www.algonquincol-
lege.com

Alian Shiveh Co.,LTD.
Technical Department
No.1.111 8th Sarvestan
Pasdaran Ave.
Tehran
16619
Iran
Tel: 98 21 2850839, 49
Fax: 98 21 2840885
Web: http://www.alianshiveh.com

Allan Hancock College
800 S. College Dr.
Santa Maria, California 93454
United States
Tel: 1-805-922-6966 ext. 3248
Fax: 1-805-928-7905
Web: http://www.hancock.cc.ca.us

American Animation Institute
4729 Lankershim Blvd.
North Hollywood, California
91602-1864
United States
Tel: 1-818-766-0521
Fax: 1-818-506-4805
Web: http://www.mpsc839.org

American Film Institute
2021 N. Western Ave.
Los Angeles, California 90027

United States
Tel: 1-323-856-7600
Fax: 1-323-467-4578
Web: http://www.afionline.org

American University
4400 Massachusetts Avenue, NW
Washington, DC 20016
United States
Tel: 1-202-885-1000
Web: http://www.american.edu

AnimAction
1529 N Cahuenga Blvd.
Hollywood, California 90028
United States
Tel: 1-323-464-1181
Fax: 1-323-464-1191
Web: http://www.animaction.com

Animathon
BP 85019
Mont St. Hilaire
Quebec
J3H 5W1
Canada
Tel: 1-514-467-8909
Fax: 1-514-467-7625
Web: http://www.animathon.com

Animation Canada
3D Department
2284 Gerrard St. E.
Toronto
Ontario
Canada
Tel: 1-416-690-1690
Fax: 1-416-690-0136
Web: http://www.animation.ca

Animation Portfolio Workshop
P.O. Box 546 Station C
Toronto
Ontario
M6J 3P6
Canada
Tel: 1-416-588-8039
Fax: 1-416-588-8039
Web: http://www.portfoliowork-
shop.com

Animation Workshop, The
34 Winthrop St.
Rochester, New York 14607
United States
Tel: 1-585-232-3949
Fax: 1-585-232-3949
Web: http://www.animatusstudio.com

Animatrix Academy of Animation
Department of Classical
Animation
Box 116
1469 Bretton Street
Halifax
Nova Scotia
B3J 3W7
Canada
Tel: 1-902-477-7052
Web: No Site

Anne Arundel Community College
Communication Arts Technology
Dept.
101 College Parkway
Arnold, Maryland 21012-1895
United States
Tel: 1-410-647-7100
Web: http://www.aacc.cc.md.us

Applied Multimedia Training
Centre
109 - 491 Portage Avenue
Winnipeg
Manitoba
R3B 2E4
Canada
Tel: 204 772 4411
Fax: 204 772 2896
Web:http://www.amtcwinnipeg.com

Applied Multimedia Training
Centres
Department of Animation
200, 7015 Macleod Trail South
West
Calgary
Alberta
T2H 2K6
Canada
Tel: 403 571 4700
Fax: 403 571 4709
Web: http://www.applied-multimedia.com

Ars Animacion
C/ Libreros, 42. Planta 1
Alcala de Henares
Madrid
28801
Spain
Tel: 34 91 883 66 37
Fax: 34 91 883 66 37
Web: http://www.arsanima.com

Art Center College of Design
1700 Lida St.
Pasadena California 91103-1999
United States
Tel: 1-626-396-2373
Fax: 1-626-405-9104
Web: http://www.artcenter.edu

Art Institute of Atlanta
6600 Peachtree Dunwoody Road
100 Embassy Row
Atlanta, Georgia 30328
United States
Tel: 1-800-275-4242
Fax: 1-770-394-0008
Web:http://www.aia.artinstitutes.edu

Art Institute of California
1170 Market St.
San Francisco, California 94102
United States
Tel: 1-888-493-3261
Fax: 1-415-863-6344
Web: http://www.aicasf.aii.edu

Art Institute of California
3601 W. Sunflower Avenue
Santa Ana, California 92704
United States
Tel: 1-888-549-3055
Fax: 1-714-556-1923
Web: www.aicaoc.aii.edu

Art Institute of Colorado
1200 Lincoln Street
Denver, Colorado 80203
United States
Tel: 1-800-275-2420
Fax: 1-303-860-8520
Web: http://www.aic.aii.edu

Art Institute of Dallas
Two NorthPark
8080 Park Lane, Ste 100
Dallas, Texas 75231-5993
United States
Tel: 1-800-275-4243
Fax: 1-214-692-6541
Web: http://www.aid.aii.edu

Art Institute of Fort Lauderdale
1799 SE 17th Street
Fort Lauderdale, Florida 33316
United States
Tel: 1-954-463-3000
Fax: 1-954-525-2602
Web: http://www.aifl.edu

Art Institute of Houston
1900 Yorktown
Houston, Texas 77056-4197
United States
Tel: 1-800-275-4244
Fax: 1-713-966-2797
Web: http://www.aih.aii.edu

Art Institute of Los Angeles
2900 31st Street
Santa Monica, California 90405
United States
Tel: 1-310-752-4700
Fax: 1-310-752-4708
Web: www.aila.artinstitutes.edu

Art Institute of Philadelphia
1622 Chestnut Street
Admissions, 1610 Chestnut Street
Philadelphia, Pennsylvania 19103
United States
Tel: 1-215-567-7080
Fax: 1-215-405-6399
Web: http://www.aiph.aii.edu

Art Institute of Phoenix
2233 W. Dunlap Ave.
Phoenix, Arizona 85021
United States
Tel: 1-800-474-2479
Fax: 1-602-216-0439
Web: http://www.aipx.edu

Art Institute of Pittsburgh
420 Boulevard of the Allies
Pittsburgh, Pennsylvania 15219
United States
Tel: 1-800-275-2470
Fax: 1-412-263-3715
Web: http://www.aip.aii.edu

Art Institute of Seattle
2323 Elliott Ave.
Seattle, Washington 98121-1622
United States
Tel: 1-206-448-0900
Fax: 1-206-269-0275
Web: http://www.ais.edu

Art Institutes International
300 Sixth Avenue
Pittsburgh, Pennsylvania 15222-2598
United States
Tel: 1-800-592-0700
Web: http://www.aii.edu

Art Institutes International Minnesota
15 South 9th Street
Minneapolis, Minnesota 55402
United States
Tel: 1-800-777-3643
Fax: 1-612-332-3934
Web: http://www.aim.artinstitutes.edu

Art Institutes International Portland
2000 SW Fifth Ave.
Portland, Oregon 97201-4972
United States
Tel: 1-888-228-6528
Fax: 1-503-228-4227
Web:http://www.aipd.artinstitutes.edu

ArtFarmAsia Animation & Digital
Exchange
Rm 907 Atlanta Centre Annapolis St.
Greenhills, San Juan Metro
Manila
Philippines
Tel: 63 2 53 502 85
Fax: 63 2 74 676 89
Web: http://www.artfarmasia.com

Associates in Art
5211 Kester Ave.

Sherman Oaks, California 91411
United States
Tel: 1-818-986-1050
Fax: 1-818-986-6363
Web: http://www.associatesinart.com

Atlanta College of Art
Woodruff Arts Center
1280 Peachtree Street N.E.
Atlanta, Georgia 30309
United States
Tel: 1-800-832-2104
Web: http://www.aca.edu

A Train Simple Company, Inc.
1334 3rd Street, 309
Santa Monica, California 90401
United States
Tel: 1-888-577-8333
Fax: 1-310-395-2151
Web: http://www.trainsimple.com

Aula do Risco
Rua Alberto Oliveira
Palacio dos Corucheus, 52 e 27
Lisbon
1700-019
Portugal
Tel: 35 1 217 979 723
Fax: 35 1 217 963 509
Web: http://www.risco.pt

Austin Community College
Department of Visual
Communication Design
11928 Stonehollow Drive
Austin, Texas 78758
United States
Tel: 1-512-223-4838
Fax: 1-512-223-4444
Web:
http://www.austin.cc.tx.us/viscom

Australian Film and Radio School
Digital Media Department
Cnr Balaclava & Epping Roads
North Ryde
New South Wales
2113
Australia
Tel: 61 2 9805 6611

Fax: 61 2 9887 1030
Web: http://www.aftrs.edu.au

AWGD Akademie Werbung Grafik
Druck
Heinrich-Gone-Steig, 4
Hamburg
D-20097
Germany
Tel: 49 40 23 06 40
Fax: 49 40 23 15 33
Web: http://www.awgd.de

Balleyfermot College of Further
Education
Ballyfermot Road
Dublin 10
Ireland
Tel: 35 31 626 9421
Fax: 35 31 626 6754
Web: http://www.bcfe.ie

Banff Centre, The
Box 1020
Banff, Alberta
Canada
T1L 1H5
Tel: 1-403-762-6100
Fax: 1-403-762-6444
Web: http://www.banffcentre.ca

Beklaedningsfagskolen
Department of Animation
Oerstedsgade 28
Odense
5000
Denmark
Tel: 45 66 12 21 45
Fax: 45 65 90 63 45
Web: http://www.bekl.dk

Bellevue Community College
Media and Technology Program
300 Landerholm Circle SE
Bellevue, Washington 98007
United States
Tel: 1-425-564-1000
Web: http://www.bcc.ctc.edu/mct

Beloit College
700 College St.
Beloit, Wisconsin 53511
United States
Tel: 1-800-356-0751
Fax: 1-608-363-2075
Web: http://www.beloit.edu

Bergen County Academy for the
Advancement of Science and
Technology
200 Hackensack Ave.
Hackensack, New Jersey 07601
United States
Tel: 1-201-343-6000
Fax: 1-201-343-2108
Web: http://www.bergen.org

Bildo akademie fuer Kunst und Medien
Postfach 41 12 68
Berlin
12122
Germany
Tel: 49 30 792 03 20
Fax: 49 30 797 00 760
Web: http://www.bildo.de

Bilkent University
Department of Art, Design,
Architecture, and Graphic Design
Bilkent
06533
Turkey
Tel: 90 312 290 1629
Fax: 90 312 266 41 36
Web: http://www.art.bilkent.edu.tr

Biola University
13800 Biola Ave.
La Mirada, California 90639-0001
United States
Tel: 1-800-OK-BIOLA
Tel: 1-800-652-4652
Web: http://www.biola.edu

Blue Sunflower Animation
Get Animated
50 Eagle Wharf Road
London
N1 7ED
United Kingdom
Tel: +44 (0) 20 7490 2990

Fax: +44 (0) 20 7336 7996
Web: http://www.getanimated.net

Bournemouth University
National Centre for Computer
Animation
School of Media Arts &
Communication
Talbot Campus, Fern Barrow
Poole
Dorset
BH12 5BB
United Kingdom
Tel: 44 1 202 595 246
Fax: 44 1 202 595 099
Web: http://ncca.bournemouth.ac.uk

Bowling Green State University
Department of Fine Arts
1000 Fine Arts Center
Bowling Green, Ohio 43403
United States
Tel: 1-866-246-6732
Fax: 1-419-372-6955
Web: http://www.bgsu.edu

Brigham Young University
Department of Visual Arts
College of Fine Arts and
Communication
C-502 HFAC
Provo, Utah 84602-6402
United States
Tel: 1-801-378-4266
Web:http://www.byu.edu/visualarts

Brooklyn College of the City
University of New York
Department of Film
2900 Bedford Ave.
0314 Plaza Building
Brooklyn, New York 11210-2889
United States
Tel: 1-718-951-5664
Fax: 1-718-951-4733
Web:
http://depthome.brooklyn.cuny.edu/film

Brooks Institute of Photography
801 Alston Road
Santa Barbara, California 93108
United States

Tel: 1-805-966-3888
Fax: 1-805-565-1386
Web: http://www.brooks.edu

Brown University
Department of Computer Science
115 Waterman St.
Providence, Rhode Island 02912
United States
Tel: 1-401-863-7600
Fax: 1-401-863-7657
Web: http://www.cs.brown.edu

Bruxelles Formation
166, avenue Louise
Bruxelles
B-1050
Belgium
Tel: 32 2 512 00 27
Fax: 32 2 513 27 50
Web:
http://www.stlouis.be/bxlformation

Burlington College
95 North Avenue
Burlington, Vermont 05401
United States
Tel: 1-802-862-9616
Tel: 1-800-862-9616
Fax: 1-802-660-4331
Web: http://www.burlingtoncollege.edu

Cal State Chico
Department of Computer
Graphics and Animation
1st. and Normal
Chico, California 95929-0005
United States
Tel: 1-530-898-4421
Fax: 1-530-898-5369
Web: http://imc.csuchico.edu

Cal State Univ., Fullerton
Department of Entertainment Art
and Animation
P.O. Box 6850
Fullerton, California 92834-6850
United States
Tel: 1-714-278-3471
Fax: 1-714-278-2390
Web: http://www.art.fullerton.edu

Cal State University Los Angeles
5151 State University Drive
Los Angeles, California 90032
United States
Tel: 1-323-343-3000
Fax: 1-323-343-4045
Web: http://www.calstatela.edu

Cal State University Northridge
18111 Nordhoff Street
Northridge, California 91330-8300
United States
Tel: 1-818-677-2242
Fax: 1-818-677-3046
Web: http://www.csun.edu/artdep

California College of Arts and Crafts
1111 Eighth Street
San Francisco, California 94107-2247
United States
Tel: 1-800-447-1ART
Tel: 1-800-447-1278
Fax: 1-415-703-9539
Web: http://www.ccac-art.edu

California Institute of the Arts
School of Film/Video
24700 McBean Parkway
Valencia, California 91355-2397
United States
Tel: 1-661-255-1050
Fax: 1-661-253-7824
Web: http://www.calarts.edu

California State University
Summer Arts Program
401 Golden Shore
Second Floor
Long Beach, California 90802
United States
Tel: 1-562-951-4060
Fax: 1-562-951-4918
Web:
http://www.calstate.edu/summerarts

California State University,
Long Beach
Department of Advanced Media
Production
1250 Bellflower Blvd.
Long Beach, California 90840
United States

Tel: 1-562-985-5471
Fax: 1-562-985-5292
Web: http://www.amp.csulb.edu

Caltech Graphics Group
MS 256-80
Computer Science Dept.
Pasadena, California 91125
United States
Tel: 1-626-395-2826
Fax: 1-626-795-1547
Web: http://www.gg.caltech.edu

Canadian Business College
Department of New Media
55 Town Centre Court
Ste. 108
Scarborough
Ontario
M4P 1X4
Canada
Tel: 888 925 9929
Fax: 416 925 9220
Web: http://www.cbstraining.com

Capilano College
Department of Commercial
Animation
2055 Purcell Way
North Vancouver
British Columbia
V7J 3H5
Canada
Tel: 604 990 7820
Fax: 604 990 7834
Web: http://www.capcollege.bc.ca

Carleton University
Department of Film Studies
423 St. Patrick's Bldg.
1125 Colonel By Drive
Ottawa, Ontario
K1S 5B6
Canada
Tel: 613 520 3993
Fax: 613 520 3575
Web:
http://www.carleton.ca/artandculture

Carnegie-Mellon University
School of Computer Science
5000 Forbes Ave.

Pittsburgh, Pennsylvania 15213
United States
Tel: 1-412-268-8525
Fax: 1-412-268-5576
Web: http://www.cs.cmu.edu

CBS Multimedia
80 Bloor Street West, 10th Floor
Suite 1000
Toronto
Ontario
M5S 2V1
Canada
Tel: 1-416-925-9929
Fax: 1-416-925-9220
Web: http://www.cbstraining.com

CDIS-Center for Digital Imaging
and Sound
3264 Beta Avenue
Burnaby
British Columbia
V5G 4K4
Canada
Tel: 800 661 1885
Fax: 604 298 5403
Web: http://www.artschool.com

Cégep du Vieux Montreal
Dessin animé
255, rue Ontario Est
Montréal
Quebec
H2X 1X6
Canada
Tel: 514 982 3437
Fax: 514 982 3448
Web: http://www.cvm.qc.ca

Centennial College
Digital Animation Program
Bell Center for Creative
Communications
951 Carlaw Ave.
Toronto, Ontario
M4K 3M2
Canada
Tel: 416 289 5100
Fax: 416 289 5106
Web: http://www.bccc.com

Center for Arts and Technology
Okanagan
Suite 100- 1632 Dickson Avenue
Kelowna BC V1Y-7T2 Canada
Tel: 1-250-860-ARTS (2787)
Tel: 1-866-860-ARTS (2787)
Fax: 1-250-712-1083
Web:http://www.digitalartschool.com

Center for Arts and Technology
Atlantic Canada
415 King Street, Fredericton
New Brunswick
Canada E3B 1E5
Tel: 1-506-460-1280
Fax: 1-506-460-1289
Tel: 1-877-369-1888
Web:http://www.digitalartschool.com

Center for Creative Studies
College of Art and Design
201 East Kirby St.
Detroit, Michigan 48202-4034
United States
Tel: 313 664 7400
Web: http://www.ccscad.edu

Center for Electronic Art
250 4th Street
San Francisco, California 94103
United States
Tel: 1-415-512-9300
Fax: 1-415-512-9260
Web: http://www.cea.edu

Central Saint Martins College of
Art and Design
Southampton Row
London
WC1B 4AP
United Kingdom
Tel: 44 1 71 514 7022
Fax: 44 1 71 514 7024
Web: http://www.csm.linst.ac.uk

Central State University
Computer Center for the Arts
1 Welsey Dr.
Wilder Force, Ohio 45384
United States
Tel: 1-937-376-6610
Web: http://www.centralstate.edu

Centre for Animation & Interactive Media
School of Creative Media
RMIT University
GPO Box 2476V
Melbourne
Victoria
3001
Australia
Tel: 61 1 9925 5206
Fax: 63 1 9925 3356
Web: http://www.rmit.edu.au/aim

Centro Integral de Cursos
Especializados
C/Alcala 155
C/Maldonado 48
Madrid
28009
Spain
Tel: 34 91 435 5843
Fax: 34 91 576 3650
Web: http://www.cicesa.com

Centro Sperimentale di
Cinematografia
Via Tuscolana 1524
Roma
00173
Italy
Tel: 39 6 72 29 41
Fax: 39 6 72 11 619
Web: http://www.snc.it

Cerro Coso Community College
100 College Parkway
Ridgecrest, California
United States
Tel: 1-760-934-2796
Tel: 1-888-537-6932
Web: http://www.coyote3d.com

CEV - Escuela Superior de
Communicacion Imagen y Sonido
Gaztambide, 65
Madrid
E-28015
Spain
Tel: 34 1 550 29 60
Web: http://www.cev.com

Chapman University
Cecile B. DeMille School of Film

and Television
333 N. Glassell
Orange, California 92866
United States
Tel: 1-714-997-6765
Fax: 1-714-997-6700
Web: http://ftv.chapman.edu

CIA - College of Interactive Arts
3D Game Design Foundation
Program
703 - 1155 Robson Street
Vancouver
Brittish Columbia
V6E 1B5
Canada
Tel: 604-689-7111
Fax: 604-689-7140
Web:http://www.gamercollege.com

Cicely Tyson School of
Performing & Fine Arts
Department of Animation
161 Elmwood Avenue
East Orange, New Jersey 07018
United States
Tel: 1-973-414-8671
Fax: 1-973-414-0154
Web: No Site

City Eye Media Centre
Northam Centre
Kent Street
Southampton
SO14 5SP
United Kingdom
Tel: 44 2 380 634 177
Web: http://www.city-eye.co.uk

City University of Hong Kong
School of Creative Media
Rm Y2656, Academic Building
83 Tat Chee Avenue
Kowloon Tong
Kowloon
Hong Kong
Tel: 27 888 049
Fax: 27 887 165
Web: http://www.cityu.edu.hk/scm

City Varsity Film & T.V. and
Multimedia School

Department of Animation
32 Kloof Street
Cape Town
South Africa
Tel: 27 21 4233 366
Fax: 27 21 4236 300
Web: http://www.cvarsity.co.za

CNBDI
121 rue de Bordeaux
Angouleme
16000
France
Tel: 33 5 45 38 65 65
Fax: 33 5 45 38 65 51
Web: http://www.cnbdi.fr

Cogswell Polytechnical College
1175 Bordeaux Drive
Sunnyvale, California 94089
United States
Tel: 1-800-264-7955
Fax: 1-408-747-0764
Web: http://www.cogswell.edu

College Boreal
Sciences Humaines, Animation
21, boulevard Lasalle
Sudbury
Ontario
P3A 6B1
Canada
Tel: 800 361 6673
Fax: 705 521 6006
Web: http://www.borealc.on.ca

College de l'Acadie
Department of Animation 2D-3D
73, Tacoma Drive, 4th Floor
Dartmouth
Nova Scotia
B2W 3Y6
Canada
Tel: 902 424 2630
Fax: 902 424 3607
Web: http://www.azimuts.ns.ca

College Inter-Dec
Department of Animation
2120, rue Ste-Catherine West
Bureau 6100
Montreal

Quebec
H3H 1M7
Canada
Tel: 514 939 4444
Fax: 514 939 3046
Web: http://www.interdec.qc.ca

College of the North Atlantic
Department of Multimedia &
Animation
P.O. Box 5400
Stephenville
Newfoundland
A2N 2Z6
Canada
Tel: 888 982 2268
Fax: 709 643 7827
Web:
http://www.northatlantic.nf.ca

Collins College
Department of Animation
1140 S Priest
Tempe, Arizona 85281
United States
Tel: 1-480-966-3000
Fax: 1-480-902-0663
Web:
http://www.collinscollege.edu

Columbia College Chicago
Film and Video Department
600 South Michigan Avenue
Chicago, Illinois 60605
United States
Tel: 1-312-663-1600
Fax: 1-312-344-8044
Web: http://www.colum.edu

Columbia College Hollywood
18618, Oxnard Street,
Tarzana, California 91356
United States
Tel: 1-800-785-0585
Tel: 1-818-345-8414
Fax: 1-818-345-9053
Web: http://www.columbiacol-
lege.edu

Columbus College of Art &
Design
107 N. 9th Street

Columbus, Ohio 43215
United States
Tel: 1-614-224-9101
Fax: 1-614-222-4040
Web: http://www.ccad.edu

Computer Master
775 Topaz Ave.
Victoria
British Columbia
V8T 4Z7
Canada
Tel: 250 380 9850
Fax: 250 380 9852
Web: http://www.computermaster.com

Concordia University
Department of Art Education
1455 De Maisoneuve Blvd. West
Montreal
Quebec
H3G 1M8
Canada
Tel: 514 848 4666
Fax: 514 848 8627
Web: http://cinema.concordia.ca

Conneticut College
Department of Studio Art
270 Mohegan Avenue
New London, Connecticut 06320
United States
Tel: 1-860-439-2200
Fax: 1-860-439-5339
Web: http://www.conncoll.edu

Consulting for Architects, Inc.
The CFA/CADD Training Center
236 Fifth Avenue
New York, New York 10001
United States
Tel: 1-800-723-8882
Fax: 1-212-696-9128
Web: http://www.cons4arch.com

Cooper Union School of Art
Film/Animation Department
266 Bleeker St. 3rd Floor
Brooklyn, New York 11237
United States
Tel: 1-718-366-2513
Web: http://www.cooper.edu

Corcoran College of Art + Design
500 17th Street, NW
Washington, DC 20006
Tel: 1-202-638-1800
Web: http://www.corcoran.edu

Cornell University
Department of Computing and
Information Science
4132 Upson Hall
Ithaca, New York 14853
United States
Tel: 1-607-255-9188
Fax: 1-607-255-4428
Web: http://www.cis.cornell.edu

Coventry School of Art and
Design
Coventry University
Priory St.
Coventry
CV1 5FB
United Kingdom
Tel: 44 24 7688 8248
Fax: 44 24 7688 8667
Web: http://www.csad.coventry.ac.uk

CSEA
Via Tempia, 6
Torino
I-10156
Italy
Tel: 39 11 222 17 00
Fax: 39 11 222 17 01
Web: http://www.csea.it

CyberTek College
Animation & CG Department
711 Kimberly Avenue
Suite 170
Placentia, California 92708
United States
Tel: 1-877-625-0555
Fax: 1-714-996-1613
Web: http://www.cybertekcollege.net

Cyclone Arts & Technologies
2D-3D animation Department
740 St-Maurice suite 108
Montreal
Quebec
H3C 1L5

Canada
Tel: 514 879 0048
Fax: 514 879 0482
Web: http://www.cyclone.qc.ca

Daikin Comtec
12 F Tokyo-Opera-City-Tower
20-2 3-Chrome Nishi-Shinjuku
Shinjuku-ku
Tokyo
163-14
Japan
Tel: 81 3 5353 7821
Web: http://www.comtec.daikin.co.jp

Danish School of Art and Design
Institute for Visual
Communication
Strandboulevarden 47
Copenhagen
DK-2100
Denmark
Tel: 45 35 27 75 00
Fax: 45 35 27 76 00
Web: http://www.dk-designskole.dk

De Anza College
Creative Arts Division
21250 Stevens Creek Blvd.
Cupertino, California 95014
United States
Tel: 1-408-864-8832
Fax: 1-408-864-8492
Web: http://www.deanza.fhda.edu

DePaul CTI
243 So. Wabash Avenue
Chicago Illinios 60604
United States
Tel: 1-312-362-8381
Web: http://www.cti.depaul.edu

De Pauw
Department of Art
110 Art Center
Greencastle, Indiana 46135
United States
Tel: 1-765-658-4336
Fax: 1-765-658-4177
Web: http://www.depauw.edu

DeMontfort University
Department of Art & Design
The Gateway
Leicester
LE1 9BH
United Kingdom
Tel: 44 116 257 7507
Fax: 44 116 250 6281
Web: http://www.dmu.ac.uk

Designskoken Kolding
Agade 10
Kolding
DK-6000
Denmark
Tel: 45 76 30 11 00
Fax: 45 76 30 11 12
Web: http://www.designskolenkolding.dk

Desktop Images
2603 W. Magnolia Blvd.
Burbank, California 91505
United States
Tel: 1-800-377-1039
Tel: 1-818-841-8980
Fax: 1-818-841-8023
Web: http://www.desktopimages.com

DH Institute of Media Arts
15657 Wilshire Blvd. Suite 470
Los Angeles, California 90036
United States
Tel: 1-323-904-1135
Fax: 1-323-904-1162
Web: http://www.dhima.com

DigiPen Institute of Technology
Department of Science - Real
Time Interactive Simulation
5001 - 150th Ave. NE
Redmond, Washington 98052
United States
Tel: 1-425-558-0299
Fax: 1-425-558-0378
Web: http://www.digipen.edu

Digital Animation & Visual Effects
School, The
1000 Universal Studios Plaza,
Suite 218, Building 22A
Orlando, Florida 32819
United States
Tel: 1-407-224-3283
Web: http://www.daveschool.com

Digital Hollywood Fukuoka
SG Bldg. 5F
2-1-5 Daimyou
Chuou-ku
Fukuoka-prefecture
810-0041
Japan
Tel: 81 92 735 7679
Fax: 81 92 735 7911
Web: http://www.dhw.co.jp

Digital Hollywood Osaka
Digital Eight Bldg., 6-5-17
Nishi Tenma Kita-Ku
Osaka
5300047
Japan
Tel: 816 316 8570
Web: http://www.dhw.co.jp

Digital Hollywood Tokyo
2-3 Kanda Surugadai
Chiyoda-Ku
DH 2001 Bldg.
Tokyo
1010062
Japan
Tel: 81 3 5281 9222
Fax: 81 3 5281 9229
Web: http://www.dhw.co.jp

Digital Hollywood Yokohama
GM21 Bldg. 2 Floor
Kitasachi 2-4-3 Nishi-Ku
Yokohama
Kanagawa
2200004
Japan
Tel: 81 45 316 6001
Web: http://www.dhw.co.jp

Digital Solutions, Inc.
Six Piedmont Center, Suite 520

Atlanta, Georgia 30305
United States
Tel: 1-404-7600-8100
Tel: 1-404-7600-8111
Tel: 1-404-7600-8112
Web: http://www.digital-solutions.com

Digital Solutions, Inc.
112 South Tryon Street, suite 1400
Charlotte, North Carolina 28284
United States
Tel: 1-704-333-4374
Fax: 1-704-333-4375
Web: http://www.digital-solutions.com

Digital Solutions, Inc.
3354 Perimeter Hill Dr., Suite 226
Nashville, Tennessee 37211
United States
Tel: 1-615-837-9767
Fax: 1-615-837-9769
Web: http://www.digital-solutions.com

Digital Training and Designs
16200 Addison Road, Suite 200
Addison, Texas 75001
United States
Tel: 1-972-407-9303
Web: http://www.digitrain.com

DOMUS Academy
Via Savona, 97
Milano
I-20144
Italy
Tel: 39 2 47 71 91 55
Fax: 39 2 42 22 525
Web: http://www.domusacademy.it

Douglas Education Center
130 Seventh Street
Monessen, Pennsylvania 15062
United States
Tel: 1-724-684-3684
Fax: 1-724-684-7463
Web: http://www.douglas-school.com

Dream Machine
505 Dovercourt Road
Toronto
Ontario

M6H 2W3
Canada
Tel: 416-513-1785
Web:
http://www.dreammachinestudio.com

Drew College Preparatory School
2901 California Street
San Francisco, California 94115
United States
Tel: 1-415-409-DREW
Tel: 1-415-409-3739
Fax: 1-415-346-0720
Web: http://www.drewschool.org

Drexel University
Department of Media Arts
33rd and Market Streets
Philadelphia, Pennsylvania 19104
United States
Tel: 1-215-895-2407
Web: http://www.drexel.edu

Dun Laoghaire College of Art,
Design and Technology
Kill Avenue, Dun Laoghaire
Dublin
Ireland
Tel: 35 31 214 4600
Fax: 35 31 214 4700
Web: http://www.iadt-dl.ie

Duncan of Jordanstone College
School of Television and Imaging
Perth Road
Dundee
DD1 4HN
United Kingdom
Tel: 44 1 382 34 52 50
Fax: 44 1 382 22 61 36
Web: http://www.imaging.dundee.ac.uk

Duquesne University
Department of Multimedia Technology
600 Forbes Ave.
Pittsburgh, Pennsylvania 15282-1702
United States
Tel: 1-412-396-5772
Web: http://mmtserver.mmt.duq.edu

Dutch Film and Television Academy
Markenplein 1
Amsterdam
1011 MV
Netherlands
Tel: 31 20 5277 333
Fax: 3120 5277 344
Web: http://www.nfta.ahk.nl

Earthlight Pictures Animation Training
520 Alan Road
Santa Barbara, California 93109
United States
Tel: 1-805-563-1242
Web: www.earthlightpictures.com

Earthlight Pictures Animation Training
Santa Monica, California
United States
Tel: 1-805-563-1242
Web: http://www.earthlightpictures.com

East Tennessee State University
Department of Technology
P.O. Box 70701
Johnson City, Tennessee
37614-0552
United States
Tel: 1-423-979-3170
Fax: 1-423-979-3160
Web: http://avl.etsu-tn.edu

EAVE
Rue de la Presse, 14
Bruxelles
B-1000
Belgium
Tel: 32 2 219 09 20
Fax: 32 2 223 00 34
Web: http://www.eave.org

Ecole Cantonale d'Art de
Lausanne
46 rue de l'industrie
Bussigny-Vaud
1030
Switzerland
Tel: 41 22 731 37 57
Fax: 41 22 731 03 13
Web: http://www.ecal.ch

Ecole de Recherche Graphique
57, rue d'Irlande
Bruxelles
B-1060
Belgium
Tel: 32 2 538 98 29
Fax: 32 2 539 33 93
Web: http://www.st-luc.be

Ecole des Metiers du Cinema
d'Animation d'Angouleme
Chateau de Dampiere
1 rue de la Charente
Angouleme
16000
France
Tel: 33 5 45 20 55 29
Fax: 33 5 45 93 60 80
Web: http://www.angouleme.cci.fr

Ecole Emile Cohl
232 rue Paul Bert
Lyon
69003
France
Tel: 33 4 72 12 01 01
Fax: 33 4 72 35 07 67
Web: http://www.ecole-emile-cohl.fr

Ecole Européenne Supérieure
d'Animation
Chateau Georges Mélies
4, Rue Pasteur
Orly
94310
France
Tel: 33 1 48 90 86 23
Web: http://www.eesan.com

Ecole Nationale Superieure
des Beaux Arts de Paris
14, rue Bonaparte
Paris
75272
France
Tel: 33 1 47 03 50 00
Fax: 33 1 47 03 50 80
Web: http://www.ensba.fr

Ecole Superieure d'Infographie
Salles de cours Sud
4, rue Parmentier

Grenoble
38000
France
Tel: 33 4 76 85 23 13
Fax: 33 4 76 85 42 64
Web: http://www.aries-esi.com

Edinboro University of
Pennsylvania
Art Department
Edinboro, Pennsylvania 16444
United States
Tel: 1-814-732-2406
Fax: 1-814-732-2629
Web: http://www.Edinboro.edu

Edinburgh College of Art
Animation Department
School of Visual Communication
74, Lauriston Place
Edinburgh
EH3 9DF
United Kingdom
Tel: 44 131 221 6000
Fax: 44 131 221 6001
Web: http://www.eca.ac.uk

EICAR-Ecole Internationale
de Création Audiovisuelle et de
Réalisation
Animated Films and Special
Effects Techniques
93 avenue d'Italie
Paris
75013
France
Tel: 33 1 53 79 10 00
Fax: 33 1 53 79 76 26
Web: http://www.eicar-international.com

Emily Carr Instiue of Art & Design
Department of Animation
1399 Johnston Street
Vancouver
British Columbia
V6H 3R9
Canada
Tel: 1-604-844-3800
Fax: 1-604-844-3801
Web: http://www.eciad.bc.ca

ENSAD - Ecole Nationale
Superieure
des Arts Decoratifs
31 rue d'Ulm
Paris
75005
France
Tel: 33 1 42 34 97 00
Fax: 33 1 46 33 97 85
Web: http://www.ensad.fr

ENSAV - La Cambre
Hogeschool, Section Animation
Abbaye de La Cambre 21
Bruxelles
B-1000
Belgium
Tel: 32 2 648 96 19
Fax: 32 2 640 96 93
Web: http://www.lacambre.be

ESAD-Ecole Superieure des Arts
Decoratif
1 rue de l'Academie
Strasbourg
67000
France
Tel: 33 3 88 35 38 58
Fax: 33 3 88 36 29 58
Web: http://www.esad-stg.org

Escape Studios
126 Westbourne Studios
242 Acklam Road
London
W10 5JJ
United Kingdom
Tel: 44 20 7524 7570
Fax: 44 20 7524 7571
Web: http://www.escapestudios.co.uk

Escola das Artes - Universidade
Catolica Portuguesa
Departamento Som e Imagem
Rua Diogo Botelho 1327- 4169-
005 Porto
Porto
Portugal
Tel: 35 1 226 196 200
Fax: 35 1 226 196 291
Web: http://www.artes.ucp.pt

Escuela de Imagen y Diseño
Department of Video-Cine-TV & 3D
Paris 143
Barcelona
E-08036
Spain
Tel: 34 93 410 85 99
Fax: 34 93 410 91 32
Web: http://www.idep.es

Escuela Superior de Dibujo
Profesional
Santa Engracia 129
Madrid
28003
Spain
Tel: 34 91 3994639
Fax: 34 91 3994815
Web: http://www.esdip.com

ETIC - Escola Técnica de
Imagem e Comunicação
Department of Animation
R. D.Luis I, no.6
Lisboa
1200-151
Portugal
Tel: 351213942547
Fax: 351213978421
Web: http://www.etic.pt

Expression Center for New Media
6601 Shellmound Street
Emeryville, California 94608
United States
Tel: 1-877-833-8800
Fax: 1-510-658-3414
Web: http://www.expression.edu

Fachhochschule Hagenberg
Medientechnik und Design
Department
Hauptstrasse 117
Hagenberg
Upper Austria
A-4232
Austria
Tel: 43 7236 3888 0
Fax: 43 7236 3888 99
Web: http://www.fhs-hagenberg.ac.at

Fachhoschule Munster
Sentmaringer Weg, 53
Munster
D-48151
Germany
Tel: 49 251 83 6 53 01
Fax: 49 251 83 6 53 02
Web: http://www.fh-muenster.de

FAMU - Faculty of Film and TV
Department of of Animation
Smetanovo Nabrezi 2
Prague
11000
Czech Republic
Tel: 42 02 24 22 13 43
Fax: 42 02 24 23 02 85
Web: http://www.f.amu.cz

Filmakademi Baden-Wurtemberg
GMBH
Department of Animation
Mathildenstrasse, 20
Ludwigsburg
D-71638
Germany
Tel: 49 7 141 969 0
Fax: 49 7 141 969 299
Web: http://www.filmakademie.de

First Interactive Computer
College
Centre for Digital Media and
Internetworking
822 Richmond Street West
Toronto
Ontario
M6J 1C9
Canada
Tel: 416 504 3614
Fax: 416 504 3760
Web: http://www.ficc.ca

Florence Design Academy
Centro di Firenze
Florence, Firenze
50100
Italy
Tel: +39.055.4223299
Web:
http://www.florencedesignacademy.com

Florida Atlantic University
Center for Electronic Communication
111 Las Olas Blvd.
Ft. Lauderdale, Florida 33301
United States
Tel: 1-954-762-5618
Fax: 1-954-762-5658
Web: http://www.animasters.com

Foundation Institute
27734 Avenue Scott, Suite 190
Valencia, California 91355
United States
Tel: 1-661-702-9240
Fax: 1-661-702-9239
Web: http://www.foundationinstitute.com

Freed-Hardeman University
School of Arts and Humanities
158 E. Main Street
Henderson, Tennessee 38340
United States
Tel: 1-800-348-3481
Fax: 1-901-989-6065
Web: http://www.fhu.edu

Freie Universitat Berlin
Center for Media Research
(CMR)
Malteserstr. 74-100
Berlin
D-12249
Germany
Tel: 49 30 838 70532
Fax: 49 30 838 70741
Web: http://www.cmr.fu-berlin.de

Full Sail Real World Education
3300 University Blvd.
Winter Park, Florida 32792
United States
Tel: 1-800-226-7625
Fax: 1-407-678-0070
Web: http://www.fullsail.com

Future Media Concepts - Mass
43 Thorndike Street
Cambridge, Massachusetts 02141
United States
Tel: 1-877-362-8724
Web: http://www.fmctraining.com

Future Media Concepts - NY
305 East 47th Street
New York, New York 10017
United States
Tel: 1-212-888-6314
Fax: 1-212-888-7531
Web: http://www.fmctraining.com

Future Media Concepts - Philadelphia
325 Chestnut Street, Suite 220
Philadelphia, Pennsylvania 19106
United States
Tel: 1-215-922-2500
Fax: 1-215-922-6383
Web: http://www.fmctraining.com

G.T.C. Amir Glinik
Softimage ATC
Habanim 7 / 24 St.
Kfar-saba
44207
Israel
Tel: 97 2 9 7661740
Fax: 97 2 9 7653145
Web: http://www.3d-files.co.il

Game Institute
New York, New York
United States
https://www.gameinstitute.com

Georgia Institute of Technology
Atlanta, Georgia 30332
United States
Tel: 1-404-894-4154
Web: http://www.gatech.edu

Gesamthochschule Kassel
Monchebergstrasse 19
Kassel
D-34109
Germany
Tel: 49 561 804 0
Fax: 49 561 804 2330
Web: http://www.uni-kassel.de

Glasgow School Of Art
Digital Design Studio
House for an Art Lover
10 Dumbreck Road
Bellahouston

Glasgow
Scotland
G41 5BW
United Kingdom
Tel: +44 (0)141 353 4424
Fax: +44 (0)141 353 4448
Web: http://www.gsa.ac.uk

Globix Corporation
Training Department
139 Centre Street
New York, New York 10013
United States
Tel: 1-800-4-GLOBIX
Tel: 1-800-445-6249
Fax: 1-212-334-8615
Web: http://www.globix.com

Gnomon School of Visual Effects
1015 N. Cahuenga Blvd.
Hollywood, California 90038
United States
Tel: 1-323-466-6663
Fax: 1-323-466-6710
Web: http://www.gnomon3d.com

Go Academy - An Animation &
Visual Effects School
Animation & Visual Effects
W10-3, Business Park,
Subang Square, Jalan SS15/4G,
Subang Jaya, Selangor
47500
Malaysia
Tel: 60 3 5621 8090
Fax: 60 3 5621 7090
Web: http://www.go-academy.com

Gobelins - l'école de l'Image
73 boulevard Saint-Marcel
Paris
75013
France
Tel: 33 1 40 79 92 79
Fax: 33 1 40 79 92 71
Web: http://www.gobelins.fr

Grande Prairie Regional College
Grande Prairie, Alberta
Canada
Tel: 1-888-539-GPRC
Web: http://www.gprc.ab.ca

Grand Valley State University
School of Communications
121 Lake Superior Hall
Allendale, Michigan 49401
United States
Tel: 1-800-748-0246
Web: http://www.gvsu.edu

Grant MacEwan College
Visual Communication Design
10045 156 Street
Edmonton, Alberta
T5P 2P7
Canada
Tel: 780 497 4315
Fax: 780 497 4330
Web: http://www.macewan.ca

Grenaa Tekniske Skole
Digital Media
Aarhusvej 49-51
Grenaa
8500
Denmark
Tel: 45 87 582200
Web: http://www.gts.dk

Griffith University
Queensland College of Art
226 Grey Street
P.O. Box 3370
South Brisbane
Queensland
Q 4101
Australia
Tel: 61 7 3875 3112
Fax: 61 7 3875 3113
Web: http://www.gu.edu.au

Groep T-Technologische
Hogeschool
Vesaliusstraat, 13
Leuven
B-3000
Belgium
Tel: 32 16 30 10 30
Fax: 32 16 30 10 40
Web: http://www.groept.be

Hamilton Adult Campus
815 Marion Rd.
Mitchell Park

South Australia
5043
Australia
Tel: 61 8 8275 8300
Fax: 61 8 8277 9380
Web: http://www.hamcoll.sa.edu.au

Harper College
1200 West Algonquin Rd
Palatine, Illinois 60067-7398
United States
Tel: 1-847-925-6000
Web: http://www.harper.cc.il.us

Harvard University
Department of VES
24 Quincy Street
Cambridge, Massachusetts
02138
United States
Tel: 1-617-495-3254
Fax: 1-617-495-8197
Web: http://www.fas.harvard.edu

Henderson State University
1100 Henderson Street
Arkadelphia, Arkansas 71999-0001
United States
Tel: 1-870-230-5000
Fax: 1-870-230-5144
Web: http://www.hsu.edu

Henry Cogswell College
School of Digital Arts
3002 Colby Avenue
Everett, Washington 98201
United States
Tel: 1-425-258-3351
Fax: 1-425-257-0405
Web: http://www.henrycogswell.edu

HFF - Academy of Film and
Television Potsdam-Babelsberg
Marlene-Dietrich-Allee 11
Potsdam-Babelsberg
14482
Germany
Tel: 49 331 6202 0
Fax: 49 331 6202 549
Web: http://www.hff-potsdam.de

Hochschule fur Grafik und
Buchkunst
Academy of Visual Arts
Wachterstrabe 11
Leipzig
D-04107
Germany
Tel: 49 341 21 35 0
Fax: 49 341 2135 166
Web: http://www.hgb-leipzig.de

Hochschule fur Kunst und Design
Neuwerk 7
Halle
06108
Germany
Tel: 49 345 77 51 50
Fax: 49 345 77 51 569
Web: http://www.burg-halle.de

Hogeschool Gent - K.A.S.K
Department of Architecture,
Audiovisual and Fine Arts
Jozef Kluyskensstraat 2
Academiestraat 2
Gent
9000
Belgium
Tel: 32 9 2660885
Fax: 32 9 2660881
Web: http://www.hogent.be

Hogskolecenter Eksjo
Department of Web Animation
Kaserngatan 24
575 35
Eksjo
575 35
Sweden
Tel: 46 381 36120
Fax: 46 381 36121
Web: http://www.eksjo.se

Holmesglen Institute
Department of Multimedia
585 Waverley Road
Glen Waverley
Victoria
3150
Australia
Tel: 61 39 5646254
Web: http://www.hitanimation.net

Hong-ik University
College of Art & Design
34-31 Shinan-Ri Chochiwon-Up
Yeonki-Gun
Chung-Nam
Seoul
339-701
South Korea
Tel: 82 41 860 2511
Fax: 82 41 866 6125
Web: http://shinan.hongik.ac.kr

Howard University
Department of Fine Arts
629 Harvard
Washington, DC 20001
United States
Tel: 1-202-806-7040
Web: http://www.howard.edu

ICARI Institute
55, Mont-Royal West
5th floor
Montreal
Quebec
H2T 2S6
Canada
Tel: 514 982 0922
Fax: 514 982 0288
Web: http://www.icari.com

IFS International Film School
Department of
Cartoons/Animation
Werderstr. 1
Cologne
Northrhine Westphalia
50672
Germany
Tel: +49 (0)221 92018810
Fax: +49 (0)221 92018899
Web: http://www.filmschule.de

Image Campus
Salta 239
Buenos Aires, Capital Federal
Argentina
C1074AAE
Tel: +54 11.43.83.22.44
Fax: +54 11.43.83.29.92
Web: http://www.imagecampus.com.ar

Indiana University
107 S. Indiana Ave.
Bloomington, Indiana 47405-7000
United States
Tel: 1-812-855-4848
Web: http://www.indiana.edu

Infocast of Digital Arts
Department of 3D Animation
#260-4351 No. 3 Road
Richmond
British Columbia
V6X 3A7
Canada
Tel: 1-866-717-8080
Fax: 1-604-717-8088
Web: http://www.idaschool.com

Information Technology Design Centre
University of Toronto
230 College Street
Toronto
Ontario
M5T 1R2
Canada
Tel: 1-416-978-0631
Fax: 1-416-971-2093
Web: www.utoronto.ca

Institut Universitari de l'Audiovisual
Passeig de Circumval-lacio, 8
Barcelona
E-08003
Spain
Tel: 34 93 542 25 00
Fax: 34 93 542 22 02
Web: http://www.iua.upf.es

Institute for Design
Department of Computer Graphics
512 Stanley Street
South Brisbane
Queensland
4101
Australia
Tel: 61 7 3846 7133
Fax: 61 7 3846 7405
Web: http://www.ifd.net.au

Integrated Groups
20, El Nasr Str.
New Maadi

Cairo
11341
Egypt
Tel: 20 2 516 8068
Fax: 20 2 516 8212
Web: http://www.is-egypt.com

International Academy of Design
5225 Memorial Highway
Tampa, Florida 33634
United States
Tel: 1-800-222-3369
Fax: 1-813-881-0008
Web: http://www.academy.edu

International Academy of Design
31 Wellesley Street East
Toronto
Ontario
M4Y 1G7
Canada
Tel: 1-416-922-3666
Fax: 1-416-922-7504
Web: http://www.iaod.com

International Fine Arts College
Department of Computer
Animation
1737 North Bayshore Drive
Miami, Florida 33132
United States
Tel: 1-800-225-9023
Fax: 1-305-374-7946
Web: http://www.ifac.edu

ISInc.
1320 National Drive
Sacramento, California 95834
United States
Tel: 1-800-877-1707
Fax: 1-916-928-9309
Web: http://isinc.com

Istituto Europeo di Design
Via Amatore Sciesa, 4
Milano
I-20135
Italy
Tel: 39 2 57 96 95 1
Fax: 39 2 55 10 37 4
Web: http://www.ied.edu

Japan Electronics College
Department of CG & Visual Arts
1-25-4 Hyakunin-cho
Shinjuku-ku
Tokyo
169-8522
Japan
Tel: 81 03 3363 7761
Fax: 81 03 3363 7685
Web: http://www.jec.ac.jp

JNT University
College of Fine Arts
Applied Art
Kukatpally
Hyderabad
Andhra Pradesh
500 072
India
Tel: 91 40 331 4282
Fax: 91 40 339 7648
Web: http://www.jntu.ac.in

Joe Kubert School of Cartoon &
Graphic Art, Inc.
37 Myrtle Avenue
Dover, New Jersey 07801
United States
Tel: 1-973-361-1327
Fax: 1-973-361-1844
Web: http://www.kubertsworld.com

John Moores University
Liverpool School of Art and
Design
68 Hope Street
Liverpool
L19 EB
United Kingdom
Tel: 44 151 231 5083
Fax: 44 151 231 5096
Web: http://www.livjm.ac.uk

K. Gibbs School of Animation & Design
Department of Digital Arts
320 South Service Road
Melville, New York 11747
United States
Tel: 1-631-370-3300
Fax: 1-631-293-1276
Web: http://www.gibbsmelville.com

Kalamazoo Valley Community College
6767 West O Avenue
P.O. Box 4070
Kalamazoo, Michigan 49053
United States
Tel: 1-269-372-5000
Web: http://www.kvcc.edu

Kansas City Art Institute
4415 Warwick Blvd.
Kansas City, Missouri 64111
United States
Tel: 1-800-522-5224
Fax: 1-816-802-3309
Web: http://www.kcai.edu

Katholieke Hogeschool Limburg
Media and Design Academy
Weg naar As 50
Genk B-3600
Belgium
Tel: 32 89 300 850
Fax: 32 89 300 859
Web: http://www.khlim.be

Kaywon School of Art and Design
Department of Animation
Naeson-dong San 125
Euiwang-shi
Kyunggi-do 437-712
South Korea
Tel: 82 31 420 1700
Fax: 82 31 424 7509
Web: http://www.kaywon.ac.kr

Kendall College of Art and Design
17 Fountain Street
Grand Rapids, Michigan 49503-3102
United States
Tel: 1-800-676-2787
Fax: 1-616-831-9687
Web: http://www.kcad.edu

Kent State University Tuscarawas
Engineering Technology
330 University Drive NE
New Philadelphia, Ohio 44663
United States
Tel: 1-330-339-3391
Fax: 1-330 339-3321
Web: http://www.tusc.kent.edu

Klik! Centre Experimental de
Mitjans Audiovisuals
Sant Medir 12, 2° 4ª
Barcelona
08028
Spain
Tel: 34 93 490 70 58
Web: http://www.klik-cema.com

Kolej Yayasan Melaka
School of Media Technology and Arts
Kolej Yayasan Melaka
No. 1, Jalan Bukit Sebukor
Melaka
Melaka
75150
Malaysia
Tel: 60 6 281 7732
Fax: 60 6 281 6845
Web: http://www.kym.edu.my

Korean Academy of Film Arts
Department of Animation
19-8 2ga Namsan-dong
Jung-gu
Seoul
South Korea
Tel: 82 2 752 0746
Fax: 82 2 752 0742
Web: http://www.kofic.or.kr

Kutztown University
College of Visual and Performing Arts
Kutztown, Pennsylvania 19530
United States
Tel: 1-610-683-4500
Fax: 1-610-683-4502
Web: http://www.kutztown.edu

L.A. City College
Department of Cinema &
Television
855 N. Vermont Avenue
Los Angeles, California 90029
United States
Tel: 1-323-953-5545
Fax: 1-323-953-4505
Web: http://www.lacc.cc.ca.us

Lake Washington Technical College
Department of Multi-Media
Design and Production
11605 132nd Ave NE
Kirkland, Washington 98034-8506
United States
Tel: 1-425-739-8100
Fax: 1-425-739-8298
Web: https://www.lwtc.ctc.edu

Lansing Community College
Art, Design & Multimedia
Program
315 North Grand Avenue
P.O. Box 40010
Lansing, Michigan 48901-7210
United States
Tel: 1-517-483-1476
Fax: 1-517-483-9781
Web: http://www.lcc.edu/vam/art

Lasalle-SIA
College of the Arts
School of Multimedia Art
90 Goodman Road
Singapore
439053
Singapore
Tel: 65 344 4300
Fax: 65 346 5708
Web: http://www.lasallesia.edu.sg

Lazi Akademie
Schlosslesweg 48-50
Stuttgart-Esslingen
D-73732
Germany
Tel: 49 711 937 83 80
Fax: 49 711 937 83 840
Web: http://www.lazi.de

Learn* Training School
3rd Floor - Standard Bank Centre
304 Oak Ave.
Randburg
Gauteng
2194
South Africa
Tel: 27 11 886 8572
Fax: 27 11 886 8574
Web: http://www.touchvision.co.za

Learning Tree University
Chatsworth Campus
20920 Knapp Street
Chatsworth, California 91311-5906
United States
Tel: 1-818-882-5599
Fax: 1-818-341-0707
Web: http://www.ltu.org

Ledet & Associates
2200 Northlake Parkway Suite 275
Tucker, Georgia 30084
United States
Tel: 1-877-819-COOL
Tel: 1-877-819-2665
Fax: 1-770-414-5661
Web: http://www.ledet.com

Ledet & Associates
5036 Yale Street Suite 203
Metairie, Louisiana 70006-3980
United States
Tel: 1-877-819-COOL
Tel: 1-877-819-2665
Fax: 1-770-414-5661
Web: http://www.ledet.com

Ledet & Associates
700 District Drive
Itasca, Illinois 60143
United States
Tel: 1-877-819-COOL
Tel: 1-877-819-2665
Fax: 1-770-414-5661
Web: http://www.ledet.com

Leeds Animation Workshop
45 Bayswater Row
Leeds
LS8 5LF
United Kingdom
Tel: 44 113 248 4997
Web:
http://www.leedsanimation.demon.co.uk

Limkokwing Institute of Creative
Technology
School of Design, Animation and
Multimedia
1 Jalan SS26/2
Taman Mayang Jaya
Petaling Jaya

Selangor Darul Ehsan
47301
Malaysia
Tel: 60 37 804 5220
Fax: 60 37 804 1520
Web: http://www.limkokwing.edu.my

London Animation Studio
Central Saint Martins College of
Art & Design
2-6 Catton St.
London
WC1R 4AA
United Kingdom
Tel: 44 20 7514 7363
Fax: 44 20 7514 7302
Web:
http://www.londonanimationstudio.tv

Los Angeles City College
Cinema-Television Department
855 N. Vermont Avenue
Los Angeles, California 90029
United States
Tel: 1-323-953-4545
Fax: 1-323-953-4505
Web: http://citywww.lacc.cc.ca.us

Los Angeles Film School, The
6363 Sunset Blvd. #400
Hollywood, California 90028
United States
Tel: 1-323-860-0789
Tel: 1-877-9LA-FILM
Web: http://www.lafilm.com

Louisville Technical Institute
Department of Computer Graphic
Design
3901 Atkinson Drive
Louisville, Kentucky 40218
United States
Tel: 1-800-844-6528
Fax: 1-502-456-2341
Web:http://www.louisvilletech.com

Loyalist College of Applied Arts &
Technology
Department of Digital Production
P.O. Box 4200 Wallbridge-Loyalist Rd.
Belleville
Ontario
K8N 5B9
Canada
Tel: 1-613-969-1913
Fax: 1-613-969-7905
Web: http://www.loyalistcollege.com

Loyola Marymount University
School of Film and Television
One LMU Drive, MC 8230
Los Angeles, California 90045-8347
United States
Tel: 1-310-338-3033
Fax: 1-310-338-3030
Web: http://www.lmu.edu/filmschool

LTU
20960 Knapp Street
Chatsworth, California 91311
United States
Tel: 1-818-882-5599
Fax: 1-818-882-1719
Web: http://www.ltuonline.com

Lycée Technique des Arts et Métiers
BTS en Dessin d'animation
19, rue Guillaume Schneider
Gr-D -Luxembourg
L-2522
Tel: 00352467616-200
Fax: 00352472991
Web: http://www.ltam.lu/ecole

Lycoming College
Department of Art
700 College Place
Williamsport, Pennsylvania 17701
United States
Tel: 1-570-321-4026
Web: http://www.lycoming.edu

MAD Academy
Studio 1
Greater Union Centre
128 Hindley Street
Adelaide SA 5000
Australia

Tel: 08 8221 5816
Fax: 08 8221 6766
Web:http://www.madacademy.com.au

MAD Academy
Fox Studios Australia
Building 220, Room 101A
(First Floor)
Pedestrian Entrance Gate 3
off Driver Avenue
Moore Park NSW 1363
Australia
Web:http://www.madacademy.com.au

MAGICA
Via Lucullo 7, int.8
Roma
I-00187
Italy
Fax: 39 6 42010898
Web: http://www.audiovisual.org

Magnet Media
New York, New York
United States
Tel: 1-877-606-5012
Fax: 1-646-486-6583
Web:http://www.digitalmediatraining.com

Maharishi University of
Management
School of the Arts
1000 N 4th Street
Fairfield, Iowa 52557
United States
Tel: 1-800-369-6480
Fax: 1-641-472-1179
Web: http://www.mum.edu

Marycrest International University
Department of
Graphic Communication and
Computer Science
1607 W. 12th St.
Davenport, Iowa 52804-4906
United States
Tel: 1-800-728-9705
Web: http://www.mcrest.edu

Massachusetts Institute of
Technology
The MIT Media Laboratory
The Program in Media Arts and
Sciences
77 Massachusetts Ave.
Cambridge, Massachusetts
02139
United States
Tel: 1-617-253-4600
Fax: 1-617-258-6264
Web: http://www.media.mit.edu

Massey University
College of Design
Private Box 756
Wellington
New Zealand
Tel: 64 4 801 2794
Fax: 64 4 801 2799
Web: http://creative.massey.ac.nz

Max The Mutt Animation Inc.
96 Spadina Avenue
Suite 907
Toronto, Ontario Canada
M5V 2J6
Tel: +1 416.703.6877
Fax: +1 416.703.3930
Web: http://www.maxthemutt.com

McKenzie College
5670 Spring Garden Rd., 10th
Floor
Halifax
Nova Scotia, Canada
B3J 1H6
Tel: 1-902-425-2015
Fax: 1-902-425-2014
Web: http://www.mckenzie.edu

Media Business School
Velazquez, 14
Madrid
E-28001
Spain
Tel: 34 91 575 9583
Fax: 34 91 431 3303
Web: http://www.mediaschool.org

Media Code
2165-D Francisco Blvd.
San Rafael, California 94901
United States
Tel: 1-415-453-9293
Fax: 1-415-454-0229
Web: http://www.media-code.com

Media Design School
Department of 3D Computer
Animation
242 Queen Street
Downtown
Auckland
North Island
New Zealand
Tel: 64 9 303 0402
Fax: 64 9 303 0646
Web: http://www.mediadesign.school.nz

Media Training
4710 Eisenhower Blvd.
Suite C6
Tampa, Florida 33634
United States
Tel: 1-888-886-7793
Fax: 1-813-886-3034
Web: http://www.medtrain.net

Mediadesign Akademie Gmbh
Berg-am-Laim-Strasse, 47
Munchen
D-81673
Germany
Tel: 49 89 450 605 0
Fax: 49 89 450 605 17
Web: http://www.mediadesign.de

Mediatek Johannesburg
83 Iris Road
PO Box 412600, Craighall, 2024
Johannesburg
South Africa
Tel: 27 11 728 7870
Fax: 27 11 728 7875
Web: http://www.mediatek.co.za

Memphis College of Art
1930 Poplar
Memphis, Tennessee 38104-2764
United States
Tel: 1-800-727-1088

Fax: 1-901-272-5122
Web: http://www.mca.edu

Mercer County Community College
P.O. Box B
Trenton, New Jersey 08690
United States
Tel: 1-609-586-4800
Fax: 1-609-586-6944
Web: http://www.mccc.edu

Mercy College
Center for Digital Arts
Computer Arts + Technology
277 Martine Avenue
White Plains, New York 10601
United States
Tel: 1-914-948-3666
Fax: 1-914-948-6732
Web: http://www.mercy.edu

Merz Akademie
Teckstrasse, 58
Stuttgart
D-70190
Germany
Tel: 49 711 268 66 0
Fax: 49 711 268 66 21
Web: http://www.merz-
akademie.de

Mesmer Animation Labs
1116 NW 54th St
Seattle, Washington 98107
United States
Tel: 1-800-237-7311
Fax: 1-206-782-8101
Web: http://www.mesmer.com

Metro New Media
35 Kingsland Road
Shoreditch
London
E2 8AA
United Kingdom
Tel: 44 20 7729 9992
Fax: 44 20 7739 7742
Web: http://www.metronewmedia.com

Michigan State University
250 Administration Building
East Lansing, Michigan 48824-0590
United States
Tel: 1-517-355-8332
Web: http://www.msu.edu

Middlesex University
White Hart Lane
London
N17 8HR
United Kingdom
Tel: 44 208 411 5000
Web: http://www.mdx.ac.uk

Minneapolis College of Art and Design
2501 Stevens Ave. South
Minneapolis, Minnesota 55404
United States
Tel: 1-612-874-3760
Web: http://www.mcad.edu

Minnesota School of Computer Imaging
Department of Animation
1401 West 76th Street, Suite 500
Richfield, Minnesota 55423-9820
United States
Tel: 1-612-861-2000
Fax: 1-612-861-5548
Web: http://www.msbcollege.com

Mission College
Department of Graphic Design
3000 Mission College Blvd.
Santa Clara, California 95054-1897
United States
Tel: 1-408-988-2200
Fax: 1-408-567-2892
Web: http://www.wvmccd.cc.ca.us

Mississippi State University
P.O. Box 5325
Mississippi State, Mississippi 39762
United States
Tel: 1-601-325-2646
Fax: 1-601-325-8740
Web: http://www.msstate.edu/dept/art

Morain Valley Community College
10900 S. 88th Ave.
Palos Hills, Illinois 60465-0937
United States
Tel: 1-708-974-4300
Web: http://www.moraine.cc.il.us

Moviola
1135 N. Mansfield Ave.
Hollywood, California 90038
United States
Tel: 1-323-467-1116
Web: http://www.moviola.com

Moviola
545 W. 45th Street
New York, New York 10036
United States
Tel: 1-212-247-0972
Web: http://www.moviola.com

MSU-Northern
Department of
Industrial/Engineering Technology
Box 7751
Havre, Montana 59501
United States
Tel: 1-406-265-4157
Fax: 1-406-265-3580
Web: http://www.msun.edu

Mt. San antonio College
1100 North Grand Avenue
Walnut, California 91789
United States
Tel: 1-909-594-5611
Fax: 1-909-468-4067
Web: http://www.mtsac.edu

Multimedia Technology Center
Red Rocks Community College
13300 W. 6th Ave.
Lakewood, Colorado 80288
United States
Tel: 1-303-914-6617
Fax: 1-303-914-6409
Web: http://www.cccoes.edu

Multimedia University
Department of Creative Multimedia
Jalan Multimedia

Cyberjaya
Selangor
63100
Malaysia
Tel: +603 8312 5555
Fax: +603 8312 5554
Web: http://www.mmu.edu.my

MUV Institute of Digital Arts
1A, I floor, TAAS MAHAL
10, Montieth Road
Egmore
Chennai
Tamil Nadu
600 008
India
Tel: 91 044 501 8111
Fax: 91 044 852 3521
Web: http://www.muvtech.com

Nanyang Polytechnic
Digital Media Design Centre
School of Design
180 Ang Mo Kio Ave 8
569830
Singapore
Tel: 65 5501600
Fax: 65 4520110
Web: http://www.nyp.edu.sg/sdn

NATFIZ
108-A Rakovsky Str.
Sofia
1000
Bulgaria
Tel: 35 92 987 9862
Fax: 35 92 986 4019
Web: http://www.art.acad.bg

National Animation and Design
Centre (NAD Centre)
Bell MediaSphere
335 de Maisonneuve East Blvd,
Suite 300
Montreal
Quebec
H2X 1K1
Canada
Tel: 1-514-288-3447
Fax: 1-514-288-5799
Web: http://www.nadcentre.com

National Film & Television School
Beaconsfield Studios
Station Road
Beaconsfield, Buckinghamshire
United Kingdom
HP9 1LG
Tel: 44 1494 671234
Fax: 44 1494 674042
Web: hhttp://www.nftsfilm-tv.ac.uk

National Institute of Design
Department of Animation Film Design
National Institute of Design, Paldi
Ahmedabad
Gujarat
380 007
India
Tel: 91 79 663 9692
Fax: 91 79 662 1167
Web: http://nid.edu

NBCC Miramichi
Department of Animation &
Graphics Technology
80 University Avenue
P. O. Box 1053
Miramichi
New Brunswick
E1N 3W4
Canada
Tel: 1-506-778-6000
Fax: 1-506-778-6379
Web:
http://animation.miramichi.nbcc.nb.ca

New Media Campus
205-2100 Airport Drive
Saskatoon
Saskatchewan
S7L 6M6
Canada
Tel: 1-306-955-4412
Fax: 1-306-955-5337
Web: http://www.newmediacam-pus.com

New York Film Academy
100 East 17th Street
New York, New York
United States
Tel: 1-212-674-4300
Web: http://www.nyfa.com

New York Institute of Technology
Department of Communication Arts
1855 Broadway
New York, New York 10023
United States
Tel: 1-800-345-NYIT
Tel: 1-800-345-6948
Web: http://www.nyit.edu

New York University
Tisch School of the Arts
721 Broadway, 8th Floor
New York, New York 10003
United States
Tel: 1-212-998-1778
Fax: 1-212-995-4062
Web: http://www.nyu.edu/tisch/filmtv

New York University
Continuing and Professional Studies
Center for Advanced Digital Applications
11 West 42nd Street
New York, New York 10036-8083
United States
Tel: 1-212-790-1370
Fax: 1-212-790-1386
Web: http://www.scps.nyu.edu/cada

Ngapartji Multimedia Centre
211 Rundle Street
Adelaide
South Australia
5000
Australia
Tel: 61 8 8235 4001
Fax: 61 8 8235 4002
Web: http://www.ngapartji.com.au

Ngee Ann Polytechnic
Department of Film and Media
Studies
535 Clementi Road
Singapore
599489
Tel: 65 460 6784
Fax: 65 462 5617
Web: http://fmsweb.np.edu.sg

Norfolk State University
Department of Fine Arts
700 Park Avenue
Norfolk, Virginia 23504

United States
Tel: 1-757-823-8396
Fax: 1-757-823-8290
Web: http://www.nsu.edu/aca-
demics/liberal/finearts

North Carolina School of the Arts
School of Design and
Production/Filmmaking
1533 South Main Street
Winston-Salem, North Carolina
27127-2188
United States
Tel: 1-336-770-3220
Fax: 1-336-770-3213
Web: http://www.ncarts.edu

North Wales School of Art and Design
Mold Road
Wrexham North Wales
LL11 2AW
United Kingdom
Tel: 44 197 829 3502
Fax: 44 197 829 0008
Web: http://www.newi.ac.uk

Northeastern University
Department of Visual Arts
239 Ryder Hall
Boston, Massachusetts 02115
United States
Tel: 1-617-373-4081
Fax: 1-617-373-8535
Web: http://www.animation.neu.edu

Northern Oklahoma College
1220 E. Grand
Tonkawa, Oklahoma 74653
United States
Tel: 1-580-628-6777
Fax: 1-580-628-6209
Web: http://www.mmdclab.com

Northwest Film Center
1219 SW Park Avenue
Portland, Oregon 97205
United States
Tel: 1-503-221-1156
Fax: 1-503-294-0874
Web: http://www.nwfilm.org

Northwestern University
Dept. of Radio/TV/Film
Annie May Swift Hall, Rm 212
1905 Sheridan Road
Evanston, Illinois 60208
United States
Tel: 1-847-491-7315
Fax: 1-847-467-2389
Web: http://www.rtvf.nwu.edu

Norwich School of Art and Design
Animation Department
St. George Street
Norwich
Norfolk
United Kingdom
Tel: +44 1603 610561
Fax: +44 1603 615728
Web: http://www.nsad.ac.uk

Nova Scotia College of Art & Design
Microcomputer Center
5163 Duke Street
Halifax
Nova Scotia
B3J 3J6
Canada
Tel: 1-902-422-7381
Fax: 1-902-425-2420
Web: http://www.nscad.ns.ca

Nuova Accademia di Belle Arti
Via Paolo Bassi 3
Milano
20159
Italy
Tel: 39 2 66 86 867
Fax: 39 2 66 84 413
Web: http://www.naba.it

Ohio State University / ACCAD
Advancd Computng Center for
the Arts/Design
1224 Kinnear Road
Columbus, Ohio 43212-1163
United States
Tel: 1-614-292-3416
Fax: 1-614-292-7776
Web: http://www.accad.ohio-state.edu

Okanagan University College
Department of Animation
#100-2899 30th Ave.
Vernon
British Columbia
V1T 8G1
Canada
Tel: 1-250-503-2650
Fax: 1-250-503-2653
Web: http://www.ouc.bc.ca

Ontario College of Art and Design
100 McCaul Street
Toronto
Ontario
M5T 1W1
Canada
Tel: 1-800-382-6516
Web: http://www.ocad.on.ca

Orange Coast College
Department of Film/Video
2701 Fairview Road
P.O. Box 5005
Costa Mesa, California 92628-5005
United States
Tel: 1-714-432-5629
Fax: 1-714-432-5072
Web: http://www.occ.cccd.edu

Oregon3D, Inc.
9875 SW Beaverton-Hillside
Highway
Beaverton, Oregon
97005-3393
United States
Tel: 1-503-626-9000
Fax: 1-503-641-5671
Web: http://www.oregon3d.com

Ostfold Regional College
Os Alle, 11
Halden
N-1750
Norway
Tel: 47 69 21 53 00
Fax: 47 69 21 53 02
Web: http://www.hiof.no

Otis College of Art & Design
9045 Lincoln Blvd.

Los Angeles, California 90045
United States
Tel: 1-800-527-OTIS
Tel: 1-800-527-6847
Fax: 1-310-665 6821
Web: http://www.otisart.edu

Ottawa School of Art
Animation Program
35 George Street
Ottawa
Ontario
K1N 8W5
Canada
Tel: 1-613-241-7471
Fax: 1-613-241-4391
Web: http://eaosa.ottawa.com

Pacific Northwest College of Art
1241 N.W. Johnson
Portland, Oregon 97205
United States
Tel: 1-800-818-7622
Web: http://www.pnca.edu

Pacific University
Department of Graphic Design
Camino del Observatoria 1464
Santiago
Chile
Web: http://www.upacifico.cl

Palomar College
1140 W. Mission Rd.
San Marcos, California 92069
United States
Tel: 1-760-744-1150
Web: http://www.palomar.edu

Parsons School of Design
66 Fifth Avenue
New York, New York 10011
United States
Tel: 1-212-229-8910
Fax: 1-212-229-5648
Web: http://www.parsons.edu

Piedmont Community College
Digital Effects and Animation
Technology
331 Piedmont Drive

Yanceyville, North Carolina 27379
United States
Tel: 1-336-694-5707
Fax: 1-336-694-7086
Web: http://www.piedmont.cc.nc

Platt College
6250 El Cajon Blvd.
San Diego, California 92115-3919
United States
Tel: 1-619-265-0107
Fax: 1-619-0265-8655
Web: http://www.platt.edu

PL Studios
P.O. Box 576
Stillwater, Oklahoma 74076
United States
Tel: 1-800-599-7201
Tel: 1-405-624-3976
Web: http://www.plstudios.com

Politecnico di Milano
Piazza Leonardo da Vinci 32
Milano
I-20133
Italy
Tel: 39 2 23 99 1
Web: http://www.polimi.it

Polycollege Stoebergasse
Stoebergasse, 11-15
Wien
A-1050
Austria
Tel: 43 1 545 32 44
Fax: 43 1 545 32 44 19
Web: http://www.polycollege.ac.at

Portsmouth School of Art, Design
and Media
Eldon Building
Winston Churchill Avenue
Portsmouth
P01 2DJ
United Kingdom
Tel: 44 23 9284 3835
Fax: 44 23 9284 3808
Web: http://www.envf.port.ac.uk

Pratt Institute
Office of Admissions
200 Willoughby Avenue
Dekalb Hall, 2nd Floor
Brooklyn, New York 11205
United States
Tel: 1-718-636-3453
Fax: 1-718-636-3670
Web: http://www.pratt.edu

Pratt Manhattan
School of Professional Studies
295 Lafayette St. 2nd Floor
New York, New York 10012-2722
United States
Tel: 1-212-461-6040
Fax: 1-212-461-6026
Web: http://ProStudies.pratt.edu

Puget Sound Center - Canyon
Park Business Center
22002 26th Ave SE
Bothell, Washington 98021
United States
Tel: 1-425-640-1950
Fax: 1-425-640-1953
Web: http://pugetsoundcenter.org

Puppets...The Animation School
400-462 Wellington Street West
Toronto
Ontario
M5V 1E3
Canada
Tel: 1-866-542-1459
Web: www.theanimationschool.com

Purdue University
Dept. of Computer Graphics
Technology
1419 Knoy Hall
West Lafayette, Indiana 47907-1419
United States
Tel: 1-765-494-7505
Fax: 1-765-494-9267
Web: http://www.tech.purdue.edu/cg

QANTM
Level 10, 138 Albert St
Brisbane Qld 4000
Australia
Tel: +61 7 3017 4333

Fax: +61 7 3003 0953
Web: http://www.qantm.com.au

Reality Horizons PTY Ltd.
3rd Floor
112 Pybus Rd.
Sandton
2196s
South Africa
Tel: 27 11 884 5570
Fax: 27 11 884 5594
Web: http://www.reality.co.za

Red River Community College
Digital Arts Dept.
400-123 Main Street
Winnipeg
Manitoba
R3C 1A3
Canada
Tel: 1-888-515-7722
Fax: 1-204-945-1636
Web: http://www.rrc.mb.ca

Regent University
College of Communication and the Arts
1000 Regent University Dr.
Virginia Beach, Virginia 23464
United States
Tel: 1-800-373-5504
Fax: 1-757-226-4381
Web: http://www.regent.edu

Replica 3D Animation School
1400 A Marsland Place
Courtenay
BC
V9N 8X7
Canada
Tel: 1-250-338-8784
Web: http://www.replica3d.ca

Rhode Island School of Design
Department of Film, Animation & Video
2 College St.
Providence, Rhode Island 02903-2791
United States
Tel: 1-401-454-6233
Fax: -1401-454-6356
Web: http://www.risd.edu

Richard Williams Animation
Masterclass
The Animation Workshop
Ll. Sct. Hans Gade 7 - 9
Viborg
DK-8800
Denmark
Tel: 45 87 25 54 00
Fax: 45 87 25 54 11
Web: http://www.animwork.dk/rwmc

Ringling School of Art and Design
Department of Computer Animation
2700 N. Tamiami Trail
Sarasota, Florida 34234
United States
Tel: 1-800-255-7695
Fax: 1-941-359-7517
Web: http://www.rsad.edu

Rochester Institute of Technology
School Of Film & Animation
Frank E. Gannett Building
70 Lomb Memorial Drive
Rochester, New York 14623-5604
United States
Tel: 1-585-475-6175
Fax: 1-585-475-7575
Web: http://www.rit.edu

Rocky Mountain College of Art & Design
6875 E. Evans Avenue
Denver, Colorado 80224-2359
United States
Tel: 1-800-888-ARTS
Tel: 1-800-888-2787
Fax: 1-303-759-4970
Web: http://www.rmcad.edu

Royal College of Art
Department of Animation
Kensington Gore
London
SW7 2EU
United Kingdom
Tel: 44 20 7590 4444
Fax: 44 20 7590 4500
Web: http://www.rca.ac.uk

Royal Danish Academy Fine Arts
School of Visual Arts
Kongens Nyrtorv 1

Copenhagen
DK-1021
Denmark
Tel: 45 33 744 606
Web: http://www.kunstakademiet.dk

Rutgers University
Department of Fine Arts
311 North Fifth Street
Camden, New Jersey 08102
United States
Tel: 1-609-757-6176
Fax: 1-609-757-6330
Web: http://finearts.camden.rutgers.edu

Ryerson University
Department of Image Arts
350 Victoria Street
Toronto
Ontario
M5B 2K3
Canada
Tel: 416 979 5167
Web: http://www.ryerson.ca

SAE Institute - Adelaide
Unit 4, Level 2
282 Gouger Street
5000 Australia
Tel: +61 (0)8 8410 6599
Fax: +61 (0)8 8410 6808
Web: http://www.sae.edu

SAE Institute - Amsterdam
Nieuwe Kerkstraat 118
1018 VM Amsterdam
The Netherlands
Tel: +31 (0)20 622 87 90
Fax: +31 (0)20 428 14 19
Web: http://www.sae.nl

SAE Institute - Athens
Nikis 28
10557 Athens
Greece
Tel: +30 210 3217661
Fax: +30 210 3217641
Web: http://www.sae.edu.gr

SAE Institute - Auckland
18 Heather St

Parnell Auckland
New Zealand
Tel: +64 (0)9 373 4712
Fax: +64 (0)9 373 4713
web: http://www.sae.co.nz

SAE Institute - Bangalore
SAE Technology College,
2nd floor, Satya Sai Complex,
224, 14th Cross,
II Main Sampige Road,
Malleswaram
Bangalore-560003
India
Tel: (+91-80) 346 6082/346
6529/346 6530
Web: http://www.saeindia.net

SAE Institute - Bangkok
46 Mahajak Building
Sokhumvit Soi 3
(Nana-Hua) Klongtoey
Nua Watana
Bangkok 10110
Thailand
Tel: +66 (0) 2655-4655 to 7
Fax: +66 (0) 2655-4660
Web: http://www.sae.edu

SAE Institute - Berlin
Kapweg 4
13405 Berlin
Germany
Tel: +49 (0)30 4986 0054
Fax: +49 (0)30 4986 0057
Web: http://www.saecollege.de

SAE Institute - Brisbane
22 Mayneview Street
Milton QLD 4064
Australia
Tel: + (61 7) 3367 0143
Fax: +(61 7) 3369 8108
Web: http://www.sae.edu

SAE Institute - Brussels
Rue Gachard 10
1050 Bruxelles
Belgique Belgium
Tel: +32 (0)2 647 92 20
Fax: +32 (0)2 648 27 19
Web: http://www.sae.edu

SAE Institute - Byron Bay
World Corporate Headquarters
373-393 Ewingsdale Rd
Byron Bay
NSW 2481
Australia
Tel: +61 (02) 6639 6000
Fax: +61 (02) 6685 6133
Web: http://www.sae.edu

SAE Institute - Chennai
SAE Technology College,
109, Parsn Apartments,
G.N.Chetty Road,
T.Nagar,
Chennai- 600017
India
Tel: (+91-44) 2820 3942
Tel: (+91-44) 2821 4045
Tel: (+91-44) 2821 4227
Web: http://www.saeindia.net

SAE Institute - Coimbatore
SAE Technology College,
2nd Floor,
Srivari Gokul Towers,
108, Race Course Road,
Coimbatore 641018
India
Tel: (+91-422) 221 8513
Tel: (+91-422) 221 8514
Web: http://www.saeindia.net

SAE Institute - Cologne
Maarweg Center
Maarweg 165
50825 Köln
Germany
Tel: +49 (0)221 954 1220
Fax: +49 (0)221 954 1221
Web: http://www.saecollege.de

SAE Institute - Frankfurt
Homburger Landstr. 182
60435 Frankfurt/ Main
Germany
Tel: +49 (0)69 543 262
Fax: +49 (0)69 548 4443
Web: http://www.saecollege.de

SAE Institute - Glasgow
85-87 Portman Street
Kinning Park
Glasgow
G41 1EJ
United Kingdom
Tel: +44 (0)141 429 1551
Fax: +44 (0)141 429 1771
Web: http://www.sae.edu

SAE Institute - Geneva
42-44, av. Cardinal-Mermillod
CH-1227 Carouge GE
Switzerland
Tel: +41 (0)22 301 10 60
Fax: +41 (0)22 301 10 65
Web: http://www.saegeneve.ch

SAE Institute - Hamburg
Heidenkampsweg 84
20097 Hamburg
Germany
Tel: +49 (0)40 2368 8080
Fax: +49 (0)40 23 36 02
Web: http://www.saecollege.de

SAE Institute - Hobart
27 Kirksway Place
Battery Point TAS 7000
Australia
Tel: +61 (0)3 6224 1416
Fax: +61 (0)3 6224 9088
Web: http://www.sae.edu

SAE Institute - Liverpool
Ground Floor
Wellington Buildings
The Strand
Liverpool
L2 0P
United Kingdom
Tel: +44 (0)151 255 1313
Fax: +44 (0)151 255 1414
Web: http://www.sae.edu

SAE Institute - London
United House
North Road
London
N7 9DP
United Kingdom
Tel: +44 (0)20 7609 2653

Fax: +44 (0)20 7609 6944
Web: http://www.saeberlin.de

SAE Institute - Madrid
Alcala, 265 - Ed. 4, 2°
28027, Madrid
Spain
Tel: +34 91 405 7059
Fax: +34 91 405 0081
Web: http://www.sae.edu

SAE Institute - Malaysia
No. 10-1,Jalan USJ 9/5R
Subang Business Centre
47620, Subang Jaya
Selangor, Malaysia
Tel: +60 03 8024 0935
Tel: +60 03 8024 9655
Fax: +60 03 8024 9650
Web: http://www.saemalaysia.com

SAE Institute - Melbourne
162 Williams, Rd Prahran
Melbourne, Vic 3181
Australia
Tel: +61 (0)3 9521 4055
Fax: +61 (0)3 9521 4455
Web: http://www.sae.edu

SAE Institute - Miami
16051 West Dixie Highway Suite 200
North Miami Beach, Florida 33160
United States
Tel: 1-305-944-7494
Fax: 1-305-944-6659
Web: http://www.sae.edu

SAE Institute - Milan
via Morimondo 19
20143 Milano
Italy
Tel: +39 02 8912 0540
WebL http://www.saeitalia.it

SAE Institute - Munich
Hoferstr. 3
81737 München
Germany
Tel: +49 (0)89 675167
Fax: +49 (0)89 6701811
Web: http://www.saecollege.de

SAE Institute- Nashville
7 Music Circle North
Nashville Tennessee 37203
United States
Tel: 1-615-244-5848
Fax: 1-615-244-3192
Web: http://www.sae.edu

SAE Institute - New Delhi
No.308, Chintels Techno Park,
A30, Kailash Colony,
New Delhi 110048
India
Tel: (+91-11) 2643 6949
Tel: (+91-11) 98106 18226
Web: http://www.saeindia.net

SAE Institute- New York
269W 40th Street
New York, New York 10018
United States
Tel: 1-212-944-9121
Fax: 1-212-944-9123
Web: http://www.sae.edu

SAE Institute - Paris
45, Av. Victor Hugo Bât. 286
93534 Aubervilliers
France
Tel: +33 1 48.11.96.96
Fax: +33 1 48.11.96.84
Web: http://www.sae-france.fr

SAE Institute - Perth
Level 1, 3-5 Bennett St
East Perth WA 6004
Australia
Tel: +61 (0)8 9325 4533
Fax: +61 (0)8 9221 4401
Web: http://www.sae.edu

SAE Institute - Rotterdam
Groot Handelsgebouw
45 Stationsplein
Postbus 29008
3001 GA Rotterdam
The Netherlands
Tel: +31 (0)10 411 7951
Fax: +31 (0)10 411 7952
Web: http://www.sae.nl

SAE Institute - Singapore
260 Sims Ave, #02-01
Singapore 387604
Tel: +65 6741 12 57
Fax: +65 67411279
Web: http://www.sae.edu

SAE Institute - Stuttgart
Leobenerstr. 32
70469 Stuttgart
Germany
Tel: +49 (0)711 615 82 76
Fax: +49 (0)711 615 82 77
Web: http://www.saecollege.de

SAE Institute - Sweden
Stockholm
Rasundavägen 45
169 57 Solna
Tel: +46 (0)8 730 5100
Fax: +46 (0)8 730 1015
Web: http://www.saestockholm.com

SAE Institute - Sydney
Level 3, 55-57 Wentworth Ave.
Surry Hills NSW 2010
Australia
Tel: +61 (0)2 9211 3711
Fax +61 (0)2 9211 3308
Web: http://www.sae.edu

SAE Institute - Trivandrum
G-11, TC-9/419, Jawahar Nagar,
Trivandrum 695041
India
Tel: (+91-471) 272 2704
Tel: (+91-471) 272 2712
Web: http://www.saeindia.net

SAE Institute - Vienna
Linke Wienzeile 130A
A-1060 Wien
Austria
Tel: +43 (0)1 961 03 03
Fax: +43 (0)1 961 05 17
Web: http://www.sae.at

SAE Institute - Zurich
Technopark Str.1
8005 Zürich
Switzerland

Tel: +41 (0)1 445 2040
Fax: +41 (0)1 445 2041
Web: http://www.saegeneve.ch

Salt Lake Community College
CAD Applications Training Center
P.O. Box 30808
Salt Lake City, Utah 84130-0808
United States
Tel: 1-801-957-4303
Fax: 1-801-957-4803
Web: http://www.slcc.edu

Samsung Art and Design Institute
Korea
Tel: 02-3438-0319
Fax: 02-3438-0319
Web: http://www.sadi.net

San Antonio College
Division of Continuing Education
1300 San Pedro Ave.
San Antonio, Texas 78212
United States
Tel: 1-210-733-2654
Web: http://www.accd.edu

San Francisco Art Institute
Advanced Technology Center
800 Chesnut
San Francisco, California 94133
United States
Fax: 1-415-749-4590
Web: http://www.sfai.edu

San Francisco State University
Department of Cinema
1600 Holloway Avenue
San Francisco, California 94132
United States
Tel: 1-415-338-1629
Web: http://www.cinema.sfsu.edu

San Francisco State University
Multimedia Studies Program
425 Market St. 2nd Floor
San Francisco, California 94105
United States
Tel: 1-415-405-3332
Fax: 1-415-405-7760
Web: http://msp.sfsu.edu

San Jose State University
Department of
Animation/Illustration
School of Art and Design
One Washington Square
San Jose, California 95192-0089
United States
Tel: 1-408-924-4340
Fax: 1-408-924-4326
Web: http://www.sjsu.edu

Santa Barbara City College
Department of Multimedia Arts
and Technologies
722 Cliff Drive
Santa Barbara, California 93109-2394
United States
Tel: 1-805-965-0581
Fax: 1-805-963-7222
Web: http://www.sbcc.net

Santa Monica College
Academy of Entertainment &
Technology
1660 Stewart Street
Santa Monica, California 90404
United States
Tel: 1-310-434-3700
Fax: 1-310-434-3709
Web: http://academy.smc.edu

Savannah College of Art & Design
548 E. Broughton St.
Savannah, Georgia 31401
United States
Tel: 1-800-869-SCAD
Tel: 1-800-869-7223
Fax: 1-912-525-5983
Web: http://www.scad.edu

SCETCH College of Art & Design
#900 - Midtown Plaza
201 - 1st Ave. North
Saskatoon
Saskatchewan
S7K 1J9
Canada
Tel: 1-306-242-8006
Fax: 1-306-242-8014
Web: www.scetch.net

School of Communication Arts
Department of Animation
3220 Spring Forest Road
Raleigh, North Carolina 27616
United States
Tel: 1-919-981-0972
Web: http://www.higherdigital.com

School of Television and Imaging
Duncan of Jordanstone College
of Art and Design
The University of Dundee
Perth Road
Dundee
DD1 4HN
United Kingdom
Tel: 44 1 382 34 52 50
Fax: 44 1 382 22 61 36
Web: http://www.imaging.dundee.ac.uk

School of the Art Institute of Chicago
Film-Making Department
112 S. Michigan 13th Floor
Chicago, Illinois 60603
United States
Tel: 1-312-345-3588
Fax: 1-312-899-1840
Web: http://www.artic.edu

School of the Museum of Fine Arts
230 The Fenway
Boston, Massachusetts 02115
United States
Tel: 1-617-267-6100
Fax: 1-617-424-6271
Web: http://www.smfa.edu

School of Visual Arts
209 East 23rd Street
New York, New York 10010
United States
Tel: 1-212-592-2100
Fax: 1-212-592-2116
Web: http://www.schoolofvisualarts.edu

Schule fur Gestaltung Zurich
Studienbereich Film/Video
Limmatstrasse 65-Postfach
Zurich
8005
Switzerland
Tel: 41 1 446 23 57

Fax: 41 1 446 23 55
Web: http://www.hgkz.ch/film-video

Scuola Nazionale di Cinema,
sede di Torino
Dipartimento di cinema d'animazione
Bonafous, strada Pecetto 34
Chieri (Torino)
10023
Italy
Tel: +39 011 947 32 84
Fax: +39 011 940 27 00
Web: http://www.snc.it

Seattle Central Community College
1701 Broadway 2BE1109
Seattle, Washington 98122
United States
Tel: 1-206-587-5448
Fax: 1-206-587-4904
Web: http://www.sccconline.com

Sejong University
Department of Film Animation
98, Gunja-Dong, Gwangjin-Gu
Seoul
143-747
South Korea
Tel: 82 2 3408 3114
Fax: 82 2 3408 3200
Web: http://www.sejong.ac.kr

Seneca College
Digital Media Centre
21 Beverly Hills Drive
Toronto
Ontario
M3L 1A2
Canada
Tel: 1-416-491-5050
Fax: 1-416-235-0462
Web: http://www.senecac.on.ca

SEPTIMA ARS. Escuela de Cine y TV
Department of Animation
C/ Fuente del Saz, 5
Madrid
28016
Spain
Tel: 34 91 457 2311, 91 457 79
Web: http://www.septima-ars.com

Sheridan College
Centre for Animation & Emerging
Technology
1430 Trafalgar Road
Oakville, Ontario
L6H 2L1
Canada
Tel: 1-905-845-9430
Fax: 1-905-815-4043
Web: http://www.sheridanc.on.ca

Siemens Nixdorf Training Center
Otto-Hahn-Ring, 6
Munchen
D-81730
Germany
Tel: 0130 845000
Fax: 0130 826589
Web: http://www.sni.de

Singapore Polytechnic
School of Info-Communications
Technology
Block 19 Level 4
500 Dover Road
Singapore
139651
Tel: 65 772 1900
Fax: 65 779 7912
Web: http://www.sp.edu.sg

Sintesys
Calle Prim, 20
2006 Donostia
Gipuzkoa
20006
Spain
Tel: 34 943 45 91 77
Fax: 34 943 45 80 70
Web: http://www.sintesys.net

Sociedad Mexicana de
Comunicadores
Independientes (AMCI)
Calle de la Loma #39 Lomas de
San Angel Inn
Distrito Federal
Mexico
Tel: 52 5 683 0532
Fax: 52 5 668 3360
Web: http://www.amci.com.mx

Socrates Digital Video
Pieter Braaijweg 77
1099 DK
Amsterdam
Netherlands
Tel: 31 20 663 4066
Fax: 31 20 663 4511
Web: http://www.socrates.nl

Sole Costa Studios
Department of Animation
Viale dei Mille, 1
Firenze
I-50131
Italy
Tel: 39 55 500 2044
Fax: 39 55 500 0342
Web: http://www.solecosta.com

Southampton Institute
Media Arts, Technology and Design
East Park Terrace
Southampton
Hampshire
SO14 0RB
United Kingdom
Tel: 44 23 80319000
Web: http://www.solent.ac.uk

Southern Illinois University
Department of Cinema & Photography
Carbondale, Illinois 62901
United States
Tel: 1-618-453-2365
Web: http://www.nmc.siu.edu/cp

Southern Polytechnic State University
1100 South Marietta Parkway
Marietta, Georgia 30060-2896
United States
Tel: 1-770-528-7200
Fax: 1-770-528-7292
Web: http://www.spsu.edu

Space Invaders
Nyhavn, 31F
Copenhagen
DK-1051
Denmark
Tel: 45 33 11 50 33
Fax: 45 33 11 50 33
Web: http://www.invaders.dk

Spencerian College
Computer Graphic Design
2355 Harrodsburg Rd
Lexington, Kentucky 40504
United States
Tel: 1-800-456-3253
Fax: 1-859-224-7744
Web: http://www.spencerian.edu

Sprott-Shaw Community College
Chilliwack Campus
#100-46165 Yale Road East
Chiilliwack
British Columbia
V2P 2P2
Canada
Tel: 1-604-795-0085
Fax: 1-604-795-2485
Web: http://www.sprottshaw.com

St. Clair College of Applied Arts
and Technology
2000 Talbot Road West
Windsor, Ontario
N9A 6S4
Canada
Tel: 1-519-966-1656
Fax: 1-519-972-3811
Web: http://www.stclairc.on.ca

St. Olaf College
Art Department
1520 St. Olaf Ave.
Northfield, Minnesota 55057
United States
Tel: 1-507-646-3248
Fax: 1-507-646-3332
Web: http://www.stolaf.edu/depts/art

Staatliche Hochschule fur
Gestaltung
Durlrsheimer Strasse, 55
Karlsruhe
D-76185
Germany
Tel: 49 721 95 41 0
Fax: 49 721 95 41 206
Web: http://www.hfg-karlsruhe.de

Stanford University
Department of Art
Stanford, California 94305-2018

United States
Tel: 1-650-723-3404
Fax: 1-650-725-0140
Web: http://www.stanford.edu/dept/art

Studio Arts
570 W. Avenue 26 Suite 425
Los Angeles, California 90065
United States
Tel: 1-323-227-8776
Fax: 1-323-227-8775
Web: http://www.studioarts.tv

Studio21
Nyugati tér 4
Budapest
1132
Hungary
Tel: +36 1 359 6410
Fax: +36 1 359 6410
Web: http://www.s21net.com

Success College of Applied Arts &
Technology
933 Salisbury Road
Moncton, New Brunswick
E1E 1C4
Canada
Tel: 1-506-855-8555
Tel: 1-800-561-9390
Fax: 1-506-852-3922
Web: http://www.ebci.ca

Sup'Infograph
135, avenue Felix Faure
Paris 75015
France
Tel: 33 1 44 25 25 25
Fax: 33 1 44 25 25 14
Web: http://www.groupesra.com

Supinfo-Ecole Supérieure
d'Informatique et Paris
Academy Of Computer Science
23, rue de Château
Landon
Paris 75010
France
Tel: 33 153 359 700
Fax: 33 153 359 701
Web: http://www.supinfo.com

SUPINFOCOM
10, av. Henri Matisse
Aulnoy lez Valenciennes
59300
France
Tel: 33 327 28 43 53
Web: http://www.supinfocom.fr

Surrey Institute of Art &
Design, University College
Farnham Campus
Falkner Road
Farnham
Surrey
GU9 7DS
United Kingdom
Tel: 44 125 2722441
Fax: 44 125 2892616
Web: http://www.surrart.ac.uk

Swinburne University
Department of Industrial
Sciences
Mail no. H49
P.O. Box 218
Hawthorn
Victoria
3122
Australia
Tel: 61 3 9214 5161
Fax: 61 3 9214 8650
Web: www.swin.edu.au

Syracuse University
Colllege of Visual &
Performing Arts
Syracuse, New York 13244
United States
Tel: 1-315-443-1870
Web: http://vpa.syr.edu

Systemhaus Munchen GmbH
Hansastr 2
Munich
D80686
Germany
Tel: 49 89 54 70 11 0
Fax: 49 89 54 70 11 34
Web: http://www.shmuc.de

Taller de Cine de Animacion
Holanda 3222 Depto.902

Nunoa
Santiago
Chile
Tel: 56 2 2698914
Fax: 56 2 2698914
Web:
http://artemiafilms.tvheaven.com

Tbdesign
207 Sagamore Ave
Portsmouth, New Hampshire 03801
United States
Tel: 1-603-431-4334
Web: http://www.tbmax.com

Technical College Slagelse
Bredahlsgade, 1
Slagelse
DK-4200
Denmark
Tel: 45 58 56 70 00
Fax: 45 58 56 73 94
Web: http://www.tss.dk

Technische Universitat
Braunschweig
Postfach 3329
Braunschweig
D-38023
Germany
Tel: 49 531 3910
Fax: 49 531 391 4577
Web: http://www.tu-bs.de

Technology Development
Center
5200 Valentine Rd.
Ventura, California 93003
United States
Tel: 1-805-676-7310
Web: http://www.vace.com

Technoz-FH-Multimedia Art
Schillerstrasse 30
Salzburg
A-5020
Austria
Tel: 43 662 46 65 0
Fax: 43 662 46 65 559
Web: http://www.fh-sbg.ac.at

Telecom Animation's Anime Juku
7-16-22
Shimorenjaku
Mitaka
Tokyo
181-0013
Japan
Tel: 81 422-42-4541
Fax: 81 422-42-4610
Web: http://www.anime-juku.com

Temasek Polytechnic
21 Tampines Avenue 1
Singapore
529757
Tel: 65 788 2000
Fax: 65 789 8220
Web: http://www.tp.edu.sg

Texas A&M
TAMU Visualization Lab
College of Architecture
A216 Langford Center
College Station, Texas 77843
United States
Tel: 1-979-845-3465
Web: http://viz.tamu.edu

Texas State Technical College
Department of Digital Media Design
3801 Campus Drive
Waco, Texas 76705
United States
Tel: 1-800-792-8784
Web: http://dmd.tstc.edu

The Animation Academy
3407 W. Olive Ave. 2nd Fl
Burbank, California 91505-4616
United States
Tel: 1-818-848-6590
Web: http://www.theanima-
tionacademy.com

The Animation Workshop
Ll. Sct. Hans Gade 7 - 9
Viborg
DK-8800
Denmark
Tel: 45 87 25 54 00
Fax: 45 87 25 54 11
Web: http://www.animwork.dk

The Art Center
Department of Animation Graphics
2525 N. Country Club Rd.
Tucson, Arizona 85716
United States
Tel: 1-800-825-8753
Fax: 1-520-325-5535
Web: http://www.theartcenter.com

The Art Institute of Atlanta
Department of Computer Animation
6600 Peachtree Dunwoody Road
100 Embassy Row
Atlanta, Georgia 30328
United States
Tel: 1-800-275-4242
Fax: 1-770-394-0008
Web:
http://www.aia.artinstitute.edu

The Art Institute of Boston at
Lesley College
700 Beacon Street
Boston, Massachusetts 02215-2598
United States
Tel: 1-800-773-0494
Web: http://www.aiboston.edu

The Art Institute of Washington
1820 N. Fort Myer Drive
Arlington, Virginia 22209
United States
Tel: 1-703-358-9550
Fax: 1-703-358-9759
Web: http://www.aiw.artinstitutes.edu

The Arts Institute at Bournemouth
School of Media
Wallisdown
Poole
Dorset
BH12 5HH
United Kingdom
Tel: 44 1 202 533 011
Fax: 44 1 202 537 729
Web: http://www.arts-inst-
bournemouth.ac.uk

The Banff Centre
Box 1020, Stn. 28
107 Tunnel Mountain Drive
Banff

Alberta
T1L 1H5
Canada
Tel: 1-800-565-9989
Fax: 1-403-762-6345
Web: http://www.banffcentre.ca/arts

The College of New Jersey
Department of Art
Holman Hall 407
PO Box 7718
2000 Pennington Rd.
Ewing, New Jersey 08628-0718
United States
Tel: 1-609-771-2652
Web: http://www.tcnj.edu

The daVinci Institute
Animation Department
1467 Brenton Street
Halifax
Nova Scotia
B3J 2K7
Canada
Tel: 1-902-429-1847
Fax: 1-902-423-5414
Web:
http://www.the-davinci-institute.com

The Digital Film School
E-Wing, 1st Floor, Abhishek Apts,
Juhu Versova Link Rd, Andheri (W)
Mumbai
Maharashtra
400053
India
Tel: (91) 690-7997
Fax: (91) 637-0041
Web: http://www.qualitycinelabs.com

THE GERMAN FILM SCHOOL
for digital production gGMBH
Demex Allee 1
Elstal
D-14627
Germany
Tel: 49 33 234 90833
Fax: 49 33 234 90834
Web: http://www.filmschool.de

The Illinois Institute of Art at Chicago
350 N. Orleans, #136
Chicago, Illinois 60654-1593
United States
Tel: 1-800-351-3450
Fax: 1-312-280-3528
Web: http://www.ilia.aii.edu

The Illinois Institute of Art at Schaumburg
1000 Plaza Drive
Shaumburg, Illinois 60173-5070
United States
Tel: 1-800-314-3450
Fax: 1-847-619-3064
Web: http://www.ilia.aii.edu

The University of the West of England
Kennel Lodge Road
Bristol
England
BS3 2JT
United Kingdom
Tel: 44 1 17 966 3411
Fax: 44 1 17 344 4820
Web: http://www.uwe.ac.uk/amd

Toon Factory
C/Cullera 73-3
Edificio Ediferia
Benimamet
Valencia
46035
Spain
Tel: 34 96 390 4253
Fax: 34 96 390 3774
Web: http://www.toonf.com

Tracor - The Arts Institute
Rosa Jardón, 1
Madrid
E-28016
Spain
Tel: 34 91 350 41 80
Fax: 34 91 350 76 51
Web: http://www.tracor.es

Trainingscape Studios Canada
5161 George street
Halifax, Nova Scotia Canada
B3J 1M7
Tel: 1-866-222-5475
Web: http://www.trainingscape.com

TSB School of Animation
419 King Street West
Oshawa
Ontario
L1J 2K5
Canada
Tel: 905 723 1163
Fax: 905 422 8962
Web:http://www.tsbosh.cnd.com

Turku Polytechnic / Arts Academy
Animation Department
Sepänkatu 3
Turku
20700
Finland
Tel: 35 8 10 55 350
Fax: 35 8 10 55 35 791
Web: http://www.turkuamk.fi

Tyrell Corporation
17-19 Foley Street
London
W1P 7LH
United Kingdom
Tel: 44 171 343 5500
Fax: 44 171 343 5501
Web: http://www.tyrell.co.uk

UCLA Animation Workshop
Department of Film & TV
P.O. Box 951622
Los Angeles, California 90095-1622
United States
Tel: 1-310-206-8441
Fax: 1-310-825-3383
Web: http://animation.filmtv.ucla.edu

UCLA Extension Visual Arts
Department of Art
Studio/Computer Graphics
10995 Le Conte Avenue, Room 414
Los Angeles, California 90024
United States
Tel: 1-310-206-1422
Fax: 1-310-206-7382
Web:
http://www.uclaextension.org/visualarts

Universal Computer Arts Academy
Department of Animation
1st Floor, Hycastle House
58 Loop Street
Cape Town
Western Cape
8001
South Africa
Tel: 27 21 424 1415
Fax: 27 21 424 1418
Web: http://www.uca.co.za

Universal Computer Arts Academy
Department of Animation
1st. Floor, Hycastle House, 58
Loop Street
Cape Town
Western Pronvince
8001
South Africa
Tel: 27 21 424 1415
Fax: 27 21 424 1418
Web: http://www.uca.co.za

Universidad de Castilla La-Mancha
Avda Alfares, 42
Cuenca
E-16002
Spain
Tel: 34 69 17 91 00
Fax: 34 69 17 91 02
Web: http://www.uclm.es

Universidad Islas Baleares
Palma de Mallorca
Baleares
Spain
Tel: 34 71 173 201
Fax: 34 71 173 003
Web: http://www.uib.es

Universidade do Algarve
Escola Superior de Educação
Campus da Penha
Faro
8000-117
Portugal
Tel: 28 9 803 561
Fax: 28 9 864 675
Web: http://www.ualg.pt/ese

Universitat Klagenfurt
Universitatstrasse, 65-67
Klagenfurt
A-9020
Austria
Tel: 43 463 27 00 383
Fax: 43 463 27 00 292
Web: http://www.uni-klu.ac.at

Universitat Tubingen
Wilhelmstrasse, 50
Tübingen
D-72074
Germany
Tel: 49 7071 29 74271
Fax: 49 7071 29 5321
Web: http://www.uni-tuebingen.de/uni/nmw

Universitat Zu Koln
Albertus-Magnus-Platz
Koln
D-50923
Germany
Tel: 49 221 470 0
Fax: 49 221 470 51 53
Web: http://www.uni-koeln.de

Universite de Liege
rue Armond-Stevart, 2-Batiment
Liege
B-4000
Belgium
Tel: 32 4 252 58 59
Fax: 32 4 254 18 99
Web: http://www.ulg.ac.be

Universite de Montreal
Etudes Cinematographiques
P.O. Box 6128
Downtown Station
Montreal
Quebec
H3C 3J7
Canada
Tel: 1-514-343-6111
Web: http://www.umontreal.ca

Universite Laval
Ecole des Arts Visuels
Edifice La Fabrique
Bureau 0100t
255 boul, Charest Est
St. Foy
Quebec
G1K 3GB
Canada
Tel: 418 656 3333
Fax: 418 656 2809
Web: http://www.ulaval.ca

Université Rennes 2 - Haute
Bretagne
Campus Villejean
6, avenue Gaston Berger
CS 24-307
Rennes
Cedex
35043
France
Tel: 33 02 99 14 10 00
Fax: 33 02 99 14 10 15
Web: http://www.uhb.fr

University Extended Education, Cal State
2600 E. Nutwood Ave. Suite 770
Fullerton, California 92831
United States
Tel: 1-714-278-2611
Fax: 1-714-278-5445
Web:
http://www.takethelead.fullerton.e
du

University of Advancing Technology
2625 West Baseline Rd.
Tempe, Arizona 85283-1042
United States
Tel: 1-800-658-5744
Fax: 1-602-383-8222
Web: http://www.uat.edu

University of Arizona
Department of Media Arts
Tucson, Arizona 85721
United States
Tel: 1-520-621-2211
Fax: 1-520-621-9662
Web: http://www.arts.arizona.edu

University of British Columbia
Faculty of the Arts
2329 West Mall
Vancouver
British Columbia
V6T 1Z4
Canada
Tel: 1-604-822-2211
Web: http://www.arts.ubc.ca/FOA

University of Calgary
2500 University Drive NW
Calgary, Alberta
Canada T2N 1N4
Tel: 1-403-220-5110
Web: www.cpsc.ucalgary.ca

University of California at Berkeley
Computer Science Division
Berkeley, California 94720-5800
United States
Tel: 1-510-642-1042
Fax: 1-510-642-5775
Web: http://www.cs.berkeley.edu

University of California
Irvine, Irvine, California 92697
United States
Tel: 1-949-824-5011
Web: http://www.uci.edu

University of Derby
School of Art and Design
Britannia Mill
Mackworth Road
Derby
DE22 3BL
United Kingdom
Tel: 44 1 33 262 2222
Fax: 44 1 33 262 2760
Web: http://vertigo.derby.ac.uk

University of Georgia
Lamar Dodd School of Art
Visual Arts Building
Athens, Georgia 30602-4102
United States
Tel: 1-706-542-1511
Fax: 1-706-542-2080
Web: http://www.visart.uga.edu

The University of Hull
Cottingham Road
Hull
HU6 7RX
United Kingdom
Tel: +44(0)1482 346311
Web: http://www.mscgames.com

University of Illinois
School of Art and Design
408 E. Peabody St.
Champaign, Illinois 61820
United States
Tel: 1-217-333-0855
Fax: 1-217-333-6632
Web: http://www.uiuc.edu

University of Illinois at Chicago
School of Art and Design
106 Jefferson Hall
929 West Harrison St.
Chicago, Illinois 60607-7038
United States
Tel: 1-312-996-3337
Fax: 1-312-413-2333
Web: http://www.uic.edu/aa/artd

University of Kentucky
College of Fine Arts
202 Fine Arts Bldg.
Lexington, Kentucky 40506-0022
United States
Tel: 1-859-257-2727
Fax: 1-859-323-1050
Web: http://www.uky.edu/FineArts

University of Louisville
College of Arts and Sciences
Louisville, Kentucky 40292
United States
Tel: 1-800-334-8635
Fax: 1-502-852-6791
Web: http://art.louisville.edu

University of Lund
Box 117, S-221 00 Lund
Helsingborg
25108
Sweden
Tel: 46 46 222 00 00
Fax: 46 46 222 47 20
Web: http://www.lu.se

University of Mary Hardin-Baylor
Department of Computer and
Information Sciences
900 College Street
Belton, Texas 76513
United States
Tel: 1-254-295-8642
Web: http://www.umhb.edu

University of Maryland, Baltimore
County
1000 Hilltop Circle
Baltimore, Maryland 21250
United States
Tel: 1-410-455-1000
Web: http://www.umbc.edu/cctc

University of Massachusetts
Amherst
Art Department
Fine Arts Center East
151 Presidents Drive
Amherst, Massachusetts 01003
United States
Tel: 1-413-545-1902
Fax: 1-413-545-3929
Web: http://www.umass.edu/art

University of
Massachusetts/Amherst
Computer Science Department
140 Governors Drive
Amherst, Massachusetts 01003
United States
Tel: 1-413-545-2744
Fax: 1-413-545-1249
Web: http://www.cs.umass.edu

University of New Orleans
Department of Drama and
Communications
New Orleans, Louisiana 70148
United States
Tel: 1-504-280-6345
Fax: 1-504-280-6318
Web: http://www.uno.edu

University of North Carolina at
Chapel Hill
250 East Franklin Street
Chapel Hill, North Carolina 27599
United States

Tel: 1-919-962-2211
Web: http://www.unc.edu

University of North Carolina
College of Arts and Sciences
PO Box 26170
Greensboro, North Carolina
27402-6170
United States
Tel: 1-336-334-5000
Web: http://www.uncg.edu

University, North Carolina State
Hillsborough Street
Raleigh, North Carolina 27695
United States
Tel: 1-919-515-2011
Web: http://www.ncsu.edu

University of Northumbria at
Newcastle
School of Art
Squires Annex.
Newcastle upon Tyne
NE1 8ST
United Kingdom
Tel: 44 1 91 227 4935
Fax: 44 1 91 227 3632
Web: http://www.northumbria.ac.uk

University of Oregon
Fine Arts Department
Eugene, Oregon 97403
United States
Tel: 1-503-346-3610
Fax: 1-503-346-3626
Web: http://www.uoregon.edu

University of Paisley
Paisley PA1 2BE
Scotland
Tel. +44 (0)141 848 3000
Web: http://www.paisley.ac.uk

University of Quebec at Montreal
Service de Formation Sur Mesure
C.P. 8888 Succursale Centre-ville
Local B3405
montreal
Quebec
H3C 3P8

Canada
Tel: 1-514-987-4068
Fax: 1-514-987-6624
Web: www.formation.uqam.ca/3d

University of South Carolina
Department of Media Arts
Columbia, South Carolina 29208
United States
Tel: 1-803-777-4236
Fax: 1-803-777-0535
Web: http://www.sc.edu

University of Teesside
School of Arts and Media
Middlesbrough
TS1 3BA
United Kingdom
Tel: 44 1 642 384 019
Fax: 44 1 642 342 067
Web:
http://www.tees.ac.uk/schools/lahs

The University of Texas at Dallas
2601 North Floyd Road
Richardson, Texas 75080
United States
Tel: 1-972-883-2111
Web: http://www.utdallas.edu

University of the Arts
Media Arts Department
320 South Broad Street
Philadelphia, Pennsylvania 19102
United States
Tel: 1-800-616-ARTS
Tel: 1-800-616-2787
Fax: 1-215-732-4832
Web: http://www.uarts.edu

University of Utah
Dept. of Computer Science-
Graphic Design
3190 Merrill Engineering Bldg.
Salt Lake City, Utah 84112
United States
Tel: 1-801-581-8224
Fax: 1-801-581-5843
Web: http://www.cs.utah.edu

University of Wales College, Newport
School of Art Media and Design
Caerleon Campus
PO Box 179
Newport, Gwent
South Wales
NP18 3YG
United Kingdom
Tel: 44 1 63 343 2182
Fax: 44 1 63 343 2610
Web: http://www.newportanimation.com

University of Washington
Seattle, Washington 98195-2350
United States
Tel: 1-206-616-3423
Fax: 1-206-543-2969
Web: http://www.washington.edu

University of Westminster
School of Computer Science
Harrow Campus
Northwick Park
Watford Road
Harrow, Middlesex
London
Middlesex
HA1 3TP
United Kingdom
Tel: 44 2 07 911 5907
Fax: 44 2 07 911 5906
Web: http://hscs.wmin.ac.uk

University of Wisconsin
6241 Humanities Building
455 North Park Street
Madison, Wisconsin 53706
United States
Tel: 1-608-262-1660
Web: http://www.wisc.edu

University of Wolverhampton
Department of Digital Media
School of Art & Design
Molineux Street
Wolverhampton
West Midlands
WV1 1SB
United Kingdom
Tel: 44 1 902 321030
Fax: 44 1 902 322517
Web: http://www.wlv.ac.uk

University of Wuppertal
Computational Design
Gausstrasse 20
Wuppertal
D-42097
Germany
Tel: 49 202 439 0
Fax: 49 202 439 2901
Web: http://www.uni-wuppertal.de

Upgrade Training Center
Corso Lodi N47
Scala D Citofono 4301
Milan
Italy
Tel: 39 02 55 17 290
Fax: 39 02 55 010 357
Web: http://www.upgrade-atc.com

USC School of Cinema-Television
Department of Animation
University Park
Los Angeles, California 90089-2211
United States
Tel: 1-213-740-3986
Fax: 1-213-740-5869
Web: http://felix.usc.edu
Web: http://www.usc.edu

Utrecht School of the Arts
Faculty of Art, Media &
Technology
P.O. Box 2471
Oude Amersfoortse weg 131
Hilversum
Noord Holland
1200 CL
Netherlands
Tel: 31 35 683 64 64
Fax: 31 35 683 64 80
Web: http://www.hku.nl

VanArts
(Vancouver Institute of Media Arts)
837 Beatty Street
Vancouver
British Columbia
V6B 2M6
Canada
Tel: 1-800-396-2787
Fax: 1-604-684-2789
Web: http://www.vanarts.com

Vancouver Film School
200-198 West Hastings Street
Vancouver
British Columbia
V6B 1H2
Canada
Tel: 1-604-685-5808
Fax: 1-604-685-5830
Web: http://www.vfs.com

Victorian College of Arts
School of Film and Television
234 St. Kilda Road
Southbank
Victoria
3006
Australia
Tel: 61 3 9685 9000
Fax: 61 3 9685 9001
Web:
http://www.vca.unimelb.edu.au/ftv

Video Symphony
731 N. Hollywood Way
Burbank, California 91505
United States
Tel: 1-818-557-7200
Fax: 1-818-845-1951
Web: http://www.videosymphony.com

Virginia College in Birmingham
Computer Aided Visualization and
Imaging
63 Bagby Drive Suite 100
Birmingham, Alabama 35209
United States
Tel: 1-205-802-1200
Fax: 1-205-802-7045
Web: http://www.vc.edu

Virtual Partners Training Center
Department of Animation
1920 Libal Street
Allouez Central Plaza, Suite 10A
Green Bay, Wisconsin 54301
United States
Tel: 1-800-701-7936
Fax: 1-920-435-7395
Web: http://www.virtualpartners.com

Vizo-Centrum Hasselt
Gv. Verwilghensingel, 40
Hasselt
B-3500
Belgium
Tel: 32 11 24 43 46
Fax: 32 11 22 98 69
Web: http://www.vch.be

VSMU - Faculty of Film and TV
Department of Animation
Venturska 3
Bratislava
813 01
Slovakia
Tel: 42 17 54 43 27 78
Fax: 42 17 54 43 01 25
Web: http://www.vsmu.sk

Washburn University
Division of Continuing Education
1700 SW College Ave.
Topeka, Kansas 66621
United States
Tel: 1-785-231-1010
Fax: 1-785-231-1028
Web: http://www.washburn.edu

West Herts College
Hempstead Road
Watford Hertfordshire
WD17 3EZ
United Kingdom
Tel: 44 192 381 2000
Fax: 44 192 381 5556
Web: http://www.westherts.ac.uk

Wifi Interactive Information
Center
Koerblergasse, 111-113
Graz
A-8021
Austria
Tel: 43 316 602 1234
Fax: 43 316 602 301
Web: http://www.iic.wifi.at

Winston-Salem State University
Fine Arts Department
601 Martin Luther King, Jr. Drive
Winston-Salem, North Carolina
27110

United States
Tel: 1-336-750-2533
Fax: 1-336-750-2522
Web: http://www.wssu.edu

Wondertoons Institute of
Animation & Media
E-Block, 1st Floor
Sri Balaji Indraprasth
1-1-508/1, Gandhi Nagar
Hyderabad
Andra Pradhesh
500080
India
Tel: 91 40 7666794
Fax: 91 40 3222211
Web: http://www.wondertoons.com

Woodbury University
7500 Glenoaks Blvd.
Burbank, California 91510-7846
United States
Tel: 1-800-784-9663
Fax: 1-818-504-9320
Web: http://www.woodbury.edu

Yale University
Art Department
1156 Chapel Street
New Haven, Connecticut 06520
United States
Tel: 1-203-432-2600
Web: http://www.yale.edu/art

GLOSSARY

ACM – The Association for Computing Machinery. It is an international scientific and educational organization dedicated to advancing the arts, sciences, and applications of information technology. With a world-wide membership ACM is a leading resource for computing professionals and students working in the various fields of Information Technology, and for interpreting the impact of information technology on society.

Ambient – Light that exists everywhere without any particular source. Ambient light does not cast shadows, but fills in the shadowed areas of a scene.

Antialiasing – The act of smoothing curves or lines on the computer screen to avoid blocky edges. On computer monitors the pixels themselves aren't curved, but they have to show curves. Using pixels to show curves in makes the edges appear jagged. The technique for smoothing out these jagged edges is called antialiasing. Antialiasing works by changing the color of pixels surrounding a the curve or line to intermediate values ranging from the color of touching areas of the background to the color of that particular curve or line.

Avi – audio/video interleave. AVI is the file format used by Video for Windows, one of three major video playback utilities used on personal computers. (The others are MPEG and QuickTime.) It is called audio/video interleave because it stores picture and sound elements in alternate interleaved chunks in the file.

Bump – As in "Bump Map." Bump mapping is a method of creating the appearance of texture or relief on a surface without modifying the underlying geometry of the model. The light and dark areas of a 2d image are interpreted as different levels of relief; 100% white or 100% black could be read by a 3D program as a high point or low point on a surface. When the renderer reads the bump map, it interprets the range of colors as highs and lows and creates a surface appearance based on that information.

CG – Short for Computer Graphic or Computer Graphics

Character Rig – See Skeleton System

Codec – Stands for coder/decoder or compression/decompression algorithm. Codecs are used to encode and decode (or compress and decompress) sound and video files.

Comping – See Compositing

Compositing – Creating an image by combining two or more images, often with the aid of mattes to mask off unwanted areas of images. The most common compositing operation is an over operation, where one image is placed over another, taking into account the matte (alpha channel information) of both images.

Concave Polygons – These are polygons that are "caved in". (Some of its sides are bent inward.) If any two points can be connected by a line that goes outside the polygon, the polygon is concave. A polygon in the shape of the letter C is would be concave.

Cross Platform – The ability of a file to run or open on more than one computer operating system, such as Mac, Windows, Irix or Linux.

Demo Reel – A compilation of work used by an artist to obtain employment.

Diffuse – Diffuse lighting assumes the light hitting an object scatters in all directions equally, so the brightness of the reflected light does not depend at all on the position of the viewer. Sunlight on a driveway is an example in the real world of diffuse lighting.

Displacement – A displacement map is an image that is used to alter the surface of an object. Unlike a bump map which only disturbs an object's surface normals, a displacement map actually distorts surface geometry.

DVD Decoder Card – DVDs use of MPEG-2 technology to compress video and sound data. It must be decoded before it is output. Many DVD players, include card whose sole function is to decode MPEG data. This is called a DVD decoder card.

Executable File – A program file that can be run (executed) by a computer. These programs usually have .exe as the extension. For example, racing.exe may be a racing game. Executables are created when their source code is compiled and bound to the operating system upon which it is to be run.

Fields – Interlaced video contains frames that are divided into 2 fields. One field contains only the odd scan lines of the frame, the other one contains only the even scan lines. Since each field contains 1/2 of the image, showing them simultaneously will trick the viewer into seeing a full image.

Interlaced Video – Interlacing is a technique used in analog TV signals to reduce the flicker perceived by the viewer while keeping frame rate low. Each video frame is sent as 2 separate fields. The first field is displayed on the odd numbered lines of the TV - the second field is displayed on the even numbered lines. There is often a time difference between the first and second fields of the video frame

Interpolation – When images are scaled up, the higher resolution is achieved by artificially filling in the gaps between the missing pixels. This process is called interpolation. It works, but the interpolation process tends to "soften" the images resulting in lowered image quality.

Live Action Footage – Footage taken that contains real persons and places, as opposed to animated or computer generated images.

Long Format Television Animation – Animation for television shows or shows that are made up entirely of animation or contain large amounts of animation per episode.

Lossless Compression – Compression is a method for storing images in fewer bits. It makes data smaller so less disk space is needed to store the files. Some image compression schemes can do this with out losing any image quality. This is called lossless compression. Image compression schemes that throw out data to save space are called lossy compression schemes.

Maquette – A small clay model created as a guide for the artists in charge of creating 3d models. Incidentally Maquette is the French word for "MOCK-UP" or "model."

Mattes – Usually a black and white image. It represents parts of an image that will be cut out or hidden. Mattes are usually derived from alpha channel, luma key or chromakey information.

Matte Painter – Artist responsible for creating painted or computer graphic imagery that did not exist in the original shot. The imagery may be added into the original shot by means of a matte or high contrast-composing element.

Motion Blur – Blur that occurs from movement of the camera or object. With traditional computer generated images, a given frame showing an object in motion will render that object with crisp, clean edges in each frame. (Unless you activate the motion blur feature in your 3d application.)When viewing a full motion version of the scene based on non motion blurred images, the result is an unrealistic strobing effect (much like watching someone move underneath a strobe light).

Mpeg – Moving Pictures Experts Group. MPEG is used to compress sound and movie files into a single MPEG movie file. It is one of three major video playback utilities used on personal computers. (The others are AVI and QuickTime.)

Non-Square Pixels – Pixels in the graphics world are just as tall as they are wide. (Square) Pixels in a television's video signal are non-square. (Rectangular.) This happened because engineers wanted to make higher resolution television images without changing the number of scan lines. In NTSC signals they are wider than they are taller. In PAL signals it the opposite.

Normals – Every polygon has an orientation. (It faces some unique direction.) This direction is defined by an imaginary ray pointing out from the surface of the polygon. This ray is called a normal.

NTSC – National Television Systems Committee. A television standard consisting of 525 lines of resolution per second for broadcasts in the United States. (However it is used in many other countries.) The NTSC standard combines blue, red, and green signals with an FM frequency for audio.

NURBs – Non-Uniform Rational B-Splines. This is a type of spline that can represent more complex shapes than most other types of splines. They are used as curves and surfaces in 3d programs.

OCR – Optical Character Recognition is the process of converting an image of text, such as a scanned paper document or electronic fax file, into computer-editable text.

Off The Shelf – Software that can be bought by anyone. As if it came off the shelf of a computer store. The opposite of proprietary software. Which often cannot be bought.

Optical Character Recognition – See OCR.

PAL – Phase Alternate Line. The television broadcast standard throughout most of Europe. This standard broadcasts 625 lines of resolution.

Particle System – Particle systems are used to simulate effects such as snow, explosions, water, dust, etc... A particle system is the collection of those particles and the controls that create (emit) them.

Planar Polygons – Planar polygons are flat. Most renderers deal with planar polygons better than non-planar polygons. Without a flat surface, objects might not be properly smoothed or render properly.

Plugins – A software program that extends the capabilities of your software in a specific way, giving you the ability to create effects with it that you were unable to do previously.

Post Houses – Short for Post Production Houses. Companies that do television, film, and video work after filming is finished.

Procedural Graphics – Graphics or graphic elements that are generated by mathematical algorithms and not manually. (By hand.)

Procedurally Generated Images – An image that is created by a mathematical algorithm, as opposed to a bit-mapped texture, which is an actual image. Procedural textures are useful for creating a random textures like noise, or automating the creation of geometric patterns.

Proprietary – Internally developed information that a company will not share or sell with individuals outside the company. For example: Proprietary software is privately developed, often to give that particular company an edge over its competition. As a result is not for sale to the public.

Proprietary Information – Privately owned knowledge or data, such as that protected by law. (Registered patent, copyright, or trademark.)

Quicktime – A method of storing sound, graphics, and movie files Developed by Apple Computer Corp. QuickTime was originally developed for the Macintosh, but has been available for Windows and other platforms for years. It is one of three major video playback utilities used on personal computers. (The others are MPEG and AVI.)

Rotoscoping – Drawing a matte on top of objects in a frame so that an effect can be applied to that part of the film. If a spaceship has to go behind a building in a live action shot, then that object can have a matte drawn on top it. This way the spaceship will not be visible in front of that object. If the camera is moving, then each frame of film would have to be rotoscoped. If the camera is still, then the same matte can probably be used for all frames in that shot.

Safe Frame – Practically every 3d and 2d video software will have this function. In some programs it is called Field Guide, in others it is called Video Safe Zone. This function will display two rectangles in the "camera view" or "render window" of your application. The outer rectangle shows how much of the image will be viewable on a television set and is called the action-safe frame. Anything outside of this rectangle runs the risk of being cut off by the bezel surrounding the picture tube. The inner rectangle shows you the area that text can reside in and still remain a safe distance from the edge of the screen. This is called the title-safe frame.

Scripts – A script is simply a text file that contains instructions for performing a task. They are not like executable programs or plugins in that they are not compiled. However, it still can be used to extend the capabilities of your 3d software in a specific way, giving you the ability to perform repetitive tasks or functions you were unable to perform previously.

SECAM – Sequential Couleur avec Mémoire. The television broadcast standard in France, the Middle East, and most of Eastern Europe. SECAM broadcasts 819 lines of resolution per second.

Shaders – Any single component that defines or alters the properties of an element in a 3d scene. Shaders can be assigned to anything. Lights, Cameras, Objects, etc... For example: A phong shader will affect the way the surface of an object looks when rendered.

Shot List – A list of shots contained on a demo reel. It will include information about what the artist did on each shot listed.

SIGGRAPH – Stands for Special Interest Group on Computer Graphics, a part of the Association for Computing Machinery. This term is also used for the SIGGRAPH Conference which takes place every summer in the USA. It is the premier conference on leading-edge theory and practice of computer graphics and interactive techniques.

Skeleton System – A set of "bones" that are used to move characters in a 3d program. They work in much the same way bones in real animals. (Deforming the skin as then rotate.)

Specular – One of the 3 major components of an objects material. (Ambient, Diffuse and Specular.) The specular component of a material is what most people think of as high-lights. It is the reflection of the light source off of the object back into the camera.

Texture Map – Unlike shading, which applies colors to the polygons of a scene, texture mapping applies a 2 dimensional bitmap image, mapped onto polygons, to simulate walls, floors, the sky, etc... For example: Texture mapping an image of bricks onto a rectangular surface will make it look like a brick wall.

Transfers – Copying animation to video. Many companies that take animation and put it on tape are called Transfer houses.

VCD – "Video Compact Disc." It is a standard Compact Disc (CD) that contains video and audio. It can hold up to 74 minutes of full-motion video with quality stereo sound. A VCD uses the MPEG-1 standard to store video and audio. Unlike a DVD (which uses MPEG-2.)

Watermark – It is a small image that is overlaid on a video sequence that is typically used to decorate and identify ownership. This technique informs the viewer that even a simple copy of the video is an action that is not permitted, so that the viewer avoids the creation and distribution of a copy.

337557

Made in the USA